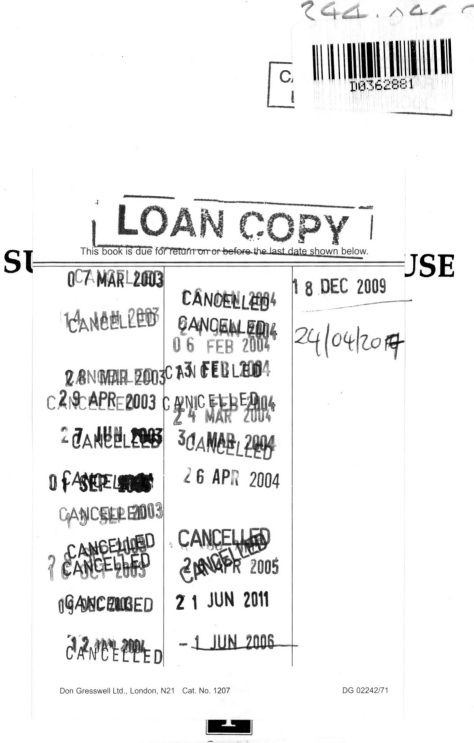

SUSTAINABILITY, LAND USE AND ENVIRONMENT

a legal analysis

London • Sydney

SUSTAINABILITY, LAND USE AND ENVIRONMENT

a legal analysis

Mark Stallworthy

BA (Oxon), LLM, Solicitor
Senior Lecturer, Norwich Law School
University of East Anglia

Cavendish
Publishing
Limited

London • Sydney

First published in Great Britain 2002 by Cavendish Publishing Limited, The Glass House, Wharton Street, London WC1X 9PX, United Kingdom

Telephone: +44 (0)20 7278 8000   Facsimile: +44 (0)20 7278 8080

Email: info@cavendishpublishing.com

Website: www.cavendishpublishing.com

© Stallworthy, Mark 2002

British Library Cataloguing in Publication Data

Sustainability, land use and environment

1 Land use – planning – law and legislation – Great Britain

2 Environmental law – Great Britain 3 Land use – environmental aspects – Great Britain

I Title

346.4'1'045

ISBN 1 85941 647 0

Printed and bound in Great Britain

For my children, Emily, Ben and Kate. And also for theirs.

PREFACE

During the project that is this book, as quick thoughts and slow legal reflexes have focused upon problems of sustainability, I have at times reminded myself of TS Eliot: speaking in *Little Gidding* of 'the last of earth left to discover' being 'that which was the beginning'. The idea that the environment is 'different' inspired the writing of the book. The consequences of our human activities are at the same time both immediate and removed, that is, whether viewed in place or time. Uncertainties at our cumulative impacts upon natural systems are reflected in much of what follows. My argument assumes that our survival as a species is under threat, and that effective solutions demand cross-disciplinary approaches. My premise is that this must be true too of the law, both in its interaction with cognate disciplines, as well as in its own internal dialogues. As with the physical sciences, legal methods tend to the reductionist: yet appropriate responses are not to be found without looking across and beyond traditional compartments.

Outside my own area, 'the law', the underlying concern for sustainability is partly a matter of lay observation. But it is at root also one of belief. Technology and innovation are moving into a new era. We are led by the biological sciences where the vanguard hitherto lay in the physical, chemical sciences. The risk society explored by Ulrich Beck is a modern expression of the consequences of humankind's detachment from the biotic community explored by Aldo Leopold, countered a half-century ago in the latter's land ethic. Reflexive responses are therefore demanded across the disciplinary spectrum. Yet even (perhaps especially) in its own era of regulation, law's approaches are highly ambivalent when viewed in the sustainability context. The law is not absolved from such questionings, and in places reinvention may be necessary.

As to this present contribution, the time to put pen to paper, or rather fingers to keyboard, became available to me courtesy of a semester's leave from Norwich Law School, from September 2000. Final additions were made at the end of 2001. But prior to the above start date the themes explored below, especially in the attention to the centrality of the question of land use in sustainability discourse, had been through a considerable period of gestation. With the help of funds from the Society of Public Teachers of Law and my own Law School, I attended an important conference in Stockholm in April 2000, *Implementation and Enforcement of EC Environmental Law*. Of a number of subsequent meetings and events, a conference at Cambridge, devoted to *Projecting Science into Society*, in March 2001, was especially provocative and stimulating. Whilst all errors are my own, I owe considerable academic thanks to the many colleagues who have been willing to discuss the themes of this book. Particular inspiration came from Bob Lee and Donald McGillivray. Ruth Massey was, I suspect, as tolerant and supportive as an editor dare be. Thanks are also due to Ben, who was introduced to the perils and joys of research, and whom I suspect will now add the academic life to boxing in his list of careers to avoid. Finally, Jill Morgan provided inestimable private law rigour at times when the public lawyer in me was threatening to cut adrift. Jill also sacrificed to this book that most precious of things: time. To her my heartfelt thanks.

What follows is therefore one lawyer's exploration of more reflexive legal approaches in the search for sustainable solutions. To return to Eliot, I am content if for some the end of the explorations in the pages that follow

> Will be to arrive where we started,
> And know the place for the first time.

Mark Stallworthy
Norwich
December 2001

CONTENTS

Contents

TABLE OF CASES

TABLE OF STATUTES

TABLE OF STATUTORY INSTRUMENTS

INTRODUCTION

The first man who, after fencing off a piece of land, took it upon himself to say 'This belongs to me' and found people simple-minded enough to believe him, was the true founder of civil society.[1]

1 SUSTAINABILITY AND LEGAL RESPONSES

The United Nations Intergovernmental Panel on Climate Change (IPCC) has now issued its report on the science and potential impacts of climate change, as brought about principally by the effects of global warming.[2] A core assumption which pervades this book is that there is an increasing predictability in the level of threat to the sustainability of humankind: that is, our survival as a species. The underlying premise is that our responses have so far proved inadequate. Sustainability must therefore be made to count for more than mere policy choice, scrabbling for attention with other, often more immediate, concerns. Meanwhile, for environmentalists, our (warmer) air is filled also with grim foreboding, given the state of denial thus far on the part of such dominant political forces as the current United States administration supported by a range of decidedly non-democratically legitimate industrial players.

The focus is therefore mostly upon questions affecting sustainability. The objective is to contribute a common lawyer's perspective of the potential role of legal mechanisms in the pursuit of sustainable solutions. The legal perspective offered here is inescapably Western in outlook: an English lawyer's approach will be conceptually redolent of common law approaches elsewhere, though such perspectives have in recent decades been gradually recalibrated towards a growing, if not always intuitive, identification with European civil law ideas. It is important from the outset to make plain the following thesis: that, whatever benefits it can bring, the discipline of law, with attention fixed mostly on the present and past, is rooted in the status quo. Ideological questions concerning the foundations of civil society, and the nature, status and acceptable extent of property rights, are an enduring theme in Western philosophy, as explicit in the headed reference above. These questions interweave at every stage with legal explanations, justifications and even capacities for change. To these indeed must be added new questions about the nature, value and efficacy of other rights systems, including human rights, recognised by law.

As its title suggests, the book is also about land use. This is put forward as being at the fulcrum of attempts to find sustainable solutions. It is also concerned with the contribution made to these attempts by planning and environmental controls; land use and development policies are 'related in fundamental ways to environmental change'.[3] By ready analogy for a lawyer, a special emphasis is laid upon relationships, although these are conceived as wider in scope than is generally the case: such as between the achievement of economic growth and sustainability; as likewise between environmental degradation and regulatory policy. To Western eyes, and seen from the United Kingdom,

---

1   Rousseau, *Discourse on Inequality*, 1755, 1962 edn.
2   United Nations, IPCC, 2001 A–C.
3   Owens, 1994, p 439.

since emerging from the tragic postwar rubble of half a century ago, we have been living in an era of regulation. The Town and Country Planning Act entered the statute book in 1947, as a key, if less heralded, part of the civilising, social democratic forces to which government then manifestly aspired. Coherent environmental regulation was some longer time coming, and economic stringency and doctrine each contributed to the time lag. Moreover, the underlying assumptions of traditional common law principles have typically proved hostile to regulatory responses in the name of environmental protection. If the processes of globalism assert the dominance of markets, then the common law has been readily identified with marketisation. It has seldom adapted appropriate responses to the resulting commodification of nature. Yet markets have implications for sustainability in profound ways. Whilst economics teaches the sensitivity of markets to traditional understandings of scarcity, there are factors that are dangerously beyond such forms of adjustment: 'there are intrinsic limits to the resources available for indefinite accumulation, and the "externalities" which the markets either do not touch or adversely influence – such as yawning global inequalities – might prove to have socially explosive implications.'[4]

For all the institutional responses explored throughout this book, globally there has been persistent environmental degradation in recent decades. As stated above, the consequences of global warming seem no longer a distant threat. Pollution continues to stretch the natural regulating capacities of ecosystems, and variously threatens the survival of biological species. There are other crises, such as continued soil erosion. This is exacerbated bizarrely by a perverse insistence upon fossil fuel energy, in manufacturing a crop dependence upon artificial fertilisers, to the detriment of natural biological cycles. A large sense of irony is needed to observe agrochemical firms now proffering solutions based upon the genetic modification of plants. In this area, as elsewhere, most environmental problems are the consequence of a myopic perception of the nature and quality of growth. Back in 1984, Porritt offered a stark assessment: 'economic growth in the future must be sustainable: that is to say it must operate within and not beyond the finite limits of the planet.'[5] Yet we operate human systems founded for the most part on resource depletion, built upon the insouciant belief that technology will continue to forestall catastrophe. The First World maintains lifestyles that accelerate resource depletion and the production of wastes, and an expanding population throughout much of the Third World aspires to much the same. Peering beyond old alliances, one of the ironies of the dismantling of the Iron Curtain is that it has illustrated a fundamental sharing of expectations with those societies formerly within the orbit of the USSR. As the scale of the global marketplace expands, there is now also a readier identification of values with rapidly developing world economies such as those in the Far East.

It is important, therefore, not to take a too-narrow view of the environment and the multiplicity of threats to it. A paradox between human aspiration and consummation emerges time and again during the sustainability argument. On the one hand, as humans we are beneficiaries of high levels of cognition, as well as capacities for abstract thought and even emotional responsiveness. On the other, wittingly pursuing a self-destructive path, our species has been described as 'uniquely capable of becoming "unbalanced" ...

---

4 Giddens, 1990, p 172.
5 Porritt, 1984, p 120.

Currently we find ourselves somewhere at the outer limit of a particularly exaggerated oscillation. It is called urban-industrialism, the wilful withdrawal of our species from the natural habitat in which it evolved'.[6] Even accepting that our developed, urban environments do indeed exemplify much of our sustainability crisis, problems are more diffuse. If environmental sciences teach us anything it is the affirmation of a core ecological message – of the mutual interdependence of natural processes. Transitions towards incorporating sustainability into policy making are grounded in a recognition that environmental policies 'affect more lives (private and collective, present and future), and to a greater extent than, arguably, any other policy area. The main reason for this is that the economy-ecology material metabolism is the most important aspect of social-environmental interaction, upon which human flourishing depends'.[7] Yet we have conspired to generate environmental threats in ways that transcend even natural boundaries, whether geographical, sectoral or jurisdictional. The dominance of global implications informs debates over sustainable development, discussed in the next section. Yet the reality of State boundaries points to externalisation of hazard, for States have 'a huge incentive to externalise hazards onto other nations and onto future generations and electorates'.[8]

It is suggested that searches for solutions must be founded upon conjoined fronts. Recurring themes here are concerned with the challenges to traditional legal processes, in facing up to what amount to crises in institutional and social response. Voices are now raised against the perceived ineffectiveness of regulatory or command-and-control solutions to bring about the necessary improvements. Developments at the European Community level are instructive. One of the tenets which had underlain the European Community's Fifth Environmental Action Programme was to move beyond reliance upon vertical, sectoral approaches by encouraging horizontal applications, taking account of all causes of pollution that contribute to identified threats, and to seek for more responsive controls, such as market-based measures, economic and fiscal arrangements and voluntary agreements.[9] Yet shared responsibility on the part of all interests, just as national responsibility, cannot simply be wished into existence. Whilst persisting with the stakeholder idea in encouraging sustainable patterns of production and consumption, the forthcoming Sixth Environmental Action Programme seeks further integration of environmental considerations into transport, energy and agriculture policies and the promotion of sustainable development in spatial planning carried out at local and regional levels, with priority given to the areas affecting climate change, health and the environment, nature and bio-diversity and natural resource management.[10]

What is now needed, therefore, goes beyond mere regulatory solutions. It is, in particular, important to consider, first, institutional approaches to the sustainability debate and the problems of unsustainable growth; and, secondly, individual tolerances and levels of acceptability accorded by the population at large. There must be purposeful efforts made to secure fuller integration of ecological principles into both policy making

---

6   Roszack, 1992, p 307.
7   Barry, 1999, p 200.
8   Macnaghten and Urry, 1998, p 270.
9   European Commission, 1993a; see also European Commission, 1996a.
10   European Commission, 2001a.

and our perceptions of environmental rights and obligations. The idea of sustainability constraints demands that we both engage with questions of culture and lifestyle changes and accept a degree of present responsibility for the welfare of future generations. Yet it has been forcefully argued that it is 'not the freakish, malicious or extreme forms of human behaviour which threaten the environment, but the everyday patterns of life of the global population, especially those in the developed North'.[11] The developed world has indeed set a demanding economic pace. Yet for all that problems are global, the present discussion cannot proceed regardless of the framework set for the debate among nations. Certain communities and societies are better placed than others to limit lifestyle aspirations, and to take a lead in the changes necessary. On the one hand, for many of the peoples of the South, our obsession with global environmental questions, climate change, ozone depletion and loss of species and habitats hardly merits attention. For them, 'these are potentially devastating dangers, but they are not so clearly a matter of priority as is the day-to-day requirement of survival as affects so many'.[12] On the other, and for developed and developing alike, the oxymoronic quality of economic 'growth', increasingly framed in global terms, retains its persistence, and engulfs the setting of policy priorities in most jurisdictions.

2 THE OBJECTIVE OF SUSTAINABLE DEVELOPMENT

If sustainable development is premised upon notions of sustainability and protection of the environment, it is necessary to offer from the first a working definition of terms. Although lawyers engaged in exposition and interpretation will reach for the elixir of definition, this has thus far worked decidedly poorly in the context of the environmental debate. Environmental questions tend to resist the cut-and-dried language that is the common currency of most legal analysis. The term 'environment' has been subjected to a wide variety of legal treatments. For instance, the contexts of domestic enactment tend to focus upon environmental protection, such as, for example, in the somewhat non-holistic 'all or any of the following media: namely the air, water and land; and the medium of air includes air within buildings and the air within other natural or man-made structures above or below ground'.[13] Amongst the offerings of the Council of Ministers of the European Community has been the fairly universal 'combination of elements whose complex interrelationships make up the settings, the surroundings and the conditions of life of the individual and of society as they are and as they are felt'.[14] As for sustainability, in the light of there being no generally agreed definition, the following useful basis has been suggested: 'doing things that can be continued over long periods without unacceptable consequences, or without unacceptable risks of unacceptable consequences.'[15] The term is fundamentally concerned with the survival of humankind as a species. The core ideas underlying sustainability discourse essentially concern quality

---

11 Wilkinson, 1999, p 37.
12 O'Riordan, 2000, p 34.
13 Environmental Protection Act (EPA) 1990, s 1(2).
14 Council Regulation 1872/84 on Action by the Community Relating to the Environment (OJ L176, 28 June 1984), p 1.
15 Heal, 2000, p 410.

of life. They challenge patterns of production and consumption, and seek to account for the availability of natural resources. They point to an engagement in the search for alternatives to economic growth, and implications for citizen involvement in such decisions. Specific themes embrace not only environmental protection measures, but also the question of efficient resource use and a concern to meet the future needs of unborn generations.

The concept of sustainable development has become central to all discussions of policy affecting development and growth. Attributing a meaning to sustainable development is no easy task. International declarations and treaties scatter the notion around today in a profligate way. Similarly, national governments make copious use of it in seemingly any policy direction that can stand the terminological strain. A fair starting point is the Brundtland Report, which in 1987 defined sustainable development as 'development that ensures the needs of the present without compromising the ability of future generations to meet their own needs'.[16] Notably, the United Nations (UN) Conference on Environment and Development (UNCED) saw in 1992, at Rio, the emergence of Agenda 21, which sought commitments to set national sustainable law making priorities, integrating issues of environment and development.[17] At the core of sustainable development, concern for future generations can be expressed through legal notions of trust and stewardship. However, on the international stage, opportunities to impose stewardship obligations appear thus far to have been deliberately avoided. This can be illustrated in the periods respectively leading up to both the seminal Stockholm Declaration in 1972 and UNCED itself. In the former instance, the UN Secretary General commended to an Intergovernmental Working Group a specific 'duty on all nations to carefully husband their natural resources and to hold in trust for present and future generations the air, water, lands, and communities of plants and animals on which all life depends'.[18] Yet no further action was taken. Similarly, in the lead-up to Rio an Experts' Working Group interpreted the preamble to the Stockholm Declaration as imposing 'the duty to hold the natural heritage of mankind in trust for future generations', which imported two basic obligations: first, the maintenance of the diversity of the resource base to the maximum extent possible; and, secondly, the prevention or abatement of pollution and other forms of degradation of the natural environment. Had it been taken up, the Group's draft Convention for the Implementation of Sustainable Development would have called upon States to 'ensure that the environment and natural resources are conserved and used for the benefit of present and future generations'.[19]

It is inevitably hard to achieve positive, sustainable responses from nation States subject to intense conflicting internal pressures. Moreover, differentials in levels of development make reaching global solutions extremely problematic. Sustainable development is therefore a collection of exercises in pragmatic response.[20] Yet it is significant that an international recognition of the global nature of the problems of

---

16   United Nations World Commission on Environment and Development, 1987, para 43.
17   UNCED Report, Agenda 21, A/CONF 151/26/Rev 1 (Vol 1), para 39.2(b)(d).
18   See Redgwell, 1999, p 119, citing UN Doc A/CONF 48/PC/SG 1/CRP 4, 13 (1971).
19   Article 2: see Munro and Lammers, 1987, p 43.
20   See Porritt, 2000, pp 103–04.

sustainable development has emerged. Indeed, in line with the growing political awareness of environmental problems, the international stage is replete with international law responses.[21] There has likewise been a growing acknowledgement of the needs of environmental justice. Concern for present generations, and especially the division between South and North, was addressed by Brundtland through the advocacy of a 'same boat' approach to environmental management. This is encapsulated in the idea that 'we all share the same finite planetary resources and means of development, and that unless we learn to co-operate as a single global entity we risk common catastrophe'.[22] The context for the discussion has been shifted, and hopefully in due course beyond a rhetorical level, to the development needs of poorer nations. It is increasingly to the rich and over-consuming, over-polluting countries that institutional processes look for responses to the challenges set by the sustainability debate. This has identified greater threats to the developing world, beset, for instance, by over-population and economic privations often exacerbated by the pressures of globalisation, as well as intensified threats from rising water levels, shifting drought zones and soil erosion, which are part products of climate change.

Questions of both inter- and intragenerational environmental justice, however, are proving extremely problematic. Three especial reasons can be given. First, there is an unwillingness within richer nations to address the structural changes needed in their own economies in order to bring about change. For instance, in pursuance of the Framework Convention on Climate Change, attempts to build upon the compromise on carbon emissions reductions reached in principle under the Kyoto Protocol in 1997 collapsed in the talks at The Hague in 2000. Such proposals continue to founder in the light of US opposition and rejection by the incoming president, confirmed at Stockholm in June 2001. A second, more immediately threatening reason concerns a sheer lack of capacity on the part of the developing world to accommodate many of the solutions advocated. Innovative improvements require investment, such as, for instance, the transfer to cleaner energy technologies. This necessitates assistance in the funding of these incremental costs. To date, the main player, the Global Environmental Facility, under the auspices of the UN Development and Environment Programmes and the World Bank, operates on a small scale relative to largely non-ecologically targeted aid flows from First to Third World. Moreover, threats to environmental integrity resulting from economic growth are exacerbated 'in those places with the most rapid growth experiences', creating 'crises in sewage disposal, toxic dumps, water supplies and transportation'.[23] Finally, at whatever jurisdictional level, the sustainability debate must confront dilemmas associated with the externalities of environmental damage. Such obstacles to the pursuit of sustainable development operate at all institutional and human levels. According to O'Riordan, 'the sustainability problematique requires millions of people to undertake hundreds of consumer and leisure choices differently, without necessarily any price signals to guide them, and with no guarantee that their own contribution will be matched by others ... It takes dedication of a high order, or a coalescence of regulatory and economic institutions, to overcome this paradox of converting micro-behaviour to macro-sustainability'.[24]

---

21   See Birnie and Boyle, 1992.
22   Macnaghten and Urry, 1998, p 214.
23   Logan and Molotch, 1987, p 96 (a case study of environmental decline in Houston, Texas).
24   O'Riordan, 2000, p 40.

3 PRESENT THEMES

The nature of the sustainability debate outlined above, in the face also of the persistent environmental crisis, demands that environmental lawyers investigate the coherence of the available conceptual tools of their trade, and suggest how legal principles and processes can themselves develop more sustainably.[25] In particular, the pursuit of sustainable development demands the encouragement of a public interest ideology, with longer term aspirations, which should inform our perceptions of both public and private law. Having outlined above the key themes to be explored, this section offers a more detailed scoping exercise, with a concise setting out of the tasks set for each chapter.

Chapters 1 to 3

The classic contribution of Aldo Leopold, through his land ethic, offers a fair point of commonality as between the early chapters. It suggests an organising ecological concept, applying an ethical basis for imposing restraints in the light of our environmental impacts, in terms especially of resource limits and ecosystem carrying capacities.[26] Chapter 1 pursues the exploration of the nature of sustainable development already introduced above. It considers problems of definition, and especially the role of the sustainable development concept on the policy making processes of today. It sets out to achieve this in the light of acknowledged dilemmas that both expectations of growth and the broad nature of available policy responses pose for natural processes. The implications of sustainable development are addressed in terms of legal doctrine, in particular by reference to intergenerational equity and the application of discounting principles. The chapter concludes with a brief consideration of ways by which a reformed economic order might contribute to the change, and of the role of certain legal mechanisms in that process.

Chapter 2 then introduces jurisdictional questions into the spatial issues that are central to the sustainability discussion. It envisages that mechanisms for the delivery of more ecological policy making must be conceived and supported at global, regional and local levels. The primary concern is to investigate how far a framework for sustainable development through international processes can be achieved. In particular, it addresses the principles underlying the development of international environmental law and the thorny issue of securing compliance, including consideration of the (currently inevitable) dominance of the World Trade Organisation in matters of international adjudication. Following a discussion of the impact of the precautionary principle in the context of sustainability, the chapter concludes with a review of problems for effective regulation, also at regional and national levels. These sustainability-related themes are then focused in Chapter 3 upon the question of control of land use, as the value and purpose of regulation of private property are examined. The starting point for any analysis of the achievement of environmental protection through legal mechanisms must lie where the common law commences, namely in private law mechanisms. Private law principles in the environmental arena are instructive, as also the recognition of limitations of the

---

25 See McAuslan, 1991, p 197.
26 Leopold, 1949.

common law as defender of environmental values. Themes drawn here are a central element toward a recognition of the broad terrain of conflicting values which underlie the sustainability debate. There is accordingly an investigation of the nature and extent of property rights by reference to the sustainability context.

Chapters 4 to 7

The concluding discussion in Chapter 3, therefore, which is concerned with the tension between property interests and regulatory demands, leads to the more detailed substantive consideration of land use regulation in the three following chapters. In the last of these, a major theme is how effectively the demands of sustainable development can be served through the formulation of land use planning policy and its delivery through the operation of development planning and controls. In preparation for this, Chapter 4 picks up the previous discussion of the question of market regulation, in the context of the impact of planning rules upon those who hold property. Land use almost invariably pervades the whole range of human activities, and therefore its regulation is fundamental to any assessment of sustainable use. The extent, therefore, to which land use planning operates under political and legal constraints is a dominant factor in resolving how effectively society can respond to the multiple environmental problems with which we are faced. Almost all development triggers the operation of the statutory planning regime, which is therefore central to problems such as those posed by the scarcity of the land resource. The chapter goes on to identify key principles underlying the English land use planning system, with attention devoted to the processes of development planning and planning control. It concludes with consideration of some of the essential quandaries of land use planning, by reference to the problems of the urban and rural environments, and the difficulties of securing sustainable solutions. The planning and environment nexus is then carried further in Chapter 5, with a discussion of the means by which planning processes can take account of anticipated environmental threats from proposed development. Consideration is given to the regulatory solution achieved through the mechanism of environmental impact assessment (EIA). The chapter looks at the premises upon which EIA is based, and the legal processes which are relevant to its being secured. Consideration of the value of EIA towards achieving greater sustainability concludes the chapter.

In the light of the regulatory arrangements with which the preceding chapters are concerned, the subject of Chapter 6 is the role of land use planning policy in delivering wider sustainable development objectives. Specific attention is focused upon the planning pressures represented by the questions of meeting development demands and securing sustainable lifestyles. The chosen contexts are the related ones of housing and transport requirements. The discussion seeks to address specific policy recognition of sustainability issues, including resource and environmental constraints. The chapter concludes with a consideration of how far a realistic sustainable rationale for land use planning control can be achieved, and includes a brief discussion of sustainability appraisal. Immediately succeeding the above chapters devoted to land use planning, Chapter 7 acknowledges the broader regulatory context, in considering more broadly environmental protection in the context of land use. This therefore turns attention to the relationship between planning and environmental controls. As the inadequacy of markets, and their related legal mechanisms, has become gradually more apparent, the response of political decision makers, as in other fields, has been to formulate a succession of regulatory approaches. For all the concern at the efficacy of command-and-control approaches, referred to above, the most recent decade has ushered in a new era of more comprehensive environmental regulation, characterised by increasingly integrated approaches to pollution control. Yet, as the chapter shows, questions affecting the siting of development cannot be described as fully integrated, although they inevitably affect the environment. Likewise, it is here that (as seen in the previous chapters devoted to planning) national, regional and local priorities may diverge. The chapter argues that these interrelationships are essential to the sustainability debate, as indeed ongoing deliberations of the Royal Commission on Environmental Pollution testify.

Chapters 8 to 10

The concluding chapters are concerned with the broader political context and its legal support structures. It is argued that the search for a fair degree of homogeneity in the acceptance of both problems and solutions should engage both political and legal processes. To this end, Chapter 8 explores the nature of risk and its assessment in the context of environmental harm. Chapter 10 addresses the ends to which political systems must aspire, and also the contribution of the legal apparatus, especially the supplementary solutions offered by adjudicative mechanisms. It must, however, be remembered that these operate not only in regulatory spheres, and so Chapter 9 first devotes consideration to the assertion of rights, in particular human rights, as a basis for securing environmental improvements. After this overview of the final themes, a little more detail is now set out.

Chapter 8 therefore discusses an abiding problem in the context of all facets of environmental protection, particularly those discussed in earlier chapters of the book. The chapter addresses the question of accommodation of issues of risk in policy making and legal approaches. It considers the notion of risk assessment and its role in setting, especially legal, regulatory frameworks. Reference is also made to counter analyses which dispute the role and value of our understandings of risk assessment. This is followed by a specific consideration of domestic approaches, citing illustrations drawn from the BSE/CJD tragedy and the new regime for clean-up of contaminated land. The chapter includes a consideration of reformed approaches in light of an emerging categorisation of a risk society, as science and its data are mediated through social institutions, with resulting transformations reflecting the priorities of policy making dynamics. In a wider context, as well as uncertainties as to risk, notions of modernity encompass displacement of the primacy of place, especially of locality, and with it bring our integration into larger communities. In such an extended context, 'the very tissue of spatial experience alters, conjoining proximity and distance in ways that have few close parallels in prior ages ... [with] our insertion into globalised cultural and information settings, which means that familiarity and place are much less consistently connected than hitherto'.[27] The age is a complex one, in which traditional reliance mechanisms are under strain, as citizens become ever-more distanced from scientific and technocratic explanations. Thus, polling

---

27 Giddens, 1990, pp 140–41.

indications suggest that, on environmental issues, 75% trust levels in scientists reduce to 46% and 43% for government and industry scientists, respectively; it is suggested that, apart from the expert/public knowledge divide, this is exacerbated by deficiencies in scientific independence, but also scientific transparency and communication.[28]

The risk assessment process has parallels in the engagement of legal processes, in so far as they seek out 'just' determinations. Whilst law may be comfortable with evidential or epistemological uncertainties, its standard approaches are likewise ill-equipped to address issues of objective, such as scientific, uncertainty, to which standard rules of causation lamentably are still often applied. The theme of political structures, to be seen in the final chapter, emerges as a key element in seeking solutions to problems such as these. However, attention turns first, in Chapter 9, to the question of the relationship between human rights notions and environmental protection. There is no logical reason to deny rights-based approaches to 'nature'. However, there are serious obstacles to the viability of such approaches in the context of human rights. The chapter commences with an overview of issues of intragenerational equity in the specific context of the environmental justice movement. Discussion then turns to broad structures of human rights protections under international instruments. The focus of the discussion is from a European regional perspective, with an analysis of the jurisprudence of the European Court of Human Rights. Amongst the myriad of political and legal consequences of the incorporation into domestic law of the terms of the European Convention, under the Human Rights Act 1998, there will surely be significant impacts in the environmental and land use context. There, decisions not only inevitably affect individual circumstances, but they also often appear to be of a quasi-judicial nature. This has already arisen in the context of planning procedures, in which challenges to the adjudicative role of the (undeniably policy making) Secretary of State have already been taken to the House of Lords. It is argued that the litigation has wider consequences in an area where administrative policy making sits cheek by jowl with administrative decision making, and is unlikely to be the last word. Indeed, whilst subject to traditional forms of judicial review, the demarcation lines as between administration and adjudication will inevitably come under renewed pressure. At a primarily legal level, this can be seen as opening up fresh possibilities for addressing inadequate delivery of regulatory controls. But it is suggested that there is more at stake than this. Sustainability demands political solutions. These solutions necessitate legal processes which are conducive to the new strategies which follow inevitably in the political wake. One consequence is that new areas of tension will inevitably arise as between political imperatives and legal principles. It would be too much (and arguably unhealthy) to expect that they will undergo necessary transformative processes co-extensively at every stage.

These considerations precipitate the discussion in Chapter 10. Together with the need for greater, informed, public involvement in risk-related issues which were earlier identified, they lead to important questions concerning both participative processes in policy making and the scope and extent of any adjudicative process. Concerning the relationship of the public with scientific issues, a recent parliamentary committee has reached similar conclusions to those referred to in the risk context. Importantly, it also

---

28 MORI/Wellcome survey, March 2001: discussed by Worcester, 2001.

urged the need for institutional changes in terms of reference to scientific issues, as well as changes in the communication of science to the public.[29] These essentially structural issues are therefore the chapter's main themes, in addressing questions affecting the amenability of democratic politics and legal processes to the genuine search for sustainable solutions. Key constraints which operate upon the policy making process in the liberal State, especially in the environmental context, are identified. This leads (as it must) to a discussion of sustainability in terms of problems within ourselves as citizens. Assuming progress towards a more reflexive process, the argument seeks to establish a link between encouraging greater accountability and addressing apparent limits to the acceptability of change.

Finally, with roots not only in the earlier part of the chapter but also throughout the book, the argument turns to the role of legal, and particularly adjudicative structures in progressing further towards greater sustainability. This encompasses some discussion of access to justice, but more importantly addresses the impact that changed structures, such as an environmental court, might have in the domestic context. If the law can no longer justify a separation from the wider political world of the constitution, then no more can it avoid the external world by sheltering within the safe, delimiting confines of common law principles and traditional processes. In whatever way modern regulation evolves, whether by extension, retrenchment, other transformation or all of these, the sustainability debate demands appropriate legal responses. These must reflect on both principle and structures, and a mutual engagement with cognate disciplinary influences upon policy making and execution. The conclusion, optimistically, asserts a potential for reformed political and legal processes to achieve improved mechanisms for imposing a sustainability, or public interest, rationale into the conflictual processes of environmental protection and land use control.

Two final points concern the scope of what follows and the limits to the understanding of domestic jurisdiction. The first is that, in deference to the chosen thematic approach and finite limits on space, it has not been possible to address all policy areas where there are environmental impacts and threats to sustainability. Inevitably such constraints have led to the omission of a detailed consideration of numerous areas. There has, for instance, been no space for an exposition of domestic environmental protection, especially pollution control and regulation, and nor has it been possible to include specific consideration of domestic conservation laws, and bio-diversity generally. The author acknowledges the irony in allowing a lack of space to induce a less than holistic approach.

Secondly, there is a jurisdictional limit to the perspective offered here. The scope of domestic law is limited to the law of England and Wales. This is a cause for regret especially given the calls for wider legal perceptions appearing throughout the work. However, reference to home jurisdiction creates especial problems for British lawyers. The United Kingdom (of Great Britain and Northern Ireland), for all its (relative) stability, is sufficiently contingent to an extent that there is an unusual layering of jurisdictions within so small a land mass and so homogeneous a society. It has been the traditional separateness of Scottish law that has been the major feature of this multilayering. Now, with the onset of devolution, including a fragile return of Northern Ireland to a level of

---

29   House of Lords, 2000.

self-rule, and the re-institution of a Scottish Parliament and creation of a Welsh Assembly, it becomes more important than ever for a lawyer professing to specialise in English law to concentrate upon England. Indeed, different domestic solutions – in Scotland, it appears, for instance, that legislative proposals are now formally assessed for environmental impact – are likely now to appear with greater regularity. Moreover, inevitably, land use and environmental protection questions will impact differently on disparate parts of the United Kingdom's land mass, and devolution will increase divergencies in approach. Nevertheless, a feature of the modern era has been that the notion of 'the UK' has become increasingly identifiable, both from within and without. The text speaks, therefore, of the UK unless there is an important jurisdictional distinction to be drawn.

CHAPTER 1

THE NATURE OF SUSTAINABLE DEVELOPMENT

The next case was that of a youth barely arrived at man's estate, who was charged with having been swindled out of large property by his guardian, who was also one of his nearest relations. ... The lad, who was undefended, pleaded that he was young, inexperienced, greatly in awe of his guardian, and without independent professional advice. 'Young man,' said the judge sternly, 'do not talk nonsense. People have no right to be young, inexperienced, greatly in awe of their guardians, and without independent professional advice. If by such indiscretions they outrage the moral sense of their friends, they must expect to suffer accordingly.'[1]

1 PROBLEMS OF DEFINITION

Sustainability should be distinguished from sustainable development. Sustainability is about respecting the processes at work in our ecosystem so as to ensure, or at least prolong, our survival as a species, and concerns our level of connectedness with future generations. Sustainability from this perspective bears close similarity with a 'principle of integrity',[2] which has been described as starting 'with the fundamental need for ecological and biological integrity and raises questions about what it would mean to institutionalize this primacy'.[3] Both ideas are necessarily tied to the precautionary principle, which is discussed in the next chapter.[4] By contrast sustainable development is about pragmatics, or ways in which we can organise ourselves politically, whether upon local, regional, national or global levels, so as to engage in habits of living which respect sustainability. The distinction has recently been most eloquently put by Porritt. The former he sees as neither elusive nor soft, but 'just about as hard-edged, uncompromising, quantifiable and scientifically rigorous a concept as exists in the indeterminate world of contemporary policy making'. In contrast, sustainable development is 'a process, not a scientifically definable capacity; it describes the journey we must undertake to arrive at the destination, which is of course sustainability itself; it is essentially driven by political and economic processes, not by science and empirical data; and it can be defined in such a way as to mean almost anything that anybody wants it to mean, which sustainability cannot'.[5]

To a marked degree, therefore, sustainable development is politically the less discomfiting notion. For its essence lies not in any non-tradability, but in those compensatory mechanisms that serve to support our social and economic systems. It is the purpose of this opening section to explore ways in which such accommodations can be reached and the priorities that should be applied within those processes.

---

1   Butler, S, from *Erewhon*, 1872, 1985 edn, p 113.
2   Westra, 1994.
3   Holland, 1998, p 6.
4   Westra, 1998, pp 13–17.
5   Porritt, 2000, pp 103–04.

1.1 'Sustainable development' as a framework for debate

It can at least be said that sustainable development is likely to inform law making across a vast range of human activities in our new century. In seeking to understand the notion, a justifiable starting point is the Brundtland Report in 1987.[6] The report established the imperative of sustainable development, which it proceeded to define as follows: 'development that meets the needs of the present generation without compromising the abilities of future generations to meet their own needs.'[7] Yet, as relatively new concepts go, 'sustainable development' has probably been defined to death. Macnaghten and Urry offer a fair approximation, in that such definitions 'share the underlying belief that economic and social change is only sustainable and thereby beneficial in the long term when it safeguards the natural resources on which all development depends'.[8] Such a view reflects a multipurpose application, for all shades of green argument, countering root causes of non-sustainability, which O'Riordan has identified as 'profoundly powerful systems of exploitation and degradation that are fostered by ignorance, greed, injustice and oppression'.[9]

The nature of the term is that it is uncertain. A universal definition is perhaps impossible, given the contradictions and variations in localised responses, for, after all, human activity reflects culture and history, as well as the geography of territory and institutions.[10] Its essential vagueness is indeed problematic. The Brundtland definition referred to above has been described by Heal as 'eloquent' though 'very thin on operational content'.[11] Cullingworth and Nadin, in a land use planning context, see it as so overworked 'that it has ceased to have any communicable meaning', though they appear at least to divine 'a broad political commitment to the idea of sustainability, even if there is no general agreement on what it means'.[12]

The evident level of broad acceptability suggests a tendency for implicit endorsement of a 'business as usual' approach.[13] O'Riordan, elaborating upon an earlier argument to the effect that it could be seen as 'a mediating term to bridge the widening gulf between "developers" and "environmentalists" ... deliberately vague and inherently self-contradictory', detects in the concept a staying power at once 'understandable, if not forgivable'.[14] There is little doubt that its potential for mixing cliché and blandness is attractive to politicians and administrators.[15] Pallemaerts refers to an 'artful vagueness' afforded by the concept to their responsibilities, illustrated by a tendency to regress to what he terms sustainable growth.[16] UK land use planning policy guidance offers a flavour of this in the following explanation: 'Sustainable development seeks to deliver the

6   United Nations World Commission on Environment and Development, 1987.
7   *Ibid*, para 43.
8   Macnaghten and Urry, 1998, p 213.
9   O'Riordan, 1993, p 37.
10   See Voisey and O'Riordan, 2001, pp 25–40.
11   Heal, 2000, p 410.
12   Cullingworth and Nadin, 1997, p 164.
13   Wilkinson, 1999, p 29.
14   O'Riordan, 1993.
15   Porritt, 1993, p 38.
16   Pallemaerts, 1994, p 14.

objective of achieving, now and in the future, economic development to secure higher living standards while protecting and enhancing the environment.'[17] The term's very fungibility can therefore support self-justificatory assertions on the part of development interests. In an analysis concerned with native peoples and their sustainable resource systems, Gedicks states that 'the cutting edge of this concept has been dulled as practically every major institution in the world economy – from multinational mining and logging companies to the World Bank – has embraced the concept. Even the International Atomic Agency claimed that "the supply of energy for economic growth in a sustainable and environmentally acceptable manner is the central activity of the Agency's programme"'.[18]

However, a search for a precise meaning is perhaps unnecessary. Jacobs has, for instance, argued that the attempt is misguided, as 'resting on a mistaken view of the nature and function of political concepts'.[19] The idea underlying such argument is that sustainable development can operate adequately as a normative though contestable concept. Thus in the circumstances of doubt as to its impact upon an ontological level, or in accordance with rights-based approaches, its value can be said to lie in encouraging argument at least broadly within its boundaries: 'resolution by reconciliation'.[20] There remains an assumption that accepted core ideas are otherwise open to dispute, and that such 'contestation constitutes the political struggle over the direction of social and economic development'.[21] Macnaghten and Urry urge a similar benefit, in that sustainability has become the new discourse, which frames the formal environmental agenda, creating in the process a common language as between environmentalists, administrators and business. On this basis it might be considered an advantage that environmental rhetoric is no longer solely the preserve of environmental groups, as corporations 'routinely advocate sustainable development, as do aid agencies, government departments, the European Union and even insurance firms'.[22] In this way sustainable development is said to be concerned with how economic growth is secured, and removing the linkage of 'materials/energy throughput' not only from pollution but also from growth.[23] It has even been argued that despite the contribution of markets to environmental damage, 'this poor record is not intrinsic on its merits' and that 'markets can be reoriented in a positive direction'.[24] Indeed, solutions increasingly look to self-regulation, or at least regulation supported by market-based systems, such as fiscal mechanisms or emissions trading.[25]

On this basis, the introduction of a level of environmental consciousness has arguably changed the terms of debate. It is necessary to bring arguments within a sustainability framework in inclusive ways that appear to have been beyond the capacities of

---

17 Department of the Environment (DoE), PPG 1, 1997a, para 4.
18 Gedicks, 1993, p 198.
19 Jacobs, 1999, p 23.
20 Myerson and Rydin, 1996, p 193.
21 Jacobs, 1999, p 26.
22 Macnaghten and Urry, 1998, p 213.
23 Pearce and Barbier, 2000, pp 29–32.
24 Heal, 2000, p 427.
25 Eg, European Commission, 2001a, para 2.3.

traditional regulatory mechanisms.[26] A dialectic has emerged, so that 'most of the emphasis is on reconceptualizing, on devising new ways of thinking (although largely from established disciplinary bases) and the details of new practice are often left to be worked out in more precise contexts, such as pollution control. The sustainable development discourse remains first and foremost a new concept aimed at altering ways of thinking'.[27] An optimistic view of more radical arguments is that they can offer 'a comprehensive set of values and objectives, an analysis of the operation of the political economy, and a strategy for political change'.[28] A perhaps more realistic view of sustainable development is that for all its apparent staying power, 'no-one can properly put it into operation, let alone define what a sustainable society would look like in terms of political democracy, social structure, norms, economic activity, settlement geography, transport, agriculture, energy use and international relations'.[29]

Calls to counter a charge of calculated vagueness, and to add substance to what is meant by sustainable development, therefore include 'better articulation of the terms, concepts, analytical methods and policy-making principles'.[30] This poses a considerable task for policy makers, administrators, and contributors from across the traditional disciplinary spectrum, as well as the individual citizen, whose way of life, real or aspirational, is at stake. An example of the kind of discussion generated by the term is that which has been encouraged by a European Union consultation paper seeking the establishment of a sustainable development strategy. Although setting neither specific objectives nor specific measures, it illustrates the kind of earnest (and urgent) debate for which the idea of sustainable development should be a catalyst. The paper includes the following:

> Although sustainable development has a very wide scope it should not be seen simply as a convenient way to bundle loosely together a collection of social, economic and environmental problems under a new label. Instead, a comprehensive perspective is needed that ensures that policies – both sectoral and horizontal – are mutually supportive rather than working against one another. Achieving this in practice will oblige policy makers to ensure that economic growth is not bought at the expense of a social divide and environmental deterioration, that social policy underpins rather than undermines economic performance, and that environmental policy is based on sound science and is cost-effective.[31]

The rest of this section explores how extensive levels of agreement as to sustainable development might be. Greater policy integration, as will be seen below, is crucial to this process, but clearly there are many gods to be assuaged in order for genuine progress to be made. Essential elements are therefore addressed, and indications given of the battleground over the kinds of change, social and economic, required in order to safeguard our future. The premise is that the notion of sustainable development can be given substance, as more than an idealistic umbrella term. It offers ground for

---

26 Eg, European Commission, 1996b.
27 Myerson and Rydin, 1996, p 99.
28 Jacobs, 1999, p 30.
29 O'Riordan, 2000, p 41.
30 Lele, 1991, p 618.
31 European Commission, 2001b, para 1.3.

engagement in important debates concerning growth and environmental protection. It is less important that solutions are contested, for that is an inevitable part of the process. The term offers an accepted basis upon which conflicting interests can acknowledge their places in the same (life)boat before exploring common ground as to how to react to the shared predicament. This amounts to a valuable framework for debate.

1.2   The relationship between natural processes and economic growth

The direction of the sustainable development argument is contested by two main groupings, with roots respectively in economic and ecological theory. The contested territory is concerned with perceptions of growth: the risks respectively posed by economic stagnation and environmental degradation. Consideration of instrumentalist perspectives upon sustainable development should therefore take place within the broader context of the ecological foundations underlying the idea of sustainability, and of its compatibility with economic growth. A sound starting point is provided by central ideas propounded in Leopold's 'land ethic' in the middle of the last century. This asserts the primacy of land use in human activities, and the implications for our survival of our exploitation of and dislocation from the natural environment. Ecology was there described as 'the science of relationships'. [32] This is ecology at its most elemental, for if evolution is the haphazard culmination of natural processes that bring life, then ecology is about how those processes maintain their existence. This approximates to fundamental notions underlying ethics, given its premising upon community interdependencies. The organising ecological concept of the land ethic, therefore, is the community of and with the land, and this mandates 'a limitation on freedom of action in the struggle for existence. An ethic, philosophically, is a differentiation of social from anti-social conduct. These are two definitions of the same thing'.[33] Expressing concern, for instance, as to the carrying capacity of ecosystems, as related to population growth, the depletion of non-renewable resources and the degradation of renewable ones, Leopold concluded that there is 'no density relationship that holds for indefinitely wide limits. All gains from density are subject to a law of diminishing returns'.[34] This indeed is the very point which underlies the second principle of thermodynamics.

Attempts to incorporate the perspectives of ecologism require a change of conceptual tools, in terms of how we approach futurity.[35] Indeed these questions raise especial difficulties for common lawyers. Two of the reasons for this are as follows: first, lawyers' preferred discourse tends to be in terms of rights and remedies, and these fit uneasily into many aspects of the sustainability debate, such as the protection of future generations discussed below; secondly, despite many years of regulatory activity, which in the environmental arena might be categorised as being in pursuit of sustainable objectives, as will be seen in Chapters 2 and 3, the basic assumptions of the common law have altered hardly at all. The implementation of an ecological approach such as the land ethic also demands a sea change in the social and economic aspirations of those individuals whom

---

32   Leopold, 1949, p 194.
33   Leopold, 1949, pp 217–18.
34   Leopold, 1949, p 236.
35   See Myerson and Rydin, 1996, pp 119–24.

the common law serves to protect, including 'massive economic reform, tantamount to a virtual revolution in prevailing attitudes and lifestyles'.[36]

Turning then to the parameters of ecologism in this context, a distinction has been drawn between shallow and deep ecology, which originates from Naess.[37] The ethics of a 'deep' ecology focus upon the needs of natural objects. Proponents reject a 'shallow' ecology categorised as the pursuit of human-centred objectives, such as those of improving the health and affluence of people in the developed world, conserving resources for development purposes and replacing with substitutes where there is depletion. The more strenuous deep ecology critiques accordingly reject human-centred approaches that have resulted in a commodified nature. The idea of a relationship marked by a strictly economic self-interest contrasts with the land ethic assertion of wider obligations within the enlarged boundaries of the natural community. There is here more than a concern to forge a critique of anthropocentrism. The near-spiritual roots of such approaches challenge the implications of our rational, experiential, reductionist perceptions of life and its processes, as closed and self-deluding. For just as the mind and body separation expressed in Cartesian dualism foundered upon the need to recognise interaction, so a rejection of mutual natural interdependence implies infinitely fragmented, self-reliant life processes. Critiques of systems of science likewise point to a reductionist approach, whereby complex systems are investigated through isolation into constituent parts. The ecological argument is that the essence of natural systems lies in interdependence, and ecological survival demands a technology that derives from scientific analysis sympathetic to the natural world.[38] More recently the alienating consequences have been expressed by such writers as Suzuki: 'Although we know who we are, where we come from, what we are for, we give that knowledge no weight; our culture tends to deny or conceal that insight, and so we are left alienated and afraid, believing the truth to be "objective" instead of embodied. A world that is raw material, resources, dead matter to be made into things, has nothing sacred in it.'[39]

The area is therefore strewn with an inevitable and at times bewildering diversity of terminology. For instance, one common distinction is the categorisation as between preservationists and conservationists, as respectively adopting approaches that are either independent or dependent upon instrumental notions of human value.[40] Seeking to reconcile such positions, Norton sees conservation and preservation as part of a spectrum of shared values: 'To conserve a resource or the productive potential of a resource-generating system is to use it wisely, with the goal of maintaining its future availability or productivity. To preserve is to protect an ecosystem or a species, to the extent possible, from the disruptions attendant upon it from human use of the species or its habitat.'[41] Moreover, given the scale of the tasks previously discussed, it has been argued that to distinguish ecologism from environmentalism is a logical necessity. Dobson categorises the latter as marked by a managerial approach which lacks a vision of 'fundamental changes in present values or patterns of production or consumption', whereas ecologism

36 Baird Callicott, 1995, p 58.
37 Naess, 1973.
38 Commoner, 1971, p 189.
39 Suzuki, 1997, p 204.
40 Passmore, 1974, p 111.
41 Norton, 1991, p 73.

requires 'radical changes in our relationship with the non-human natural world, and in our mode of social and political life'.[42]

Thus, as will be seen below, and especially in the discussion of risk and cost-benefit analysis in Chapter 8, a charge levied against what is termed environmentalism is that it compromises too readily with competing ideologies.[43] In contrast, ecologism affects more radical priorities. Implicit in a basic norm of 'self-realisation', these, for instance, include interest in smaller, more self-reliant and less mobile population units.[44] It thus asserts that sustainable society 'is substantially about living "in place" and developing an intimacy with it and the people who live there'.[45] From this perspective, ecologism mandates not only an acceptance of greater limitation upon mobility but also a level of protectionism. The former characteristically reflects Leopold's ecological warning, in the context of preserving the wilderness, against 'the expansion of transport without a corresponding growth of perception'.[46] As to the latter, Porritt has argued that the complex patterns of world trade need to be rejected, and suggested that sustainability requires increased self-sufficiency and selective protection of the domestic market.[47] Similarly within a framework of protectionist policies, it has been suggested that, with a view to encouraging a healthy life and hopefully technological advances, use of non-renewable resources must be planned, with support measures (including fiscal policies) to decrease fossil fuel dependence and production of waste.[48] Such approaches are inevitably a long way from fruition. As will be seen in the next chapter, the World Trade Organisation increasingly dominates the relationship between environment and trade. The impacts of global markets, including on domestic production and consumption patterns and practices, are felt everywhere. This can be seen in the travails of the UK livestock industry during 2001's arguably market induced (or exacerbated) crisis of Foot and Mouth disease, but can be particularly severe for vulnerable economies in the developing world.

There are nevertheless opposing views that paradoxically offer a critique of the malleability of ethical arguments underlying sustainability. It has been asserted, for example, that sustainable development amounts to a technical rather than an ethical injunction, and is less convincing than what amounts to the normative concept of optimality, namely the highest welfare of society.[49] This further suggests a wider critique of the perspectives of modern environmentalism. It is argued, for instance, that deep ecological concerns at anthropocentrism derive from a distrust of human nature, and of man as a social and political being, and that the effects of pollution and land use controls can be 'fundamentally disruptive to the entire individual and commercial system'.[50] This brings the argument once again to the core terrain of conflict between natural and economic processes of growth, and the search for common ground.

---

42 Dobson, 2000, p 2.
43 Dobson, 2000, p 7.
44 Naess, 1973.
45 Dobson, 2000, p 91.
46 Leopold, 1949, p 269.
47 Porritt, 1984, p 135.
48 See Daly and Cobb, 1989, pp 259–64.
49 Beckerman, 1995, pp 126–29.
50 Smith, 1974, p 8.

1.3 Sustainable development and policy integration

A key issue in achieving progress is to determine whether there are acceptable bases for reconciling the conflicting priorities. Two fundamentally linked areas of debate and re-evaluation emerge: not only the inimical nature of notions of growth and sustainability, but also the question of integration of environmental policy into the wider field of decision making. The potential contribution of sustainable development lies in two directions. First, it offers a foundation for mandating the integration of environmental and economic considerations into decision making. Secondly it offers a means of ensuring that developmental costs are internalised.[51] Despite the problems of definition, therefore, 'it must mean that in every developmental decision the environmental costs are internalised. This will require that laws be modified to include environmental externalities and establish concrete management criteria against which to judge the sustainability of each project'.[52]

The movement within the European Union towards greater integration exemplifies the problems encountered in 'greening' policies more broadly. Since 1992 there has been a Treaty requirement to integrate environmental policies across policy making processes, now updated under the Treaty of Amsterdam.[53] Integration is accordingly expressed as a general objective, within Article 6: 'Environmental protection requirements must be integrated into the definition and implementation of the Community policies and activities referred to in Article 3, in particular with a view to promoting sustainable development.' The European Commission has subsequently instigated the production of sectoral reports concerning integration of environmental factors into policy making. These cover in particular transport, energy, agriculture and regional policy.[54] A draft Sixth Environment Action Programme proposes taking this forward in explicit ways, as in tackling climate change: for example, by shifting energy production away from fossil fuels (especially coal and oil), and towards renewable energy resources and combined heat and power stations (respectively to produce 12% and 18% of electricity by 2010), by reducing nitrous oxide and methane emissions in agriculture, and (somewhat vaguer) inducing 'structural changes' in the transport sector.[55]

Yet growth is the essential problematic area of the green debate, and must dominate integration arguments. Norton states that 'the problem of growth, and of devising a national response to it, represents the greatest challenge of modern environmentalism'.[56] The essential dilemma concerns the growth imperative upon which all modern economies depend. It may be that the United States produces 25% of world carbon dioxide emissions with 7% of the population, but pollution is but one incident of a global marketplace where transnational frontiers mean little. Signs of a US economic downturn at about the time of the 2001 inauguration of President George W Bush have led to widespread concerns in Europe and elsewhere among the developed economies. The

---

51 See Smith, 1995.

52 Hodas, 1998, p 6.

53 OJ C340/42, 10 November, 1997a.

54 Eg, European Commission, 2000b; European Commission, 2001a, para 2.2.

55 European Commission, 2001a, para 3.3.

56 Norton, 1991, p 119.

social consequences of economic recession are extremely painful (especially for those already disadvantaged) and political responses tend to be economics based and market led. More combative ecological theorists focus their concerns upon the dilution through political discourse of behaviour regarded as sustainable. Green politics essentially differs from conventional approaches in its interpretation of the nature of scarcity, as being 'rooted in the biophysical realities of a finite planet, ruled and limited by entropy and ecology'.[57] It demands changed lifestyles through alternative patterns of resource use, fundamental to which is respect for the carrying capacities of natural processes. It thus argues for the necessity to achieve 'a comprehensive revision of policies and practices that perpetuate growth in material consumption and in population ... (and) a rapid, drastic increase in the efficiency with which materials and energy are used'.[58] This requires a revision of the dominance of such indices as gross national product in policy debate, along with traditional measures of wealth, efficiency and cost. Limits to growth are accordingly a fundamental tenet, in order to reduce the external costs imposed by our industrial society, expressed in the 'belief that quantitative demand must be *reduced*, not expanded'.[59]

Yet changed paradigms also raise fundamental issues of justice.[60] In particular it has been pointed out that environmental concerns can threaten social justice, for the argument for 'a "no-growth" or "steady-state" economy ... in its articulation, raises questions of equality and distribution'.[61] Indeed much of the context of the international sustainable development process commenced at Rio in 1992, and, as discussed in the next chapter, lay in a mutual recognition of the comparative vulnerability of the developing world to the consequences of more effective international environmental measures.[62]

That there are limits to growth is being whispered in certain political quarters. At a regional level, the European Commission is seeking to progress the debate beyond the lip service to which the definitional problems discussed above otherwise point. Thus its proposed Sixth Environment Action Programme, fixing upon priority areas for action, headlines 'The Sustainable Use of Natural Resources and Management of Wastes'. The expressed objective is to ensure that consumption of renewable and non-renewable resources and the associated impacts do not exceed the carrying capacity of the environment and to achieve a decoupling of resource use from economic growth through significantly improved resource efficiency, dematerialisation of the economy, and waste prevention.[63] Inevitably the criticism can be raised that as yet there are few signs of progress in significant areas, such as carbon taxation and sustainable transport systems. Further, optimism should perhaps be moderated in view of the distinctly conservative view of the European Commission concerning its proposals to secure protection against climate change: 'The prevention of climate change does not have to mean a reduction in growth or prosperity levels. Rather, it means reshaping the economy so that emissions are

---

57 Irvine and Ponton, 1988, p 26.
58 Meadows, Meadows and Randers, 1992, p 20.
59 Porritt, 1984, p 136.
60 See Commoner, 1971.
61 Smith, 1974, p 13.
62 Bunyard and Morgan-Grenville, 1987, pp 246–76.
63 European Commission, 2001a, para 6.1.2.

decoupled from economic growth. Climate change is a powerful force for technological innovation and higher economic efficiency.'[64]

The value of 'sustainable' initiatives such as these appears to lie in the willingness of the powerful European trading block to attempt to devise more sustainable policies, and in the resulting shifts in the terms of debate. This in turn demands the kind of long term, inclusive perspectives akin to those demanded by ecological approaches. If contested areas are to be resolved, then it is essential that long term interests of future generations are asserted and accorded protection. It is to this aspect that the argument now turns.

2 A LEGAL BASIS FOR THE PROTECTION OF FUTURE GENERATIONS

2.1 Recognising intergenerational equity

As the chapter head indicates, reparations for misfortune in the Erewhon society depicted by Samuel Butler would be levied upon victims. This comic parable on the limitations in our social behaviour is in one respect nearly imitated by reality. For a similar paradox manifestly applies in the continuing aversion to factoring future generational interests into our own law and policy making processes. As will be seen below, the principle of intergenerational equity is an established ethical approach. The argument is however concerned with legal protection. It discusses whether there are grounds for asserting that a normative scheme exists, and whether an extension of traditional trust doctrine is appropriate. At each stage, it is necessary to confront the question of whether it can be said that there can be rights, and correlative obligations, to a certain quality of environment.

The notion of sustainable development is marked by its close connection with the idea of inter- as well as intragenerational equity. The latter is concerned with equitable allocation in the present. Moreover, distribution questions should arise in discussions both within and across jurisdictions. Yet a temporal aspect is central to the concept of sustainability. It has been said that sustainable development is 'inherently intergenerational'.[65] Developed economies in particular have been driven by an accelerating level of depletion of finite resources, with the consequence that 'benefits are largely distributed in the present and the risks for the most part displaced to the future'.[66] In deploying intergenerational obligations in the cause of sustainable development, intergenerational equity is a useful conceptual vehicle for seeking to unlock community responses to environmental threats.[67]

---

64 European Commission, 2001a, para 3.1.
65 Weiss, 2000, p 369.
66 Rosenbaum, 1991, p 164.
67 Redgwell, 1999, p 184.

Such ideas have the potential to extend beyond the individualism and market orientation of liberal theories in seeking to address core concerns of sustainable living. These include the following: first, an intensification in global ecological interdependence; secondly, an historic inequality of resource use; and thirdly, a growing pressure on limits in ecological carrying capacity.[68] The focus for debate has therefore been greatly broadened beyond long-standing (and likewise suspect) theories of intragenerational mutuality. Any 'trickle down' benefit to those disadvantaged as wealth increases has a tendency to indefinite delay and, more crudely still, is vulnerable to subsequent removal. Intragenerational inequality poses questions for those who seek sustainable solutions post-Rio, and will be returned to in the next chapter. Otherwise, the strength of commitment to sustainable development may ultimately depend upon the coherence of arguments for empowering a protection of the interests of future generations.

The notion of protecting unborn generations is an ethical one, and instances of its expression in terms of law have thus far been limited both in scope and purpose. Weiss optimistically suggests the emergence of a fundamental norm 'concerning our relationship with present, past and future generations. Until recently, international law has addressed intertemporal issues mainly by relating the present to the past. Increasingly, intertemporal issues relate the present to the future, as in economic development, environmental and natural resource protection, and cultural heritage issues'.[69] This can perhaps be seen in the explicit recognition of future generations gradually being introduced into international treaties, as will be seen in the next chapter. The emergence of temporal principles in international law has been described as a process of 'creeping intergenerationalisation'.[70]

Numerous national jurisdictions make provision in their constitutional enactments, although it is debatable how far even then substantive norms are sufficiently robust to fix policy makers with obligations of an enforceable nature. The most notable concrete application remains a judgment of the Philippine Supreme Court.[71] The case of *Minors Oposa* arose out of a challenge to the granting of logging licences, and applicants purported to act as representatives of both present and future generations.[72] The action had been based upon a constitutional provision, requiring the State 'to protect and advance the right of the people to a balanced and healthful ecology in accord with the rhythm and harmony of nature'.[73] The applicants were successful on an interlocutory appeal against a striking out on the basis that there was no cause of action. The Supreme Court accepted the existence of an 'obligation to ensure the protection of that right for the generations to come'.[74] Subsequently, in the International Court of Justice, Judge Weeramantry has argued for fuller recognition, even divining that 'the rights of future generations have passed the stage when they were merely an embryonic right struggling for recognition. They have woven themselves into international law through major

---

68 See Langhelle, 2000, especially pp 306–10.
69 Weiss, 2000, p 369.
70 Redgwell, 1999, p 126.
71 See Allen, 1994.
72 *Minors Oposa v Secretary of the Department of Environment and Natural Resources* (1994) 33 ILM173.
73 Philippines Constitution 1987, Art II.
74 (1994) 33 ILM 173, 185.

treaties, through juristic opinion and through general principles of law recognized by civilized nations'.[75]

The appearance of such concerns in international law reflects a heightened global awareness of the need to create structures to achieve a balance between the interests of present and future generations. However, whilst it has been argued that the idea of intergenerational equity should be viewed as especially significant to further development towards sustainable development under international law, little progress has been made towards a recognition of binding obligations.[76] Further progress toward transforming any moral obligations into enforceable norms remains problematic. In order to address this, Weiss has pioneered arguments to the effect that principles of intergenerational equity are 'potentially unifying norms to counter alienation associated with fragmentation'.[77] The underlying premise is that each generation is both a custodian of the planet for future generations and a beneficiary of its fruits. Thus all States have an obligation to ensure that 'each generation must pass the planet on in no worse condition than it received it and provide equitable access to its resources and benefits'.[78]

In order to encourage movements toward enforceable intergenerational obligations, Weiss has proposed a set of normative principles, which rely upon the conservation respectively of options, of quality, and of access.[79] The conservation of future options accordingly emphasises diversity of the resource base. This may allow for the creation of substitutes, just as trade-offs are seen as inevitable in determining whether a generation is conserving the quality of the environment. Development of these principles is stated to be informed by four criteria. First, there should be equality among generations, so as neither to exploit resources to the exclusion of future generations nor to impose unreasonable burdens upon the present; secondly, the generations must be accorded the flexibility to achieve their goals according to their own values; thirdly, the principles should be generally shared across cultures within different political and economic systems; and, fourthly, there should be reasonable clarity as to application of principles in foreseeable situations. Duties imposed under the above would need to be sufficiently wide ranging so as to embrace the conservation of resources, ensuring equitable use, avoiding adverse impacts, preventing disasters, minimising damage, providing emergency assistance, and compensating for environmental harm: with resource management plans operating 'on the assumption that resources should be conserved and managed on a sustainable basis unless there are compelling reasons not to do so'.[80] The essence therefore is that development needs would only be accepted conditionally upon a balancing process requiring 'the development of predictive indices of resource diversity and resource quality, establishment of baseline measures, and an improved capacity to predict technological change'.[81]

---

75 *Advisory Opinion on the Legality of the Threat or Use of Nuclear Weapons* (1996) 35 ILM 809, 888 (dissenting opinion).
76 Redgwell, 1999, p 127.
77 Weiss, 2000, p 370.
78 Weiss, 1989, p 24.
79 Weiss, 1989, p 87.
80 Weiss, 1989, p 51.
81 Weiss, 1989, p 43.

Yet whilst the needs of future generations are yet to be fully articulated in legal terms, an expression in terms of the notion of intergenerational equity has recognisable analogies with established notions of trust. It may come to be interpreted most effectively through existing trust doctrine, along lines considered below.

2.2 Notions of trust

The idea of the 'trust' is essentially an equitable mechanism, whereby legal and beneficial entitlements are maintained as recognisably separate. Resulting obligations placed upon the trustee, as legal titleholder, include a strict obligation to deal with trust property in accordance with the terms of the trust, for the benefit of defined persons, purposes or objects. Fiduciary duties placed upon trustees expose them to potential liability to the beneficiaries for breach, and that liability may bind the trust property.[82] Trust approaches have the advantage of making available such notion of fiduciary obligation towards future generations. Thus, in pursuit of a trust-based formulation, Redgwell suggests that the approach of the Philippine Supreme Court in *Minors Oposa* 'may lead to the imprinting of an *inter vivos* trust on the present generation'.[83] This amounts to a duty based upon an idea of stewardship, namely 'to take care of land and preserve it for the sake of the future, not waste and destroy it'.[84] The impact on property owners would be to deny 'any valid claim to degrade, unsustainably consume, or destroy resources in which future persons have an important stake'.[85] The profound implications of this are further considered in Chapter 3.

There is perhaps an analogy with the public trust notion in the United States. This arguably common law notion, with roots in Roman law, has made some headway in American jurisprudence.[86] Its essence lies in the assertion that judicial protection may be accorded in the wider public interest to the safeguarding of natural resources from degradation.[87] Jurisprudentially, the notion is a house with many mansions. Where an interest is recognised, it may be used to limit governmental action or to restrict the range of actions normally available under private property rules. A thin skein of principle has thus far emerged in a series of judicial pronouncements, defended by Sax on the basis of an assertion of judicial restraint upon 'potential abuses' of democratic processes.[88] This justification begs questions of the effectiveness of democratic controls, but the public trust idea is not explored further here. It should however be noted that its inchoate nature leads to valid questions as to its relationship with the existence of explicit regulatory powers which are vested in the environmental interest. Moreover, it is unclear what its relationship might be with present administrative law arguments on behalf of those who endeavour to persuade the courts of the standing of individuals and groups to represent

---

82 Oakley, 1996, pp 14–17.
83 Redgwell, 1999, p 93.
84 McGregor, 1999, p 434.
85 McGregor, 1999, p 435.
86 Sax, 1970.
87 Eg, *National Audubon Society v Superior Court*, 658 P 2d 709, 732 (Cal 1983).
88 Sax, 1970, pp 521–23.

the general interest themselves.[89] Besides, such proactivity is unlikely to commend itself to what might be termed, subject to recent developments discussed in Chapter 9, an English judiciary by culture and tradition constitutionally repressed.

Yet an advantage of a public trust is that it can arise without express declaration. Without going so far, but still in the context of intergenerational equity, Redgwell suggests two specific trust mechanisms that might be worth pursuing: the charitable trust and the statutory trust. Weiss's notion of the 'planetary trust' appears to draw implicitly upon the former concept, the value of which lies in its relationship with purposes. It avoids limitations inherent in ordinary trust doctrine, which demand certainty of objects, including as to the class of beneficiaries, as well as temporal limits (as under the rule against perpetuities). The notion of charitable trust also utilises the doctrine of *cy près* in the event of a failure of purposes, thereby saving the trust. Charitable trusts are expressed in terms of purposes related to community benefit and are 'an inherently more democratic and public-spirited mechanism than the private trust, and less exclusionary in scope'.[90] Environmental objects have come within the categories of acceptable charitable purposes,[91] under either educational purposes or the residual category of purposes for the benefit of the community. The anthropocentric nature of the endeavour remains essential. Whilst, for instance, trusts for the purposes of humane treatment of other species may be acceptable on grounds of the uplifting effect upon mankind,[92] the tendency has been to subject this to a further requirement, whereby the protection accorded must be of human utility value.[93] Whilst this approach might be philosophically well rooted, including within Kant and otherwise, it contrasts with more expansive views elsewhere, where it appears that a specific concern with the protection of bio-diversity may prove acceptable.[94] A further restriction is that the pursuit of political objects – broadly construed as to bring about law reform – may result in a failure of the public benefit requirement.[95]

The alternative vehicle for trust doctrine referred to above is that of statutory trust funding.[96] Such a trust can be established in the public interest to facilitate an identified environmental interest, or in the event of permitted development then at least to provide equivalent protection. Illustrations of compensatory trust funds include those US federal statutory clean-up arrangements, under Superfund provisions, for sites contaminated by hazardous waste,[97] as well as the Oil Spill Liability Trust Fund, for oil spills.[98] In each

---

89 Lazarus, 1986.
90 Redgwell, 1999, p 14.
91 Originating under the 1601 Statute of Elizabeth.
92 *In Re Wedgwood* [1915] 1 Ch 113.
93 *Re Grove-Grady* [1929] 1 Ch 557.
94 See Redgwell, 1999, p 18, citing *Attorney-General (NSW) v Sawtell* [1978] 2 NSWLR 200.
95 See *National Anti-Vivisection Society v Inland Revenue Commissioners* [1948] AC 31; *McGovern v Attorney-General* [1982] Ch 321.
96 See Redgwell, 1999, Chapter 2.
97 Comprehensive Environmental Response, Compensation and Liability Act 1980, Superfund Amendment and Reauthorization Act 1986.
98 Oil Pollution Act 1990; see also the more limited terms of the Brussels Convention on the Establishment of an International Fund for Compensation for Oil Pollution Damage (1972) 11 ILM 284, discussed by Birnie and Boyle, 1992, pp 292–97.

case, revenues derive *inter alia* from taxation on oil products. There is some comparability in Europe with the Lugano Convention on Civil Liability, which would require that 'operators conducting a dangerous activity on its territory be required to participate in a financial security scheme or have and maintain a financial guarantee up to a certain limit, of such type and terms as specified by internal law, to cover the liability under this Convention'.[99] A comparable idea was first proposed by the European Commission in its review of civil liability arrangements in the context of environmental damage. It had tentatively proposed 'joint compensation schemes to cover the costs of environmental restoration. This would enable responsibility for costs to be shared fairly within the economic sector most closely connected to the presumed source of the damage'.[100] In contrast, in the most recent Commission white paper, the proposal appears to have been put to one side. Instead, financial security appears to depend on the encouragement of the insurance industry into the market, supported by tight formulations of what constitutes environmental damage, and the development of qualitative and quantitative criteria to improve the evaluation of risk.[101] Otherwise the Commission confines itself to an oblique reference to 'insurance being one of the possible ways of having financial security, alongside, among others, bank guarantees, internal reserves or sector-wise pooling systems'.[102] The large scale withdrawal of the insurance industry from this area of the public liability market remains notoriously intractable.[103] It is, moreover, doubtful whether continuing problems of non-insurability may be satisfactorily resolved by such stratagems as the rejection of retrospective liability, allowing a specific defence based upon regulatory compliance, and retaining a fault liability requirement where 'significant' damage to bio-diversity arises from non-dangerous activities.[104]

Aside from the practicalities of funding constraint, numerous advantages can be claimed for exploring the use of trust doctrine. It offers, first, an intertemporal approach; secondly, an acknowledgment of the need to recognise present standing on behalf of future generations; and, finally, a potential for institutional and financial mechanisms for protecting future concerns. Paradoxically, therefore, its utility may now become as adaptable in the cause of environmental protection as it has traditionally been in the more worldly pursuit of preserving private wealth. According to Gray, the trust 'is philosophically and logically compatible with principles of conservation of biological diversity and ecological integrity, sustainable use and waste minimization, proper resource valuation, social equity, community participation, and intergenerational equity'.[105] Nevertheless, such views have attracted powerful opposition. Therefore, before investigating whether any broader rights-based approach to the protection of future generations might succeed, it is necessary to consider a range of critiques of such a project.

---

99 Council of Europe, 1993.
100 European Commission, 1993b, para 4.2.
101 European Commission, 2000b, para 4.9.
102 European Commission, 2000b, p 23.
103 Cf Faure and Grimeaud, 2000.
104 European Commission, 2000b, paras 4.1–4.3, 4.51.
105 Gray, 1996a, p 235.

2.3   Questioning legal protection of the unborn

Main critiques of the effort to accord legal protection tend to focus upon divergent ethical and even sociobiological rationales. Deriving little support from ethical foundations, sociobiological perspectives focus upon the idea that the group approach is inappropriate. This involves a rejection of the possibility of incorporating group values, and a reassertion of individualistic notions. Applying neo-Darwinian argument, it can be asserted that the only justification for caring about future generations lies in the field of biology, for 'evolution has hard-wired our brains so that we have no choice but to care about future generations ... albeit in a strictly circumscribed sense'.[106] The complexities of human culture therefore tend to reinforce biology, that is, in favour of a predisposition at best to care for individuals depending upon 'how closely we perceive the individual of concern to be related to us'.[107] However unethical the argument, a practical weakness lies in its inability to accommodate the social interreliances to which modern evolutionists for the most part subscribe.[108]

The ethical rationale is more considerable, precisely because it accepts, indeed insists upon, the notion of moral obligation to future generations.[109] Attfield speaks of a 'tradition of stewardship' without necessary reference to future generations, and which simply 'requires humans to care for the earth on which they live'.[110] D'Amato also disconnects the putative beneficiaries, arguing that 'we should cultivate our natural sense of obligation not to act wastefully or wantonly even when we cannot calculate how such acts would make any present or future persons worse off'.[111] Gaba sees rights in this context as 'futile', opting for an ethical protection of 'moral subjects'.[112] The reasons offered are that not only are rights not absolute, but there is no consensus as to the content of relevant rights and obligations, beyond the idea of preserving humanity as a whole.[113] Norton suggests that our obligations to future generations are owed not to individuals. Instead, as regards the future, 'we are morally required to undertake stabilising actions ... just as we are indebted to our forefathers, not individually but collectively, for our cultural heritage; these obligations derive from faith in the value of the human struggle, the axiom of future value'.[114] Such an ethical perspective is reflected in Sagoff's view that the present generation is under a moral obligation to our present environmental ideals, which will be of benefit to future generations.[115]

A further problem concerns how many generations into the future should be considered. However termed, there remains a problem in perception of the future, and such unpredictability may defeat attempts at projection. There is, for instance, a utilitarian

---

106 Barresi, 1997, p 70.
107 Barresi, 1997, p 75.
108 Dawkins, 1989, Chapter 12.
109 Feinberg, 1980, p 181.
110 Attfield, 1983, p 194.
111 D'Amato, 1990, p 198.
112 Gaba, 1999, p 279.
113 Gaba, 1999, pp 261–62.
114 Norton, 1991, p 218.
115 Sagoff, 1988, pp 61–63.

argument to the effect that the evaluation of the impact of distant events upon present behaviour should be negligible.[116] Rawls' analysis of duties to the future suggests a 'motivational assumption', whereby the present generation can accept looking to the interests of the two generations to come.[117] Even where such assertions require revision in the light of developing understanding of threats to sustainability, just as the future cannot exhibit a current preference, future needs are themselves uncertain. For instance, there is uncertainty in the sense of future adaptive preferences, which arguably means that future generations will be programmed to accept the world that they inherit.[118] Gaba concludes that mankind can 'make "investment" decisions that alter the environment, in effect providing other forms of wealth to our descendants, and that we are therefore free to consume existing resources'.[119] Without going so far, Passmore concludes that our obligations are limited, in that 'we ought to try to improve the world so that we shall be able to hand it over to our immediate successors in a better condition, and that is all'.[120]

It may furthermore be argued that any expression of a moral duty to future generations in terms of rights is inimical to the individualism which pervades traditional liberal notions of rights.[121] Moreover, the extension of notions of individual rights, especially under Western legal systems, as under contractarian theory, may founder upon problems of competency at an intergenerational level. Barresi suggests that individuals in the present generation are interested in ensuring use on a sustainable basis, but only to ensure 'that his or her descendants will have an appropriate amount of natural and cultural resources'.[122] In contrast, notions of rights and duties at an intragenerational level are understandable within recognised legal conceptions and jurisdictions. A major obstacle lies therefore in the so-called identity problem: the lack of identifiable, existing, individuals as rights-holders. For instance, the very existence and composition of future generations is necessarily contingent.[123]

Yet whilst accepting that rights are at best conditional, it is possible to assert a revised liberal theory, to the effect that duties arise out of present intentions to bring future generations into being. Ackerman would therefore impose a present obligation to behave 'in a way which will withstand the inevitable questions that the young will raise about their upbringing' ('because I say so' is presumably insufficient in this instance).[124] He goes on to express this in terms of trusteeship, to the extent that each generation must not 'deplete the per capita share of capital available to the next'.[125] Barry asserts as a minimum 'the notion that those alive at any time are custodians rather than owners of the planet, and ought to pass it on in at least no worse shape than they found it in'.[126] Rawls' just savings principle imposes obligations on each generation to preserve more than

---

116 See Moore, 1959, pp 152–54.

117 Rawls, 1973, p 128.

118 Gaba, 1999, p 265.

119 Gaba, 1999, p 287.

120 Passmore, 1974, p 91.

121 See Norton, 1982, pp 335–36.

122 Barresi, 1997, p 79.

123 Parfit, 1983.

124 Ackerman, 1980, p 222.

125 Ackerman, 1980, p 227.

126 Barry, 1977, p 284.

established institutions and other gains of culture and civilisation, adding 'in each period of time a suitable amount of real capital accumulation'.[127] Yet in assuming conditions of 'moderate scarcity',[128] the just savings principle does not appear to pay much regard to the severity of environmental threats with which the global community is now faced (although it has been pointed out that *A Theory of Justice* predated the seminal Stockholm conference, discussed in the next chapter).[129] Such modern contributions therefore contain little specificity concerning what should be put aside. There is even some analogy with traditional Lockean analysis. On its face, as seen in Chapter 3, Locke's civil society was founded upon an original annexation of land for private use. Yet this was premised upon there being 'land enough in the world to suffice double the inhabitants'.[130] Moreover, his sufficiency condition suggests a forerunner of a sustainable argument, in that whilst society might appear to enable a 'dishonest' man 'to carve himself too much, or take more than he needed', there was likewise no harm in another accessing part of this 'where there is enough'.[131] Despite this somewhat anarchical solution, Lockean standards retain their influence, as for instance in a modern application, whereby present physical resource use should be limited to as far as technology allows for 'recycling or depletion of such resources without net loss in their output capacity'.[132]

2.4   Obligations and rights discourse

It is accordingly difficult to find a future voice, despite wide recognition of threats to biological diversity and climate, risks posed by artificial chemicals and accumulations of wastes, and (though most scientists would probably not agree, next, perhaps) consequences of developments in biological science. Weiss challenges the above critiques, largely on the basis of what she sees as planetary rights which necessarily 'inhere to all generations. There is no theoretical basis for limiting such rights to immediately successive generations; indeed to do so would in some cases offer little or no protection to more distant future generations'.[133] She accepts that prediction is near impossible, 'either because their values, and hence their preferences, will change over time, or because technological developments may change the options available to them upon which they will base their preferences. The proposed principles try at a minimum to ensure a reasonably secure and flexible natural and cultural resource base for future generations and a reasonably decent and healthy human environment for the present generation'.[134] Therefore, a principle of equitable access seeks to address the above uncertainties by arguing the value-neutrality of intergenerational equity, thereby preserving sufficient in trust to enable later generational values, similarly constrained by their own future, to be applied.

---

127 Rawls, 1973, p 285.
128 Rawls, 1973, pp 127–29.
129 Redgwell, 1999, p 107.
130 Locke, 1690, 1924 edn, Chapter 5, para 36.
131 Locke, 1690, 1924 edn, Chapter 5, paras 51, 32.
132 Kavka, 1978, p 201.
133 Weiss, 1989, p 97.
134 Weiss, 1989, p 39.

Considering briefly how far a rights discourse can be applied,[135] given the interrelationships explored above, the notion of a right must for this purpose accord with the idea of Hohfeld's claim-rights as correlative to duties.[136] Yet questions arise as to whether it makes sense to speak of a right at all. Indeed, if so, it is unclear on what basis such right might be enforceable. Conceptual limitations also remain: for instance, discussion in terms of rights inevitably tends toward anthropocentrism.[137] In the somewhat narrower discussion of trust mechanisms, Matthews' trenchant analysis concludes that these 'did not come into existence because animals, or trees in California, complained to the Chancellor that property given to trustees for their benefit was being misapplied. They were called into existence because *people* complained'.[138] Moreover, rights do not exist *in vacuo*, and tensions typically arise between those that are available, instances of which are discussed in Chapter 3.

The ascribing of rights to future generations as set out above therefore remains problematic. Indeed, accepting the doubtful nature of the application of a principle of intergenerational equity as a matter of law, Redgwell notes that 'it is of critical importance to develop a clear definition. Is it a substantive right(s) or merely an interest to be taken into account? Is it a principle to influence decision makers in setting and applying standards, or does it extend to liability for breach of substantive trust obligations? If substantive obligations can be breached, what is the remedy?'[139] Her conclusion is that the best that intergenerational equity can offer is as a principle guiding developing norms of international law. For the present, therefore, the inchoate idea of environmental rights contrasts with human rights provisions, discussion of which is deferred until Chapter 9, but which are 'imbedded much more deeply in western culture and legal traditions'.[140] Merrills categorises future generations as shadowy rights-holders, and counsels a concentration on the present, as to both claims and moral responsibilities 'which may of course include responsibilities in respect of future generations'.[141] The solution offered by Weiss is founded on the distinctly awkward notion of group entitlement. In so far as the idea underlying intergenerational trusts is the public good, analogous, as discussed above, to the inherent flexibility of the charitable trust, this suggests rights notwithstanding a lack of beneficiaries. In this way, she proposes that her idea of planetary rights suggests not individuals but 'generational rights, which can only be usefully conceived at a group level'.[142]

If such an approach once again suggests trust-based solutions, then the difficulty in identifying members of future generations as rights-holding beneficiaries of sustainability is compounded by problems in recognising representative competence or agency.[143] This might be resolved by legal measures to secure the appointment of trustees or

---

135 See, generally, Waldron, 1984, pp 1–20.
136 Hohfeld, 1919.
137 Cf Redgwell, 1996.
138 Matthews, 1996, p 1; see Redgwell, 1999, p 12.
139 Redgwell, 1999, p 143.
140 Barresi, 1997, p 87.
141 Merrills, 1996, p 33.
142 Weiss, 1989, p 96.
143 Merrills, 1996, pp 32–33.

ombudsmen, to represent the group, rather than indeterminate individuals.[144] An ombudsman in particular would require the institution of a public appointment. In view of the obstacles to representation, an ombudsman must be both independent and empowered to act beyond mere reliance upon informal, advisory processes, and must have powers to bring enforcement proceedings.[145] Similar formal appointment of trustees should be considered, for the more implicit arrangements as under, for instance, public trust doctrine are unlikely to emerge. Stone has likewise contemplated an extended approach to representation of the environmental interest that is more broadly non-anthropocentric.[146] Drawing comparisons with what has been achieved with the law affecting persons lacking capacity, as also artificial corporations, he argues for the recognition of 'rights' in grant to the natural environment. For the purposes of legal arrangements for enforcement, he proposes the creation of a form of guardianship by court order. In the context of domestic administrative challenge, this approach has been echoed by Alder. In order to overcome a personal interest requirement, which otherwise tends to deflect attention away from the environmental interest, he suggests the representation of the environmental interest by an agent. This would allow the court to focus on 'the real issue of identifying and scoping the environmental claim rather than upon the characteristics of the human surrogate'.[147] There is some international comparability with a proposal endorsed by the Brundtland Commission's Group of Experts.[148] Yet to date no institutional apparatus has emerged. It cannot be said that the creation under the Rio process of the Commission on Sustainable Development, referred to in the next chapter, largely in a reporting and monitoring role, has met this objective.

There are thus significant obstacles in the way of formalising a role for future generations, whether in legislative or administrative processes. Perhaps a realistic objective would be to press for a formally recognised custodianship, which may yet emerge through the kind of environmental tribunal referred to in later chapters. With a structure in place, arguments might then move on towards issues of empowerment and enforcement.

3 DISCOUNT CONCEPTS AND SUSTAINABILITY

The final section of this chapter therefore concerns the methods of securing a balance between the demands for growth and the need for sustainability. A feature of much of the above discussion has been the tendency in the present to discount future needs. Yet sustainability is about the threat to the survival of humankind, rather than the need gradually to accommodate lifestyles to changed resources. Back in 1972, a seminal report to the Club of Rome's *Project on the Predicament of Mankind* expressed the threat in terms of a time disparity masking the growing crisis. Thus, more immediately felt positive

---

144 See, eg, Sands, 1989, p 394.
145 Allen, 1994, p 740.
146 Stone, 1972.
147 Alder, 1998, p 187.
148 See Munro and Lammers, 1987.

feedback loops (which produce growth of industrial capital, and population, exponentially) are constrained only in the long term by negative feedback loops (pollution, depletion of non-renewable resources, famine).[149] The conclusion was that whilst the crisis continues to be delayed, its proportions upon arrival will be such that it may be too late to take any effective protective action.

The extent of the willingness of the present generation(s) to forgo immediate economic benefits, and to introduce mechanisms aimed at securing environmental benefit into the future, is a fundamental question. Simple as this seems, it creates serious difficulties, many of which are explored in subsequent chapters. For instance, while the formal decision as to a fifth terminal at London's Heathrow Airport is awaited, following a uniquely lengthy planning inquiry, it now seems widely accepted that for reasons of market position and responding to (what amounts to heavily subsidised) customer demand, Heathrow must also have a third runway.[150] Any counter to the ruling social and economic paradigm therefore demands that, before we can even agree on more sustainable mechanisms, society needs to be able to formulate with greater clarity what it is that it wants.

3.1 Problems of value

On a functional level, sustainability needs to find a voice as a tool of policy. The factoring in of a wider scale of values by reference to sustainable development requires agreement as to what the content of reformed indicators should be. This will inevitably involve a wide rejection of the dominance of producer and consumer values that persist today. It inevitably makes arriving at a workable classification more difficult. Yet it has been pointed out that 'development' does not simply mean growth, for 'most advocates of sustainable development include sociopolitical objectives in their view of "development" – it is held to mean more than mere continued or accelerated economic growth. So justice is a part of the content of "sustainable development" as a social, economic and political strategy'.[151] Old dogmas can be challenged, so that goals, instead of being 'based on quantitative measures of gross national product ... should be ecologically centred and qualitative'.[152] Sustainability has accordingly been defined as natural value, that is, the value of things created by natural processes rather than artificial ones. But any theory based upon natural resources must address issues of both recognised 'irreplaceability' and also some limited form of discounting of future needs. What has been termed a green theory of value must therefore seek to link value 'to some naturally occurring properties of the objects themselves'.[153]

Alternative approaches are available. Different economic perceptions can be somewhat crudely distinguished, as between so-called 'strong' and 'weak' versions of sustainable development. The underlying idea mirrors the deep and shallow approaches to ecology referred to previously. The emphasis of strong sustainability is upon the

---

149 Meadows, Meadows, Randers and Behrens, 1972, pp 156–57.
150 (2001) *The Guardian*, 25 June.
151 Benton, 1997, p 23.
152 Wall, 1994, p 126.
153 Goodin, 1992, pp 69–73.

maintenance of natural capital. It regards the environment as inviolable, or near-inviolable. This places emphasis upon maximum sustainable yield, with the precautionary protection of ecosystems, and a commitment to holding within the carrying capacities of the biosphere. Given a world of finite resources and without limitless capacities such as to absorb the waste generated, it challenges the consumption imperative consequent upon industrialisation.[154] This is far removed from traditional notions of valuation, and also contrasts with weaker sustainability notions, which broadly look to preserve what is termed critical natural capital. In accounting for total capital stock, this allows, for instance, for substitution between the natural and human-made capital. By its nature it is accordingly more amenable to the idea of trade-off of environmental costs against economic benefits of development.

The task is to seek a realistic accommodation between the disjunctive views outlined above. It does seem possible to endorse a qualitative evaluation process which is resistant to purely exploitative resource valuations but still pays heed to the 'real' world. Norton supports an environmental approach to resource use as a two-stage process 'which first determines constraints to natural scientific models of ecological communities and only then proceeds to apply economic reasoning'.[155] Also searching for a convergence, Benton describes a secular point of view, which refuses to evaluate nature separately from 'human cultural practices through which value is assigned'.[156] Such an approach therefore asserts that it is necessary to enter into a 'practical engagement with the world we inhabit', for of greatest value is 'the outcome (both intended and unintended) of past generations of human interaction with the biological and physical environment'.[157]

A pragmatic policy option may be to seek a convergence between growth and environmental protection through forms of 'ecological modernisation', which include the impact of future innovation.[158] Thus, just as humankind needs to reinvent itself, and new ways of city (and rural) living need to be found, so too there are positive signs that growth may be achievable. This would extend to the development of products which enable travel and trade without the devastating effects of carbon dioxide emissions.[159] Moreover, there is a growing political consensus in favour of environmental protection mechanisms encouraging employment. For instance, the European Commission is seeking strategies to ensure that environmental and employment policies are mutually beneficial, as well as emphasising competitiveness through energy-saving technologies and environmentally sound products and services.[160] Closer to an optimistic highest common denominator approach, it has even been argued that market competition leads to a general uplift in environmental standards, as 'determined by the country with the most stringent pollution control standards' with an economy dependent upon 'high-value, high-quality products with stringent environmental standards enforced'.[161]

---

154 Dobson, 2000, p 27.
155 Norton, 1991, p 118.
156 Benton, 1997, p 34.
157 Benton, 1997, p 35.
158 Discussed by Dobson, 2000, pp 206–14.
159 See European Commission, 2001a, para 1.
160 See European Commission, 1997a, 1999.
161 Weale, 1992, p 77.

Transposing such sanguinity to human nature, Norton's notion of convergence posits that an 'integrated system of value' can emerge, which given implicit constraints in human behaviour will accord respect to 'cross-temporal obligations to protect a healthy, complex, and autonomously functioning system for the benefit of future generations of humans'.[162]

This prognosis therefore makes vast assumptions about the perfectibility of the nature of competition (as well as human nature). The global nature of the environmental threats now facing humankind rather suggest that our adaptive capacities have been pushed to uncertain limits. However, as Johnston has pointed out, 'time has become a scarce commodity. The rapid pace of change in population, way of life, and environment has caused a redefinition of the notion of environmental constraint. Humans no longer have the luxury of time to adjust to changing conditions'.[163] The related problem of human behaviour is a theme appearing in subsequent chapters, and the political repercussions of a lack of convergence between citizen and consumer is considered in Chapter 10.

3.2   Validity of structured notions of trade-off

Cost benefit analysis is key to the process of identifying acceptable levels of trade-off. It suffers from many limitations, and most especially in that it is necessary also to arrive at an assessment of risk on the basis of available objective information. Detailed discussion of the problems of risk assessment in an environmental context is deferred until Chapter 8. For the present, assuming that the idea of discount is accepted at all, valuing future needs leads inevitably to argument as to discount methods. Accepted utilitarian approaches resolve themselves into forms of cost benefit analysis. Williams asserts that modern utilitarian principles can accommodate the notion of maximum sustainable yield. Thus, in the context of renewables, the aim must be to counter 'destructive utilization', in order to pass on 'interest-bearing resources which are not all at their maximum sustainable yield'.[164] Indeed, the past will otherwise appear confounded at every stage, given the present's domination of future choices. Future generations will therefore require access to key resources (water, air, and land would seem fairly non-contentious examples), including perhaps a fair opportunity to access non-renewable resources to some degree. It is after all less realistic to expect cultural changes, processed even through dozens of generations, to result in wholly alien and non-identifiable needs.

By contrast, pure ethical perspectives offer rather less protection. Gaba offers the rather nebulous notion of 'virtue ethics', by reference to present values and preferences, subject to a 'futurity discount factor'.[165] This purports to allow us to protect the future both as an end in itself and by focusing on our own mental qualities as decision makers. Just as the same author has rejected the idea of enforceable intergenerational obligations, it is unclear as to how far such virtue ethics could be regarded as immutable. There is an inevitable danger of an over-valuation of the present, especially given the suggestion of a moral obligation to ensure that present actions 'properly represent an expression of our

---

162 Norton, 1991, p 226.
163 Johnston, 1994, p 8.
164 Williams, 1995, p 26.
165 Gaba, 1999, pp 271–74.

best moral character'.[166] Likewise Norton presents the rather vaguer 'axiom of future value', which has its roots in the premise that 'the continuance and thriving of the human species is a good thing, and every generation is obliged to do what is necessary to perpetuate that good'.[167]

Returning to the search for an agenda for more active engagement with future interests, the role of risk assessment is at the crux of this debate. Just as economic questions are premised upon resource scarcity, cost benefit analysis essentially involves a negotiation of trade-offs. There is a specific advantage in a structured calculation where the unsatisfactory alternative seems to be to rely mainly upon intuition.[168] Rose sees it as valid to seek 'to bridge the gap, to dramatise the value of things that are too easily ignored, to invite a discussion of things we value ... So what if we borrow that market language? We have to use what we have, and this talk may help to disarm those who would simply ignore environmental value'.[169] On an epistemological level, an analogy with the polluter pays principle may be drawn, which through 'connecting scientific and economic measurement ... rearranges the cultural context ... The result is "optimal", a better trade-off between the costs and benefits of economic activity'.[170]

Difficulties caused by scientific uncertainty and lack of data will inevitably qualify calculations as to the nature of harm as well as the likelihood of its occurrence. A long-standing implicit acceptance has existed and Alder and Wilkinson, for instance, point to the courts endorsing a form of weak sustainability: 'in effect saying that environmental damage can be traded off against benefits of a different kind leaving it to the executive to deal with the problem of valuation.'[171] Courts indeed are engaged in such assessments all the time, and in cases of public law challenge this applies just as much to failures of judicial intervention.[172] Farber cites two examples from US jurisprudence, respectively concerning the legality of a riparian undertaking's discharge of mineral waste containing asbestos into Lake Superior and a blanket regulatory ban on the use of asbestos, in each case where harm to human health could not be established.[173]

Without offering a detailed analysis of economic approaches to sustainability, it can be said that constraint is supported there by reference to market conduct, as also in economic approaches to explaining legal support mechanisms.[174] Yet in this context complexities are especially notable where non-use values require consideration.[175] As an economic tool, therefore, the application of contingency valuation offers the dual advantages of being preference based and producing quantifiable data. But such a valuation process, especially where cast within an artificial framework for analysis premised upon

---

166 Gaba, 1999, p 287.

167 Norton, 1991, p 216.

168 Farber, 1999, p 10.

169 Rose, 1989, p 1645.

170 Myerson and Rydin, 1996, p 197.

171 Alder and Wilkinson, 1999, p 264.

172 *R v Secretary of State for the Environment ex p Kingston-upon-Hull CC, Bristol CC* (1996) 8 JEL 336; cf *R v Secretary of State for Environment ex p FoE* [1994] CMLR 760.

173 *Reserve Mining Company v United States*, 514 F 2d 492 (8th Cir 1975); *Corrosive Proof Fittings v EPA*, 947 F 2d 1201 (5th Cir 1991): see Farber, 1999, pp 15–38.

174 See especially Posner, 1992, especially Chapter 6.

175 See Tietenberg, 2000, especially Chapter 3.

willingness to pay, is contentious. For instance, it is criticised for making assumptions which account for environmental values on an equivalent utilitarian basis to other goods and services, ignoring the nature of value systems and their potential relationship with rights.[176] Farber categorises resulting disputes as being 'between tree huggers and bean counters ... over the legitimacy of the market-based method as a mechanism for social choice'.[177] Others less sanguine as to what can be achieved include Sagoff, who objects fundamentally to what he terms the 'shadow-pricing' of environmental values by bringing them into market calculations at all. He challenges the idea at root on grounds that environmental values are of a higher order and concerned with the collective values of citizens.[178] This is to be contrasted with what amount to the mere personal preferences of consumers.[179] Moreover, the spatial implications of environmental threats are seen by Westra as the greatest stumbling block to the use of contingent valuations. She points to the inaccuracy inherent in an assumption of environmental harm being 'localised, so that if only locals are affected, they and they alone ought to have a voice on decisions about acceptability of environmental risks'.[180] In reality, environmental harm is potentially without boundaries, and can be externalised well beyond sites of origin and local communities.

The task of achieving a reconciliation of opposing interests should not be at the cost of environmental integrity. Farber strikes a conciliatory note, espousing a 'pragmatic shade of green' philosophy, seeking out prudent precautions against potentially serious risks, with cost benefit analysis as a necessary 'restraint on over-zealous regulation, without allowing it to become a straitjacket'.[181] However, such pragmatism may lead nowhere (this sentence is written the day after President George W Bush released power stations in the US from carbon emission controls, seriously disabling prospects for further progress in the Kyoto process, discussed in Chapter 2).[182] Moreover, discount factors may be expressed in terms which barely adjust the status quo, as where not significantly exceeding long term growth rates. Mirroring the critiques of intergenerational equity above, this amounts to a discount factor for the next generation or so, and thereafter a mere intention to 'avoid substantial risks of future disaster to remote descendants'.[183] A more challenging suggestion lies in the potential for valuation of what have been described as ecosystem services. These can be regarded as public goods, for they cannot be exclusively controlled, and Salzman identifies them as having indirect non-market uses, being neither directly consumed nor traded.[184] Assuming that their elemental nature does not produce a value of infinity, it has been suggested that imposition at the margins (that is, in cases of specific threat) would encourage public access to data; it

---

176 See Hanley and Milne, 1996, pp 257–58.
177 Farber, 1999, p 41.
178 Sagoff, 1988, pp 16–17.
179 See also Sunstein, 1997.
180 Westra, 2000, p 155.
181 Farber, 1999, pp 203.
182 (2001) *The Independent*, 15 March.
183 Farber, 1999, p 155.
184 Salzman, 1997, p 893.

might also assist challenge before the courts, by support for a broader 'ecosystem nexus' basis for standing.[185]

Solutions point to regulatory, and ultimately political, processes. Yet, however satisfactorily discount factors can be applied, political processes may prove unreliable, a theme explored more fully in subsequent chapters. Two major criticisms remain. First, a tendency to externalise, as across boundaries, is likely to persist. Contingent valuations are no sure answer to problems in meeting public policy goals of protecting the citizen from immediate and long term harm, 'while ensuring that no serious harm is vested upon other populations, geographically (and maybe even temporally) removed from the community at issue'.[186] Secondly, more traditional political goals may continue implicitly to dominate. It has been charged that the discounting process under cost benefit analysis 'attracts an entirely specious authority. Worse still is the lust for short term returns ... with which ... decisions are usually made, and the confidence in progress which seems to give assurance that all other considerations can look after themselves'.[187] In this, politicians and administrators are not necessarily removed from the majority public mood. As a consequence, standard public law solutions, based upon participatory techniques, require careful appraisal. It is to such externalities, and potential resistance to reform, that the final section in this chapter now turns.

3.3   Post-scarcity approaches and the ruling economic order

Sustainable development accordingly requires that we move towards a more coherent admission of the externalities of market failure. This amounts to a challenge to the necessary identification of progress with production, for 'neglect of the various social and ecological costs of industrial progress is the key to understanding the green critique of contemporary industrial societies'.[188] At their poles, the two main strains in discourse on sustainability which therefore emerge are: first, a pragmatic response to the recent recognition of environmental crisis; and, secondly, a rejection of all solutions premised upon economic growth.[189]

The first, therefore, is the arguably dominant force of 'ecological modernisation', which covers a range of preferences, but is premised upon the need to protect both economic growth and the environment.[190] The underlying premise is an unlikely win-win situation, or positive sum game, with development and the environment perceived as, if not quite symbiotic, then at least mutually beneficial. The significance of the Brundtland Report, aside from a placing of sustainable development on the agenda of world governments, lies in its imperative for making the Rio process all-inclusive. The report set as one of the objectives for environment and development policy the need to revive growth and to change its quality, as well as to 'merge' the environment and economics as factors in decision making. Thus Brundtland herself would not accept such

---

185 Salzman, 1997, pp 898–900; also, *Lujan v Defenders of Wildlife*, 504 US 555, 594 (1992), Justice Blackmun (dissenting).

186 Westra, 2000, p 169.

187 Attfield, 1983, p 194.

188 Barry, 1999, p 209.

189 See Davoudi, 2000, pp 127–30.

190 See Hajer, 1997, pp 24–41.

endemic tension. She has since described protectionism as 'one of the aspects of confrontation which needs to be abolished ... The advantages of free trade for the countries of the North and South ought to be evident'.[191] The idea appears to embrace a high degree of confidence in humankind's technocratic capacities in continually finding solutions as problems unfold. This broad discourse has some distant relationship with the more extreme technocratic fix theories, such as the factor four proposition, which suggests increasing productivity by sufficient magnitude to achieve a doubling of wealth whilst halving depletion.[192] Even more extreme, some commentators suggest that solutions can still be found in economic efficiency and the advance of technology, even factoring in, as a future benefit, the value of non-environmental investments through development.[193]

The second, alternative approach seeks to challenge the growth-dependent cycle of production and market processes. Even the Rio process, for instance, has been criticised as a cynical exercise, which has 'legitimized the process of increased industrial development'.[194] Citing the Brundtland Report, Ost warns of the ambiguity of holding sustainable development out as:

> ... able to mobilize diverse economic and political forces, though on the basis of a false reconciliation of environment and development, of ecology and economy, of North and South. The inevitable oppositions of interest and ideological struggles seem to have been transcended by the representation of a future of reconciliation, thanks to the progress of science and the reign of national planning. The apocalyptic discourse calling for a cessation of growth is replaced by the mobilizing discourse of responsible, shared progress.[195]

An alternative path is to distinguish investment from consumptive behaviour. Jacobs, for instance, pursues the need for changed mechanisms to alter views of economic development in terms of public investment rather than year-on-year increases in personal disposable income.[196] A similar reformed paradigm was offered by the authors of the *Limits to Growth* report, in the idea of the equilibrium state, with opposing forces in a state of balance.[197] This is based upon an admission that our technological achievements have resulted in 'crowding, deterioration of the environment, and greater social inequality because greater productivity has been absorbed by population and capital growth'.[198] The key to their argument is that, in order to escape the consequences of the incentive of material growth, social value must be ascribed to quality of life. The equilibrium state would be based upon the creation of stability in population and capital over a period, so as to ensure a longer time frame, by lower investment levels, taking account of resource sustainability. The change required – to bring levels of capital and population into accord with what is termed social value – would be premised upon all inputs (births and investment) and outputs (deaths, depreciation) being kept to a minimum.[199] In this way,

---

191 Brundtland, 1999, p 5, cited by Dobson, 2000, p 91.
192 von Weizsacker, Lovins and Lovins, 1997.
193 See Farber, 1999, pp 157–60.
194 Finger, 1993, p 36.
195 Ost, 1994, pp 343–44.
196 Jacobs, 1996.
197 See Daly, 1971.
198 Meadows, Meadows, Randers and Behrens, 1972, pp 177–78.
199 Meadows, Meadows, Randers and Behrens, 1972, pp 170–73.

such a society, 'released from struggling with the many problems caused by growth, may have more energy and ingenuity available for solving other problems'.[200]

Yet a root of the difficulty in finding solutions, and the counterpart of prevailing perceptions of growth, is the problem of power having shifted away from political institutions, especially in the global market place. Addressing the question from the perspective of production, Korten argues that it is necessary to interfere with the operations of transnational corporations and their financial markets. Such a view suggests that corporate power, buttressed by support systems created under the Bretton Woods institutions of the World Bank and International Monetary Fund, as well now as the World Trade Organisation (WTO), is disproportionate to available restraining mechanisms through either markets or regulation. This concerns more than the corrupting influences of power and of money. Corporate power tends to dominate policy agendae, at all levels, and even of international bodies.[201] It is corporate interests which benefit where growth becomes 'the organizing principle of public policy'.[202]

The global marketplace, and its dominance by transnational corporate interest, demands the excessive levels of consumption, pollution and waste that so intensify the ecological crisis. In its train, it also leads to low levels of subsistence and population explosions, as well as severe disruption of the livelihood base of poorer communities, such as the diversion of agricultural resources in the South towards export crops for the rich nations. This Korten likens to the displacement of the agrarian economy, through enclosures, after 1750 in England.[203] Green proposals are therefore antithetical to trade-dominated dialogues, such as those within the WTO, and challenge the consequent impacts upon national, especially less developed, economies.[204] Dobson cites four grounds for ecological concern at the assumptions underlying trade: the waste of resources caused by trade patterns; the turning of wants into needs; the vulnerability of economies to worsening terms of trade; and the dependence consequent upon the exercise of political and economic power.[205]

The sustainability debate can be categorised as a conflict over modernism. This may be compared with the discourse following the emergence of a risk society, discussed in Chapter 8, which is likewise central to responses to environmental threats.[206] Thus, Beck propounds newly evolving societal arrangements in response to a growing awareness of the unintended consequences of industrial modernisation.[207] These include an exponential growth in risk and associated uncertainties, with technology viewed as not only saviour but also threat. Such uncertainties afflict expert and technocrat, as well as the citizen. Likewise in the context of social organisation, therefore, Giddens states that markets 'provide the signalling devices implied in complex systems of exchange, but they

---

200 Note 198 above, pp 174–75.
201 Korten, 1995, p 54.
202 Korten, 1995, p 50.
203 Korten, 1995, pp 44–47.
204 Cf Juniper and Denny, 2000.
205 Dobson, 2000, p 90.
206 Beck, 1992.
207 See Durkheim, 1973.

also sustain, or actively cause, major forms of deprivation'.[208] He concludes that there is a need for a 'post-scarcity system' of politics. This would offer an opportunity to extend the definition of 'life circumstances of human beings' beyond economic criteria.[209] Indeed, the economic system, premised upon responses to limited scarcity, through pricing mechanisms and increased production, probably breaks down where essential sources of supply are endemically squeezed, and the existence of substitutes becomes questionable. Giddens' premise, for a reconsideration of 'the major goods of life' as being no longer scarce, has much in common with broader critical reconsideration of ideas as to progress.[210] The related challenges for a post-scarcity order would demand significant changes in expectations and modes of social life, and – arguably most radically – a questioning of distribution of wealth.[211] This latter consideration is an inevitable consequence of any diluting of corporate power through terms of trade by the encouragement of increased local self-reliance and accountability.[212]

Striking a reformed power balance necessitates reformed legal approaches. Yet traditional legal mechanisms tend presumptively to adopt traditional market paradigms. Thus, externalities have been described by Hodas as 'only an afterthought in a legal system driven by an individual/market-oriented paradigm', who proceeds to argue for 'a law of environmentally costed decision making', which amounts to an integration of economic interests and ecological values in order fully to account for external effects.[213] At project level, green accounting techniques can be applied, both in integrated resource planning and in contingent valuation for damage assessment, scope for which in developing discounting techniques has already been referred to. Reformed accounting systems would include such matters as efficient resource use and waste.[214] Pointing to standard financial accounting as deducting an amount from income to represent depreciation of capital assets, Korten questions the lack of comparable adjustment for the depletion and natural capital.[215] Hodas suggests the development of natural resource accounting, under which national economic accounting indicators must be adjusted to take account of related environmental degradation costs.[216] In response, such resource-based activities with a potential for environmental damage could be internalised through financial mechanisms, such as insurance or performance bonds.[217]

In conclusion, much of this chapter has been concerned with the task of according greater transparency to the implications of our choices. The lesson is that these extend far beyond the limited choices as predominantly defined by markets. The above discussion suggests that the sustainable development discourse should not deflect from the ultimately conflictual and political nature of choices available in the practical search for

---

208 Giddens, 1990, pp 164–65.
209 Note 208 above, p 165.
210 See Miles and Irvine, 1982.
211 Ophuls, 1977, p 163.
212 Korten, 1995, Chapter 22.
213 Hodas, 1998, p 25.
214 See MacGillivray and Zadek, 1995.
215 See Korten, 1995, Chapter 3.
216 Hodas, 1998, p 50.
217 Hodas, 1998, pp 51–55.

sustainability. It is ultimately about harnessing the impacts of market ideology, and the necessity of recognising that 'environmental risks are produced industrially, externalised economically, individualised judicially, legitimised scientifically and minimised politically'.[218] Moreover, for all the concern over outcomes, it has been pointed out that sustainability is best understood in terms of decision making processes.[219] It is about how far processes, in the hands of administrators who, as posited by McAuslan, embody their own public interest ideology, should be supplemented by a more inclusive paradigm.[220] It is therefore about engaging the citizen in the debate. Yet the trend towards stakeholding approaches also carries dangers. For instance, discussing the idea of self-responsibility on the part of enterprises, Ost refers to apparent consensus in partnerships which create 'the real risk that external constraints would weaken, that the *show* of action would replace action itself, that *representation* of ecological concern would mask the reality of strategies of market occupation. At the same time, the need for legal intervention would be questioned, in favour of strategies of persuading the public that have more to do with conditioning to publicity and political marketing'.[221] Indeed, the underlying premises on which the socio-economic system is based place severe obstacles in the way of the search for environmental solutions. For all the growing awareness of sustainability issues, presumptions in favour of the exploitation of resources and the maximisation of production and consumption continue to dominate political and social agendas.

Notwithstanding the contested nature of interests referred to in this chapter, however, it is possible to move towards sustainable policies. The idea of an equilibrium society, already referred to, has been described as having to 'weigh the trade-offs engendered by a finite earth not only with considerations of present human values but also with consideration of future generations'.[222] The task is to produce policies, through such institutional arrangements as a liberal democracy affords, with the objective of a (relatively speedy) movement towards a sustainable society.[223] Such policies will have to deliver effective control of polluting emissions, a shift in energy extraction and use from fossil fuels and nuclear power to renewable sources, related changes in agricultural practices, and assurance of water quality and supply. It is the nature of these issues that they interrelate, as they relate also to the need to address gross wealth disparities and for meeting the challenge of population control. As we shall see in the next chapter, issues of sustainable development must encompass such questions.

Aside from finding legal mechanisms in support of new normative arrangements, policy responses include appropriate regulatory efforts, buttressed by financial and fiscal measures, respectively, to incentivise sustainable and penalise non-sustainable behaviour.[224] Most of all, the growing recognition of a need for solutions based upon sustainable development, whilst not of direct threat to the dominance of markets accepted now in most economies, presupposes an acceptance of the need for restraint through

---

218 Beck, 1998, p 26.
219 See Buckingham-Hatfield and Evans, 1996, pp 5–6.
220 McAuslan, 1980, pp 2–6.
221 Ost, 1994, p 343.
222 Meadows, Meadows, Randers and Behrens, 1972, p 182.
223 Hajer, 1997, especially Chapter 6.
224 See, eg, European Commission, 2001a, para 2.3.

planning. Moffatt encapsulates this by calling for a Keynesian approach which 'allows micro-economic matters to be conducted through market mechanisms whilst the broader macro-economic and ecological problems can be managed by political intervention'.[225] Legal mechanisms must operate upon global, regional, and local levels – frequently upon all together – and are essential to securing both the articulation and delivery of a reformed paradigm.

225 Moffatt, 1996, pp 181–82.

CHAPTER 2

SUSTAINABILITY AND LEGAL PRINCIPLE

Things are tougher than we are, just
As earth will always respond
However we mess it about;
Chuck filth in the sea, if you must:
The tides will be clean beyond.
But what do I feel now? Doubt?[1]

It will be recalled from the Introduction that ecological interdependencies within ecosystems, of which humankind forms but part, and to which national and regional boundaries are for the most part an irrelevance, is a main theme for sustainable approaches. This calls for collaboration upon an international scale. In this chapter it is proposed to consider the basis for legal enforcement of those policies which purport to foster sustainable development. The discussion seeks to review it as a response to the environmental crisis, especially in international environmental law. Some consideration will also be given to the legal provenance of other, related environmental principles, which may in due course develop more substantial content, such as the precautionary principle. An overview of how policy making structures are starting to focus upon achieving sustainability will be followed by some concluding thoughts as to how far legal analysis is pertinent to the achievement of a framework for sustainable development.

1 INTERNATIONAL PROCESSES

1.1 The Rio framework for sustainable development

In the environmental sphere, as in other fields of international law, activities within a State's boundaries may pose a threat to the interests of neighbouring States. As discussed in the previous chapter, it is in the nature of externalities that they are not shaped by human boundaries. It is now accepted that impacts may be more diffuse and threaten the unowned environment, such as the atmosphere and high seas: locations which justify classification under the global commons.

The main impetus for sustainability to become a political issue has been through international fora. The seminal moment was the holding in Stockholm in 1972 of the United Nations Conference on the Human Environment.[2] The foundations laid in the Stockholm Declaration produced a tentative start in response to growing scientific disquiet, and could be described as an expression of ethical approaches by which humankind might confront the dilemmas of environmental degradation.[3] Principle 1 of

---

1   Larkin, P, from 'Going, going', 1972, 1990 edn, p 189.
2   UN Conference on the Human Environment, Stockholm, UN Doc A/CONF/48/14/REV 1 (1972).
3   See Hodas, 1998, pp 8–9.

the Stockholm Declaration expressed sustainable development in terms of rights and duties: 'Man has the fundamental right to freedom, equality and adequate conditions of life, in an environment of a quality that permits a life of dignity and well-being, and he bears a solemn responsibility to protect and improve the environment for present and future generations.' The extent of these obligations was broadened in Principle 2, as follows: 'Natural resources of the earth, including the air, water, land, flora and fauna and especially representative samples of ecosystems must be safeguarded for the benefit of present and future generations through careful planning or management, as appropriate.' In like vein, the World Charter for Nature in 1981 placed emphasis upon the need to achieve a wise use of resources and to secure optimum sustainable productivity without endangering co-existing ecosystems and species.[4] Again, even if it were intended that the Charter should contribute to the creation of binding international law, as Birnie and Boyle point out, 'it is difficult to argue that in relation to conservation of resources it has any binding legal status'.[5] Similarly, in 1991, the World Conservation Union, revisiting its 1980 World Conservation Strategy, expressed the same principle in terms of an obligation to improve the quality of life 'whilst living within the carrying capacity of supporting ecosystems'.[6] Emergent principles such as these, along with similar approaches appearing in a range of environmental treaties, exemplify the soft law nature at most of much international commitment to sustainability.[7] Thus, typically, a declaratory stage is reached, unencumbered by more than token attention to the mechanics of enforcement. In other words, related rights and obligations remain largely inchoate.

The mounting international concern at the global nature of environmental problems, and their close relationship with economic development, led to the emblematic United Nations Conference on Environment and Development (UNCED), in Rio in 1992.[8] The conference took place in the wider context of suspicions on the part of developing States that, in a continuation of historic trends, they were now to be squeezed between the twin forces of market globalism and a developing environmental agenda. Importantly, there was a linking of sustainability and development, and commitments under the Rio process were premised upon principles of a right to equitable development and 'common but differentiated responsibilities', under which, for instance, the principle of lower compliance standards applicable to developing countries was accepted.[9] However, the sovereign right of States was explicitly recognised in respect of the exploitation of their own resources 'pursuant to their own environmental and developmental policies'. Yet this was made subject to 'the responsibility to ensure that activities within that jurisdiction or control do not cause damage to the environment of other States or of areas

---

4   UN General Assembly Resolution, UN Doc A/RES/37/7 (1982), (1983) 23 ILM 455, especially Articles 10, 11.

5   Birnie and Boyle, 1992, p 431.

6   See International Union for Conservation of Nature and Natural Resources, 1980, 1991; a draft Covenant on Environment and Development was further produced in 1995.

7   Eg, the London Convention on the Prevention of Marine Pollution by Dumping of Wastes and Other Matter (1972) 11 ILM 1294; Convention Concerning the Protection of the World Cultural and Natural Heritage (1972) 11 ILM 1358; Washington Convention on International Trade in Endangered Species of Wild Fauna and Flora (1973) 12 ILM 1085.

8   UN Conference on Environment and Development, Rio, UN Doc A/CONF 151/5/REV 1 (1992) 31 ILM 874.

9   Rio Declaration, Principle 7.

beyond the limits of national jurisdiction'.[10] It was further expressly declared that States would co-operate 'in the further development of international law in the field of sustainable development'.[11]

Sustainable development was therefore the common theme underlying the UNCED process. Principle 1 of the Declaration was more limited than its 1972 precursor: 'Human beings are at the centre of concerns for sustainable development. They are entitled to a healthy and productive life in harmony with nature.' Principle 3 explicitly addressed the development-environment nexus: 'The right to development must be fulfilled so as to equitably meet developmental and environmental needs of future generations.' The ground had been laid by the preparatory Brundtland Report, produced by the World Commission on Environment and Development in 1987.[12] As a result, sustainable development was introduced into the policy making agenda, through the setting of objectives and formulation of issues such as changing the quality of growth, meeting essential needs of life, controlling population levels, conserving resources, encouraging technological development and managing risk.[13] It has, however, been pointed out that the report was limited by an inability to 'go beyond identifying categories that need to be addressed to transform the idea of sustainable development into reality'.[14]

Nevertheless, affirmation of the Brundtland Report at the Rio Conference resulted in two significant treaties, namely the Framework Convention on Climate Change and the Convention on Biological Diversity.[15] Moreover, what emerged from the Rio process was perhaps limited, but a clarification of pressing environmental issues was achieved, as well as the beginnings of an institutional structure to take initiatives further, with a UN commitment to a five-yearly progress review. Further, the process produced Agenda 21.[16] This was particularly significant, in that it mandated 'socially responsible development while protecting the resource base and environment for the benefit of future generations'.[17] It amounted to a detailed expression of the environmental threats facing the international community, as well as methods to be employed in addressing the crisis, and respective objectives and priorities for action (at national and local level). A central element of Agenda 21 was the linkage between environmental and social and economic problems, such as poverty, over-population, disease and housing.[18] It called for the production of national Sustainable Development Strategies; and the UN Commission on Sustainable Development was established as a review, monitoring and co-ordinating body.[19] In this respect, concerns have arisen at problems in procurement of reliable information to underpin the process, especially in those economies which are under greatest pressure. However, as O'Riordan has noted, 'at least the concept is laid down. These chapters are fundamental for the future of active environmental science and the

10   Principle 2.
11   Principle 27.
12   United Nations World Commission on Environment and Development, 1987.
13   See paras 29–65.
14   Hodas, 1998, p 10.
15   See (1992) 31 ILM 849; (1992) 31 ILM 818.
16   UN Conference on Environment and Development, Agenda 21, UN Doc A/CONF 151/26 (1992).
17   Agenda 21, para 8.7.
18   Agenda 21, Chapters 3–7.
19   Agenda 21, para 38.11.

promotion of global citizenship – a community that is both knowledgeable and has the tools to alter societies and economies towards greater sustainability.'[20]

Overall, the Rio process constituted an important new development in the creation of core international principles of law and policy focused upon global issues that threaten sustainability.[21] It has been said that the significance of the Rio Declaration can be attributed to the obligatory nature of its wording, and a real consensus as to the need for generally agreed norms of international environmental protection.[22] Whilst recognising its formally non-binding nature, Boyle has felt sufficiently confident to conclude that the Declaration was 'overtly intended to initiate new law for the international community of States; for this reason many of its provisions are formulated in normative and obligatory terms'.[23] The process, therefore, as well as setting out certain key substantive principles and procedures, manifested an acceptance of the relationship between sustainable development and development, especially in the link between environmental degradation and underdevelopment. The earlier report of the UNCED Experts' Group had cited the 'nefarious impact of poverty and underdevelopment', concluding that 'irrational use of natural resources and degradation of the environment which is the result of poverty and underdevelopment will ... be a formidable obstacle to sustainable development itself'.[24] The importance of Rio, therefore, is that it assured a degree of global consensus concerning a 'linkage between the global economy and environmental degradation that lies at the heart of theories about sustainable development'.[25]

However, a fundamental weakness of the Rio process lies at the heart of the development-environment nexus. Subsequently, throughout the first half of 2001, the United States has adopted stances towards the continuing Kyoto Protocol process in respect of global warming that indicate that insufficient burdens are placed upon developing States. Thus a major foundation of the UNCED scheme, even before any large-scale ratifications, is already under considerable strain. In this light, it is unsurprising that the Rio process had already come under more pronounced criticism in the light of subsequent failures to progress agreed initiatives, with the possible exception of the growth of local Agenda 21 plans. This reflects structural weaknesses at an institutional level. An early low point was encountered in 1997 at Earth Summit II: the UN General Assembly Special Session on Sustainable Development.[26] Of the many problems encountered, perhaps the most severe, was the post-1992 fall in developed States' official development assistance to the developing States, with an average contribution out of Gross Domestic Product, targeted long term at a figure of 0.7%, actually reducing, from around a half to little over a third of that target. Jordan and Voisey offer the crumb of comfort that the 1997 Session has at least 'brought home the

---

20 O'Riordan, 2000, p 43.

21 See also the Vienna Convention for the Protection of the Ozone Layer (1985), (1987) 26 ILM 1529, together with the Montreal Protocol on Substances that Deplete the Ozone Layer (1987) 26 ILM 1550.

22 Boyle and Freestone, 1999, pp 3–4.

23 Boyle, 1999, p 69.

24 Munro and Lammers, 1987, p 66.

25 Bell and McGillivray, 2000, p 90.

26 See O'Riordan, 2000, Chapter 2.

uncomfortable truth that sustainability requires changes to deeply rooted modes of political behaviour, although it undoubtedly strained North-South relations. Politicians now know just how much work needs to be done. Flimsily patched up compromises made at Rio were shown to be just that'.[27]

1.2 Securing sustainable development through principles of international law

Before offering an analysis of prospects for fuller implementation of sustainable development, it is necessary to consider the status of international environmental law and the nature of existing commitments. Binding sources of international environmental law derive from international law generally, as traditionally contained in treaties, custom, UN resolutions and declarations, and subsidiary sources such as court decisions and juristic writings.[28] Although there is some recognition by the International Court of Justice on the basis of 'general practice accepted as law',[29] it remains unclear how far customary international law can be said to accommodate environmental principles. Arguments in favour of general inter-State obligations can be found.[30] Though numerous discrete environmental treaties appear to have binding effects upon States,[31] generally it is the nature of such treaties that they are declaratory. However, even soft law instruments entered into by States and international organisations, both informal and formal, can be identified as having normative features. There is in any event some advantage of soft law over hard law in that 'as occasion demands, it can either enable States to take on obligations that otherwise they would not, because these are expressed in vaguer terms, or conversely ... may enable them to formulate the obligations in a precise and restrictive form which would not be acceptable in a binding treaty'.[32] That States should also pursue this as a path of least resistance should be no great surprise, given similar difficulties encountered within the domestic spheres of Nation States. Sands' analysis of the UNCED process leads to the conclusion that States are 'not prepared to set in motion a radical transformation of the international legal order. International law in the field of sustainable development points to a body of principles and rules drawn from traditional approaches, evolutionary rather than revolutionary'.[33]

It is necessary, therefore, to pursue the potentiality of sustainable development as a principle of international law. The term has been categorised by Sands as having four, related objectives. The first three are referable to natural resources and the interests of present and future generations: a commitment to preserve; the application of appropriate

---

27 Jordan and Voisey, 1998.

28 Birnie and Boyle, 1992, pp 9–26.

29 See Statute of the International Court of Justice, Article 38.

30 Eg, *Nuclear Tests II Case: Request for an Examination of the Situation in Accordance with Paragraph 63 of the Court's 1974 Judgment in the Nuclear Tests Case (New Zealand v France)* [1995] ICJ Rep 288.

31 For instance, the Convention on Wetlands of International Importance (Ramsar) 1971, (1972) 11 ILM 963; Washington Convention on International Trade in Endangered Species of Wild Fauna and Flora (1973) 12 ILM 1085; UN Convention on the Law of the Sea (UNCLOS) (1982) 21 ILM 1261.

32 Birnie and Boyle, 1992, p 27.

33 Sands, 2000, p 381.

standards for exploitation; and equitable use, bearing in mind other States and peoples. The fourth requires that environmental considerations be integrated into economic and other development plans, programmes and projects, and conversely that development needs are taken into account in the pursuit of those environmental considerations.[34] It cannot however be said that significant progress has yet been made in translating the recognition of moral obligations to future generations into binding international legal norms. As well as being contained in declarations such as Principles 1 and 2 of the Stockholm Declaration, soft law commitments to sustainable development are present in a broad swathe of treaties. These now routinely contain (commonly preambular) references to the welfare of future generations.[35] Numerous references likewise appear in non-binding instruments in a variety of contexts, as, for instance: 'The present generations have the responsibility of ensuring the needs and interests of future generations are fully safeguarded.'[36]

Notwithstanding the attempts being made, as illustrated above, to respond to global environment threats through international negotiative and legal processes, pervasive problems remain in the way of finding solutions. However innovative and precautionary international environmental regimes may appear to be, if not implemented effectively, 'they may be worse than worthless if they give the impression that all is well when the opposite is in fact true'.[37] Genuine progress in the field of international law would improve the prospect of solutions to many of the most serious environmental threats. However, it would be inaccurate to suggest that the range of available measures discussed below offer a thematic coherence, either from the point of view of substantive subject matter or expectation of enforcement. Sands has pointed to a lack of co-ordination between initiatives, which also tend to be both reactive and ad hoc: 'Limited implementation and enforcement suggests that international environmental law is in its formative stages.'[38]

Legal and institutional structures, whether in legislative or judicial contexts, have failed therefore to build upon the normative characteristics which can arguably be ascribed to sustainable development.[39] It has been said that, along with an absence of judicial standards for review, there are no substantive international obligations placed upon governments to ensure that development is sustainable.[40] Lowe goes so far as to assert that a lack of norm-constraining characteristics disables sustainable development from even soft law status. What remains is 'a convenient, if imprecise, label for a general policy goal which may be adopted by States unilaterally, bilaterally, or multilaterally. It is

---

34 Sands, 2000, pp 374–75.

35 See eg the preambles to the Convention on International Trade in Endangered Species of Wild Fauna and Flora (1973) 12 ILM 1085; Convention on Biological Diversity (1992) 31 ILM 818; Framework Convention on Climate Change (1992) 31 ILM 849; Helsinki Convention on the Transboundary Effects of Industrial Accidents (1992) 31 ILM 1330; Paris Convention for the Protection of the Marine Environment of the North East Atlantic (OSPAR, 1992) (1993) 32 ILM 1068.

36 UNESCO Declaration on the Responsibilities of the Present Generations Towards Future Generations, UNESCO General Conference, 29th Session (12 November 1997), Art 1.

37 Freestone, 1999, p 360.

38 Sands, 2000, p 372.

39 Sands, 2000, pp 408–09.

40 Boyle and Freestone, 1999, p 16.

clearly entitled to a place in the Pantheon of concepts that are not to be questioned in polite company, along with democracy, human rights, and the sovereign equality of States'.[41] Yet even this argument concludes that it may still have value in a resolution of conflicts between recognised legal norms, as what is termed a modifying norm.[42] Such a mediating role suggests a potential for integration into the processes of international law, especially if available in judicial fora. Progress remains generally reliant therefore upon the idea that international sources do inform national policy making. International law is after all important for the development of such principles, for they 'often develop precisely because of their non-binding origins'.[43] Sands at least feels able to conclude that 'the complex societal, technical, and cultural matters' which sustainable development addresses are 'now being addressed holistically for the first time'.[44] The task of achieving consensus and clarifying frameworks for sustainable development may no longer be beyond the conceptual and institutional apparatus of international law.

2 IMPLEMENTING SUSTAINABLE DEVELOPMENT WITHIN INTERNATIONAL ENVIRONMENTAL LAW

2.1 Strategies for securing compliance

Given the growth of environmental commitments in international documents, and the disquiet previously discussed as to binding status, the question of securing compliance through international processes is now considered. Most environmental rules, given the vagaries of evidential requirements and problems of general interest and the unowned environment, raise particular problems of implementation. Outside the jurisdiction of national legal systems, such problems multiply. Lawyers are perhaps prone to the promotion of legal texts as evidence *per se* of compliance (especially where structures exist either for adjudication, or at least for applying political pressures). Nevertheless, there is wide scepticism as to the value of international law in influencing State behaviour.[45] There is also substantial evidence that a wide range of compliance strategies for international law is available once the hardest task is achieved, namely ensuring its general acceptability within the international community.[46] In this task, for instance, the principle of reciprocity should be crucial as an aid to international understanding of the implications of environmental externalities. Fisher encapsulates this by asserting that no breach 'could result in a benefit which would be sufficiently large to outweigh the detriment of having all other countries violate all of the nation's other rights protected by international law'.[47] After all, the principles and rules of international law provide 'a framework within which the various members of the international community may co-

---

41 Lowe, 1999, pp 30–31.

42 Lowe, 1999, p 34.

43 Bell and McGillivray, 2000, p 85.

44 Sands, 2000, p 409.

45 For instance, Waltz, 1979, especially Chapter 9.

46 Fisher, 1981.

47 Fisher, 1981, p 135.

operate, establish norms of behaviour and resolve their differences',[48] and this is necessarily a mutually beneficial process. Yet, in the nature of international law, securing such compliance is based upon co-operation, ultimately reinforced through the political process. This applies also in circumstances of bilateral dispute and even where an adjudicative body such as the International Court of Justice (ICJ) is involved.

Such general delimitations are still more acute in the environmental field, where the overarching purpose has been described as the protection of 'common interests, common property or the interests of future generations, peoples or non-human species ... No other model offers useful solutions to the problem of controlling phenomena of global character, such as global warming or ozone depletion, where no single State's acts are responsible and where the interests of all are at stake'.[49] In principle, institutional machinery is required for the co-ordination of policy, development of law, monitoring of performance, and adjudication of disputes. Whilst there are numerous examples of treaties putting institutional machinery in place, these often lack sanctioning (or even monitoring and investigative) teeth. Their success is constrained by deficiencies in meeting support criteria, such as independent status, community of interest amongst States, publicity and encouragement of interest group participation.[50] It appears that institutional deficiencies lie at the heart of delivery under the Rio process. As seen in the previous section, the creation of the UN Commission on Sustainable Development was significant especially as a focal point for broadening the sustainability debate, increasing the availability of information and providing a locus for sustainability issues at the UN. However, its influence will remain limited whilst the scope of its remit remains constrained. There is, for instance, no evaluative control over national sustainable development reports received. O'Riordan has pointed to 'a lack of clarity on what the whole reporting process is meant to achieve and the best means to get there'.[51]

Three essential compliance mechanisms under international law are traditionally identified. These have been described as consisting of primary rule systems, compliance information systems, and non-compliance response systems. Primary systems focus upon provision for pressures and incentives with a view to regulating behaviour. Information systems consist of the collection, interpretation and wider dissemination of data. Non-compliance response systems produce formal or informal forms of sanction. First, therefore, primary rule systems encourage compliance especially by setting appropriate criteria. For all the caution which must accompany the discussion of the value of legal solutions, compliance objectives presuppose the existence of rules systems, hard and soft, emerging from the international law process. Moreover, rules tend to alter the value systems which underlie the processes of negotiation and debate, and thereby foster behavioural change.[52]

Secondly, information systems potentially contribute transparency to assuring the monitoring and discovery of violations. These typically consist of reporting requirements or rules for information access for third parties. Information processes and complaints

48   Sands, 1995, p 14.
49   Boyle, 1991, p 230.
50   Boyle, 1991, p 245.
51   O'Riordan, 2000, p 45.
52   See Mitchell, 1996, pp 16–24.

procedures especially empower non-governmental organisations in their political and lobbying roles.[53] Although national compliance levels appear to show mixed success,[54] reporting requirements are increasingly imposed in international treaties.[55] Effectiveness is enhanced where the object of control is an identifiable sector or range of undertakings, as, for instance, CFC producers for the purposes of the Vienna Convention and Montreal Protocol. In contrast, diffuse contributions to environmental degradation are more resistant to such mechanisms: 'technical capabilities will make verification of point-source pollution, like power plants, far easier than aerial polluters, such as logging or rice farming.'[56] Here international fora are essential. Mitchell points to treaty rules regarding Mediterranean pollution, whereby increased compliance has followed the provision and dissemination of pollution information (as well, interestingly, as the placing of scientists in 'dominant policy positions', a problematic issue to be considered further in Chapter 8).[57] Access in national and regional arenas may be achieved in numerous ways, and is usually enhanced where regulatory bodies may be responsible for the receipt and co-ordination function.[58] As stated above, measures may be more straightforward in the regulation of individual pollution sources, as rules are commonly imposed for licensing systems, and related publicly available information. For instance, UK laws for transparency of environmental information have largely followed the terms of a European Community Directive, which had the objective of ensuring public access to information in the hands of public authorities and set out the essential terms and conditions on which information should be made available (and which is currently under review).[59] Self-reporting systems may also assist, as under environmental management and audit schemes or product eco-labelling.[60]

The final form of compliance system, namely non-compliance response, is the most difficult to achieve. A wide variety of approaches include negative and positive mechanisms. Negative, or penalty, mechanisms are little developed at an international level. For instance, the idea of the imposition of State liability for environmental damage, in the absence of specific international obligations, has thus far made no substantial impact in the international arena.[61] At a regional level, within the European Union a carbon tax has been proposed, based upon a levy upon fossil fuels by reference to energy content and carbon dioxide emissions.[62] However, further progress for the proposal faces

---

53 Sands, 1996c, pp 65–66, 68.

54 See, eg, US General Accounting Office Report, *International Environment: International Agreements Are Not Well Monitored*, GAO/RCED-92-43.

55 And see United Nations Economic Commission for Europe (UNECE), Convention on Access to Information, Public Participation in Decision-Making and Access to Justice on Environmental Matters, 1998.

56 Mitchell, 1996, p 19.

57 Mitchell, 1996, p 34.

58 Eg, the European Environment Agency: see EC Regulation 1210/90.

59 See EC Directive 90/313 on Public Access to Information on the Environment (OJ L158/56, 23 June 1990); transposed in the UK under the Environmental Information Regulations 1992, SI 1992/3240; the Commission has proposed extensions to public information and participation rights: see draft Directive COM (2000) 839.

60 Eg, EC Regulation 1836/93 on Eco-Management and Audit Scheme (EMAS) (OJ L168, 10 July 1993); EC Regulation 880/92 on Eco-Labelling (OJ L99, 11 April 1992).

61 See Boyle, 1999, pp 76–79.

62 See proposed Directive to Introduce a Tax on CO_2 Emissions and Energy COM(95) 172 final (10 May 1995): especially draft Arts 1, 7.

substantial obstacles in the light of national reluctance to cede exclusive jurisdiction over policies of taxation. Individual Member States have made considerable progress in introducing environmentally related economic instruments, including taxes and levies.[63] Yet tensions with economic and trading interests are evident also at the regional level, as in the European Commission's stated emphasis upon the 'importance of the legal framework related to the functioning of the single market which has to be respected by Member States when introducing environmental taxes and charges'.[64] In contrast, the imposition of trade sanctions under the Montreal Protocol is an illustration of an established negative mechanism.[65] This area is generally rendered complex by problems of compatibility with regional trade association rules, as well as the dominance of the World Trade Organisation (WTO) and the WTO Appellate Body, referred to below. Otherwise, recourse to adjudicative mechanisms is subject to the limitations inherent in the international law process. As well as those established under the procedures under the Montreal Protocol, a range of adjudicative bodies exist, such as the ICJ (which now comprises an Environmental Chamber) and the International Tribunal for the Law of the Sea under UNCLOS. There may also be a cross-over into the jurisdiction of other judicial bodies, which may have an overlap with the environment, either regionally, such as the European Court of Justice, or under distinct remits, such as the European Court of Human Rights. The risks of incompatible approaches being pursued have led to suggestions for a specialist international body, with 'an overarching jurisdiction, able to integrate the various approaches and meld them into a coherent whole'.[66]

More positive inducements to compliance extend to incentives for the prevention of violation. Financial mechanisms are increasingly applied, and include the revised Global Environment Facility, under the auspices of the World Bank, the UN Environment Programme and the UN Development Programme. Certain treaties now require that incremental costs for developing countries are met by developed States, and this was on the face of it a key element of the Rio process.[67] The Global Environment Facility supports the commitment to common but differentiated responsibilities, and has the objective of assisting poorer States to meet the incremental costs of introducing sustainable policies.[68] Accordingly, financial support is supplemented by education and technological aid. The nature and extent of incremental costs remains, however, contested.[69] But even so, having such mechanisms in place is particularly important given the UNCED emphasis upon the link between environment and development.

The creation of other incentives-based mechanisms for achieving international enforcement is at an early stage. For the future, these may include economic instruments to encourage greener technologies. Progress has been made toward a broader application

---

63 The Commission website has posted a Database on Environmental Taxes in the EU Member States: see www.europa.eu.int/comm/environment/enveco/env_database/ database.htm.

64 European Commission, 1997B, para 52; eg, ENDS Report, 314, 'UK waits for EC state aids clearance for climate levy', p 5 (March 2001).

65 Article 4.

66 Sands, 1998, p 3.

67 Eg, Climate Change Convention, Article 4(7); Kyoto Protocol, Article 11(2): full text at www.unfccc.de/resource/convkp.html.

68 See O'Riordan, 2000, pp 48–51; Freestone, 1999, pp 360–64.

69 Sjoberg, 1996; also, Jordan and Werksman, 1996.

under the Climate Change Convention, through the proposal to develop an emissions trading regime contained in the Kyoto Protocol in 1997.[70] A by-product of the process would be the availability of pollution credits ostensibly for improved performance. However the commitments reached as to carbon reductions have become mired in controversy, and a follow-up 2000 conference at The Hague failed to secure an agreement. The treaty is due to be ratified during 2002, although President Bush announced soon after his inauguration that the United States did not intend to ratify.[71] The US view, that the treaty is fundamentally flawed by virtue of unrealistic targets and the imbalance between developed and developing States, has subsequently led to its rejection of the implementation rules agreed by other signatory States at Bonn in July 2001.[72] As French commented post-Kyoto, 'for a number of influential States, traditional economic growth dependent upon fossil fuels is still the imperative consideration'.[73]

2.2 The limitations of State sovereignty and trade dominance

Two particular obstacles to securing environmental improvements operate on respectively national and international planes: nationally, in the light of the traditional incidents of territorial sovereignty, and internationally, in the face of other, at times conflicting, commitments. As to the former, the notion of exclusive jurisdiction is fundamental to the recognition of the sovereignty of States under international law.[74] Moreover, in so far as sustainable development emerged from the Rio process as a legal principle, it needs to be mediated through national governments, as thus far there appears to be 'only a limited role for international definition and oversight'.[75] Yet the transboundary implications of environmental problems challenge the assumptions underlying State sovereignty, as well as the international law processes in which States engage. For instance, an essential problematic that confronts international environmental law lies in achieving a meaningful response to the growing awareness that changes are necessary in cycles of production and consumption. In a classic illustration of the problem affecting the global commons, despite the benefits to be gained in restraining our external impacts, each State and individual 'lacks any market-based "rational" incentive to reduce emissions'.[76]

The achievement of an alleviation in those externalities which lead to environmental degradation will surely fail without the development of a new dynamic which counters traditional views of State territorial and sovereign claims in this field. Whether through recognition in treaty or custom, it is necessary to facilitate challenge from neighbouring and other States.[77] This explains the importance of international co-operation for, as Sands puts it, 'the challenge for international law in the world of sovereign States is to

---

70   Article 16.
71   (2001) *The Guardian*, 30 March.
72   (2001) *The Independent*, 24 and 25 July.
73   French, 1998, p 239.
74   Brownlie, 1990, p 287.
75   Boyle and Freestone, 1999, p 7.
76   Hodas, 1998, p 17.
77   Boyle and Freestone, 1999, p 2.

reconcile the fundamental independence of each State with the inherent and fundamental interdependence of the environment'.[78] Thus, arguably the most revolutionary aspect of the Rio process has been that 'it makes a State's management of its own domestic environment and resources a matter of international concern for the first time in a systematic way'.[79] Thus, Agenda 21 plots further ways forward in addressing this issue.[80] Solutions may increasingly be focused upon the micro-level, that is, altering individual behaviour in devolved contexts. Where primary rules address this, enforcement at the appropriate level will demand the co-operation of the national jurisdiction and international supervision.

Yet, as seen above, a crucial limitation is that even where the body of international law contains rules recognised by States as having a binding nature, compliance issues are hard to resolve. Indeed, few treaties provide for executive agencies with policing responsibilities.[81] Any enforcement is generally achieved by reliance upon informal dispute settlement. Although there are few instances of States seeking recourse in the ICJ, an opportunity to consider the notion of sustainable development arose in a dispute between Hungary and Slovakia. The court was called upon to construe treaty obligations concerning a hydroelectric dam project, and specifically upon the question of a lack of entitlement on the part of Hungary to suspend bilateral treaty obligations, alleging ecological necessity, as well as the disproportionate nature of Slovakia's response.[82] The ruling is remarkable for the interposition of the notion of sustainable development into consideration of substantive law affecting resource issues. The judgment contained the following:

> Owing to new scientific insights and to a growing awareness of the risks for mankind – for present and future generations – of pursuit of such interventions (upon nature) at an unconsidered and unabated pace, new norms and standards have been developed, set forth in a great number of instruments during the last two decades. Such new norms have to be taken into consideration, and such new standards given proper weight, not only when States contemplate new activities but also when continuing with activities begun in the past. This need to reconcile economic development with protection of the environment is aptly expressed in the concept of sustainable development.[83]

There is therefore a potential for application of the principle within the context of evolving international law. Commenting upon the judgment, Higgins detects 'the change in focus from disputes about concessions and control of natural resources to disputes about sustainability and the limits of resource use'.[84]

---

78 Sands, 1995, p 16.

79 Boyle and Freestone, 1999, p 6.

80 Agenda 21, Chapter 4.

81 But see, eg, the Washington CITES Convention on International Trade in Endangered Species of Wild Fauna and Flora; and the Paris Convention for the Protection of the Marine Environment of the North East Atlantic.

82 *Case concerning the Gabcikovo-Nagymaros dam project (Hungary v Slovakia)* (1998) 37 ILM 162.

83 *Ibid*, para 140.

84 Higgins, 1999, p 111.

The international obstacles should arguably be easier to address, but perversely show every sign of persistence. This problem draws upon the considerable tensions between the extension of environmental protection measures and the liberal order's formalised global commitments to free trade. Grounds for conflict may therefore arise where trade is restricted by unilateral measures, on grounds either of protecting the domestic or global environment or designed to influence the domestic policies of other States. Such restrictions might even be prescribed in accordance with international environmental law. Yet other treaty frameworks often make reference to trade priorities. For instance, the Framework Convention on Climate Change states that measures taken, 'including unilateral ones, should not constitute a means of arbitrary or unjustifiable discrimination or a disguised restriction on international trade'.[85] Likewise, Agenda 21 devotes some attention to the socio-economic nexus that international trade has with the environment.[86]

For the future, the integration of environment and development issues raises barely explored questions of trade and protection. The WTO is now responsible for the operation of a host of multilateral trade and related agreements. Its commitment to the benefits of free trade, and to securing economic growth and stable economic relations through the multilateral trading system, derive from the General Agreement on Tariffs and Trade (GATT) process, adopted in 1947. They are based upon the prohibition of 'arbitrary discrimination between products from different countries' and of national measures which 'constitute disguised restrictions to trade'.[87] Unsurprisingly, at least for its time, GATT made scant reference to environmental concerns, save for limited references to national measures necessary to protect human, animal or plant life or health, and relating to natural resource conservation.[88] Although criticised as the face of globalised markets, its defenders argue that the WTO protects the poorer nations. Grounds offered for this view include the assertion that immediate priorities of developing countries include 'escape from poverty, rather than ending child labour or clearing up air pollution. To ban their imports because they do not have labour and environmental standards as high as rich countries is to deny them any hope of development – and the ability to afford such high standards in future'.[89] Such acceptance of short-termism is the antithesis of sustainability. Yet, notwithstanding that politico-economic activities (including aid packages) can destabilise primary producer markets elsewhere, there is a substantial political constituency among nations which is sceptical of further environmental incursions into world trade law.[90]

Whilst the GATT process was originally supported by mere negotiative and diplomatic techniques, enforcement processes have become increasingly effective. In 1995, following the Uruguay Round, a new adjudicative system emerged, under the auspices of the Dispute Settlement Understanding (DSU), and as a consequence the framework provides for an adjudicative structure. Paradoxically, it can therefore be said

---

85 Article 3(5); see Cameron and Makuch, 1996.

86 Agenda 21, Chapter 2.

87 See Article XX of GATT, as amended, following the Uruguay Round of Multilateral Trade Negotiations (1994) 33 ILM 13.

88 Article XX, paras (b), (g); and see Cromer, 1995.

89 Legrain, 2000, p 35.

90 See Biermann, 2001.

that upon the wider international stage environment-related disputes now fall for resolution under the auspices of the WTO.[91] The settlement of disputes through the DSU has teeth: for instance, failure to implement recommendations may lead to requests for compensation or suspensions of concessions, as well as imposition of sanctions against defaulting States. References in the preamble to the post-1995 WTO Agreement make it possible for the objective of sustainable development to be cited in support of environmental arguments. The Appellate Body has itself ruled that just as under the WTO 'the optimal use of the world's resources should be made in accordance with the objectives of sustainable development ... we believe it must add colour, texture and shading to our interpretation of the agreements annexed to the WTO agreement'.[92]

More specifically, it appears that two tests are to apply to disputes concerning the application of environmental standards alleged to be beyond GATT rules: namely scientific justification or risk assessment.[93] These tests have been applied by the GATT panel hearing the dispute and by the Appellate Body.[94] Some commentators therefore conclude that the WTO is capable of more fully integrating environmental and developmental considerations into its pursuit of further trade liberalisation and economic growth.[95] This process is said to afford a pooling of knowledge and resources, and a counterweight to disproportionate national pressures, which 'may help to structure and systemize regulatory decision making'.[96] Reviewing the major environmental adjudications to date, Cameron and Campbell are optimistic that environmental objectives are gradually being incorporated into the world trade system, and emphasise the need for further integration of principles of international law into its processes.[97]

Yet there are problems for State and regional policy makers, where compliance is likely to detract from regulatory activities despite what they perceive to be best advice. Jordan and Voisey conclude that the point of balance between the two is likely to be determined in bodies such as the WTO, expressed to be 'more powerful' than the UN.[98] Moreover, its adjudicative procedures appear, at least at global level, to be the only significant ones in place: 'The WTO has a dispute settlement mechanism which is envied and feared in about equal measure by those that participate in the policy making arena. Compulsory, swift, rule-based, and backed by the kind of sanctions which make politicians and business leaders think again, the WTO has already attracted cases which would not have been heard anywhere else and which involve environmental protection'.[99] Indeed, Earth Summit II in 1997 drew back from declaring that measures under environmental agreements should not be challenged in the WTO, preferring to emphasise the need to seek to incorporate sustainable development and environmental protection into trade regimes.

---

91 See Cameron and Campbell, 1998, Parts I and II.

92 *Shrimp/Turtle Dispute* (1998) 37 ILM 832; (1999) 38 ILM 118, 153.

93 See, eg, WTO Agreement on Sanitary and Phytosanitary Measures, Art 3(3).

94 See *European Communities – Measures Affecting Meat/Livestock and Meat Products (Hormones) Case*, WT/DS26/AB/R, WT/DS48/AB/R.

95 Galizzi, 2000, p 119.

96 Breyer and Heyvaert, 2000, pp 347–48.

97 Cameron and Campbell, 1998, especially pp 215–18.

98 Jordan and Voisey, 1998, p 96.

99 Cameron and Campbell, 1998, p 204.

The acceptability of such an adjudicative forum, however, appears questionable. As Breyer and Heyvaert have put it, the WTO procedures 'will play an important role in evaluating, sanctioning, or condemning risk regulation, an activity for which ... they are perhaps not optimally equipped'.[100] Moreover, fundamental issues will inevitably require determination in circumstances of acknowledged technical or scientific uncertainty. Yet, as genetic biology disputes between the United States and the European Union surface before the WTO, it is that body's adjudication processes which appear to be charged with what amounts essentially to a surrogate political role. Concerns arise as to policy orientation, given the circumstances of the WTO process 'taking the lead in deciding ... where the balance between global free trade and environmental protection lies'.[101] Its appropriateness for this task must be questioned. From the environmental perspective there is a threat of myopia towards sustainability constraints which demands more integrative adjudicative processes.[102] In contrast, on a regional basis, the European Union has sought to develop a more inclusive approach. The European Court of Justice some time ago accepted that the application of principles of free movement of goods, under Article 28 of the Treaty of Rome, is subject to limitation on grounds of protection of the environment as a mandatory requirement.[103] Sands has even felt able to conclude that, by such recognition, the ECJ 'has given (on occasion) environmental protection objectives an equal (or occasionally greater) weight over entrenched economic and trade objectives. And it has demonstrated a willingness to recognise and act upon some of the special characteristics of environmental issues'.[104]

3 THE PRECAUTIONARY PRINCIPLE

Indeed the flow of gradual, normative incursions of environmental ideas through European Community processes into UK domestic law is under way. The founding treaty now provides a framework for responses to the wider implications for the environment of policy making and economic activities. The idea of sustainable development shares a common genus with numerous other emergent principles in the arena of environmental protection. For instance, prospectively, in the search for sustainable solutions, the incorporation of the notion of integration into the treaty is likely to become increasingly significant, and appears in the discussion below. The link between sustainable development and the precautionary principle appears especially powerful, and prior consideration is therefore given to this principle.

---

100 Breyer and Heyvaert, 2000, p 349; also, Oesterle, 2001.
101 Bell and McGillivray, 2000, p 106; and see *Tuna/Dolphin Dispute* (1992) 30 ILM 1594 and Shrimp/Turtle Dispute (1998) 37 ILM 832; (1999) 38 ILM 118.
102 See Mugwanya, 1999.
103 Case 302/86, *EC v Denmark* [1988] ECR 4627, para 9.
104 Sands, 1996a, p 227.

3.1   The nature of the precautionary principle

The successful application of the precautionary principle is central to a successful balancing of other policy demands against the risks of unacceptable levels of environmental degradation. The principle has been formulated primarily in response to a problem of policy formulation in the face of scientific uncertainty. The underlying premise is that 'the damaging effects of human activities may become irreversible before the scientific community can agree the precise nature or scope of their impact; taking precautionary action can help avoid this'.[105] Impacts include those concerning whether there will be environmental damage from certain activities, if so, its extent, or indeed the likelihood of its occurrence. The principle is therefore one response to temporal and spatial difficulties connected with determining the nature and extent of environmental harm. It is commonly accepted that the principle derives from the German notion of *vorsorgeprinzip*, which encapsulates a duty owed to citizens in the context of uncertainty as to risk, in contrast with *gefahrenabwehr*, or duty to afford protection against identifiable risks.[106]

Seeking a workable definition is, however, more problematic. The Council of Europe's independent group of experts produced model provisions for an environmental protection code in 1994.[107] The aim was to offer a scheme for integrated environmental protection and promotion of an ecologically stable and healthy environment, by reference to the promotion of sustainable resource use.[108] Amongst a range of general principles,[109] the precautionary principle is defined there as follows:

> When planning or implementing any action, measures shall be taken beforehand in order to avoid or reduce any risk or danger to the environment. Everyone whose activities are likely to have a significant impact on the environment shall, before taking any action, take into consideration the interests of others as well as the need to protect the environment. If, in the light of experience or scientific knowledge, an action is likely to cause a risk or danger to the environment, it shall be carried out only after prior assessment indicating that it will have no adverse impact on the environment.[110]

Applying some flesh to the conceptual bones, O'Riordan and Cameron have pointed to a range of core elements, namely: preventative anticipation, in a willingness to act in advance of definite scientific proof, on grounds that it is better to pay a little now than much more later, thereby affording a breathing space for earth's resources and systems; a concession to our ignorance as to tolerance thresholds; shifting the burden of proof onto those proposing developments or changes; concern for future generations and in recognition of their interests or rights; accepting responsibility for former ecological debts; requiring greater caution from those who have committed the most damage to date; and applying proportionality, so restraints are not unduly costly.[111]

---

105 Holder, 1997, p 123.
106 von Moltke, 1988, pp 57–70.
107 Council of Europe Model Act on the Protection of the Environment, 1994.
108 Article 2.
109 Articles 4–11.
110 Article 5.
111 O'Riordan and Cameron, 1994.

On the face of it, the precautionary principle presupposes a fine shift in the balance of environmental debate, so that 'once a *prima facie* case is made that a risk exists, then scientific uncertainty works against the potential polluter rather than, as in the past, in his/her favour'.[112] It is unlikely, however, that any applications of the principle are likely to move quite so far, without a mandating of formal requirements. A pragmatic view is offered by von Moltke, who describes the principle as 'a guide for policy development. In this respect, it always incorporates some notion of practical feasibility, including economic capacity. At the same time, it clearly goes beyond a "no regrets" policy which is based on realising all environmental gains which can be achieved without additional cost'.[113] A more specific role for the principle has been ascertained by Gray, in two essential respects, namely, where knowledge is insufficient either as to a chemical or its effects within the biogeochemical cycle and where concentrations are approaching quality standard or critical load limits.[114] However, many scientists are critical, for instance, perceiving the principle as shifting the power balance away from 'sound science' and into the realm of political and social factors.[115] It is also suggested that demands for greater caution will result in hidden economic costs, through the relegation of other interests, such as a slowing down in innovation.[116] It is moreover politically problematic, as it indicates collision with established economic freedoms which are supported by limitations upon the range of legal liability. It is therefore unclear how far proactive legal measures, including the imposition of further precautionary regulation, or even liability without proof of damage, might be politically acceptable.

3.2 Recognition of the precautionary principle

Yet it is argued that the principle is intrinsic to a wide range of environmental measures, particularly at the international level.[117] It indeed enjoys a widespread recognition in international law documents, and its ubiquity suggests that it was seen as a major plank of the Rio process. Thus, for instance, Principle 15 of the Rio Declaration 1992 provides: 'Where there are threats of serious or irretrievable damage, lack of full scientific certainty shall not be used as a reason for postponing cost-effective measures to prevent environmental degradation.' Likewise, the preamble to the Convention on Biological Diversity states: 'Where there is a threat of significant reduction or loss of biological diversity, lack of full scientific certainty should not be used as a reason for postponing measures to avoid or minimize such a threat.' The Climate Change Convention holds that 'Parties should take precautionary measures to anticipate, prevent or minimize the causes of climate change and mitigate its adverse effects. Where there are threats of serious or irreversible damage, lack of full scientific research shall not be used as a reason for postponing such measures, taking into account the policies and measures to deal with climate change should be cost-effective so as to ensure global benefits at the lowest

---

112 Freestone and Hey, 1996, p 13.
113 Von Moltke, 1996, p 106.
114 Gray, 1996b, p 135.
115 Freestone and Hey, 1996, p 13.
116 Cf Porritt, 2000, p 43.
117 Freestone and Hey, 1996, p 3.

cost.'[118] To complete the set, and whilst non-binding, Agenda 21 states: 'A precautionary and anticipatory rather than a reactive approach is necessary to prevent the degradation of the marine environment.'[119]

The principle is, however, a contestable concept. Its status at international law remains unclear. Citing the Rio process, Cameron and Abouchar argue that it has achieved the status of custom,[120] pointing out that the precautionary principle 'is no less vague than most principles of international law'.[121] Its prevalence, however, in international documents does not prompt other jurists to go so far. It suffers from a fundamental lack of specificity. Sands accepts that an argument can be made for its becoming a principle of customary law,[122] but holds that whilst 'potentially the most radical and far-reaching of environmental principles, its meaning and effect are unclear and remain mired in controversy'.[123] Birnie and Boyle see both normative character and practical utility of the principle undermined by unanswered questions 'concerning the point at which it becomes applicable to any given activity'.[124]

There has moreover been but limited judicial recognition of any legal normative approach. Judge Weeramantry, former Vice President of the ICJ, has argued that the Stockholm Declaration led to the emergence of a new principle, based upon the protection of present and future generations and the precautionary principle. Thus in the light of evidence problems facing claimants, especially as to availability of information, the law 'cannot function in respect of the environment unless a legal principle is evolved ... and environmental law has responded with what has come to be described as the precautionary principle'. On such basis it was said to become possible to seek 'to prevent on a provisional basis, the threatened environmental degradation, until such time as the full scientific evidence becomes available in refutation'.[125] There is also limited national authority applying the principle, for instance in the New South Wales Land and Environment Court, where it has been described as 'a statement of common sense' for the purposes of interpretation of wildlife conservation legislation.[126]

At a regional level, the adoption of the principle within the European Union, together with a commitment to sustainable development and related principles, is of significance for the UK's policy making machinery. Article 174 of the revised founding treaty now sets out certain key environmental principles upon which environmental policies shall be based: these include the precautionary principle, and the principles of the polluter pays, preventive action and rectification of damage at source.[127] These are all formally linked to a general aim of a high level of environmental protection. The Treaty on European Union

---

118 Article 3.
119 Chapter 17, para 17.21.
120 Cameron and Abouchar, 1996, p 52.
121 Cameron and Abouchar, 1996, p 46.
122 Sands, 1995, p 213.
123 Sands, 2000, pp 375–76.
124 Birnie and Boyle, 1992, p 98.
125 *Nuclear Tests II Case: Request for an Examination of the Situation in Accordance with Paragraph 63 of the Court's 1974 Judgment in the Nuclear Tests Case (New Zealand v France)* [1995] ICJ Rep 288 (dissenting opinion).
126 Cited by Cameron and Abouchar, 1996, p 47.
127 Article 174(2); and see European Commission, 2000c.

(TEU), negotiated at Maastricht in 1992, states that the European Union 'shall set itself the following objectives: – to promote economic and social progress and a high level of employment and to achieve balanced and sustainable development'.[128] Sustainable development became a fundamental objective upon amendment of the founding treaty at Amsterdam in 1997: 'implementing common policies or activities ... to promote throughout the Community a harmonious, balanced and sustainable development of economic activities' within the Community's remit.[129] Whilst this does not appear to be a justiciable concept, its major influence will be with reference to the principle of integration, discussed below, as well perhaps as a principle of interpretation where Community legislation is the subject of dispute.

It remains, however, unclear as to how far such principles can derive legal status within Community law, beyond a role in informing policy making priorities.[130] Their development is largely dependent upon follow-up legislative process.[131] This suggests an expression of political will, and at most a non-binding norm: in so far as the precautionary principle becomes 'a general indication of what might be desirable policy'.[132] Such difficulties are unsurprising, and accord with Dworkin's point that a principle, unlike a rule, 'states a reason that argues in one direction, but does not necessitate a particular decision'.[133] The concept of the polluter pays is likewise problematic, beyond perhaps somewhat amorphous ideas such as internalising environmental costs, or guiding those responsible for regulatory compliance, or even as a potential policy pointer in dealing with toxic tort claims. Whilst, as seen previously, policy approaches must increasingly take account of externalities, true external costs of environmental damage are however difficult to assess. Moreover, there are likely to be others, such as employees, consumers, creditors, or indeed taxpayers, upon whom the real burden of payment falls. To an extent, this mimics the idea of environment as a public 'good'. Thus, whether activities are operated privately (as, in the UK, for the present, are the railways) or publicly (as, for instance, are the police and other regulators), economic costs incurred due to necessary investment, or indeed in meeting legal liabilities, may ultimately be a matter for the public purse.

Such principles may however be brought within recognisably legal structures in accordance with developing European jurisprudential approaches to interpretation. For instance, it has been established by the European Court of Justice (ECJ) that it may be possible to rely upon the principle of rectification at source where an action is apparently otherwise taken in defiance of Community law.[134] It is further possible to illustrate the interpretative process by reference to proceedings brought in the wake of the BSE crisis. Following the imposition by the European Commission of a Community- and world-wide ban on the export of beef and derived products from the UK, the UK Government

---

128 TEU, Article 2.
129 Founding Treaty, Article 2.
130 Indeed, their application would in any event be subject to the proportionality principle: see Purdue, 1991, p 535.
131 Hession and Macrory, 1994, pp 151–67.
132 Holder, 1997, p 130.
133 Dworkin, 1977, p 24.
134 Such as the upon a refusal to grant a licence for the import of certain waste from another Member State: Case C-2/90, *EC v Belgium* [1993] 1 CMLR 365, 397 (the *Wallonia Waste Case*).

brought proceedings alleging illegality. The ruling of the ECJ was based explicitly upon the question of the proportionality of the Commission's action.[135] Addressing the provisions of Article 174, the ECJ ruled that 'Community policy on the environment is to pursue the objective *inter alia* of protecting human health ... (and) provides that that policy is to aim at a high level of protection and is to be based in particular on the principles that preventive action should be taken and that environmental protection requirements must be integrated into the definition and implementation of other Community policies'.[136] The basis of the judgment can therefore be seen to be analogous to the precautionary principle, as in the unambiguous statement that in the event of 'uncertainty as to the existence or extent of risks to human health, the institutions may take protective measures without having to wait until the reality and seriousness of those risks become fully apparent'.[137]

Further legal development in respect of the Article 174 principles will depend upon future legislative action within the Community. The English courts have implicitly recognised this, in the course of considering whether a minister was required to apply the precautionary principle, in exercising delegated powers to authorise electricity cable laying, with potential for risks due to ensuing high local electromagnetic impacts. By reference to the appearance of the principle in Article 174, it was held in the High Court that 'it is not intended that a statement of policy or, still less, a statement of the principles which will underlie a policy should in itself create an obligation upon a Member State'.[138]

3.3 Effectiveness of the precautionary principle

The effective application of the precautionary principle is therefore in large measure dependent upon explicit political and adjudicative determinations. For the UK, as for other Member States, it is likely that any significant developments will come through Community processes. In default of any such substantive developments, applying a precautionary approach may operate merely to point the process in a particular direction. It enables 'a balanced approach to risks. It serves the interest of risk-aversion; yet it means that the precautionary principle is not a trump card that *a priori* overrides other considerations'.[139] Porritt suggests contrasting weak and strong formulations for such a balancing process, which to an extent mirror similar approaches to sustainability already discussed. The weak formulation gives a higher weighting to environmental factors in standard cost benefit calculations, and tougher regulations to take account of uncertainties, whilst the strong version requires strict measures in order to protect critical natural capital, and potentially encompasses the abandonment of otherwise viable economic activities.[140] Yet, weak or strong, the principle does not necessarily operate on absolute terms. Nollkaemper points to mitigation of the principle by such factors as the

---

135 Paragraphs 110–11.

136 Paragraph 100.

137 Paragraph 99.

138 *R v Secretary of State for Trade and Industry ex p Duddridge* [1995] Env LR 151, 168 (*per* Smith LJ) (approved by Court of Appeal at [1996] Env LR 325).

139 Nollkaemper, 1996, p 81.

140 Porritt, 2000, p 44.

typical balancing of risks as between pollution of different media, and the balancing of cost benefit.[141] This may be expressed through the establishment of thresholds, such as 'threats of serious or irreversible damage' or 'reasonable grounds for concern that pollution may be caused'.[142] Such pragmatic precautionary tests are duly constrained by 'indeterminacy of threshold levels, the insufficiently developed procedures to address risks below threshold levels and the allocation of the burden of proof'.[143]

The rate of further progress in producing a coherent application of the precautionary principle is therefore uncertain. A significant related development is the inclusion now within the European Community's founding treaty of a formal commitment to integration. In 1992, at Maastricht, a requirement to integrate environmental policies into the EC policy making processes was inserted into the treaty. As was seen in the preceding chapter, amendments negotiated at Amsterdam,[144] have promoted this provision into a general objective of the treaty, with a view to promoting sustainable development.[145] The principle of integration has arguably graduated to a central (if not pre-eminent) role in the policy making hierarchy.[146] It is indicative of moves towards protection extending beyond regulatory constraints, within a structure referred to by Winter as 'emancipatory law' which is duly 'inoculated with ecological considerations'.[147] On a broader policy level, the council meeting at Helsinki in December 1999 announced that integration of environmental issues and sustainable development into the definition and implementation of policies is a central factor in the fulfilment of Europe's commitments under Kyoto, which is due to be ratified in 2002. The Commission was further invited to prepare by June 2001 a proposal for a long term strategy for integration of policies for economically, socially and ecologically sustainable development, with an eye to the Community's contribution to the 10-year Rio process review in 2002.[148]

The Commission has since embarked upon a series of sectoral strategies: initial strategies were agreed for energy, transport and agriculture at Helsinki;[149] and other sectors for which strategies have been mandated include the internal market, industry, development and fisheries.[150] The focusing of strategies more prospectively has advantages in terms of enhanced recognition of impacts on sustainability, as for instance in the long-overdue setting of long term targets for sustainable transport. Schedules for strategic compliance will lean heavily on the production of sectoral indicators, which

---

141 Eg, Best Available Techniques, under Art 2(3) OSPAR Convention 1992.

142 Climate Change Convention, Art 3(3); OSPAR Convention 1992, Art 2(2).

143 Nollkaemper, 1996, p 94.

144 OJ C340/42, 10 November 1997.

145 Article 6.

146 van Calster and Deketelaere, 1998; and see O'Riordan and Voisey, 1998.

147 Winter, 1989, p 45.

148 See European Commission, 2001b, discussed in Chapter 1.

149 Council Reports: *Strategy for Integrating Environmental Aspects and Sustainable Development into Energy Policy*, 13773/99; *Transport and Environment*, 11717/99; *Strategy on the Environment Integration and Sustainable Development in Common Agriculture Policy*, 13078/99.

150 See, eg, *Integration of Environmental Protection and Sustainable Development into the Internal Market Policy*, 13622/99; *Integrating Sustainable Development into the Industry Policy of the European Union*, 13549/1/99/REV 1; *Integration of Environment in the Community's Development Policies*, 13644/99.

have also been under development by the Commission.[151] These are intended to function as contact points between policy makers and the various sectors, supported by reporting structures. Sectoral policy statements will be required to address such matters as the setting up of monitoring arrangements, assessment methods, evaluation, and follow-up strategies.[152]

The required take-up is to be variously achieved in Member States, and likewise the UK is moving towards the production of policy integration indicators and objectives within its overall sustainable development strategy referred to in the next section. Regional and national strategies are also expected to coincide with relevant policy initiatives. For instance, in agriculture, reform of the common agricultural policy (under Agenda 2000 mechanisms) is to be linked to integration strategy, so as to contribute to environmental objectives for reductions in chemicals and in emissions, protection of bio-diversity and soil, and improvements in water quality.[153]

The integration principle is therefore a high motivational factor for the policy agenda. Justified doubts otherwise as to the legal status of the integration principle, for reasons similar to those explored above, have nevertheless been challenged. It has for instance been forcefully argued that where an objective is achievable in a variety of ways, the integration principle entails a choice in accordance with the proportionality principle for the least environmentally harmful.[154] This suggests an analogy with the approach taken by the ECJ when addressing the issue of environmental protection for the first time, accepting it as an essential objective of the Community: 'the principle of freedom of trade is not to be viewed in absolute terms but is subject to certain limits justified by the objectives of general interest pursued by the Community provided that the rights in question are not substantially impaired.'[155]

In contrast, internationally, a narrower view appears to be emerging through the institutional apparatus of the WTO.[156] This may not be surprising, given the paucity of specific referencing to the environment in formal documents. However, there is provision in the Agreement on Sanitary and Phytosanitary Measures to the following effect: 'in cases where relevant scientific evidence is insufficient, a Member may provisionally adopt sanitary or phytosanitary measures on the basis of available or pertinent information ... In such circumstances, Members shall seek to obtain the additional information necessary for a more objective assessment of risk and review the sanitary or phytosanitary measure accordingly within a reasonable period of time.'[157] In resolving the Beef Hormone dispute between Europe and the United States, both the adjudicating panel and Appellate Body rejected an interpretation through a standard based upon the recognised principle of deference. This principle accepts the exercise of discretionary authority by local

---

151 European Commission, *Coordinated Report on Environmental Indicators*, 13598/99.

152 Eg, European Commission, *Communication on Indicators for the Integration of Environmental Concerns into the Common Agricultural Policy*, COM (00) 20 final (2000).

153 European Commission, *Communication on Directions Towards Sustainable Agriculture*, COM (99) 22 (1999).

154 Jans, 2000, pp 17–23.

155 See Case 240/83, *Procureur de la République v Association de Défense des Brûleurs d'Huiles Usagées* [1985] ECR 531, para 120.

156 Cf Cameron and Campbell, 1998, pp 218–19.

157 Article 5(7).

administrations – provided that the exercise can be construed as reasonable. Whilst perhaps less non-invasive than the *Wednesbury* principles under English law, this does at least constrain WTO bodies from engaging in *de novo* reviews. Although the panel emphasised that it was necessary to reach an objective assessment, by application to both facts and quantitative scientific evidence, the Appellate Body appeared to favour a standard of assessment which might enable the leading of broader arguments, of a non-quantitative nature. However, the nuances of such an approach appear quite subtle. They have thus been compared to another form of *de novo* review, which 'reduces to the following rule of thumb: 'as long as a WTO panel's interpretation of scientific evidence is plausible, it may set aside any regulatory measure based on a different interpretation.'[158] Separately from the issue of appropriate international adjudicative bodies and structures referred to above, therefore, it will become increasingly important that emerging sustainable development principles can be factored into WTO arrangements.

Finally, it remains unclear how extensively the precautionary principle is capable of applications within a coherent legal framework. As will be seen in Chapter 8, the role of science is essential in understanding risk. Balancing processes must respond to objections raised to changes which will veer somewhere between the frankly Luddite (say, seeking a total prohibition on stem cell research) and the near-convincing (as for example in the case of the use of the chemical DDT).[159] Referring to some of the arguments concerning the testing of genetically modified crops, it has been stated that if the principle 'is used not just to constrain risky innovation, but to halt even the gathering of data on which any rational decision making process must rest, then it is dead in the political water as a serious policy tool. And with it our claim to be as concerned about "sound science" as anyone employed by government or big business'.[160] At the other extreme, perhaps only around 3% of (over 75,000) synthetic chemicals in industrial production and use have been subjected to comprehensive testing for toxicity. Progress is slow, given the limitations on toxicological analysis, the implications of which will also be considered further in Chapter 8. Indeed, Porritt describes the current control process as 'deeply politicized', in that the chemical industry has made sure that environmental regulations are written in such a way that the burden of proof rests on the regulator to prove each individual chemical, in isolation, is harmful'.[161]

The precautionary principle therefore operates in a terrain beyond that of conventional risk assessment, which applies a systematic, procedural approach on the basis of available, quantifiable data. A more pre-emptive process, such as the precautionary principle, should be closely allied with a principle of reverse onus for industrial chemicals which 'shifts the burden of proof off the shoulders of the public and onto those who produce, import, or use the substance in question'.[162] An illustration is the approach in Sweden, which is moving away from regulation on a substance-by-substance basis, requiring that by 2007 all products sold must be free from substances that are persistent and liable to bio-accumulate.[163] In the light of continuing high levels of

158 Breyer and Heyvaert, 2000, p 351.
159 Carson, 1965, pp 35–38.
160 Porritt, 2000, p 79; also, Rosenbaum, 1991, pp 45–46.
161 Porritt, 2000, p 94.
162 Steingraber, 1999, p 270.
163 Discussed by Porritt, 2000, pp 100–01.

scientific uncertainty, and *a fortiori* legal uncertainty, a heavy political onus falls upon policy makers (and, through the political process, citizens). Indeed, 'the conflict between social institutions – both legal and economic institutions which correspond to human norms giving expression to the social contract – and the natural environment – which most certainly does not respond to social norms – remains the central dilemma in defining effective environmental policy'.[164] Yet, for all the positive signs referred to above, the opportunities for effective environmental planning may become increasingly restricted. Admittedly, in Europe it is explicitly provided that measures adopted under the environmental article 'shall not prevent any Member State from maintaining or introducing more stringent protective measures. Such measures must be compatible with this Treaty. They shall be notified to the Commission'.[165] Yet, given the need to consider real changes in how we run world economies, the importance of the WTO in hearing challenges to environmental 'protectionism', in effect as a primary adjudication mechanism on domestic, regional and international law principles, is a profound cause for disquiet.

4 SUSTAINABLE APPLICATIONS FOR NATIONAL POLICY AND LAW

Whereas it was appropriate that consideration of the precautionary principle in the previous section could be developed at a stage removed from domestic legal mechanisms, attention is now given to questions affecting the translation of sustainable solutions into national policy and law. Indeed, in view of the constraints referred to earlier in this chapter, it is important to consider domestic, as well as regional, regulatory and policy making regimes as a primary focus for the delivery of sustainable development. Progress towards sustainable solutions demands changes in legal processes, and perhaps too our understandings of liability triggers in the context of environmental harm. This exercise must extend over traditional areas of law, as well as by recourse to reformed policy approaches discussed previously. In particular, by reference to regional initiatives, moves towards integrated strategies are being mirrored in national processes.

4.1   Private law and review mechanisms

The relevance of private law mechanisms is discussed more fully in Chapter 3, and for the present, three points are noted. First, it is necessary to recognise that private property has an entrenched status in the common law, the liberal traditions of which do not so readily accommodate wider notions of public interest. Indeed, in some jurisdictions, such as US federal law, there are closely related constitutional guarantees which for the most part render private rights inviolable, at least to the extent that full market value compensation will adhere in the event of disruption.[166] The tendency of private rights to trump welfare considerations continues to prevail.[167]

---

164 von Moltke, 1996, p 97.
165 Article 176.
166 See *Lucas v South Carolina Coastal Council*, 505 US 1003 (1992).
167 Dworkin, 1977.

Secondly, as a vehicle for cohesive, structured environmental improvement, the private law has inevitably been found wanting. Reasons for this centre on the very nature of private legal processes, and especially in their reliance upon litigation, which tends to be both sporadic and reactive, whereas continuing and injunctive approaches are more likely to bring about change. Moreover, access to private law is limited by the availability and scope of a recognised cause of action, as well as by any restraining terms.[168] In this latter respect, English law generally requires a claimant to establish fault, and specifically foreseeability of the relevant type of harm.[169] Liability is moreover likely to be avoided upon compliance by the defendant with state-of-the-art practice.[170] Also problematic in this context is that it is necessary for the claimant to have suffered recognised harm.[171] Even in this event, it is in the nature of environmental threats that it may be difficult to adduce technical evidence which is sufficient to establish a causative nexus leading to that harm, and indeed as to whether the defendant is a sufficient part of that causative link.[172] The law's adjudicative processes apply burdens of proof, but are in reality looking to reduce facts to an acceptable level of certainty. It is by contrast uncomfortable with problems of objective uncertainty. Acceptance of the existence of substantial scientific doubt is not conducive to tests which are based upon whether it is more probable than not that a defendant's conduct caused the harm.[173] This is so even where the nature of the evidential task is mitigated by reference to the idea of substantial increase in risk of harm.[174] Such problems are particularly evident in cases of diffuse or chronic pollution.

Thirdly, any environmental public interest litigation will inevitably raise difficult policy considerations. In private law, courts are traditionally quick to staunch potential floodgate repercussions. The English High Court case of *Merlin v British Nuclear Fuels*[175] is a simple illustration of the point. The case arose out of a strict liability claim for damage resulting from the nuclear energy process emissions from the Sellafield power plant.[176] The value of the claimant's house was severely reduced due to public awareness of high levels of radionuclide background radiation in the vicinity. The claimant could not however establish a link to long term damage to health. In respect of property damage, the court refused a remedy on grounds of there being no physical damage to the fabric of the building. This therefore placed circumstances such as these firmly within the economic loss category, which is generally disastrous for a claimant in English tort law.[177] Moreover, the conclusion was that 'it is in the nature of nuclear installations that there will be some additional radionuclides present and if mere presence of this additional source is enough to constitute damage ... the result would inevitably be that the defendants were indeed in breach of their statutory duty every day to possibly thousands of citizens, each of whom have a claim for compensation'.[178]

---

168 *Hunter v Canary Wharf Ltd* [1997] AC 655.

169 *Cambridge Water Company v Eastern Counties Leather plc* [1994] 2 AC 264.

170 *Savage v Fairclough* [2000] Env LR 183.

171 *Reay and Hope v BNFL* [1994] Env LR 320.

172 *Graham and Graham v Rechem* [1996] Env LR 158; cf *Margereson and Hancock v JW Roberts* [1996] Env LR 304, discussed by Steele and Wikeley, 1997.

173 *Wilsher v Essex Area Health Authority* [1988] AC 1074.

174 *McGhee v NCB* [1972] 3 All ER 1008.

175 [1990] 2 QB 557.

176 Under s 12 of the Nuclear Installations Act 1965.

177 Cf *Blue Circle Industries v Ministry of Defence* [1998] 3 All ER 385.

178 [1990] 2 QB 557, 572 (*per* Gatehouse J).

Private enforcement may on the face of it be more appropriate in the public law realm. Regulatory incursion, discussed below, presupposes forms of governmental-administrative control, which include enforcement processes and sanctioning arrangements. However, it also brings other legal consequences in its train. Thus, related rights which are inherent in the process may arise. For instance, parties engaged in the regulatory process may have to take account of procedural protections which are not necessarily environmental, in the sense that they may operate in other contexts. An illustration of this is the privilege against self-incrimination, discussed in Chapter 9. Yet certain important domestic legal provisions do attach procedural requirements to environmental measures; this was one notable aim of the European Community's 1985 Directive on environmental impact assessment, to which the argument returns in Chapter 5.[179]

Further rights of challenge may arise through the general application of administrative law principles. A double hurdle lies in wait for the litigant bringing an environmental judicial review application. First, the challenge must come within a recognised head of substantive challenge, which we may call a justiciable issue. Secondly, the courts must be willing to accept the applicant's standing to bring the action. In this latter respect, it is typically difficult for an individual or group to maintain a challenge in defence of the unowned aspects of the environment, or where it cannot otherwise be said that they are victims of an alleged breach. Nevertheless, English courts have shown increased flexibility in recent times, as in the wider interpretation accorded to the 'sufficient interest' test.[180] However, for all such developments, certain other jurisdictions have gone further and allowed a genuine 'citizen suit' right of action pursuant to protection of an asserted environmental interest.[181] Moreover, some jurisdictions have put in place legislation for vesting general environmental rights in citizens.[182] Although there is no space to consider enforcement questions here, a myriad of State constitutional provisions now contain express statements of rights to a clean environment.[183]

As regards substantive rights, although the English courts are relatively at ease with those of a procedural nature, rights of challenge to the exercise of administrative discretion are traditionally constrained within the confines of *Wednesbury* irrelevance and irrationality based principles.[184] However, particular impetus towards more purposive interpretations has come from the European Court of Justice, in its interpretation of the nature of individual rights which can arise under environmental directives.[185] Despite a lack of consistency in approaches,[186] members of the English bench are arguably

---

179 Directive 85/337 on the Assessment of the Effects of Certain Public and Private Projects on the Environment (OJ 1175/40, 5 July 1985; and amending Directive 97/11 (OJ L73/5, 14 March 1997)).

180 See *R v HMIP ex p Greenpeace (No 2)* [1994] Env LR 76.

181 Eg, Morelli, 1997.

182 For instance, the Yukon Territory, s 6 Environment Act 1991: 'The people ... have the right to a healthful natural environment'; Quebec, s 19 Environment Quality Act, RSQ 1977, c Q-2: 'Every person has the right to a healthy environment and to its protection.'

183 For examples see Weiss, 1989.

184 *Associated Provincial Picture Houses Ltd v Wednesbury Corporation* [1948] 1 KB 223.

185 See, for instance, Case C-72/95 *Aannemersbedrijf PK Kraaijevelt BV v Gedeputeerde Staten van Zuid-Holland* [1996] ECR I-5403.

186 See, eg, Alder, 1998.

increasingly in step with such approaches.[187] Aside from this, there has been but patchy progress in the according of substantive rights in national laws, and the English domestic jurisdiction exemplifies this.

4.2   Regulatory impacts

It is through public sector regulation that efforts to impose land use and environmental controls have traditionally progressed. Modern regulation can be imposed in pursuance of either economic or non-economic objectives.[188] Much of this book is concerned with the problem of securing environmental protection in the context of other policy interests. How ensuing conflicts are resolved is indicative of values placed by society upon the environment and land resources. The separation may of course be more apparent than real. For instance, prior to 1986 there was no European Community competence to enact environmental legislative measures at all.[189] The justification for the enactment of over 200 environmental instruments in the area was based on one of two articles: enabling either the harmonisation of laws directly affecting the operation of the common market,[190] or the exercise of residual powers for attainment of objectives of the Community.[191] Indeed, even after an environmental power had first become explicitly available, the Commission (thereby benefiting from easier passage upon qualified majority vote) purported for a time to apply an Article which authorised measures to achieve the objective of a single market.[192] Since 1992 there has been no need for such stratagems, given that equivalent voting procedures now apply.[193]

The idea of environmental regulation is, however, a highly contested area. With the general demise of the heavily State-directed economies, regulatory processes operate against an endemic tension between free and social marketeers. The former embrace regulation in response to failures of markets, and otherwise place reliance upon private law to accord sufficient protection to competition. They demand that regulatory adjustments otherwise do as little damage as possible to the market structure.[194] The latter, embracing the market mechanism where possible, further seek a distributional impact to alleviate the results of market forces, as for instance 'for purposes of social integration and the achievement of other non-economic values, such as social solidarity and equity'.[195] Certain more hopeful public law commentators argue that a third, more functionalist approach is now in the ascendant, emphasising 'good governance, proper procedural proprieties, and the accountability of regulators'.[196] Arguably, an emerging

---

187 *R v Secretary of State for Environment ex p Kingston-upon-Hull, Bristol City Councils* (1996) 8 JEL 336.

188 See Ogus, 1994, Chapter 3.

189 The Single European Act 1986 originally inserted what has now become Article 174.

190 Under Article 94 (ex-100): eg, Directive 85/337 on the Assessment of the Effects of Certain Public and Private Projects on the Environment.

191 Under Article 178 (ex-235): eg, Council Directive (79/409/EEC) on Wild Birds (OJ L103 79, p 1).

192 Under Article 95 (ex-100a); this was sanctioned initially by the ECJ in the *Titanium Oxide Case*: Case C-300/89, *Commission v Council* [1991] ECR I-2827.

193 Article 175(1).

194 See Smith, 1996, pp 257–59, 274–82.

195 McCrudden, 1999, p 276.

196 McCrudden, 1999, p 277.

modern liberal consensus tends to the acceptance of such a free market perspective. But what has been described as increased marketisation has resulted in a growth of private forms of power,[197] which has in turn caused complex problems for regulators.[198] Moreover, national regulation is beset by a multiplicity of public and quasi-public bodies. This carries the risk of a general confusion of accountabilities, as in newly privatised service sectors. Due to what Marr has described as the unbundling of the State, it becomes increasingly difficult to identify especially public accountability but even genuine responsibility for operational matters.[199] For instance the rail sector crisis in 2000, following the fatal derailment at Hatfield, has led to widespread criticism of the structural arrangements for the privatised rail industry.[200] These concern numerous features, including multiplicity of operators and contracting out of track maintenance, but it is notable that there the regulatory system arguably discourages proper maintenance through seeking to apply market solutions, as in compulsory transfer payments to operators on the basis of closure times even for repairs.[201] Problems of accountability are more fully considered in Chapter 10.

The environmental context exemplifies certain 'goods' that markets cannot effectively provide. The past 30 years have been a time of burgeoning environmental regulation. However, recent years have also seen severe pressures brought to bear as to how far the liberal establishment was prepared generally to accept regulatory activity. Even so, concerns over the problem of the 'free rider' have led liberal commentators to approve of legislation to achieve the 'regulation of common pool resources'.[202] However, whilst Epstein appears willing to accommodate the regulation of air pollution and toxic substances, he offers a critique of regulation affecting land under development. This is on the somewhat narrow basis that this can only harm the citizen's own property, and otherwise merely removes the property from the general ecological balance, a matter at most of economic and aesthetic losses.[203] In such circumstances he demands compensation, on the basis of an inflexible distinction between regulation being categorised as either good or bad, that is, either 'an attempt to control the defendant's wrong or to provide a public benefit'.[204] Likewise, markets have not prioritised sustainable solutions. Indeed they tend to encourage short term thinking and a tendency to devalue future impacts.[205] In contrast, in the context of environmental protection, distributional justice demands some form of temporal adjustment. According to Ogus, the 'use or consumption of some resources may vitally affect what is available in the distant future. This applies particularly to non-renewable sources of energy but extends more generally to assets which are the subject of irreversible decisions (allowing animal species or cultural monuments to be destroyed). The market system of allocation obviously fails

197 Hutton, 1996, p 176.
198 Ayres and Braithwaite, 1993.
199 Marr, 1996, pp 252–65.
200 See interview with Transport Minister (2000) New Statesman, 11 December, p 18.
201 Increasing reliance by Railtrack plc upon additional government subsidy in support of its role suggests the possibility of further review.
202 Epstein, 1985, p 345.
203 Epstein, 1985, p 123.
204 Epstein, 1985, p 121.
205 Hutton, 1996, pp 243–56.

to deal with this problem since the preferences of future generations for the relevant resources are not reflected in current demand'.[206] Such arguments echo the numerous intergenerational difficulties discussed in the previous chapter, including methods of assessing future need, the appropriate redistributional timescale, and how far the existence of alternative solutions might be available in any event.[207]

In the UK, as elsewhere, the public interest nature of environmental protection suggests a need for proactive management processes. Sustainability customarily appears in policy statements affecting land use planning control. However, a cautionary note should be struck, for Rydin has asserted that 'British planning has sought fairly systematically to engage with environmental or sustainability issues over the 1990s, if only at the level of rhetoric'.[208] Nevertheless, given its broadly inclusive nature, discussed below, it is especially useful to discuss land use planning in the context of sustainability. Planning is derivative of early incursions of the law into other areas, such as housing and health. There is in turn a broad sweep of policy making which impacts symbiotically together with land use planning. A substantial range of cognate policy and regulation is therefore relevant to the planning process, and it retains a central place in the policy making process. As well as housing and public health, transport, urban and rural policies, and pollution necessarily have particular relationships with planning, and each of these areas will fall under discussion in ensuing chapters.

However, context is vital, and planning control operates within a determinedly free market system. UK strategy commences from the premise that in principle 'the free market in land should operate to achieve an efficient basic allocation of land between competing uses, but the land market is an imperfect one in various ways ... The planning system, in particular, has been a powerful instrument for protecting those aspects of the environment' whose value is not adequately reflected through a free market'.[209] Within the market economy, the relationship of the public and private sectors has proved essential to the success of regulation. It is likewise essential to the successful achievement of policy priorities in the field of sustainability. The picture thus far, in terms of achievement, is patchy, though Bell and McGillivray feel able to point to 'some evidence of emerging policies based on sustainability thinking', though in relatively limited areas, citing minerals planning and out-of-town shopping centres, rather than more generally.[210] The regulation of land use planning control in such a system is inevitably a political battleground. In public sector terms, planning can be a transparent form of social engineering, its foundations rooted in the idea that attitudes and behaviour are responsive to physical surroundings. The concerns of planning are many and varied, but they cannot be said to be bound together in a coherent way. In this, planning reflects policy tensions within the political structures of the State. The concerns of planning with the urban and rural environment, indeed for a wide range of economic and social impacts, and its ability to respond to periods of growth or decline, are considered especially in Chapters 4 and 6 below. There will be consideration of the capacity to

---

206 Ogus, 1994, p 49.
207 For an overview of ethical perspectives, see, eg, Partridge, 1981.
208 Rydin, 1998, p 4.
209 UK Government, 1994, para 41.
210 See Bell and McGillivray, 2000, pp 86–87.

respond through planning to environmental degradation, given the deteriorating condition of our environment for all the vast extension in the panoply of environmental regulation now in place.

As to wider environmental regulation, the UK has a traditionally more closed approach to regulation than pertains in the US.[211] Indeed, our legislation is characterised by the vesting of wide powers in regulatory bodies. Proactive regulatory approaches can be seen in the development of pollution controls. The UK's scheme falls for the most part under the Environmental Protection Act 1990. Nevertheless, controls in respect of air pollution were introduced as early as the Alkali Act 1863. Attempts to tackle water pollution, now contained under the Water Resources Act 1991, originate from the Rivers Pollution Prevention Act 1876. A highly discretionary administration of regulation, supported by legal powers of control and enforcement, traditionally relies upon a strong compliance-based ethos. Such an approach is increasingly augmented by broad central powers of direction, as under the compulsory scheme for the clean-up of contaminated land introduced under the Environment Act 1995. This generally obliges regulators to comply with detailed, mandatory 'guidelines' imposed by central government.[212] Typical compliance approaches reflect a 'community benefit' approach, encouraging corporate concurrence in compliance mechanisms, with an emphasis upon harm prevention and co-operation, with enforcement, especially by prosecution only as a last resort, and only where there has been evidence of intentional, flagrant or continual misbehaviour. Such a benign enforcement approach has been described as 'systematically less orientated to prosecution as the favoured means of securing compliance with the law ... Persuasion works best, however, when the government negotiates against the background of a demonstrated capacity for tough criminal enforcement against companies that resist good-faith negotiation or that perpetrate unusually evil crimes'.[213]

Much of the blame for continuing underachievement in environmental policy terms, despite pervasive regulatory structures, has however been placed upon the command-and-control basis of regulatory regimes. Thus, for instance, the European Community's Fifth Environment Action Programme called for the development of a wider range of strategies in order to secure sustainable development, to include fiscal measures, improved access to environmental information and individual access to justice, more extensive interagency co-operation throughout the Community, and an extension of voluntary measures such as environmental audits and voluntary agreements.[214] Economic instruments have the environmental advantages that they incentivise environmentally responsible behaviour. Price signals may alter market behaviour or otherwise internalise costs in ways that support the polluter pays principle.[215] Though taxation has proved an extremely difficult area to progress at Community level, resort is being had to an increased range of economic instruments at the domestic level.[216] In the

211 Smith, 1996.

212 Contained in Circular 2/2000, *Contaminated Land: Implementation of Part IIA Environmental Protection Act 1990* (Part IIA was inserted into the EPA by s 57 Environment Act 1995).

213 Braithwaite and Pettit, 1992, p 146.

214 European Commission, 1993a.

215 UK Round Table on Sustainable Development, 2000a.

216 See De Souza and Snape, 2000.

UK, an established landfill levy was in 2001 followed by a climate change levy (on certain commercial forms of fossil energy use); and aggregates tax and selective road charging schemes are awaited.[217]

Just as the efficacy of regulation has been seen to require a co-operative culture, then the introduction of broader instruments has been formally linked to the encouragement of stakeholding on the part of various interests. In an attempt to broaden acceptance, especially on the part of business, the Fifth Programme had tentatively addressed this, and the approach reaches something of an apotheosis in the newly proposed Sixth Environment Action Programme, which will also provide the environmental component of the Community's forthcoming strategy for sustainable development.[218] The underlying premise is that a wider constituency is to be addressed in the search for sustainable solutions, and policy makers should therefore seek to work closely with business and consumers, seeking solutions through involvement – and accountability – on the part of all sections of society. As seen in the previous chapter, the programme will maintain commitments to growth and environmental protection, although whether it makes any lasting impact will depend on the success with which economic expectations are altered.

The UK, likewise influenced by the impetus of regional European developments, has sought a formal introduction of sustainability into domestic policy processes. The importance of emerging strategy is that it contains a framework for guiding policy, emphasising policy integration, to include both promoting a competitive economy and combating poverty and social exclusion. The process commenced in a 1990 white paper, which outlined current policies and future policy directions affecting the environment.[219] Following UNCED, in particular the requirement under Agenda 21 for production of national sustainable development strategies, the government has sought to set out general commitments in successive strategy documents: *Sustainable Development: The UK Strategy*, produced in 1994,[220] and a revised version, *A Better Quality of Life: A Strategy for Sustainable Development for the UK*, in 1999.[221] There is a commitment to annual national progress reporting against fifteen headline indicators,[222] and full strategic reviews every five years.[223] The importance of the most current strategy lies in its attempt to scope the sustainability debate, encouraging stakeholding and assuring continued levels of transparency. The document sets objectives for sustainable development: social progress which recognises the needs of everyone; effective protection of the environment; prudent use of natural resources; and maintenance of high and stable levels of economic growth and employment. Without any particular specificity as to the status or applicability of particular elements, the objectives are broken down into ten guiding 'principles and approaches'. These are as follows: putting people at the centre; taking a long term perspective; taking account of costs and benefits; creating an open and supportive

---

217 See ENDS Report 314, *The End of a First Term's Environmental Tax Reforms*, pp 21–23 (March 2001).
218 European Commission, 2001a.
219 UK Government, 1990.
220 UK Government, 1994.
221 UK Government, 1999.
222 UK Government, 1999, at para 10.11.
223 UK Government, 1999, at para 10.12.

economic system; combating poverty and social exclusion; respecting environmental limits; the precautionary principle; using scientific knowledge; transparency, information, participation and access to justice; and making the polluter pay.[224] The most substantial section of the document sets headline indicators for sustainable development in order to measure progress and inform policy decisions.[225] There is no space here to provide an extensive review of such indicators, although they include the following: climate change; energy supply; development assistance; air quality and the atmosphere; water quality; marine activities; water bio-diversity; fisheries; coastal areas; soil; contaminated land; landscape and wildlife; forests and woodland; and minerals.

There is, however, concern as to how integration is to be achieved. Much may depend upon the impact of integrative developments at the European level previously discussed.[226] For instance, the UK strategy does not appear to set 'over-riding objectives, targets and timetables which other government departments, regional and local authorities must meet. In fact, there are no new quantitative targets or timetables. This reflects the very broad scope of the document, and the consequent need to secure the approval of other ministers for specific new policy commitments'.[227] Integration must also in the future take account of UK regional developments. Not only are there separate initiatives in Northern Ireland and under the new devolved institutional arrangements for Scotland and Wales, but, in line with the Agenda 21 philosophy, strategic documents are being produced especially for the newly created English regions. There are eight such regions outside London and regional assemblies are drawn from local authorities. The national strategy requires the production of sustainable development 'frameworks' for all English regions. This to be achieved through either voluntary regional chambers, as designated by central government for a regional development agency area and with wider membership, or regional sustainable development Round Tables, which are rather more grass roots initiatives.[228] Meanwhile, at the most local level, the great majority of local authorities, with participation of local communities, have produced Local Agenda 21 sustainability plans. This is innovative, especially in the sense that its object is 'to extend participation in planning to groups often excluded from the formal land use planning process, through meetings, workshops, etc'.[229]

5 DEVELOPING STRUCTURES FOR SUSTAINABLE DEVELOPMENT

The nature of environmental problems demands progress towards the creation of obligations that are not only rational responses but also subject to coherent legal strategies for exposition and enforcement. Internationally, the process towards a universal set of

---

224 UK Government, 1999, para 4.1.
225 See UK Government 1999, chapter 8.
226 See section 3.3 above.
227 Farmer, Skinner, Wilkinson and Bishop, 1999, para 2.2.
228 See Regional Development Agencies Act 1998, s 8.
229 Farmer, Skinner, Wilkinson and Bishop, 1999, para 2.14.

legislative and institutional arrangements remains in a very early stage of development, and there is little sign as yet of any coherent framework. Yet appropriate responses are also required at regional and national levels, where indeed more immediate impacts may be expected. The European Union's commitment to proceed with Kyoto despite the United States' withdrawal is, paradoxically, a positive sign of a willingness to engage with problems of climate warming without an insistence upon multilateral action. Yet these events may also lead to conflicts as terms of trade are perceived to be impacted upon by differentials in response. There are nevertheless grounds for arguing that environmental protection and competition are not mutually exclusive. Gaines describes as a shared myth of conflict the common belief that environmental compliance costs threaten competitiveness. Arguing that there is good reason to seek co-operation between environmental and development interests, he refers to supporting evidence that takes account of both longer term impacts and measurement of benefits on the output side, that is, net of environmental degradation.[230] Hodas suggests that sustainable development through legal constraint be supported by natural accounting to better reflect the value of ecosystems services and natural capital.[231]

Growing levels of agreement amongst scientists as to many of the global environmental issues may assist in this process, as in the case of global warming. Yet three priority needs identified by Sands remain to be convincingly addressed:

> To establish improved mechanisms for identifying critical issues and priorities for law making; to ensure that all relevant actors are able to participate fully and effectively in the international law making process (in particular developing countries), including the negotiation, implementation, review and governance of international environmental agreements or instruments; and to rationalise the international law making process by improving co-ordination between international organisations and their secretariats, in particular those established by environmental agreements.[232]

A useful contribution in the search for a coherent set of legal principles was made by the UNCED Experts' Group on Environmental Law. In 1986, the group produced a draft Convention on Environmental Protection and Sustainable Development.[233] Whilst the mandate underlying its production was that such principles should be in place in or before the year 2000, the report retains more than historic interest. Such a convention would create a binding, universal set of 'rights and responsibilities of States individually and collectively for securing environmental protection and sustainable development'.[234] The responsibilities on the part of States would embrace future generations, other species and ecosystems. Thus Article 2 would require that States 'ensure that the environment and natural resources are conserved and used for the benefit of present and future generations'. Sustainability was explicitly addressed in Article 3, which would place obligations upon States in respect of ecosystems, genetic diversity and (by reference to living natural resources and ecosystems) the limits of optimum sustainable yield. The

---

230 Gaines, 1997.

231 Hodas, 1998; see also Gray, 1993 and Collison, 1998.

232 Sands, 1995, p 137.

233 See Munro and Lammers, 1987, p 235 *et seq*; see also, UNEP Expert Group, *Report on Identification of Principles of International Law for Sustainable Development*, 1996, presented to the UN Commission on Sustainable Development.

234 Munro and Lammers, 1987, p 15.

draft Convention devoted considerable attention to problems of compliance discussed above. As well as the creation of a Commission for Sustainable Development referred to above, the group proposed further structural reform, including an international ombudsman and an institutional framework geared to avoidance and adjudication of disputes, by negotiative arrangements and ultimately binding settlement through a Permanent Court of Arbitration or the ICJ.[235]

Once again, at regional and national levels, it is likewise necessary to concentrate on developing convincing structures. Yet, in terms of delivery, with a view to achieving increased policy integration, it is necessary to move beyond current UK strategy commitments to headline indicators in the various sectors referred to in the previous section and to develop detailed compliance strategies.[236] Moffatt outlines the variety of measuring indicators that have been proposed,[237] and makes the point that they are required not only for ethical reasons, but also for pragmatic ones, for scientists and decision makers: 'both as a guide to specific environmental management projects and as a broad guide to evaluating the ways in which a nation's or region's economy and ecology are moving.'[238]

The devil is in the detail, as Americans say, and the development of realistic constraints and strategies based upon normative values of the kind mentioned in these first two chapters will assist in the urgent task of moving towards sustainable solutions. For all the reservations charted above, a shift in stance has been achieved. For instance, in its 2000 rural white paper, discussing the further development of Regional Development Strategies, the government stated that these would be expected to 'encourage sustainable development' through measures including recognition of 'the value of the environment as an economic asset to be used sustainably', and by ensuring that 'development is appropriate and occurs in areas which are able to support it'.[239]

How far these good offices can be translated beyond the obvious rhetoric will greatly depend upon creating structures, both to formulate and deliver on policy, in an integrated fashion, and to ensure wider understanding and acceptability of the difficult choices that are necessary. In particular, the need to translate the strategic approach into other policies and programmes is crucial to the eventual level of success of these approaches. A new development for the UK is the newly created Sustainable Development Commission, under the chairmanship of ecologist Jonathan Porritt. The Commission is charged with review of the UK's achievement of sustainable development in all relevant fields, and identification of processes or policies which may be undermining this; identification of important unsustainable trends which will not be reversed on the basis of current or planned action, and suggesting action to reverse such trends; deepening understanding of the concept of sustainable development, increasing awareness of the issues it raises, and building agreement on them; and the encouragement and stimulation of good practice. A key role for the Commission will be to review the state of sustainable development in the UK as revealed by the indicators referred to above, the monitoring of

235 Munro and Lammers, 1987, pp 16–18.
236 Moffatt, 1996, p 57.
237 Moffatt, 1996, Chapters 4–7.
238 Moffatt, 1996, p 58.
239 DETR/MAFF, 2000, para 7.3.6.

progress in sustainable development reporting at all levels and deciding on required sectoral responses.[240]

Finally, it has been said that 'we bequeath social institutions, as well as an "environment", to future generations. Most of these institutions were devised within a context of unsustainable growth'.[241] The significance of sustainable development may therefore appear more hortatory than relevant to the creation of obligations. Wood has asserted that for all the rhetoric the European Union 'is premised on a fundamentally misguided driving force or ethos of economic growth and competitiveness ... [as a] key player in the global phase of capitalist industrialism'.[242] Indeed, this has official echoes in an opinion of the EC's Economic and Social Committee, which has voiced a need to address 'very basic issues' such as 'under what conditions economic growth and environmental protection are compatible and how the massive use of resources is to be avoided'.[243]

Yet the problems are not only institutional. The population has to be confronted with the implications of resisting changes in lifestyle. This is in large measure a question of education and information, as well as political leadership. A former government advisory body in the UK, reporting in 2000 on the concept of sustainable development indicators, commented upon a 'still widespread ignorance about the nature of some of these problems and the need for more sustainable solutions. The headline indicators could and should play a part in helping to explain some of the issues and challenges more widely. The government needs to promote the use of the indicators in public debate and in the media'.[244] Political acceptability will determine the scope and effectiveness of each of the notions of sustainable development and the precautionary principle. Acceptable levels of resource depletion and environmental risk are ultimately matters for genuine political responsibility.[245]

---

240 UK Government, 1999, para 10.13.

241 Redclift, 1997, p 266.

242 Wood, 1999, p 51.

243 European Economic and Social Committee, 1999, para 3.4.2.

244 UK Round Table on Sustainable Development, 2000b, para 41.

245 European Commission, 2000c, para 7.

CHAPTER 3

REGULATION AND PRIVATE PROPERTY

> Meanwhile the ground, formerly free to all
> As the air or sunlight,
> Was portioned by surveyors into patches,
> Between boundary markers, fences, ditches.
> Earth's natural plenty no longer sufficed.
> Man tore upon the earth, and rummaged in her bowels.[1]

This chapter considers the impact of private property (and common law) ideologies upon the cause of environmental protection and arrangements for land use planning. These regulatory regimes must operate within a culture dominated by the intractability of an economic system the foundations of which challenge notions of sustainability. It has been cogently argued that human rights perspectives are not necessarily useful in most contexts of environmental protection.[2] Little attention is given in this context to traditional rights-based approaches, and a discussion of human rights is deferred until Chapter 9. That said, the new-found applicability of human rights perspectives under UK law, with the coming into force of the Human Rights Act 1998, will assist lawyers, perhaps especially both in the conception and drafting of laws, as well as in the context of administrative law challenge, to adjust the ideological balance discussed below.

1 IDEOLOGIES OF THE MINIMAL STATE

1.1   Property and values of the liberal State

There is at heart a conflict between the fundamentally market-based, liberal principles upon which society transacts its business and a transition to greater sustainability through ecological reform and more holistic approaches. Ranged against prevailing economic and legal notions are those of environmental ethics, which place emphasis upon the interdependence of ecosystems, and urge more precautionary approaches in the light of lack of knowledge as to long term effects of toxic substances and polluting emissions, seeking to create a deeper notion of what is a public good.

By contrast, the classical version of the modern liberal State mandates State action only in those circumstances where agreement can be obtained, and then only to the minimum extent compatible with individual freedom.[3] This discussion moreover occurs against a background of a property law with roots still clearly defined in 17th century philosophy and 19th century political science. Such principles are not surprisingly

---

1   Hughes, from 'Creation', 1997, pp 11–12.
2   See Miller, 1998, Chapter 9.
3   See Hayek, 1949.

anthropocentric. They are also rooted in the importance of the individual and the pursuit of individual happiness, and closely connect with cultural notions of liberty. For all the ubiquity of modern regulation, a fundamentally static ideology of private property persists. For the purposes of the law of property, 'it is the owner who counts, not the land itself. If the land is damaged by an outsider, the injury is to the owner, not to the land itself, and the remedy extracted by the law is the payment of money to that owner. Boundary lines are respected in the law, in defiance if not ignorance of nature's true interconnection ... Both the owner and the owner's land exist in legal separation from the rest of the natural world'.[4]

It is not the place here to offer a detailed analysis of either economic principles or the nature of property. However, it is necessary to challenge assertions by proponents of private property rights of an essential symbiosis with individual autonomy, as expressed through ownership and the opportunity to take part in market transactions. On this basis property rights can be said to 'tie the welfare of individuals to the value consequences of their choices, they provide decision makers with the incentive to take these consequences into account by co-operating with others and specializing in those productive activities in which they have a comparative advantage ... and discovering new opportunities for gain, including technological and institutional innovations'.[5] For their part, markets are generally perceived as the most efficient systems for the facilitation of production and exchange, producing incentives through price, enabling participators to respond as circumstances change. The efficiency argument can be succinctly put as follows: 'rights to the use of resources flow to their highest-valued uses, as judged by consumers, and the welfare of individuals depends on their success in making others better off through voluntary exchange.'[6]

The conflict of a property ideology with ecological approaches goes to the root of the difficulties facing environmental protection measures. Private notions of property still conceive of it as a resource, abetted by the often physically displaced nature of degradation, and by its own normative scale, which regards degradation as a matter of reduced economic valuations. Thus, an absolutist view of property rights is an assertion of immutable dominance on the part of the private interest in decisions affecting the property resource. This involves a wide-ranging package, including rights to 'possession, use and disposition'.[7] The element of excludability in particular, as well as the right of alienation, can be categorised as representing an exercise in 'psycho-spatial' self-affirmation, and broadly described as 'property as socially constituted fact'.[8] This appears to owe some debt to the Hegelian notion of man creating nature, in the assertion that the 'normal bundle of property rights contains no priority for land in its natural condition; it regards use, including development, as one of the standard incidents of ownership'.[9] Sustenance is derived from a free market economy, which conceptually accommodates 'commodified land and natural resources'.[10] Such arguments tend to propound an

---

4   Freyfogle, 1994, p 836.
5   De Alessi, 1999, p 15.
6   De Alessi, 1999, p 1.
7   See the exposition in Epstein, 1985, p 59.
8   See Gray and Gray, 2001, pp 111–13.
9   Epstein, 1985, p 123.
10 McGregor, 1999, p 392.

argument that is rooted in Locke, and based upon a form of natural law theory, which asserts pre-existing property rights 'independent of agreement and prior to the formation of the State'.[11] Here it is said lie the roots of absolutist doctrine: enjoyment of property uninhibited by social controls.

Yet one looks in vain for anything representing a satisfactory concept of legitimacy in the highly static and unrealistic idea of natural rights resulting from the original commons. By contrast, for Hobbes it was the state of nature itself that was marked by a lack of the constraints necessary to order a civilised society; and which justified a vesting of absolute authority in the sovereign State. Transposed to today's conditions, this implies acceptance of the regulatory purpose: the central feature of property, perceived as a right to exclude others, yet not constraining the sovereign, acting in its role as the personification of 'the common peace and security'.[12] For his part, Locke, focusing horizontally, made certain assumptions for a necessary right to exclude others from one's property: all had liberty to first appropriate, although a form of justification was found in a right to the produce on grounds of the mixing of labour.[13] Even this justification appears to have been jettisoned by modern Lockeans.[14] Proponents of an absolute property ideology are close to those who espouse a minimal State, defending its legitimacy on grounds that 'no more extensive State could be morally justified, that any more extensive State would violate the rights of individuals'.[15] This suggests an immutable nexus between the freedom of the individual and the institutions of private property.[16]

Certainly property ideologies are identified with the capacity of individuals to develop as independent members of civil society. Thus it lends independence to individuals in enabling the exercise of 'the autonomous judgment necessary for their common self-rule'.[17] Indeed, Rawls, accepting that exclusive use of property affords 'a sufficient material basis for a sense of personal independence and self-respect, both of which are essential for the development and exercise of the moral powers', would not extend this basic liberty to either individual or equal control of the means of production or natural resources.[18] Yet in significant ways, certain absolutist proponents have gone beyond even Lockean analysis, for instance arguing that there is no such thing as society, or, at its kindest, that individuals develop independently from their social situation.[19]

Most doctrinal resistance in Anglo-American jurisprudence rejects regulation as representing unjustified assault upon property. The argument is to the fore amongst certain United States jurists, for two main reasons. First, there is a constitutional context, especially in the role of compensable takings there, which attracts a level of constitutional discourse to a greater extent than seen in our own jurisdiction.[20] For instance, the Fifth

---

11   Epstein, 1985, p 334.
12   Hobbes, 1651, 1996 edn, Chapter 24, p 172.
13   Locke, 1690, 1924 edn, Chapter 5, para 27.
14   Eg, Nozick, 1974; Gauthier, 1986.
15   Nozick, 1974, p 333.
16   See Rowley, 1993.
17   Rose, 1994, p 61.
18   Rawls, 1993, p 298.
19   Eg, Friedman, 1962.
20   *Pennsylvania Coal Co v Mahon*, 260 US 393, 414 (Holmes J).

Amendment provides: 'No person shall ... be deprived of life, liberty or property, without due process of law; nor shall private property be taken for public use without just compensation.' It is but a short step for absolutists to insist that the regulation of property, and specifically through land use controls, is tantamount to at least a partial taking.[21] Given that the context for such arguments is the availability of compensation, there is an element of self-fulfilment in the assertion that the result is a negative-sum game, where 'transaction cost barriers are likely to exceed the gains that otherwise are obtainable from any shift in land use or ownership'.[22]

In resource terms, a key issue is how far autonomy extends to an unrestrained right of profit maximisation as an incident of ownership.[23] The ideological conflict in the United States has been especially marked over litigation concerning the right to develop property situated upon wetlands. There is some irony for English eyes, in view of the arguably under-regulated protection of wetlands from development, as discussed in Chapter 6. In a landmark ruling, the Wisconsin Supreme Court held that a landowner 'has no absolute and unlimited right to change the essential character of the land so as to use it for a purpose for which it was unsuited in its natural state and which injures the rights of others'.[24] Further, such development controls have been held not to amount to a taking unless substantial and justified expectations have been thwarted and the regulation is unreasonably onerous.[25] Yet the United States Supreme Court has in recent years adopted a position more closely akin to that of the absolute property lobby.[26] Writing prior to the emergence of such majority view,[27] Byrne described the approach as a non-normative commodification of public values.[28] He went on to identify numerous incidents of what were (at the time) dissenting opinions in favour of extending the takings doctrine.[29] Thus, unencumbered rights of property might be identified with individual liberty and with the opportunity for economic development.[30] A refusal of development permission was equated with a physical invasion of the applicant's property.[31] Indeed, adopting the approach of classical economics, the inefficiency of wealth transfers was propounded, on the basis of public unwillingness to pay for its competing needs.[32] Such judicial arguments resonate with those of Locke, who at least had the justification of writing in a time when the beneficence of the earth's resources appeared unending (with, ironically, the resources of North America then newly available for plunder).

---

21 Epstein, 1985, pp 100–01.
22 Epstein, 1985, p 265.
23 McGregor, 1999, pp 420–21.
24 *Just v Marinette County*, 201 NW 2d 761, 768 (Wis 1972).
25 *Claridge v New Hampshire Wetlands Board*, 485 A2d 287 (1984); see also *Village of Euclid v Ambler Realty Co*, 272 US 365 (1926), where zoning ordinances were upheld; *Hodel v Virginia Surface Mining and Reclamation Association*, 452 US 264 (1981), where the impacts of strip mining regulation were held to be non-compensable.
26 *Lucas v South Carolina Coastal Council*, 505 US 1003 (1992).
27 Ie, *Lucas, ibid.*
28 Byrne, 1990, p 248.
29 See further Sax, 1996.
30 See *Penn Cent Transp Co v New York City*, 438 US 104 (1978); *Nollan v California Coastal Commission*, 483 US 825 (1987).
31 See *Fresh Pond Shopping Center Inc v Callahan*, 464 US 875 (1983).
32 *Pennell v City of San Jose*, 485 US 1 (1988).

Secondly, and rooted in a related historical context, it is said that the foundations for a post-colonial society reflected the rise of a mercantile class with a practical need to curtail government power.[33] This rationale leads today to those arguments which extol the commodification of real, just as of personal, property. Thus it has been contended that 'a land use policy which is socially equitable and environmentally sensitive is not resolved simply by labelling as a "resource" rather than a "commodity". Instead ... land transactions and land use should ... be scrutinized in a manner not unlike the treatment extended to a multitude of other commodities no more "affected with a public interest" than is land'.[34] Epstein likewise argues that private property rights operate as barriers to State power and, albeit undefined within the US Constitution, that they should be decisive in the constitutional context. The burden of this theory, based upon the constitutional eminent domain clause, is that the State may force property exchanges for public uses, but then only upon payment of compensation: 'by demanding that losers in the legislative process retain rights that leave them as well off as they were before.'[35]

The minimal State argument therefore engages with environmental (as perhaps other social) problems with reluctance, and insists upon a strategy of minimal response. It may see justification in the lack of available private law consequences. Thus, in considering the possibility of restraint upon building on flood plains, discussed in the next section, Epstein points to the lack of 'invasive conduct by the individual landowner, so the most that can be said is a taking of development rights for public use'.[36] Likewise, in confronting pollution, it is claimed to be preferable that the State stays its hand, so that even a market solution such as tradable pollution rights 'unfortunately involves central decision as to the desirable *total* amount of pollution'.[37] Such critiques of communal responses to pollution are closely tied to liberal economic perspectives. On this basis, applying a rudimentary cost benefit analysis, society should allow polluting activities if there is a net benefit, the test for which is 'whether the activity could pay its way, whether those who benefit from it would be willing to pay enough ... to cover the costs of compensating those ill affected by it'.[38] Where applicable, compensation methods offered are somewhat limited, ranging from say soundproofing and compensating for reduced property values in the vicinity of airports, to the vaguer notion of lawyers and courts being made responsible for distributing compensation in complex class actions. This may be an unstated reference to the problems caused by cumulative pollution, but if so the logistics of arriving at compensatory arrangements, let alone putting them in place, would be gargantuan.

An extreme version of such ideology charges that regulation is a modern-day successor to feudalism in its unjust interference with property rights, threatening to emasculate the notion of private property so that it 'increasingly approximates conditional tenure'.[39] In contrast, the market-based approach claims to offer a non-feudal

---

33 Freyfogle, 1985, p 728.
34 Babcock and Feurer, 1977, p 290.
35 Epstein, 1985, p 346.
36 Epstein, 1985, p 124.
37 Nozick, 1974, p 81.
38 Nozick, 1974, p 79.
39 Pipes, 1999, p 231.

world where property transactions can take place.[40] Such liberal strands of thought abjure not only the top-down tyranny of government, but also modern, bottom-up approaches, such as Reich's willingness to attach new forms of conditional property right to the assertion of welfare rights.[41] Furthermore, such ideologists devote considerable energies into challenging any reordering of priorities. Thus, for instance, Epstein cites the egotism underlying evolution, arguing that such an approach 'strikes at the very heart of personal self-identification and individual self-expression. It presupposes the kind of detachment from, and impartiality toward, self that no human being emerging from his evolutionary past of remorseless self-interest can hope to emulate'.[42] The argument is analogous to the less strident reference by Adam Smith to the 'invisible hand' whereby, accorded an opportunity for specialisation by the market, the individual's contribution, in pursuit of individual interests, also promotes the public interest.[43]

Without entering the field of social biology, it nevertheless appears dangerous to apply genetic predisposition in the context of determining the nature of rights and obligations.[44] Interestingly, long before the current incursions of genetic science, at the heart of Hobbes' social contract lay the idea that the selfishness of individuals gives way to the mutuality of benefit and protection arising from co-operative political arrangements. Dawkins, though often challenged for alleged genetic determinism, appears content to recognise that humans have 'a capacity for genuine, disinterested, true altruism', which he categorises as the ability to rebel against the genetic 'tyranny of the selfish replicators'.[45] In any event, a Darwinian approach rooted in an idea of the selfish gene can view ostensibly co-operative decisions as being based upon self-interest across a longer timeframe. Thus it can be said that 'altruism economizes on costs of policing and enforcing agreements' through patterns of mutual aid.[46] But even without going this far, it seems that it can be accepted that 'it is perfectly possible to hold that genes exert a statistical influence on human behaviour while at the same time believing that this influence can be modified, overridden or reversed by other influences'.[47] Proponents of collective ownership might not derive much comfort from a view that theirs is no less a manifestation of genetic selfishness, but ardent property ideologues will on these grounds be even less satisfied.

Such reference to a sociobiological rationale, in support of the liberal economic one, is disconcerting on a broader level. At the time of writing, the genome project is within sight of completion of its first mapping phase. Increased genetic engineering activity, however regulated in individual jurisdictions, appears now a certainty, and amongst the myriad of ethical consequences we are likely to see determinist arguments renewed and refreshed. This is causing a major rethink in most disciplines, and it must in law also, whether our concern is with human rights, with issues of capacity and responsibility, or, as here, with public law conceptions of social organisation.

---

40   Sanders, 1987, pp 386–87.
41   Reich, 1964, p 768; cf Pipes, 1999, pp 289–90.
42   Epstein, 1985, p 341.
43   Smith, 1776, 1976 edn, Book IV, *Of Systems of Political Economy*, pp 477–78.
44   See, eg, Wells, 1998.
45   Dawkins, 1989, pp 200–01.
46   Hirschliefer, 1977, p 28.
47   Dawkins, 1989, p 331.

1.2   Regulation and public interest ideologies

Standard property paradigms appear to engage in sustainability discourse barely at all. They are especially unpersuasive over the question of external effects, previously discussed, and which in this context are those consequences which are not borne by the market participator. The market-property-rights nexus has nevertheless afforded the classical Coasian solution, which asserts that transaction (or non-transaction) choices are available to address the essentially reciprocal nature of negative effects.[48] Such traditional rationale further tends rhetorically to diminish the scale of externalities. Thus proponents of markets and property solutions adopt a wide range of supporting justifications: as in the reliance upon innovation and substitution to resolve resource problems, along with challenges even to scientific consensus, whereby uncertainty is maintained as a reason to persist in status quo, as opposed to precautionary, approaches.[49] For example, adopting Hardin's approach to the commons, Demetzhas argued that private property, with the power to exclude others, incentivises more efficient resource utilisation, internalises costs onto owners, and thereby even encourages conservation.[50] Concerning the question of accessibility (and declining productivity caused by over- or under-use) of the commons, Hardin's tragedy of the commons has bolstered the proposition that private property is essential in the face of scarcity of resources. The alternative he described as follows: 'Ruin is the destination to which all men rush, each pursuing his own interest in a society that believes in the freedom of the commons. Freedom in a commons brings ruin to all.'[51] The theory makes a valid point about the dangers of unconstrained access to limited resources, but sweeping conclusions as to the dangers of the commons seem misplaced. However, it is necessary to distinguish between unowned property and a regime for common property, for given finite resources, 'the open access that necessarily results from the absence of a property regime risks the danger of exploitation'.[52] Indeed, Freyfogle reaches the same result by analogy with usufruct allocating limited rights to individuals 'while retaining public ownership of the resource'.[53]

It can likewise be argued that regulation disables the mutual reciprocity between owners inherent in the law of nuisance, the value of which as an environmental mechanism is discussed later in this chapter. For instance, Brubaker has linked the creation of pollution control regimes with the erosion in property rights, as through such stratagems (ironically) as statutory authority defences, property owners 'have been forced to underwrite the activities which harm them'.[54] She appears to conclude that sole reliance upon regulatory activity to ensure environmental protection is illusionary, for 'government-made laws and regulations, designed to protect particular industries and promulgated in the name of the public good, are environmental culprits'.[55] This is an interesting perspective, although it amounts to a reminder that licence and consent

---

48   Coase, 1960.
49   See Dejevsky, Connor and McCarthy, 2001.
50   Demetz, 1967, p 351.
51   Hardin, 1998, Chapter 1, p 7.
52   Kohler, 1999, pp 232–33.
53   Freyfogle, 1985, p 736.
54   Brubaker, 1999, p 109.
55   Brubaker, 1999, p 110.

regimes are the means by which politicians and administrators enable economic activity not by preventing pollution but by determining those pollution levels that are deemed acceptable. Moreover, property arguments appear even less justified where seeking to 'tie the welfare of individuals to their success in internalising external harms and benefits, encouraging the development of new technologies and new institutional arrangements and the prompt adaptation to changes in circumstances'.[56] This purported link between reduced restrictions on private property and achieving viable environmental solutions appears without serious foundation. It is surely unrealistic to seek solutions based upon new institutional arrangements deriving from traditional property ideology.

And yet, the onset of regulation has not moreover challenged fundamentally the dominant perceptions underlying liberal, market notions of property rights. That is not to say that private property notions have not been constrained by law, as under environmental protection and land use planning controls. Yet the dominance of private property ideology has been retained at the core of our scheme of values as translated through law and regulation. Instead, as McAuslan has argued, those who make policy and administer regulatory arrangements have pursued a compromise ideology of public interest. A highly centrist public interest ideology has served to maintain the status quo, and to bolster 'the existing state of property relations in society, the existing capitalist system with its emphasis on private property and a functioning market for that property'.[57] The technocratic consequences have placed obstacles in the way of any more radical, participative approaches. The common law, described as 'a partisan participator in the struggle for control over power and resources and not a neutral referee policing the struggle',[58] has likewise accommodated this ethos, and is thus a prime force in maintaining that status quo. Indeed, throughout what has been since the early 1980s a deregulatory era, there has been a steady flow of regulation aimed broadly at environmental protection, it is difficult to identify significant changes in ideology. The public interest is filtered by administrative priorities, and questions of land use which are central to the notion of sustainability, as will be seen in the next following chapters, are leavened by that process. Pollution control, as will be seen in Chapter 7, can likewise be categorised as partly misplaced, for the problem is not pollution alone but rather 'the jarring discontinuity between the ways people live and the natural functioning of the earth's systems'.[59]

That a private property ideology persists can also be seen in the environmental agenda becoming increasingly about stakeholding, discussed in the previous chapter. This emphasises shared responsibility, and encouragement of the market to work for the environment, especially through voluntary mechanisms.[60] This, depending upon the exercise of political will, may be a sign of surer sustainable policy making to come. Yet it carries the risk that entrenched, growth-related priorities will continue to head the agenda. As already seen, considerable doubts exist as to how effectively these adjustments can be achieved. Thus, for instance, in the UK there is considerable

---

56 De Alessi, 1999, p 30.
57 McAuslan, 1980, p 268.
58 McAuslan, 1980, p 270.
59 Freyfogle, 1994, p 837.
60 Eg, European Commission, 2001a, para 2.3.

opposition on the part of much of industry to the introduction of the climate change levy. A further example connected with climate change, on the international stage, is the current danger of the strategy agreed originally at Kyoto in 1997 to achieve cuts (or, rather, reductions in growth rates) in atmospheric pollution, falling apart.

2 CONSTRAINING ACTIVITIES THROUGH REGULATION

2.1 The contingent status of property rights

The choices available in resolving conflicts between property and environmental restraint are explored further in the concluding section to this chapter. For the present, it is necessary to offer a brief discussion of the nature of contingent approaches to property rights. Regulation, according to a key argument of proponents of property-based approaches, leads to the subordination of individual to community, and ultimately the destruction of the substance of the notion of property right.[61] Yet the question of what level of freedom should be accorded to the fostering of individual autonomy through rights in property is one of the major political questions in any society. These debates have persisted since the Enlightenment, and echo those into how far the expression of Rousseau's general will can guarantee civil freedom in circumstances of restraint. The acceptance of the role of the State in civil society, and that rights acquired from the State include private property rights, does not necessarily require a denial of restraint as an article of faith. To be sure, the social contract (appropriately, unfinished) was an idealistic hypothesis, which sought to counter Hobbes' assertion that being free and being ruled were inimical. On the other hand, Rousseau also implicitly recognised the threat of private property ideology to questions of reform. In this respect he concluded that the real political system had tended to impose the order of the rich and powerful in order to protect their claims to possession: 'the origin of civil society and laws ... fixed for all time the law of property and inequality, transformed shrewd usurpation into settled right.'[62]

The reciprocity of arrangements which underlies modern notions of property is greatly more complex than absolutist approaches allow. This can be seen in the description of the concept of property as 'rules governing access to and control of material resources, and such a system of rules may assign to several people rights in the same resources'.[63] Hart's classic exposition distinguishes general from special rights, the former including freedom from interference and the latter arising from specific transactions and relationships.[64] Thus, in either respect, in terms of abstract entitlement it appears that there is no single, indivisible right of ownership, but rather a bundle of rights.[65] This view has gained widespread acceptance, at least in common law jurisdictions,[66] that though part of a broader taxonomy of entitlements, rights can also be

---

61 McGregor, 1999, pp 391–92.
62 Rousseau, 1743, 1968 edn, p 178.
63 Waldron, 1988 edn, p 35.
64 Hart, 1984, p 84.
65 Honore, 1961, p 107.
66 Gray and Gray, 2001, pp 113–15.

identified as correlative to obligations, a problem encountered in the discussion of sustainability in Chapter 1.[67]

By analogy, the common rights to land inherent in the feudal system could be described as 'a conditional tenure and imposing particular obligations in return for the privilege of receiving rent'.[68] There may appear to be an irony in the feudal ideal operating as a bulwark for less property-orientated thought. Yet it was based on the contention that 'all property was held subject to the performance of duties – not a few of them public'.[69] Moreover, the duty aspects underlying feudal arrangements have influenced those who have argued for a rejection of private property, in favour of 'the security of improvements', as opposed to land values (represented by rent).[70] This compares with the original Lockean conception founded upon value in use and improvement.

In any age or scheme, therefore, limits are doctrinal, as in the sense of the primacy of relationships, in respect of things, but between persons.[71] Kelsen made the similar point that just as 'law as a social order regulates the behaviour of citizens, property too, can legally consist only in a certain relation between one individual and other individuals'.[72] It is accordingly not at all inimical to the notion of rights *in rem* that those relationships are explored, for 'despite intuitive assumptions to the contrary, property is concerned not with relationships to a thing (which is after all simply a fetish), but with relationships between people'.[73] Thus property rights are socially constructed, and neither natural nor predetermined. In other words, a society's 'exact mixture of private and common property rights will differ as the result of the historical, economic, ideological and sociological pressures that have arisen within that particular community'.[74] The resulting regime will reflect implicitly custom and convention, regulated from time to time by decisions reached through the political process.[75] So just as for Locke an original labouring on the commons accorded a prescriptive claim to title, then society may retain a right to recognise subsequent adjustments.[76]

Ultimately therefore the extent of private property is contingent. Certain rights should have a prior call upon protection, such as the right of exclusion, than will others, such as an unrestrained right to develop. Indeed, although classical economics insists intuitively that private conceptions of property are conducive to efficiency, even there, in certain circumstances departures are acceptable. In particular, this applies to market failure, as where socially optimal uses are prejudiced by unacceptable externalities, such as monopolistic behaviour. It also applies to public goods, namely those that cannot be readily accessed, partly related to their abundant supply. Rose has gone further and

67   See Hohfeld, 1919.
68   George, 1884, p 292.
69   Philbrick, 1938, p 710.
70   George, 1884, pp 308–10.
71   See Hohfeld, 1919.
72   Kelsen, 1970, p 131.
73   Kohler, 1999, p 225.
74   Kohler, 1999, p 230.
75   McGregor, 1999, p 423.
76   McGregor, 1999, pp 412–13.

argued that there are precedents for notions of 'inherently public property'. This would include customary rights, rights by prescription, such rights as easements of necessity, and forms of public trust. Thus it has been suggested that the private property regime can be viewed in its entirety 'as a "public property" owned and managed by governmental bodies'.[77] She categorises as important to 'inherently public property' that it is based upon the idea of socialising activities, which increase the greater the levels of participation. Though the balance is now under postindustrial challenge, commerce has been the dominant factor in the development of support infrastructures, thus socialising by reference to expansion of wealth.[78]

It is remarkable that, for all the compelling arguments concerning the contingency of property rights discussed above, as supported by the property, planning and other regulatory reforms through the past century, the conceptual premises upon which such rights are based continue to subsist, impervious to more than incremental reform. Regulation can also be said to reflect the reciprocities between different interests referred to above. Moreover, it has been pointed out that regulation is not necessarily restrictive of rights, given that, as a result of mutuality, 'the overall bundle of rights is no smaller in size, only different in composition'.[79] Communitarian perspectives emphasise social, or public interest, rules that 'provide some support for communities in which individuals choose to develop'.[80] The tentative development of such rules has been termed, by reference to land use planning, 'community rights', as an extension of an indeterminate public interest ideology in preference to (though to a large degree overlapping) McAuslan's ideology of public participation.[81]

Moreover, Gray and Gray go so far as to suggest that State regulation of property has created 'an overarching criterion of publicly defined responsibility. It is in reality, this model which most closely corresponds to the State-directed control of land which dominates the law of real property today'.[82] This appears to reflect the conception of 'property as propriety', which connotes the responsibility of trust to a larger community, which was discussed in Chapter 1.[83] Whilst Rose's argument referred to above is developed without a detailed ecological examination, she recognises that such aesthetic and normative preferences are incommensurable with normal market preferences. This can be seen in their resistance to traditional forms of measurement.[84] It is precisely because the law of property is concerned with what Byrne calls 'relational rights' that it is to do with the allocation of social benefit. In this way, it sets 'the boundaries between private and public control of things'.[85]

The radical perspectives discussed above posit that individual self-respect and freedom derives from more than the pursuit of economic advantage. Early in the last

---

77   Rose, 1986, pp 719–20.
78   Rose, 1986, p 774.
79   Freyfogle, 1996a, p 181.
80   McGregor, 1999, p 421.
81   Millichap, 1998, p 428.
82   Gray and Gray, 2001, p 115.
83   See Rose, 1994, pp 65–66.
84   See Sagoff, 1981, p 1402 *et seq*.
85   Byrne, 1990, p 244.

century, Tawney criticised the idea that the attainment of material wealth was the foremost objective of human endeavour, citing 'the smiling illusion of progress won from the mastery of the material environment by a race too selfish to determine the purpose to which its triumphalism shall be applied'.[86] This has modern echoes in the work of O'Riordan, who describes the concept of sustainable development as 'rooted in human supremacy over peoples and places, and emerged with the paternalistic air of decaying colonialism'. This is where the political focus lies, rather than upon the more pluralistic ideas embraced by sustainability. O'Riordan concludes that lying at its heart 'is self-regeneration and self-reliance – of the soul, as well as of the economy, ecology and society. When the soul embraces the recognition of caring and sharing so that enterprising livelihoods are enabled to flourish in millions of cultures and spaces, then the transition might move forward'.[87]

2.2 Justifications for planning and environmental controls

Once the essential contingency of property rights is accepted, it is necessary to consider how and when community interest may justifiably impinge on those rights. The resolution of this question is highly relevant to the efficacy of regulation which is premised upon levels of constraint. In particular, the encouragement of legitimate uses, together with procedures to achieve such goals, are the stuff of land use planning and environmental regulation. Recent years have seen increased public regulation of activities, especially in response to perceived environmental threats. However, the historical development of property rights, for all the incremental reforms which have taken place, is the nearest that we come to a conceptual basis. Caldwell points to the inadequacy of philosophic foundations and concludes that 'laws and practices pertaining to land ownership and use are beneficial primarily to persons interested in exploitation or litigation'.[88] Traditional models of property law therefore fail satisfactorily to address from first principles how far property uses should be protected, on public interest, especially environmental grounds This suggests a need to provide for 'defensive "rights" in the sense that no person has the right to abuse, exhaust, or destroy the item of property'.[89] Given that gap in our jurisprudence, it is unsurprising that, as in other fields of activity, political solutions have looked to a continued bolstering of the edifices of regulation.

Constraints have nevertheless been successfully, if incrementally, applied to many uses of property, as will be seen in the following chapters, albeit without challenge to the foundations of the system of ownership. Indeed, though not dealt with in any detail here, pressures (and abuses) are often exacerbated by regulatory interference. An illustration of this can be seen in the profits available to landowners arising out of increases in development values, and the weak failure of early attempts by government in the UK to recapture some of this value for the community. Moreover, 'the sale or trading in land is relatively immune from regulation, and unlike regulation of other commodities, land use

---

86 Tawney, 1984, p 277.
87 O'Riordan, 2000, pp 52–53.
88 See Caldwell, 1974, p 759.
89 Freyfogle, 1985, p 741.

policy shows little concern for a broad social interest'.[90] On the other hand, in terms of achieving wider social goals, to which the incursions of planning and environmental regulation are directed, conceptual deficiencies in the common law and property apparatus have been bypassed in crucial respects.

Thus, as indicated above, implicit in most attempts to conceptualise property, whatever its nature, is the notion of constraint. Property, just as other fundamental legal constructs, such as contract, is subjected sporadically to processes whereby the public interest may be engaged. This prevents a placing of 'unlimited power on owners to use and exploit resources as they wish'.[91] Property notions must address broader terms of public good, for the question as to 'how material resources are to be controlled and their use allocated is one that arises in every society'.[92] This can only partly be achieved by private law conceptions. For instance, Ogus states that 'the principles governing the extent of property rights can be refined to deal with the externality problem by limiting use to accord with what would have been contained in a contract between the owner and the affected third parties if transaction costs had not prevented them from reaching such an agreement'.[93]

Restriction of land use amounts to a paradigm application of notions of community interest. Put crudely, unless there are restrictions in place, 'one owner could hold hostage whole communities by her obnoxious use of her land'.[94] Assertions of private rights remains quite proper, but their acceptability requires testing within a fuller, informed process. For instance, as will be seen in Chapter 9, a planning enforcement against an owner living on her own land in a caravan without benefit of planning permission, was held to be lawful, and not to breach Article 8(2) of the European Convention on Human Rights.[95] Other balancing questions may require resolution, as, for example, in considering whether traditional private law mechanisms such as nuisance can assure the necessary levels of social protection. This theme is discussed in the following section, although it should be noted that a *prima facie* criticism may be raised in that ownership rights 'must generally be qualified if any degree of action in the interests of the collective welfare is to be possible: given that nuisance law is frequently seen as promoting property rights against the general welfare, to give those rights priority at common law might smack of individualism in the worst sense'.[96]

Indeed the notion of individualised interests, which lies at the root of private law remedies, can sit uneasily in the face of assertions of collective interest. For instance, McAuslan has described the court as a poor regulator, however responsive in certain individual circumstances: 'What the courts are attempting to do in considering nuisance claims is a simplistic form of cost benefit analysis but the approaches they adopt ... are not so different to the much more sophisticated analysis used by environmental consultants, inspectors conducting public inquiries into major proposals for development, or indeed

---

90 Babcock and Feurer, 1977, p 304.
91 Ogus, 1994, p 20.
92 Waldron, 1988, p 34.
93 Note 91 above.
94 McGregor, 1999, p 420.
95 *Buckley v UK* [1996] JPL 1018.
96 Steele, 1995, p 241.

civil servants advising ministers.'[97] Environmental protection accordingly suggests the need for management and proactive processes, with a view to seeking out collective ends. Woolf has concluded that the 'primary focus of environmental law is not on the protection of private rights but on the protection of the environment for the public in general'.[98] Private law does not offer a viable rationale for addressing problems which 'demand collective action'.[99] Four especial obstacles persist. First, private law rights, including those based upon property, may not reflect the wider environmental interest. Secondly, wherever a particular jurisdiction draws the balance, the terms of engagement for a private cause of action are necessarily limited. Thirdly, objective uncertainty as to harm is likely to severely undermine private law action. Fourthly, there will inevitably be only selective enforcement. This problem is both more pervasive and different in quality from what amounts to discretionary decision making in respect of enforcement on the part of regulators as they pursue compliance strategies, discussed in the previous chapter.

However, not only because of the survival of common law principles affecting property and obligations, questions affecting the environment will inevitably arise in the context of private law. Indeed, the balance of environmental good may not always lodge with public bodies where conflicts arise between regulatory determinations and private rights. Attention now turns to this question.

3 PRIVATE LAW PROTECTION OF ENVIRONMENTAL INTERESTS

3.1   Toxic tort in an era of environmental regulation

As will be seen throughout this book, the catalyst for political and regulatory responses often lies in the face of an uncertain nature and scope of environmental threat. We rely upon regulation to fix levels of acceptability. Consideration is given, for instance, to planning controls in the following chapters, together with a discussion of the environmental impact assessment regime and of the relationship between planning and pollution controls. Perhaps the most important point of reference for any consideration of regulation, however, is the discussion of risk in Chapter 8. We live in a risk society, in which we struggle to understand the nature of risk, confronted by an extreme pace and complexity of technological development, in a world where cumulatively, humankind is exacerbating risks beyond the capacity of most individuals (and institutions) to engage.[100] Indeed, as was seen in the previous section, policy makers, administrators and courts have all encountered 'difficulty adapting property rules fast enough to continue to serve society's new needs at times of rapid social change'.[101] Thus given the extent of change (as well as systemic institutional limitations), it has been cautioned that 'regulation is never really a prospective task'.[102] Yet regulatory controls continue to

---

97   McAuslan, 1991, p 198.
98   Woolf, 1992, p 4.
99   Elworthy and Holder, 1997, p 59.
100 Beck, 1992.
101 Frazier, 1998, p 58.
102 Lee, 2000a, p 89.

dominate, notwithstanding that there is currently a shift in policy strategies towards alternative market-based regimes, with perhaps other ways being found to compensate for environmental harm, whether through insurance, sectoral levies, or underwriting by the taxpayer.[103]

The existence of regulation inevitably impacts upon the perceived role of the common law in circumstances of environmental damage. The approach in the English courts to private disputes appears to amount to an acceptance that regulation and the common law may be travelling in different directions, or rather as the former grows in invasiveness the latter will seek to balance this by roughly staying still. Thus, according to Lord Goff, 'given that so much well-informed and carefully structured legislation is now being put in place for this purpose (that is, liability for pollution), there is less need for the courts to develop a common law principle to achieve the same end, and indeed it may well be undesirable that they should do so'. [104] Likewise concerned with the limitations of the common law, the New York Court of Appeals, hearing a nuisance claim on grounds of noise and vibration against the operator of a cement plant, admitted that 'the judicial establishment is neither equipped in the limited nature of any judgment it can pronounce nor prepared to lay down and implement an effective policy for the elimination of air pollution. That is an area beyond the circumference of one private lawsuit'.[105]

Private legal processes are indeed limited by inherent restraints, as indicated in the previous chapter and further discussed in this section. Thus successful enforcement follows recognised processes for establishing liability. This requires, for example, both a recognised cause of action and a recognition that a claimant has suffered a form of harm for which the defendant should be liable.[106] The availability of private forms of action at least in part reflects Dworkin's notion that legislatures and judges are respectively concerned with policies and principles, and in the latter case rules applicable to rights and remedies, in dispensing individual justice, place inherent limits on the adaptive abilities of the common law.[107] There is a dislocation in environmental matters, accentuated by technical limitations. Bruggemeier characterises the problems in this context as follows: problems of identification (does an event constitute pollution?); problems of source (whence does pollution emanate?); problems of boundaries (what are the effects?); and problems of common interests (how might the unowned environment be protected?).[108]

Such limitations are more pronounced in view of the problems encountered in matching legal mechanisms to the nature of environmental harm. Yet traditional legal liability restrictions within domestic tort doctrine remain locked into fault-based requirements. Determining questions of fault may not be the most appropriate or efficient compensation mechanism. The Council of Europe in 1993 proposed rules incorporating strict liability into the civil law, with the aim of ensuring adequate compensation and also prevention and reinstatement.[109] This has been recognised by the European Commission

---

103 European Commission, 1993b, 2000b.

104 *Cambridge Water Company v Eastern Counties Leather plc* [1994] 2 AC 264.

105 257 NE 2d 870, 871 (1970).

106 *Merlin v BNFL* [1990] 2 QB 557.

107 See, eg, Dworkin, 1975.

108 Bruggemeier, 1994; also, Rabin, 1987, pp 29–33.

109 Council of Europe, Lugano Convention on Civil Liability for Damage Resulting from Activities Dangerous to the Environment, European Treaty Series/150, 21 June 1993.

in its white paper on environmental liability, which proposes a limited form of strict, prospective liability.[110] Similar problems affect related principles, such as foreseeability, proof of damage and causation. For instance, the foreseeability requirements in negligence have now been transposed into circumstances of nuisance and the dangerous escapes doctrine contained in *Rylands v Fletcher*, at least as far as foreseeability of harm is concerned.[111] Moreover, issues of causation may be terminal in toxic tort litigation.[112] The claimant must satisfy the burden of proof in establishing that causation can be traced to a particular defendant.[113] This requirement is alleviated generally by tests categorised by reference to 'substantial increase in risk',[114] or the notion of it being 'more probable than not that D's conduct caused the harm'.[115] Yet causation in the context of the objective uncertainties often associated with environmental harms is greatly more problematic.[116] Such problems may typically be exacerbated by temporal problems where harmful exposure might have occurred long in the past.

In the context of property use, therefore, much environmental harm challenges our understanding of activities which are still regarded as quite lawful. Moreover, the law of tort, for all that the consequences of the development of negligence over the past century has created a revolution in risk reallocations, is extremely uncomfortable in the realms of environmental damage. By their nature, environmental harms tend to be disjunctive in time and place. Cumulatively, we are capable of causing damage far removed from locality and the present. The point has been made by comparing traditional local perceptions of causal influences with the Newtonian 'compartmentalising' approach to natural science: 'Locality means that entities in any system can only be influenced by causes that are effective in the nearby spatial domain'.[117] Thus the suggestion of non-local, even global, harms takes us far beyond easily comprehensible conceptions. Here once again externalities appear, as illustrated by global warming, for 'present legal and economic systems provide no incentive to minimise CO_2 emissions. On the contrary for each person, the benefit of present emissions exceeds the cost of emission reductions and the harms to that person in the future, even though the cumulative effect on the world of rapid climate change could be catastrophic'.[118]

With the above problems in mind, it is necessary to remind ourselves that there is a corpus of private law mechanisms which can relate to the perceived ends of environmental protection. The tort of nuisance has a fair claim to lie at the root of traditional English law legal responses to environmental threats. Nuisance is about threats to the enjoyment of land, based on the principle *sic utere tuo ut alienum non laedas*, namely that every person should so use property without causing harm to that of another. In part, the role of nuisance has been facilitative in accommodating the industrial

---

110 European Commission, 2000b.

111 *Cambridge Water Company v Eastern Counties Leather plc* [1994] 2 AC 264.

112 *Graham and Graham v Rechem* [1996] Env LR 158.

113 See Lord Cranworth, *St Helen's Smelting Co v Tipping* (1865) 11 HL Cas 642; also, Ogus and Richardson, 1977, p 300; Hart and Honore, 1985, Chapter 5.

114 *McGhee v NCB* [1972] 3 All ER 1008.

115 *Wilsher v Essex Area Health Authority* [1988] AC 1074.

116 *Reay and Hope v BNFL* [1994] Env LR 320.

117 Svedin, O'Riordan and Jordan, 2001, p 49.

118 Hodas, 1998, p 24.

age, enforcing a resiting of rights boundaries as between the owners and occupiers of land to something less than a mutual equivalence of threatening activities. Thus, McAuslan, has concluded that: 'judges subtly altered the balance in nuisance law so as to facilitate the industrial revolution and reduce the scope for challenges to urban and industrial activities. The point is important: courts can and do reshape and redefine the law in the light of the changing goals and needs of society.'[119] Nuisance consists of either unreasonable, indirect injury to land or unreasonable interference of a substantial nature with the use and enjoyment of land. Whilst in principle injunctive, seeking such relief against the operations of on-going enterprise is inevitably problematic.[120] Note that economic value is prejudiced, in the former instance by physical injury, and in the latter by reference to a diminution in amenity value.[121] In the latter instance, as in the case of noise, vibrations, fumes or smoke, a major delimiter upon liability is the need to establish an unreasonable interference with the user.[122] The question of reasonableness of interference with the plaintiff's amenity will also be subject to the locality doctrine, by reference to the character of the neighbourhood, with deleterious consequences for those in certain areas and with low property values.[123]

The tort of nuisance is illustrative of conceptual deficiencies generally found in toxic torts and referred to previously. Moreover, its basis in property has a further restrictive effect, for as a cause of action, it offers limited access to justice for those without a right or interest in property. Prospects of increasing the potential of the remedy have been severely restricted by the ruling of the House of Lords, where it has been made clear that nuisance is a tort against property and not against the person.[124] Such retrenchment in the conceptualisation of nuisance very much limits its role as a remedy. This is especially so in the context of gradual unfolding of awareness of environmental consequences. As one commentator has put it: 'Insults to the sensibilities of land occupiers from smoke, noise and foul odors have been overshadowed by a chemical revolution that seems to portend a multitude of unseen risks in everyday life from the synthetic products that we routinely encounter.'[125] Paradoxically, it is the property right nexus within the tort of nuisance that has at least in the United States made it the focus for a wider debate, as to how far for instance land use control is justified in extending beyond nuisance in constraining the landowner.[126] This has its source in the contested territory between regulation and private law. Partly by way of political backlash to perceptions of over-regulation, principles underlying the tort are in the United States enjoying something of a renaissance. It has, for instance, been argued that its value lies in its individualistic foundations, its relationship to private property and market transactions, and to the efficiency of polluters being required to internalise pollution costs as 'least-cost' avoiders.

---

119 McAuslan, 1991, p 198.

120 *Halsey v Esso Petroleum* [1961] 2 All ER 145; cf *St Helen's Smelting Co v Tipping* (1865) 11 HL Cas 642.

121 *Halsey v Esso Petroleum, ibid.*

122 See, eg, Ogus and Richardson, 1977, pp 297–300; though it is arguable that the test of unreasonableness applies across the board: see Steele, 1995, p 252.

123 Lee, 2000a, p 87.

124 *Hunter v Canary Wharf Ltd* [1997] AC 655; also *Pride of Derby & Derbyshire Angling Association Ltd v British Celanese* [1953] Ch 149.

125 Rabin, 1987, p 28.

126 Epstein, 1985, p 265.

Green goes as far as to contrast statutory regulation as 'the product of a more politicised and less informed rule making process'.[127] Such views echo market analyses of nuisance, and the view that pollution is ultimately a conflict in land use, to be resolved on a transactional basis through land values.[128] This reflects an underlying view of tort as distributing losses through market pricing, even as far as bringing about in consequence the internalisation of social costs on the part of the polluter.[129]

In so far as civil liability frameworks secure compensatory adjustments, this is an illustration of their poor fit with the objectives of environmental protection. It has been pointed out that 'environmental protection is generally an incidental feature, rather than the *sine qua non* of private law rights and obligations'.[130] Indeed, compensation may not lead to environmental improvement at all. Himsworth sees 'tort law as a very low-ranking priority on the environmental lawyer's agenda' and nuisance as being 'no more than a system which is an adjunct to the general law of property and which serves as a protection for the rights of property owners *inter se*'.[131] As discussed previously, the fact of primary reliance upon regulatory mechanisms is in part due to the deficiencies attending upon private action.[132] The genesis of legislation, originally for public health purposes, and subsequently more broadly for purposes of land use planning and environmental protection, lies in the need to find credible responses to the threats posed by urbanisation and industrialisation, as also, now, industrialised agricultural practices. Moreover, other rights have arisen in consequence, especially in the public law arena.[133]

Nuisance has been superseded by regulation because of its inadequacy for the task of addressing problems of cumulative or diffuse harm, damage to the unowned environment, and the complexities of increased risk caused by scientific uncertainty.[134] As seen above, its limited value further derives from the restrictive approach to any extension of nuisance beyond the twin nexus of actual property damage and damage to amenity so as to encompass damage to health and the physical integrity of the person.[135] Otherwise, the distinction between nuisance and negligence, narrowed in recent authority in the context of foreseeability of harm,[136] may shrink still further in the face of the established impact of accepted, or prescribed, standards for the purposes of negligence actions.[137] All such factors suggest an inevitable conclusion that nuisance must have at best a supplementary role in response environmental threats.[138]

---

127 Green, 1997, p 543.

128 Coase, 1960; a critique of the inappropriateness of the efficiency of a bargaining process in the context of environmental damage is offered by Ogus and Richardson, 1977, pp 314–17.

129 For instance, Klemma, 1976.

130 Redgwell, 1999, p 3.

131 Himsworth, 1997, p 171.

132 McLaren, 1983.

133 See Miller, 1998, Chapter 1.

134 Frazier, 1998, p 93.

135 *Hunter v Canary Wharf* [1997] AC 655.

136 Following to its logical conclusion the principle in *Wagon Mound (No 2), Overseas Tankship (UK) Ltd v Miller Steamship Co Pty* [1967] 1 AC 617.

137 See *Albery & Budden v BP Oil & Shell Oil* [1980] JPL 586; also, *Scott-Whitehead v NCB* (1987) 53 P & CR 263.

138 See, further, Ogus and Richardson, 1977.

3.2 Nuisance, planning law and the assertion of the public interest

It is now necessary to consider how conflicts between regulatory and private law mechanisms referred to above are resolved. In particular, conflict can arise between the 'public' decision making process leading to permitted development and the 'private' rights of the aggrieved neighbour. However, in the UK, there is no clear enunciation of principles to be applied in the resolution of these tensions. Regulatory processes have been developed without formal regard for the common law, even where a private law challenge might raise persuasive environmental arguments.

A limited defence of statutory authorisation has been recognised by the courts. An activity or use, which might otherwise give rise to a claim in nuisance, is rendered lawful, in principle, where it can be said to be on the basis of the will of Parliament. In respect of specific statutory provisions, this is arguably merely an expression of the non-availability of judicial review of Acts of Parliament. The principle appears to be limited so that an otherwise unlawful act must be no greater than necessary for the fulfilment of the statutory purpose, as well as carried out in a non-negligent manner.[139] A claim may therefore lie 'only to the extent that the actual nuisance (if any) caused ... exceeds that for which immunity is conferred'.[140] The authority granted must accordingly be strictly interpreted.[141] The approach has been criticised for failing to pay due regard to the question of damages in lieu, where the court is unwilling on policy grounds to make a discretionary injunctive award.[142] The main concern in the present context, however, is that the approach pays insufficient regard to the resulting externalisation of pollution costs.[143]

In any event the principle outlined above applies at best *mutatis mutandis* to the grant of planning permission under the land use control regime. In principle, a planning authority has no jurisdiction to authorise a nuisance, and thereby to preclude a subsequent challenge by way of nuisance.[144] Nevertheless, rejecting a claim in nuisance, the High Court has ruled that this issue is 'a planning problem, not a question for the courts'.[145] The judgment appeared in places to suggest a broad principle, conclusions being based upon a view that 'Parliament is presumed to have considered the interests of those who will be affected ... I believe that principle should be utilised in respect of planning permission'.[146] It was, however, further suggested that a planning permission may alter the character of the neighbourhood. The Court of Appeal has subsequently applied a narrow construction to the earlier authority.[147] The court was unimpressed that in the earlier case the local authority seeking an injunction in public nuisance had as planning authority granted planning permission in the first place. Further, it was stated

---

139 *Allen v Gulf Oil Refining Ltd* [1981] AC 1001.
140 *Ibid*, at p 1014 (*per* Lord Wilberforce).
141 *Ibid*, at p 1007; note that the case concerned a private Act of Parliament.
142 See Tromans, 1982, pp 106–08.
143 Cf *Tock v St John's Metropolitan Area Board* (1989) 64 DLR (4th) 620.
144 *R v Exeter CC ex p JL Thomas & Co Ltd* [1990] 1 All ER 413.
145 *Gillingham BC v Medway (Chatham) Dock Co Ltd* [1992] 3 All ER 923.
146 *Ibid*, at p 934 (*per* Buckley J).
147 *Wheeler v JJ Saunders Ltd* [1995] 2 All ER 697.

categorically that 'the court should be slow to acquiesce in the extinction of private rights without compensation as a result of administrative decisions which cannot be appealed and are difficult to challenge'.[148] There appeared to be agreement on the bench that the change of use which had the benefit of permission was 'not a strategic planning decision affected by considerations of public interest'.[149] An assenting judgment was likewise based primarily on all the interests at stake here being private interests.[150] In a later case, in the context of pollution control, noxious gases and odours arising from the operation of a landfill site were held to constitute an unreasonable user.[151] The site was licensed by the Environment Agency under the Environmental Protection Act 1990 Part II, and whilst it seemed clear that regulatory breaches had probably occurred (but not enforced), it seems that this was not an essential element in the nuisance finding. The case is interesting, therefore, in that private law nuisance was available to seek redress for defects ordinarily subject to judicial review.

The courts therefore retain jurisdiction as to whether the private interest underlying an assertion of nuisance should take priority over any public interest expressed through the planning or other regulatory process. Regulatory regimes enabling certain activities may therefore be held not to legitimate a nuisance, although distinctions between land use decisions and ongoing pollution controls may require further elaboration. It remains the case, however, that the chances of successful proceedings are subject to the determination of the question as to whether a planning authority has permitted a change in the 'character of the neighbourhood'. The authorities point to the neighbourhood test as being determined with the permitted development in mind. It appears that the principle involves the application of an informal test of public interest or benefit before the private law question of unreasonable interference can be decided. Although the utility of activities is seldom commented on explicitly in nuisance cases, the courts are duly called upon to review location and operation in the context of the permitted use. A view of public utility must inevitably inform determination of unreasonable interference.[152] The overlap between land use planning and the law of nuisance is therefore resolved by a balancing process of the sort that on the face of it the doctrines of nuisance well understand. However, it remains unclear on what basis the threshold for a reasonable activity may be altered by the award of a planning permission, and how far this might constitute a fair basis for prejudicing private rights: 'the role of public or community interests in nuisance remains marginal and ill-defined.'[153] Even if it is admitted that locations will differ (though this should raise questions of environment justice), planning procedures should already have addressed the issue of public benefit. In view of the potential conflict of values, it has been said that the 'difficulty is that nuisance has typically protected the kind of interests which environmental regulation must inevitably qualify in some circumstances'.[154] As a consequence, 'the temptation will be for judges to

---

148 *Wheeler v JJ Saunders Ltd* [1995] 2 All ER 697, p 711 (*per* Peter Gibson LJ).

149 *Ibid*, p 707 (*per* Staughton LJ).

150 *Ibid*, p 712 (*per* Peter Gibson LJ).

151 *Blackburn v ARC Ltd* [1998] Env LR 469.

152 Penner, 1993, pp 3–4.

153 Steele and Jewell, 1993, p 573.

154 Steele, 1995, p 258.

regard the results which flow naturally from planned developments as "reasonable"'.[155] Thus, transposing the context, as discussed above, most commentators would agree with Lord Goff as to the effectiveness of collective action and the recognition through regulation of community interests. This after all further satisfies testing by reference to democratic mandate, and on the face of it, the private law action has the worst of the argument here.[156]

Yet even accepting that planning consent may affect the character of a neighbourhood, it can be argued that such standard 'simply adorns this weakening of protection with a spurious democratic legitimacy'.[157] Crawford has maintained that planning permission is itself ultimately an administrative function. If so, this must apply *a fortiori* in the case of regulatory consents given where procedures are less participative, as in the case of Environment Agency authorisation systems.[158] Moreover, in the public law context, where planning permission is applied for, an aggrieved person has limited opportunities to object. If there is an inquiry, it may be possible to give evidence to the inspector. Yet upon grant of permission, there is no third party right of appeal to the Secretary of State.[159] This leaves a residual possibility of challenge by way of an application for leave to seek a judicial review, albeit on distinctly limited grounds. However the public interest can be best represented, there is a need for an explicit consideration of potential harm to the competing interests of neighbours during the regulatory process. Without this, it would therefore be unwise to discount the value of the residual role for private law in this context.

If planning permission cannot therefore be determinative,[160] when is the balancing of interests to be carried out? It can be argued from the authorities that this occurs at the planning stage. Whilst the question of any balancing of interests may be opened at a later stage, inevitably the nature of any nuisance will be defined by the planning permission granted. The question of terms of removal of private rights has not been considered by the courts. Lord Hoffmann has merely concluded that the land use planning system 'is a far more appropriate form of control, from the point of view of both the developer and the public, than enlarging the right to bring actions for nuisance at common law. It enables the issues to be debated before an expert at a planning inquiry and gives the developer the advantage of certainty as to what he is entitled to build'.[161] Paradoxically, however, a feature of the case the report of which contains the above *dicta* was that planning controls had largely been lifted. Deemed consents applied in accordance with highly flexible urban development area/enterprise zone procedures. In such circumstances, justifications based upon planning rules having been followed, in granting an effective right to develop, have an oxymoronic quality.[162]

---

155 Steele, 1995, p 255.
156 See, eg Himsworth, 1997, p 168.
157 Penner, 1993, p 14.
158 Crawford, 1992.
159 See Purdue, 2001.
160 See Miller, 1998, p 50.
161 *Hunter v Canary Wharf Ltd* [1997] AC 655, 710.
162 Cf *Hunter, ibid*, pp 700–01.

In contrast, the recognition of a residual category of rights in a system otherwise dominated by regulation would afford the possibility of challenging the public interest perceptions of regulators. Thus it has been argued that the private law action 'contains the potential to prize open issues about the desirability of the development and its impact on a locality, thereby increasing the accountability of and participation in the overall decision making process'.[163] In this way, nuisance amounts to a potential challenge to regulatory failure, in the sense of 'shortcomings of the applicable systems of control and enforcement'.[164] Moreover, judicial solutions outlined above are unsatisfactory in failing to give due account to the feature of land use control that it is more generally a regulatory response to an assertion of a developer's private interest.

Given the importance of the integrity of the planning process, it is necessary to recognise that it cannot offer a perfect indicator of the public interest. That the planning process should not necessarily be determinative, McGillivray and Wightman ascribe to spatial variability and the flexible consequences within the regulatory scheme. They accordingly contrast the ability of private action to 'foster a wider and more informed debate about a proposed or existing development than may typically be found within routine planning permissions'.[165] It has thus been suggested that in such circumstances the status quo receives an increased level of protection, against which they categorise private law claims as 'protective of an existing local distribution of land use'.[166] This suggests a 'twin-track' approach – to counter a suggested 'single-track' near inevitability of private law yielding to regulation – which would permit different answers even where an activity is allowed by regulation. Such a challenge would presumably be available not only at the time of the original development and commencement of use. Thus, albeit that the onus on the claimant might be more difficult to meet, a nuisance claim may be raised also in the face of changes in the locality, including altered lawful use on the part of a third party.[167] Viewing nuisance as a potentially effective environmental ground of challenge, Steele's optimistic conclusion is that its use 'might take the law beyond the development-friendly era of negligence'.[168]

Yet a problem persists as to the justified extent of private law in the face of regulation. It also remains to be considered whether opportunities for challenge are more effectively located in the field of public law. For instance, as discussed further in Chapter 5, it is apparent that the efficacy of the formal scheme in place for requiring environmental assessment to a crucial degree depends on adequate access to justice for third parties. Whilst inevitable doubts continue to surround the extent of public law rights of challenge, especially in the context of environmental harm, the principles underlying nuisance offer at best a supplementary ground for action.

In the context of the planning process, the fact that wider interests exist, many of which fall within a category traditionally bounded by the notion of nuisance, should perhaps be expressly recognised as a material consideration. Moreover, current levels of

---

163 McGillivray and Wightman, 1997, p 145.
164 Steele, 1995, pp 239–40.
165 McGillivray and Wightman, 1997, p 154.
166 McGillivray and Wightman, 1997, p 156.
167 *Sturges v Bridgman* (1879) 11 Ch D 85.
168 Steele, 1995, p 258.

involvement of third parties, in particular those objecting to development, could be augmented by express rights of challenge by way of appeal. However, concerning the broader point raised above, to the effect that nuisance offers a 'current use' protection, this question surely demands more rigorous application through the regulatory process. It is inherent in much of the environmental critiques of current approaches to land use that owner expectations should be restrained. It remains necessary to assert more pronounced public control over private decisions affecting land and the environment. Commending a 'rights to use' approach for the purposes of vesting rights and obligations on all holdings through a more powerful planned process, Caldwell argues that the result 'would direct public action away from litigation and toward planning and administration'.[169] Concerns at Brave New World implications must be countered by open, participatory processes and such questions are further addressed in Chapter 10. In the meantime, the concluding section to this chapter considers the value of exploring further possibilities for reforming conceptions of private interests for the purposes of environmental protection.

4 INCORPORATING ENVIRONMENTAL VALUES

4.1 Addressing limitations in the common law

Regulation is central in any attempts to find convincing environmental protection mechanisms. The scale of environmental threats has overtaken common law conceptions of control. In a risk society, harm's 'destructive ripples are difficult even for the trained ecologist to trace. A landowner simply cannot be permitted to look away when the harm he causes is imposed, not on some single neighbour who comes over the fence to complain, but on a hundred or a thousand landowners miles downstream or downwind, who lack the time and ability to trace the problem back'.[170]

Private action is subject to a variety of limitations, but crucially 'perspectives represented in the litigation process may not coincide with the larger community's views on the reasonableness of a resource owner's expectations'.[171] As seen above, property law and common law support structures together afford some limited protections, but seldom address problems of environmental degradation other than where immediate neighbours are affected.

Yet in light of the close interrelationship of environmental issues, effective protection requires some equivalence as between public and common law approaches. Answers lie in the expression and enforcement of fundamental values, and defining their limits. This means, in particular, that common law mechanisms should not fall too far out of step with the cognate aspirations of public law and regulation. Subject to the maintenance of acceptable normative constraints, therefore, effective responses to environmental threat require a doctrinal compatibility. The implications for the role of the common law in an era of environmental regulation have been considered by Lee, who points to a danger of dislocation between the two regimes, concluding that unless a level of harmonisation can

---

169 Caldwell, 1974, p 772.
170 Freyfogle, 1996a, pp 186–87.
171 Frazier, 1998, p 68.

be achieved, the daunting alternative for the courts will be that they 'will face claims in the realm of the environment which are not susceptible to effective determination in the light of scientific uncertainty'.[172] The importance goes beyond concerns for the coherence and purity of the common law, for such ossification suggests an ever declining role for tort doctrines in this area.

It is not easy however to suggest ways in which the ordinary courts can develop what would amount to new ways of looking at the world. In any event the deterrent role of liability is threatened by 'insurmountable problems of discontinuity in enterprise management, unforeseeability of the parameters of risk, doubts about the contributory fault of others, speculativeness in discounting to present value'.[173] Though less directly than is public law, the common law has to engage with resolving issues of public interest. Some writers have argued that the influence of statutory provisions should empower common lawyers in the pursuit of public values.[174] More generalised principles of interpretation would for instance be a way of seeking greater consonance. However, given broad principles of legality and reasonable expectations of litigants, the need for clarity and coherence would limit reform opportunities. It is at present difficult to see how our domestic courts could begin to address specific problems caused by environmental toxic tort actions referred to previously, even assuming that the processes of litigation could be rendered more conducive to this process. Lee counters over-pessimism by reference to illustrations of recognised tests being interpreted quite expansively.[175] Moreover, as testimony to the pervasive impact of European Community law on the domestic law of the Member States, the contents of the 2000 white paper on environmental liability indicate the kind of thorough review which domestic processes have seemed unable to generate.[176] For instance, a greatly expanded legislative view of the nature of recognised harm, as well as of causation requirements, might emerge.[177] There would also be an obligation on Member State governments to incorporate into domestic liability rules a considerable extension in notions of standing, extending into the context of private law actions becoming available to interest groups.[178]

Another way of putting this is to say that the categories of externalities which require legal redress should not be closed. The consequences of such compatibility on the part of the common law would be beneficial also for the quality and acceptability of regulation: 'Regulations that address loss of bio-diversity and habitat destruction will make much more sense when we become more accustomed to recognising protection of ecological integrity as an important community interest to be harmonised with other principles in the balancing function of property law.'[179] In other words, such movement in the common law would encompass a higher level of recognition of obligations towards the community.

---

172 Lee, 2000a, p 91.

172 Rabin, 1987, p 43.

174 Farber and Frickey, 1991, p 906.

175 *Griffiths v British Coal Corporation* (1998) unreported, 23 January, High Court.

176 European Commission, 2000b.

177 See Hedemann-Robinson and Wilde, 2000, p 211 *et seq.*

178 See Betlem, 1995.

179 Frazier, 1998, p 108.

4.2   Property rights and ecological reform

Despite the growth of regulation, lawmakers have failed to create a new conception of private property, which retains a presumption of freedom as its benchmark. Although what amounts to a 'property backlash' in the United States against regulations which are invasive of real property interests has no direct comparison elsewhere, Raff has pointed to wider threats posed to the environment by current conceptions: 'Without acceptance of the obligations lying embedded in property, when applying the presumption in favour of freedom of property, it is doubtful that environmental reform legislation can achieve its intended goals. This is a very weighty consideration at any time, but especially when that legislation implements solutions to international concerns about environmental degradation expressed in international agreements and commitments.'[180] As part of a much larger reform project Freyfogle goes further still, calling for 'elements of self-discipline and community' to be introduced into a reconstructed institution of private ownership. Frazier has likewise attempted to express a more reformist agenda, so that property obligations 'more closely reflect prevailing community standards', suggesting that legislators and courts 'focus more explicitly on the principles that guide the balancing process by which such institutions create, interpret, or apply property rules'.[181] He categorises a mix of principles that guide the balancing function of property law: individual principles, such as stability, reliability, individual liberty, and civil rights; and community principles, such as the police power (or regulatory authority), and nuisance. Given that he asserts that a flexibility principle operates so as to keep rules 'from stagnating and losing touch with the society they serve', he proposes the institution of an 'ecological integrity principle', which would encompass the protection of humans, borrowing from public trust doctrine.[182] The intent is that this would prompt the recognition of ecological integrity as an important community interest.

The task is to create institutions capable of achieving sustainability objectives in line with reformed approaches to the public interest. Ideological property arguments are unable to engage with those sustainability issues which must come to dominate political and legal discourse. In particular, arguments that environmental protection requires protection from State encroachment, property rights 'restored to the maximum degree possible to their original, comprehensive meaning' must be rejected.[183] In contrast, we should investigate ways in which we can go further than encouraging incremental changes to the doctrinal status quo. Freyfogle has argued for example for a movement towards reducing the perceived divergence between land ethics and private property. The basis for this is the assertion that the ownership paradigm elevates the individual over the communal well-being is anthropocentric and is dominated by market rights and ideas of economic growth. He suggests a series of guiding norms, including a recognition that property is interconnected, that land, as well as persons, deserves redress, and that just as

---

180 Raff, 1998, pp 691–92.
181 Frazier, 1998, p 56.
182 Frazier, 1998, pp 101–09.
183 Pipes, 1999, p 288.

the nature of parcels differs then so should uses to which they may wisely be put.[184] Whilst such an argument calls for a retention of the structural framework of private property norms, these would be incorporated into 'a land ethic and be based on the durable wisdom of ecology'.[185]

Such reformist arguments import a primacy to a concern for future welfare. The objective would be to mitigate the loss of a sense of temporal continuity, linking ourselves with the future as well as the past.[186] This is analogous with the modernist approach of commentators such as Korten, who urges that life post-capitalism depends on a fundamental rethinking and restructuring of ownership rights to move toward stakeholder ownership and human-scale enterprises.[187] He attributes the lack of an ethos of stewardship to the loss of identity with locality, for reasons which include the fractured nature of interests encouraged by markets; our urbanisation, mobility and lack of a sense of place as a society; and the global nature of competitive pressures affecting those working on the land. Seeking an approach based on inherent limits, he argues that property rights lack moral legitimacy when used by those who have more than they need to exclude others from access to a basic means of living; likewise where they absolve themselves from responsibility for an equitable sharing and stewarding of resources that are the common heritage of all.

This concern reflects Locke's original notion of property being made subject to the so-called proviso, or 'sufficiency limitation'. This in effect provided that there must be 'still enough and as good left, and more that the yet unprovided could use'.[188] Despite its potential value as a theoretical compromise, even the proviso falls foul of certain absolutist notions. For instance, Sanders has argued that the proviso, by constraining what is available for initial acquisition, undermines property transfer rules.[189] Yet the original approach supports those of regulatory theorists and environmentalists, the main distinction being its expression at a time when the earth's bounty appeared unending. Although a reading of Locke offers no explicit indications of a commitment to future generations, Waldron has interpreted the proviso as implying that property rights must never stand in the way of sustenance.[190]

To return to the earlier themes of this chapter, an essential question is therefore whether the demands of sustainability can be captured within a changed view of the nature of property. According to Caldwell, 'the changes which have been occurring in modern society have made the present land ownership system increasingly dysfunctional to rational economic and ecological perspectives'.[191] Ecological perspectives make different assumptions to those which underlie those of the free market in allocating resources. It has been said for example that they do not 'take the health and aesthetic integrity of the human environment for granted'.[192] In order to constrain damaging

---

184 Freyfogle, 1996b, pp 648–50.
185 Freyfogle, 1996b, p 661.
186 See Macnaghten and Urry, 1998, p 273.
187 See Korten, 1999, Chapter 9.
188 Locke, 1690, 1924 edn, para 32.
189 Sanders, 1987, pp 380–87.
190 Waldron, 1988, p 216.
191 Caldwell, 1974, p 774.
192 Frazier, 1995, p 369.

activities, a proposed green alternative might look for a reworking of what reasonable expectations are to be made of property owners. Thus it might impose an 'obligation to use private property responsibly, society's reasonable expectations for the responsible use of common property, the interests of future generations in access to good-quality resources, and respect for government's role as trustee of some elements of public and common property'.[193] This amounts to a reorientation of conceptions of private property rights by reference to the public interest.[194] In contrast, the weight of cultural history, as also the core values of the common law, are ranged against such reformist conceptions.

That such a project may be beyond the evolutionary capacities of the common law may not matter, however, provided coherent and responsive regulatory pressures can be justified and maintained. Effective environmental regulation should seek to factor ecological and social responsibility into the political process. A radical, modernist approach is offered by Byrne, who applies Leopold's land ethic through the imposition of a new regulatory framework for land use. For instance, any change in the character of land that impairs its natural value would require a permit; no permit would be granted unless a development served a compelling human need; if specific harm to the environment would follow, but which regulation does not otherwise prohibit, then it can be permitted provided that it will be accomplished with the minimum of environmental damage, is further subject to monetary compensation representing environmental damage, and human gains substantially exceed the environmental harm.[195]

Such questions lie at the very core of the sustainability debate, and demand that ways be found to secure their introduction and to 'sustain' them in a democratic, non-oppressive sense. In particular, participatory processes would be essential to securing acceptance on the part of those whose rights would be more formally constrained. This can also assist in the education process, as also in encouraging understanding of the mutual benefits obtained by environmental protection.[196] Therefore, alongside the long term public interest, the legitimate interests of individuals, where 'socially and environmentally harmless' would also require protection.[197] As will be seen in the following chapters, such processes may also counter NIMBYism (or, the 'Not in my backyard' motivation), and likewise strengthen the resolve of planning authorities 'to resist the blandishments and political pressure from interests seeking to use land for their personal gain'.[198]

However, even without asserting a new dynamic, the problems inherent in the current conflict between statutory consequences and common law expectations explored above require urgent review. Such conflicts may best be determined by a specialist environmental tribunal. Further impetus has recently been given to the general question of setting up an environmental court, and this is discussed in Chapter 10. Such a specialist body might for instance enable review of the merits of administrative decisions in defined circumstances. This would achieve a mechanism for asserting a public interest rationale in

---

193 Frazier, 1995, p 346.
194 Caldwell, 1974, p 775.
195 Byrne, 1990, p 243.
196 Freyfogle, 1998, pp 306–07.
197 Caldwell, 1974, p 769.
198 Babcock and Feurer, 1977, pp 308–09.

environmental and land use controls in ways which the constraints explored above currently prevent.[199] Generally, as McAuslan has pointed out, such a body would offer an antidote to 'the dissatisfaction of the too cosy relations between regulator and regulated'.[200] There is however no reason in principle why its remit should be restricted to public law disputes, and its jurisdiction could extend to private law adjudications. If this were to happen, then certain of the reformist ideas explored above as to the nature of harm and questions of compensability might become integrated into the process. But more than this, it would offer a coherent means by which development and other activities, which now appear pitted against a range of regulatory regimes, might lawfully be contained within sustainability constraints. The following chapters consider essential issues concerned with the rationale and impact of those regimes in the context of land use and the environment.

---

199 See Woolf, 1992, pp 13–14; Crawford, 1992, p 271.
200 McAuslan, 1991, p 205.

CHAPTER 4

THE REMIT OF ENGLISH LAND USE PLANNING LAW

> We spray the fields and scatter
> The poison on the ground
> So that no wicked wild flowers
> Upon our farm be found. ...
> We give no compensation
> The earth is ours today,
> And if we lose on arable,
> Then bungalows will pay.[1]

These next, central chapters carry discussion of arguments concerning sustainability into domestic regulatory contexts. The particular focus in this (and the succeeding) chapter, in light of the previous discussion, is the nature and extent of land use restrictions which can justifiably be imposed upon those with property entitlements, especially in the face of environmental threats. As will be seen also in Chapter 6, the question as to how far the freedoms of private property owners as to use and development of land can be permitted is of crucial importance to securing greater sustainability.

1 THE TASK OF LAND USE PLANNING

This first section is devoted to the fundamental features underlying land use planning regulation. Town and country planning laws constitute that body of rules which regulate the right to develop land, including changes in its use. The means by which this objective is fulfilled are essentially twofold. First, development planning is the public, proactive process, by which planning authorities produce and review strategic plans (in both broad and detailed terms) for their localities. Secondly, development control is the process whereby individual proposals for specific development are either permitted or rejected by the planning authority. The effectiveness and appropriateness with which land is released into the development process are matters which are crucial to sustainable development objectives.

1.1 The roots of modern planning

Whilst there is no space to offer a full history, it is important to understand the origins of modern planning law, as well as its major contours. The Town and Country Planning Act 1947, presently superseded by the Town and Country Planning Act 1990 (TCPA), has been described as 'a comprehensive code imposed in the public interest'.[2] Planning has

---

1   Betjeman, 'Harvest hymn', 1966, 1970 edn, pp 350–51.
2   *Pioneer Aggregates (UK) Ltd v Secretary of State for the Environment* [1985] AC 132, 141 (*per* Lord Scarman).

long been politically contested territory, due to a traditional role as emblematic of an interventionist State. It is, however, worth briefly exploring the incremental development of planning, and its evolution from a scheme which was partial and permissive to one which became near universal and mandatory in nature. Although a broader remit for planning emerged slowly, town planning for the most part came about in response to the dislocating consequences of 19th century industrialisation and urbanisation; and 'could be represented as a logical extension, in accordance with changing aims and conditions, of earlier legislation concerned with housing and public health'.[3] Its public health roots derive from the introduction in 1848 of central and local boards of health concerned with sanitary conditions.[4] Provisions for the clearance of unfit housing followed,[5] and a consolidation empowered the passage of bylaws for minimum building standards.[6] An explicit statutory reference to 'planning' appeared only in 1909, in a statute amounting to little more than an enabling provision.[7] At about the same time, the idealist movements, emerging at the turn of the 20th century,[8] led to developments which bore the hallmark of social reform.[9] Employment-related model towns such as Saltaire, Bourneville and Port Sunlight were respectively inaugurated in 1853, 1878 and 1887. Under the impetus of the earliest visionaries, such as Ebenezer Howard, the Garden City Association was set up in 1899,[10] the Garden City Pioneer Company in 1902, and First Garden City Limited in 1903. Soon after, the earliest garden cities – precursors to the idea of New Towns – appeared.[11]

Aside from the idealist movement, general planning emerged from legislation in the aftermath of the Great War, largely as an incident of housing reform. Following two 1917 Royal Commission reports, concerned respectively with Industrial Unrest, and the Housing of the Industrial Population in Scotland, legislation introduced into housing municipal provision and State subsidy, along with tighter standards.[12] Compulsory purchase arrangements were also introduced.[13] A further prong of this legislation was the introduction of rudimentary 'planning schemes', which can fairly be described as the direct antecedent to modern planning. These were required of larger urban authorities with populations in excess of 20,000 and were subject to ministerial approval. Importantly, these were permissive, and in response to the spread of unchecked development there were limited attempts to control development through the 1930s.[14] Planning schemes were upgraded so as to empower coverage over any land, including built-up areas and areas likely to be developed. This control of development remained residual, and still permissive, although developers had an incentive to apply for interim

3   Ashworth, 1954, p 181.
4   Public Health Act 1848.
5   See, eg, Shaftesbury Act 1851; Artisans and Labourers' Dwellings Act 1868; Artisans and Labourers' Dwellings Improvement Act 1875.
6   Public Health Act 1875; London Building Act 1894.
7   Housing, Town Planning etc Act 1909.
8   Howard, 1902; Geddes, 1915.
9   See Ward, 1994, especially Chapter 2.
10   Subsequently the Town and Country Planning Association.
11   The forerunners, Letchworth and Welwyn Garden City, had been instituted by 1919.
12   The Housing and Town Planning Act 1919.
13   Acquisition of Land (Assessment of Compensation) Act 1919.
14   See TCPA 1932; Restriction of Ribbon Development Act 1935.

development orders, which protected compensation rights in case a zoning process failed them.[15] Thus, with no control over individual developments and the risk of incurring a duty to compensate, a legally tortuous, bureaucratic system of confirming existing trends persisted; the Uthwatt Committee noted the existence by 1937 of zones sufficient to house approaching 300 million people.[16]

An indirect consequence of the introduction of housing standards, and in its slipstream the painfully slow growth of planning and concern as to spatial policy, was that new estates were diverted onto the periphery of towns, on to what came to be known as suburban land. This, together with improvements in energy supply and transportation, led to an outward expansion of both public and private building. Paradoxically given close connections between housing growth and planning's concern for the land resource, the statutory separation of planning from housing after 1925 was arguably misplaced.[17] Thus, by 1939 the picture was of a restricted planning regime manifestly incapable of addressing an era of rapid development. Echoing admittedly more limited policy rethinking during the earlier war, the 1939–45 war even today appears to have been a time of unusual reordering of priorities. Three influential and radical expert committees were set up in 1941: the Beveridge Committee on Social Insurance and Allied Services, Uthwatt Committee on Compensation and Betterment, and Scott Committee on Land Utilisation in Rural Areas. A 1944 white paper, *The Control of Land Use*, was a sea change: 'Provision for the right use of land, in accordance with a considered policy, is an essential requirement of the government's programme of postwar reconstruction.'[18]

The underlying premise of the statutory regime introduced in 1947 could be described as the nationalisation of private development rights, through the operation of development control.[19] The legislation introduced a mandatory planning duty on local authorities for the first time. In principle, all land, excluding agricultural development, was brought under regulatory control, requiring prior planning permission.[20] Development planning was based on the universal preparation by planning authorities of Development Plans, to include allocation of main uses, main transport routes, minerals, woodlands, green belts, reservoirs, water supply and sewage disposal. These could be supplemented by Town Maps, detailing plans for urban areas, including designated comprehensive development areas, for slum clearance and redevelopment programmes. The responsible authorities were to be the then higher tier, county and county borough authorities. But the seeds of what has since become a strongly centralised policy direction lay in the creation of a new co-ordinating department of State (then, the Ministry of Town and Country Planning).

The system remains in many of its essential features similar today, and is discussed further in the next section. However, the identity of the department responsible has metamorphosed many times. In 1997, the incoming government created the Department of Environment, Transport and the Regions (DETR), succeeding (and enlarging the scope

---

15 See Cullingworth and Nadin, 1997, p 3.
16 See Grant, 1982, p 21, citing Barlow Report; see UK Government, 1940, para 143.
17 Town Planning Act 1925.
18 See Cullingworth and Nadin, 1997, p 8.
19 See Vogel, 1986, p 35.
20 TCPA 1990, s 57(1).

of) its predecessor, the Department of the Environment (DoE). Following the 2001 general election, the nearest responsible ministry is now the Department of Transport, Local Government and the Regions (less poetically, DTLGR). Ironically, given the arguments here concerning the close relation between environment and land use planning, an effective demerger has been secured at the stroke of the Prime Ministerial pen. The 'environment' rump has been placed in a new Department of Environment, Food and Rural Affairs (DEFRA). Thus it has become grafted onto the old Ministry of Agriculture, Fisheries and Food (MAFF), of which more will be said in Chapter 8. A first impression of the reorganisation, at its kindest, appears to show a high degree of concentration upon dismantling and refocusing MAFF, with rather less attention to securing a coherent strategic place for 'the environment' in the delivery of national administration.

1.2   The scope of planning

It is now necessary to consider how broadly, or how narrowly, the remit of our planning regime extends. The traditional land use concerns of planning can be described as generally including 'the need to protect public health, to prevent unplanned (physical) development, to protect nature as a refuge from modern life, to provide for the public interest, to manage the environment, and to find a fair balance between competing demands'.[21] The boundaries between planning and environmental protection are at times hard to distinguish. This is inevitable, given that planning 'is implicitly environmental in the sense that its *raison d'être* is to regulate our immediate surroundings, allowing for a rational allocation of land uses among competing demands. It can also influence "hard" issues like air quality, water pollution and the siting of hazardous installations which attract a narrower sense of the term'.[22] Planning can be a proactive policy tool, which likewise can be seen as having an ideological role, Rydin referring to its seeking 'a more acceptable pattern of use of our built and natural environment' thereby 'easing the pain' of a postmodern, fragmented, flexible economy.[23] It also has a conservational role, especially in respect of 'the broad structures within which we live, work and exist'.[24] The potential range of the planning process is such that it can claim an inclusiveness that is not apparent in other areas of the policy process. Thus an argument for the role of planning is that it is the main means of expression of policy integration. As Steeley has put it, 'there are not enough good models of the relationships between things: economics, culture, space and causality models each having drawbacks, it was necessary to seek a way of integrating these models to help strategically plan the city as the basic unit of management'.[25]

However, the dominance of national policy making within the planning regime has traditionally tended to downplay the aspirational, or integrative, aspect of planning, in favour of an emphasis upon the physical land use implications, guardedly extended by reference to locational and amenity elements. The system in many respects has also been

---

21   Macnaghten and Pinfield, 1999, p 20.
22   Miller, 1998, p 47.
23   Rydin, 1998, pp 351–52; see also Lash and Urry, 1987.
24   Rydin, 1998, p 353.
25   Royal Commission on Environmental Pollution, Seminar, 2000.

called upon to promote growth, to the extent even of the ordinary planning process being withdrawn or severely modified.[26] This has meant that planning has not provided a consistent, land use-focused platform for a more integrated policy process. Instead, beset by constraints and isolated by discrete policy powers vested elsewhere, it has often appeared to be failing, as for instance in terms of deficiencies in securing appropriate housing provision and transport infrastructure, and responding to urban and rural deprivation. Such issues are further discussed below. The plain and obvious truth, however, is that land use planning cannot be isolated from a vast range of public policy questions. The expectation that planning can work without a broader policy integration emphasis has been made possible by a combination of insistence upon the sanctity of market forces and a central dominance of policy issues. As we will see below, it must be hoped that sustainable development objectives can offer a suitable platform for a more open and integrated process.

The sustainability discourse indeed suggests that a more expansive approach can be justified. Certainly, notions of sustainable development can readily be assimilated into an integrated perspective of planning. Its remit has been described to extend to environmental objectives, which include 'the redistribution of resources to disadvantaged inner city groups; the longevity of the built stock; the conservation of wildlife; or the encouragement of urban development. A composite goal – such as sustainable development – may guide the planning process. The common strand is the focus on the use of the built and natural environment, and as strategies which can alter that use'.[27] The modern environmental agenda, and the wider implications of land use decisions, regionally, nationally and globally, has the potential to bring about a change in planning priorities. Owens has pointed to the gradual injection of broader concerns 'exemplified by global warming and the consumption of non-renewable resources', such as transport and pollution, although in 1994 she was unable to assert with any confidence that there had been more than a little practical impact.[28]

The role of planning has thus been circumscribed in one key respect, for it is concerned mainly with the locus of development activity, rather than questioning development viability. Though traditionally implicit, the central idea underlying planning is that it addresses the instabilities caused by the market system, including threats caused to both natural and built environments and the overexploitation and underutilisation of resources. Planning therefore operates at a crucial interface of market activities and public regulatory controls. The balance between the two shifts over time and the scope of planning as a regulatory response 'at any particular time will relate to the currently accepted limits of the public sector's role in devising strategies for the physical environment. It is important to recognise that as social and economic change occurs, the area shaded by the planning umbrella will alter'.[29] Operating in the context of market forces, and in pursuit of its role 'to regulate, stimulate and impose order and structure', planning has features of an ideological nature, as well as addressing practical issues of

---

26 See Owens, 1994, p 440.
27 Rydin, 1998, pp 1–2.
28 Owens, 1994, pp 441–42.
29 Rydin, 1998, p 2.

land value.[30] Seen thus, at its most proactive, it can be said to have a redistributional impact in addressing the externalities of economic activity: with dual tasks relating to negative externalities, by seeking to protect areas and communities against adverse consequences, and positive externalities, by seeking to divert resources into preferred land uses and facilities.[31]

1.3   The private retention of development value

A further respect in which the role of planning has been circumscribed concerns land values. Despite the original objectives for planning, increases in land value have generally accrued for the private benefit. Although battles have been lost by public interest agencies long ago, the private driving of the development process has had significant implications for the state of national infrastructure, and now the ability to respond positively to the challenge of sustainability. As will be seen in the next section, land use planning has the consequence of restricting the range of rights available to those who own property. Ideological and other implications of this have already been discussed in the previous chapter. Now that the discussion is moving towards an explanation of the land use planning system, it is necessary from the outset to be clear as to the conditions under which planning rules are required to operate.

Two particular problems have dogged the planning process. They are each related to resources. First, there has been little replacement of the private sector by the public sector as the primary agency for development. Much land has passed through the hands of local government, especially during the era of council house building (an era that has been in gradual, terminal decline since the 1980s).[32] However, the resources have not been available to these authorities for the purposes of building up land banks to prime the development process, also in directions and especially locations decided upon by regulatory decision.[33] Moreover, without the creation of consistent conditions enabling public bodies to obtain lands at existing value, obstacles (especially as to cost) are placed in the way of both public development of land and public provision of essential infrastructure, as property values rise inexorably in areas where either development land is already at a premium or new development is otherwise permitted.

A second, related problem concerns the development value of land. Major structural problems have been created by the endemic inability of politicians to grasp the nettle of ownership of development land values in a system based upon development constraint. The notion of development value cannot be disentangled from its impact upon the planning process and vice versa. Planning policies and planning control decisions generate important movements in land values, and in value differentials between different landholdings. Significant movements in value can derive from the mere holding of land, as opposed to its development. Indeed, in the right conditions, non-release of land otherwise earmarked for development can have the effect of pushing values further

30   Rydin, 1998, pp 7–8.
31   Rydin, 1998, pp 352–54.
32   See Burnett, 1978 and Merrett, 1979; cf Driscoll, 1997, pp 824–25.
33   See Ward, 1994, pp 196–97.

upwards. Development value has been described as being 'neither deserved nor earned and which is largely inequitable'.[34]

Yet the story of attempts to harness development value to community purposes, just as to enable public control of development in accordance with the needs of the community, suggests that no serious experiment has ever been in place. The Uthwatt Committee in 1942 reviewed the chaos of the pre-war system, in which development values were partially nationalised but the obligation to compensate at market value produced chronic over-designation. Its report concluded that the value of development rights should be vested in the State (and indeed that increases in site value should be taxed annually). The idea of development value was understood in terms of 'betterment' and represented value added by public investment or the application of public regulation.[35] In some respects the 1947 Act went further, a radical component of development control being that it would encompass the compulsory purchase of all development rights, under which owners would only retain existing values as well as existing use rights. Therefore, what has been described as the 'compensation bogey' was simply abolished: 'henceforth development would take place according to good planning principles.'[36] A fund (set at £300 million) was established in a Central Land Board, in order to respond to claims through making once-and-for-all payments for development rights foregone. The system purported to be a comprehensive one, whereby there would be no compensation for planning refusals (still the position today), any compulsory purchase of land would be at existing use value, and in the event of permitted development a development charge would apply. The development charge was set at a rate of 100% on the development value accruing to land by virtue of planning permission or otherwise.[37] This was to ensure that all market transfers would take effect also at existing use values.[38]

The measure was probably doomed from the start. The Conservative opposition pledged repeal of development charges, the expectation of which could therefore be 'planned' for by landowners and developers. With their abolition in 1953, the 1947 legislation therefore lost one of its essential foundations. This emasculated the planning role. It also opened up other discrepancies. For instance, differentials between landowners were widened inequitably for compulsory purchase remained at existing use value, until amending legislation substituted (with certain exceptions, such as new towns) market value compensation. Other than partial attempts through fiscal strategy to recoup a proportion of these gains, there were two further attempts at 'planning' (albeit centrally administered) solutions. The first, through the creation of a Land Commission, the introduction of a less punitive betterment levy, originally at 40% of development value, and levied upon vendors (thereby obviating the vulnerability of purchasers to paying twice over), which was repealed in 1971. The final attempt was the introduction of a community land scheme under the Community Land Act in 1975. This was aimed at

---

34 Grant, 1982, p 18; also Grant, 1999, especially pp 62–67.

35 UK Government 1942a, para 260.

36 Cullingworth and Nadin, 1997, p 10.

37 Town and Country Planning (Development Charge) Rules 1948 (SI 1948/1189).

38 TCPA 1932 had provided for a 75% charge in respect of increases arising under its restricted scheme of planning controls.

improving land availability. The system was complex but in the first instance authorities were able to purchase land and sell at market prices, benefiting from an exemption from a new Development Land Tax (originally at 80%). Others would be taxed on realised development value. The system was introduced at a time of economic crisis and failed largely due to chronic underfunding of authorities (unable to build more than a derisory level of land stock despite the opportunity in principle to retain profits upon subsequent sale). Once again, there was also the spectre of repeal and the incoming government obliged through the Local Government Planning and Land Act 1980.

Financial benefits derived from development value therefore remain a private matter, which is where most of the land resource resides. The idea of nationalising development value has been lost. It has been said that this loss 'is more than a matter of land taxation or even equity. The so-called "financial provisions" of the 1947 Act underpinned the whole system, and made positive planning a real possibility. Though it seems unlikely that the issue will return to the political agenda in the foreseeable future, it should not be forgotten that this vital piece of the planning machinery is missing'.[39] These factors have contributed significantly to the domination of the planning system by market forces. This is achieved in numerous ways: in instituting development proposals, in negotiating with planning authorities, and in litigating in response to refusals of planning permission or imposition of planning conditions. In driving the development process, the private sector brings all the perceived advantages of efficiency. But in the course of this, negative consequences follow.

There are three particular consequences of the above. First, the existence of planning constraint creates the conditions for windfall profit. It results in 'a planned scarcity of development land, and ... local plans become speculators' guides and the increase in values becomes, in effect, a highly regressive form of indirect taxation on homeowners and others who eventually use the land after it has been developed'.[40] Secondly, as a consequence of private sector domination over land availability, the land use planning system is hindered in its allocative role in anticipating and responding to identified need. Thirdly, planners accordingly operate a negotiative process with parallels to the compliance approaches of the pollution control authorities, discussed in Chapter 2.[41] The implications for the utility of planning have therefore been significant. It has contributed, as Grant has stated, 'to reduce the role of planning into a largely regulatory function and to reassert private sector initiative as the primary means for plan implementation'.[42] Thus the fight over, and to increase, development values is big business, offering more immediate priorities than the environment. As a part of the development control equation, assertions of sustainable development are inevitably vulnerable. As will be seen below, it remains too early to say whether its role in the sustainability debate will change this, but there must be serious misgiving over the viability of introducing broader public interest constraints in circumstances of the continuation of private betterment windfalls to the present extent. Ironically, the idea of planning gain, generally supported by developer interests, has gone some way to alleviating this defect, and it is considered in the

---

39 Cullingworth and Nadin, 1997, p 10.
40 Newby, 1979, pp 232–33.
41 See Vogel, 1986, Chapter 3; also Cullingworth and Nadin, 1997, p 19.
42 Grant, 1982, p 33.

discussion of the planning system below. However, with the question of sustainability in mind, some consideration is now given to a further, this time essentially 'spatial', problem of the planning regime.

1.4   Local, central and technocratic priorities

An essential element of the character of a community is that it is defined by place, and there is a legitimate community interest in the control of land use.[43] Development control is therefore for the most part justifiably a local function. However, just as the planning regime is administered by local government, planning concerns have tended to be narrowly focused on localities. This has arguably encouraged a pro-development bias, given the economic needs of local communities. As was seen in the conclusion to the previous chapter, calls for increased community participation in land use decisions can be largely driven by resistance not being reflected in local political priorities: 'the regulation of the use of land should not be left to the caprice and parochial intents of multitudes of local governments, each defining the public welfare in its own image, or in the image of a clutch of neighboring property owners.'[44] Even where there has been local resistance, the refused applicant's right of planning appeal to the Secretary of State, referred to below, has traditionally led to more development-friendly policy decisions.

Moreover, due in large part to the lack of an holistic policy process, discussed above, there is wide scepticism as to the extent to which planning has been able to contribute to social and environmental progress. Davoudi contrasts an early visionary perspective from a subsequent regulatory one. Whereas the former encompassed reformist visions and an emphatically strategic role, she argues that the latter is technical, bureaucratic and concerned with tactical conflict mediation: 'the mounting activities of the private sector have shifted the focus of the system towards its regulatory mode of action. The demand for site-specific conflict management has succeeded the need for strategic action.'[45] The era which evidences a more technocratic age dates from around 1970, categorised by the above changed paradigm,[46] in which a 'systems' approach has been applied to planning processes.[47]

Not only is the impress of central control a pervasive feature, therefore, but the planning process is culturally largely reactive to private sector proposals. Again, according to Davoudi, the negotiative nature of these tactical responses to (predominantly) private sector projects became all too readily subsumed into the 1980s' central government commitment to rolling back the State, with planners expected to oil the wheels of development.[48] She sums up the more recent state of planning as largely unchanged, administering the system and 'mediating between competing interests', with one essential change due to plan-led planning, whereby 'the arena of conflict mediation has increasingly moved away from the individual development control cases towards the

---

43   McGregor, 1999, p 426.
44   Babcock and Feurer, 1977, p 312.
45   Davoudi, 2000, p 127.
46   See Hall, 1994, Chapters 7 and 8.
47   Davoudi, 2000, pp 124–25; also, Macloughlin, 1969.
48   Thornley, 1991.

plan preparation stage. The plans themselves, however, have become development control manuals, stuffed with central government's regulatory norms and criteria for land use development ... the planning profession (having) retreated to the status of managing the semi-judicial process of planning legislation'.[49] This raises interesting questions, aside from any quasi-judicialisation of the process considered below.

A major theme of this book is that broad strategic levels of co-ordination are essential for progress towards greater sustainability. The limitations of local planning in the sustainability context must also be borne in mind. The process is responsive to proposals for development, and localities will inevitably be subject to a wide spectrum of social, economic and environmental pressures. Furthermore, the distributional consequences of regional discrepancies require a broader planning framework, best addressed at national (or regional) level.[50] By analogy, though not pursued here, it is in relation to regional economic disparities that the European Union made initial incursions into spatial planning issues, through structural fund and other financial aid mechanisms under the European Regional Development Fund.[51] Environmental harm, however, as we have seen, can arise in ways that are far removed from spatial and temporal frames of reference. This has long been the case for planning, and despite the genuine attractions of the local autonomy which underpins the system of local delivery of development control, to parcel off according to administrative boundaries is unrealistic. Given the transnational concerns of say climate change, the adequacy of responses at the local community level, (also even at a national level), must be identified and redressed. It may be too that local planning authority roles in strategic decision making and policy applications will in the future be further restrained. If so, there are consequences for participative processes that must be addressed.

Yet whilst the implications of policies in terms of sustainability will in certain key respects serve to confirm the need for strategies on broader spatial levels, the importance of locality should not be dismissed in the wider sustainability debate. Reliance upon Development Plans encourages positive planning policies, and the development of Regional Planning Guidance (RPG), discussed below, may in due course create a more balanced process with a reduced degree of domination by central government.[52] It is, however, important to remember that solutions, especially where there are implications for local economic activity, must be found locally. This is the experience under Local Agenda 21, where there have been considerable successes in encouraging levels of local engagement in the preparation of Local Sustainable Development Strategies.[53] Local initiatives, and increasing citizen participation, to be discussed in Chapter 10, are an essential element in progress toward sustainability. The task of persuasion towards, and acceptance of, more sustainable lifestyles must in the first instance involve communities at local levels.

---

49 Davoudi, 2000, p 126.
50 See Cullingworth and Nadin, pp 4–6, citing Barlow and Uthwatt Reports: see UK Government, 1940 and 1942a.
51 Bachtler and Twok, 1997.
52 See DETR, *Strengthening Regional Accountability*, March 2001, especially paras 2.7, 4.
53 Local Government Management Board, 1998.

2 THE SYSTEM OF STRATEGIC LAND USE PLANNING

2.1 Development presumptions and constraints

In this section, attention is now given to a consideration of the more essential features of the modern system of planning. It is not appropriate to offer a blow-by-blow account of the English planning law regime, and readers are referred to the main texts on the subject.[54] It is however proposed to offer an account of the operation of the essential features of development planning and development control. Furthermore, what follows must be considered in light of a persistent and generally prevailing presumption in favour of development. This, during the 1980s, was encapsulated in the following approach: 'There is always a presumption in favour of allowing applications for development, having regard to all material considerations, unless that development would cause demonstrable harm to interests of acknowledged importance.'[55] As will be seen below, there has recently been a shift in statutory and policy emphasis, at least in formal terms, especially in the modern presumption in favour of the Development Plan. However, this process could go further, and Grant has pointed to there being no legal obstacle, given the political will to overcome vested interests, to specifying a requirement in such plans for only developments good enough to accept.[56]

The planning system has an extremely wide remit, and as Bell and McGillivray point out, 'in balancing economic, social and environmental factors to do with development in a democratic context it ought to be a key mechanism for making development more sustainable'.[57] Development planning is in principle anticipatory, although development control as a process tends to be reactive to (largely, private sector) development proposals. The relationship between developers and planning authorities can be described as negotiative, as may be seen in the prevalence of such features as pre-application consultations between the parties and the entry by larger developers into planning agreements delivering further local benefit.[58] This negotiative feature derives from a system which is fundamentally policy-based, according a high degree of discretion to planning regulators. For all its discretionary basis, however, it is a statutory scheme, now contained in the consolidating Town and Country Planning Act 1990.[59]

The fundamental premise therefore is that there is no legal right to develop. This is formally achieved through the requirement that development cannot be undertaken without planning permission. In this way, the system seeks to balance the conflicting interests at stake. According to government guidance, the value of development control is that it 'can help to secure economy, efficiency and amenity in the development and use of land'.[60] To this end, development is defined as 'the carrying out of any building, engineering, mining or other operations in, on, over or under land; or the making of any

---

54 Eg, Moore, 2000; Duxbury, 1999; Greenwood, 1999; Hockman, Trimbos et al, 1999; Heap, 1996.
55 DoE, Circular 14/85, 1985, since withdrawn.
56 RCEP, Seminar, 2000.
57 Bell and McGillivray, 2000, p 293.
58 Bell and McGillivray, 2000, pp 293–94; and see Vogel, 1986.
59 As amended, especially under the Planning and Compensation Act (PCA) 1991.
60 DoE, PPG1, 1997a, para 3.

material change in the use of any buildings or other land'.[61] There are exceptions to the requirement that in principle all development is subject to the grant of planning permission by the local planning authority. For instance, this is accomplished by the grant of deemed consents to a range of developments within acceptable classes, known as 'permitted development',[62] and the exclusion of certain changes of use from the definition of development.[63] The range of circumstances accorded exceptional treatment is important, in the sense that ruling boundaries will reflect policy approaches of the government of the day. As will be seen in Chapter 5, wider consequences may follow, as where apparent exemption from the planning process might appear to obviate the need for an environmental assessment that might otherwise be required.

It is necessary to consider precisely what is meant by the loss of a right to develop. In reality, this amounts to a shift in onus, at which point the regulatory system becomes engaged. Yet the system, as will be seen below, provides a decision making process based largely upon the exercise of policy discretions. This creates two issues of consequence for legal analysis. The first is that land use planning is a classic example of a public process operating somewhere between the executive-administrative and the judicial-adjudicative functions. Thus, in so far as the process contains procedures to ensure neutral and fair determination of disputes over planning decisions, both development aspirations and objections will be dealt with by way of policy application, extension or restriction. The implications of this are referred to below, and once again in the context of the assertion of individual rights, in Chapter 9. The second issue likewise relates to the policy determination as to whether a development is acceptable, but is more elemental. Whether or not it can be said that a presumption in favour of development formally applies, the system is culturally predisposed towards development, unless a reason informing rejection can be justified.[64] Indeed, a true understanding of planning law demands that this be recognised as a first principle, for intuitively a planning question will be 'not so much one of law as of practice. Law is only the framework for action'.[65]

With a precautionary eye to the above, therefore, the discussion now turns to the essential features of the system of development planning and planning control.

2.2 Strategic policy making and development planning

The system is plan-led, though its strategic influences are surprisingly disparate. The production of Development Plans is the responsibility of local planning authorities. As stated above, central direction is a fundamental feature of the scheme. Whilst there remains no national development plan, central government influence is extremely powerful. Policy guidance, mainly issued by central government (now, DTLGR), provides the framework for planning decisions. In particular, Planning Policy Guidance Notes (PPGs) set out central government policy across (currently) 24 policy areas, including

---

61 TCPA 1990, s 55.
62 See Town and Country Planning (General Permitted Development) Order 1995 (SI 1995/418).
63 See Town and Country Planning (Use Classes) Order 1987 (SI 1987/764).
64 Harrison, 1992.
65 Cullingworth and Nadin, 1997, p 121.

general principles for the preparation of Development Plans.[66] Other thematic guidance include Minerals Planning Guidance Notes (MPGs), issued to assist in the preparation of local mineral plans.

The strategic foundation at the local level is based upon the preparation of Development Plans. These plans have been described as 'the mechanism by which the land use implications of various social and economic policies within a defined locality are addressed'.[67] As Miller points out, a development plan is environmental in the sense that 'it influences the allocation of all land uses within its area', contrasting an amenity-led approach, such as protecting an area of outstanding natural beauty, with one which is pollution-led, such as applying a presumption against residential development near an industrial area with especial hazards.[68] All local planning authorities are required to produce Development Plans for their areas, on a continuing basis. The system has been founded since 1968 upon a dual plan scheme: Structure Plans and Local Plans. Consequent upon the abolition of the metropolitan counties,[69] and subsequent reorganisation of selected non-metropolitan counties,[70] all land use policies for certain areas are to be contained in a Unitary Development Plan. Structure Plans, prepared by upper tier, county authorities, are statements of general policy for the county area.[71] Under policy guidance, their scope is restricted to land use issues, expressed to include housing, green belts, conservation, the economy, transport, minerals issues, waste treatment and disposal, land reclamation, tourism, leisure and recreation and energy generation.[72] The generality is expressed through a written statement, containing broad statements of policy and proposed measures to improve the physical environment, also supported by an explanatory memorandum. Local Plans, prepared by lower tier, district authorities, are more detailed. They specifically relate to land use in the sense that they identify sites as being suitable for particular purposes. Policies and land allocations are contained in a detailed written statement, supported for identification purposes by a proposals map. Local Plans must accord with the broader policies of the relevant Structure Plan.[73] The Local Plan will however prevail, unless listed as non-conforming by the Structure Plan.[74]

Development Plans are today of pivotal importance in the scheme of development control. It is specifically provided that where, 'in making any determination under the planning Acts, regard is to be had to the Development Plan, determination shall be made in accordance with the Development Plan, unless material considerations indicate otherwise'.[75] This amounts to a presumption in favour of development subject to correspondence with the plan and subject to conflicting material considerations,

---

66 DETR, PPG 12, 1999c.
67 Miller, 1998, p 52.
68 Miller, 1998, p 52.
69 Local Government Act 1986.
70 A partial scheme for unitary authorities was created by the Local Government Act 1992.
71 See TCPA 1990, ss 30–31.
72 DETR, PPG12, 1999c.
73 TCPA 1990, s 46.
74 TCPA 1990, s 48.
75 TCPA 1990, s 54A (inserted by PCA 1991).

discussed below.[76] Applications not in accordance with the Development Plan will therefore fail unless material considerations justify the grant of permission. Whilst Development Plans are therefore permissive in the sense that decisions may depart from them, they are a powerful indicator as to what a planning authority will find acceptable upon an application for permission to develop; conversely, departure from it in refusing permission exposes the planning authority to overturning on appeal (and possibly costs).

A constraining requirement for central approval for Structure Plans has been abolished, subject to central intervention powers, and there is consequently greater local autonomy in the production of Structure and Unitary Plans.[77] In line with the plan-led system, the preparation of Local Plans upon a district-wide basis has become mandatory. Assertions of reduced central control must, however, be tempered. As will be seen below, and in subsequent chapters, central policy guidance for the preparation and content of Development Plans is in numerous respects quite prescriptive. For instance, as will be seen in Chapter 6, government guidance has recognised the need for Development Plans to accommodate sustainability issues. Moreover, the strategic base was extended by requiring counties to produce minerals plans and waste plans for their areas,[78] which in the latter instance must have regard to the eventual national waste strategy.[79] Moreover, centrally adopted Regional Planning Guidance Notes (RPGs) are growing in importance. It is necessary to discuss the role of RPGs before moving on to consider the operation of development control.

2.3   Strategic policy making and regional planning

Planning at a regional level partly fills the void left by the lack of an overall national plan. Its increasing importance in strategic thinking was emphasised in the report of the Urban Task Force, set up to advise especially upon issues of urban regeneration.[80] In terms of the environment, the great potential of RPG is that it extends beyond the locality. Whilst regional foundations in England are at an early stage, especially in institutional and accountability terms, they offer the opportunity for wider co-operation already experienced between neighbouring authorities in the preparation of Unitary Development Plans.

Whilst space constrains fuller consideration here, the regional initiative also encompasses future urban and rural regeneration. Each of the eight Regional Development Agencies (RDAs) established under the Regional Development Agencies Act 1998, was required to include regeneration when producing a Regional Strategy by the end of 1999.[81] The government has pump primed RDAs with significant sums (£1.7 billion over the period 2001–04), and a major task concerns the development of policies

---

76 See DoE, PPG1, 1997a, para 40; also, *City of Edinburgh Council v Secretary of State for Scotland* [1998] JPL 224.

77 TCPA 1990, s 35 (since the PCA 1991).

78 The national waste strategy replaces waste disposal plans, under the repealed s 50 Environmental Protection Act (EPA) 1990.

79 Town and Country Planning (Development Plan) (Amendment) Regulations 1997 (SI 1997/531).

80 Rogers, 1999, recommendations 42–48.

81 Eg, RPG6, East of England (Cambridgeshire, Norfolk, Suffolk), 23 November 2000 (see www.eeda.org.uk).

for regeneration. In terms of sustainability, RDAs should provide a more strategic approach than the relatively small local planning authority units. However, save in respect of London, so far they are non-elected, representation being made up from local councillors and appointees from other sectors of the community. They have been described as 'business-led quangos designed to improve the economic performance of underperforming regions'.[82]

Although further consideration of sustainable development approaches required at a regional level are considered in Chapter 6, two illustrations of strategic impact, filtered through RPGs, are offered here. First, with regard to housing, the government has stated that the eventual RPGs will set the overall level of provision to be made for housing in each region and a distribution to constituent structure (and unitary development) planning authorities. According to policy guidance for regional planning, housing strategy should be formulated as part of a regional spatial strategy, with the objective of producing 'an integrated, strategic, approach to planning housing development which supports an urban renaissance and delivers sustainable development. RPG should define the spatial objectives for the region, consistent with the regional sustainable development framework ... and with the government's objectives for housing'.[83] Planning authorities have moreover been placed on notice that, in preparing their plans, they 'must have regard to this guidance and should avoid, wherever possible, re-opening consideration of the level of housing provision for their areas which has been considered in full within the RPG process'.[84] In the preparation of both draft RPGs and Development Plans, in order to determine housing sufficiency, account must be taken of 'government household projections, the needs of the regional economy, the capacity of urban areas to accommodate more housing, the environmental implications, and the capacity of the existing or planned infrastructure'.[85]

A second example concerns the availability of water resources. This is another factor in spatial strategy which must be taken into account in preparing proposals in RPG for the distribution of regional development: 'The availability of water resources should be taken into account in framing policies, and RPBs (Regional Planning Bodies) must bear in mind that the implications of planning policies in neighbouring regions will also need to be taken into account. RPBs should consider, with the Environment Agency and the water industry, what the implications of different policy or spatial options are for the provision of major new water resources and in turn what their environmental effects may be in order to ensure sustainable development'.[86] This reflects the notion of river basin management which likewise informs the approach taken in the EU's new Water Framework Directive'.[87] For their part, local planning authorities are required to consider the availability of water resources when determining the distribution of development, and early consultation with water companies and the Environment Agency is advised in order to 'help local authorities ensure that new developments are located in ways that

---

82 Hetherington, 2001.
83 DETR, PPG11, 2000B, para 5.1.
84 DETR, PPG3, 2000A, para 7.
85 DETR, PPG3, 2000A, para 5.
86 DETR, PPG11, 2000B, para 2.34.
87 Council Directive 2000/60, on Establishing a Framework for Community Action in the Field of Water Policy, OJ L327/1, 22 December 2000.

will minimise or eliminate the environmental impact of additional demand for water and sewage services, thereby contributing to a more sustainable development process'.[88]

A new era of regional planning, with plans to be prepared regionally rather than from the centre, has been instituted. Central government is currently producing a series of new RPGs, following preparation and submission by the Regional Planning Bodies; and separately, following the 2000 election, the London Mayor and new Greater London Authority are required to prepare a 'Spatial Development Strategy'. Although arrangements are to be contained in separate RPGs, the objective of the new regional framework is to achieve greater planning co-ordination. They are to set out a broad development framework on a regional basis, over a period of 15–20 years. The broad remit is to consider strategic questions, including the scale and distribution of new housing and transport, infrastructure, economic development, agriculture, and waste matters, as well as environmental priorities. It will aim to provide an integrated spatial framework for planning, economic development, housing and transport policies, which steers development towards more effective uses of land and buildings that are accessible by sustainable forms of transport. [89]

3 PLANNING APPLICATIONS AND DEVELOPMENT CONTROL

Given that the system is premised upon the requirement that development of land be subject to permission, strategic questions of the sort discussed above need to be translated into an operational control process. As previously stated, space constraints mean that readers requiring detailed accounts should refer to standard planning law texts. The intention here is to explain key elements within the system of planning control, in particular, material considerations, planning conditions, and planning obligations. Then opportunities for challenge are considered, both by disappointed developers and third parties. Although strictly a strategic question, the section closes with a brief review of accountability questions by reference to public involvement in plan formulation through the inquiry process. Its appearance here is because of a close procedural referability to inquiries upon appeal. Indeed, as will be seen in Chapter 9, the role of central administration in resolving issues in all such cases raises shared questions of due process.

3.1   Policy and material considerations

Planning guidance is of great significance in a system so marked by administrative discretion. Indeed, guidance has previously defined planning matters as formally limited to those relating directly to the physical development and use of land. Recent years have seen a change of emphasis: 'The planning system regulates the development and use of land in the public interest. The system as a whole, and the preparation of Development Plans in particular, is the most effective way of reconciling the demand for development and the protection of the environment. Thus it has a key role to play in contributing to the

---

88 DETR, PPG12, 1999c, para 6.20.
89 See DETR, PPG11, 2000b.

Government's strategy for sustainable development in locations which do not compromise the ability of future generations to meet their needs.'[90] In support of the limited visions of the traditional planning remit, legal interpretations of planning concerns by reference to the statutory arrangements have been traditionally narrow. This approach has been driven by judicial attitudes in interpreting the limits of administrative discretion.

The primary requirement upon planning authorities concerns the treatment of material considerations. In dealing with planning applications, a planning authority has a duty to 'have regard to the provisions of the Development Plan, so far as material to the application, and to any other material considerations'.[91] Unsurprisingly, there is ample authority for requiring the planning authority to take relevant central guidance into account.[92] It is these factors that essentially determine the scope of the discretion available to the authority. Whilst there is no statutory definition of material considerations, a broad test has emerged to the following effect: 'whether ... it serves a planning purpose ... which relates to the character and use of the land.'[93] On the question of content, guidance states that there must be 'genuine planning considerations, ie, they must be related to the purpose of planning legislation, which is to regulate the development and use of land in the public interest'.[94] It has, however, been held that these might extend to amenity, social and economic factors, and 'any consideration which relates to the use of land and development of land is capable of being a planning consideration'.[95] The breadth of approach in individual cases will be a significant pointer to the relevance of issues such as environmental ones. Thus, for instance, disturbance to other occupiers of land is a relevant consideration, regardless of controls under other legislation.[96]

It has been accepted that material considerations may include financial considerations. Thus where a proposed planning project is acceptable, but a related or enabling element of the scheme, in order to generate funds, involves further development for which permission would not otherwise have been granted, the whole may be acceptable. The test to be applied by the courts appears to be that the decision will not be invalid solely on the basis that account has been taken of the financial realities of the overall situation, provided it is made ultimately on planning grounds, rather than for an ulterior motive, and that it is not irrational.[97] The balancing process, therefore, whereby an unacceptable proposal can nevertheless be approved in this way, may in some circumstances appear strained. Such a flexible approach leaves much scope for argument: deals after all are held together by financial realities and this will be especially transparent in such cases of enabling but otherwise unacceptable development. There may be circumstances where such enabling projects will generate funds for environmental ends.

---

90 See DoE, PPG1, 1997a, para 39.
91 TCPA 1990, s 70(2).
92 *JA Pye (Oxford) Estates Ltd v West Oxfordshire DC* [1982] JPL 577.
93 *Westminster CC v Great Portland Estates plc* [1985] AC 661, 670 (*per* Lord Scarman).
94 DoE, PPG1, 1997a, para 50.
95 See *Stringer v Minister of Housing and Local Government* [1971] 1 All ER 65, 77.
96 *Ladbroke (Rentals) Ltd v Secretary of State for the Environment* [1981] JPL 427.
97 *R v Westminster City Council ex p Monahan* [1988] JPL 107; *Wansdyke District Council v Secretary of State for the Environment* [1992] JPL 1168.

Thus, for instance, clean up of contaminated land on a primary development site, either voluntarily or in pursuance of statutory obligations, may be paid for in this way.[98] This is part of the same balancing process referred to above. However, it suggests that inequities between owners might arise, for an owner subject to the statutory enforcement process, where it is determined that land contamination is such that it is not suitable for current use, would be unable to generate funds in this way.

More generally, it has been accepted that the existence and adequacy of pollution controls are material considerations.[99] Miller concludes that where an environmental issue can be shown 'to relate fairly and reasonably to the character and use of the land, then the courts would be unlikely to declare it an abuse of discretionary power'.[100] The views of regulatory bodies with responsibilities under other regimes, as required by statutory instrument as statutory consultees,[101] are implicitly material considerations.[102] The Environment Agency must be consulted for those developments which involve any of a wide range of issues.[103] These include mining operations; operations to the bed or banks of a river or stream; storage or refining of oil or its derivatives; treatment or disposal of sewage, trade waste, slurry or sludge; cemetery use refuse or waste deposit; and developments affecting land within 250 metres of land used for deposit of refuse or waste in the previous 30 years. There is also non-statutory consultation, as advised by circular, and for instance consultation with the Agency is advised for developments within 500 metres of an Integrated Pollution Control process, and with the local authority for developments within 250 metres of a process subject to local authority air pollution control.[104]

Environmental regulation is not *per se* concerned with land use issues, but only with the extent to which activities on a site are likely to meet its requirements and to continue to do so. Many of the problematic issues confronting environmental protection controls are relevant to sustainable planning. Environmental regulation, especially in the sphere of conservation, will directly affect land uses. Moreover performance by those required to be registered under environmental regulation, such as waste management licensing, will impact upon available land uses elsewhere. There will inevitably be overlap, and conflicts may arise between those operating the regimes, as considered further in Chapter 7.

3.2   Planning conditions

The rationale for planning conditions is that development is a process which extends beyond completion and into methods of implementation. The Act allows the imposition of conditions by the planning authority 'as it thinks fit'.[105] The courts have, however, set restrictive interpretative tests for their validity. A three-part judicial test for this is based

---

98   See Moore, 2000, p 227.
99   See *Gateshead MBC v Secretary of State for the Environment* [1995] Env LR 37.
100 Miller, 1998, p 52.
101 Town and Country Planning (General Development Procedure) Order 1995 (SI 1995/419), Art 10.
102 See Miller, 1998, pp 53–54.
103 Though time constraints on the planning process are extremely tight.
104 DoE Circular 9/95, Appendix B.
105 TCPA 1990, s 70(1).

upon the following: reasonableness, relation to the permitted development, and planning purpose.[106] Applying *Wednesbury* principles, conditions must not be so unreasonable that no reasonable authority could have imposed them.[107] Moreover, planning authorities cannot 'use their power for an ulterior object, however desirable that object may seem to them to be in the public interest. If they mistake or misuse their powers, however *bona fide*, the court can interfere by declaration and injunction'.[108] Whilst planning conditions must fairly and reasonably relate to the development, negatively constructed 'pre-conditions' (to be met before a permission can be implemented), have been held to be valid.[109] Under these so-called 'Grampian conditions', for instance, certain conditions operating off-site have been found to be acceptable where they concern infrastructure work related to the site. There remains some doubt, however, as to whether there must be reasonable prospects of their being met.[110]

Ministerial guidelines have sought to extend the judicial test into six requirements. This extended test is as follows: necessity; relevance to planning; relevance to the development; enforceability; precision; and reasonableness in all other respects.[111] The guidelines lay emphasis upon grant of permission, so that conditions should only be imposed in order to render an otherwise objectionable application for permission acceptable. The planning authority will be expected to provide a particular and precise justification for a decision that is not in accord with this requirement.

Yet the requirement that a condition should meet a planning purpose looks on its face to be especially problematic for an authority seeking to impose conditions.[112] There appear therefore to be unnecessary tensions in the system owing to a lack of certainty. Few challenges appear to have arisen under this head.[113] The courts have struck down conditions on grounds of their being of a social nature, as in prioritising protected housing occupation for those assessed as needy by the authority.[114] Although such interpretation may recur, it sits ill in light of modern conditions affecting housing, as mentioned below, with even central guidance now emphasising a need for affordable housing provision. Moreover, as seen in the previous section, what constitutes a planning purpose has become an area of considerable movement.

Overall, an extended consensus view of the planners' remit appears to have emerged at greater speed than the courts might otherwise have accepted. Thus it appears clear that

---

106 See *Newbury DC v Secretary of State for the Environment* [1981] AC 578, 599–600 (*per* Viscount Dilhorne).

107 *Associated Provincial Picture Houses Ltd v Wednesbury Corporation* [1948] 1 KB 223; eg, *Hall & Co Ltd v Shoreham-by-Sea UDC* [1964] 1 WLR 240.

108 *Pyx Granite Co Ltd v Minister for Housing and Local Government* [1958] QB 554, 572 (*per* Lord Denning MR).

109 *Grampian Regional Council v Aberdeen District Council* (1984) 47 P & CR 633.

110 DoE, 1995a, para 40; cf *Millington v Secretary of State for Environment, Transport and the Regions and Shrewsbury and Atcham BC* [1999] JPL 644, *Merritt v Secretary of State for Environment, Transport and the Regions and Mendip DC* [2000] JPL 371.

111 DoE, 1995a.

112 *R v Bristol CC ex p Anderson* [2000] PLC 104.

113 See Bell and McGillivray, 2000, p 327.

114 *R v Hillingdon LBC ex p Royco Homes Ltd* [1974] 2 All ER 643; also, *Chertsey UDC v Maixnam's Properties Ltd* [1965] AC 735.

acceptable conditions include the provision of environmental amenities,[115] and compensation for environmental damage.[116] There are also increasingly explicit policy requirements that planning authorities consider issues of sustainability in a widening range of circumstances. This perhaps illustrates a gradualist judicial approach in new regulatory circumstances discussed in the previous chapter. More likely however, it reflects the prevalence of a negotiative process over what might in other circumstances be litigious leanings on the part of commercial entities. A powerful illustration of this lies in the growth of planning obligations, to which attention now turns.

3.3   Planning obligations

In order to remove barriers to development, planning authorities may enter into planning agreements, or accept unilateral developer undertakings.[117] The putative basis for this lies in recognition that development may reflect additional costs to the locality. The system has come to be known as 'planning gain': an instance of positive planning, whereby some wider community benefit can be secured from the developer as a condition of being able to proceed. The benefits to be derived can be considerable. Planning obligations enable beneficial contributions to infrastructure or community beyond the close concerns of the development. They also illustrate a further form of private sector sponsorship increasingly prevalent in a political society grown cynically weary of the need to persuade citizens of the benefits that can accrue from taxation.

The legal status remains open to doubt, especially towards the outer boundaries of the community contributions that might be required. Whilst when compared with planning conditions it is accepted that the legality of planning obligations is more reliable, doubts persist as to precisely where planning agreements differ from conditions. The legal requirements affecting agreements must necessarily be less restrictive, in order for there to be any purpose in developers accepting them.[118] Respecting this distinctiveness, the House of Lords has ruled that the tests for validity are to be compared with those for planning conditions in as much as the planning obligation must have a planning purpose and must not be perverse or unreasonable. It seems therefore that its validity does not require satisfying the further test of fair and reasonable relation to the development referred to above.[119] This clarification has brought considerable relief to planning authorities, and even to developers (for offers of planning gains may assist in the resolution of residual concerns, or even competing proposals). Yet subsequent policy guidance indicated that a closer relationship is required as between community benefit and the development for which permission is sought.[120] Applicable tests for this purpose are expressed to include those of necessity; relevance to planning; direct relationship to the proposed development; fair and reasonable relationship to the development in scale and kind to the proposed; and reasonableness in other respects. It therefore appears to

115 *R v Plymouth CC* [1993] JPL 1099.
116 *Tesco Stores Ltd v Secretary of State for the Environment* [1995] 2 All ER 636.
117 TCPA 1990, s 106, as revised under PCA 1991.
118 See, eg, *Good v Epping Forest DC* [1994] JPL 372.
119 *Tesco Stores Ltd v Secretary of State for the Environment* [1995] 2 All ER 636.
120 DoE, 1997b.

remain necessary that there is some connection with the development, although it is unclear in what circumstances this is unlikely to be met. It has in consequence been suggested that planning obligations 'can be used to offset the loss or impact of any resource present on a site prior to development, but they cannot be used to secure a list or range of desirable benefits from developers, even if the local planning authority consider such benefits to be related in some way to the proposed development'.[121]

The notion of wider benefits appears, however, to be commonly accepted.[122] Indeed, references in the 2000 rural and urban white papers suggest that the government appears to have assumed that unrelated forms of gain, such as social housing or play areas, are integral to the process. Clarification is awaited as to suitable types of improvements that might be requested in terms of environmental consequences. A more direct approach to off-site effects is likely to emerge. This may come through either offsetting (such as establishing nature reserves as 'cover' for a greenfield development elsewhere) or payment of impact fees (on a schedule of charges seeking to reflect external effects such as habitat loss or demands on other services).[123] The Urban Task Force suggested that standardised impact fees might be introduced in place of negotiation in the case of smaller urban schemes.[124]

The resulting arrangements have the advantage of mutual benefit and acceptance, seldom seen by comparison where permissions are not forthcoming, especially on environmental grounds. Yet for all that, the legal foundations for the acceptability of planning gain remain conventionally opaque. Thus, in the light of the heavy policy basis of the scheme, Bell and McGillivray conclude that two systems appear to apply: first, where a dispute arises as to an authority's demand, in which case central policy may protect the developer; and, secondly, where agreement has been reached, in which event judicial intervention appears unlikely.[125] Yet numerous concerns arise, relating to the ethics of bargaining and the visibility of the system.[126]

First, there are dangers of unjustifiable pressure being brought to bear upon developers (perhaps also on authorities although only in marginal cases as they should have been satisfied as to the proposal on planning grounds). Indeed, the circumstances may amount to unequal treatment as between competing development applications, and lead to at least the suspicion of abuse.[127] Secondly, as a matter of process, there is the question of low public visibility of a transaction in which 'bargaining is a closed, private activity which sits uneasily astride the current emphasis on open government and public participation'.[128] Thirdly, perhaps the most potent criticism is that there is a possibility that planning authorities might themselves be subjected to improper political pressure

---

121 Land Use Consultants, 1999, para 4.70.
122 See Rowan-Robinson and Durman, 1992.
123 DETR/MAFF, 2000, para 9.2.4; DETR, 2000c, p 48.
124 Rogers, 1999, recommendation 51; and see Grant, 2000b, discussing developer contributions, including impact fees, at pp 176–79.
125 Bell and McGillivray, 2000, p 333.
126 See the discussion in Cullingworth and Nadin, 1997, pp 143–46.
127 Even where unjustified, suspicions are arguably encouraged by discretionary elements regarding material considerations.
128 Cullingworth and Nadin, 1997, p 146.

due to the promised gain as part of the package. After all, there are always risks inherent in an applicant's right of appeal, and an offer of a unilateral undertaking would be a material consideration in any appeal. The first two concerns are likely to be resolved in part by the inclusion of details of agreed obligations onto planning registers.

The last element is more intractable in that, for all its concrete advantages, a system of planning gain allows private developer interests to dictate the process. Given the departure, already charted, of planning law from its 1947 foundations, in the loss of public ownership of increases in development value consequent upon grant of permission, there is much hidden private planning 'gain' underlying the process. Accordingly, just as development values are privately owned, as discussed earlier in this chapter, planning gain offers 'a means of capturing some of this value for the public benefit'.[129] Indeed, the relationship between financial stringency in the public sector and problems in the way of services and infrastructure provision may be directly linked to the readiness of developers to contribute under these arrangements. After all, 'their ability to do so is closely related to anticipated resulting increases in land values'.[130]

3.4   Participation in the planning process

The plan-led system described above allows for a range of opportunities for wider involvement in policy making. In particular, the public inquiry is available in connection with the production of draft Local Plans. There is also resort to inquiries at the planning control stage in respect of controversial proposals. The Secretary of State has power to call in certain planning applications. Likewise, applicants have a right of statutory appeal to the Secretary of State in the event of refusals or the imposition of conditions.[131] The form of an appeal will in most cases be determined by the Planning Inspectorate, in consultation with the parties, and more than four-fifths of appeals are heard by written representations.[132] Of those that proceed to inquiry, in most cases, so called transfer cases, the final decision will be a matter for the inspector. However, for those appeals which are of major national importance, so-called reserved cases, the inspector will report to the Secretary of State who will make the eventual decision.

Thus a counter ethos to a closed administrative and technocratic system is suggested by the introduction of such opportunities for public participation. In the context of plan preparation and approval, this challenges what might otherwise remain closed, bilateral accommodations. It also introduces a public recognition of political conflict. Statutory planning procedures were paradoxically a later accretion to the 1947 Act scheme.[133] The pre-planning stages, in which draft plans are prepared, are extremely lengthy processes that can take over five years. The public has the right to make initial representations. More direct contributions may be made as Local Plans go to inquiry and Structure Plans

129 Cullingworth and Nadin, 1997.

130 Grant, 1982, p 34.

131 TCPA 1990, s 78.

132 Town and Country Planning (Inquiries Procedure) (England) Rules 2000 (SI 2000/1624); Town and Country Planning (Determination by Inspectors) (Inquiries Procedure) (England) Rules 2000 (SI 2000/1625); Town and Country Planning (Appeals) (Written Representations Procedure) (England) 2000 (SI 2000/1628).

133 See Skeffington Report, 1969, and TCPA 1968.

to examination in public.[134] The latter is a limited inquiry process, for attendance is by invitation, and its terms are effectively determined by the local planning authority. Though central approval is no longer required for Structure Plans, the Secretary of State has authority to direct modifications or even to call in.[135] A similar (and unlikely) right of call-in is available in the case of Local Plans.[136] There is a right to appear at the inquiry in the case of the less strategic, more detailed Local Plan process,[137] and likewise in the case of Unitary Development Plans.[138] Objections may therefore be placed before the inspector, and there is a further right to present a case.[139]

There is no doubt that considerable opportunities are afforded within the system to third parties. They may lodge an objection to draft Development Plans. They also have a general right to be heard at public inquiries. Then, in exercise of its control functions, where a local planning authority proposes to depart from the plan, it is subject to more stringent publication requirements and must notify the Secretary of State, with a view to a possible call-in. However, unlike for applicants in the event of refusal, third parties opposing grants of planning permission have no rights of appeal.[140] Subsequent to the decision of the Secretary of State, there are limited rights of access to the court for the benefit of 'persons aggrieved'. These include such persons as the applicant, local planning authority and those who appeared at an inquiry and made representations.[141] The specified grounds are that either the decision is beyond the powers contained in the legislation or a failure to comply with procedures has created substantial prejudice.[142] In the case of Development Plans, grounds are similar, as for instance in the event of failure by the local planning authority properly to consider an inspector's report.[143] The basis of such appeals against planning decisions by the Secretary of State are therefore to some extent referable to those for judicial review.[144] The statutory six week time limit for commencement of proceedings is, however, a strict one.[145] Successful appeal leads to a quashing of the original decision, and the matter is remitted once again to the authority or minister.

Although the planning regime compares favourably with other schemes of public regulation, there are substantial questions that must therefore be raised as to the value of the current participatory arrangements.[146] Two major factors can be identified. The first relates to the relegation of planning into a regulatory function as explored above; and the

---

134 TCPA 1990, ss 31–35C.
135 TCPA 1990, ss 35, 35A; *West Sussex CC v Secretary of State for Environment Transport and the Regions* [1999] PLCR 365.
136 TCPA 1990, ss 44, 45.
137 TCPA 1990, ss 36–52.
138 Local Government Act 1985, ss 12–28.
139 Town and Country (Development Plan) (England) Rules 1999 (SI 1999/3280).
140 See Brown, 2001; Purdue, 2001.
141 *Turner v Secretary of State for the Environment* (1973) 28 P & CR 123; *Westminster CC v Great Portland Estates plc* [1985] AC 661.
142 TCPA 1990, s 288.
143 TCPA 1990, s 287.
144 *Warren v Uttlesford DC* [1997] JPL 1130.
145 *Smith v East Elloe RDC* [1956] AC 736.
146 See, eg, Stanley, 2000; also, as to environmental assessment, see Parkin, 1993.

second concerns the problems of the centre in producing effective arrangements for strategic decision making, and doing so in an accountable way. As has been said of most institutions conceived by humankind, including environmental regulators, the planning process can be accused of being captured in the sense of servicing entrenched interests.[147] And the extent of substantive limits upon third party involvement, irrespective of form, will determine the value of the participatory process. Moreover, opportunities afforded for challenge and conflict at inquiries produce such levels of delay and expense as seem to run counter to sensible, 'planned' policy making. Participation is limited by what is a non-participatory style of executive government at the centre. This issue is linked with the paradox of domination of central government priorities, initiatives and funding restraints, which combine to influence both the framing of legislation as well as the development of planning policy. And yet in planning matters a high level of indecisiveness exists at the centre, which is arguably reflected in the nature of inquiry processes.

Within a plan-led system, it is scarcely surprising that local inquiries induce high levels of conflict. The form and content of the Local Plan itself is likely to engender fierce debate. Moreover, the importance of the plan for future decision making under planning control has been said by Grant to impose 'greater strain on development plans than they are capable of bearing, because the temptation is to include a level of detail that makes it impossible for the plan to provide a robust framework for taking subsequent decisions in a manner sufficiently flexible to accommodate unforeseen changes in local circumstances'.[148] In respect of inquiries following in the wake of planning applications, perhaps especially upon call-in, similar conflicts can take off.

Not surprisingly such set piece events can be extremely lengthy inquiries, and problems of dispute, delay and expense all have their roots in both politicisation of conflict and gaps in strategic thinking. An example of delay, albeit extreme, is the inquiry into a Terminal 5 for Heathrow airport. The inquiry was completed in March 1999, having lasted for almost four years, and the inspector's final report is currently awaited. Grant indicates a cost of perhaps £200 million, with £14.5 million the cost to public funds (indeed local authorities' contributions appear to have been incapacitated on grounds of cost).[149]

Reasons for lengthy inquiries can be reduced into issues of scope and content, and the ethos of contesting parties. A useful summary is contained in Grant's report upon the feasibility of an environmental court. As to the former, there has been an increased focus upon particularly environmental issues. More information is likely to be available, including formal environmental statements, and generally more sophisticated scientific methods and data. Moreover, quite apart from an ethos that seeks to accord fairness, openness and impartiality, the heavily policy-based discretionary features of the planning system encourage a high degree of caution as to whether to exclude submissions as non-material. Such judicial review as is available is at its most effective in disputes concerning exclusion of relevant matters. Those making representations, especially where organised, are likely to introduce the wider implications of proposed developments and relevant

---

147 See Gunningham, 1974, p 69 *et seq*; also, Cullingworth and Nadin, 1997, pp 280–81.
148 Grant, 2000a, para 12.8.
149 Grant, 2000a, para 12.9.

policies, and may be equipped to raise technical objections or to lead their own technical evidence. In particular, in the risk society, expert evidence is more likely to be challenged.[150]

At the heart of the argument therefore is the pervasive schizophrenia of centre political arrangements, and the unbalanced accountability that this creates. Inquiries occur often in contentious circumstances, and whilst our politicians are generally complaisant in retaining overweening constitutional powers, they are curiously uneasy about manifestations of discontent.[151] On the one hand, in face of core conflicts between national and local interests, central government is dominant, and as will be seen in Chapter 10, constitutional balancing processes (as through the courts) are limited.[152] On the other, central government needs to convince as to its capability institutionally to operate a coherent framework for decision making.

As to the question of effective policy making, there are discontinuities (which would seriously threaten emerging sustainability strategies) in central abdication of responsibility. Inquiries into roads have been particularly contentious, and their value is checked in circumstances where wider strategic discussions have not taken place at national level. Wood points out that the various impacts 'upon public expenditure, the deployment of natural resources, land use and land management can only be handled centrally by government ministers'.[153] Grant likewise expresses concern that public local inquiries can become the procedure for the making of government policy. He concludes that this can be 'quite inappropriate, because it converts a public local inquiry into a national event, and it assumes that the parties will bring all the evidence necessary to the making of national policy before the inquiry. It can, nonetheless, provide a very good mechanism for informing the government in an open and unbiased way about a range of issues which might influence policy making'.[154] A significant change may have been signalled following the inquiry into a proposed bypass for Hastings (Sussex), which brought environmental and economic conflicts into sharp focus. Despite unanimous support for a new road from the South-East Regional Assembly and county and district councils, the Secretary of State for DTLGR ruled against the proposed development on grounds that the arguments in favour were insufficient to outweigh very strong environmental interests.[155] This is an illustration perhaps of the current vogue for more strategic sustainability-related policy approaches leading to greater central responsibility. These issues and their accountability implications are considered in Chapter 10.

There may in the future be central pressure to 'institutionalise' the process through existing representative institutions and away from public participation. There are clear political concerns at issues of cost and delay, and certain procedural changes are being introduced.[156] For the present, new guidance seeks to produce more rigorous pre-inquiry

---

150 Grant, 2000a, para 12.9.

151 Witness the bizarre petrol tax revolt in late 2000; see ENDS Report 308, 'Climate and transport strategies at risk in fall-out from fuel crisis', September 2000, 19–21; also Grayling, 2001.

152 Grant, 2000a, para 12.10.12.

153 Wood, 1995, p 71.

154 Grant, 2000a, para 12.9.

155 (2001) *The Independent*, 13 July.

156 DETR, 'Streamlining the processing of major infrastructure projects and other major projects of national significance', 1999.

case management, speedier timetables, and also measures to reduce delays, duplication and unnecessary withholding of evidence.[157] Answers may be found in more effective arrangements for setting clear, limited scope and objectives for inquiries in the light of coherent predetermined national policy and appropriate risk assessments. Here, however, as will be seen in the next chapter, a formal preliminary procedure might unhelpfully predispose those chairing a later public inquiry, even if the advantages of speed can be established.

Problems of inefficiency are inevitable given the nature of the system which produces the policies and the controls which are expected to match. As stated above, the process also lays bare the political tensions, including those between local perceptions and meeting wider, national strategic needs and particularly the demands of sustainability. As has been stated in a report to the Royal Commission on Environmental Pollution, with reference to Local Plans:

> Government *has* tried to require local plans to achieve, overall, at least an approximation to national targets for land allocation for housing, minerals extraction and waste. This has resulted in immense and continuing controversy and tedious iteration of proposals, counterproposals, objections, inquiries and directions. This seems likely to get worse because almost by definition, the less contentious sites for housing, minerals extraction and waste disposal will tend to be used first, so each round of planning will need to grapple with increasingly 'difficult' sites and decisions, making the local consequences of national principles increasingly unpopular.[158]

With problems of delay and securing acceptable levels of participation and rights of challenge, the solution proffered by Grant is that of a specialist court. Whilst discussed more fully in Chapter 10, in this context the burden of the Grant Report is that just as administrative bodies preside over hearings, an Environmental Court may be involved in policy making, provided that it operates at a supervisory level. This would classically apply to inquiries into draft Development Plans or into major proposals for development, subject to the careful caveat that 'no sufficient policy has been adopted by government'.[159] It would also allow for integration with the wider judicial process, to accord increasing access to opportunities of challenge where legal disputes arise. In the specific context of inquiries, however, the report suggests that the proposed Environmental Court would provide a tighter focus upon issues to be resolved. Procedurally, it suggests judicial case management techniques, such as more proactive adjudication, and consultation conferences or seminars for objectors or experts in order to determine the extent of dispute.[160] The benefit of such a focused judicialisation (of an already quasi-judicial administrative process) should be reflected in the quality of both report back to the decision maker, and the decision itself, made within a coherent strategic (and sustainable) framework.

---

157 DETR, Circular 05/2000, *Planning Appeals: including Inquiries into Called-in Planning Applications;* also, Town and Country Planning (Hearings Procedure) (England) Rules 2000 (SI 2000/1626).

158 CAG Consultants, 1999, para 5.27.

159 Grant, 2000a, para 1.4.5.

160 Grant, 2000a, para 13.14.5.

4 PLANNING AND SPATIAL CONFLICT

Before the argument more broadly considers issues of sustainability in the planning context in Chapter 6, the next chapter looks at a newly formalised mechanism reflecting the symbiosis between planning and the environment. Chapter 5 seeks to set out the effect that the introduction of environmental impact assessment has had upon planning, and to offer some thoughts on its potential influence for the future. In order to introduce these themes, however, the closing section of the present chapter looks at endemic problems which continue to confront the planning system, and which can now be understood as at the root of most threats to sustainable planning. The many diverse consequences illustrate the holistic contexts which planners, but also honest and responsible policy makers, must address.

4.1   Scarcity and the land resource

Planning is ultimately concerned with the living conditions of the community.[161] It is unsurprising therefore that the roots of planning control originated in the problems of the urban environment, with 80% of the UK's population living in urban areas of over 10,000 population, covering 7% of the land mass.[162] These areas account for 90% of economic activity and most pollution.[163] It was the plight of the cities that informed much of the 19th and earlier 20th century legislation, originally in the field of health, and latterly, more symptomatically, in housing, and then planning. The urban white paper indicates a modern physical pattern of settlement as follows: urban core, 9%; suburban/urban, 23%; suburban, 43%; suburban/rural, 20%; and rural, 5%.[164] These patterns are described by government as a 'complex interaction between natural growth, the impact of changing transport, people's preferences and planning'.[165] What amounts to a population exodus (from the urban, and now also suburban areas) has placed significant pressures on the land resource, an issue picked up in detail in the consideration of housing in Chapter 6. There are numerous social consequences, including polarisation in urban areas and pressures on rural communities. However, of specific relevance are two exacerbating factors: first, continued pressures on the land resource, with underused urban land and extensions of development into greenfield sites; and, secondly, increased wastage of resources and higher levels of pollution, as for instance car dependence increases and journeys become longer. Both these issues are discussed more fully below.[166]

Instances of tension between urban and rural interests, whilst endemic, appear to have become especially marked at the turn of the new century, including accusations of a government more wholeheartedly committed to urban interests. The farming crisis is essentially an economic one, with its roots in global markets and reduced values of European subsidies (prospectively to decrease further under Agenda 2000). Moreover, in

---

161 See Pepper, 1984, pp 110–13.
162 DETR, 2000c, para 1.7.
163 RCEP, Seminar, 2000.
164 DETR, 2000c, para 1.15.
165 DETR, 2000c, para 1.16.
166 DETR, 2000c, paras 2.10, 2.28-2.30.

the case of the UK, food safety has become a major issue, in light of the BSE crisis following 1997. Voices are now heard questioning a heavily subsidised, agri-industrial system, in light of the consequences of intensive production and the allied use of chemicals and pharmaceuticals, for nutrition, health, and animal suffering, as well as a range of threats to ecosystems, through organic and resource depletion and degradation. The 2001 outbreak of Foot and Mouth Disease is arguably symptomatic, a crisis exacerbated by intensive production methods and insufficiently charted (and profit-related) movements of livestock. The political response has been said to have showered resources into 'a virus which harms little but the profits of agri-business'.[167] This appears largely to have dictated the (albeit effective) policy of large-scale culling of stock on contiguous premises (and resort to vast pyres and burial pits for speedy destruction), rather than recourse to innoculation strategies. The crisis has in turn exacerbated a much wider rural crisis, as access to the countryside was for some time restricted, generating severe problems for businesses reliant on tourism.

Tensions between rural interests and urban 'consumers' are not however new, and have traditionally been most problematic in respect of land use, with urban sprawl being perceived as an especial threat.[168] Such concerns were identified in 1942 by the Scott Committee, whose seminal report proposed that planning permission should only be available in rural areas to prospective developers who were able to demonstrate 'need'.[169] The eventual planning scheme manifestly did not do this; contrasting approaches were introduced for rural and non-rural development, respectively. In particular, the designation of areas of land to act as buffer zones was introduced in the policy of green belts, discussed below. A rural/urban antagonism built into the planning system, largely to do with protection against urban encroachment, has however ceased to be meaningful according to Newby, given the rate of social, landscape and agricultural change affecting the countryside.[170] The 2000 rural white paper recognises that a 'key challenge is to get right the relationship between our towns and cities and the countryside'.[171] Two main aims are set out, namely to stem migration from urban areas, through regeneration initiatives, improved services and design, and more efficient land use, and to ensure that rural development is of 'good quality and well planned'.[172] This rather vague idea is supported by reference to minimised land take, utilisation of previously developed land and existing buildings, reduced transport need, and respect for local character and environment. Especially problematic is the housing context, in the face of a massive further accretion in projected numbers of separate households.[173] A main response to this problem can be seen in pressure to decontaminate land and encourage the development of brownfield sites. There is now a national target that 60% of additional housing should be provided on previously developed land and through conversions of existing buildings by 2008.[174]

---

167 Harvey, 2001.
168 UK Government 1942b; see also Newby, 1979, p 237.
169 Newby, 1979, p 231.
170 Newby, 1979, pp 239–40.
171 DETR/MAFF, 2000, para 9.2.1.
172 DETR/MAFF, 2000, para 9.2.2.
173 See, eg, DoE, 1996a.
174 See DETR, 2000c, para 4.17.

4.2   The concept of the green belt

As seen in the opening section of this chapter, the Second World War proved a fertile time politically for commencing deeper engagement with social problems. The 1940 Barlow Report has been described as providing 'the philosophical basis of the postwar planning system: a humane desire to improve the living conditions of the city, combined with a strict preservationist approach to the countryside'.[175] Thus it sought to address the perennial tasks of urban regeneration (especially in the north of England) and preventing urban encroachment into rural areas. This has been exacerbated by the idea that rural areas are havens for traditional ways of living which should be protected accordingly, as will be seen in the next section.

The policy of green belts dates from the 1950s, and marked a specific response to the long-standing land use problem of urban sprawl.[176] The essential rationale for the notion lies in the objective of checking urban encroachment by development into open countryside.[177] Green belts are designations of areas of land to act as buffer zones: central policy guidance states that the 'fundamental aim of green belt policy is to prevent urban sprawl by keeping land permanently open ... They can assist in moving towards more sustainable patterns of urban development'.[178] They are established through Development Plans, Structure Plans providing the strategic context for more detailed definition under Local Plans. In 1995, green belts approved under Structure Plans covered around 1,540,000 hectares, that is, around 12% of England,[179] and this area continues to be gradually extended.[180]

Development planning for green belts involves significant constraints at the level of development control. Restrictive countryside development policies are augmented by 'a general presumption against inappropriate development' within the green belt; and 'development should not be approved, except in very special circumstances'.[181] An onus is placed upon the applicant to establish why permission should be granted. Such circumstances required to justify inappropriate development, subject to limited exceptions for certain new buildings or alterations or extensions to existing buildings, 'will not exist unless the harm by reason of inappropriateness, and any other harm, is clearly outweighed by other considerations'.[182] A restrictive approach to fulfilment of this test is pursued by inspectors and the Secretary of State, as well as by planning authorities.[183]

As a policy based upon designation, green belt policy is therefore inevitably closely related to other planning policies. An illustration of the prevailing presumption derives from the pressure on land use caused by the insatiable demand for housing provision.

---

175 Macnaghten and Urry, 1998, p 39; UK Government, 1940.
176 See DoE, PPG2, 1995b, para 1.1.
177 See *Northavon DC v Secretary of State for the Environment* [1993] JPL 761.
178 DoE, PPG2, 1995b, para 1.4.
179 See DoE, PPG2, 1995b, para 1.3.
180 See DETR/MAFF, 2000, para 9.2.4.
181 DoE, PPG2, 1995b, para 3.1.
182 DoE, PPG2, 1995b, paras 3.2–3.4.
183 See Elson and Ford, 1994.

Green belt policy generally prevails. In housing guidance, it is stated that the exceptional rural policy of allowing so-called exception housing, discussed in Chapter 6, 'does not alter the general presumption against inappropriate development in the green belt'.[184] The justification given for this approach is that exception housing is not appropriate to these areas, being 'by their nature close to the main conurbations where conditions are not typical of the generality of rural areas. However, exceptionally, very limited development of affordable housing within or adjoining existing villages or other small settlements may be acceptable and consistent with the function of the green belt'.[185] Guidance suggests that this might be in some of the more extensive areas of green belt away from the urban fringe, especially where there are many small settlements. Emphasis is placed on local planning authorities' judgment as to whether very limited development within existing settlements will be acceptable and consistent with the function of the green belt. Thus low-cost housing development, which would not normally be considered for development under such policies, may be permitted, having regard to all material considerations, including green belt objectives and evidence of local need.[186]

Two persistent criticisms are made of green belts. First, it is asserted that designation has created intensive pressure upon urban areas. This has resulted in deterioration and artificial windfalls through urban land price inflation.[187] Secondly, designation is ineffective in containing development pressures, but encourages displaced urban sprawl. It has been suggested that the consequent displacement places countryside elsewhere under more intense development pressures.[188] This is an illustration of a problematic phenomenon in this context, in which overall changes are inevitably the sum of individual changes. The comparison of planning with the squeezing of a balloon has been coined for this process: 'effective at changing the shape at the point squeezed, but only by causing bulges elsewhere, and with little effect on the overall size of the balloon.'[189] The effect is exacerbated by the local nature of planning control. In environmental terms, for example:

> ... an overall reduction in car traffic or greenhouse emissions requires that any local increases in these in some places are more than offset by reductions in other places. This is significant because planning regimes often currently only displace pressures. Development stopped in one form or place happens in a different form or place. For example, new development "leapfrogs" over green belts. Employers and housebuilders denied greenfield sites with unlimited parking by one planning authority move to a more accommodating one. More thorough designation and protection of the most special environments has diverted development pressure to the rest.[190]

Yet a green belt principle appears fairly readily to comply with ideas commonly associated with the general notion of sustainability. Thus policy guidance states: 'The essential characteristic of green belts is their permanence. Their protection must be

184 DETR, PPG3, 2000a, Annex B, para 5.
185 DETR, PPG3, 2000a, Annex B, para 5.
186 DETR, PPG3, 2000B, Annex 3.
187 Elson, Walker and Macdonald, 1993.
188 Elson, Steenberg and Mendham, 1996.
189 Land Use Consultants, 1999, para 5.21.
190 Land Use Consultants, 1999, para 5.20.

maintained as far as can be seen ahead.'[191] As a matter of designation, guidance requires that following approval of its general extent, a green belt 'should be altered only in exceptional circumstances'.[192] The guidance sets out an explicit sustainability objective as follows: 'When drawing green belt boundaries in Development Plans, local planning authorities should take account of the need to promote sustainable patterns of development. They should consider the consequences for sustainable development (for example in terms of the effects on car travel) of channelling development towards urban areas inside the inner green belt boundary, towards towns and villages inset within the green belt, or towards locations beyond the outer green belt boundary.'[193] Moreover, where any large-scale development occurs within the green belt, including mineral extraction, waste tipping, roads and other infrastructure developments or improvements, then that development must as far as possible contribute to the achievement of the objectives for the use of land in green belts.[194]

However, there may be a conflict with sustainable development objectives. Reverting to the above metaphor, the Land Use Consultants Report points out that sustainability requires:

... the _reversal of many trends_ – that is, making the balloon *smaller overall* and not just a different shape. We still want to protect the most outstanding sites – but without development then eroding the qualities of the less 'special' areas; we want less traffic and energy use overall, not just a smaller increase or in different places; we want our countryside protected, but without our towns crammed, or people prevented from living in the households of their choice. In all these areas, planning is caught between rising expectations (both consumerist and policy) and diminishing room to manoeuvre. Literally as well as metaphorically: many of the locations to which development pressures could previously be deflected are now occupied.[195]

This is a graphic illustration of the essentially limited nature of the land resource. Its diversion to new development activities requires a high degree of strategic planning not provided by the currently segmented scheme. An example in resource terms is the encouragement of increased use of brownfield sites. This should in principle reduce development pressure on rural areas, but it remains necessary to arm planners with policy guidance that explicitly accords priority to brownfield sites. This could be achieved perhaps by requiring environmental impact assessments of developers (including consideration of alternative sites) who propose otherwise. Some indication of recognition of this seems to have been made in the 2000 rural white paper.[196]

4.3   Problems of urban and rural planning

Discussion of brownfields leads inevitably to consideration of urban planning policies. The Urban Task Force, set up by government under the chairmanship of Lord Rogers,

191 DoE, PPG2, 1995b, para 2.1.
192 DoE, PPG2, 1995b, para 2.6.
193 DoE, PPG 2, 1995b, para 2.10.
194 DoE, PPG2, 1995b, para 3.13; objectives are listed in para 1.6.
195 Land Use Consultants, 1999, para 5.21.
196 DETR/MAFF, 2000, para 9.2.4.

was concerned to consider the causes of urban decline in England and to recommend practical solutions.[197] The Task Force recommendations, including as to brownfield development,[198] are specifically addressed in the 2000 urban white paper, and referred to further in Chapter 6.[199] The white paper has castigated the unsustainable implications of past planning policies, such as the encouragement of major new shopping developments outside urban areas. These have led to reduced competitiveness and viability of town and city centres. The government continually emphasises communities (as in the objective of mixed development patterns), and such out-of-town development has arguably exacerbated community fragmentation, as well as a separation of places where people shop, work and spend their leisure time, from where they live. They have also encouraged poor-quality design and layouts and unnecessary travel.[200]

There have been significant pockets of failure in urban policy, not least of which is the sheer scale of social deprivation.[201] Accordingly much urban and regional policy purports to achieve regeneration, especially of the inner cities. This involves a progression of measures, ranging from public investment, through market-based approaches, to the current vogue for public-private partnerships.[202] It has been said that 'mainstream land use planning and urban policy ... essentially evolved during the 1990s towards a partnership approach without any significant new initiatives in the planning field, in contrast with a growth in pollution control legislative activity'.[203] This was extended more widely under the general Private Sector Finance Initiative under the Finance Act 1992,[204] with the private sector accorded access to benefit from public funds for key infrastructure projects, with a return through market prices, rents, and public sector service payments. Also, regeneration mechanisms have been directed towards bids by partnerships between public sector and outside bodies for inner city funds, as under the Single Regeneration Budget.[205] External trade pressures however cannot be discounted, as seen in Chapter 2, and the recent Partnership Investment Programme was placed on hold following a 1999 European Commission decision that it breached treaty rules on State aids.[206]

A political consensus seems however to have coalesced around a public-private approach, though a somewhat different agenda was suggested by the creation in 1997 of the Social Exclusion Unit. Moreover, funds are now channelled through the eight Regional Development Agencies (RDAs) referred to above, which bodies have assumed the role of the Rural Development Commission,[207] together with the London Development Agency and English Partnerships. As well as having economic,

---

197 Rogers, 1999.
198 Rogers, 1999, recommendations 61–64.
199 DETR, 2000c, paras 4.6–4.10.
200 DETR, 2000c, para 4.18.
201 See, eg, Walker, 2000.
202 For fuller treatment, see Rydin, 1998, Chapter 13.
203 See Rydin, 1998, p 78.
204 Eg, the new Norfolk and Norwich Hospital; also some private sector roadbuilding, such as the Birmingham Northern Relief Road.
205 DETR, 2000c, paras 5.25–5.27.
206 DETR, 2000c, p 65.
207 DETR, 1997a.

employment and business efficiency objectives, the RDAs are required to 'contribute to the achievement of sustainable development in the UK'.[208] Indeed, the new governmental strategy for seeking sustainable economic development also proposes to utilise Local Strategic Partnerships to bring together local authorities, RDAs, other service providers, business and community groups, and the voluntary sector. The purpose of the exercise will be to develop Community Strategies and agree priorities for action and monitoring of local performance against agreed local indicators, taking into account national and regional targets.[209] In bringing together economic, social and environmental issues, they will be asked to integrate the results of existing initiatives, including progress made in developing local sustainable development strategies by Local Agenda 21 Groups.[210]

The twin issues of land use and its availability for sustainable development are crucial to addressing the problems outlined above. Related challenges have been identified by government as follows: 'The first is about achieving sustainable economic and social renewal in declining areas to reclaim land, restore economic activity and improve services. The second is about planning for sustainable economic growth in areas which are expanding but which may have problems such as land shortages.'[211] It is notable that both in expanding (and therefore economically successful) and declining areas, pressures are placed upon land.

In contrast to urban approaches, the ruling ethos ever since the modern planning system emerged in 1947 has respected the establishment's perceptions of essentially homogeneous rural interests within an Arcadian countryside which acts as some sort of repository for our communal soul. There are still indications that this pervades, as in the apparent solidarity represented by the Countryside Alliance,[212] and the signs of communal rural frustrations during the 2001 Foot and Mouth crisis (as well as the high level of emotive media coverage). However, in reality countryside interests are highly disparate.[213] This can be seen in the debate about stewardship, and the protection of bio-diversity. Whilst not a main theme of this book, much conservation law in the UK is based upon voluntary arrangements, and conservation bodies, severely constrained as to funding, accordingly struggle to be effective, as in the protection of areas such as sites of special scientific interest.[214]

Conversely, less clearly the subject of positive planning, the traditional approach to the countryside has been concentrated upon control of the extent of the urban built environment and a relatively non-regulated policy towards agricultural development.[215] Thus, following on from Barlow, referred to above, the Scott Committee was emphatic in its concentration upon the physical control of urban growth. Newby has concluded that this 'sanctified the prior claim of agriculture over both land use and labour in rural

---

208 See DETR, 2000c, paras 5.22–5.27.
209 DETR, 2000c, paras 3.24–3.27.
210 DETR, 2000c, paras 3.28, 5.28–5.31.
211 DETR, 2000c, p 65; committed spending up to 2003–04 is £1.7 billion.
212 Eg, a mass rally in central London, March 1998.
213 See Murdoch and Marsden, 1994.
214 See Wildlife and Countryside Act 1981.
215 See Curry and Owens, 1996.

areas'.[216] The result has been a planning policy for rural England which reflects a discreditable, Faustian compact between powerful landed interests (increasingly major corporations) and postwar reformer urbanites. The latter have been described as possessing 'a hopelessly sentimental vision of rural life ... Consequently the 1947 Act framed the objectives of rural planning in terms of the protection of an inherently changeless countryside and the consensual "rural way of life" which overlooked important social differences within the rural population'.[217] The result has been that it is 'the most privileged members of English rural society who have benefited the most from the operation of the planning system in rural areas, while the poor and the deprived have gained comparatively little'.[218] In contrast, other rural inhabitants have been long-standing victims of the decline in employment opportunities and service provision in their local economy. Lifestyle opportunities have been squeezed further by the flow of immigration into the countryside of 'commuters, ex-urbanites and second home owners', resulting in 'considerable pressure on rural housing markets, pressures which land use planning policies have been unable to deal with to ensure affordable housing for local needs'.[219]

However, in recent years, there has been recognition of particular social and economic problems facing rural communities, as evidenced in recent rural white papers.[220] The 2000 document, in particular, refers to development pressures, deprivation (in employment, income levels and transport), threats to bio-diversity, as well as the strategic problems of the farming sector. A MAFF census for the year to June 2000 charted 24,000 job losses in the farming industry.[221] As for housing, the white paper further contains a partial response to the severe shortage in affordable rural homes, with extra allocations to the Housing Corporation, looking to increasing the number of new house builds by up to about 9,000 per annum in small rural settlements.[222] Indeed, further funds to alleviate the housing shortage may be generated by any local authorities that avail themselves of a proposal enabling a charge of full rates of council tax on second homes. This, together with other recent changes in planning guidance, which have also been aimed at increasing land release for purposes of building of affordable homes, is discussed in Chapter 6 below.[223]

Planning guidance includes a heightened commitment to achieving diversification of the rural economy.[224] However, the rural white paper suggests that planning authorities are insufficiently flexible in considering such development applications, and a revision to the content of guidance is anticipated.[225] Indeed, together with freedom from planning restrictions, funding support arrangements have traditionally reflected policies to protect productive agricultural land, with regeneration funding hitherto targeted at designated

---

216 Newby, 1979, p 230; UK Government, 1942b.
217 Newby, 1979, p 239.
218 Newby, 1979, p 237.
219 Rydin, 1998, p 344; also, Shucksmith, 1990; Symes, 1990.
220 DoE/MAFF, 1995; DETR/MAFF 2000.
221 (2000) *The Guardian*, 19 December.
222 DETR/MAFF, 2000.
223 Eg, DETR, PPG11, 2000b, para 9.
224 DoE, PPG7, 1997c; cf Elson, Macdonald and Steenberg, 1995.
225 See DETR/MAFF, 2000, para 8.4.

Rural Development Areas. Funds are now to be directed through the RDAs.[226] The rural white paper has confirmed £1.6 billion of support for the rural economy up to 2006 under the Rural Development Programme.[227] Importantly, the emphasis is shifting towards a diversion of funding support from production aid to agri-environmental schemes, including support for countryside stewardship, organic farming schemes, and environmentally sensitive areas.

4.4 Sustainable lifestyles and polarisation

The government's sustainability strategy of 1999 referred to the idea of mixed use, high-density development, related to transport corridors. There was accordingly emphasis upon the need to strengthen urban and rural communities through the land use planning system, by the promotion of the 'siting of high-density developments near existing transport corridors and town centres. The government is also encouraging mixed use development which integrates housing – including affordable housing – with shops and employment opportunities'.[228] Across most of the country, urban areas are sources of development demand. This must inevitably lead to urban extensions, assuming that development in rural areas will continue to be constrained. Particularly in view of demographic trends mandating a need for new home builds referred to above (Cambridge and its sub-region alone, for example, must provide for 2,800 additional new homes annually over the 20 year period ending in 2016), stark choices must be faced. First, spare urban land can be made available. But the finite nature of the resource (even including appropriate brownfield sites) suggests that especially in growth areas this will be insufficient. Next, spare land can be found at the edges of urban areas. This brings considerable conflict with green belt policies. The only other realistic alternative, having sought opportunities to develop smaller urban areas, such as market towns, further, is to look to build subsidiary urban areas – in other words, a new generation of new towns, clustered around existing urban settlements.

In this context, and in the light of the various pressures referred to above, the unavoidable conclusion is that the planning system is bedevilled by built-in polarisations. These are almost all traceable to problems of space and lifestyle expectations. The pressure points have been caused by the related social phenomena of urban dispersal (mainly, for those who could afford it), motor car use (and reliance), and extraordinary increases in numbers of households. The green belt system at its most inflexible (that is, most of the time) polarises divisions between rural and urban dwellers and their respective lifestyles, exemplified by the warfare which ensues where major incursions are proposed (and often more silently – plenty of money may be at stake – where there is some nibbling at the edges). Meanwhile, successful urban areas nevertheless contain a growing base of population which may be excluded from reasonable lifestyle expectations as property prices remain artificially high, leading to stretching of regions through wider population dispersal and (to complete the vicious circle) pressure on

---

226 For a discussion of domestic and EC funding, see Shaw, 1999, pp 59–67.
227 DETR/MAFF, 2000, para 8.2.5–8.2.6.
228 UK Government, 1999, para 7.58.

will advance sustainable development with what he terms the reality: 'a false sense of environmental security'. Instead of advancing sustainability, EIS (Environmental Impact Statement) laws have created a false sense of environmental security.[8] Ost suggests what he terms two logics: on the one hand, there is a logic of publicity and right to information, which affords an independent, public service-style environmental study; on the other, a private logic emphasises commercial freedom, with simplified procedures and an environmental study viewed as an administrative formality or publicity exercise.[9] He has accordingly identified three purposes which the assessment exercise should have. As well as offering a tool for informing the public, and a tool of decision making for the administrative decision maker, it is also a conceptual tool, to inspire the project's director. In order for this latter effect it must be carried out as early as possible, for 'if done too far downstream from the decision its role risks being reduced to that of justifying the option taken'.[10]

1.2   The relationship of planning and environmental impact assessment

Planning law has been described as 'in many respects a model of what an open democratic system of public administration should be'.[11] The objectives underlying EIA are in principle compatible, given that they are directed toward the production of detailed information to inform the planning process.

As has been seen in previous chapters, development is a hitherto relatively uncontrolled area in terms of environmental controls. This is especially so given the tension between environmental and traditionally conceived economic interests, able to drive the planning process, with access to rights of appeal not available to third parties. EIA offers a means of redressing this by imposing constraints upon both regulator and developer. The process has therefore been described as an important innovation in a land use planning system which previously lacked any 'legal guarantee that environmental implications would be considered; at least in any depth or in a systematic way'.[12] Formal requirements for permission operate as a preventative check upon development. EIA supplements the process through multimedia approaches which reflect those increasingly prevalent in pollution control mechanisms.[13]

Environmental assessment, at a project level, therefore, affords an opportunity to integrate environmental interests into circumstances where affirmative consent is already required, in order to proceed with a proposal affecting land use. Its underlying philosophy accordingly embodies McAuslan's delineation of a radical, or populist, approach to planning, which emphasised a link between procedural and substantive aspects, identifying a requirement for 'new structures and processes of government which deliberately and significantly alter the balance' in order to ensure 'greater attention

---

8   Hodas, 1998, p 7.
9   Ost, 1994, p 351.
10   Ost, 1994, p 350.
11   McAuslan, 1991, p 200.
12   Purdue, 1997, p 244.
13   See, eg, Pollution Prevention and Control Act 1999.

to social, community and ecological factors' in the process. [14] However, as will be seen below, since its introduction into the UK, EIA has been undermined by narrow approaches to its application, doubts as to its extent, and problems in its enforcement.

2 LEGAL PROCESSES FOR SECURING ENVIRONMENTAL ASSESSMENT

2.1 The EIA Directive

In the same way that Strategic Environmental Assessment (SEA) is being forged at the European level, as discussed in the following chapter, the principle of environmental assessment for projects was introduced into European legal processes following the adoption in 1985 of the founding EIA Directive.[15] Its rationale is to subject to environmental assessment the approval of those private and public developments that are likely to have significant effects on the environment.[16] It is project based, and attaches to grants of development consent. These are defined as 'the decision of the competent authority or authorities which entitles the developer to proceed with the project'.[17] Note that the term 'project' is not readily translatable into English planning law, and has contributed to concerns as to how far the courts can take account of the 'salami' effect of separate, though related planning applications. The English High Court has for example in the context of highways distinguished in this context a new road from improvements. The former 'may inevitably be said to be a project in its entirety not capable of being dealt with by separate stages', whereas for the latter 'the nature and ordinary meaning of the word "project" is that which is about to be done'.[18]

The measure therefore fulfils a preventative role, requiring an assessment at a time when a land use decision is made in principle. The preamble to the Directive affirms 'the need to take effects on the environment into account at the earliest possible stage in all technical planning and decision making processes'. Member States were accordingly required to adopt all necessary measures to ensure assessment of projects likely to have significant effects on the environment by virtue, inter alia, of their nature, size or location, before grant of development consent.[19] The Directive goes on to distinguish between certain types of major project for which an assessment is mandatory and others which require assessment where the Member State considers that their characteristics so require. Projects for mandatory assessment are set out in Annex I of the Directive.[20] Annex II projects are subject to evaluation by individual Member States as to whether assessment

---

14 McAuslan, 1980, p 6.
15 Council Directive 85/337 on the Assessment of the Effects of Certain Public and Private Projects on the Environment (OJ L175/40, 5 July 1985); also amending Directive 97/11 (OJ L73/5, 14 March 1997).
16 Article 1(1).
17 Article 1(2).
18 *R v Secretary of State for Transport ex p Surrey CC* (1993) unreported, 24 November, Co–2929–93 (Macpherson J).
19 Article 2(1).
20 Article 4(1).

is required, on the basis of likelihood of having significant environmental effects, by virtue of their nature, size or location.[21] The system is founded upon the provision of an environmental statement by the developer, and the types of information to be supplied for this purpose are set out in Annex IV.[22] Since the adoption of the revised Directive guidance is provided to assist the evaluation process, which is made subject to selection criteria set out in Annex III.

An essential element of the Directive is contained in the further provision for procedural rights to consultation and a level of public participation.[23] Appropriate information must be provided, in a comprehensible form, to promote public awareness of environmental implications, within a reasonable time in order to give the public an opportunity to express opinion before the development consent is granted.[24] The provision of such participative arrangements is significant for two reasons. First, it ascribes a broader role to citizens in a manner regarded as essential to acceptance of both appropriate development and the regulatory arrangements applicable. Secondly, the arrangements enable citizens to seek enforcement through judicial procedures. Indeed, such 'rights' as attach can secure avoidance of what amount to significant constraints upon access to justice for those seeking to rely on the terms of environmental legislation.[25] Environmental law tends to protect general interests,[26] not clearly amenable to individual claims. Moreover, representation of a general interest is especially problematic given the programmatic nature of many environmental directives.[27]

Considerable discretion is therefore vested in Member States, in particular in deciding whether non-mandatory projects are likely to have a significant effect on the environment.[28] One of the changes introduced under the 1997 amending Directive is that, whilst retaining due recognition of thresholds and criteria-based approaches, a more systematic approach to the question of requiring an assessment on the basis of significant environmental effects is encouraged. The Directive therefore now sets out selection criteria to be applied in determining that question, and such screening criteria should succeed in introducing greater certainty of response.[29] A related change concerns environmental statements themselves, where a form of scoping is formalised, by the placing of a duty on a requested authority to advise developers as to the nature and extent of a required statement.[30] The nature of such statements has been something of a regulatory no-go area, and led to criticisms as to the availability and contents of environmental statements.[31] The new measure nevertheless largely retains the current,

---

21 Article 4(2).

22 Article 5.

23 Article 6.

24 Article 6(2).

25 See Case C-72/95, *Aannemersbedrijf PK Kraaijevelt BV v Gedeputeerde Staten van Zuid-Holland* [1996] ECR I-5403.

26 See Advocate General Jacobs, Case C-58/89, *Commission v Germany* [1991] ECR I-4983, 5008; also, Macrory, 1996.

27 Case C-236/92, *Comitato di Coordinamento per la Difesa della Cava v Regione Lombardia* [1994] ECR I-483.

28 Article 4(2).

29 Cf original DoE Circular 15/88, on determining the question of significance.

30 Article 5(2).

flexible arrangements.[32] This is so even to the extent that an outline of the main alternatives to the project proposed and reasons for its choice taking into account the environmental effects need only be provided where alternatives have in fact been studied.[33] That said, it is within the discretion of the planning authority to require a statement concerning alternatives in the scoping process.

A two-tier system is applied to the question of the likelihood of significant effects, for the purposes of Annex II projects, with exclusive thresholds or criteria and otherwise screening upon a case-by-case basis to determine potential EIA developments under Schedule 2.[34] These screening procedures are to be applied with the aid of indicative thresholds or criteria as to when an EIA is more likely to be required on grounds of likelihood and environmental significance.[35] These are non-determinative, although permission may be invalidated by defects in the screening process.[36] The authority is required to place on the planning register a reasoned explanation of its screening opinion as to whether an assessment is required of the developer. There is no requirement to give reasons where EIA is not required for a development.[37] However, a statement of the main reasons and considerations must now be given for a decision concerning applications which have been subject to EIA, and where appropriate measures are required to minimise environmental effects.[38]

2.2 Securing legal compliance with the EIA Directive in the UK

The terms of the transposing regulations have closely followed the terms of the Directive. The basis of the UK's implementation of the Directive (in its original form, in 1988) was by way of an incremental augmentation of the existing planning system, rather than the introduction of discrete EIA arrangements.[39] The context within which the domestic EIA regulatory scheme operates is accordingly founded upon planning principles. The domestic process is therefore focused upon planning decision making, on the basis of maximising information as to the environmental implications of development proposals. Planning decisions themselves remain based upon securing the balancing process as between material considerations, which as we have seen in the previous chapter include wider economic and social objectives. To that extent the process is neutral, but its major contribution is the incorporation of transparency and wider participatory opportunities into the decision making process. The preventative objective referred to above is also present, in the sense that negative impacts can be addressed at an early project stage.

---

31 See Jones and Bull, 1997; also, Oxford Brookes *et al*, *Survey of Environmental Statements*, reported at ENDS 270, p 10 (July 1997). Compare the more formalised position in the US: Sheate, 1994, Chapter 4; and Mertz, 1989, pp 484–88.

32 The previous Annex III becomes Annex IV for this purpose.

33 Article 5(3).

34 Part II, reg 4.

35 DETR, Circular 2/99, 1999e, Annex A.

36 *R v St Edmundsbury BC ex p Walton* [1999] Env LR 879.

37 *R v Secretary of State ex p Marson* [1998] 3 PLR 90; and see regulation 4(6) of Regulations 1999 (SI 1999/293).

38 Directive 97/11, Art 9(1); also, Regulations 1999/293, reg 21.

39 Town and Country Planning (Assessment of Environmental Effects) Regulations 1988 (SI 1988/1199); see now Town and Country Planning (Environmental Impact Assessment) (England and Wales) Regulations 1999 (SI 1999/293).

There is insufficient space to offer a review of procedural aspects in any detail.[40] In circumstances where a project falls within the requirements for EIA, whether as mandatory or as determined by the planning authority, developers are required to carry out a systematic analysis of the predicted environmental effects of development projects. This is likely to necessitate detailed surveys of the site and project. The procedure requires developers to produce an environmental statement to the planning authority, containing an assessment of likely adverse effects on the environment, and any proposed measures by way of mitigation.[41] Before reaching a decision, the authority must consult bodies such as the Environment Agency, and may also consult with other specialist groups. As seen in the previous section, an important factor, especially for its opening up the possibility of wider legal recourse, is that information provided must be available to the public, to enable an opportunity to respond to the environmental statement.

The incremental approach to implementation, through additions to the planning system, has given rise to a series of difficulties in transposition. These include, for example, the relationship between EIA requirements for development proposals which require planning permission and the implications of permitted development status, under General Development Orders, which obviate the requirement for planning permission at all.[42] Similar implications arose as to successful appeals against enforcement proceedings against breach of planning control, resulting in deemed applications for permission.[43] Likewise, so-called pipeline breaches were considerable sources of controversy at the time of the coming into force of the transposing regulations.[44] As a consequence of the chosen method of transposition, in excess of 40 sets of domestic regulations have eventually been required in an effort to complete the process of implementation.[45]

The European Commission has recognised that it is difficult to ensure enforcement of the directive.[46] Aside from the Commission's lack of policing powers in support of this part of the Treaty, there are no explicit powers to investigate the quality of the assessments or to monitor the results of the assessment process. The availability of private enforcement mechanisms, including potentially through the doctrine of direct effect, briefly considered below, is therefore crucial. Here, it remains unclear how far the notion of general environmental interest can be developed under European jurisprudence as

---

40 See DETR, *Guidance: Environmental Assessment* (1998, updated September 2000); DETR, *EIA: A Guide to Procedures*, February 2001.

41 See further, DETR, *Guidance: The New Environmental Impact Assessment (EIA) Regulations*, March 1999.

42 Grant, 1991, p 152.

43 *Cheshire CC v Secretary of State for Environment* [1996] JPL 410.

44 Highways Act 1980, s 105A(7), introduced by the Highways (Assessment of Environmental Effects) Regulations 1988 (SI 1988/1241), expressly excluded circumstances 'where a draft order or scheme relating to construction or a draft order is published before the coming into force of the Regulations'.

45 Eg, Environmental Assessment (Afforestation) Regulations 1988 (SI 1988/1207) (see *In the Petition of Richard Swan* [1998] Env LR 251); Electricity and Pipeline Works (Assessment of Environmental Effects) Regulations 1990 (SI 1990/442); Highways (Assessment of Environmental Effects) Regulations 1994 (SI 1994/1002); Town and Country Planning (General Permitted Development) Order 1995 (SI 1995/418); Town and Country Planning (Environmental Assessment and Unauthorised Development) Regulations 1995 (SI 1995/2258).

46 European Commission, 1996b, Annex II.

currently conceived. Yet EIA's procedural nature, particularly in demanding affirmative action on the part of the Member State as to the establishment of rights to participation and to consultation, renders regulatory performance in principle amenable to review proceedings, at the instigation of individuals and groups. Indeed, the according of such rights is itself premised upon wider conceptions of the public interest. It is arguable that the Directive is in certain respects sufficiently clear and precise so as to enable individual enforcement.[47] The European Court of Justice has placed emphasis upon the wide scope and broad purpose of the Directive, in order to encourage the availability of assessment where there may be significant environmental effects, even extending the range of what must be considered as potentially assessable projects under Annex II. As a general principle, therefore, the Directive appears to lay down 'an unequivocal obligation', as to which discretionary features relating to whether an assessment is required are matters of detail.[48] The court has accordingly been unwilling to accept that administrative discretions are absolute, and has required interpretation in the light of legislative purpose on the basis of objective criteria. For instance it has held that the Directive allows for no discretion for the exemption of whole classes, without review on the merits, unless such projects can be seen as not likely to have significant environmental effects, when the relevant criteria are applied.[49] It has likewise rejected the imposition of assessment thresholds that inevitably exclude projects within an identifiable class.[50]

The main justification for challenge therefore appears to rely upon the notion of review of the exercise of administrative discretion, by reference to the terms of the Directive. As a matter of principle, the ECJ has concluded that where the discretion conferred has been exceeded by legislative or administrative authorities, then 'individuals may rely on those provisions before a court of that Member State against the national authorities and thus obtain from the latter the setting aside of the national rules or measures incompatible with those provisions'.[51]

2.3   Enforcement of environmental assessment requirements

One consequence of its procedural foundations is that the Directive has been the source of considerable litigation in the courts of Member States. Despite the passage of transposing legislation and the potential for judicial review (and perhaps assertion of rights under the principle of direct effect), individuals seeking to assert a right to require administrative compliance with the Directive have faced considerable obstacles where mandatory provisions do not apply. The English High Court has consistently resisted purposive interpretations towards claims in reliance on the Directive, preferring to place emphasis upon available administrative discretion.[52] This has been matched by a tendency to fall

---

47   Case C-72/95, *Aannemersbedrijf PK Kraaijevelt BV v Gedeputeerde Staten van Zuid-Holland* [1996] ECR I-5403, Opinion of Elmer AG, paras 68–70; and see, generally, Case 41/74, *van Duyn v Home Office* [1974] ECR 1337.

48   Case C-431/92, *Commission v Germany* [1995] ECR-I 2189, paras 39–40.

49   Case C-133/94, *Commission v Belgium* [1996] ECR I-2323.

50   Case C-72/95, *Aannemersbedrijf P K Kraaijevelt BV v Gedeputeerde Staten van Zuid-Holland* [1996] ECR I-5403, para 31.

51   Case C-435/97, *World Wildlife Fund v Autonome Provinz Bozen* [2000] 1 CMLR 149, para 68.

52   For example, *R v Swale BC ex p RSPB* (1991) 3 JEL 135.

back on the _Wednesbury_ review doctrine.[53] The roots of this approach are deeply entrenched, especially in light of the pervasiveness of administrative discretion under UK planning law. This is manifested in the highly flexible notion of material considerations, as seen in the previous chapter. Thus, for instance, 'any consideration which relates to the use and development of land is capable of being a planning consideration. Whether a particular consideration falling within that broad class in any given case is material will depend on the circumstances'.[54] Whilst 'materiality' is a question of law, the weight to be attributed to it by the administrator is 'a question of judgment, which is entirely a matter for the planning authority. Provided that the planning authority has regard to all material considerations, it is at liberty (provided it does not lapse into _Wednesbury_ irrationality) to give whatever weight [it] ... thinks fit or no weight at all'.[55] Indeed, disputed matters have often been categorised as questions of fact rather than law. In one application, therefore, it has been held that 'whether any particular development is or is not within the schedule descriptions is exclusively for the planning authority in question subject only to _Wednesbury_ challenge. Questions of classification are essentially questions of fact and degree not of law ... [and the court was not] entitled upon judicial review to act effectively as an appeal court and to reach its own decision so as to ensure that our EEC Treaty obligations are properly discharged'.[56] Moreover, the lack of a statutory requirement to give reasons for permission has been treated as the basis for an implication that such decisions were not intended by Parliament to be the subject of challenge.[57] Private applicants have therefore found considerable obstacles in their way in also having to challenge traditional judicial perceptions of State authorities as repositories of the public interest.[58] Alder refers to such public interest perceived as being in 'the custody of the Secretary of State rather than one of direct procedural recognition'.[59] Judicial deference to the administration has the inevitable consequence of avoidance, at least on its face, of being seen to transgress into merits questions, as being the business of policy makers and administrators.[60]

Moreover, the doctrine of direct effect enables a right to be maintained against a State, in circumstances of State default in implementation or enforcement according to obligations arising under a Directive. In order for a right to arise against the State, the following criteria must be met: namely, that there is a clear, sufficiently precise obligation, which is not subject to condition or limitation, and the State has no real discretion as to whether to comply. Yet, in the context of possible resort to the doctrine of direct effect, domestic rulings, in reliance upon the breadth of available discretion, have tended to resist. One commentator has concluded that this approach 'shows the heavy reliance placed by the Community legal system upon the willingness of national courts to enforce Community obligations', and this is especially problematic 'when new controversies in

---

53   _Associated Provincial Picture Houses Ltd v Wednesbury Corporation_ [1948] 1 KB 223.

54   _Stringer v Minister of Housing and Local Government_ [1971] 1 All ER 65, 77, _per_ Cooke J.

55   _Tesco Stores v Secretary of State for the Environment_ [1995] 2 All ER 636, 657, _per_ Lord Hoffmann.

56   _R v Swale BC ex p RSPB_ (1991) 3 JEL 135, pp 142–43; see Ward, 1993, p 237.

57   See _R v Poole BC ex p Beebee_ (1991) 3 JEL 293, 298.

58   For instance, _Twyford PC v Secretary of State for the Environment_ (1992) 4 JEL 273.

59   Alder, 1993, p 213.

60   Wade and Forsyth, 2000, pp 33–34.

environmental law are raised'.[61] For instance, direct effect has been rejected on grounds that not all the Directive's provisions were sufficiently clear and precise, although there appears to be no ECJ authority requiring that all such terms be clear and precise for such purposes.[62] The Court of Session has also held that direct effect could not apply to an Annex II project, in view of the discretionary nature of the decision as to whether assessment is required, this being 'not a discretion as to the means of implementation, but a discretion as to whether steps should be taken at all in the particular context'.[63]

There are now signs of change, however, as English appellate courts have had an opportunity to construe obligations arising under the Directive. Thus, despite the apparent ambivalence even within the ECJ as seen above, the issue of direct effect seems to have been side-stepped, as arguments have proceeded without challenge as to its application.[64] The House of Lords has had to consider whether a planning authority should have required an EIA under a customised procedure, added under the Planning and Compensation Act 1991, which enabled the imposition of conditions upon extant 'old minerals permissions' or 'interim development orders'.[65] Whilst no EIA requirement was contained in the domestic statute and accompanying guidance, the Directive's wide definition of development extended to the subject of the case, extraction of mineral resources, and the process was also listed in Annex II. It was held that such procedure, though permission had already been given, was a 'development consent' within the meaning of the Directive and that consideration must therefore be given to whether an EIA was required. According to Lord Hoffmann, the purpose of the procedure:

> ... was to give the mineral planning authority a power to assess the likely environmental effects of old mining permissions which had been granted without, to modern ways of thinking, any serious consideration of the environment at all. It is true that the power to deal with these effects was limited to the imposition of conditions rather than complete prohibition. But the procedure was nevertheless a new and free-standing examination of the issues and could therefore, in my opinion, require the information provided by an environmental impact assessment.[66]

2.4   The potentially horizontal effect of the Directive

Given that transparency and public participatory objectives are, as we have seen, central to the notion of EIA, the quality of legal mechanisms for individual access to justice is important for the achievement of substantial compliance. However, as we have likewise seen, although fuller consideration will be accorded in Chapter 9 below, according 'rights' to persons and other bodies is problematic in the environmental context. Perceived

61 Fitzpatrick, 1994, p 368.

62 *Wychavon DC v Secretary of State for the Environment ex p Velcourt* (1994) 6 JEL 351; cf *Twyford PC v Secretary of State for the Environment* (1992) 4 JEL 273, p 279.

63 *Petition of Kincardine and Deeside DC* (1992) 4 JEL 289: see Macrory, 1992, p 297.

64 *R v North Yorkshire CC ex p Brown* [1998] Env LR 623; *Berkeley v Secretary of State for the Environment and Fulham Football Club* [2001] Env LR 303.

65 Planning and Compensation Act (PCA) 1991, s 22; see now Town and Country Planning (Environmental Impact Assessment) (England and Wales) (Amendment) Regulations 2000 (SI 2000/2867).

66 *R v North Yorkshire CC ex p Brown* [1998] Env LR 623, pp 630–31.

human interests, and legal rights structures which support them, will often be inimical to environmental interests. The amenability of a directive such as the present one to enforcement by reference to individual interests (by resort to classic public law grounds of challenge such as abuse of authority) can be threatened by doctrinal limitations in defence of other interests. Moreover, individuals can only rely upon the terms of an asserted requirement of a directive before a national court against Member States to which the directive has been addressed.[67]

The policy thus far of the ECJ has been that a directive 'may not impose obligations on an individual and that a provision of a directive may not be relied upon as such against such a person'.[68] The ECJ has on numerous occasions declined to extend horizontal application to the doctrine of direct effect.[69] There is a long-running debate on the question of whether such constraint is justified. One justification is that direct effect enables 'rights to be claimed by individuals against the State in default. The State cannot rely on its own failure to confer those rights. ... To give what is called "horizontal effect" to directives would totally blur the distinction between regulations and directives which the EEC Treaty establishes'.[70] Another is that 'the national court's obligation to interpret domestic law in conformity with a relevant directive is limited by the general principles of law which form part of Community law and in particular the principles of legal certainty and non-retroactivity. Thus, a directive cannot, of itself and independently of a national law adopted by a Member State for its implementation, have the effect of determining or aggravating the liability in criminal law of persons who act in contravention of the provisions of that directive'.[71] Thus a failure to implement an environmental directive had resulted in an unlawful prosecution of a private party who had acted on the assumption of transposition.[72]

A successful challenge under the terms of the EIA Directive may well impact upon third parties, given the potential impact upon development. By contrast, doctrinal limitations (such as the avoidance of incidental horizontal effect) would disable access to justice – say to seek a quashing of a grant of permission for unsatisfactory compliance with EIA requirements by an authority. Yet the success of actions pursued on the basis of direct effect will often be at some cost to third parties. A dispute of this nature has arisen in the English courts, in another case concerning an old mining permission.[73] Under the domestic procedure, upon failure by the mineral authority to make a determination in the designated time, a deemed determination would arise.[74] The House of Lords had previously left open the question whether the deeming provision might be disapplied on the ground that it would enable an authority to avoid its obligations under the

---

67 Case C-168/95, *Luciano Arcaro* [1996] ECR I-4705, para 36.
68 Case C-152/84, *Marshall v Southampton and South-West AHA (No 1)* [1986] QB 401, p 422.
69 Case C-91/92, *Faccini Dori v Recreb Srl* [1994] ECR-I 3325; Case 14/86, *Pretore di Salo* [1987] ECR 2545.
70 *Marshall v Southampton AHA (No 1)*, Slynn AG, pp 412–13; *R v Somerset CC ex p Morris & Perry (Gurney Slate Quarry) Ltd* [2000] Env LR 585.
71 Case-80/86, *Officier van Justitie v Kolpinghuis Nijmegen BV* [1989] CMLR 18.
72 Case C-168/95, *Luciano Arcaro* [1996] ECR I-4705.
73 *R v Durham CC, Sherburn Stone Company and Secretary of State for the Environment ex p Huddleston* [2000] Env LR 488.
74 PCA 1991, Sched 2, para 2(6)(b).

Directive.[75] The applicant, an individual living nearby, asserted that he had been denied the opportunity to express a properly informed opinion before consent, the State being obliged to make available to the public any information gathered by the authority. The developer raised the horizontal effect question, arguing that direct effect would result in obligations being imposed upon it in breach of the principles of Community law. The Court of Appeal ruled, however, that the authority was required to treat the deemed permission as ineffective. The result was expressed in terms of vertical effect, which, according to Sedley LJ, did not 'interpose a new obligation in the relations between individuals or retrospectively to criminalise the activity of one of them. It is to prevent the State, when asked by a citizen to give effect to the unambiguous requirements of a Directive, from taking refuge in its own neglect to transpose them into national law'.[76] Moreover, the application did not offend against the principles against imposition of obligations or sanctions, for 'to read "the imposition on an individual of an obligation laid down by a directive which has not been transposed" as including the application to an individual of conditions laid down by such a directive for the grant of a necessary permission by the State would be to nullify the court's decisions and reasoning' in other extensive jurisprudence of the ECJ.[77]

The interpretation of whether a particular challenge threatens horizontal effect must accordingly be viewed in its precise context. For instance, in an employment context of a prospective claim for unfair dismissal by part-time employees against employers being precluded by a national qualifying period, the courts have declined to give direct effect to the Equal Treatment Directive.[78] The House has held that such individuals cannot seek disapplication of a national law against the State in order to assist a claim against the employer. Lord Hoffman stated that this would otherwise 'give the Directive, by an easy two-stage process, the very effect which the jurisprudence of the Court of Justice says it cannot have, namely to impose obligations upon an individual'.[79] Sedley LJ was able to distinguish the earlier authority as the case before him was 'not one in which treating an environmental impact statement as a uniform prerequisite of a determination touches any legal relationship between' the individual parties. The distinction could be expressed in terms of benefit, there being 'a fundamental difference between imposing legal obligations on an individual which limit his freedom of action vis à vis other individuals and placing conditions upon that individual's entitlement to secure a benefit from the State. The latter ... seems to me to come in the category of permitted transposition from Community to domestic law as surely as the former does not'.[80] For Sedley LJ, therefore, the principle may be wider, for 'enforcement of a directive by an individual against the State is not rendered inadmissible solely by its consequential effect on other individuals'.

---

75 See Article 6(2).

76 *R v Durham CC, Sherburn Stone Company and Secretary of State for the Environment ex p Huddleston* [2000] Env LR 488, p 505 (Sedley LJ).

77 *Ibid*, per Sedley LJ, p 502; see Case C-441/93, *Pafitis v Trapeza Kentrikis Ellados AE* [1996] 2 CMLR 551; Case C-201/94, *R v Medicines Control Agency ex p Smith and Nephew Pharmaceuticals Ltd* [1996] ECR 5819; Case 103/88, *Fratelli Constanzo v Comune di Milano* [1989] ECR 1839; Case C-435/97, *World Wildlife Fund v Autonome Provinz Bozen* [2000] 1 CMLR 149.

78 *R v Secretary of State for Employment ex p Seymour-Smith* [1997] 1 WLR 473.

79 *Ibid*, para 47.

80 *R v Durham CC, Sherburn Stone Company and Secretary of State for the Environment ex p Huddleston* [2000] Env LR 488; and see *Marshall v Southampton AHA (No 1)* [1986] QB 401, pp 411–14 (Slynn AG).

There is, for instance, authority in which an applicant excluded from domestic tender procedures in breach of a directive's terms was entitled to rely on the direct effect doctrine although the contract had been awarded elsewhere.[81] Similarly, there is ECJ authority enabling an individual to call the State to account for non-implementation of the EIA Directive, even though a developer was adversely affected as a consequence.[82]

Finding a coherent dividing line between horizontal and vertical direct effect remains conceptually problematic, albeit that private individuals may suffer indirectly as a result of say a successful administrative law challenge. It has been said that it as 'difficult to avoid the conclusion that the saga of horizontal direct effect is not yet dead, and that there is further confusion ahead before anything like a clear position on the permissible legal effects of a non-implemented directive will be reached'.[83] Perhaps inevitably resort is made to 'an equally subtle distinction (and ultimately one that may be difficult to sustain) between the impermissible imposition of an obligation contained in a non-transposed directive, and the permissible adverse effects of a non-transposed directive on an individual may have to be made'.[84] Between the two poles of permitted and impermissible effect, according to Sedley LJ, 'lies a variety of problematic situations'.[85] Sedley LJ accepted that the case would have been more problematic had the developer gone ahead with quarrying and been prosecuted.[86] A unifying principle was proposed, whereby treating the State as having done what the Directive calls upon it to do stops short both of modifying the legal relations between private persons and of criminalising what they have done.

In the context of planning and the environment, what has been termed the tripartite problem is especially acute, involving an essential contradiction 'between giving rights to some private individuals to stop environmental damage, at the cost of imposing obligations on others'.[87] The Court of Appeal seems therefore to have attempted a rationalisation that extends beyond ECJ jurisprudence to date. The risk of a creeping horizontal effect requires clarification. In the environmental field, albeit that there may be problems of standing, just as the review process classically asserts notions of (public) benefit rather than rights, corresponding disbenefit will inevitably be challenged on grounds of unacceptable horizontal application. Sedley LJ's solution appears to argue for the delineation of permissible effect in public law terms. An essential distinction can therefore be drawn between a public law which 'is concerned essentially with wrongs, in the sense that the State's powers are circumscribed by laws which a person with a sufficient interest may seek to enforce so long as anybody potentially affected also has a say; while private law, concerned essentially with rights, governs the relations of persons with each other'. Thus here private law rights or interests can here be contrasted with the point at issue, namely 'a pure question of public law: that is to say, a question of the limits of the State's powers in a field where authority has been delegated by Parliament to what

---

81 Case 103/88, *Fratelli Constanzo v Comune di Milano* [1989] ECR 1839, para 31.

82 Case C-435/97, *World Wildlife Fund v Autonome Provinz Bozen* [2000] 1 CMLR 149.

83 Craig and de Búrca, 1998, p 210.

84 Craig and de Búrca, 1998, p 206.

85 *R v Durham CC, Sherburn Stone Company and Secretary of State for the Environment ex p Huddleston* [2000] Env LR 488, p 491.

86 Cf *R v Somerset CC ex p Morris & Perry (Gurney Slate Quarry) Ltd* [2000] Env LR 585.

87 Ward, 1993, p 242; see also Jans, 2000, pp 198–200.

is now the European Union. The ... entitlement to seek judicial review depends not upon his physical propinquity to the site, though that is no doubt a stimulus, but upon his interest in the legal protection of the environment. While this may not be the acid test of all horizontal direct effect issues, in my view it casts useful light upon a case such as this one, underscoring the same primary distinction as can be seen in the case law of the European Court of Justice'.[88] Yet, determining principles in the blurred territory between horizontal and vertical effect may in the end be a matter for political resolution.[89]

Once applicants such as Huddleston are perceived as representing the public interest then doctrinal limitations to direct effect would fall away.[90] The environmental context demands new public interest solutions to assertions of rights and the judgment suggests that answers may best be found in a realignment of the public/private law divide. In the light of looking at the purpose of the EIA Directive, a right of challenge in the courts lies at its core, on the basis of a defined public interest in compliance with the EIA process. In an equivalent context it has been stated that 'the public/private law divide is not an easy one to draw and this will inevitably give rise to uncertainty if this is indeed the route down which the Court (of Justice) is travelling'.[91] Indeed, this partial rationalising of the current status of ECJ jurisprudence raises hard questions as to the nature of horizontal effect. Yet in our context, the Court of Appeal's disinclination to see the purposes of the EIA Directive averted suggests a fertile area for future challenge in domestic courts.[92]

2.5 The exercise of residual judicial discretion

Despite what therefore appears to be a more expansive view of implementation issues taking root in domestic courts, other factors inherent in the process have limited expectations of formal assessment. In particular, the courts retain an equitable discretion to withhold a remedy upon review, even where the challenged decision was outside statutory grant of powers or where an applicant's interests might be substantially prejudiced by non-compliance.[93] The discretion may for instance be exercised by refusing to quash a planning consent in circumstances that such failure had no practical consequence.

High Court litigation concerning EIA has been replete with just such conclusions. Thus, it has been held that the court would 'of necessity' refuse a remedy where 'material available to the inspector, which although not put in the form of an environmental impact assessment, covered all matters that such a statement would have provided'.[94] A similar conclusion was drawn where the authority 'had in their possession the substance of what they would have had if they had applied their minds to the 1988 Regulations and had prepared such an environmental statement. The substance of all the environmental information which was likely to emerge from going through the formal process envisaged

---

88 *R v Durham CC, Sherburn Stone Company and Secretary of State for the Environment ex p Huddleston* [2000] Env LR 488, at p 503.

89 de Witte, 1999, p 193 *et seq.*

90 Alder, 1993, p 209.

91 Hilson and Downes, 1999, p 127.

92 See further *R v Somerset CC ex p Dixon* [1997] JPL 1030.

93 Confirmed by statute: see TCPA 1990, s 288(5)(b).

94 *Wychavon DC v Secretary of State for the Environment ex p Velcourt* (1994) 6 JEL 351, p 357 (Tucker J).

by the Regulations had already emerged and was apparently present in the Council's mind'.[95] Going to the root of the discretion, this has been categorised as a distinction 'of form, not substance. None of the applicants has asserted that there was any relevant piece of environmental information of which he was in ignorance or which was made available in too complex a form so that he could not understand it or its significance. None alleges that he was prevented from making the case that he would had the requirements of the Directive become part of national law'.[96]

A similar approach had been successful before the Court of Appeal in a case where environmental issues had been investigated by local planning authority officers as well as being part of a public inquiry into a development. The Secretary of State had confirmed the recommendation of the inspector, and granted permission, but had failed to consider the question as to whether an environmental statement was required as part of an EIA process. It was accepted by the Court of Appeal that a *prima facie* breach had occurred, for 'had the point been considered, there is a real prospect that the first respondent would have required an environmental statement'.[97] However, in light of its residual discretion as to whether to award a remedy, the court ruled that 'Community law does not require the elimination of the discretion available'.[98] The approach of the court was to consider how far such failure could be categorised as a matter merely of form, rather than substance. It concluded that the objectives of the Directive were in substance achieved by the procedure followed taken as a whole and the information available to those concerned with the proposed development.

However, the House of Lords has pursued a more purposive approach and allowed the applicant's appeal in that case.[99] Thus the failure to follow the EIA process was seen to lead to an *ultra vires* decision on the application, and it would be exceptional to withhold an order to quash. Moreover, given the duty under Article 10 of the Treaty whereby the courts must ensure fulfilment of obligations arising under the Treaty, the courts were 'not entitled retrospectively to dispense with the requirements of an EIA on the ground that the outcome would have been the same'.[100] Lord Hoffmann contrasted the situation where a procedural step would be superfluous. The discretion it appears may therefore only be exercised in circumstances where there had been compliance substantially with the terms of the Directive, and this could not be envisaged where no environmental statement, including non-technical summary, had been made publicly available. This appears to accord with the view of the ECJ in an earlier case, where the Court appeared to have been satisfied that equivalent procedures may be acceptable. There, pre-existing national provisions for assessment had been applied and the court held that the Commission had failed to specify in what respects the Directive had not been complied with.[101] However, the Court was also satisfied that 'the objective of

---

95 *R v Poole BC ex p Beebee* (1991) 3 JEL 293, p 299 (Schiemann J); see Harte, 1991, pp 306–07.

96 *Twyford PC v Secretary of State for the Environment* (1992) 4 JEL 273, p 281 (McCullogh J); and see Bryant, 1996, p 266.

97 *Berkeley v Secretary of State for the Environment and Fulham FC* [1998] Env LR 741, p 752 (Pill LJ).

98 *Ibid*, p 756.

99 *Berkeley v Secretary of State for the Environment and Fulham FC* [2001] Env LR 303.

100 *Ibid*, pp 304–05.

101 Case C-431/92, *Commission v Germany* [1995] ECR I-2189, para 45.

making the public aware of the environmental implications of a project on the basis of specific information provided by the developer was attained'.[102] There, a structured assessment had been produced, for the authority had 'integrated the information gathered and the reactions of the sectors concerned in the consent procedure, and took that into account in its decision approving the project'.[103]

The House of Lords' insistence upon a narrow interpretation of the residual judicial discretion to withhold a remedy places emphasis where it should lie, namely upon EIA as a process, a point which is discussed below. The value of EIA is that it is a process, its essence being to require that a procedure be followed. The formal requirements encourage objectivity and transparency, and are not evaluative in the sense of determinative of outcome.[104] Whilst there is a balancing of interests to be achieved in such cases, it must be recalled that in this case there had been a failure both by the developer to produce, and by the regulatory agencies to consider requiring, an environmental statement in terms envisaged by the Directive. It is not at all apparent on what basis the event of a planning inquiry, following a calling in by the Secretary of State, and subsequent determination having received an inspector's report, would justify obviating the obligations under the Directive by exercise of the judicial discretion. This is therefore referable to rights of the citizen being central to the purposes of the Directive. This according to Lord Hoffmann should mean:

> ... not merely a right to a fully informed decision on the substantive issue. It must have been adopted on an appropriate basis and that requires the inclusive and democratic procedure prescribed by the Directive in which the public, however misguided or wrongheaded its views may be, is given an opportunity to express its opinion on the environmental issues ... A court is therefore not entitled retrospectively to dispense with the requirement of an EIA on the ground that the outcome would have been the same or that the local planning authority or Secretary of State had all the information necessary to enable them to reach a proper decision on the environmental issues.[105]

3 THE CONTRIBUTION OF ENVIRONMENTAL IMPACT ASSESSMENT TO SUSTAINABILITY

3.1 The preventative role of environmental assessment

Normative arrangements within the Treaty are essentially policy based, and although there has been some limited judicial recognition of Article 174 principles as an aid to interpretation,[106] this weighs against justiciability.[107] Nevertheless, the policy arrangements under the revised Treaty point to the value of integration under Article 6, as discussed in Chapter 2, in addressing sustainable solutions. It has accordingly been

---

102 Case C-431/92, *Commission v Germany* [1995] ECR I-2189, para 43.

103 *Ibid*, para 44.

104 *Ibid*, Elmer AG, para 35(3).

105 *Berkeley v Secretary of State for the Environment and Fulham FC* [2001] Env LR 303, pp 304–05.

106 Eg, Case 2/90, *EC v Belgium* [1993] 1 CMLR 365; *R v London Boroughs Transport Committee ex p Freight Transport Association* [1992] 1 CMLR 5.

107 *R v Secretary of State for Trade and Industry ex p Duddridge* [1995] 7 Env LR 151.

argued that where 'a government has committed itself in terms of policy to sustainable development and to regard for the legitimate needs and aspirations of future citizens, then it ought not to be able to disregard that policy on commercial grounds, however attractive; at the very least it should justify its departure from that policy'.[108] This would represent a legal response to 'the idea of limitations imposed by the state of technology and social organisations on the environment's ability to meet present and future needs'.[109] In the context of land use development projects, EIA fulfils a preventive role. Indeed, the First Environmental Action Plan asserted that the best environmental policy 'consists in preventing the creation of pollution or nuisance at source, rather than subsequently trying to counteract their effects ... Effects on the environment should be taken into account at the earliest possible stage in all the technical planning and decision making processes'.[110] Formalised requirements for planning permission, operating as a check *ex ante* on development, exemplify the preventive approach contained in Article 174.

Planning can be said to be at the 'sharp end' of delivering sustainable land use, a phrase used by McAuslan in the analogous contested context of the relationship of planning laws with private property interests.[111] EIA, as stated above, embodies a multimedia approach akin to those approaches which have emerged to regulate polluting processes.[112] Assessment is fundamentally concerned with a balancing of such interests, on a political, but nevertheless informed, basis. It is scarcely surprising that, given the endemic tension between environmental and often more immediate economic interests and pressures, there remains resistance to the advantages offered by EIA. Problems in this exercise appear throughout the planning process, albeit often implicitly. Thus, contractors and others inevitably incur costs at various stages of commitment, evident from the design and pre-application stage onwards. The courts have clearly treated such costs as influential factors.[113]

Yet central to sustainability objectives is the recognition that development inevitably imposes both internal and external costs. Assessment is an essential means by which especially externalities can be identified, and then either avoided or mitigated.[114] Constraints imposed by assessment may be accordingly justified 'by limits inherent in the need for long-term sustainability'.[115] The procedure right at the heart of assessment is an expression of this belief, and in turn challenges the presupposition that decisions need only be identified in terms of profitability and balance sheet. Furthermore, it is arguable that assessment, just as clean technologies in pollution control, incentivises wider economic benefits, including marketing opportunities, the transfer of technology and

---

108 Tromans, 1995, p 793.

109 United Nations, World Commission on Environment and Development, 1987, p 43.

110 1973, OJ C/112, p 6.

111 McAuslan, 1980, coining the phrase used, p 145.

112 Eg, Integrated Pollution Prevention and Control Directive 96/61, OJ L257/6; also, European Commission, 1993a.

113 See *Twyford PC v Secretary of State for the Environment* (1992) 4 JEL 273; *R v Swale BC ex p RSPB*(1991) 3 JEL 135.

114 Brown, 1981.

115 Paehlke, 1989, p 252.

techniques, and the benefits of reassuring providers of financial and insurance services.[116]

The Directive affixes the duties relating to EIA upon 'the decision of the competent authority or authorities which entitles the developer to proceed with the project'.[117] In accordance with the general preventive objective, the public interest requires an assessment to take place at a time when a land use decision is made in principle. Thus, in the preamble to the Directive, the Council 'affirm the need to take effects on the environment into account at the earliest possible stage in all technical planning and decision making processes'. Whilst the National Environmental Policy Act of 1969 (NEPA) in the United States can be contrasted in that it imposes a form of SEA for federal government authorities, criticisms of its operation are instructive. A dissenting opinion in the Supreme Court has warned that 'an early start on the statement is more than a procedural necessity. Early consideration of environmental consequences through production of an environmental impact statement is the whole point of NEPA ... (and) allows the decision maker to take environmental factors into account when he is making decisions, at a time when he has an open mind and is more likely to be receptive to such considerations'.[118] Endorsing this approach, Hodas has criticised the majority view in the Supreme Court sharing a narrow interpretation of the procedural requirements of NEPA which does not require preparation of an environmental statement until the eleventh hour. This has 'clearly signalled its hostility towards advancement of the statute's sustainable development goals, even in a requirement as minor as allowing courts to order agencies to begin preparation of EISs early enough so they can provide meaningful input'.[119]

This, however, has an unusual consequence when applied to UK planning law, where the planning regime, especially in respect of larger developments, commonly operates by way of outline applications for permission. An outline grant of permission assures entitlement to proceed subject to approval of reserved matters upon a detailed application stage.[120] It has been accepted that in principle any assessment should take place at the earlier stage, which constitutes the decision entitling the development to proceed.[121] Given the nature of outline applications, in the context of EIA a lack of information may present problems for both developers and potential challengers. It is therefore necessary that the description of a proposed development is sufficient at that stage to enable the main effects likely to be caused to the environment to be identified and assessed, otherwise refusal must follow.[122]

---

116 Welford and Gouldson, 1993, Chapter 3.

117 Article 1(2).

118 *Marshall J, Kleppe v Sierra Club*, 427 US 390 (1976), 417–18.

119 Hodas, 1998, p 41.

120 *R v London Borough of Bromley ex p Barker* [2001] Env LR 1.

121 *R v London Borough of Hammersmith and Fulham ex p Council for the Protection of Rural England London Branch* [2000] Env LR 549.

122 *R v Rochdale MBC ex p Tew* [2000] Env LR 1.

An analogous line of argument arose in a case referred to above, concerning a minerals permission, where conditions had been set by the authority in breach of the requirement for an EIA. There, the authority had originally unsuccessfully argued that, as with so-called pipeline projects, where development consent procedures had been initiated before the Directive took effect, no EIA was required.[123] This was argued before the Court of Appeal and rejected.[124] Whilst EIA was usually required at the earlier stage of outline permission, when an assessment is most relevant, any such principle had to be flexibly interpreted. Thus, in the context of old mining permissions, the subsequent statutory requirement for registration and affixing of conditions, under the 1991 Act, constituted 'the decision which entitles the developer to proceed with the project in the terms of the Directive'.[125] It was emphasised that the ruling was 'not intended to apply generally to schemes in which, in the interests of orderly planning, a series of consents is required before development can proceed. The last of the decisions giving consent is not necessarily or universally the relevant decision for the purposes of Articles 1 and 2 of the Directive'.[126]

Indeed, in the event of separate applications forming part of a larger project, over a lengthy period, difficult questions may arise as to what level of information to require at the early stage.[127] However, generally, as stated above, assessment must be dealt with at the stage of outline application for a development. An alternative view can be propounded to the effect that the nature of EIA as a process suggests the appropriateness of phasing in the same way as occurs where outline and detailed permissions are sought. In this event it would be necessary specifically to require a further environmental statement at the later stage, pursuant to outline conditions or in reserved matters applications.[128] But, subject to such a change, the realistic conclusion must be that compliance requires that all information as can reasonably be required be made available at the earlier stage.[129] Government guidance appears to accept this, and as a consequence developers must seek to provide more detailed treatment in outline applications as to environmental impacts than might otherwise be the case. Even in that event, however, a considerable onus lies upon a planning authority that has already granted outline permission, for at the detailed application stage, an informal updating exercise must surely be attempted.

3.2 The value of environmental assessment as a process

The imposition of such process can be described as neutral in the sense that it is essentially not about questions of outcome. It has been described as 'only a small step towards environmentally sensitive decision making. Requiring developers to gather

---

123 *Twyford PC v Secretary of State for the Environment* (1992) 4 JEL 273.

124 *R v North Yorkshire CC ex p Brown* [1998] Env LR 385.

125 *Ibid*, p 392 (Pill LJ).

126 *Ibid*, p 393 (Pill LJ).

127 See Elvin and Robinson, 2000, pp 882–83; also Case C-396/92, *Bund Naturschutz Case* [1994] ECR I-3717.

128 Lea, 2000, p 134.

129 See *R v Rochdale MBC ex p Milne* [2001] Env LR 22.

environmental information, consult, and finally place that information in the public arena, does not ensure that the final decision is itself environmentally sensitive, nor that the developer has really made that decision on the basis of the environmental information'.[130] Legal control is indirect, providing 'a conduit by which information may enter decision making procedures' and will not necessarily be determinative of outcome.[131] On a radical view, such a notion of EIA can be criticised for its having a delimiting procedural nature. Thus Freyfogle has asserted that in the United States a reason why 'the information-based approach of NEPA has made so little headway is that it did little to dismantle the legal tradition that has most forcefully shaped our interactions with the land – our inherited property-law notion of what it means to own land'.[132] The broader implications of such an argument were considered in Chapter 3.

Yet the procedural underpinnings, provided interpretation by the courts is sensitive to the purposes underlying the rationale for assessment, bring significant advantages. Thus the EIA process has been described as more than the performance of discrete environmental studies, amounting to 'an iterative process of decision making, involving the production of information and consultation, intended to influence the process at every stage'.[133] Indeed, formal assessment 'objectivises' the process. Thus the developer, as the most appropriate person, is required to produce the environmental statement upon which the process depends, which then becomes more fully integrated into project formulation.[134] Judicial decisions are increasingly asserting the substance underlying a rigorous application of procedures. For instance, the High Court, ruling that the approval of a new road scheme without an EIA was defective, has pointed out that 'one of the dangers of a planning application which ... presents two choices – "new roads" or "heavy lorries continuing to use the old town" – is that in the absence of a thorough environmental assessment of the "new road" it is too easy to choose the "new road"'.[135]

The objectivisation has been implicitly endorsed by the House of Lords' narrow interpretation of residual powers to refuse relief. According to Lord Hoffmann, 'I do not accept that this paper chase can be treated as the equivalent of an environmental statement ... The point about the environmental statement contemplated by the Directive is that it constitutes a single and accessible compilation, produced by the applicant at the very start of the application process, of the relevant environmental information and the summary in non-technical language'.[136] It is through such rigorous enforcement that procedural measures can have a substantive effect on processes. The effect of the decision will be profound, as developers and planning authorities are required in consequence to confront the question of EIA and where it is appropriate secure compliance with its requirements. The situation cannot now be finessed with any confidence that, save on technical grounds such as delay in applications for review, the courts will decline to intervene. On the contrary, purposive interpretations of the obligations contained in the Directive seem likely to continue.

130 Donson, 1997.
131 Elworthy and Holder, 1997, p 390.
132 Freyfogle, 1994, pp 835–36.
133 Macrory, 1992, p 300; see *Bund Naturschutz Case* [1994] ECR I-3717, Gulmans AG, paras 31–36.
134 Wathern, 1988, Chapter 1.
135 *R v St Edmundsbury BC ex p Walton* [1999] Env LR 879, 894 (Hooper J).
136 *Berkeley v Secretary of State for the Environment and Fulham FC* [2001] Env LR 303, p 318.

Overall, therefore, there are considerable potential gains involved in applying formalised requirements. First, EIA contributes to a climate of objectivity and transparency. Participation and consultation rights are premised upon broader conceptions of the public interest discussed above. They counterbalance the potential for abuse, where information in the public domain is strictly curtailed. Sheate accordingly points to 'the important procedural differences introduced by EIA, including the importance of public participation and the formal consideration of specific environmental information'.[137] The quality of information and level of participation accorded requires sympathetic, purposive judicial support upon recourse to enforcement of rights arising under the Directive.[138] Despite criticisms of the sort referred to above, assessment is more firmly established in the US; it is strongly arguable that this is a consequence in part of a readier availability of challenge through the courts.[139] Moreover, the participatory nature of this process leads not only to opportunities to bring legal challenges based upon procedural defects, but also to the benefits of a wider community involvement in the decision making process.[140] Secondly, EIA constitutes a coherent mechanism for placing reasonable restraints upon regulators. Regulators must assure the integrity of the process by ensuring that sufficient detail is produced to enable informed decisions to be made.[141] This may be especially important where regulators themselves have an interest in proposed development, as where decisions as to process are within the discretion of a developer/authority.[142] But more generally, the EIA statutory process encourages adherence to the required procedures save in the most exceptional circumstances. Thirdly, EIA offers a mechanism for placing obligations upon those applying for planning consent. This offers a counterweight to the influential role of development interests in the planning process. The potential for the dominance of such interests goes beyond the pressure to support economic activity which is traditionally important in the planning process. This perspective reflects a view that the imposition of environmental regulation is largely justified by externalities imposed by market failure, where the task of legal regulation is at least to restructure 'in the most efficient and least market-disruptive manner', as discussed in Chapter 3.[143] There is also the influence which direct representation of those interests within the process brings. Participation for the proposed developer is assured: 'no interest has exercised this right to take part in governmental process more pervasively or successfully than has business.'[144]

3.3   Potential for reform

The current process does contain significant limitations. The Royal Commission on Environmental Pollution, investigating wider issues of the relationship of planning and

---

137 Sheate, 1994, p 119.
138 See Vogel, 1986, p 126.
139 Sheate, 1994, pp 98–99.
140 See Tilleman, 1995.
141 Holland, 1985.
142 *R v Poole BC ex p Beebee* (1991) 3 JEL 293, 298.
143 See Smith, 1996, p 258; cf Sagoff, 1997.
144 Rosenbaum, 1991, p 163.

environmental protection, has given a preliminary indication of experts' concerns at EIA. These highlight in particular the need for research into the effectiveness of the consequences of planning decisions post-EIA for the environment; and the need for EIA to include consideration of the human health impact of development. Most importantly, the Commission emphasises the importance of sound methodology and availability of appropriate expertise, whether in formal EIA or informal processes, to ensure that the necessary skills and data are available for planners to apply appropriate techniques and understand the answers.[145]

As to procedures, provision for a duty to consider alternatives would not be excessively onerous. Another deficiency in the framework is the lack of structured requirements in respect of administrative response to the participatory processes required by the Directive, save that such information must be taken into consideration in the development consent procedure.[146] Given the discretionary elements underlying much of the EIA regime, it may therefore be that insufficient is done to assure the impact of the participation process. Contrasting this arrangement with that under NEPA, Tabb warns against participation becoming 'just a hollow promise. In order for public involvement to be truly meaningful, there must be some specific procedural mechanism to guide the developer and the competent authority to evaluate the comments generated'.[147] This is, however, counterbalanced, as has been seen above, by the availability of third party legal challenge by way of review, and in the United States by the statutory opportunities for citizen suits.[148] This will inevitably concentrate the minds of developers and regulators alike in circumscribing the nature of both the environmental statement and, more generally, the whole EIA process.

It may be that the process would be enhanced by other changes, such as where EIA takes place and development proceeds, it may be appropriate to accord follow-up procedures through the planning system, perhaps through conditions attaching to actual environmental impact. Where no EIA has been required, transparency would be enhanced by extending duties of explanation on the part of regulators. This might be augmented by specific third party rights of appeal. Such disputes as arise might then usefully be considered by an Environmental Court of the type suggested in Chapter 10.[149] Such a body might monitor compliance with environmental obligations through advisory and investigative processes. It might also exercise a quasi-judicial function, in which decisions on the merits might further become available, in connection with such matters as requirement for and content of assessment.[150]

In 1991, in a review of the early days of EIA rules in the UK, Carnwath pointed to the potential significance of 'the policy approach implicit in EA [EIA]'.[151] He saw the process as countering a presumption in favour of allowing development, so that 'the developer is

---

145 RCEP website, Environmental Planning Study, Themes, 2000, paras 29–31 (at www.rcep.org.uk/epissues.html).
146 Article 8.
147 Tabb, 1999, p 959.
148 Morelli, 1997; cf Greve, 1990.
149 And see Sheate, 1994, Chapter 7.
150 Alder, 1993, p 220.
151 Carnwath, 1991, p 62.

required to describe and justify the environmental effects of his scheme. Implicitly the onus has shifted to him. Common sense suggests that, under this code, if he fails to provide adequate information to show that his project is acceptable, the authority may refuse permission for that reason alone'.[152] With the emphasis today upon determinations in compliance with the Development Plan,[153] the interpretation of environmental considerations appearing there will increasingly inform planning decision making in this area. Indeed, the imposition of both EIA and less formal consideration of environmental matters as material considerations are already affected by the introduction, as discussed in the next chapter, of sustainability appraisal into the Development Plan process.[154] At the same time, the enforcement powers available to the European Commission are likely to place formidable obstacles in the way of policies geared towards diluting assessment requirements in the face of major projects.[155]

The scope for any reforms will inevitably be influenced by expected progress within the European Union toward an SEA regime, discussed in the following chapter. The discussion also now turns to a fuller consideration of the extent to which there is realisable potential for developing a sustainable framework into planning law.

---

152 Carnwath, 1991, p 63.

153 TCPA 1990, s 54A.

154 DETR, PPG12, 1999c, paras 4.16–4.22.

155 See, eg, Commission enforcement against the UK (IP/01/1166, 1 August 2000); also (2001) *Independent on Sunday*, 26 August.

CHAPTER 6

SEEKING A SUSTAINABLE FRAMEWORK FOR LAND USE PLANNING

Isn't it a pity about the Inner City?
People leave who shouldn't ought
And that affects the rate support
If only those who stayed behind
Had left instead, no one would mind.[1]

1 FORMAL POLICY RECOGNITION OF SUSTAINABILITY

The two preceding chapters have considered the general principles upon which domestic land use planning law is founded, as well as the bolt-on arrangement of the environmental impact assessment process. The central themes have therefore sought to address the impact of the increasing range of environmental issues which call for consideration in the planning context, both strategically and within development control, as also through adjudicative and participatory structures. As we have already seen, in whatever political, administrative or judicial guise (or mix) the players appear, institutions and citizens face substantial challenges in the broader context of sustainability. The discussion now turns to the role of planning as a mechanism for the achievement of sustainable development.

1.1   Sustainability strategies

The purpose of the land use planning regime is linked with the achievement of sustainable development in general planning guidance:

> The planning system regulates the development and use of land in the public interest. The system as a whole, and the preparation of development plans in particular, is the most effective way of reconciling the demand for development and the protection of the environment. Thus it has a key role to play in contributing to the government's strategy for sustainable development by helping to provide for necessary development in locations which do not compromise the ability of future generations to meet their needs.[2]

In response to commitments reached at UNCED in 1992, discussed in earlier chapters, central government has produced two versions of a Sustainable Development Strategy for the UK.[3] The broad thrust of the most recent document was discussed in Chapter 1. For planning purposes, whilst there is no national plan, the Sustainable Development Strategy, together with individual sector-specific strategies, such as in respect of waste and air quality, goes some way to providing the conditions for a strategic framework. Within the realms of land use planning, there is a quandary for the centre in delivering

---

1   Stephen Holley; sadly unpublished, but extracted from Ward, 2000.
2   DoE, PPG1, 1997a, para 39.
3   UK Government, 1994 and 1999.

targets for sustainable development, for delivery of the process, albeit under the ultimate policy direction of the centre, in generally the hands of local planning authorities. However, as will be seen below, strategic structures are now developing upon regional levels.

Two significant features, which seek to draw together policy in accordance with national political priorities, can be identified. First, since 1999 the conditions for an increased regional influence on the policy process within England have been established (following devolution in Scotland and Wales), with the development of regional planning under Regional Planning Bodies (RPBs). These have to date been drawn from regional conferences of local authorities, although the Secretary of State has designated Regional Chambers, with community (that is, non-local government) membership of at least 30%, including business and voluntary sectors.[4] These chambers will in due course oversee the eight Regional Development Agencies (RDAs) whose role was discussed in Chapter 4.

Secondly, following the lead contained in the 1990 white paper, planning policy guidance is increasingly expressed as founded upon sustainable development objectives.[5] This emphasises, for instance, issues of interconnectedness, as between policies such as transport, housing, out-of-town developments, and building on flood plains. Formal regard to the notion of sustainable development can be divined in the modern day proliferation of sustainability indicators, as discussed in Chapter 2. The purpose is to derive indications of progress as expressed through statistical analysis, specification and quantification. The rationale underlying their development is therefore 'to measure how sustainable a nation's economy is. Sustainability indicators are not intended to be snapshots of the environmental situation but to be normative'.[6] Target-led planning is now the norm for locally produced plans as, for instance, in connection with protection of sites, air quality, and waste recycling. However, a recent report for the Royal Commission on Environmental Pollution (RCEP) has pointed to central government reluctance 'to set concrete targets in some sectors or areas at a national level. Some national targets are relatively efficiently translated to local action (such as from the Bio-Diversity Action Plan). Others meet with significant resistance (such as housing targets)'.[7]

Sustainability appraisal has accordingly emerged as part of a strategic approach towards integrating sustainable development into the consideration of strategic options and their impacts. Planning guidance for regional planning (RPG) requires that RPBs should carry out a sustainability appraisal as an integral part of the preparation of draft RPG. The process is commended by government as enabling 'the emerging RPG to play its part in assisting the economy, reducing social exclusion, enhancing the environment and ensuring the prudent use of natural resources. It should also help avoid, reduce or mitigate any adverse impacts in these key areas. The potential direct, indirect and cumulative impacts of different strategic options need to be appraised in order to integrate sustainable development objectives in the formulation of policies and inform

4   Regional Development Agencies Act 1998.
5   UK Government, 1990.
6   See Myerson and Rydin, 1996, p 100.
7   Farmer, Skinner, Wilkinson and Bishop, 1999, para 14.7.

decisions on which options should be promoted in the draft strategy'.[8] The principles are also expected to inform preparation of Development Plans.[9]

Such strategic appraisal necessitates that methodological standards be set, and further guidance has been produced to this end. The guidance offers a definition of sustainability appraisal, as 'a systematic and iterative process undertaken during the preparation of a plan or strategy, which identifies and reports on the extent to which the implementation of the plan or strategy would achieve the environmental, economic and social objectives by which sustainable development can be defined, in order that the performance of the strategy and policies is improved'.[10] The approach is essentially objectives based, so that whilst appraisal is to operate independently of strategy making, it is to inform it at key points (rather in the same way that science and policy making should co-exist, as discussed in Chapter 8). Indeed the setting out of objectives has the advantage of putting some flesh on the subjectively slim body cage of the idea of sustainable development: 'The methodology for appraisal ... promotes precision through use of objectives and targets to define sustainable development benchmarks, against which the emerging regional strategy can be iteratively appraised.'[11] Whilst the strategy purports to contain a framework for action, with headline indicators to help measure progress and to inform policy decisions, delivery of integrated commitments, especially across departments, is more problematic. The report to the RCEP referred to above concludes that the RPG sustainability appraisal guidance points to 'the relationship of these targets to national and local objectives which will need to be observed closely in the near future in order to determine how different interests are integrated in the final production of plans. In many areas there needs to be a greater range of targets, with clear strategies for their implementation'.[12]

1.2   Resource and environmental considerations

Whilst the planning system accords formal recognition to decision making at local (and now regional) levels, mandatory national guidance, augmented increasingly by national target setting, is a dominant feature of the system. Planning guidance generally confirms the key role of the planning system in the pursuit of sustainability: 'to enable the provision of homes and buildings, investment and jobs in a way which is consistent with the principles of sustainable development. It needs to be positive in promoting competitiveness while being protective towards the environment and amenity.'[13] Likewise, sustainable development emerges as the expression of commitment to 'a new rural vision' in the rural white paper. It purports to recognise 'the value of the environment as an economic asset to be used sustainably; ensuring development is appropriate and occurs in areas which are able to support it, supporting sustainable best practice through funding, example and guidance'.[14] A sustainable planning framework,

---

8   DETR, PPG11, 2000b, para 2.26.
9   DETR, PPG12, 1999c, paras 4.16–4.21; also DOE, 1993a.
10   DETR, 2000f, para 2.1.
11   DETR, 2000f, para 2.6.
12   Farmer, Skinner, Wilkinson and Bishop, 1999, para 14.7.
13   DoE, PPG1, 1997a, para 1.
14   DETR/MAFF, 2000, para 7.3.6.

in recognition of the public interest role of planning in regulating development and land use, should 'provide for the nation's needs for commercial and industrial development, food production, minerals extraction, new homes and other buildings, while respecting environmental objectives; use already developed areas in the most efficient way'.[15] The guidance goes on to illustrate this by reference to numerous areas, although in some places, as in soil quality and travel minimisation, this appears something of a 'wish list'. These areas are as follows: use of already developed areas in the most efficient way, while making them more attractive places in which to live and work; conservation of both the cultural heritage and natural resources (including wildlife, landscape, water, soil and air quality), taking particular care to safeguard designations of national and international importance; and shaping new development patterns in a way which minimises the need to travel.

Important questions arise, namely, as to what environmental considerations are to be relevant; and as to what criteria will be used to determine prudent use of resources. Guidance on Development Plans sets out considerations which authorities are required to take 'comprehensively and consistently into account (either as policies/proposals or as part of the explanatory memorandum/reasoned justification of plans)'.[16] These range across most policy influences upon the planning process and include the following: improving the physical and natural environment in urban areas, including maintaining the character and vitality of town centres, providing for tree planting and open spaces, and generally revitalising urban areas;[17] conservation of the built and archaeological heritage;[18] landscape quality, conservation of the natural beauty and amenity of the land, including tree and hedgerow protection, and the character and diversity of the countryside and undeveloped coasts;[19] conservation and enhancement of wildlife habitats and species, and the promotion of bio-diversity;[20] waste and mineral extraction, processing and tipping operations;[21] the need to avoid development on unstable land;[22] coastal protection, flood defence, and land drainage issues;[23] energy conservation, global warming, and reduction in greenhouse gases;[24] air quality and pollution;[25] noise and light pollution;[26] and the protection of groundwater resources from contamination or overexploitation.

The commitment to prudent use of natural resources is inevitably more problematic.[27] An overview as to availability of resources is mandated for the explanatory memorandum of a Structure Plan or the reasoned justification of any Local

---

15 DoE, PPG1, 1997a, para 5.
16 DETR, PPG12, 1999c, para 4.4.
17 DETR, PPG3, 2000a; DoE, PPG6, 1996b.
18 DoE, PPG15, 1994b; DoE, PPG16, 1990a.
19 DoE, PPG7, 1997c; DoE, PPG20, 1992.
20 DoE, PPG9, 1994c.
21 DETR, PPG10, 1999b; also, Mineral Planning Guidance Notes.
22 DoE, PPG14, 1990b.
23 DoE, PPG20, 1992.
24 DoE, PPG22, 1993b; DETR, PPG13, 2001a.
25 DoE, PPG23, 1994a; also, DoE, 1997d.
26 DoE, PPG23, 1994a.
27 DETR, PPG12, 1999c, para 4.5.

Plan or Unitary Development Plan. Guidance states that it must include 'an indication of the assumptions made about the resources likely to be available for carrying out the policies and proposals formulated, and for the associated infrastructure. It should have particular regard to the conservation of finite or non-renewable resources such as land and energy, the need for more sustainable development, and the implications for public sector capital expenditure. Assumptions should be in broad terms and should not attempt an unrealistic degree of precision'.[28] Considerations to which the authority must pay regard include the following: the availability and protection of water sources; the need to re-use previously developed sites wherever possible; the protection of the best agricultural land;[29] soil protection;[30] the need to conserve mineral resources, whilst ensuring an adequate supply, encouraging efficient use of materials and recycling of wastes, and prevention of unnecessary sterilisation of areas of high-quality resources by development location decisions.[31]

Planning is a particularly open-ended area of policy, as emphasised with the arrival of a sustainability discourse. Given the broader themes that are the subject of this book, there is no space to devote detailed attention to a full selection of land use planning issues here. The purpose next is therefore to give an indication of certain key issues that must be addressed by the planning process in the broader context of sustainability. Growing concerns amongst scientists over the likely catastrophic consequences for humankind of global warming demand responses through radical changes in the way we live. Pollution from industrial processes is increasingly regulated, as in the UK under the Environmental Protection Act 1990. Nationally and regionally, in particular, wider ranges of instruments are being found to supplement traditional regulatory techniques. As we have seen there are hopes of genuine international progress towards more sustainable activities. What is thus far missing is any genuine commitment to lifestyle changes. As for all solutions, structures are required for translating environmental demands into workable policies set within rational legal frameworks, then for their enforcement, and importantly also for their acceptance. As well as more widespread awareness and understanding of ecological approaches, spatial issues and locality are key factors in seeking sustainable solutions to lifestyle questions.

2 SUSTAINABILITY AND THE NEED FOR SPACE

2.1   Development planning

The planning system has the considerable advantage of being premised on the forward arrangements of the Development Plan process. The strategic response to meeting housing needs is dependent upon the preparation by planning authorities of Development Plans and RPG. Relevant factors must include government household projections, regional economic needs, urban capacity to accommodate more housing,

---

28   DETR, PPG12, 1999c, para 6.28.
29   DoE, PPG7, 1997c.
30   See DETR, Draft Soil Protection Strategy, March 2001.
31   Further guidance is contained in Minerals Planning Guidance Notes.

environmental implications, and infrastructure capacity.[32] Guidance subjects sustainable patterns of housing development to stated criteria. These include concentration of most additional development within urban areas. The assessment of housing capacity is made subject to certain efficiency criteria, recognising that land is 'a finite resource. Urban land and buildings can often be significantly underused. In order to establish how much additional housing can be accommodated within urban areas and therefore how much greenfield land may be needed for development, all local planning authorities should undertake urban housing capacity studies'.[33] Maximising the re-use of previously developed land extends to empty properties and the conversion of non-residential buildings for housing.[34] A presumption of resort first to re-use is, however, subject to failure to meet set criteria on infrastructure or physical and environmental constraints such as contamination, instability or flood risk. Moreover, the government has made it clear that priority must be given to brownfield sites at the development control stage, and that major greenfield developments are not to be given planning permission without the Secretary of State first being given an opportunity to consider whether housing policy guidance has been complied with.[35] This, on the face of it, suggests a less development-friendly centre than in the past.

The new regional framework aims for a greater degree of co-ordination. Co-ordination through both RPGs and Development Plan processes is also expected for the prioritising of diversion of development to previously developed land. Moreover, issue of RPGs by the Secretary of State assumes major significance in setting overall levels of housing provision for 'each region and a distribution to constituent Structure Plan and unitary development plan (UDP) authorities. In preparing Structure Plans and UDPs, authorities must have regard to this guidance and should avoid, wherever possible, re-opening consideration of the level of housing provision for their areas which has been considered in full within the RPG process'.[36] Planning is therefore to become subject to regional recycling targets, set in RPG, with structure planning/UDP and Local Planning Authorities required to adopt land recycling targets in Development Plans.[37] For the purposes of identifying specific sites allocated for housing in plans, authorities are required to operate sequentially. This involves starting with the re-use of previously developed land and buildings within urban areas identified by the urban housing capacity study, then urban extensions, and finally new development around nodes in good public transport corridors.[38]

2.2   Land, market pressures and social needs

Discussion of this topic is dictated by housing provision being perhaps the most basic individual requirement for every individual, and directly and immediately a matter of

---

32 DETR, PPG3, 2000a, paras 4–5.
33 DETR, PPG3, 2000a, para 24.
34 See DETR, PPG3, 2000a, paras 21–22.
35 See DETR, 2000d.
36 DETR, PPG3, 2000a, paras 6–7.
37 DETR, PPG3, 2000a, para 23; Annex C defines previously developed land.
38 DETR, PPG3, 2000a, paras 30–32.

land use. Housing provision is inevitably a prime demand upon the planning system. Moreover, as previously discussed, there is in this area both linkage, and inevitable tension, between economic demands and sustainability. In revised policy guidance, the government explicitly recognises its importance: 'Economic growth should not be frustrated by a lack of homes for those wishing to take up new employment opportunities: but to promote sustainable development, the need for economic growth has to be reconciled with social and environmental considerations, particularly those of conserving and enhancing the quality of our environment in both town and country.'[39]

It is important to recognise that housing provision is now overwhelmingly met by the market. At one level, this makes for a close relationship between developer and development control, which process, for all the support of strategic and local planning, operates as a largely reactive support system. The relationships between planning and the market are complex. Even outside the social sector, discussed below, planning constraints can be significant factors in a burgeoning housing need.[40] A restrictive approach to releasing land for development can reduce development opportunity and also contribute to rising property prices.[41] In carrying out its role, modifying the market to general policy outcomes, the planning system affects the quantity of land available. Opportunities for benefiting from increased development values provide incentives to alter behaviour. It can be argued that planners can use price to influence allocations of land and types of development.[42] More transparent illustrations of this can be seen in respect of planning gain and affordable housing provision.

Current government projections for England for a 20 year period to 2016 are for an increase of around 4.4 million (subsequently revised to 4.1 million) households requiring to be housed, representing an increase of around 23%.[43] The main reason for the increase is a demographic one, not accounted for by population alone. An increase in population of around 7%, or 3.4 million, is expected for the quarter-century 1996–2021, whilst over that same period a growth in the number of households is anticipated from a figure of around 20 million to 24 million.[44] The picture appears complicated by figures available for empty houses. The Empty Homes Agency figures indicate 3.64% of total housing stock in England was empty as at April 1999.[45] Government figures have since confirmed totals of around 355,000 homes in the private sector and 470,000 homes in the social rented sector.[46] Such properties cannot however readily be diverted toward meeting the problem. They are often in areas of low demand or otherwise unpopular, and the overall picture may not respond significantly to possible use of fiscal incentives to encourage fuller use of such properties.[47]

---

39 DETR, PPG3, 2000a, para 3.
40 See Jones and Watkins, 1999, p 97.
41 See Bramley and Watkins, 1996.
42 Monk, Whitehead, Jarvis and Russell, 1999, p 14.
43 DoE, 1996a.
44 DETR, 2000c, para 2.3.
45 Based upon DETR HIP1 returns by local authorities: see www.emptyhomes.com/nstats.htm.
46 DETR, 2000c, p 57.
47 DETR 2000c, p 56.

Moreover, planning in this field is confronted inescapably by underlying influences in the pattern of land use, especially 'housing-led urban dispersal and high levels of owner occupation'.[48] This has traditionally been supported by fiscal benefits such as mortgage interest tax relief, an ostensibly middle class benefit introduced in the Housing Act 1923, which has been now removed. Yet housing needs cannot all be met by the market processes referred to above, for there is a considerable portion of the population that cannot engage in the market. The government accepts that since the 1980s, the UK 'has seen a rise in income inequality almost unique among developed countries. Closing the gap between the poorest communities and the rest is a particular challenge. Around 65 local authority areas in England have high levels of deprivation, many more contain pockets of severe deprivation'.[49] Further pressures arise from a severe backlog in social housing provision, such that some commentators argue that government figures for household needs should be increased to around 5 million.[50] Indeed, housing problems are perhaps dwarfed by the apparently insoluble problem of social housing. Central policies since the 1980s have seen a virtual withdrawal of local government from new housing provision. Following introduction of the right to buy, around 2.7 million homes, representing 30% of council housing stock, were sold off between 1979 and 1997. New building mostly ceased following restrictions from 1980 on housing allocations and freezing of sale receipts (though the latter was lifted in 1997).[51] Remaining council housing provision is still at around 19% in England and Wales, and contains severe pockets of social deprivation for those trapped in 'sink' estates.[52] Social housing needs are increasingly met by registered social landlords, especially housing associations, themselves increasingly reliant upon private funding. For all the improvements in building and estate design, reliance on private capital has also contributed to higher, low-subsidy rent levels. This brings familiar problems, and 'new entrants to housing association properties are increasingly likely to be dependent on welfare benefits: those in work would find the rent commitment an impossible burden. So ultimately, large areas of residential properties are occupied only by those who are economically inactive: unemployment becomes a norm for that area'.[53]

The most obvious concern for planning has been the need to provide for efficient and habitable settlements. Yet the need for planning constraints, as seen above, contributes its own problems in areas of highest demand and greatest pressure on the land resource. The inexorable rise in development pressures on the South East is an endemic problem, and continues a process which commenced well before the Second World War. Employment demand there is expected to increase by as much as 6% by 2006.[54] Likewise, planning restrictions aimed at urban containment have contributed to the pressures on rural localities, where affordable housing opportunities for local people are further prejudiced by inward population movements. Moreover, second homes continue to be assessed to

48 Jones and Watkins, 1999, p 101.
49 UK Government, 1999, para 7.13.
50 Jones and Watkins, 1999, p 103, citing Holmans, 1996.
51 Jones and Watkins, 1999, p 93.
52 Lee, Murie and Marsh, 1995.
53 Kettle and Moran, 1999, p 235.
54 DoE, 1996a; and see Wintour, 2000.

council tax at just 50% of the full rate, which it is estimated by the Rural Housing Trust costs local authorities some £150 million annually in income foregone.[55] The 2000 rural white paper has (surprisingly tentatively) proposed a consultation exercise which may lead to charges at full rates at the option of local councils, and this has been criticised by *inter alios* the Countryside Agency and Rural Housing Trust as a weak response.[56] The planning system is therefore under severe strain in areas of high housing demand.

2.3 Urban land availability

New housing guidance has been described by the government as 'central to our drive for an urban renaissance and its effective implementation by all local authorities is vital'. Certain policies are extremely problematic. For instance, in a section of housing guidance devoted to social issues, not only are authorities required to 'take account of assessments of local housing need in determining the type and size of additional housing for which they should plan', they must also 'encourage the development of mixed and balanced communities'.[57] Despite laudable aims, *inter alia* the tackling of exclusion, there are substantial (and not only tenurial) obstacles in the way of creating such mixed urban communities.[58]

As for location, as well as continued efforts to avoid urban encroachment into rural areas, as seen above, emphasis is now laid upon the re-use of brownfield sites. Site contamination on many sites is a major factor in re-use decisions, and the scale at which clean-up under the contaminated land regulatory regime takes place will influence the pace of release of suitable development land. In 1998 there were around 58,000 hectares of brownfield land in England, either vacant or derelict or otherwise available for development.[59] In an effort to encourage the re-use of brownfield sites, government has combined with the Ordnance Survey, English Partnerships, and local authorities through the Local Government Improvement and Development Agency to produce a new National Land Use Database.[60] Its objective is to give an indication of land availability. A further layer of regeneration strategy is to be introduced, in order to bring brownfield sites back into use. Pilot Urban Regeneration Companies are to be set up, also along public/private sector partnership lines, together with new Local Strategic Partnerships, investing in selected areas where the private sector might be unwilling to tread, following a joint venture between English Partnerships and the Royal Bank of Scotland (Priority Sites Ltd).[61] Four pilots already exist, with an anticipated 12 more to be created annually. The aim of sustainable economic growth however continues to lean more towards the traditional focus on economic regeneration.

---

55 See Hetherington, 2000a; indeed Exmoor National Park Authority has proposed changes to its Local Plan seeking to restrict second home ownership in its area: see, eg, (2001) *The Guardian*, 5 September.
56 See Hetherington, 2000b.
57 DETR, PPG3, 2000a, para 10.
58 See discussion, 'Balanced, mixed or sustainable communities?', in Kettle and Moran, pp 233–35.
59 DETR, 2000c, para 4.29.
60 See www.nlud.org.uk.
61 DETR, 2000c, pp 62–63.

However, the Urban Task Force would have been more radical. It proposed statutory duties to release redundant land and buildings to Regional Development Agencies and local authorities in order to secure locally determined regeneration objectives. Such duties would be placed on public bodies and utilities with significant urban landholdings, extending for instance to the portfolios of the Ministry of Defence and NHS Estates. The report further proposed that vacant land be taxed, in order to deter owners seeking to hold onto land unnecessarily.[62] However, subject to the availability already of compulsory purchase arrangements, the government has stated that it is unwilling to mandate private sector release, and likewise to introduce taxation.[63] Whilst accounting requirements may encourage public sector organisations to dispose of redundant assets, the government response appears to be limited to encouraging local authorities for instance to make use of empty properties.[64]

High urban population levels appear crucial to the process of efficient land recycling. New approaches will increasingly lay emphasis upon the efficiency with which land is developed, including improved building design and the need for high densities. The urban white paper indicates that whilst older suburban densities are at around 35–40 dwellings per hectare, recent housing development is at densities of 25.[65] Planning authorities are accordingly advised to encourage housing development which makes more efficient use of land (at between 30 and 50 dwellings per hectare) and to seek greater density of development around places with good public transport accessibility.[66] Guidance states that plans 'avoid housing development which makes inefficient use of land and provide for more intensive housing development in and around existing centres and close to public transport nodes'.[67] Such policies have received the broad *imprimatur* of the Rogers Committee, suggesting that planning authorities be discouraged from refusing permission on grounds of density and overdevelopment, and that a presumption be applied against excessively low densities for urban development.[68]

A cautionary note should be sounded, however, as such matters remain contentious, and there is every reason to suppose that arguments will find their way into planning appeals. Thus, Ward has recently warned that increasing urban density levels may carry the risk of repeating past failures.[69] Perhaps foremost amongst these have been postwar high-rise housing policies that have recently been reversed.[70] Ward states that in the decades following 1945, 'urban regeneration was design-led. It tore the cities apart', as a result of destruction of housing, rather than improvement, and caused 'enormous disruption, physical and social'.[71] He cites a prescient contemporary warning against the failure to 'realise the strength and the impulse towards the family house and garden as

---

62 Rogers, 1999, Recommendations 61–64.

63 DETR, 2000c, p 148.

64 DETR, 2000c, p 56.

65 DETR 2000c, para 4.15.

66 DETR, PPG3, 2000a, paras 25, 58.

67 DETR, PPG3, 2000a, para 11.

68 Rogers, 1999, Recommendation 3.

69 Ward, 2000.

70 See O'Hagan, 1999, for a fictionalised account of the pressures and consequences.

71 Ward, 2000, p 40.

prosperity increases; they think the suburban trend can be reversed by large-scale multistorey buildings in the downtown districts. This is not merely a pernicious belief from the human point of view, but a delusion ... In a few years, the multistorey method will prove unpopular and will peter out ... Damage will be done to society by the trial ... the damage may amount to a disaster'.[72]

2.4   Extending beyond urban settlements

Responses to the previous generation's land availability pressures had been found after 1945 in the new towns policy, which built upon ideas of the idealist movement and early garden cities such as Letchworth, already referred to in Chapter 4. Indeed, a century ago, Howard's desire for a movement out of the city was partly to improve living standards (and, ironically, at the time also to repopulate rural areas) and partly (as a consequence of lower urban densities) to lower unearned urban site values and so to enable a 'greening' of the city.[73] As has been seen, choices for development of an urban area present the following alternatives: find spare land internally; take land on the urban periphery; rely upon a growth potential of smaller existing centres; or create a cluster of 'new towns'. It will be recalled that a major delimiter on any broad range of solutions is the green belt. Some of the pressures attendant upon these choices, as also the polarisation of debate, were referred to in Chapter 4.[74]

The radical alternative of a new generation of new towns brings further pressures. The new towns idea has a distinguished past, and reference needs to be made to the historic context.[75] The main incarnation of (in the event, 32) new towns was seen over a period of between three and four decades from 1946. Unusually, the process was a public one, and not driven by the private sector. This was accordingly an idea of positive planning, although schemes fell largely outside the planning process, with permissions granted by special development orders. The New Towns Act 1946 had vested designation powers in central government for identification of new town sites and the appointment of development corporations (latterly the Commission for New Towns).[76] These public bodies had wide powers to produce a master plan, develop land, acquire land (including by compulsory purchase), dispose of land and secure funds through borrowings. The legislation enabled the development of new towns, initially from scratch, and latterly by expanding existing large towns.[77] The reasons for the ending of the policy are many, and include a downward slide in population projections (though we have since discovered that these do not accurately correlate with household numbers). Most importantly, however, traditional public support weakened as funding commitments were perceived as denying traditionally distressed conurbations.[78]

---

72   Frederick Osborn, quoted by Ward, 2000, p 40.

73   Howard, 1902.

74   See further Hall, Gracey, Drewett and Thomas, 1973.

75   See further Schaffer, 1970.

76   New Towns Act 1959.

77   Town Development Act 1972.

78   Cullingworth and Nadin, 1997, p 26.

In light of the need for development, and the lack of suitable sites to make a repeat of earlier policy realistic, a new generation of new towns – clustered in sub-regions around existing urban centres – is an alternative to rethinking the scope and role of green belt policy. Pointing to the relative success of the ensuing new towns movement, Ward's proposed solution for today is that new households

> ... should go into new and expanded settlements along viable public transport corridors in the places where people want to live (or have to live, for their jobs). This is where they are going, mainly in the South East. Behind all the rhetoric and posturing about rural values, the planning authorities are working together to accommodate the new households in towns such as Milton Keynes and Ashford, or along the M11 corridor and the Thames gateway extending to Southend. Many of these new growth zones cluster around New Towns like Milton Keynes, Corby, Harlow and Basildon. Indeed, one of the best-kept secrets of social policy is that the postwar New Towns, by comparison with suburban expansion or high-density inner city development, were a social and financial success and were far more economical in land use than any other form of urban expansion.[79]

Policies of urban regeneration were conceived in large part to redress this, but may prove insufficient for the task. Given levels of likely housing need, then, even looking to increased efficiency of land use and urban capacity, considerable development will need to extend beyond urban areas. In considering urban extension, village expansion or new settlement, guidance requires that planning authorities 'utilise the most sustainable option'.[80] Villages are in principle better protected from extension than urban areas. These are required to be by way of infill or otherwise subject to extremely limited criteria.[81] Jones and Watkins conclude that 'the current passive approach will not be able to impose constraints on rural development without high-density development and unacceptable piling-up in some cities, especially those where brownfield sites are now dwindling, and an increase in problems for local country dwellers'.[82] Indeed, Breheny and Hall argue realistically, if apocalyptically, that 50% of projected housing demands must be met by allocation of greenfield sites. These writers echo Ward in suggesting the need for new settlements, together with outward extension of green belts.[83]

Whilst the new towns era is as yet unlikely to return, guidance recognises at least the possibility in principle of new settlements, premised upon significant shortfall in regional housing provision. Such development, whether large-scale additions to existing settlements or free-standing, would be required to meet sustainability criteria, including lack of a more sustainable alternative, sufficient size to support a range of local services, including schools, shops and employment; use of previously developed land; exploitation and improvement of existing or proposed public transport; and use of public transport is encouraged through design and layout, According to the guidance, 'the cost of developing a new community from scratch, including the full range of new services and infrastructure, means that they will only infrequently be a viable option due to their scale and the time required to develop them. New settlements will not be acceptable if they

---

79 Ward, 2000, p 41.
80 DETR, PPG3, 2000a, para 65.
81 DETR, PPG3, 2000a, para 69.
82 Jones and Watkins, 1999, p 102.
83 Breheny and Hall, 1996.

will simply function as a dormitory of an existing larger settlement'.[84] This places a considerable onus on the preparation of Development Plans and RPG. It is hard to believe that new settlement policies could come otherwise than from the centre, given the implications for location of jobs, and the pressures on transport and other public services.

Still the next favoured alternative after urban development is to seek urban extensions. These are stated to be 'likely to prove the next most sustainable option especially where it is possible to utilise existing physical and social infrastructure, there is good access to public transport (or where new public transport provision can be planned into the development), and there is good access to jobs, schools, shopping and leisure facilities'.[85] This may result in depletion of the green belt, and the government, specifically recognising the problem of the leapfrog effect discussed above, accepts that a review of green belt boundaries may be 'the most sustainable of the available options. An extension of an urban area into the green belt may, for example, be preferable to new development taking place on a greenfield in a less sustainable location. Nonetheless, the government regards this as an exceptional policy that should not compromise the objectives for which green belts were designated'.[86] With these alternatives in view, the likely conflict and slow, incremental pace of incursion into the green belt (as well as steep costs) suggest that revised enabling procedures facilitating either such urban extensions or new urban settlements (assuming appropriate locations can be found) may be necessary to meet the scale of the problem. An interesting illustration of the tenacious political hold of the green belt can be seen in the revised planning guidance on transport, referred to below. An annex amends guidance on green belts,[87] with advice on the circumstances where park-and-ride schemes may be acceptable in the green belt.[88]

2.5 Building on flood plains

Any specific illustration of the difficulties caused by the factors of land availability pressures and a system reliant upon private sector development within a negotiated regulatory framework has been the tendency to build on flood plains. Such pressures, alleviated somewhat by local authority acceding generally to Environment Agency objections, continue.[89] To date, there is little relevant policy guidance. For instance, that on housing refers to land permeability in extremely vague terms of greening initiatives which 'can enhance quality, assist the permeability of land for storm drainage and contribute to biodiversity'.[90] Development Plans are often quite inadequate, and would have to be overridden in the light of new specific guidance.[91] The problem has been exacerbated by serious flooding witnessed in 1998 and 2000 – even affecting historic river basin settlements especially in Yorkshire and the Severn Valley – and which most

---

84 DETR, PPG3, 2000a, paras 72–73.
85 DETR, PPG3, 2000a, para 67.
86 DETR, PPG3, 2000a, para 68.
87 DoE, PPG2, 1995b.
88 DETR, PPG13, 2001a, para 62; Annex E.
89 House of Commons Select Committee, 2000b, para 8.
90 See DETR, 2000a, para 52.
91 House of Commons Select Committee, 2000b, paras 25–27.

commentators suggest is linked to global warming. However, this is not the only threat to flood plains. Agriculture, for instance, remains outside planning controls. According to evidence provided by the Council for the Protection of Rural England, 'Extensive ploughing of meadows, land drainage, field enlargement and other land management practices can all significantly increase flood risk'.[92] The contribution of the (former) Ministry of Agriculture Fisheries and Food was witheringly criticised by a Select Committee, citing its exacerbation of the situation through a traditional long-standing availability of grants for land drainage and ploughing up of meadows, and its role in the delay of the application of environmental impact assessment to agriculture: 'It is salutary to consider that a contributory cause of the recent floods may have been the determination of MAFF over many years not to implement the Environmental Impact Assessment Directive. This is a grave condemnation of this Ministry.'[93] Diversion of grant aid towards sustainable agri-environmental schemes mentioned in Chapter 4 could also be used to address this issue. The problem would be further alleviated by the introduction of environmental impact assessments.

The government has for the first time produced planning policy guidance on considerations of flood risk in the development planning and control process.[94] During consultation, the government acceded to demands for a firming up of the guidance. This now emphasises the need for application of the precautionary principle in lessening the risks of flooding, and assessment on the basis of a sequential test, from low- to high-risk areas.[95] There should not be inappropriate development on flood plains, subject to wholly exceptional circumstances. What is described as a balanced, flexible approach should be applied to previously developed land, in recognition of the wider sustainability objectives for brownfield sites.[96] The Select Committee recommended local solutions in light of local considerations, including alternative locations for development, the scope for design solutions, and degree of risk, with a clearer allowance for urban areas protected by flood defences. The tension between laudable aims is an inevitable part of the sustainability process. Indeed the Select Committee pointed out that works associated with diversification and re-use of buildings, such as provision of hard-standing, can increase the risk of flooding.[97] Otherwise, where development is allowed, developers should be required to meet the expense of provision and maintenance of adequate defences, as under planning obligations discussed in Chapter 4 above. Measures such as improved design minimising water run-off will be included. The issue of continued maintenance will in some circumstances be problematic. Despite the guidance being explicitly based upon the precautionary principle and sustainable development, it is recognised that long term maintenance responsibilities will devolve onto the wider local community, at local level or indeed the taxpayer (through, for example, the part-funding of the activities of the Environment Agency). This will be either on the basis of developers having contributed in part to defences or because it is considered appropriate for

---

92 House of Commons Select Committee, 2000b, para 43.
93 House of Commons Select Committee, 2000b, para 44.
94 DTLGR, draft PPG25, 2001, replacing DoE Circular 30/92, *Development and Flood Risk*.
95 See DTLGR, PPG 25, 2001, para 30.
96 DTLGR, PPG25, 2001, paras 55, 35.
97 House of Commons Select Committee, 2000b, paras 25, 46.

defences to vest in the authority, with maintenance contributions capitalised over a longer, say 30 year, period.

3 PROBLEMS OF RURAL HOUSING

3.1 The problem of affordable housing

Despite a traditional reluctance to allow special non-market considerations into the process, especially in view of the risks of legal challenge,[98] affordable housing is now recognised as a material planning consideration to be taken into account in formulating Development Plan policies and in deciding planning applications involving housing. There has nevertheless been criticism of a lack of response in Local Plan provision.[99] An exception to the generally restrictive approach to allowing village development is provided for affordable houses to meet local needs, and to help to secure a mixed and balanced community, and planning authorities are therefore required to 'make sufficient land available either within or adjoining existing villages to enable these local requirements to be met'.[100]

Guidance now provides that in the event of 'a demonstrable lack of affordable housing to meet local needs – as assessed by up-to-date surveys and other information – Local Plans and UDPs should include a policy for seeking affordable housing in suitable housing developments'.[101] The role of RPG (a broader regional context also appears in Regional Housing Statements) and Structure Plans/UDPs is 'to provide advice and information on those factors which local authorities should take into account in preparing their plans, informed by local housing need assessments. This should reflect the particular needs and circumstances of different areas, such as those of low demand for housing and rural areas. Estimates for affordable housing set out in RPG should be regarded as indicative and should not be presented as targets or quotas for local planning authorities to achieve'.[102] Local plan policies for affordable housing should define what the authority considers to be affordable in the local plan; indicate how many affordable homes need to be provided; and identify suitable areas and sites on which affordable housing is to be provided. In turn, underpinning local housing strategies and Local Plan policies, local assessments of housing need, including affordable housing, 'should consider not only the need for new housing but ways in which the existing stock might be better utilised to meet the needs of the community'.[103] This might, as discussed above, involve the use of existing empty houses and conversion of non-residential property.

Given the continuing importance of the private sector in delivery, it is required that development control decisions as to affordable housing 'reflect local housing need and individual site suitability and be a matter for agreement between the parties. Local

98 Kirkwood and Edwards, 1993.
99 See Barlow, Cocks and Parker, 1994.
100 DETR, PPG3, 2000a, paras 70–71.
101 DETR, PPG3, 2000a, para 14.
102 DETR, PPG3, 2000a, para 12.
103 DETR, PPG3, 2000a, paras 15, 13.

Planning Authorities and developers should be reasonably flexible in deciding the types of affordable housing most appropriate to a particular site. The objective should be to ensure that the affordable housing secured will contribute to satisfying local housing needs as demonstrated by a rigorous assessment'.[104] However, there is provision for a stick, whereby a decision by a planning authority that affordable housing should be provided in development of a site, creates 'a presumption that such housing should be provided as part of the proposed development of the site. Failure to apply this policy could justify the refusal of planning permission'.[105] Specific provision is made for visibility of affordable housing decisions. These 'should be transparent and accountable: all parties should know the full basis for planning decisions, including planning obligations agreed in order to make housing proposals acceptable. Therefore ... local planning authorities should ensure that full information about planning obligations involving affordable housing contributions is placed on the statutory planning register'.[106] This feature is set to become more prevalent in developer-planner negotiation, and as discussed in Chapter 4, an extension of greater visibility to planning gain generally is overdue.

3.2   Exception housing

A somewhat hybrid scheme allows 'exception housing' in rural areas.[107] This scheme augments the above policy structure, by enabling a planning authority to grant permission on an exceptional basis. In effect the approach to identification of areas and to meet rural housing requirements, including affordable housing needs, is plan-led. Local Plans and UDPs are required to state whether such a policy exists and how it will be applied. The basis for the exception is that it applies to 'land within or adjoining existing villages which would not normally be released for housing, so as to provide affordable housing to meet local needs in perpetuity'.[108]

The effect therefore is, exceptionally, to allow planning permission for small sites, within and adjoining existing villages, which would otherwise be 'subject to policies of restraint, such as green belt, and which the local plan would not otherwise release for housing'.[109] Legal enforceability to ensure unbroken availability as affordable housing for local needs may be through either planning conditions or planning obligations. Care may need to be taken, however, as past pointers are ambivalent. For instance Cullingworth and Nadin point to an earlier circular on affordable housing,[110] which confined itself to stating that whilst these methods 'cannot normally be used to impose restrictions on tenure, price or ownership ... they can properly be used to restrict the occupation of property to people falling within particular categories of need'.[111] Under the exception

104 DETR, PPG3, 2000a, para 16.
105 DETR, PPG3, 2000a, para 17; see criteria set out in DETR, 1998d, para 10.
106 DETR, PPG3, 2000a, para 20.
107 See Williams, Bell and Russell, 1991.
108 DETR, PPG 3, 2000a, para 18; also Annex B, 'Providing for Rural Exception Housing'.
109 DETR, PPG3, 2000a, Annex B, para 2.
110 DoE, 1991.
111 Cullingworth and Nadin, 1997, p 145.

arrangements, it is explicitly stated however that any 'inclusion of clauses in planning obligations which would enable lenders of private finance to dispose of property on the open market as a last resort if a borrower were to get into financial difficulties, are unacceptable in respect of housing schemes on exception sites'.[112] Further, such clauses should be unnecessary in circumstances of lending to registered social landlords, partly because of statutory safeguards to private lenders.

Due to the exceptional nature of the sites, the usually popular mechanism for market housing, with mixed development allowing cross-subsidy on the same site, are stated to be inappropriate. Whilst this may make political sense, it serves to reinforce the problem of finding suitable land, as well as the nature and impact of the resulting developments. There will be extensive arrangements required for community deliberation, but no identification of sites (or indeed allocation for local needs or affordable housing only) is allowed: 'housing provided on exception sites should be regarded as additional to the provision in the Development Plan.'[113]

4 TRANSPORT ISSUES AND SUSTAINABLE USE OF LAND

4.1 Transport and sustainability

A related, but broader, sustainability issue concerns transport strategies. Transport questions are closely linked with sustainability. Motor car and freight vehicles are significant contributors of the carbon emissions that contribute to global warming,[114] as well as local air pollution levels.[115] There has been significant EC activity in this area,[116] and there are domestic product standard controls for both vehicles and fuel, concerned with issues such as fuel content, emission limits and maintenance tests.[117] However, a system premised upon market growth and insistent upon the importance of private transport for the wider economy has neglected necessary policy adjustments, especially to restrict less essential uses. Reductions can be achieved. By analogy, in discussing the environmental threat of current growth levels in the aviation industry, Grayling has pointed out that growth can be curtailed by targeting the more price-sensitive leisure travel market, and by measures to more accurately reflect the environmental costs of flying, such as noise, air pollution, airport infrastructure, and road and rail links.[118]

The benefits of reducing travel miles, especially in terms of the UK meeting its projected commitments to emissions reductions in the cause of forestalling climate change, are considerable. In view of the major industrial changes undergone by the UK economy in the past two decades, as well as the success of environmental measures in

---

112 DETR, PPG3, 2000a, Annex B, para 6; see further DETR, 1998d, paras 27–29.
113 DETR, PPG3, 2000a, Annex B, para 4.
114 See Adams, 1999.
115 McCarthy, 2000b.
116 Stemming from Directive 70/20, including 99/102, setting limits for emissions from cars and light vans; and 99/52, setting procedures for checking roadworthiness of private cars.
117 See Motor Vehicles (Type Approval) (Great Britain) Regulations 1994 (SI 1994/981); and various Road Vehicle (Construction and Use) Regulations.
118 Grayling, 2000.

bringing about significant reductions in ambient pollution from major installations, the inexorable rise in road traffic emissions has become the greatest cause for environmental concern. The threats posed by fuel emissions bring other threats in their wake, in terms of use of non-renewable resources and threats to human health, especially in urban settings. They also open up debate about policies which have not been success stories in the past: such as the attractiveness and vitality of urban areas as places to live (and even to work and to shop). If problems are caused in large part by a lack of satisfactory public transport facilities, then this failure is exacerbated by the impact of urban migration discussed above. Yet the picture is one in which even central government is constrained. Since the mid-1980s, bus transport has been partially deregulated,[119] and the rail network and operating companies have been privatised according to methods which, especially as regards the former, have seemed on the verge of systems breakdown.[120] Moreover, a so-called taxpayers' revolt in September 2000 led to distinctly non-environmental fiscal concessions on the part of central government.[121]

Transport issues impact upon related policy areas such as housing provision. As seen above, planning guidance is devoted to sustainable residential environments, the criteria for which include the promotion of development linked to public transport. This linkage is required 'in order to reduce the need for travel by car' by reference to siting 'larger housing developments around major nodes along good-quality public transport corridors' and to seeking 'to ensure that all housing developments are accessible by a range of non-car modes'.[122] Moreover, guidance refers to access to public transport as a priority. In this respect the guidance appears more committed to such prioritising than the revised transport guidance which appeared subsequently. Housing guidance states that public transport 'should be used positively to shape the pattern of development: equally, new housing development can be used to make public transport services more viable'.[123] Despite such words, however, and even assuming satisfactory levels of public transport were in place, the success of such a policy approach is dependent also upon provisions to limit other transport uses, especially the car.

4.2   Transport and land use planning

As will have been clear from the earlier discussion, therefore, land use planning can hardly be otherwise than integrally concerned with the question of road traffic movements, and the beneficial effect on air pollution from reduced traffic and free-flowing traffic are generally accepted.[124] Miller's 1999 Report for the Royal Commission on Environmental Pollution has considered the current impact of law on this question in some depth, and concludes that the aim of pollution reduction is at best an incidental factor. He further points to other concerns such as 'accidents, anxiety, intimidation by

---

119 See Transport Act 1986.

120 Hutton, 2000a.

121 (2001) *The Independent*, 22 February.

122 DETR, PPG3, 2000a, para 47.

123 DETR, PPG3, 2000a, para 48; further guidance on identifying the potential of public transport is contained in *Planning for Sustainable Development: Towards Better Practice*, replicated as Annex D to PPG3.

124 See DETR, 1997b, para 1.10.

large or fast vehicles that are out of scale with the surroundings, noise, fumes, vibration, dirt and visual intrusion on a vast scale'.[125] Whilst air pollution issues are material considerations, and most Development Plans do make reference to air pollution, it remains the case that these 'have tended to consist of little more than bland statements of good intent'.[126] Certainly revised planning guidance on transport and planning makes only slight reference to pollution.[127]

In 1994 the Royal Commission on Environmental Pollution recommended that whenever a change of land use generated 'appreciably higher levels of traffic', then application for a new planning permission should be obligatory. Yet no such policy has ever been taken up.[128] However, there are signs of a shift in policy approach under the guidance newly issued. It does generally seek to encourage land use policies and transport programmes which help to reduce growth in the length and number of motorised journeys; encourage alternative means of travel with less environmental impact; and reduce reliance on the private car. Previous policy guidance has aimed to reverse the trend towards out-of-town retail parks. Between 1979 and 1997, 13 million square metres of out-of-town shopping floor space were developed. Policy guidance on town centres and retail developments, recognising the need to avoid pollution in congested town centres and to promote the vitality of town centres, at last produced in response in 1996, and this has recently been strengthened by requiring that there should be no such development if there is an option of developing nearer to a centre.[129]

The revised transport guidance has the aim of improved integration of transport and planning policies, at a local level, with a view to sustainable development and delivery of the government's 10 year transport plan. The objectives are stated to be to integrate planning and transport at the national, regional, strategic and local level, with a view to promoting more sustainable transport choices, promoting accessibility by public transport, walking and cycling to jobs, shopping, leisure facilities and services, and reducing the need to travel, especially by car.[130] The central element appears to be the active management of the pattern of urban growth by integrating transport investment decisions with location decisions on major land uses. Local Planning Authorities will be required to make the fullest use of public transport, and focus major generators of travel demand in city, town and district centres and near to major public transport interchanges. They should ensure that development comprising jobs, shopping, leisure and services offers a realistic choice of access by public transport, especially in urban areas. Indeed, in rural areas, most development for housing, jobs, shopping, leisure and services should be located in local service centres to be designated in the Development Plan to act as focal points for housing, transport and other services.[131] Transport Assessments (replacing Traffic Impact Assessments) are to be required alongside planning applications with significant transport implications.[132] For major proposals, the assessments should

125 Miller, 1999, para 3.4.
126 Miller, 1999, para 3.
127 DETR, PPG13, 2001a, para 66.
128 RCEP, 1994, para 9.66.
129 DoE, PPG6, 1996b.
130 DETR, PPG13, 2001a, para 4.
131 DETR, PPG13, 2001a, para 6.
132 DETR, PPG13, 2001a, para 23.

illustrate access to the site by all transport modes and proposed measures to improve access by public transport.

The Transport Act 2000 required the preparation of Local Transport Plans by Local Highway Authorities, with an integrated transport strategy for each area, with a costed programme of measures to improve local transport over the five years to 2006 (supported by a capital settlement of £8.4 billion). The Act contains enabling provisions for tackling urban congestion, through road charging schemes and workplace parking levies, and these would also be integrated into Transport Plans.[133] The Transport Act 2000 further mandates local submission of Bus Strategies. Under the guidance, planning authorities are required to ensure that Development Plan strategies and the Local Transport Plan complement one another, and that land use allocations and local transport investment and priorities are closely linked.[134] Parking, transport and demand management strategies must be consistent with the overall strategy for planning and transport.[135] Planning policies (including maximum parking restrictions), alongside other planning and transport measures, are to be used to promote sustainable transport choices and reduce reliance on the car for work and other journeys. Sites and routes critical in developing infrastructure to widen transport choices for both passenger and freight movements must be protected.[136] Planning obligations may involve infrastructure improvements such as to the road network in the vicinity of a large development. Planning conditions attached to commercial use developments often limit car parking space. National maximum parking standards apply to developments unless the applicant has demonstrated that a higher level of parking is needed, in which event measures are to minimise the need for parking. The standards will not for the present apply to small developments, and authorities may further loosen the requirements for retail and leisure developments located in town centre or edge of centre sites, where the parking will serve the town centre as a whole.

The major task for the new integrated regime appears to concern the question of changing patterns of transport use. It may be found wanting, in two respects. First, choice remains an important commitment. Thus reference is made to 'reducing the physical separation of key land uses' so as to reduce the need for car journeys, through enabling 'people to make sustainable travel choices'.[137] Moreover, designation for development is not to be 'on the assumption that the car will represent the only realistic means of access for the vast majority of people'.[138] There are already indications of local resistance to road charging schemes. Secondly, a related form of the softly-softly approach, though arguably democratically less justifiable, applies in the case of freight transport. The guidance refers to 'sustainable distribution, including where feasible the movement of freight by rail and water', supported by encouragement of road/rail interchanges and for large freight-generating developments to be served by rail. These may not in most cases be realistic, but there is no further indication as to how necessary transformations in demand are to be managed.[139]

---

133 Transport Act 2000, Part III.
134 DETR, PPG13, 2001a, para 20.
135 DETR, PPG13, 2001a, paras 49–58.
136 DETR, PPG13, 2001a, para 48.
137 DETR, PPG13, 2001a, para 3.
138 DETR, PPG13, 2001a, para 26.
139 DETR, PPG13, 2001a, para 45.

5 A SUSTAINABLE RATIONALE FOR LAND USE PLANNING CONTROL?

5.1 Incorporating sustainable development objectives

Were we starting from here, then the legal framework for land use planning and wider environmental controls might be premised upon an accepted, coherent notion of sustainable development. Indeed, the cynicism which widely prevails in this context, discussed from the outset, pervades in this context also. Sustainable development has, for instance, been described as 'a rallying cry, a demand that environmental issues need to be taken into account; but it provides little guide to action'.[140] Yet, as has been seen above, 'sustainable development' appears to be seeping into the policy consciousness, and revised planning guidance in particular is replete with references to sustainable development. Government, in stating its commitment to the principles of sustainable development, accepts that planning 'and development plans in particular, can make a major contribution to the achievement of the government's objectives for sustainable development'.[141] It further recognises that progress 'can only be made if the various objectives are considered in a holistic way'.[142] Development Plan policies 'should implement the land use planning aspects of sustainable development and must be capable of being addressed through the land use planning system'.[143] It remains unclear how far 'legally enforceable conditions and (planning) obligations can give practical expression to planning's new and broader roles – beyond land use and development control'.[144] If, as Grant has recently argued, the incorporation of policy objectives such as sustainable development has narrowed the range of political options available to planners,[145] then we will have to wait to see how disputes are resolved in the event of challenges to restrictive planning approaches taken upon sustainability grounds.

Yet land use is arguably at the core of sustainability concepts, and the nexus between planning aspirations and those apparent in conceptions of sustainable development should be a relatively close one. Numerous key areas of planning can be said already to have a macro-spatial focus.[146] A good illustration of this lies in the policy relationships between planning and housing, transport, and green belt protection, and some of these have been discussed. But the range of relevant policy areas is much wider, and Millichap points to relevant planning constraints affecting agricultural land, mineral resources, the conservation of the historic built environment, and habitat protection.[147] Moreover, temporal as well as spatial issues lie at the core of land use planning. Writing of the specific context of the well-being of future generations, Macnaghten and Pinfield have argued that planning is well placed to deliver sustainable development which 'now clearly provides the new context for framing public policy on land use and

---

140 Cullingworth and Nadin, 1997, p 165.
141 DETR, PPG12, 1999c, para 4.1.
142 DETR, PPG12, 1999c, para 4.3; see further themes explored in DETR, 1998c.
143 DETR, PPG12, 1999c, para 4.2.
144 Elworthy and Holder, 1997, p 297.
145 RCEP, Seminar, 2000.
146 See Millichap, 1993, pp 112–13.
147 Millichap, 1993, pp 113–18.

environment'.[148] Norton sees land as 'the moral thread that links past, present, and future individuals in a common culture. That culture can be perpetuated only if it respects limits inherent in the land context – for continuity in that land context gives shared meaning to cultures as they unfold through time'.[149]

General planning guidance does include within its key policy objectives commitments to sustainable patterns of development which are more broadly environmental in principle: as in the context of the integration of transport programmes into land use policies, the location of housing, and a refocusing upon town centre development.[150] However, it has been overtaken by more recent revisions in discrete areas, such as housing and transport, and importantly affecting the Development Plan process. This is especially so of the revised guidance for Development Plans, requiring a more strategic view of their role within the planning system, and emphasising the integration of sustainable development issues.

The difficult area of demarcation (and dealing with numerous relevant issues at the planning stage would be a remarkable feat of bottom-up policy making) is dealt with as follows: 'Whilst Development Plans should not contain policies for matters other than the development and use of land (and should not contain policies which duplicate provisions in other legislative regimes, for example in environmental health, building regulation and health and safety legislation) it is important that they have regard to wider sustainable development objectives ... To justify and explain the plan it may be necessary to refer to environmental, economic, social, and other relevant considerations in the explanatory memorandum of a Structure Plan or reasoned justification to a UDP or Local Plan. It may also be appropriate to include references to other local authority strategies, as well as to strategies of other bodies (for example, Regional Development Agencies) where they are relevant in the formulation of a particular land use policy.'[151] The guidance has moreover anticipated greater integration of transport and land use policies, in particular as to procedures and also the relationship with new Local Transport Plans.[152]

Some attempt is therefore made to encourage broad co-ordination in the development planning process. Thus Planning Authorities 'should ensure that interactions between policies are fully considered; that the policies formulated ... form an integrated whole (for example, by forming an overall strategy for a coastal area); and that full account is taken of their environmental, economic and social effects'.[153] The Structure Plan and UDP Part I 'should provide a statement of the overall strategy for development and the use of land in the area within the context of sustainable development objectives ... and indicate how development will be served by transport and other infrastructure. Structure Plan policies should therefore be limited to strategic policies and proposals which provide an appropriate framework for Local Plans and development control'.[154] This is part of a wider process, confirmed in generalised powers granted to local authorities under the

---

148 Macnaghten and Pinfield, 1999, p 17.
149 Norton, 1991, p 219.
150 DoE, PPG1, 1997a, paras 23–27.
151 DETR, PPG12, 1999c, para 3.5.
152 DETR, PPG12, 1999c, chapter 5; also DETR, 1998b.
153 DETR, PPG12, 1999c, para 3.10.
154 DETR, PPG12, 1999c, para 3.9.

Local Government Act 2000, namely 'to do anything which they consider is likely to achieve any one or more of the following objects: (a) the promotion or improvement of the economic well-being of their area; (b) the promotion or improvement of the social well-being of their area; and (c) the promotion or improvement of the environmental well-being of their area'.[155] This is supported by a strategic requirement, whereby each local authority must prepare a 'community strategy' for the purpose of 'promoting or improving the economic, social and environmental well-being of their area and contributing to the achievement of sustainable development in the United Kingdom'.[156] In preparing or modifying such strategies, authorities must 'must consult and seek the participation of such persons as they consider appropriate', as well as have regard to central guidance.[157]

5.2   Sustainability appraisal and strategic environmental assessment

Reference was made earlier in this chapter to the emergence of the notion of 'sustainability appraisal' as part of a strategic approach toward integrating sustainable development into the consideration of strategic options in RPG and Development Plans.[158] Moreover, the usefulness of local initiatives, in accordance with Local Agenda 21 and otherwise, in the production of sustainability plans is widely accepted.[159] Yet there is concern at the value of central government efforts in the crucial areas of integration, co-ordination and implementation of sustainability strategic planning.[160] To this end, Levett has pointed to a lack of outcome criteria for both environmental and social aspects of sustainability, such as explicit sustainability targets and integrative indicators, under the planning regime.[161] There is a need to address broader issues, such as the procedural and institutional arrangements for the setting and apportioning of sustainability targets, along with appraisal of planning policy and guidance. Levett would go still further and suggests two further issues for consideration: namely, the capturing of betterment and planning gain, and consideration as to how to determine the balance between public and private rights.[162] Each of these would be likely to offer considerable challenges to a developer-led system, unsuccessful attempts at a realignment of which were seen in Chapter 4.

Planning guidance now emphasises the contribution of sustainability appraisal towards Development Plan strategies, indicating issues that may be addressed there, either as land use policies or as considerations which influence policies in the plan.[163] Prior to the incorporation of sustainable development objectives in recent strategy documents and policy guidance, land use planning contained few such strategic environmental objectives. Sustainability appraisal is to accord with the broad objectives

---

155 Local Government Act (LGA) 2000, s 2(1).
156 LGA 2000, s 4(1).
157 LGA 2000, s 4(3).
158 Eg DETR, PPG11, 2000b, para 2.26; DETR, PPG12, 1999c, paras 4.16–4.21.
159 Farmer, Skinner, Wilkinson and Bishop, 1999, para 14.8.
160 Farmer, Skinner, Wilkinson and Bishop, 1999, para 14.5.
161 RCEP, Seminar, 2000.
162 RCEP, Seminar, 2000.
163 DETR, PPG12, 1999c, chapter 4.

for sustainable development contained in the 1999 general strategy document, namely: effective protection of the environment and prudent use of natural resources; maintenance of high and stable levels of economic growth and employment; and social progress which recognises the needs of everyone. Moreover, a holistic approach is required, seeking to apply the same methodologies used for environmental appraisal to encompass the other, economic and social, issues.[164]

The underlying principle of an emerging process known as Strategic Environmental Assessment (SEA) is that it concentrates upon plans, programmes and even policies. SEA is an illustration of preventive environmental protection.[165] It therefore extends beyond specific projects, considered in the previous chapter. Just as with project-based assessment, it is essentially concerned with processes. An advantage of SEA is that it therefore offers a procedural means in which to resolve tensions between environment and development interests.[166] In particular, it demands transparency of decision making from an early moment in the decision making process. SEA is of value especially where project assessment is not appropriate, as where problems extend across sectors and across political boundaries. SEA 'enables informed choices to be made, at the earliest decision making levels and when it matters most, as to the relative role different options and development patterns should play within an overall sectoral policy'.[167] Moffatt illustrates the effect by reference to automobile and power plant emissions, advocating SEA as part of a Keynesian approach which would allow 'micro-economic matters to be conducted through market mechanisms whilst broader macro-economic and ecological problems can be managed by political intervention'.[168]

It is unclear how SEA might relate to sustainability appraisal, and there is no reference to SEA in current planning guidance. There are similarities between sustainability appraisal and SEA, for both are objectives based. However, the distinctiveness of SEA is twofold. First, it can incorporate a sustainability-based element within the policy making process itself: 'SEA would require sustainable principles to underlie all policy formulation so that the objectives of a policy would have to be environmentally-led.'[169] Secondly, it introduces participative mechanisms into the process, and indeed from that early stage. This would perhaps be the most radical element of SEA. Revised planning guidance does not increase participative approaches beyond the statutory requirements that apply to the production of plans. Sustainability appraisal does go a considerable way towards introducing detailed objectives and other criteria and may become a process akin to SEA. However, policy formulation by the centre, and its interpretation across a wide range of sectors (even under the broad planning head), does not suggest a commitment to participation from the early stages. Sheate has indeed suggested that there is a danger of losing environmental considerations in sustainability appraisal, as disjointed tiers of government produce complex relationships between sustainable development policies

164 DETR, PPG12, 1999c, para 4.1; DETR, 1998c.
165 See Wathern, 1988, p 207.
166 Therivel, Wilson, Thompson, Heaney and Protchard, 1992.
167 Sheate, 1994, p 153.
168 Moffatt, 1996, p 181.
169 Sheate, 1994, p 172.

and planning. He also cites a need for further links between environmental and planning decision making tools, such as post-project monitoring processes.[170]

It is likely that a form of SEA will soon emerge from the European law making process. Progress towards finalisation of the long-standing proposal for an SEA Directive is awaited.[171] A different dynamic would be put in place once the Directive is adopted.[172] This would require assessment of environmental effects of strategic documents across the range of legislation and administration, once the authority had chosen its preferred option, but before adoption or submission to Parliament. Planning documents would be included, such as Development Plans and planning policy guidance. Its sectoral range would be extensive, including land use planning, industry, agriculture, fisheries, waste, water, transport, energy, and conservation of habitats. Beyond this there will be a discretionary element attaching to plans and programmes that set the framework for future project development consent. A key element in all SEA approaches would be the introduction of participatory features. These would enable input on the part of environmental authorities, citizens and groups (and in cases of transboundary significance, any affected Member State and its public likewise). The effect would be extensive, embracing early scoping as to the shape and extent of the environmental report to be produced and post-adoption information about the decision and the way in which it was made. This will extend to information as to how reasonable alternatives were investigated and reasons for choices made.

SEA would form a part of a range of measures concerned to integrate environmental concerns into planning and policy making. It would therefore need to be understood in the context of integration strategies pursued elsewhere in the European Union as discussed in Chapter 2, as also within individual Member States.[173] It would also go some way towards compliance with obligations set out in the Aarhus Convention. There parties are required to publish facts and analysis as to questions of relevance and importance in framing major environmental policy proposals; and to provide in an appropriate form information on the performance of public functions or the provision of public services relating to the environment by government at all levels.[174] Originally proposed in 1996, the proposed SEA Directive has been contentious. One consequence has been a narrowing of scope. Its purpose has been modified so that policy has been excluded, and it is likely to extend only to assessment of plans and programmes for their environmental consequences during preparation and prior to adoption. This appears to reflect experience in those Member States, such as the Netherlands and Denmark, which have introduced forms of SEA. There, SEA has broadly been applied to sectoral plans and programmes rather than to policy proposals and related law making. The latter processes are considered inappropriate to the types of participative approach demanded by SEA, and reliance instead is placed upon informal, non-statutory, administrative procedures.

---

170 RCEP, Seminar, 2000.
171 See draft Directive, The Assessment of the Effects of Certain Plans and Programmes on the Environment [1997] OJ C129/8.
172 Farmer, Skinner, Wilkinson and Bishop, 1999, para 14.9.
173 Applying Article 6 of the Treaty.
174 United Nations Economic Commission for Europe (UNECE), Convention on Access to Information, Public Participation in Decision-Making and Access to Justice on Environmental Matters 1998, Article 7(a)(c).

Nevertheless, progress has been made towards an agreed form of SEA. A common position was finally agreed by the council in March 2000, and following further Parliamentary amendments a further opinion was produced by the Commission in October 2000.[175] At the time of writing, the text is once again under revision following political agreement in March 2001.

5.3   Balancing processes and sustainability

All planning concerns involve matters of compromise. Regulatory intervention under principles of sustainability has other difficult constituencies to meet, including how far the economy must be planned centrally and what levels of autonomy are to be accorded to localities or regions. The priorities of development and market (indeed, consumer) interests have traditionally dominated planning policy- and decision making. It has generally been the case that a preponderant significance is accorded to the needs of economic growth. Indeed, as Owens points out, sustainability 'rhetoric in planning policy guidance is accompanied by reiteration of the necessity and desirability of economic growth, exhibiting a confusion which will inevitably manifest itself in the planning process'.[176] Indeed emphasis on growth appears unremitting in the revised guidance on Development Plans. In a section headed 'Maintenance of high and stable levels of economic growth and employment', it provides for instance that a key objective is to encourage continued economic development and growth.[177] Thus the planning system is said to be able to 'help create the right conditions in which businesses can thrive and prosper. In preparing Development Plans, local authorities should take account of the need to revitalise and broaden the local economy, the need to stimulate employment opportunities, and the importance of encouraging industrial and commercial development'.[178]

Inevitably sustainability in land use has to balance development against leaving alone. Because of the relative grassroots nature of the planning process, such tensions can arise in circumstances where a central agency is empowered to make the final policy decision. Not only are contentious planning applications more likely to be called in for determination by the Secretary of State, but in the significant cognate area of trunk road development, a separate (traditionally transport-led) regime operates.[179] Moreover, in circumstances where pollution controls are called into question, as discussed in Chapter 7, conflict may arise as between objectors, or even the custodians of the planning process, and those bodies charged with the regulation of environmental pollution.[180] Miller has concluded that 'the planning system is driven by calculations of aggregate utility, with the desires and preferences of third parties, no matter how firmly held, counting for little if they cannot be translated into tangible reasons for negating the presumption in favour of development'.[181]

---

175 See Commission proposal, COM (1999) 73 final; Communication to the European Parliament Concerning the Common Position, SEC (2000) 568 final.

176 Owens, 1994, p 441.

177 DETR, PPG12, 1999c, para 4.7; and see DTI, White Paper, 1998.

178 DETR, PPG12, 1999c, para 4.9.

179 Bryant, 1996.

180 See *Gateshead MBC v Secretary of State for the Environment* [1995] Env LR 37.

181 Miller, 1998, p 71.

A gap in any event remains between the potentially powerful impact of planning processes on sustainable development and a central ethos which has in recent years pursued a largely deregulatory agenda, looking for outright sale, or latterly public-private partnerships, in respect of erstwhile 'public' utilities.[182] This has led to widespread scepticism as to what governments can achieve, and to increasingly opaque accountability structures. Meanwhile, governments face considerable political obstacles in looking beyond the next election. An incident of this is the obsession of utility regulatory arrangements with pricing, thus meeting perceived consumer demands, rather than delivering on questions such as resource conservation.[183] This, together with the universal political perception that it is the state of the economy that wins elections (a remarkable exception to this appears to have been the Bush-Gore US presidential election in November 2000), suggests that proactive planning policies will face central intransigence (on both Development Plan approvals and planning determinations and appeals).

Unsurprisingly, movement toward specific recognition of sustainability considerations, such as carrying capacity, has been slow. Given the traditionally somewhat restricted role for planning, privileging economic activities and narrowing the environmental (at times even the planning) agenda, it would be hard to disagree when Owens cautions against overstating the role of planning as an instrument of environmental policy: 'planning is contained within, and constrained by, economic and political forces and priorities on a wider stage.'[184] These constraints have been supported by restrictive judicial interpretations of for instance planning purposes. Moreover, given the mixed messages from higher echelons of the political hierarchies, inured obstacles at planning authority level should not be underestimated. For instance, whilst pointing to the 'enhanced purpose and credibility' given by the sustainable development concept to the planning system, Macdonald and Heaney accept that 'the planning profession's interpretation of sustainable development is narrow, still focused on economic development as opposed to environmental and social impacts'.[185] If this is so, then it should be no cause for surprise, given the limitations built into the planning role, by reference to industrial, agricultural and transport activities.[186]

In contrast, sustainability principles, as Owens has pointed out, 'challenge the presumption in favour of development and sit uneasily with the utilitarian ethos of "balance" that has dominated planning decisions'.[187] It might therefore be inappropriate to speak of balancing factors, as the emphasis should lean the other way. This suggests a need to develop an alternative ethical basis, especially for the problem of defining 'critical natural capital', of the sort discussed in earlier chapters. Owens suggests that the process of defining sustainability will expose conflict more starkly and at an earlier stage in the planning process. This will require legal resolution in due course as developers would challenge the inevitable loss of development rights.

---

182 Despite a partial rearguard action under EC law, as in the principle of emanations of the State: see
   Foster v British Gas plc [1990] ECR I-3313; *Gibbons v South West Water* [1995] IRLR 15.

183 See Jenkins, 1995.

184 Owens, 1994, p 440.

185 Macdonald and Heaney, 1999, p 40.

186 Hall, Hebbert and Lusser, 1993, p 20.

187 Owens, 1994, p 440.

5.4   Towards a sustainable agenda for planning

It remains to be seen whether 'sustainability' provides a new alchemy, ensuring new resolutions of resource issues such as carrying capacity and a reordering of value systems, or proves unable to influence existing power constraints in any meaningful way. Tensions between traditional planning approaches and a sustainability rationale require resolution. These have been illustrated as follows: 'Most fundamental are issues of definition concerning whether a "deep green" preservationist, "techno-green" technical fix or "shallow green" growth-based strategy are employed. Further, as a consensus-building exercise on the need to tackle global environmental issues sustainability, has been spectacularly successful – but this masks the difficult choices that will and are emerging, such as the balance between environmental protection and economic growth. Planning practice has been ill-equipped to deal with these issues – can a Local Plan effectively resolve issues of jobs and environmental protection? If brownfield development is now the priority, how will developers be encouraged to re-use land and who will pick up the costs of restoration?'[188]

The wider problem, however, as seen throughout this book, also lies in ourselves. As will be seen in Chapter 10, both politicians and citizens together resolutely aspire to the short term. There may be signs of a readiness to commence educative processes, or at least a broader debate. For instance, the government apparently intends to further revise general planning guidance in order to explain ways to plan for sustainable communities in the context of economic, social and environmental demands.[189] Community strategies referred to above will supplement this process. But guidance persists in the vindication of the status quo of choice. For instance, the commitment to the principle of improved integration contained in the revised Development Plan guidance is stated to be 'a key element in supporting more sustainable travel choices and in reducing the need to travel'.[190] Much depends both on investment towards sustainable choices and also on finding democratic formulae for setting out just how hard (by current perceptions) such choices are.

There are, however, recent wider trends that may create a constituency eventually to mobilise disparate pressures for change. For instance, whilst not especially sanguine, Davoudi is able to point to the risk society, as discussed in Chapter 8, which either fears or witnesses the unintended consequences of scientific and technological development. This contributes to a wider crisis in democracy, as seen in growing cultural and environmental concerns and reduced trust in politicians and other authorities. At a more local level, this manifests itself in concern at the erosion of local identities, through both globalisation and environmental degradation. Here, Davoudi categorises 'what is often maliciously called NIMBYism ... (but, rather) an increasing distrust of the capacity of expert systems and government institutions in managing the risks involved'.[191] These considerations suggest a need for planning arrangements to reinterpret the balancing debate referred to above by seeking means to introduce ecological perspectives, including

---

188 Allmendinger and Chapman, 1999, p 8.
189 DETR, 2000c, para 4.26.
190 DETR, PPG12, 1999c, para 5.1.
191 Davoudi, 2000, p 132; see further Giddens, 1998.

greater reflexivity towards environmental risk. The increased recognition of sustainability as a factor in the formal or technocratic sense (of objectives, targets and indicators) needs to be augmented with progress by reference to more normative sustainable criteria, such as carrying capacities and critical natural capital.

A deeper commitment to sustainability demands a considerable change of ethos, changing the dynamics of both institutional constraints and legal approaches to rights and obligations inherent in the processes discussed in this and preceding chapters.[192] If not quite a return to visionary approaches, progress towards a sustainable agenda requires an adjustment of priorities at work in the planning process, as in the interpretation and implementation of determined objectives, standards and indicators.[193] Yet it is strongly arguable that the conceptual framework in place is sufficient to enable sustainability priorities to play a fuller role.[194] Healey and Shaw categorise such an adjustment as one towards 'a regulatory regime which focuses explicitly and specifically on assessing and mitigating the adverse impacts of development projects within a framework of precautionary limits informed by an argumentative approach to planning debate allowing both technical and moral/aesthetic issues to be discussed in an open, democratic way'.[195] They conclude that the impact on the planning system 'could be to encourage not a reinforcement of traditional strategies and policies but a fundamental rethinking of the form and content of the system in terms of conceptions, technical methods and policy processes ... (which) could also lead to significant institutional changes, to allow, for example, intersectoral co-ordination and a stronger emphasis on regional strategy'.[196]

Proposals can be made, all on recognisable legal territory, being substantive and procedural in nature. Procedural suggestions are inevitably more readily comprehensible. First, by reference to rethinking public-private relationships, the balance inherent in the liberal economic prioritisation underlying the discretionary nature of administrative decision making should be adjusted. The law has perhaps failed in such a task, as evidenced by problems in conceptualising the type of public interest challenges required and indeed (without a push) in satisfactorily accommodating environmental considerations at all. More purposive interpretations are required, and could be accommodated within the broader jurisdictional remit for an Environmental Court considered in Chapter 10. Secondly, applying McAuslan's radical typology once again, as seen in numerous themes discussed above, including most especially SEA, it becomes necessary to look to more coherent participative processes. The rationale for further participation has been succinctly justified as follows: 'legalized argumentation, like economic reasoning is reductionist in its treatment of the diverse concerns people have about environmental issues. This suggests that the development of discursive, communicative approaches to exploring the form and content of Development Plans is more likely to reflect the breadth of contemporary understanding of environmental issues

---

192 See Barry, 1999, pp 129–37.
193 Blowers, 1997.
194 See Rowan-Robinson, Ross and Walton, 1995.
195 Healey and Shaw, 1994, p 435.
196 Healey and Shaw, 1994, p 436.

than the calculative approaches being addressed by government.'[197] Thirdly, and in support of the previous measures, consideration should be given to according rights of challenge to planning decisions to third parties, beyond the current restrictions of applications for judicial review. This, it is argued, 'would create pressures to encourage broadly based consensus-building around the dilemmas of combining economic development and environmental objectives'.[198]

In substantive terms, first, there should be an insistence upon greater specificity as to recurrent sustainability issues in development planning and control processes. Following the 1999 sustainability strategy document, central guidance is now producing more detailed advice and specification as to policy criteria. This is feeding relevant sustainability issues into planning consideration at both regional and local levels. Secondly, the view of planning as a process needs to be broadened. This would extend, for example, to the introduction of planning aftercare in terms of monitoring and continued control. An analogy can be drawn with the handling of the 2001 Foot and Mouth disease crisis. Here, conflict arose between environmental landfill operators and the government that sought to augment an overstretched incineration policy by requiring the disposal of cattle carcasses by burial. Although the landfill industry pointed to BSE rules otherwise requiring the destruction by incineration of cattle over 30 months old, and notwithstanding its view that there was no risk to human health, the government held out against providing any indemnity against liability in the event against spread of infection.[199] In the planning sector, aftercare requirements might contribute to the satisfactory resolution of problems concerning unwanted or redundant activities and installations. The nature of powers that this would require would need clear setting out, but such a reform would address the once and for all nature of the operation of the planning system. It might also meet a criticism of the present system that it leads to inappropriate trade-offs between environmental assets and economic gains from development. For instance, an idea of 'developer obligations' has been suggested, whereby a specific requirement would arise for the replacement of, or compensation for, 'lost assets, according to their significance'.[200]

Thirdly, sustainable notions need to be upgraded within the process, for instance through requirements to maintain and enhance the carrying capacity of ecosystems or a general requirement of environmental care.[201] If this is somewhat generalised, then, more assertively, 'true sustainability indicators' have been proposed. The rationale underlying the proposal is the need for widespread acceptance of a fundamental reordering of priorities. This has been referred to as a recognition that 'there is no free lunch. Planning as a tool can and must be central to sustainability. Current planning practices and techniques can be developed to enable this. But for this to happen, planning as a value must be re-established. This implies a need for a fundamental rethink of the relationship between public and private interests. Planning cannot deliver sustainability, or even halt many anti-sustainable trends so long as it is construed and operated as a reactive tool to

---

197 Healey and Shaw, 1994, p 435; also, Sager, 1994.
198 Healey and Shaw, 1994, p 435.
199 Reported in *The Guardian*, 18 April 2001.
200 See UK Round Table on Sustainable Development, 2000c, pp 10–12.
201 Healey and Shaw, 1994; also, Macnaghten and Pinfield, 1999, pp 31–32.

limit and redirect certain categories of private decision, and where every intervention in them has to be justified as an exceptional trespass on private rights'.[202] Cultural indications of an unwillingness to truly engage with these issues are everywhere. For instance the UK Round Table on Sustainable Development voiced concerns at a lack of integration between land use plans and public investment policies. For instance, decisions in principle on public funding for infrastructure projects appear to pre-empt planning decision making. Likewise, a number of new hospitals have been developed on greenfield sites, often as part of the Private Finance Initiative.[203] The position even today is of a regulatory salami slicing effect, and it seems that a *sine qua non* for many of the changes considered above must be the introduction of an effective regime of strategic environmental assessment.

As has been seen above, land use planning policies can do much to allay the unnecessary environmental degradation associated with development. They should accordingly play a central role in determining the terms of acceptable location of major traffic-generating uses. Planners may even be empowered to seek beneficial environmental consequences upon a proactive basis, in collaboration with other regulators and representatives from all sides of the community. For instance, they can afford opportunities for activities on a localised basis. The full potential for securing sustainable patterns of development demands not only increased specificity as to what sustainability requires, discussed above, but also a prioritising as against other policy demands (such as ruling perceptions of global free trade). This demands that substantial responses, upon an integrated basis, need to be delivered. An OECD report discussed land use planning in the context of transport and traffic demands in urban areas in 1995, and concluded as follows: 'People and firms do what is best for themselves and not necessarily what is best for the city, the country or even the planet. Everyone optimising one's own situation does not automatically lead to an overall optimum – this has to be reached by careful land use management and a knowledge of how people respond to changing conditions. Policy makers should therefore try to ensure through a variety of measures, including regulatory and economic instruments, that the rational responses of travellers, residents and firms are compatible with those which lead to more sustainable patterns of development.'[204]

As in other contexts referred to in this chapter, profound questions as to culture and behavioural change lie at the core of the problem of whether real progress can be made towards sustainable development. It is essential that the land use planning regime is able to engage with the questions of choice and lifestyle that are crucial to this process. Yet even then, land use planning is but one of a mass of cognate regulatory schemes which are likely to persist through even deregulatory eras. Institutional problems of inter-agency relationship and conflict inevitably arise, and it is to the implications of this that attention now turns.

---

202 CAG Consultants, 1999, para 5.47.
203 UK Round Table on Sustainable Development, 2000c, pp 12–13.
204 OECD/European Conference of Ministers of Transport, 1995, p 19.

CHAPTER 7

THE RELATIONSHIP BETWEEN SEPARATE REGULATORY REGIMES

> Coketown ... where Nature was as strongly bricked out as killing airs and gases were bricked in ... had come into existence piecemeal, every piece in a violent hurry for some man's purpose, and the whole an unnatural family, shouldering, and trampling, and pressing one another to death.[1]

The objective underlying this chapter is to offer a discussion of key interactions between land use planning and environmental controls. These relationships are essential to the sustainability debate. We live, as stated above, at a time of specialist, indeed multiplicitous, regulation. Although the era of increased environmental concerns and legal control structures has grown independently of the land use planning regime, it is necessary to recognise and clarify the nature and scale of impacts upon planning law. This chapter therefore tackles the question of the role of planning in view of the wider regulatory context. The focus provided in previous chapters is however retained. It is beyond the scope of this book to chart the burgeoning areas of regulatory responses to environmental threats, whether on a media-by-media basis or in more integrated forms. For this purpose, the reader is referred to English environmental law texts such as Bell and McGillivray, and likewise Miller's excellent analysis of the scope of environmental 'rights'.[2]

1 RECONCILING REGULATORY OBJECTIVES

1.1   Planning as enabler and constraint

Referring once again to the land use planning system, it can be said that its hallmark in principle lies in its anticipatory role: as a process of preventive control. This encompasses not only the more strategic role at work in the preparation of Development Plans, but also the operational system of development control. Yet, as has been seen in the preceding chapters, given the commercial dynamics of the property development industry in the UK, the role of planning authorities is also a reactive one in terms of the generation of appropriate development. Thereafter, upon any grant of permission 'the only practical continuing control exercised is when conditions have been attached to the grant'.[3] There are therefore numerous ways in which permitted development affects the environment, as for instance, in 'the scale of development, its location, design, interaction with neighbouring land uses, and in its use of resources (for example, use of raw materials in construction, water, production processes, etc) and its output of waste and other emissions (during both construction and operation)'.[4]

---

1   Dickens, from *Hard Times*, 1854, 1989 edn, p 83.
2   Miller, 1998.
3   Purdue, 1999, p 585.
4   Land Use Consultants, 1999, para 4.3.

There has been a process of considerable assimilation of environmental matters into a variety of regulatory regimes. Some commentators go so far as to suggest a primacy for environmental considerations. Thus procedures can be said to shift the onus away, from one of grant of permission 'unless there are good reasons for refusal' to one where 'the developer's proposals have to be demonstrably acceptable, and permission can be refused if they are not. Though official pronouncements and advice are coy in acknowledging this, it is clear that environmental factors can be decisive in a planning decision and that applicants may even be required to discuss the merits of alternative sites'.[5] Given the pervasiveness of notions such as sustainability, any such trend is likely to intensify. This therefore suggests a more generally extended remit for planning, beyond the more obvious circumstances of environmental impact assessment, discussed in Chapter 5, as environmental issues have penetrated into the planning lexicon.

However, a cautionary note should be struck, in two respects. First, the broad range of factors to be taken into account in determining planning applications may not, taken together, be conducive to meeting environmental needs. Matters of policy broadly in the 'public interest' are generally mapped out in discussions *inter partes* by planners and developers. Issues raised for instance in the context of planning gain, as discussed in Chapter 4, are not necessarily of an environmental nature, and moreover the purpose is primarily compensatory.[6] A report produced to the Royal Commission on Environmental Pollution has criticised this consequence, on grounds that development decisions can be based upon potential compensation rather than acceptability according to agreed sustainability criteria: 'Where developments with negative impacts are approved, mitigation and/or replacement of lost assets must be openly agreed; some assets should remain non-negotiable.'[7] That said, the process can be diverted towards securing environmental improvements, as where a development site is contaminated, the authority might justifiably seek extra clean-up (beyond the criteria set under the regime under Part IIA EPA 1990), or even indeed clean-up elsewhere. At present, however, as already seen, how far guidance on planning gain enables such wider benefits is unclear. The report referred to above duly concluded that it is necessary to counter the fact that 'planning legislation provides little leverage in securing financial investment from developers into environmental initiatives, as a means of recompense for environmental damage caused', and endorsed the recommendation of the Urban Task Force Report that guidance should enable 'revenue expenditure contributions to help improve the quality and management of the urban environment'.[8]

Secondly, in circumstances where another regulatory body has responsibilities towards an activity or process, demarcation issues arise. As a 'front line' regulator, it is essential that the local planning authority is clear as to the extent of its powers in determining applications for development. This aspect is considered further below.

---

5   Cullingworth and Nadin, 1997, p 163.
6   Healey, Purdue and Ennis, 1995.
7   Land Use Consultants, 1999, para 4.73.
8   Land Use Consultants, 1999, para 4.71.

1.2   Environmental objectives and diffuse regulatory mechanisms

Since July 1999, an important review has been conducted by the Royal Commission on Environmental Pollution as to whether current arrangements for environmental planning are capable of achieving necessary environmental policy objectives. It is to consider whether radical reform of planning systems would help to deliver more effective, accountable and transparent environmental protection with a view to achieving sustainable development. The current land use planning system is rightly perceived as central to the investigation, as also other relevant regimes, such as pollution control, air quality, waste, water, agri-environment and bio-diversity, and especially the interactions between them. The study has concentrated upon five main themes, concerning environmental sustainability, boundaries, integration or co-ordination between regulatory functions, subsidiarity and democracy, and approaches to assessment.[9] It is worth briefly recounting the main features of these themes.

First, as to sustainability, the review will seek to identify the extent to which current environmental planning systems promote or prejudice environmental sustainability. Such an investigation must therefore address endemic problems considered in earlier chapters, and to recur especially in Chapter 8, namely the extent to which environmental objectives can, or should be, balanced against those of an economic or social nature. In addition, the reactive nature of planning systems must be scrutinised, as for instance, how far the present plan-led system has moved away from what remains an effective presumption in favour of development (provided that an application is in accord with the Development Plan). Furthermore, there have been changes in terminology, from, say, predict and provide to plan, monitor and manage, which appear inapposite in the face of more pressing practical difficulties, such as the need for extensive new residential building programmes previously discussed. Likewise, the planning structure, for the greater part embedded in its locational roots, is subject to pressures (whether for or against development) that are often far removed from environmental priorities. This can be seen in connection with the opposition to waste treatment facilities, and even to attempts to rethink waste strategy, referred to below.

There are further difficulties in imposing positive planning measures. It may for instance be difficult to exercise control over the cumulative impacts of discrete projects, even although Development Plans are required to identify where further development is constrained by the cumulative effect of existing and future polluting uses of land.[10] Permission is also generally of a once-and-for-all nature, with a lack of any real conditionality as to subsequent monitoring and review of a permitted use. This is not unexceptionable, for where a proposed source of pollution would not require a pollution control permit, 'local planning authorities might, in some circumstances, consider adding conditions to the planning permission, to tackle the source's possible effect on land use or amenity. These conditions might require a scheme of monitoring and mitigation, covering planning concerns to be approved by local planning authorities before the development went ahead'.[11] Generally, however, it is unsurprising that, as will be seen below, planning

---

9   RCEP, news release, 11 April 2000.
10   DoE, PPG23, 1994a, para 2.12.
11   DETR, Guidance, *Air Quality and Land Use Planning*, LAQM G4(00), para 20.

has little room for manoeuvre in addressing potential pollution consequential upon development. This is so, as to both point source industrial emissions (which are generally regulated by other bodies) and more diffuse threats, such as to air quality due to traffic (which are regulated hardly at all). The system inevitably has difficulty engaging in questions posed by longer-term risks from such by-products of human activities as production of waste and global warming.

The second theme concerns boundaries, which the Royal Commission has translated into a question as to whether current division of administrative units and between policy areas is conducive to environmental sustainability. The ramifications of such a debate are extremely broad, especially as there was no shared objective at work when boundaries were delineated and responsibilities handed out. From the land use planning perspective, there are important questions as to the effectiveness in assisting toward meeting policy targets in such crucial environmental fields as transport, fossil fuel use and climate change. Indeed the Commission produced a report on energy sources and use during 2000, which warned *inter alia* that persistent trends in energy use render achievement of scientifically prudent emission reductions over the next half century greatly problematic.[12] There are more localised boundary areas also, such as nature conservation, linking development to sustainable water provision, and flood protection, especially in the context of river and coastal flood plain development. This may also be affected by agriculture, and more generally this is a major gap in the planning scheme, which requires rethinking especially in the light of the pollution threats posed by modern industrial farming processes.

The question of boundaries is closely related to a third theme, introduced earlier in this section, concerning the relationship between planning and pollution control. The separate nature of the systems can lead potentially to duplication and uncertainty. One especial point of intersection which has not been made, save through the required consultative process, is that of environmental impact assessment. As seen in Chapter 5, this is a part of the planning process, even where a separate assessment process conducted under pollution control for industrial emissions applies. Indeed, although the linkages are not drawn with high definition, guidance does expect that environmental statements 'should include broadly similar information to an application for Integrated Pollution Control authorisation'.[13] Generally, the planning system also relies upon the efficiency by which the Environment Agency, as pollution regulator, is able to respond to consultation. Increased integration, especially between planning and pollution control, would affect strategic planning mechanisms as well as control processes. There are further systemic differences between the regimes in terms of the amount of participation they allow in the process, and the possibilities accorded under the planning regime, charted in Chapter 4, are not replicated in the generally more technical approaches to environmental regulation. This may become a larger issue as wider means of securing environmental objectives are found outside regulatory regimes, as through economic instruments: for instance, encouraging the viability of development of brownfield sites, in 2001 a 150% accelerated payable tax credit was introduced for owners and investors who incur clean-up costs. Further examples of non-regulatory approaches are (inevitably)

---

12   RCEP, 2000.
13   DETR Guidance, *Air Quality and Land Use Planning*, LAQM G4(00), para 19.

forms of self-regulation, which may be supplemented by opportunities for voluntary environmental agreements.

If stakeholding is of its nature participative, then the question of participation is likewise inherent in the fourth theme, of subsidiarity – delivering decisions at the lowest level consistent with achieving the common welfare – and democracy. The delivery of national policy targets may well be in tension with ensuring adequate local accountability, as well as perceived local interests. Local planning regimes can conversely prejudice national targets. Indeed, contrary to the principle of subsidiarity, strategic decisions on such matters as transport are for 'decision making at the highest level of government. It is quite inimical to the concept of local democracy or devolved government. The very serious impact these questions have upon public expenditure, the deployment of natural resources, land use and land management can only be handled centrally by government ministers'.[14] The current development of a regional planning base may provide solutions to some of the inevitable pressures, for all that questions of accountability – far from resolved even nationally given the limited reform thus far of the House of Lords – remain to be resolved. Moreover, these are a part of broader questions introduced from the first in Chapter 1: for environmental issues cannot be confined within the arbitrary boundaries of local, regional or even national frameworks, but must be viewed in the context of transnational threats and international law commitments. This creates dilemmas for not only appropriate levels of decision making but also for effective and inclusive ways to involve the wider community in the process.

Questions of accountability and transparency inevitably arise in considering all sides of the process. Thus it is important to consider the stages, if any, at which it is appropriate that the decision making apparatus, informed by scientists and other technical experts, be required to take account of public representations within a transparent process. Participation can be factored into processes in a number of ways. Thus informal focus groups are increasingly used by political researchers, although traditionally in planning more formal rights to consultation exist. These contributions may be direct (as in planning inquiry) or indirect (as introduced for RPG). The benefits of public involvement can lead to greater public acceptance, an especially important matter where issues of environmental justice arise. Moreover, in terms of ensuring sustainability, the identification of the citizen with difficult environmental dilemmas and to their resolution is essential to the process. The participation of the citizen may be more effective in land use planning than in pollution regulation, but there are gaps, as already discussed in Chapter 4. In particular, there are limits on access to justice, not only as to cost but also most noticeably in the lack of a statutory third party right of appeal against planning determinations. As already seen, many of the above issues might be solved by the creation of a specialist Environmental Court, and further consideration of this topic is deferred until Chapter 10.

The fifth theme, that of approaches to assessment, is a technical one, though central to the success of the idea of environmental constraints, and concerns the ability of regulators to carry out necessary appraisal, as well as appropriate assessment methodologies. These questions relate to the various regulatory functions, including requirements for the production of environmental plans and the assessment of their environmental impacts. It

14   Wood, 1995, p 71.

is necessary to consider how universal environmental assessment should be, and the level of detail required. The very balancing process is problematic, as seen previously, and this is especially so where environmental values may be regarded as non-negotiable, so that mitigation arrangements may not lead to sustainable solutions. Likewise health impacts are seldom enunciated in areas of planning policy, despite the growing evidence of the detriment in terms of health costs and accelerated deaths for vulnerable people.[15] Nevertheless, there are a range of species of assessment tools, such as sustainability appraisal, already a requisite contributory part of Development Plans and RPG. Other bases include those upon the valuation of environmental benefits foregone through notions of environmental capital. Related to this, ecological footprinting offers a radical sustainability indicator, through the calculation of what is required to sustain current levels of resource and energy consumption. Although this has not been introduced into the UK's Sustainability Strategy, it has been announced that it is to be included in the Welsh Assembly's action plan for future policy appraisals.[16]

1.3   Air quality and land use regulation

The final parts of this section contain a review of the kind of limitations under which a land use planning regime is required to operate in respect of potential conflict between development and environmental consequences. The areas of air quality and waste control have been selected for explanatory purposes. Then, for completeness, the section closes with a consideration of judicial approaches to resolving disputes which have arisen between regulators concerned respectively with highways control and planning.

With an eye to the relationship between planning and air quality, it has to be said that this has been relevant, where at all, on a largely indirect basis. A fundamental limitation is that land use planning is not concerned with challenging ruling patterns of production and consumption.[17] This arguably reflects a planning system forced into a narrow understanding of land use, as with policy formulation reliant upon predict-and-provide techniques, especially where national targets drive the planning process to the detriment of local consultation and decision making and lock local authorities into unsustainable patterns of development.[18] There has traditionally been a lack of policy integration in the context of air quality, with little role for land use planning in securing reductions in air pollution, save through location policies and allocating space to different types of transport.[19]

There was discussion of the relationships between transport and land use planning in Chapter 6. Any consideration by public agencies of related issues must be seen against the seemingly inexorable growth in private transport.[20] Apart from the implications for global warming, traffic is recognised as perhaps the most significant threat to air

15   Laurance, 2000.
16   ENDS Report 314, March 2001, pp 40–41.
17   Hine, 1999, pp 166–67.
18   Farmer, Skinner, Wilkinson and Bishop, 1999, paras 4.28–4.30.
19   Hine, 1999, pp 151–52.
20   See, eg, RCEP, 1994.

quality.[21] Technological improvements, such as design changes to vehicles, increases in fuel efficiency and future advances towards alternative hydrogen fuel cells, may limit the extent of pollution and in the longer term even alter trends.[22] Yet, as the recent fuel price 'crisis' in the UK has shown, little of substance has been achieved in the UK since the oil crisis in the mid-1970s to shift transport use patterns away from reliance upon oil. Anticipation of technical fixes still appear inappropriate in this context, and Roszak has described technological optimism as 'the snake oil of urban industrialism'.[23]

The control of air pollution, according to Bell and McGillivray, has been 'the classic example of the use of reactive legal controls to regulate specific problems as they arise. Policy approaches had hitherto been sparse and incoherent. Although the legal controls had been modernised and broadened, it was only in the 1990s that a coherent strategy was developed to deal with the problem of atmospheric pollution', and indeed it was only in 1995 that 'the first steps were taken towards a coherent air quality management system'.[24] A regulatory scheme imposes operational controls upon an extended range of industrial activities. Integrated Pollution Control regulation, originally contained in Part I of the Environmental Protection Act 1990, transposed the requirements of numerous European Directives concerning industrial emissions.[25] This has been superseded by Integrated Pollution Prevention and Control under the Pollution Prevention and Control 1999 Act, which is being phased in upon a sectoral basis up to 2001.[26] Control is premised upon the regulation of prescribed processes by prior authorisation.[27] The basis of control is that prescribed activities and processes are made subject to standards in order to limit the emission of harmful pollutants into the atmosphere, as also to land and water, in accord with the principle of Best Available Techniques. These integrated controls are now being extended to cover energy use, waste reduction and site restoration. Regulation of polluting processes is the responsibility of either the Environment Agency or local authorities.[28] A related regime, applying to less polluting processes, and focusing on emissions to air, falls under Local Air Pollution Prevention and Control, administered by local authorities.[29] In contrast with traffic emissions, technological developments have enabled significant reductions in air pollution from industry, with increasingly stringent demands being set. Miller for instance has stated that even waste incinerators, regulated increasingly through requirements for arrestment equipment, make small contributions to air pollution compared to that made by road traffic, where in contrast 'a narrower range

---

21 DETR, 1997c, p 8.

22 Ward and Tindale, 2000.

23 Roszak, 1972, Chapter 2.

24 Bell and McGillivray, 2000, pp 413–14.

25 See Framework Directive on Emissions from Industrial Plant 84/360 EEC/84/360, (1984) OJ L188/20; and daughter directives concerning emissions of sulphur dioxide, nitrous oxide and dust from Large Combustion Plants 88/609, and Incinerators, 94/67 and 89/369.

26 See Council Directive 96/61/EC on Integrated Pollution Prevention and Control.

27 Under EPA 1990, s 2; see Environmental Protection (Prescribed Processes and Substances) Regulations 1991 (SI 1991/472).

28 Part A(1) and (2) processes: see Pollution Prevention and Control (England and Wales) Regulations 2000 (SI 2000/1953).

29 Part B processes: see Pollution Prevention and Control (England and Wales) Regulations 2000 (SI 2000/1953).

of controls applies'.[30] Indeed, it is even argued that incinerators might produce fewer greenhouse gasses than disposal to landfill.[31]

A framework directive on air quality management appeared in 1996.[32] It is to be followed by a new generation of daughter directives setting limits for, in the first instance, 12 major pollutants. Following its proposed Acidification Strategy in 1997, the Commission has moved towards setting quality limits, through national emission ceilings for such substances. Compliance is to be achieved through objectives, frameworks, and specific targets set under the National Air Quality Strategy.[33] In turn, local authorities are required to review and assess air quality in their areas and designate management plans.[34] Guidance is produced to assist this, and also for the purpose of securing links between air quality and land use planning under Development Plans and RPG.[35] Where air quality objectives are unlikely to be met, authorities must designate Local Air Quality Management Plans, with proposals for action to comply with targets and objectives for local areas.[36] Authorities are to be placed under a duty to comply with directions from the centre to take specific action in furtherance of set objectives.[37] In order to achieve objectives, local authorities must rely upon planning and traffic management powers, as well as controlling those emissions which fall under local air pollution control. Strategy also sets down standards and objectives within which other regulatory activity regarding air quality policy must operate. Thus the Environment Agency in exercising pollution control functions must have regard to these standards, and for instance designate Air Quality Action Areas where objectives are not likely to be met within periods specified.[38]

Whilst planning guidance has made limited reference to air quality, this is now at least recognised as a key consideration in the integration between planning and transport.[39] Thus, securing sustained improvements in air quality through reduced private traffic miles calls for greater integration, in support of target driven strategies so as to conform with national and regional targets.[40] This requires translation into planning through the establishment of appropriate powers and duties, in order to develop a role that extends beyond largely confirming existing trends. We are now seeing increasing attempts at integration. This was seen in the previous chapter, especially in attempts to secure the integration of transport issues through Development Plans. This is especially the case through such policies as encouraging developments that involve reduced travel, and reasonable distances, linked to improved public transport nodes and interchanges.[41]

---

30 Miller, 1999, pp 8, 15.

31 ENDS Report 292, March 1999, pp 15–16; cf (2001) *The Guardian*, 22 May, 'Incinerator breaches go unpunished'.

32 Framework Directive on Ambient Air Quality Assessment and Management 96/62/EC.

33 DETR, 2000g.

34 Part IV Environment Act 1995.

35 DETR Guidance, *Air Quality and Land Use Planning*, LAQM G4(00); *Air Quality and Transport*, LAQM G3(00).

36 DETR, 1997c; Air Quality (England) Regulations 2000 (SI 2000/928).

37 Consultation Paper, *Proposed Regulations Transposing the EC Air Quality Framework Directive and the First Daughter Directive*, March 2001.

38 Environment Act 1995, s 81.

39 DETR, PPG 13, 2001a, para 11.

40 Hine, 1999, p 173.

41 DETR, PPG12, 1999c, Chapter 5; see Hine, 1999, pp 168–73.

Likewise, integration is now further focused upon regional planning, as for instance in RPG treatment of housing and transport issues.[42] Indeed, policy guidance devotes specific attention to air quality, and the role of RPG in helping to meet national air quality objectives. Regional Planning Bodies are required to take account of regional air quality considerations in reviewing RPGs. Here, sustainability appraisal can be informed by local authority air quality reviews and assessments, and addressed at the level of RPG, through 'advising on the location of regionally significant development, reducing the need to travel and promoting public transport'.[43]

The processes of integration have been enhanced by a series of transport management initiatives appearing in recent years. Strategically, integrated transport strategies have been encouraged under the Transport Act 2000 through the introduction of Local Transport Plans. Authorities are required to have regard to such matters as Air Quality Strategy in exercising their powers. There is a duty on local traffic authorities to review existing and forecast traffic levels and set targets for reductions.[44] There has been increasing pressure for more radical measures especially to tackle urban congestion, by encouragement of public transport, and particularly the extension of financial mechanisms into road use and parking charges.[45] Schemes are now gradually being introduced, although there appear to be high levels of local resistance. As seen in Chapter 6, legislative enabling provisions are now in place for such measures as road charging schemes and workplace parking levies, which would also be integrated into Transport Plans.[46] It appears likely that a charging scheme will be introduced in London in the foreseeable future.[47] More limited measures include spatial measures such as calming and parking controls.[48] Traffic calming powers enable restrictions through narrow gateways into urban centres.[49] Authorities also have powers outside the planning legislation to close roads for short periods.[50] For instance, there are powers of selective prohibition or restriction of road traffic in order to meet air quality objectives and to close roads where exceptionally high pollution levels are of likely danger to the public.[51] The High Court has, however, ruled that a temporary ban was not available where there is an occasional episode of high pollution.[52]

Overall, however, even as these measures come on stream, they are unlikely to counter the prevalence of private travel modes in a significant way. According to Hine, 'individuals' transport decisions do not relate to the environmental and social costs that such transport decisions produce, even though there has been a move towards adopting pricing mechanisms which reflect those wider concerns'.[53] In planning terms the focus remains a long term one of encouraging greater integration of transport and development

---

42 DETR, PPG11, 2000b, especially Chapter 6, and paras 2.33, 9.4.
43 DETR, PPG11, 2000b, para 15.2.
44 Road Traffic Reduction Act 1997; also Road Traffic Reduction (National Targets) Act 1999.
45 DETR, 1998b; see MVA Consultancy, 1996.
46 Transport Act 2000, Part III.
47 (2001) *The Guardian*, 11 July.
48 See Roberts, Cleary, Hamilton and Hanna, 1992.
49 Highways (Traffic Calming) Regulations 1999 (SI 1999/1026).
50 See Miller, 1999, Appendix 8.
51 Road Traffic Regulation Act 1984, especially s 14.
52 *R v Greenwich LBC ex p Williams* [1997] JPL 62; and see Miller, 1999, paras 5.10–5.13.
53 Hine, 1999, p 152.

needs, with for instance policies of urban containment and higher density, mixed developments. Whilst air pollution is 'one among a number of adverse impacts which motivates, at the strategic level, both the integrated transport policy and the review of the road building programme', there appears to be no evidence of air pollution considerations leading to rejection of road proposals.[54] In one instance, a planning authority had refused permission for a supermarket development within the Bath Conservation Area, which decision was overturned on appeal, the Secretary of State dismissing the impact on local air quality objectives as matters to be achieved nationally. For all that the pollution impact was a material consideration, Miller has concluded that 'planners ultimately have little opportunity to intervene, especially when refusal runs the risk of an appeal and the decision being taken by a central executive less sympathetic to local sensitivities'.[55] This may indeed be an instance of the tensions that can arise between the centre and the locality, where the centre is concerned with securing a 'healthy' economy (and under pressure from concerned interests). Yet the desensitising towards environmental factors can cut both ways, and the willingness of either to accept a development proposal will likely ensure permission.

1.4   Waste and land use regulation

By contrast to the above, the role of planning has been a central contributory part of formulating waste policies, in a way which has not hitherto been the case in respect of air pollution. Changed approaches to waste creation and disposal are outlined below. The impact of altered approaches especially to waste disposal will be felt in a demand for new, improved waste facilities.[56] There are two particular factors which threaten necessary changes. First, there are few signs as yet that achievement of the scale of envisaged reductions in waste generation is realistic, given the need not only for structural change but also for altered expectations and behaviour on the part of consumers and producers. The second factor is that planning permission is required for the deposit of waste to land, as well as for new waste management uses, and widespread opposition is common. The necessary level of new provision will therefore inevitably lead to opposition in public consultative processes and to legal challenge.[57] Doubtless incineration will generate the greatest likelihood of challenge, especially on health grounds.

Before considering the issues which will affect planning decisions, an outline of the waste regulatory regime is now set out. As in the case of air quality, environmental regulation is in the hands of specialist pollution control bodies. Waste regulation is largely the responsibility of the Environment Agency. Permitting powers in respect of waste disposal of the Environment Agencies are contained in the waste management licensing regime under Part II EPA. Yet even here overlaps occur, and waste processes, such as large incinerators, are regulated, generally by the Agency, under the IPC regime

---

54 Miller, 1999, para 3.
55 Miller, 1999, para 3.4.
56 House of Commons Select Committee, 2000a.
57 Eg, *R v Derbyshire CC ex p Murray* [2001] Env LR 26 (Kay J); *R v Leicestershire CC ex p Blackfordby and Boothorpe Action Group* [2001] Env LR 2 (Richards J).

contained in Part I EPA, the process being exempt from Part II control.[58] Indeed the onset of IPPC will see a wider range of waste facilities, such as larger landfill sites, transferred into the IPPC permitting system. However, permits may only be granted where a site has received planning permission, if this is required under planning legislation. Planning guidance requires waste planning authorities to take the Agency's advice into account when developing policies and taking development control decisions, both as to specific sites and broader considerations such as Best Practicable Environmental Option (BPEO) for different waste streams.[59]

As in the case of air quality, planning in connection with waste treatment and disposal operates in a context of developing national and local strategies. European and national initiatives increasingly reflect a consensus that sustainable development requires more sustainable production and consumption patterns, including as to resource consumption and waste management. The Waste Framework Directive sets out a series of principles with a view to more sustainable management of waste.[60] Overall there is an obligation to apply BPEO in managing waste. For instance, management is to be in accordance with the 'waste hierarchy', ranking (in reducing order of desirability) waste reduction, re-use, recovery (such as recycling, composting, waste-to-energy), and disposal. There are therefore specific measures for reducing the amount of waste produced, for ensuring the best use of waste once created, and for minimising health and environmental risks associated with waste. In order to achieve sustainable management, the Directive requires Member States to develop waste management plans, and an integrated network of disposal installations. Moreover, the Landfill Directive has set demanding, staged targets (through 2020) for the reduction of disposals to landfill, especially of biodegradable municipal wastes.[61] This Directive further provides for enhanced standards of operation and aftercare of landfill sites, prohibiting co-disposal of hazardous, non-hazardous and inert wastes, requiring pre-treatment prior to disposal, and enhanced controls over gas and leachate produced, and requiring financial provision for long term maintenance and aftercare.[62]

The UK's main response has been the production of a National Waste Strategy, in accordance with obligations laid upon the Secretary of State under the Environment Act 1995.[63] This sets out an overall framework for waste management, including both management issues and national targets for preferred treatment methods, and the context for the preparation of a wide variety of land use and waste management plans. For instance, it has added supplementary staged requirements for 'value' recovery (through 2015) from municipal waste, through such measures as recycling, composting and energy recovery, and for landfill reduction (through 2005) for industrial and commercial wastes.[64] As with air quality, concerns remain as to how targets will be filtered effectively through the various regional and local levels of responsibility. Support mechanisms will be crucial to this process. Viewed through the lens of externalities, transferring the true

---

58 Waste Management Licensing Regulations 1994, reg 16(1)(a).
59 DETR, PPG10, 1999B.
60 Council Directive 91/156.
61 Council Directive 99/31 on Landfill of Waste.
62 See DETR, 2000j.
63 DETR, 2000i.
64 See DETR, 1999d.

environmental costs of waste management practices will be increasingly addressed through economic instruments. The attention to waste streams incorporates an approach based upon producer responsibility, with obligations to recycle, recover or re-use materials or products.[65] This now extends for instance to targets in connection with packaging waste.[66] The UK already has a landfill tax, introduced under the Finance Act 1996, with a limited environmental hypothecation element under its Landfill Tax Credit Scheme.[67]

Thus development control is crucial to the success of the strategic approaches outlined above. In the first place, planning guidance indicates how the land use planning system should contribute to sustainable waste management through the provision of the required waste management facilities. Detailed consideration of location of facilities is to be contained in Development Plans and policies contained in waste local plans.[68] Waste planning authorities are required to take account of regional policies in producing waste Development Plans.[69] They are required to consult the Environment Agency and take into account National Strategy. Waste planning guidance therefore requires plans to be consistent with forecasts of local and regional waste requirements as well as other considerations. It further requires planning authorities to comply with numerous principles, including BPEO in respect of waste streams, regional self-sufficiency, the proximity principle and the waste hierarchy.[70] National Strategy is to be supported by a new generation of Waste Local Plans to be prepared by county councils (or Part II of UDPs), to provide a more detailed picture through mandatory municipal waste planning strategies, including statutory performance standards for recycling by local authorities.

Regional planning appears cast in the future role of main generator for creating structures to ensure the meeting of targets under the National Strategy. The government seeks the development of regional strategies for meeting likely demands for waste management, as an integral part of RPG, and then reflected waste development plan policies.[71] Waste management decisions should therefore take account of the need for regional self-sufficiency and the proximity principle, in accommodating treatment and disposal. RPG is required in the guidance to meet the following objectives: 'set regional waste capacity and disposal targets, including for the recycling and recovery of waste, to promote sustainable waste management, waste minimisation and alternatives to landfill. The targets should be consistent with local authorities achieving statutory performance standards for household waste recycling and composting. In general they should promote the moving of waste up the hierarchy of treatment methods (reduction, re-use, material recycling and composting, energy recovery, and disposal without energy recovery); set indicators for the measurement of progress against these targets, which can be regularly monitored; in line with the national strategy and the Best Practicable Environmental

---

65 See Environment Act 1995, s 93.

66 Council Directive 94/62/EC on Packaging and Packaging Waste; also, Producer Responsibility Obligations (Packaging Waste) Regulations 1997 (SI 1997/648).

67 See HM Customs and Excise, 1998.

68 DETR, PPG10, 1999b, paras 33–35.

69 Town and Country (Development Plan) (England) Regulations 1999 (SI 1999/3280).

70 DETR, PPG10, 1999b.

71 DETR, PPG11, 2000b, para 13.2.

Option principle, specify the number and capacity of the different types of waste management facilities required, identify their broad locations in the region, supported, where appropriate, by a criteria-based approach; and assess the need for any facilities to deal with special/hazardous waste in the region.'[72] Regional Planning Bodies are to be assisted by new Regional Technical Advisory Bodies (RTABs), whose role is to advise on regional strategy, and specifically on options for the management of waste within the region with a duty to incorporate planning policies for regional waste management capacity into RPG.[73] In support, the Environment Agency is required to produce Strategic Waste Management Assessments, addressing present and future waste management needs also upon a regional basis.

In principle, the hope is that the above structures produce solutions which meet the requirements both under the ruling Directives and in accordance with the proximity principle. However, local waste authorities are under pressure to comply with duties laid upon them.[74] This has been introduced through guidance mandating the preparation of municipal waste strategies indicating how landfill and recycling targets are to be met.[75] Much depends upon the production of workable strategic waste management assessments and the creation then of viable RPG concerning waste, taking account of National Strategy and municipal waste management strategies, and even community strategies for sustainable development under the Local Government Act 2000.[76] The newly regionalised process is therefore at risk of lagging behind the quite burdensome demands which have been set. Producing a national policy framework does not however ensure delivery, and Tromans has pointed to the danger that:

> ... driven by financial penalties and the need to cater for the waste arisings for which they are responsible, local authorities may be tempted to short-term solutions which do not represent the BPEO and do not achieve a coherent national strategy ... Will waste planning authorities be willing through the development planning process to sacrifice their own interests where necessary in the regional interest so far as major and locally unwelcome facilities are concerned? ... How, if at all, are the public to be brought round to some degree of acceptance of the waste facilities needed? Whose task is this – the government, RTABs, local authorities, the industry, or all of them?[77]

The tasks are daunting. As seen in the case of air quality, novel demands need to be made both upon institutions as well as upon citizens, and which are likely to encounter severe resistance. The plans referred to in this section barely go beyond recognising the difficulties.[78] If this is the best that can be expected from central government then a massive onus will be placed upon Regional Planning Bodies in the future, for which democratic credentials to date appear singularly ill-equipped.

---

72 DETR, PPG11, 2000b, para 13.4.
73 DETR, PPG10, 1999b, Annex B.
74 Tromans, 2001, pp 261–63.
75 DETR, 2001b; see also, Local Government (Best Value) Performance Indicators 2001/724.
76 See s 4.
77 Tromans, 2001, pp 263–64.
78 Eg, DETR, 2000i, Vol I, paras 4.12–4.13.

1.5 Highways controls and land use

A further area where regulatory objectives can come into conflict is where a highways authority purports to exercise powers in apparent conflict with a relevant planning determination. This may occur particularly where material considerations relate to safety and the public interest.[79] Yet a planning authority's original determination, in accord with the views of the Highways Authority as statutory consultee, may be overturned on appeal by the Secretary of State. The balance of power between these regimes has surprisingly required judicial resolution. The courts have adopted the position that the highways authority's statutory discretion, as to whether it was willing to proceed to enter into a highways agreement with the developer, may be deemed to have been negated by the planning process.[80] Thus, the High Court has ruled that a highways authority's subsequent refusal resulted from an error of law in determining its statutory powers. Its discretion was deemed to have been limited by the fact that the disputed issue had been fully considered during the planning process, ultimately, following an inquiry, by the Secretary of State.[81] The Court of Appeal has pursued an even more restrictive line, to the effect that the conflicting approach by the highways authority was unreasonable under *Wednesbury* principles. It was accordingly found to be necessarily unreasonable 'where road safety objections have been fully heard and rejected on appeal, then (for a highways authority) quite inconsistently with the inspector's factual judgment on the issue, nevertheless to maintain its own original view'.[82] For this purpose, the court considered important factors to be that the Secretary of State, and not just the planning authority, had resolved the planning issue, and that neither new facts nor changed circumstances had emerged to inform the highways question.[83]

The case may on this ground be contrasted with a later High Court decision, where the planning permission had been granted and thus the developer had not been to appeal.[84] There, the highways authority's subsequent refusal to enter into a highways agreement was in light of apparently changed circumstances (over the course of a four year period which had elapsed following the grant of planning permission). In consequence, the authority was held not to be bound. However, Carnwath J ruled that 'a formal decision ... made on a particular subject matter or issue affecting private rights by a competent public authority ... will be regarded as binding on other public authorities directly involved, unless and until circumstances change in a way which can be reasonably found to undermine the basis of the original decision'.[85] For all its continued formal discretion, therefore, an earlier loss of the highways authority's statutory power, to direct a refusal of planning permission on highways grounds, has now been augmented by a deemed restriction on the exercise of remaining powers. The consequence has been expressed in terms of an apparent estoppel, whereby 'the grant of planning permission ...

---

79 See Town and Country Planning Act 1990, s 78.
80 Cf Highways Act 1980, s 278.
81 *R v Warwickshire CC ex p Powergen plc* [1997] JPL 843, 851 (Forbes J).
82 *R v Warwickshire CC, ex p Powergen plc* [1998] JPL 131, 136 (*per* Simon Brown LJ).
83 *Ibid*, at pp 136–67.
84 *R v Cardiff CC ex p Sears Group Properties Ltd* [1998] 3 PLR 55.
85 *Ibid*, at p 64.

and the exercise of discretion by the planning inspector in determining that the highways works are for the public benefit will be final and conclusive'.[86]

It is perhaps unsatisfactory that statutory arrangements leave such conflicts to be resolved by judicial fashioning of a rule as to which is the dominant statutory regime. This is especially so, as the 'losing' highways regulator appeared in these instances to have been insistent upon its stance. If justified on the basis that it protects the integrity of the planning regime,[87] then this suggests an according of priority which, as discussed in the following section, is not evident where a conflict with pollution control appears to arise.

2 THE CO-ORDINATION OF LAND USE AND POLLUTION CONTROL FUNCTIONS

2.1 The separate nature of the regulatory regimes

With the above issues in mind, therefore, it is unsurprising that the relationship between land use planning and pollution control, even today, can be described as 'not particularly clear'.[88] The opaque nature owes much to the discretionary nature of the planning policy process: 'the weight to be given to environmental issues and the power to control them under pollution legislation in determining applications for planning permission is a matter for the particular decision maker, be it local planning authority or Secretary of State'.[89] Moreover, co-ordination is called into question by the need for a developer to make separate applications under planning and pollution control. The resolution of conflicts between perceived public interests can be especially problematic where discrete statutory powers are vested in separate regulatory authorities. There is authority for the relatively unhelpful proposition that whilst a public body, in exercise of its powers, may make one determination, another is not thereby prevented from taking a conflicting position on the same issue.[90]

The 1990s therefore saw a significant increase in the incidence of regulation of industrial processes. The regulation which was installed for polluting processes and waste control, respectively under Parts I and II of the EPA, was based on pre-emptive measures, requiring authorisation in advance of regulated activities. Inevitably, the imposition of greater pollution regulation has resulted in a complex regulatory picture, and this applies particularly where a developer is required to apply for permission under planning control. Early in that decade the government had refused to support amendments to its then Planning and Compensation Bill, which would arguably have upgraded the role of planning authorities in the environmental arena, by such measures as placing duties upon them to impose planning conditions in order to counter adverse environmental effects, as well as to have regard both to conservation interests and to the

---

86   Note 81 above, at p 853.
87   Note 82 above, at pp 134–35.
88   Moore, 2000, p 228.
89   Moore, 2000, p 229.
90   *Parker v Secretary of State for Transport* [1997] JPL 635.

desirability of securing sustainable development. Yet, as discussed in the previous chapters, planning perceptions have shifted in recognition of a wider process whereby environmental protection considerations have been increasingly assimilated into a range of regulatory controls.[91] Thus, given that the central concern of planning is the acceptability of activities the subject of development applications, it is well established that environmental impacts are material considerations to be brought into the balance in planning determinations.[92]

By its nature, planning control purports to be an application of strategic thinking. Development of land may lead to environmental damage in indirect as well as direct ways. Indirect damage can come about singly or as a result of cumulative development, in the sense of 'unwanted secondary effects of developments, namely the waste substances and surplus energy generated by the development once in operation'.[93] Indeed, the Royal Commission back in 1971 had pointed out that, whilst certain forms of development may not be themselves polluting, 'without adequate planning, their overall effect could be a grave deterioration in the quality of the environment which would outweigh the benefit of efficient anti-pollution measures'.[94] For its part, it was further inevitable that the planning system was to cast its eye with greater concern at the environmental implications of proposed development. As Tromans had it in 1991, such a 'web of control is becoming increasingly complex, and what were thought of as established lines of demarcation, based on traditional approaches, may become increasingly difficult to hold'.[95]

2.2 The impact of pollution controls

The obvious connections between pollution and planning controls was recognised in 1976, when the Royal Commission produced a report summarising concerns at the failure to address these issues.[96] The report came in the aftermath of the then groundbreaking Control of Pollution Act 1974. A key instance of potential conflict concerns whether the local planning authority can prevent the location of a potential source of pollution at the development stage. Conversely, pollution problems may be exacerbated if planning decisions enable the siting of developments in close proximity both to one another and to sites already committed to different uses.[97] The Royal Commission's view was in essence that planning decisions must follow careful consideration of planning effects, and must therefore lead to a refusal – and not a conditional consent – if the authority considers a development unacceptable on pollution grounds. Central government had broadly adopted the same view. The approach would moreover absolve the planners from detailed involvement in setting conditions, clearly more appropriate for the pollution control bodies.

---

91 Jewell and Steele, 1998, p 78.
92 See eg *Gateshead MBC v Secretary of State for the Environment* [1995] Env LR 37.
93 Tromans, 1991a, p 13.
94 RCEP, 1971, at para 11.
95 Tromans, 1991b, p 514.
96 RCEP, 1976.
97 *R v Exeter CC ex p Thomas* [1990] 1 WLR 100.

Regulators are nevertheless engaged in different tasks. Indeed a subsequent Royal Commission Report, concerning the operation of BPEO, in terms of pollution control, recognised the limits within which the planning system operates, and that control of day-to-day industrial operations was best achieved in other ways.[98] As has been seen above in the discussion of air quality, the basis of IPC, now superseded by IPPC, has been the setting of integrated standards for emissions of pollutants to air, land and water, in accord with the principle of Best Available Techniques. In addition, where an IPC process is likely to involve the release of substances into more than one environmental medium, regard must be had to BPEO. The BPEO scheme has been based upon a requirement that authorisation conditions must comply with policies specified by the Secretary of State relating to specific processes or substances and such matters as emission limits, quality standards or objectives. In determining the conditions of any authorisation, the pollution control authority is under a duty to ensure that Best Available Techniques Not Entailing Excessive Cost (BATNEEC) is applied in preventing, or where not practicable, reducing to a minimum and rendering harmless, any release of prescribed substances into any environmental medium, and rendering harmless any other potentially harmful substances released.[99] Yet concern remained that pollution 'is often dealt with inadequately, or sometimes forgotten altogether, in the planning process. In part this stems from a lack of guidance and advice. Planning officers and committees are not pollution experts and they are necessarily dependent on advice on pollution matters'.[100]

Central government has so far sought to address such gaps through planning policy guidance, the implications of which approach are discussed in the next section. In particular, as already seen in Chapter 4, on being required to determine a planning application, the first consideration for the local planning authority will be the Development Plan.[101] Albeit that it will be relevant to the question of addressing environmental impact, this may not be especially helpful, given the inevitability of its being expressed in general terms, and with numerous other policy purposes in mind. Moreover, as suggested above, other regulatory constraints may apply, and this must affect the approach of planning control in respect of prospective pollution impacts.

2.3 Reconciling planning and pollution controls

As seen in the previous section, where conflicts arise, it is to the courts that the regulators have looked for a determination. Two important cases have arisen. The first concerned a planning application for a clinical waste incinerator, and the planning authority sought a review of the Secretary of State's decision to allow the developer's appeal. The second case arose from a challenge made by an individual, following a grant of permission for the purposes of a development concerning a municipal waste incinerator. Turning to the first case, reported as *Gateshead MBC v Secretary of State for the Environment*,[102] the relevant Development Plan set out certain criteria which were required to be met for the purposes

---

98 RCEP, 1988, paras 4.4, 4.5.
99 See EPA 1990, s 7.
100 RCEP, 1988, para 3.35.
101 See TCPA, s 54A.
102 *Gateshead MBC v Secretary of State for the Environment* [1995] Env LR 37.

of approval of 'planning applications for development with potentially noxious or hazardous consequences'.[103] These included the following: adequate separation from other development to ensure both comfort and amenity; availability of transport routes to national networks to avoid densely built-up areas and provide for a safe passage of hazardous materials; and acceptable consequences in terms of environmental impact. At issue was the question as to whether the proposal had acceptable consequences in terms of environmental impact.

The planning authority had refused the application, and the appeal went to an inquiry. Although satisfied that pollution controls would ensure there would be no unacceptable impact on adjacent land, the inspector recommended refusal.[104] His main concern had been a lack of sufficient definition of the air quality impact of the development, and an insufficient allaying of public disquiet over dioxin emissions.[105] The Secretary of State allowed the appeal, and subsequent challenges were dismissed by both the High Court and the Court of Appeal. In the latter, Glidewell LJ ruled that 'it is not the role of the planning system to duplicate controls under the EPA 1990. Whilst it is necessary to take account of potential emissions on neighbouring land uses when considering whether or not to grant planning permission, control of those emissions should be regulated by HMIP (Her Majesty's Inspectorate of Pollution, forerunners to the Environment Agency) ... The controls available ... are adequate to deal with emissions from the proposed plant and the risk of harm to human health'.[106] The court accepted that the environmental impact of emissions in such circumstances raised material considerations to be addressed by the planning authority. However, in connection with the regulatory overlap, the Court of Appeal endorsed the views of the first instance judge,[107] to the effect that a further material consideration was 'the existence of a stringent regime under the EPA for preventing or mitigating that impact for rendering any emissions harmless. It is too simplistic to say: "The Secretary of State cannot leave the question of pollution to the EPA"'.[108] There are therefore potentially conflicting material considerations to be resolved in accordance with the placing of such weight as can be justified. In such circumstances, the courts have traditionally regarded the contents of available planning guidance as important factors.

The decision, however, raises unresolved issues. It is notable that counsel for the planning authority had argued that the Secretary of State had misunderstood the powers and functions under pollution control, and that once planning permission were granted there would be almost no prospect that the Agency would use its powers to refuse authorisation.[109] Thereafter the regulatory task would presumably be to seek to ensure that pollution is kept at an acceptable level. For instance, by way of damage limitation, the Agency would presumably seek to ensure that BATNEEC applied. The planning authority may realistically only refuse planning permission in this respect on grounds that unacceptable harm to the environment is likely to be caused. Generally, it is unlikely

---

103 Policy EN16 of the approved Tyne and Wear Structure Plan.

104 *Gateshead MBC v Secretary of State for the Environment* [1995] Env LR 37, p 45 (Inspector's Report, para 507).

105 *Ibid*, at p 45 (Inspector's Report, para 506).

106 *Ibid*, at p 46.

107 Reported at [1994] 3 Env LR 11.

108 *Gateshead MBC v Secretary of State for the Environment* [1995] Env LR 37, at p 44.

109 *Ibid*, at p 48.

to depart from any views of the Environment Agency upon consultation. However, it seems that it is not necessarily an objective assessment.[110] There is Court of Appeal authority that accepts that a refusal of permission, notwithstanding one based upon public concerns that could not be objectively justified, may still in certain circumstances be valid as a matter of law.[111] The extent of this principle is unclear, especially in the context of weighting against other considerations. It should be remembered that those proceedings arose out of an application for an order for costs on grounds of unreasonable behaviour by the planning authority following a successful appeal.[112] Moreover, in *Gateshead*, Glidewell LJ, whilst accepting that public concern is a material consideration, 'if in the end that public concern is not justified, it cannot be conclusive'.[113] The question of weighting of public concern against other evidence is considered further in the next chapter during the discussion of risk assessment.

Under current approaches, therefore, a planning authority refusal of permission on grounds of unacceptable harm to the environment, as a planning ground (that is, independent of pollution controls), is unlikely to survive appeal. The judgment in *Gateshead*, as well as its explicit endorsement in planning guidance, suggests a more limited role for the planning stage in cases of potential overlap. Thus, according to Purdue, 'while the existence of the specialist pollution controls has not cut down the scope of "material considerations", such controls have constrained how planning authorities exercise their powers in the context of environmental protection'.[114] This has a further effect, for those who might wish to challenge an authority's grant of planning permission in such circumstances. It has been suggested that it 'makes further challenges – especially by third parties against a local planning authority which is supportive of the orthodoxy – far more difficult'.[115] Likewise, the pollution control agency might itself be in a bind, limited as it is to securing the statutory objectives. These objectives are expressed to include in particular 'ensuring that, in carrying on a prescribed process, the best available techniques not entailing excessive cost will be used (i) for preventing the release of substances prescribed for any environmental medium into that medium or, where that is not practicable by such means, for reducing the release of such substances to a minimum and for rendering harmless any such substances which are so released; and (ii) for rendering harmless any other substances which might cause harm if released into any environmental medium'.[116] The vital decision as to the acceptability of such development would already have been determined, at the planning stage, and in the circumscribed planning context.

The second case likewise come before the Court of Appeal, and highlighted the potential overlap with waste disposal provisions. The decision in *R v Bolton MBC ex p Kirkman* suggests that the role of planning decision making is still further confined in this

---

110 Piatt, 1997.

111 *Newport MBC v Secretary of State for Wales and Browning Ferris Limited* [1998] JPL 377, 384.

112 TCPA 1990, s 302(2).

113 Note 92 above, at p 49.

114 Purdue, 1999, p 588.

115 Miller, 1999, p 16.

116 See EPA 1990, s 7(2); also, enabling provision, Pollution Prevention and Control Act 1999, Schedule I; and draft Pollution Prevention and Control Regulations 2000, Schedule 2 (Best Available Techniques).

context. It will be recalled that no licence can be determined by the Environment Agency unless any planning permission required has been granted.[117] There, a nearby resident unsuccessfully challenged by way of judicial review a grant of planning permission for a municipal waste incinerator.[118] The application was largely based upon national waste management regulations,[119] under which the relevant waste Directive had been transposed.[120] As seen above, when determining planning applications for waste disposal sites, planning authorities are now required to fulfil specific obligations, including that waste will be recovered or disposed of without endangering human health or the environment.[121] The regulations further require the planning authority to consider the 'waste hierarchy', which ranks recycling as the priority method of disposal (above both energy recovery and landfill).[122] Three questions arose. These related to the question of regulatory overlap and the nature of the duties laid upon the authority.

First, concerning environmental threats posed by atmospheric discharges from the development, both local planning authority and Environment Agency were interested. The Agency had been consulted on the application and had indicated its intention to accept the pollution control application in principle. In its view equipment and technology were available to ensure that releases would comply with legislative requirements, and be rendered harmless to the environment. Schiemann LJ was not convinced that ceding responsibility to the Agency would constitute a breach of duty by the planning authority: 'while the dual system of control permits an LPA (local planning authority) to exercise a greater control and conduct a greater degree of investigation that this LPA saw fit to do, it does not render this legally obligatory.'[123] The second and more complex issue concerned the nature of the duties laid upon the authority. The Court of Appeal accepted that, in the light of *Gateshead* and the domestic regulations, the planning authority was required to satisfy itself that a proposed waste installation could be operated without danger to human health or the environment. Although reasons are not required to be given upon grant of planning permission, the court was content that a review could be carried out, based upon material available to the planning authority. The court was duly satisfied that the authority had complied with that duty. Moreover, no duties were imposed in respect of the waste hierarchy.[124] Whilst there was a requirement in the regulations to take account so far as material of any plan, and the local waste plan repeated a presumption in favour of recycling, the authority was not bound to refuse planning consent in any given instance. This appears to be on the basis that decisions affecting the waste hierarchy are at a relatively inchoate stage, and to endorse the views of the first instance judge that no obligation can as yet be said to exist.[125] Difficult questions may arise in the future when mandatory waste management policies have been imposed, and developed through the Development Plan and RPG process.

---

117 See, eg, EPA 1990, s 36(2).
118 [1998] Env LR 719; [1998] Env LR 560.
119 Waste Management Licensing Regulations 1994 (SI 1994/1056).
120 Framework Directive on Waste 75/442/EEC, as amended by 91/156.
121 Article 4.
122 As also under the Greater Manchester Waste Plan, 1996.
123 [1998] Env LR 719, 725.
124 Framework Directive, Art 3(1)(a); also EPA, s 50.
125 [1998] Env LR 560, 576–77.

The third issue concerned how far the authority was under a duty to require a BPEO assessment in respect of the method of disposal of the waste. BPEO provisions appear in planning policy guidance, as being the outcome of a systematic consultative and decision making procedure which emphasises the protection of the environment across land, air and water.[126] The procedure should establish the option that provides the most benefits or the least damage to the environment, as a whole, at acceptable costs, in the long term as well as the short term. The first instance judge had pointed out that no statutory requirement existed whereby the authority must demonstrate that the proposed waste treatment represents the BPEO. Once more, the local waste plan could not be seen as creating a binding obligation. However, just as in the case of a statutory environmental statement for the purposes of assessment, and the nature of any environmental threat to air quality, the issues of waste hierarchy and of BPEO are capable of being material considerations. The Court of Appeal accepted that BPEO 'as an objective, is clearly capable of being a material planning consideration, and has been so treated by this Council. To say that it is "not a planning test" is possibly misleading. While it may not be the planning authority's primary duty to carry out a BPEO test, and they may be guided by the views of the authorities more directly responsible, it remains a potential planning issue to which they need to have regard in the overall balance'.[127] However, as seen above, the weight to be attached to material considerations is a matter for the discretion of the planning authority, and challenge remains enmeshed in the restrictive *Wednesbury* principles.[128] The provisions of revised waste guidance have since replaced general guidance in respect of planning and waste, and these point out that BPEO for each waste stream is one of the key principles on which the government seeks waste management principles to be based.[129] It has been held that the BPEO assessment is required to be site-specific, but that its detail is a matter for the planning authority.[130]

It cannot be said therefore that the commitment to a waste hierarchy has yet become a justiciable principle. In contrast, by reference to the terms of the Directive, Miller has argued that 'effective commitment to a strong notion of sustainability would require the empowerment of some state body to refuse to authorise a waste installation deemed to be operating at an unduly low level in the hierarchy. Under Part II of the Environmental Protection Act 1990, the Environment Agency currently has no power to refuse a waste management licence on those grounds; although it is possible that implementation of (the IPPC Directive) ... will require legislation empowering the Agency to ensure that the authorisation of individual plants is consistent with overall waste strategy. In the interim, planning refusal (and the absence of an appropriate planning consent automatically entails refusal of a waste licence) could achieve that objective'.[131] Overall, the resolution of the BPEO question therefore appears to leave its own 'regulatory hierarchy' at work. The BPEO obligation laid upon the Environment Agency is directed at releases caught within the pollution control process. Any BPEO at the planning stage, unlike the more

---

126 DoE, PPG23, 1994a.
127 [1998] Env LR 560, 580.
128 *Associated Provincial Picture Houses Ltd v Wednesbury Corporation* [1948] 1 KB 223.
129 DETR, PPG10, 1999b.
130 *R v Derbyshire CC ex p Murray* [2001] Env LR 26.
131 Miller, 1999, p 15.

technical environmental assessment, must presumably be directed at wider questions affecting the nature and location of the development, including a consideration of the waste hierarchy alternatives referred to above. Yet, strangely, the Court of Appeal appears to accept a rather abstract view of its having taken place, albeit for instance lacking specific costings. Despite an apparent duty to identify suitable sites in Development Plans, further guidance might indicate how planning authorities can encourage the use of options higher up the waste hierarchy.[132]

It has been suggested that it may be possible to build on the pollution control principles of BPEO. Thus, in the case of waste, assuming that recycling is the best overall option within the waste management hierarchy,

> BPEO methodology should inform the development of a strategy (or planning policy) to deliver recycling facilities. A strategy might include, for example, either a single large recycling facility, or a number of smaller ones, as well as encouragement of on-site recycling. This is probably best considered initially at the regional level (through RPG) filtering down through the planning system as guidance for development plans. However, to be effective, the existing BPEO methodology (which was originally developed for use in potentially polluting 'process' industries) would have to be extended to take into account a much wider range of environmental, social and economic considerations.[133]

It is notable that, since 1999, planning guidance cautions, restrictively, against plans assuming the achievement of waste targets towards the upper end of the waste hierarchy by excluding disposal facilities such as landfill and incineration.[134] This suggests concern at central government level at the strategic implications of refusals, in an area where public concern is a prevalent feature. Yet that is not to say that challenges to waste site permissions can be dismissed as simply NIMBYism. Stanley, for instance, has cited three factors that are prevalent in contentious planning issues, and which he terms 'local policy', 'bad bargain' and 'risk perception and response' problems.[135] The first involves a systemic weakness in the planning process that only effectively engages the public in the siting decision stage, and he compares a consensus-building policy experiment by one county authority. The second is a justice question, which concerns the inequity of a siting decision process that concentrates costs upon a single community as host. Here, he offers possible incentive and mitigation schemes which might overcome the problem of inadequate compensation. The third derives from failures of communication, and suggests a need for developers to respond more positively to community concerns in regard to risks generated by proposals. In particular, it is necessary to recognise that such concerns extend beyond notions of objective risk.[136] He concludes that conflict resolution requires 'the use of consensual and co-operative techniques rather than the traditional adversarial, decide-announce-defend approach to conflict resolution'.[137] Yet, where a planning authority engages with such local concerns, in order once again to resolve inter-agency issues, its only realistic recourse is to judicial review.

---

132 ENDS Report 288, January 1999, p 43.
133 Land Use Consultants, 1999, para 5.21.
134 DETR, PPG10, 1999b.
135 Stanley, 2000.
136 See, further, Sandman, 1993.
137 Stanley, 2000, p 1239.

2.4   Planning, the precautionary principle and statutory frameworks

In an area of decision making so replete with discretionary exercise of delegated powers, it is unsurprising that the Secretary of State seeks to impose consistency, also where issues of regulatory authority overlap arise. The constraints under which planning authorities are now to operate, therefore, are underscored by the steadily encroaching comprehensiveness of pollution control regimes. Moreover, as has been seen in previous chapters, references to environmental implications for planning purposes now appear in a range of planning guidance papers. Policy guidance, available only in draft form at the time of the *Gateshead* judgment, recognises the increased interest on the part of planning authorities in controlling potentially polluting activities. It amounts to an attempt to address the relationship between planning and pollution control, described as 'separate but complementary in that they are designed to protect the environment from the potential harm caused by development and operations, but with different objectives'.[138] There is specific recognition of the possibility of refusal of permission 'on planning grounds, despite the grant, or potential grant, of a pollution control authorisation or licence'. Planners, facing the question of material considerations for purposes of their own regime, are therefore advised that the weight to be attached to such matters will depend on the scope of the pollution control system in each particular case.[139] The guidance goes on to clarify the nature of material considerations in such circumstances, the list including matters such as location, amenity impact, the risk and impact on the use of other land, the prevention of nuisance, impact upon road or other transport networks and the surrounding environment, as well as the need for and feasibility of site restoration sufficient for an appropriate afteruse.

An assumed limitation upon the planning process which appears in guidance is that decisions on planning grounds are to be made on 'land-use grounds'. There is therefore express reference to the application of the authority of *Gateshead*, in that the planning system 'should not be operated so as to duplicate controls which are the statutory responsibility of other bodies (including local authorities in their non-planning functions). Planning controls, except where they are applied in the context of hazardous substances, are not an appropriate means of regulating the detailed characteristics of potentially polluting activities'.[140] Moreover, there is explicit reference to clear demarcation lines: 'Lack of confidence in the effectiveness of controls imposed under pollution control legislation (IPC) is not a legitimate ground for the refusal of planning permission or for the imposition of conditions on a planning permission that merely duplicates such controls.'[141] Whilst planning authorities will need to consult pollution control authorities 'in order that they can take account of the scope and requirements of the relevant pollution controls', they 'should work on the assumption that the pollution control regimes will be properly applied and enforced. They should not seek to substitute their own judgment on pollution control for that of the bodies with the relevant expertise and the statutory responsibility for that control'.[142]

---

138 DoE, PPG23, 1994a, para 1.2.
139 *Ibid*, at para 1.36.
140 *Ibid*, at para 1.3.
141 *Ibid*, at para 3.23.
142 *Ibid*, at para 1.34.

As to whether a planning refusal is an available response where the planning authority considers that pollution control is inadequate, Miller has concluded that whilst guidance 'does not totally exclude the possibility of refusing planning consent for an IPC process by reference to its effects on atmospheric quality ... it clearly makes such a challenge far more difficult'.[143] The same author offers an early illustration of where a planning decision received short shrift in the light of an overlapping environmental pollution jurisdiction. Inquiries had followed an appeal against refusal of planning permission for the installation of a gas turbine, fuelled by coke oven gas from its pre-existing coking plant at the Monkton Works on Tyneside, by National Smokeless Fuels Ltd. The appeal was in due course allowed by the Secretary of State, against the recommendation of the inspector.[144] Whilst there would not be an increase in sulphur emissions (indeed a new stack might have led to slightly lower local emissions) the residents' action group had argued a breach of European legislation, due to inappropriate preventive measures using BATNEEC.[145] The Minister ruled that the operation was regulated under pollution control legislation. Moreover, no rights were conferred on individuals under the European legislation, and there was no duty upon him as an emanation of the State under Article 10 of the Treaty. Miller suggests that the decision is contrary to the doctrine of sympathetic interpretation.[146]

Other commentators are more non-committal as to the implications of *Gateshead* for reduced planning discretion. One leading text concludes that 'the weight to be given to environmental issues and the power to control them under pollution legislation in determining applications for planning permission is a matter for the particular decision maker, be it local planning authority or Secretary of State'.[147] Bell and McGillivray conclude that it affirms the view of there being 'no definite dividing line between planning and pollution control and that each decision maker is entitled to arrive at different conclusions if it exercises its discretion reasonably'.[148] This gap may become more stark as IPPC becomes fully operational, for the pollution control scheme should offer a more holistic exercise, which is more concerned with general environmental impacts. Thus extended definitions apply to 'environmental pollution', to mean pollution of the air, water or land which may give rise to any harm, including to the health of human beings or other living organisms, and harm to the quality of the environment, taken as a whole, or as to the quality of the air, water or land, and other impairment of, or interference with, the ecological systems of which any living organisms form part, as well as offence to the senses of human beings, damage to property, or impairment of, or interference with, amenities or other legitimate uses of the environment.[149]

Whilst the post-*Gateshead* guidance assists with the interpretation of lawful exercise of discretionary powers by the authorities concerned, what is missing is a recognition of the

---

143 Miller, 1999, p 10.

144 DoE, Decision Letter: Appeal by National Smokeless Fuels Ltd and Coal Products Ltd (Ref No APP/A4520/A87/075692), 1991, DoE Northern Regional Ofiice.

145 See Framework Directive 86/340, Art 4.1.

146 Case 14/83, *von Colson v Land Nordrhein-Westfalen* [1984] ECR 1891; Case C-106/89, *Marleasing SA v La Comercial* [1990] ECR I-4135.

147 Moore, 2000, p 229.

148 Bell and McGillivray, 2000, p 392.

149 See Pollution Prevention and Control Act 1999, s 1(2)(3).

contested nature of such issues, that is, how such decisions should be arrived at, and by whom. Yet it is surely the planning process which is most appropriate to engage in the primary exercise of considering acceptability in a range of circumstances. For instance, the role of planning control as primary regulator is recognised in the encouragement of imposition of conditions upon any grant of permission for the development of contaminated land.[150] In this sense, positive planning can integrate obligations which might otherwise arise upon a later enforcement of statutory clean-up under Part IIA EPA 1990. In a similar sense, the planning regime is well placed to address wider needs, whether in terms of the wider implications of development or compliance with related obligations, as under the waste hierarchy or air quality targets.

A fundamental ecological critique of regulatory approaches relates to the assumptions underlying such controls, and the continued emphasis upon technocentric and efficiency-led approaches. In this context, Alder and Wilkinson point out that the 'problem is directed at efficiency concerns but does not address the problem of conflicting ethical priorities'.[151] Elsewhere, Wilkinson has challenged the ethical foundations which underlie the anthropocentric and utilitarian emphasis of such measures: in effect, the well-being of human populations and the lack of concern at cumulative, synergistic and long term effects upon ecosystems. This results, for instance, in standard setting taking its lead from a narrow scientific focus upon toxic effect upon individual organisms, scarcely justifying BPEO methodology. Discretionary powers are accordingly vested in the regulator-expert, operating under a 'complex formula which attempts to compare mathematically, across media, the ratios of released substances to legal maximum allowable concentrations for those media and to combine these into the numerical "integrated environmental index"'.[152] This once again goes to the root of the difficulties in accommodating environmental perspectives into sanctioning apparatus, and suggests a lack of congruence between our conceptions of environmental law and ethics as pollution controls 'provide the minimum degree of protection necessary to continue maximum economic growth and material consumption'.[153] Priorities can be detected in techniques which, through cost benefit analysis, lean towards economic valuations, and can be described as a commodification of values.[154] The broader questions which arise, seen in earlier chapters, are further discussed in the next chapter.

What therefore are realistic parameters for planning authority concern? According to policy guidance, its role is to focus 'on whether the development itself is an acceptable use of the land rather than the control of the processes or substances themselves. It also assumes that the pollution control regime will operate effectively'.[155] This raises very serious questions concerning the culture of the respective regulatory bodies, and how they reflect public values, including levels of public participation and other forms of democratic involvement in their processes. As to the role of the Environment Agency, it appears to be confirmed in *Gateshead* that there can be no question of an estoppel

---

150 See Purdue, 1999, p 592.
151 Alder and Wilkinson, 1999, p 202.
152 Wilkinson, 1999, p 28.
153 Wilkinson, 1999, p 29.
154 See Hanley and Milne, 1996.
155 DoE, PPG23, 1994a, para 1.33.

operating, Glidewell LJ merely indicating that it was a matter of certainty that the Agency 'should not consider that the grant of planning permission inhibits them from refusing authorisation if they decide in their discretion that this is the proper course'.[156] This reinforces the custom and practice by which, as the Secretary of State indicated, a pollution control application for authorisation would normally be made by the time the planning inquiry began, but determination would wait upon it. All parties must therefore enter into a form of limbo as the planning process works through. The *Gateshead* case suggests a serious lack of convergence as between planning control and the precautionary principle. The Court of Appeal appeared to accept that only if expected emissions were certain to be in breach should a refusal of planning permission follow. This would be on the basis that the planning decision (in this instance, on the basis of an inspector's report) would pre-empt a refusal under pollution control regulation, there on grounds that there was at that stage no clear evidence about the quality of the air in the vicinity of the site.[157] The conclusion must be that, given that operational aspects fall within the remit of the Environment Agency, then the planning authority can only refuse permission if the Agency certainly would, even though the inspector had there found that 'the discharge data is only theoretical and insufficient practical experience is available for forecasts to be entirely credible'.[158] This removes a key precautionary role from the planning authority, a conclusion the more likely in view of the extended notion of environmental harm for the purposes of the pollution control stage of regulation under IPPC.

3 RECONCILING CONFLICTS

3.1   Establishing policy priorities

Planning constraints operate therefore under a considerably restrictive remit in the context of environmental pollution. Nevertheless, the planning system will need to address environmental protection issues in a growing range of circumstances, as applications for development permission will be the primary focus for proponents of a proposed new activity. For instance, the basis of definition of contaminated land in the new regime under Part II EPA ensures that it will only be where a new use is proposed that remediation obligations may arise. The planning system should have recourse to local contaminated land policies as set out in Development Plans. As seen above, there may also be opportunities to impose conditions which mandate prior remediation. Aside from reliance upon a response from the Environment Agency under the planning consultation process, it seems that planning guidance will be required in the specific context of contaminated land.[159]

---

156 [1995] Env LR 37, 50.
157 *Ibid*, at p 49.
158 *Ibid*, at p 45, quoting para 505(7).
159 DETR, 2000c, p 60.

The siting and locational issues which are the stuff of planning should extend more generally to the allocation of environmental risk. Especially in circumstances where environmental impact assessment does not apply, therefore, but where some consideration of environmental risk has taken place, a refusal of grant of permission is likely to lead to an appeal.[160] It has been argued that the process must achieve three aims, namely, to take all relevant issues into account; to enable all interested parties to have an informed input into the decision making process; and to equip the decision maker with the skills to adjudicate fully and fairly upon all the issues.[161] In order to produce just decisions, the planning authority must be able to access appropriate information. Yet, incongruously given the above limitations, the government has indicated that the planning process should have an increased role in addressing problems of climate change. It has suggested the introduction of a good practice guide on the implications of climate change for the planning process, by reference for instance to 'strengthening Planning Policy Guidance to take more account of environmental hazards such as flooding'.[162]

Planning is, however, not an unalloyed good in terms of environmental protection. The local basis of the planning process is likely to come into conflict with wider, including national, policy considerations. As we have seen, there are significant limitations on local competencies to address environmental questions. These may be technical, but more importantly, environmental issues are likely to have impacts on wider stages than the local. As Woolf has pointed out, 'multi-jurisdictional regulation is often required because many environmental externalities such as acid deposition, groundwater pollution, and oil spills fail to respect artificial political boundaries'.[163]

Moreover, the planning system operates in an area where national and regional policy targets are increasingly being promulgated, for instance, as discussed above as to air quality and transport planning, as well as waste treatment and disposal. Central demands will often come into conflict with local community perspectives, which are in turn likely to put planning decision making procedures under extreme pressure.[164] There is a wide-ranging literature on this subject.[165] Public law challenges are seldom framed in the 'why me' mode, although such is likely to be a subtext (and may be justified). For instance, a ground of challenge to the extension of a landfill site, by way of an application for judicial review, was that in applying the objectives of waste disposal (without risk to water, air, soil, plants and animals), under Article 4 of the Framework Directive, a special status must be given to local need. As these were already provided for, it was argued that the proposal did not meet a specific local need.[166] Although the court agreed that such obligations for national implementation were material considerations, they were of unquantifiable weight and there moreover appeared to be no precedent for the idea of a special category of consideration.

---

160 Eg, *Envirocor Waste Holdings Ltd v Secretary of State for the Environment* [1996] JPL 489.

161 Stanley, 1997, p 1.

162 DETR, 2000c, p 73.

163 Wolf, 1996, pp 43–44.

164 McCarthy, 2000a.

165 See eg Cowell and Owens, 1998.

166 *R v Derbyshire CC ex p Murray* [2001] Env LR 26.

On the other hand, policy may dictate otherwise. In the contentious siting of incinerators, the proximity principle, whilst only a material consideration in planning terms, is likely to be a factor, and may be seen as a *quid pro quo* for funding provided to local authorities under the national waste strategy. Somewhat archly, a minister has been quoted as saying: '*Daily Mail* and *Daily Telegraph* readers cannot expect that their waste will be disposed of in the back yards of *Sun* and *Mirror* readers. We expect people who produce the waste to take some responsibility for its disposal.'[167] A further example of how local decision making will increasingly cede to national strategy is in the area of transport. The new strategic national plan has provided high levels of funding (£180 billion in total) for various projects aimed at infrastructure improvements.[168] National multimodal plans will be expected to inform regional strategies and the Local Transport Plans that will set out priorities and plans to deal with pollution and congestion in greater detail, requiring central approval. Integration will be assisted through the creation of a Commission for Integrated Transport.[169] Even if the national strategy gives little indication of being aimed at reduced traffic levels, this is in any event traditionally a difficult task also for land use planning. Indeed, the area has illustrated the dangers of fragmentation in policy delivery, as localities have competed with one another. There can be justifiable fears for instance that other areas will enable development of 'cheaper peripheral sites', and it is also difficult for developers to place reliance upon future levels of public transport provision.[170] Against this there appears to be a greater commitment to the co-ordination of transport and planning in the revised versions of regional and development planning guidance as well as guidance on housing and transport, discussed in the previous chapter.

3.2   Synthesising regulatory objectives

In its current review, referred to earlier in this chapter, the Royal Commission has indicated that the planning process is crucial to the effective delivery of environmental protection. This is especially the case as to whether the shift to a plan-led system would more effectively promote sustainability, and the question of whether there should still be an effective presumption in favour of development.[171] The separation of planning permission and pollution authorisations is an obvious example of where greater integration might lead to more coherent forms of control. It is interesting, but no less problematic, that the ruling directives allow environmental impact and IPPC assessments to be combined. Decision making processes must operate in the light of an awareness of potential conflicts. These cannot be wished away, and processes such as BPEO and environmental impact assessment differ in both scope and purpose.

A rational response is to ensure that appropriate procedures are in place to assist in their resolution. The Urban Task Force recommended that it was necessary to resolve conflicts and inconsistencies between regulations which cover contaminated land, water

---

167 ENDS Report 310, November 2000, p 33.
168 DETR, 2000h.
169 See, eg, 1999 Reports on National Road Traffic Targets, and Provisional Road Transport Plans.
170 Brearley, 1999, p 408.
171 ENDS Report 303, April 2000, pp 11–12.

and waste, and that for instance site owners should have just one set of standards to work to when resolving problems of site contamination.[172]

Consultation was emphasised by the Royal Commission in 1976, in order that planning authorities seek advice from pollution authorities on specific proposals, and that the latter, likewise, in drawing up its long term policies, should act in consultation with planners. The significance of consultation has been emphasised by a House of Commons Select Committee in its report on developments affecting the flood plain, referring to the importance that the Environmental Agency 'play a leading role in all stages of the planning process. It should devote adequate resources to pressing its case before Regional Planning Guidance and Structure Plan Panels, at Local Plan and Unitary Development Plan Inquiries, and in response to consultation on planning applications. Local Planning Authorities will be assisted by the Environment Agency taking a consistent approach at each stage of the consideration of development of individual sites – at the land allocation stage in the Development Plan, when an outline plan is submitted, and at the consideration of the details'.[173] The Environment Agency is expected under the new Guidance to respond within 21 days, and where the authority is minded to grant permission the Agency must have an opportunity to make further representations (though is further advised to bear in mind that objections must stand scrutiny on appeal).[174]

Yet this raises questions as to the effectiveness of the Environment Agency's responses to consultation under the planning system. There are also dissonances as between the greater degrees of accountability and participation under planning controls, than under pollution legislation. On the one hand, as seen above, there must inevitably be questions raised as to the purpose of participation in these processes. This impacts upon levels of public involvement and participation which can be incorporated into the system. As the range of targets and indicators increases there is greater emphasis upon central dictation. It has been argued that coherent strategic planning of land use and land management will inevitably override local discretion and wider participation, for both as to transport and housing 'local decisions and market responses will provide no answer. The intensifying conflict between city centre and countryside, between personal freedom and care for the environment cannot otherwise be properly arbitrated'.[175] However, environmental solutions called for in this book demand effective forms of participation. In 1988, discussing BPEO, the Royal Commission stated that in difficult cases decisions 'cannot be left to scientists, industrialists and regulatory experts alone. Public involvement is needed so that the public values underlying the choice of BPEO are identified and clearly understood'.[176]

Yet it was suggested above, especially in the context of waste planning, that it may be possible to build on the principles of BPEO.[177] If land use planning has failed to contribute sustained impetus for environmental improvement, this may be due to the

---

172 Rogers, 1999, recommendation 72.
173 House of Commons, 2000b, para 28.
174 DTLGR, 2001, paras 64–66; cf House of Commons, 2000b, para 29.
175 Wood, 1995, p 73.
176 RCEP, 1988, p 18.
177 And see Tromans and Guruswamy, 1986.

failure of legal principles and institutional structures to deliver a coherent and integrated protective regime. Planning is ideally suited to be the fulcrum of an approach that recognises the policy dictates of sustainable development.[178] This is demonstrably happening in those areas covered by environmental impact assessment, where data is more readily available to authorities, and further matters such as alternative considerations can be factored in. The development planning stage, with its inclusive consultative process, is crucial to creating a broader role for environmental protection priorities. Using the language of BPEO, Tromans stated in 1987: 'Good planning can reduce, if not eliminate, adverse environmental impact ... Potential conflicts might be resolved, BPEO-type problems identified, technical expertise built into land use policies, and a genuinely vigorous multimedia approach to pollution problems at a level of local responsibility.'[179] Sustainable development can be seen to be another way of expressing a broad notion of BPEO. At the development planning stage, it offers a strategic basis for considering land use problems in a wider context, with the development control process performing a more specified preventative role. In each respect, it offers the best opportunity for an integration of approaches, at the level of policy making and co-ordination of technical data and advice.

Going beyond inter-agency relations, the importance of effective participatory techniques and transparency, together with a related need for access to justice, is considered more fully in Chapter 10. It is necessary in particular, as suggested in Chapter 4, that there be a review of whether there should be third-party rights of appeal against planning decisions. Moreover, in the event of challenge, it is necessary to consider the structures and institutional arrangements. Grant has pointed to the drawbacks of a system in which judicial review is available in tandem with the operation of separate regulatory processes, leading to judicial restrictions being placed upon the time in which proceedings may be brought to challenge the grant of a planning permission. The proposal for a separate Environmental Court might partly address this problem of overlap and delay, through a strict approach to case management, as well as the combining of judicial review and third party merits appeals, 'in a fast-track procedure, which would allow all the issues to be combined in a single hearing'.[180]

The planning regime, accordingly, has the capacity to offer an effective strategic role in seeking sustainable solutions in the development context. In its final report, the UK Round Table on Sustainable Development saw the strength of planning to lie in 'the discretion in the hands of decision takers to weigh all the aspects of the development – social, economic and environmental – in reaching a decision. But that discretion can be constrained by other, more detailed, codes and regulatory regimes'.[181] The report concluded that the land use planning system has a crucial part to play in securing sustainable development, as developments by building and changes of use:

> ... shape the physical world of the future and influence the way people will live their lives in it. The planning system is one of the few current mechanisms which clearly links national goals with local ones; which gives an opportunity for issues to be examined 'in the round';

---

178 Cf New South Wales Planning and Assessment Act, s 90.
179 Tromans, 1987, pp 107–08.
180 Grant, 2000a, para 13.14.7.
181 UK Round Table on Sustainable Development, Fifth (and final) Annual Report, 2000, para 2.13.

and which allows, indeed encourages, public participation in decision making. These positive existing traits of the system reflect the concept and purpose of sustainable development. It is important that they are retained and developed further.[182]

The participatory base of planning, and the growing emphasis on development planning, together with the emergence of a regional framework, suggest that appropriate structures can be put in place to bring about the array of changes required, especially in urban living and in social, even economic, expectations. Pollution control is an essential tool, and should be seen as an integral, supplementary element of a regulatory regime concerned with the planning and control of land use.

---

182 UK Round Table on Sustainable Development, Fifth (and final) Annual Report, 2000, para 2.10.

CHAPTER 8

ENVIRONMENTAL PROTECTION AND SCIENTIFIC UNCERTAINTY

The cloud had gone over where the reindeer grazed, poison had come down in the rain, the lichen became radioactive, the reindeer had eaten the lichen and got radioactive themselves. What did I tell you, she thought, everything is connected ... When the accident happened the Norwegian government had to decide what amount of radiation in meat was safe, and they came up with a figure of 600 becquerels. But people didn't like the idea of their meat being poisoned, and the Norwegian butchers didn't do such good business, and the one sort of meat no-one would buy was reindeer, which was hardly surprising. So this is what the government did. They said that as people obviously weren't going to eat reindeer very often because they were so scared, then it would be just as safe for them to eat meat that was more contaminated every once in a while as to eat less contaminated meat more often. So they raised the permitted limit for reindeer meat to 6,000 becquerels. Hey presto! One day it's harmful to eat meat with 600 becquerels in it, the next day it's safe with ten times that amount.[1]

These concluding chapters address questions of sustainability in the broader context of political decision making and the relationship between policy and supporting legal arrangements. This chapter is concerned with the nature of risk and its assessment in the context of environmental harm. Risk is a typically pervasive question in most areas affecting environmental policy and law. The extent of environmental threat can often be hard to assess, and a lack of objective certainty impacts also on the value of legal solutions. Moreover, risk has to be accommodated within broader social structures, and it is suggested should only be justified upon grounds of informed acceptability. It is argued that levels of reliance upon technical assistance, especially where mediated by policy makers, should be conditional. Indeed, the idea of risk assessment is fraught with difficulties. It raises questions which mirror those which affect environmental problems generally in the policy process: to do with the weighting of conflicting demands.

1 THE MEANING AND ROLE OF RISK ASSESSMENT

The first section seeks to identify the pervasive influence of risk upon environmental policy making. It further considers the reasonable expectations of a risk assessment process, as well as the need to identify more appropriate responses to the management of risk. In the first part, issues of objective uncertainty and the limits of science are addressed.

1.1   Setting objective frameworks

Risk has been described as 'the organising concept that gives meaning and direction to environmental regulation', with regulators 'increasingly required to base their actions on

---

1   Barnes, *The Survivor*, 1989, pp 85–86.

risk assessment'.[2] Rosenbaum describes environmental policy making as 'a volatile mixture of politics and science that readily erupts into controversy among politicians, bureaucrats and scientists over their appropriate roles in the process, as well as over the proper interpretation and use of scientific data in policy questions'.[3] Yet scientists and other experts are in an invidious position, as scientific advice will often clothe (even shield) the administrator or politician with a scientific authority. This incident has contributed to the wide governmental acceptance of environmental protection. With reference to policy making in the United States, Hornstein has pointed to risk assessment being blessed with the key advantage that 'it offered something for everyone'.[4] When politicians speak therefore of 'sound science' it is inevitably, wittingly or otherwise, apt to mislead. The discussion which follows concludes by considering how far ultimate responsibility should be a matter of political judgment, on the basis that 'science cannot relieve public officials and institutions from making many difficult and controversial environmental decisions'.[5]

Risk assessment is a structured response to uncertainty as to the effects of human activities. It raises fundamental questions as to how society addresses uncertainty. Its foundations lie in processes involving both those with technical knowledge of relevant fields and those responsible for policy formulation. In the UK, a group convened under the then Chief Scientific Adviser, Sir Robert May, produced during 2000 a report on risk procedures in the context of food safety. This pointed to two methods of risk assessment practice in use, respectively termed formally structured assessments and reliance upon expert judgment. The report concluded with the view that 'while no single risk assessment formula can be applied to all problems, we believe that carrying out a systematic risk assessment is the best way of approaching risk'.[6] The rationale given for this lay in 'the rigour with which the hazards and the populations exposed are identified, risks are estimated and uncertainties exposed'.[7] But in defining the process, it remains important not to lose sight of inherent uncertainties. The former head of the United States Federal Environmental Protection Agency has defined risk assessment as 'the attempt to quantify the degree of hazard that might result from human activities – for example, the risks to human health and the environment from industrial chemicals. Essentially, it is a kind of pretence; to avoid the paralysis of protective action that would result from waiting for "definitive" data, we assume that we have greater knowledge than scientists actually possess and make decisions based on those assumptions'.[8]

Thus circumscribed, risk assessment may be contrasted with risk management, which is the exercise of decision making responsibilities. The latter can be described as the process by which an administrative agency decides upon action or inaction in the light of estimates of risk emerging from the assessment process.[9] Cost benefit analysis has

---

2   Jasanoff, 1997, p 1; see also Jasanoff, 1999.
3   Rosenbaum, 1991, p 68.
4   Hornstein, 1992, p 565.
5   Rosenbaum, 1991, p 166.
6   Office of Science and Technology, 2000, para 6.
7   Office of Science and Technology, 2000, para 7.
8   Ruckelshaus, 1997, p 48.
9   Ruckelshaus, 1997, p 50.

assumed a pivotal role in approaches to risk management, offering an accepted framework for making regulatory decisions in the face of the existence of risk. As a result it appears necessary to find a mutual language. Cost benefit analysis can be variously defined, as discussed in Chapter 2, but it essentially requires a factoring of environmental values into decision making apparatuses. It may be inevitable that, in order to bridge the lack of comparable measurability, recourse must be had to the language of the market. This process is a pragmatic, structured response to decision making dilemmas. It has likewise been criticised for its implications in diluting environmental values, as discussed below.

It is important that all concerned in the processes recognise the proper roles which can be ascribed to science and other technical experts. It is for instance the concern of scientists to predict both the nature and levels of risk with as much accuracy as possible. They are not concerned with the acceptability of risk. Their role is therefore not even to eliminate risk, but to produce verifiable information which is sufficiently accessible for use in the decision making process. Whatever the arguments as to objective validity or subjectivity of content, it is inevitable that risk assessment must rely upon expert analysis of risk. Citing the (eventual) success following the accumulation of a body of scientific knowledge on the dangers of DDT pesticides and asbestos, Rosenbaum concludes that scientific data 'enable officials to define more carefully and clearly the range of options, risks and benefits involved in regulating a substance even when the data cannot answer all risk questions conclusively'.[10]

Science methodologies, especially in the physical sciences, can be criticised for their reductive nature. Yet this is perhaps inevitable, given the rate of progress and the demands upon specialisation, and can even be seen as a continuation of the process that dates from the schism post-Newton between the disciplines of science and philosophy. Control traditionally relies upon peer review: the idea of science as a process of disconfirmation.[11] Mee has criticised what he describes as a post mortem approach, at odds with the demands of the precautionary principle, for whilst 'sufficiently reliable techniques are currently available to give early warning signs of pollution ... no single technique or group of techniques can ensure a fully anticipatory approach'.[12] The argument is therefore that this indicates a need for a broader conceptual framework, such as by formulating responses on the basis of investigation for adverse effects, rather than identification of likely pollutants. This implies for instance a need for a restrictive approach to the introduction of new substances. Risk assessments, say in the case of pollutants, must inevitably be concerned with investigating the presence and impact of suspected pollutants. Yet the limitations are legion. The relative uncertainties confronting arguably all scientific hypotheses are especially significant in the area of environmental degradation and related threats to human health. Percentage claims vary, but Rosenbaum for instance suggests that there is no information available on the toxic effects of an estimate approaching 80% of chemicals used in industrial processes.[13]

---

10   Rosenbaum, 1991, p 155.
11   Popper, 1962.
12   Mee, 1996, p 130.
13   Rosenbaum, 1991, p 149.

Even where the toxicity of substances has been identified, there are limitations inherent in dose-response assessment methods, especially as to the question of impact on human beings.[14] The problems in epidemiology include limits upon the validity of experimental conditions, the representative nature of the organisms tested, whether all toxic substances are accounted for, and the impact upon toxicity of other factors such as site disturbance. Alongside observable impacts, there are particular uncertainties associated with low-level, long term risks, whether to individuals, their successors, or to whole ecosystems, and which testing at high levels cannot satisfactorily replicate. The valuing of human life is especially prone to distortions in cost benefit calculations, as discussed in the context of sustainability in Chapter 2. Mee concludes that 'there is not enough information available to conduct proper risk assessments and to estimate the human cost benefit associated with such contaminants in the environment'.[15]

These issues often lie at the frontiers of science, as in the emerging debate concerning genetically modified organisms.[16] Closely tied to the question of sustainability, having largely agreed on the question of global warming, the scientific community is only gradually reaching agreement upon predictions as to its timescale and effects.[17] It has been pointed out that an essential drawback of risk assessment is that it 'may appear to provide clear and precise information about the risk, when this is not the case. If little hard scientific data was available for the risk assessment process, then the outcome will be as imprecise as the assumptions and judgments that went into it'.[18] The generic approach represented by quantitative or numeric guidance in principle offers structure and consistency. Yet despite apparent objectivity, the value of measurement through quantitative values is likewise afflicted by the problem of input data. Policy makers should look to translate such assessments in ways that recognise such possibilities. For instance, central guidance under the new contaminated land regime requires that consideration be applied to the assumptions underlying the numerical values, together with any conditions relevant to their use, and any adjustments that need to be made to reflect site-specific circumstances.[19]

Quantitative analysis, according to Piller, 'promises certainty in a haze of intimidating numerical specificity. It is a false premise, however, because scientific abilities develop unevenly. The science of measurement, for instance, has recently yielded ways to detect the presence of some toxic substances down to parts per million. Yet the sciences of assessment – toxicology and epidemiology – lag far behind'.[20] A key factor, such as latency, prevalent in low exposure levels and long timescales, challenges the effectiveness of research capacities. Likewise, other consequences follow on the limitations of risk assessment, as in the question of potential liability for environmental harm due to the development of genetically modified plant technology.[21] By contrast, opportunities for

---

14 Mee, 1996, pp 119–23.
15 Mee, 1996, p 123.
16 See, eg, Vidal, 2000.
17 See United Nations, IPCC, 2001; cf Morris, 1997.
18 Office of Science and Technology, 2000, para 7.
19 DETR, 2000k, Explanatory Memorandum, Annex 3, para B48.
20 Piller, 1991, p 176.
21 See Rifkin, 1999.

legal challenge, which remain particularly reliant upon causality being established, are reduced.

1.2 Principles of risk response

Progress towards greater sustainability must both confront problems of environmental risk and address the appropriateness of responses. Identifying the nature of harm is closely allied to problems of risk assessment. Environmental protection, whether in terms of reactive or proactive law and policy responses, requires the assistance of predictive science. Three especial difficulties can be identified. The first two are concerned with the nature of the relationship of assessment to decision and the validity of the assessment. First, degrees of reliance on expert analysis may stray into the area of choice as to acceptability of risk. For instance, in the context of contaminated sites, it is said that 'site specific or quantified risk assessment leans heavily on professional judgment as to what is an acceptable level of risk'.[22]

Secondly, scientific methodology is the more vulnerable the more that probabilities and outcomes cannot be readily defined. Pursuing the contaminated sites illustration, risk assessment in this area has been described as an 'art' where there are 'abundant opportunities for personal interpretation and bias. The latter can be detrimental to the outcome, but also provide the underpinning professional judgments that are inherent to an effective process. Risk assessment cannot be reduced to standardised institutions and guidelines'.[23] A prescient conclusion is that especially where 'we typically have little knowledge about the impact of new technologies, it is impossible fully to quantify any associated risks: we are dealing with uncertainty. Moreover, where we do not even know the range and character of potential impacts and the different combinations in which these might occur, we are dealing with both uncertainty and ignorance'.[24] This can also be seen in the traditional UK approach to the licensing of polluting discharges, with a preference to be based upon assimilative capacities of receiving media. Yet it has been pointed out that as a result acceptable limits reflect a limited number of observable results, excluding the possibility of other indirect and interactive effects. Indeed we are often engaged upon a 'good guess' leap into the darkness.[25] This suggests that our culture of 'good science' is 'so narrowly construed that it cannot accommodate ignorance and the complex actions of the environment. This has led policy makers to an inbuilt bias against the environment'.[26]

Thirdly, difficulties also apply in the legal domain. In addressing questions of harm and uncertainty, lawyers have their own approaches. Uncertainties are resolved by rules, as in demanding that certain standards of proof are met, and by whom. However, as has been seen in Chapter 3, where uncertainty is of an objective (rather than epistemological) nature, resolution is very much more awkward for the lawyer.[27] Moreover, causes of

---

22 Tromans and Turrall-Clarke, 2000, p 34.
23 Petts, Cairney and Smith, 1997, p 301.
24 Global Environmental Change Programme, 1999, p 6.
25 Hencke, 2000.
26 Wynne and Mayer, 1993.
27 See Cohen, 1977.

action are relatively inflexible in content, and relationships with property interests create difficulties in respect of the unowned environment. Questions as to the incidence of risk and its adjustment, traditionally falling to be considered under claims in private law, are resolved through the often arbitrary lens of causation. Yet endemic difficulties in defining the nature of harm, and whether interests of identifiable individuals or groups have been prejudiced, now also occur in the contexts of public law responses. The constraints of legal methodologies have become apparent: environmental degradation may have long timeframes and may be subject to a high degree of uncertainty. Indeed in the public law sphere, whilst powers of action are policy-driven and therefore more broadly based, similar problems may attach to regulatory and related compliance approaches. As efforts are therefore made to shift environmental protection away from reliance upon so-called command-and-control approaches, to be replaced or supplemented by alternative, incentivised strategies, the identification of harmful environmental impacts continues to be important.

Yet, whatever the cultural limitations, risk responses are crucial to the quality of the sustainability debate, discussed in earlier chapters. For instance, upon an international level, discussing obligations upon States to reduce adverse impacts, Weiss suggests an obligation to engage in necessary scientific research, in order to better evaluate threats to the well-being of present and future generations. As to the level of risk to be passed on, it is accordingly necessary 'to develop objective criteria, based on the diversity and quality of our natural and cultural environment and on the sustainable use of our biosphere, to determine whether risks that we foresee for future generations are appropriate or whether they may be minimized at acceptable cost. A major difficulty in assessing risks to future generations is the scientific uncertainty that often surrounds the question of whether there will be any adverse impacts and, if so, how severe'.[28] In the context of sustainability, pointing to encouraging signs in the Montreal Protocol on Ozone Depletion, Weiss concludes that an obligation is owed by the present generation 'to proceed extremely cautiously in the face of scientific uncertainty about risks of serious irreversible harm to future generations'.[29]

This accords with the advocacy of the precautionary approach for taking preventive action before the availability of conclusive or at least definitive evidence of harm. There is a fundamental tension between those who demand realistic identification of risks and those who advocate a more precautionary line. The former, technical rationalist approach, urges 'caution to avoid overestimating risks in ways that create obstacles to profitability'.[30] Ruckelshaus explains this as the view that 'regulation ought not to be based on a set of unprovable assumptions but only on connections between pollutants and health effects that can be demonstrated under the canons of science in the strict sense'.[31] The meaning of 'strict sense' can be explained by reference once again to Wynne and Mayer's critique of 'good science'. This is accordingly delineated as an institutional construct arising as 'a product of culture as well as intellectual principles. In Britain the culture which has predominated, inevitably influencing environmental policies, has been

---

28   Weiss, 1989, p 67.
29   Weiss, 1989, p 69.
30   Piller, 1991, p 181.
31   Ruckelshaus, 1997, p 49.

largely reductionist – that is breaking down an area into its smallest components in the belief that only those directly observable and measurable parts matter. It often takes the view that factors have no significance unless they can be tied into a cause-and-effect relationship'.[32] Political and legal approaches share certain of these inherent limitations, and likewise accord preference to the status quo, whether expressed in terms of industrial or lifestyle imperatives. It also accords with the views of those concerned to restrict unnecessary regulation. Thus the chairman of the UK's Better Regulation Task Force, in expounding its five principles of good regulation, namely transparency, accountability, proportionality, consistency and targeting, in an immediate response to the publication of the report of the Philips Inquiry into BSE, warns against 'excessively cautious' approaches.[33] Yet Ruckelshaus holds that waiting for firm evidence of human health effects is morally unacceptable: 'far from overestimating the risks from toxic substances, conventional risk assessments underestimate them, for there may be effects from chemicals in combination that are greater than would be expected from the sum effects of all chemicals acting independently. While approving of risk assessment as a priority-setting tool, this viewpoint rejects the idea that we can use risk assessment to distinguish between "significant" and "insignificant" risks. Any identifiable risk ought to be eliminated up to the capacity of available technology to do so.'[34]

2 CRITIQUES OF RISK ASSESSMENT

Risk assessment is therefore subject to strenuous critiques. These centre upon the determination of values which underlie the calculation process. The main issue pursued here concerns the role of the technical expert as separable from those of policy makers and administrators: those who must assume responsibility for managing risk. In terms of sustainability, given that the stakes can be extremely high, it is essential that risk management be based upon institutional structures which acknowledge the conflictual nature of risk, especially within its wider social construction. It is argued that a presumption of openness is essential.

2.1   Whose environmental values?

There are two essential critiques in the face of the seeming advantages of objectivity and the search for a neutral process described above. The first is rooted in ethics, in what might be termed the indivisibility of environmental values. It maintains an opposition to cost benefit approaches on grounds that the process unacceptably creates a commodification of essentially non-marketable values, or of 'shadow-pricing' of such values.[35] Gauna states that 'agencies should recognise that health and healthy ecosystems have an ethical dimension that cannot be addressed adequately within a benefit cost approach', and even goes on to refer to 'the pretence of objectivity in quantifying,

---

32   Wynne and Mayer, 1993.
33   Haskins, 2000.
34   Ruckelshaus, 1997, pp 49–50.
35   Sagoff, 1988, Chapter 4.

comparing, and managing risk and (agencies should) instead consider normative concerns to inform regulation'.[36] This has support from Shere, who argues that environmental improvements such as reduced pollution have not been achieved through risk assessment, but are the result of improvements in technology: in other words, practice-based controls which inevitably closely relate to the regulatory process. He accordingly argues that regulators should be refocused on environmental protection, based upon quality of life and ethics arguments, which 'have been almost entirely removed from the regulatory agenda by the focus on risk assessment'.[37]

Sagoff posits a more inclusive ethical approach to risk, which lies somewhere between restraining on the basis of a no-risk society, and allowing economic goals to achieve allocatory efficiency. This entails an approach based upon reasonable steps towards the elimination of harm, achieved through cooperation by regulators, industry, consumers and environmental groups: the idea of regulatory ends being ethically motivated but conforming to the means available to achieve them.[38] This is compatible with views of the Royal Commission on Environmental Pollution. Values have been defined by the commission as 'beliefs, either individual or social, about what is important in life, and thus about the ends and objectives which should govern and change public policies'.[39] It will be argued below that values must be more effectively transposed into policy making processes with a view to achieving sustainability. Not only should policy makers seek to encourage debate around such values, they should also aim to ensure their articulation and to find appropriate responses.[40] Whilst values are relatively fixed, as compared with preferences, the need to encourage more 'sustainable' values – or at any rate behaviour which more clearly correlates – is discussed in Chapter 10.

The second critique more pragmatically argues that a concentration upon quantitative methods of valuation results in confusion, by legitimating a process of bringing environmental values into market calculations. It has been suggested that it is inherent in instrumental valuation that it tends to favour environmental degradation.[41] Moreover, the process can mask what are properly regarded as contingent features, for not only is the process of comparing different types of risk itself problematic, but as seen above the task is limited by data availability. Thus uncertainties are unavoidably built into both definitions of risk and ranges of attributed value.[42] Given problems in valuation of environmental factors, it is therefore inevitable that emphasis will be placed upon those that are more receptive to quantitative representation, such as economic costs and benefits. Cost benefit analysis may in consequence disadvantage more contingent environmental interests. This incumbrance is not applied (at least not openly) in the case of other public interests. Wilkinson compares the allocation of law and order resources or medical treatment, which is not on the basis of the 'value' attached to individuals by other individuals. 'By analogy, legal protection or remediation for species and ecosystems cannot be properly determined by economic criteria.'[43]

---

36   Gauna, 1998, pp 52–53.
37   Shere, 1995, p 416.
38   Sagoff, 1988, especially Chapter 9.
39   RCEP, 1998, para 7.4.
40   House of Lords, 2000, para 2.60.
41   See Kelman, 1997, pp 94–96.
42   See Applegate, 1995.
43   Wilkinson, 1999, p 28.

On this view, an emerging numbers game results in a tendency to trump more qualitative public interest notions, such as ecosystem protection, intergenerational and intragenerational equity, and even cultural values. Numbers have been described as 'seductive: they apply a degree of accuracy and certainty that is often unjustified'.[44] Likewise, whilst the administrator is shielded by the acceptance of the assessment exercise as valid, results can be spectacularly arbitrary. Dramatically changing projections illustrate this, as for instance the risk of members of the population of the UK contracting new variant CJD as a result of the BSE crisis. Figures issued by the Department of Health state that in January 1998 there were 23 confirmed cases,[45] and in February 2001, 98 cases.[46] This suggests that the chances of contracting CJD have moved from around 1 in 5 million to around 1 in 650,000 during the intervening period. A more common instance is the bewildering variety of values resulting from processes of attributing a money value to lives saved. It has for instance been pointed out that in 1985 'three federal agencies variously estimated a life to be worth from \$400,000 to \$3.5 million'.[47] Two further illustrations of this point can be made by reference to Rosenbaum's analysis. First, discussing data concerning deaths resulting from emissions from electric power plants, he points out that the process is 'a politically perilous act sure to seem arbitrary, if not morally repugnant, no matter what value is assigned'.[48] Secondly, discussing valuation of human lives in the context of environmental threat generally, he quotes an aide to former President Nixon, to the effect that protagonists would often agree to halve any numeric difference. He concludes that many decisions are made 'ultimately on the basis of political, administrative or other considerations and later sanctified with economics for credibility'.[49]

2.2   Use and abuse of the role of experts

For their part, when called upon to advise government, scientists are 'frequently faced with thinking about issues that are not usually at the forefront of their reflection. The advice is solicited in response to government or social problems and therefore must be contextualised in social worlds not always so familiar to the advisors'.[50] In other words, the reality of scientific contingency will often be by-passed by the question parameters set by administrators and policy makers. It has therefore been asserted that risk assessment institutionalises the dangers of non-neutrality, in allowing the ideological restrictions to be imposed upon environmental protection, especially 'by controlling the way in which "technical decisions" are made'.[51] Those who construct models often have excessive faith in their own predictions.[52] Moreover, according to Piller, experts' statements are 'social

---

44   Applegate, 1995, p 1671.
45   See Department of Health, 1998.
46   See Department of Health, 2001.
47   Piller, 1991, 177.
48   Rosenbaum, 1991, p 131.
49   Rosenbaum, 1991, p 134.
50   Mukerji, 1989, p 200.
51   Brown, 1988, p 196, cited by Shere, 1995, p 490.
52   RCEP, 1998, para 2.56.

and political choices defined as technical choices'.[53] Institutional factors are influential, as also the subjective perceptions of the experts, as human as the rest of us. Thus, for them also, 'coalitions solidify and disagreements become polarised as conflict becomes more acrimonious'.[54] It would be idle to ignore that scientists too have values. Yet as discussed below, they are subject to funding and other pressures which threaten independence of contribution to wider policy debate. Whilst there are ways in which such problems can be addressed (as in encouragement of timely publication and the operation of peer review), solutions lie in recognising these constraints, especially in the setting of the scientific agenda. The House of Lords Select Committee has concluded that public support for scientists is more likely where values are openly declared and there is engagement with the wider public.[55]

Thus mandating cost benefit analyses of regulatory bodies not only imposes costs upon tight administrative budgets but also operates a bias given the generally greater difficulty in calculating environmental, as opposed to business, costs and benefits. Scott argues that efficiency-based cost benefit approaches carry the implication of '"right" answers, not only in respect of the level of governance issue, but in relation to the setting and stringency of standards and to the choice of policy instruments. It militates in the direction of government by expert'.[56] It can also be said to militate against action to protect the environment, Latin concluding that 'a requirement for formal analyses may introduce a systematic bias against government action'.[57] This is endorsed by the Global Environmental Change Programme, which has pointed to those areas of high uncertainty where science cannot provide definitive answers: 'the policy of relying on claims of "sound science" may, ironically, itself be unsound. Ethical issues are central.'[58]

The use of cost benefit approaches, and the statutory duties likewise imposed, tends to reflect dominant economic and political priorities, as discussed in Chapter 2. This symbiosis is reflected in broader discussions of regulatory roles, such as the tension between free market economics and the objectives of governmental regulation. Smith, for instance, cites the proper limits of regulation as follows: first, as only properly justified by '"market failure", which in the case of most health, safety and environmental regulation is caused by the existence of "externalities" – costs that one economic unit imposes on others and need not reckon with itself (or benefits that accrue to all and which no single actor has an incentive to provide)'; and, secondly, as a legal restructuring of 'a market system so as to achieve desired ends that the market has heretofore failed to serve, but to do so in the most efficient and least market-disruptive manner'.[59] Yet transposing this role into risk comparisons, there is a danger that we 'ignore the economic underpinnings of the equation. Corporations do not profit from lightning strikes but they make a fortune from polluting industries'.[60]

---

53 Piller, 1991, p 179.
54 See Mazur, 1981, p 29.
55 House of Lords, 2000, para 2.65.
56 Scott, 1998, p 18.
57 Latin, 1982, p 188.
58 Global Environmental Change Programme, 1999, p 4.
59 See Smith, 1996, p 258.
60 Piller, 1991, p 175.

If it is necessary to weigh benefit against cost, the resulting analysis of risk, as Piller explains, 'rejects value judgments regarding social need, lifestyle, or community preservation. In other words, it subtly limits debate. It evolves easily to acceptable risk'.[61] This is achieved by either ignoring or treating as mere technical uncertainties the deeper problems underlying risk assessment, including institutional pressures and cultural expectations, as well as inadequate data; indeed, the basis for assessment, such as whether worst case or conservative values, may create a high degree of variability. Statistical risk is thus limited by the input data, as seen above, and in circumstances of paucity of evidence, as in low-frequency, high-impact occurrences, figures seem more likely to confuse than to enlighten.[62] Society (like individuals), whilst being remarkably risk averse in certain circumstances, even leading to panic, can be strangely sanguine in others. It is important to recognise that the framework for social debate is affected by both awareness of risk and choice of interests, along with values accorded to them.

2.3 Risk as a social construct

The notion of a risk society has already been referred to. As propounded by Beck, it is argued that society's post-industrial phase is evolving into a new modernity.[63] This is marked by a heightening of risk, as to both sources and extent, incorporating global impacts upon the environment and consequences also for future generations. Beck refers to an experimental society in which there is an unregulated, unaccountable technological and scientific establishment. This society is one in which the protective role of science has been exposed as inadequate, with technology and innovation indeed generating not only solutions but also new forms of risk. Likewise, citing the otherwise diverse examples of nuclear power and quieter highways, Piller points out that 'a technical fix rarely eliminates a problem at its social or economic roots; technology often changes the intensity, form or location of undesirable side effects'.[64] The concept of the risk society therefore describes a state in which 'hazards produced in the growth of industrial society become predominant. That both poses the question of the self-limitation of this development and sets the task of redefining previously attained standards (of responsibility, safety, control, damage limitation and distribution of the consequence of loss) with reference to potential dangers. These, however, not only elude sensory perception and the powers of the imagination, but also scientific determination'.[65]

Beck describes the idea of reflexive modernity as a process of self-contradiction, for 'the more modern a society becomes, the more unintended consequences it produces, and as these become known and acknowledged, they call the foundations of industrial modernisation into question'.[66] The lack of certainty inherent in reflexivity has a number of incidents. Giddens points to three factors, each fundamental to the nature of risk, and to our assessment of it, in a technocratic age: differential power, changing values, and the

---

61   Piller, 1991, p 176.
62   See, eg, Radford, 1997, 1999.
63   See Beck, 1992.
64   Piller, 1991, p 188.
65   Beck, 1996, pp 28–29.
66   Beck, 1998, p 91.

impact of unintended consequences. He suggests a new risk profile, with ecological threats 'the outcome of socially organised knowledge, mediated by the impact of industrialism upon the material environment'.[67] He suggests that whilst 'the disembedding mechanisms have provided large areas of security in the present-day world, the new array of risks which have thereby been brought into being are truly formidable'.[68] Thus the scope of risk has extended in terms of both intensity and the expansion in contingent events, especially in transforming nature.

The implications of this indicate a need to re-examine commercial modes of production and to challenge science, politics and legal approaches to risk management. The roots of such risk theory therefore call into question basic norms of decision making in civil society, in the context of these new, especially environmental, uncertainties. Revised approaches to decision making would recognise risks as a by-product of industrial society where expert and non-expert alike lack understanding. This further strand is embedded in the idea of the risk society is the notion that trust in experts and in institutions has been lost. In political terms, citizens now discover the weakness of many scientific foundations: 'what is in question is not only the limits of, or the gaps in, expert knowledge, but an inadequacy which compromises the very idea of expertise.'[69] A different perspective on this is that the change is less clear cut. According to Wynne, public perceptions have in a variety of areas always been 'qualified by the experience of dependency, possible alienation, and lack of agency'.[70] In contrast, as seen above, it is not necessarily accurate to categorise scientific assumptions as realist, for 'expert knowledge embodies social assumptions and models framing its objectivist language and ... lay people have legitimate claim to debate those assumptions'.[71] Moreover, citing empirical observation of the workings of lay knowledge in response to environmental threats, Wynne concludes that the boundaries between experts and non-experts are more fluid and that 'constructive kinds of interaction and mutual inspiration or dependency ... may exist between them'.[72]

Pursuing the above arguments as to social construction of risk a little further, social science commentators generally caution against risk being seen as solely a technical matter, for determination by, or sometimes even by reference to, experts.[73] Technical expectations of the risk assessment process are challenged in numerous ways. A central critique concerns the tendency towards reliance upon assumed science at the expense of wider sociopolitical factors. In an analogous discussion of risk and the development of a blame culture, Douglas has categorised the avoidance of charges of bias as a main objective of the expert. This leads to a perceived search for 'the real essence of risk perception before it is polluted by interests and ideology ... they exclude the whole subject of politics and morals. To see them studying risk taking and risk aversion in some imaginary pure state is disappointing to anyone who has been attracted to the dirty side of the subject'.[74] Likewise, the Global Environmental Change Programme has pointed to

67 Giddens, 1990, p 110.
68 Giddens, 1990, pp 124–25.
69 Giddens, 1990, p 131; and see Jouhar, 1984.
70 Wynne, 1996, p 52.
71 Wynne, 1996, p 59.
72 Wynne, 1996, p 62.
73 See Adams, 1995, especially Chapter 11.
74 Douglas, 1994, p 11.

the source of uncertainty in many cases as being 'inherently social and economic in character, and may never be resolved by conducting more scientific research ... Yet there appears to be little familiarity with, or at least acceptance of, this knowledge in policy circles. Scientific judgments on risks and uncertainties are underpinned and framed by unavoidably subjective assumptions about the nature, magnitude and relative importance of these uncertainties. These "framing assumptions" can have an overwhelming effect on the results obtained in risk assessments. This partly explains why different risk assessments on the same issue can obtain widely varying results, even though each has apparently been conducted in accordance with the tenets of "sound science"'.[75]

Three especial consequences follow. First, risk perceptions may alter in the face of circumstances that intensify awareness of uncertainty, and thus a lack of control. We all engage in balancing behaviour in response to perceived risks, and responses will depend upon what Adams terms a 'risk thermostat' which responds to our own 'cultural filters'.[76] Especially in terms of health and environmental protection, he has pursued this idea, pointing to 'virtual risk', where individuals are unable to indulge in balancing behaviour to adjust risk thresholds, but are more at the mercy of unknown, and often far-distant consequences, which may even be intergenerational in their effect.[77] A simple example of subjective filtering is the paradox in the UK public having expectations of the railway system – which, although privatised, is to receive £60 billion worth of subsidies under a Ten-Year Transport Plan[78] – that are not required of private activities. Thus differential responses are made as to the acceptability of railway compared with road fatalities, though cars have been described as being '1000 times more dangerous than trains'.[79] Yet the cultural filters as applied to road travel arguably perceive it more acceptably as 'a private activity where we assess our own risks'.[80] Likewise, Porritt notes less concern at low-risk, high-frequency events such as road accidents than at high-risk, low-frequency events, such as nuclear accidents. The public therefore appears to register statistical probability produced by scientists by 'only as much ... as fits with their personalized, pre-existing risk framework, which is in turn shaped by a whole host of different factors depending on attitudes to the wider world and people's perceived place in it'.[81] Risk perceptions can therefore conflict dramatically: 'what is a relative risk to experts may appear as an absolute risk to citizens. It does not matter that the same citizens overlook (through denial, rationalization, or other distortions) an even greater threat from a source presumably under their control. Conversely, what is a significant threat to officials may be only a relative threat to citizens.'[82] The result can be either reckless pragmatism or unattainable risk aversion on the part of the citizen.[83]

---

75   Global Environmental Change Programme, 1999, p 7.
76   Adams, 1995, pp 42–45.
77   Adams, 1996.
78   DETR, 2000h.
79   Wolmar, 2001.
80   Coward, 2000.
81   Porritt, 2000, p 37.
82   Edelstein, 1988, pp 133–34.
83   House of Lords, 2000, para 2.58.

Secondly, problems of risk can be approached from numerous broader policy perspectives, and perceptions are influenced by cultural relativism. A cultural perspective, offered by Giddens, suggests four 'adaptive reactions', from pragmatic acceptance, through sustained optimism, cynical pessimism, and (his preference) radical engagement.[84] Likewise, Jasanoff points out that different societies have different tolerances as to what levels of risk may or may not be acceptable.[85] This may result in wider conflicts, as in the implications of European and North American perceptions of the debate on GMOs. Yet for all such differences it has been said that the public generally understands risk in a commonsense way, based upon everyday experience.[86] Safety is a relative term, and tolerances are affected by a variety of factors, including levels of availability of public information and opportunities for public participation in the context of these issues.

Thirdly, the presumptive objective approaches of governing hierarchies have become more readily contested. For instance, irrespective of whether absolute or relative criteria underlie the imposition of environmental standards, risk assessment has even been dismissed as 'a purely legalistic response and does not reflect the minimal support for the scientific basis behind these standards'.[87] The assessment of risk becomes ultimately a political question, in which technical solutions are on their own inadequate. Thus a premise underlying the risk society, that there is a growing distrust of technocracy, is widely shared. Inherent risks simply assume new forms, as a chemicals revolution of the last century has given way to one of biotechnology in this. Areas of concern include genetic modification and genetic engineering, as well as food safety.[88] Distrust of scientists has grown, especially those working for government or industry.[89] Thus, in the face of continued systemic failure to accommodate decision making to reflect precautionary responses to uncertainties, as seen above, fundamental changes in the structuring of decision making processes are debated. This is considered below, and further, in Chapter 10.

3 RISK ASSESSMENT WITHIN THE UK'S POLICY MAKING PROCESS

As risk assessments, however crude, are the stuff of everyday life, so likewise institutions, even the courts, engage in assessment within their own frameworks and for their own purposes. This section applies the already discussed issues of acknowledgment of risk and appropriate responses to selected circumstances, both explicit and implicit, within UK regulatory and policy making structures.

---

84 Giddens, 1990, pp 134–37.
85 Jasanoff, 1997, p 2.
86 Irwin and Wynne, 1996.
87 Edelstein, 1988, p 134.
88 See House of Lords, 2000, paras 2.11, 2.44.
89 See Worcester, 2001, pp 17, 12: citing MORI/Cabinet Office Better Regulation Unit, 1999, MORI/BMA, 2000.

3.1 Legal frameworks

The assessment of risk has a distinct relevance in the determination of questions of legal liability. As has been seen above, in the determination of whether actionable harm can be established, there is some comparability to the connection of causation issues with degrees of risk as traditionally encountered in private law. According to Kimblin, 'the courts' determination of the standard of care in negligence is risk assessment after the fact ... (which) determines the degree to which harm from a hazard may be foreseen; when harm has occurred the claimant must prove that the harm was foreseeable in order to succeed'.[90] In the area of public law and policy, risk analysis impacts upon both the delivery of policy and the extent and availability of legal challenge. The growth of formal techniques for risk assessment is likely increasingly to require adjudication. Yet whilst assessment is finding its way into legal mechanisms, it appears that by its nature expression of risk criteria is ultimately a discretionary exercise on the part of regulators, taking account of such guidance as to scientific evidence as may be available.[91] Outside the question of EIA, where applicable, risk assessment is an uncertain area for planners. Often it is encountered in the context of the assumed need to defer to pollution control, as discussed in the previous chapter, although (BATNEEC notwithstanding) there may still be risks or perceived risks of environmental harm, which may be material.[92]

An illustration of a need for adjudication arising in the context of risk and probability can be seen in the High Court decision of *Envirocor Waste Holdings*.[93] This was an appeal against a decision of an inspector to reject an appeal against refusal of planning permission for a waste transfer facility. There was a potential impact upon the processes of a food manufacturer with premises some 250 metres from the appeal site. The main issue was whether there was an element of risk that could fairly be regarded as serious or substantial, but which could not be prevented by safeguards imposed under planning or licensing legislation. Brooke J held that 'probabilistic risk assessment was not a precise science, or art form, and the evidence before the inspector was extremely incomplete ... it was only one part of the evidence that a decision maker should take into account when evaluating the merits of a proposal like the instant one and provided that he made it clear that he had understood the effect of that part of the evidence the inspector was of course entitled to disregard it if he found other parts of the evidence more cogent or of greater value in assisting him to his final conclusion'.[94] However, allowing the appeal, Brooke J concluded that the inspector had not given sufficiently clear and intelligible reasons when dealing with evidence as to risk factors. The court considered that there was 'no evidence at all that a tainting incident would be likely to occur', seemingly on the basis of a presupposition of likelihood as 'an annual risk of such an incident at 1 in 30' over an assumed 30-year timespan.[95] In contrast, the inspector's view appeared to have been that the appeal must fail because there was always some risk of spillage causing a 'tainting

---

90   Kimblin, 2000, p 361.
91   Eg, *R v Tandridge DC ex p al Fayed* [1999] 1 PLR 104.
92   See, eg, DoE, PPG23, 1994a, para 3.18.
93   *Envirocor Waste Holdings Ltd v Secretary of State for the Environment* [1996] JPL 489.
94   *Ibid,* at p 493.
95   *Ibid,* at p 495.

incident', whatever precautions were taken. The figures on expert evidence were that a risk was in the order of between one in 100,000 and one in 300,000 per year, over a 30 year period. The inspector concluded that 'the proposed development would create a situation where a tainting incident ... would, sooner or later, be likely to occur. The divergence of views on risk assessment allow for a wide variation between "trivial" and "substantial" but even at the lower end it does not mean that the risk should be ignored. It is clearly apparent to me that the potential for taint could be created by the spillage of a very small quantity of waste and that, once spilt, there would be little that could be done to prevent contaminated air from reaching the BCM factory ... Clearly the greater the amount of tainting compound spilt, the greater the possibility of tainting would be, and it seems to me that whatever precautions are taken to minimise the risks, there could be no circumstances in which that risk was not present, even if the drum unloading and loading areas were to be enclosed'.[96] Yet Health and Safety Executive (HSE) criteria in the context of involuntary risk to life created by a new development were cited. Whilst these are not necessarily comparable in terms of degree of risk, they suggested that an annual risk of 'a dangerous dose or worse' of one in 3 million or less could be regarded as 'trivial', whereas one in 100,000 or more would automatically indicate 'substantial risk'.[97] Brooke J was happy to apply those figures to level of risk of occurrence. The agreed range 'would unquestionably have fallen for the most part outside the area of "substantial risk" according to the HSE criteria'; indeed, *a fortiori*, as experts had agreed that as a result of further proposed measures (affecting unloading at the site), 'the frequency of any incident ... would be "greatly reduced", a conclusion which would be self-evident to a layman who knew little about risk analysis but merely used his common sense'.[98] Thus he considered that it had been beholden upon the inspector to explain what it meant to say that a risk of an incident of the above order could not be ignored, and to assess likely frequency at which incidents of varying degrees of seriousness might occur, taking account of anticipated reductions.

Clearly, numerous conclusions were reached by the inspector which the High Court concluded were in error, and Brooke J was able to conclude as follows: 'If he really meant that he was entitled to take into account any risk, however exiguous, that might be posed by an otherwise desirable development, then in his judgment the inspector had misdirected himself. The inspector was, of course, at liberty to take into account accident scenarios ... but ... had made no effort to estimate the likely frequency of the worst-case scenario which had impressed him so much. If he had started by making his own assessment of the risk set out in the original plans, had then estimated the extent to which that risk would be reduced by the inclusion of the covered enclosure, and had gone on to assess the risk of worst-case scenario occurring on that hypothesis, then it would have been possible to follow his reasoning and to reach a judgment as to whether the inspector had reached a conclusion that was open to him on the evidence. But he had done none of those things.'[99] In other words, some level of discounting is required.

Moreover, however much deciding upon acceptability of risk appears to be a discretionary exercise on the part of regulators, objective foundations for assessment may

---

96 *Envirocor Waste Holdings Ltd v Secretary of State for the Environment* [1996] JPL 489, referring to para 43, reported at pp 494–95.
97 See Health and Safety Executive, 1989.
98 *Envirocor Waste Holdings Ltd v Secretary of State for the Environment* [1996] JPL 489, at p 494.
99 *Ibid,* at pp 494, 495–96.

be demanded at the adjudication stage. This may have wider consequences, as objective criteria have been required for the exercise of administrative discretions afforded under Community Directives. As was discussed in Chapter 5, the Court of Justice has been unwilling to regard administrative discretions as absolute and required interpretation in light of legislative purpose and in reliance upon objective criteria.[100] Thus, in the case of waste disposal, the Directive is of a framework nature and it has been held that this militates against direct effect.[101] Yet under its terms, in making decisions on waste facilities, Member States are required to take necessary measures to ensure that waste is recovered or disposed of without endangering human health, and without using processes or methods which could harm the environment. The latter is broadly defined to be without risk to water, air, soil, plants and animals, without causing a nuisance through noise or odours, and without adversely affecting the countryside or places of special interest.[102] Despite the framework nature of the Directive, therefore, a court may be required to review the exercise of administrative discretion in reaching conclusions as to acceptability of risk.

Moreover, acceptability of risk may not solely be a concern of objective science established by expert evidence. One further factor, in the planning sphere, may survive the objectivisation of decision making through risk assessment. In the previous chapter, reference was made to the conclusion that planning decisions need not necessarily be based upon objective assessment.[103] Stanley has reviewed those cases where public concern has been in issue in the planning context. There is no doubt, as mentioned previously, in cases connected respectively with the installation of a waste incinerator and a chemical waste recycling plant, that public concern amounts to a material consideration.[104] Likewise, the Court of Appeal has further ruled that public concern at the impact for nearby neighbouring land uses of extending permission for a bail hostel was a material consideration.[105] Stanley has argued that no objective basis should be required for evidence as to public concern, for such factors are by their nature multifaceted, albeit varying in degree, especially when categorised as 'outrage' reaction, in the face of perceived 'dread' risks (involving for instance lack of control, inequitable distribution, catastrophic potential), as well as 'unknown' (say, unobservable) impacts.[106]

The question of weighting of public concern against other evidence is problematic, however, in circumstances where the balance of expert evidence is supported by relevant risk assessment. If this points to objective assessment of 'acceptable' impacts upon health and the environment, then it is difficult to see how it can in principle be anything other than a trump. However, it is undeniable that public and experts may be looking through different ends of a risk telescope. This is risk society territory, and, moreover, recalling

---

100 Case C-133/94, *Commission v Belgium* [1996] ECR I-2323; also Case C-72/95, *Aannemersbedrijf PK Kraaijevelt BV v Gedeputeerde Staten van Zuid-Holland* [1996] ECR I-5403, para 31.

101 Case C-236/92, *Comitato di Coordinamento per la Difesa della Cava v Reg Lombardia* [1994] ECR I-483.

102 Framework Directive on Waste, 75/442, Art 4.

103 See Piatt, 1997.

104 *Gateshead MBC v Secretary of State for the Environment* [1995] Env LR 37; *Newport MBC v Secretary of State for Wales and Browning Ferris Limited* [1998] JPL 377, 384.

105 *West Midlands Probation Committee v Secretary of State for the Environment and Walsall MBC* [1998] JPL 388.

106 Discussed by Stanley, 1998, pp 920–28.

Wynne earlier in this chapter, upon comparing scientific assumptions and lay knowledge, in neither case do objective and subjective estimations appear to lie wholly one way.[107] This leads to a difficulty for the decision maker, and by extension the adjudicator, in deciding upon the degree of weight that should be, or should have been, accorded to public fears or concerns. Perhaps the best that can be said is that it is necessary for the decision maker to have 'an adequate understanding of the factors, influences, and processes which together operate to create "public concern"'.[108] As seen in the previous chapter, the strategic planning process should explicitly address such issues, to some extent pre-emptively. The more that this can be achieved, then explosions of genuine public concern could be largely confined to those in response to new (and unforeseen) demands and to those generated by emergency-type (as opposed to infrastructure) situations, such as the resort to mass burnings (concern at dioxins) and mass burials (concern at soil and water contamination) of cattle, pigs and sheep, during the 2001 Foot and Mouth disease crisis.[109]

3.2   Structuring risk assessment for policy makers

The growing debate about uncertainty and risk has led to attempts to encourage greater coherence in the presentation and use of scientific advice in policy making. The administration had doubtless received a serious jolt by the findings of the Phillips Inquiry into Bovine Spongiform Encephalopathy (BSE), discussed below. At central government level, a coherent attempt has been made by the office of the Chief Scientific Adviser to introduce guidelines for government policy makers in approaching risk assessment.[110] Three main ruling principles have been set out, namely: that departmental procedures should allow the early identification of issues for which scientific advice will be needed; that policy making should draw on the best available scientific advice; and that there should be a clear presumption towards openness in explaining scientific advice. Departments were required to report annually to the Chief Scientific Adviser, and in follow-up reports have given indications of the procedures that had been put in place and reviewed departmental progress.[111] Key features are emphasised as being the assimilation of the guidelines into departmental practice, raising awareness of the principles in a positive way, and monitoring compliance by policy makers.[112]

In these further reports, there has also been an explicit recognition of the difficulties where scientific advice is uncertain or divided, and of the importance of advice being seen to be impartial. As a consequence, emphasis has been placed upon the importance of release into the public domain, at the earliest opportunity; and the involvement of a sufficiently wide range of best expert sources representing a diversity of views. This bears out a central finding of the Phillips Inquiry into BSE. In commenting upon instances of scientific ignorance and failures of communication, the report voiced concern at the

---

107 Wynne, 1996, p 59.

108 Stanley, 1998, p 931.

109 (2001) *The Guardian*, 25 May.

110 Office of Science and Technology, 1997.

111 Office of Science and Technology, 1998 and 1999.

112 Eg, Office of Science and Technology, 1997, sets out 'key principles'.

inappropriate use of advisory committees. For instance, expert committee conclusions were not reviewed, such recommendations being taken as definitive rather than advisory despite surrounding uncertainty (even after some of the premises had been demonstrated to be unsound), and advice was sought upon policy decisions without targeting or identifying those aspects upon which the experts were regarded as qualified.[113] Indeed, on important occasions matters were placed before experts where information was available not to the experts but only to the administrators, making the latter better placed to perform.[114]

Further joint guidance has continued the process instigated by the former Chief Scientific Adviser and sought to establish risk assessment, risk management and risk communication as essential elements of structured decision making processes across government. It also seeks to provide a framework for the development of functional risk assessment guidance, including social aspects of risk, including participatory and stakeholder solutions, and dealing with uncertainty.[115] There are now developments elsewhere in public administration. For instance, the Environment Agency produced a document concerned with environmental risks connected with BSE.[116] In connection with the subsequent GMO scare, the Advisory Committee on Releases into the Environment has sought to produce guidance on the assessment of risk connected with bio-diversity and genetically modified crops.[117]

3.3 Statutory application of cost benefit analysis to agency risk assessment

Such is the prevalence of criteria now being applied to the measurement of risk – it is for instance integral to the whole BATNEEC process – that it is not intended to list all the areas where assessment is called for in environmental matters.[118] Additionally, recent formal incursions of cost benefit analysis into UK environmental legislation indicates a tendency toward a higher degree of commitment to detailed content. Although this suggests limitations upon discretion, a cautious view would point to the general lack of prioritising of values, which suggests retention of a high degree of administrative autonomy. This may be limited in other ways, as under general deregulatory requirements that may be imposed. It is difficult to form general conclusions as a matter of law, for whilst such requirements are routinely applied in reaching regulatory decisions, there has as yet been a notable lack of recourse to challenge by way of judicial review. The onset of the contaminated land regime, as discussed later in this section, may signal a change in this quietus.

There is now a statutory provision, under the Environment Act 1995 that the Environment Agency '(a) in considering whether or not to exercise any power conferred upon it by or under any enactment, or (b) in deciding the manner in which to exercise any such power, shall, unless and to the extent that it is unreasonable for it to do so in view of

---

113 Phillips Report, 2000, Vol 1, para 1221.
114 Phillips Report, 2000, Vol 1, para 1222.
115 DETR/Environment Agency/Institute for Environment and Health, 2000, especially Chapters 3, 6.
116 Environment Agency, 1997.
117 Advisory Committee on Releases into the Environment, 2000.
118 See eg DoE, 1995c.

the nature or purpose of the power or in the circumstances of the particular case, take into account the likely costs and benefits of the exercise or non-exercise of the power or its exercise in the manner in question'.[119] This amounts therefore to a quite novel general duty on the regulator to take into account the likely costs and benefits of any proposed exercise of powers, unless unreasonable in view of the nature and purpose of the power or the particular facts. This is subject to a balancing provision, in that the duty imposed does not affect its obligation nevertheless to discharge any duties, comply with any requirements, or pursue any objectives, imposed upon or given to it otherwise than under this section.[120] As to the question of unreasonableness, central government guidance has suggested that it would include circumstances where it 'would frustrate the need for rapid action', as where there is imminent danger of serious harm.[121] The guidance proceeds to set out the environmental matters that must generally be brought into the account. Accordingly, the Agency is required to take account of certain 'needs'. These are expressed to include a holistic approach to the environment (especially cross-media impacts); long term perspectives (especially if effects are irreversible, or where high costs of restoration are involved); bio-diversity; the encouragement of improved technologies; the development of close and responsive relationships with the general public, local communities and regulated organisations, working in partnership with central and local government; and the provision of high-quality information and advice on the environment, both to the regulated and to the wider public. Moreover, in the consideration of costs and benefits, account must be taken of environmental threats, namely risks of irreversible damage; the impact upon the global environment; and the effect upon future generations.

In determining cost, further criteria require that certain quantifications should be applied as to the best available scientific information; risk assessment to underpin a decision; and the identification of areas of uncertainty, to take account of this under the precautionary principle. However, given the inevitable problems in determining such quantifications, guiding principles are set out which must in such circumstances apply to the required cost benefit approaches which are taken. These include the avoidance of disproportionately large economic cuts; the use of all available risk analysis techniques; the exercise of judgment where risks are not easily quantifiable or susceptible to monetary valuation; the assessment of impacts on society as a whole, as well as the environment by taking account of the effect on human health, impacts on the industrial sector and on particular groups of people; trying to assess longer-term implications; and establishing adequate procedures for staff charged with the consideration of cost benefit questions, to ensure consistence within the principles established in government guidance. Statutory guidance as to the discharge of the Agency's functions under section 4 of the 1995 Act underpin this, setting out aims and objectives that the Agency is required to follow with respect to its sustainable development objective. The guidance seeks to justify a role for cost benefit analysis, in placing values on environmental impacts and standard setting. It emphasises the need to encourage responses which minimise costs and help to exploit competitive advantages, basing decisions upon sound science and analysis of impacts,

---

119 Environment Act 1995, s 39(1).

120 At s 39(2).

121 See DETR, Guidance to the Environment Act, 1995.

risks, costs and benefits, to ensure that actions to achieve compliance are proportionate to the objectives concerned. The Agency is required primarily to concern itself with the effects for society as a whole, on the welfare of people and business, changes in the use of resources and impacts on the environment. For instance, decisions about economic development are required to take account of the costs of potential pollution and waste and the value of resources that are consumed and, conversely, of the value of any environmental improvements made. The guidance therefore, in its generality at least, purports to ensure that environmental costs and benefits are properly and fully taken into account in public and private sector decisions alongside economic costs and benefits.

3.4   Contaminated land and risk assessment

Assessment arrangements of greater specificity have been incorporated into the new UK regime for contaminated land, contributing to the designation of land as contaminated and levels of remediation required. The legislation itself was an enabling measure and for operational context for the new scheme resort must be had to the circular containing the detailed statutory guidance. Such guidance is authorised in respect of the definition of contaminated land, its identification, its remediation, liability exclusions and apportionment arrangements, and recovery of the costs.[122] Cost benefit questions are set out in considerable detail within this essential policy document, and dominate the operation of the arrangements. The guidance ensures that relevant information is factored into the decision making processes. Government guidance does not require a cost benefit assessment by responsible agencies, but rather places them under a duty to take account of likely costs and benefits. Thus the duty generally involves assessments about whether or not to take action, appropriate levels of control, and options for achieving environmental objectives. Guidance points to risk analysis techniques in appropriate cases. Costs and benefits which are either unquantifiable or not readily quantifiable are to be included, and the duty is expressed ultimately to require the exercise of judgment by the Agency.[123] Costs include costs to individuals and to the environment.[124] In considering costs of remediation, the authority is required to take account of those which are incurred at the outset (such as feasibility studies), ongoing management and maintenance, and disruption costs, as well as losses resulting from remedial action, including land value depreciation.[125] Benefits are not defined, and presumably refer to benefits of all kinds whether environmental or otherwise.

The effect of the policy guidance is to restrict the potentially heavy remediation liabilities which might apply to polluters and current owners of contaminated land. Inevitably, the regime reflects policy decisions as to the burden placed upon the private sector and the ruling concern for minimising impact on the public purse. The guidance, for instance, sets out three central elements of site-specific risk assessment as follows: suitability for current use; suitability for any new use, should development be planned;

---

122 EPA 1990, Part II A, ss 78A(2)(5), 78B(2), 78E(5), 78(F)(6)(7), 78P(2).
123 See, eg, DETR, 2000k, Annex 3, Chapter A, for a setting out of risk assessment principles.
124 See s 56(1) and Part I definition.
125 DETR, 2000k, Annex 3, para C.34–35.

and (on either basis) a limitation of remediation requirements to such work as is necessary to prevent unacceptable risks to human health or the environment. Limitations are reflected in the treatment of whether it is reasonable to require remediation.[126] The guidance describes this as 'reasonable having regard to the cost which is likely to be involved and the seriousness of the harm or of the pollution'.[127] The remedial action shall be regarded as reasonable,[128] in circumstances where 'an assessment of the costs likely to be involved and of the resulting benefits justify incurring those costs. Such assessment should include the preparation of an estimate of the costs likely to be involved and of a statement of the benefits likely to result. This latter statement need not necessarily attempt to ascribe a financial value to those benefits'.[129] Timing issues must also be addressed, with a view to delimiting required action, as where the costs can be delayed, or even reduced over time, as where natural processes are likely to assist or new techniques or wider development schemes come into play.[130]

On this basis, work is avoided which is either premature – 'so distorting priorities' – or unnecessary 'so wasting resources'.[131] It has therefore been said that the scheme seeks 'to avoid wasting resources by cleaning up land so as to make it fit for any purpose for which it might conceivably be needed in future. At one level, this is about risk assessment, but more fundamentally it is about the differing philosophical approaches of pragmatically doing enough for present purposes as against a complete and comprehensive solution here and now'.[132] The issue of public cost thus appears the more transparent in the law making process. Yet this transparency can be used as an obfuscatory political device. Upon the introduction of the Bill which contained the contaminated land clean-up regime, the government's explanatory and financial memorandum suggested that there were no financial implications, by reference, despite its wholesale inappropriateness, to a pre-existing statutory nuisance enforcement regime. Subsequently, following the incoming government's 1998 Comprehensive Spending Review, real, albeit limited, central resource commitments were made up to 2002, in support of set-up costs, including strategic development, site inspections, enforcement actions and remediation.[133]

Detailed circumstances are set out in the guidance as to enforcement requirements. Thus, for instance, the process of definition of contaminated land must accord with principles of risk assessment, in accord with established (contaminant/source – pathway – receptor) approaches.[134] Risk is defined as a combination of two elements: namely, the probability or frequency of occurrence of a defined hazard, such as exposure by a substance with the potential to cause harm, and the magnitude including the seriousness of the consequences.[135] The guidance proceeds to identify risk assessment in the context

---

126 EPA, Part IIA, s 78E(4), (5).
127 DETR, 2000k, Annex 3, para C.29.
128 EPA Part II, s 78E(4).
129 DETR, 2000k, Annex 3, para C.30.
130 DETR, 2000k, Annex 3, para C.32.
131 DETR, 2000k, Explanatory Memorandum, para 10.
132 Tromans and Turrall-Clarke, 2000, p 12.
133 DETR, 2000k, Explanatory Memorandum, para 10.
134 DETR, 2000k, Annex 3, paras A.9–21.
135 DETR, 2000k, Annex 3, para A.9.

of key statutory limiting concepts of significant harm and significant possibility of significant harm.[136] For such a determination to be made, the regulator must accordingly be satisfied that there is a significant possibility of significant harm, on the basis of adequate scientific assessment of available information using appropriate, authoritative and scientifically based guideline values for pollutant concentrations.[137] In the face of constraining technical demands such as those illustrated above, regulators face considerable burdens in justifying their clean-up demands or actions in connection with contaminated land. Inevitably, both courts and the Planning Inspectorate (in the case of the most potentially contaminated 'special sites') will be drawn into adjudication where statutory rights of appeal come to be exercised. Acceptability of levels of risk in appropriate circumstances, through such guideline values as are produced from time to time by central government, will generally be determinative. Nevertheless, as seen above, the technical demands upon adjudicators are likely to be greatest where objective uncertainty survives the process of expert submissions.

3.5 Balancing conflicting legal frameworks in the risk context

This section discusses the stark illustration of both policy and (so far limited) legal responses to risk issues connected with the BSE/CJD tragedy. Following the government announcement in March 1996 that a probable link existed between exposure to BSE-infected meat and new variant Creuzfeldt-Jacob Disease, the European Commission placed a ban upon UK beef exports.[138] Legal challenges to the ban illustrate the divergent cultural perspectives underlying the treatment of risk in the decision making process, as well as ways in which such issues can be opened to adjudication.[139] They further illustrate the potential for the precautionary principle to be influential in the determination of the extent of regulatory powers. The UK sought annulment on grounds that the Commission lacked legal competence in the area; that its decision breached the principle of proportionality; and that it was inconsistent with the Treaty objectives of the Common Agricultural Policy. The UK further argued that under the terms of the Treaty, the range of exceptions to the principle of free movement of goods (enshrined in what are now Articles 28 and 30), were insufficient to justify Commission action, allegedly for economic reasons. The Commission argued that the UK sought to draw an artificial distinction between public health and the proper operation of the internal market, and that the measures taken were necessary over the long term in order to fulfil the aims of protection of public and animal health in the context of the proper operation of the internal market.[140] In its final judgment, the ECJ made two essential rulings. First, it held that the Commission was authorised to adopt safeguard measures in response to new information which significantly altered the perception of risks to human health, including a worldwide ban on exports; and that the Commission had neither failed to meet

---

136 DETR, 2000k, Annex 3, chapter 3.
137 DETR, 2000k, Annex 3, para A.28.
138 Commission Decision 96/239.
139 See Cases C-157/96; C-180/96, *NFU v MAFF, UK v Commission* [1998] ECR I-2265; and Case C-180/96R, *UK v Commission* [1996] ECR I-3903 (interim proceedings).
140 Under Directives 90/425 and 89/662.

legislative conditions imposed, nor used its powers for an improper purpose. Secondly, in the context of the Common Agricultural Policy, where there was a discretionary exercise of powers (under what are now Articles 34 and 37), the principle of proportionality would only be breached by adopting measures 'manifestly inappropriate having regard to the objective which the competent institution is seeking to pursue'.[141] As to the imposition of the temporary ban, pending further scientific examination, whilst alternative measures might have been available, the Commission had not acted in breach of the principle. This was in light of two factors: namely, the seriousness of the risks involved; and the urgency of the situation. The objectives of the Common Agricultural Policy could not be pursued at the cost of public interest considerations such as the protection of health.

The judgment was overwhelmingly influenced by issues of uncertainty, translated into the slightly awkward fit of Community law principles of interpretation. Thus in ruling that the Commission had not exceeded its discretionary powers, in order to contain the disease within the territory of the UK, the Court had regard 'first, to the uncertainty as to the adequacy and effectiveness of the measures previously adopted by the United Kingdom and the Community and, second, to the risks regarded as a serious hazard to public health'.[142] Further, on the allegation that the decision, as being unsupported by scientific evidence, was to reassure consumers and the market, and not to protect health, the Court noted that a 'high level of health protection' is an objective under the Treaty,[143] and that health is also expressed to be a constituent part of other EC policies. Thus, following earlier authority,[144] as stated in the interim judgment, 'efforts to achieve the objectives of the Common Agricultural Policy cannot disregard requirements of public interest such as the protection of consumers or of the health and life of humans and animals, which the Community institutions must take into account in exercising their powers'.[145] The Court further stated that 'the circumstances show that it (the Commission) had regard above all to protecting public health in the context of the internal market' and that there was 'nothing to suggest that the Commission acted, as the UK claims, solely for economic reasons in order to stabilize the beef and veal market'.[146] The Court was scathing on the question of uncertain scientific evidence. Pointing out that scientists 'have as yet only an imperfect knowledge of Creuzfeldt-Jacob Disease and, more particularly, its recently discussed variant ... There is at present no cure for it; death ensues several months after diagnosis. Since the most likely explanation of this fatal disease is exposure to BSE, there can be no hesitation. Whilst acknowledging the economic and social difficulties caused by the Commission's decision in the UK, the Court cannot but recognise the paramount importance to be accorded to the protection of health'.[147]

---

141 Cases C-157/96; C-180/96, final judgment, at para 97.
142 *Ibid,* at para 62; and see para 63 of the judgment in interim proceedings.
143 Eg, now Article 3(p); also, Article 174.
144 Case 68/86, *UK v Commission* [1988] ECR 855, para 12.
145 Cases C-157/96; C-180/96, interim judgment, para 63.
146 *Ibid,* para 62.
147 *Ibid,* para 93.

The Court found that the plea, alleging that the Commission's response failed to satisfy the principle of proportionality, was unfounded.[148] Under that general principle of EC law, it is necessary that measures adopted by Community institutions do not exceed the limits of what is appropriate and necessary in order to attain the objectives legitimately pursued by the legislation in question; when there is a choice between several appropriate measures, recourse must be had to the least onerous; and the disadvantages caused must not be disproportionate to the aims pursued.[149] Concerning the response of the Commission, the Court recognised numerous continuing uncertainties, such as the mode of transmission within cattle. Thus 'the ban has a legitimate aim – the protection of health – and, as a containment measure prior to eradication measures, it was essential to the achievement of that aim'.[150] The Court accepted that UK measures had had positive results, although 'there are serious doubts as to their effectiveness'.[151] The effect upon the free movement of goods was accordingly held to be in conformity with the general principles of Community law, especially the principle of proportionality, and indeed accorded with the objective to ensure the free movement of agricultural products.[152]

Whilst the wording may not have been apposite in the circumstances, the above approach was analagous to an application of the precautionary principle. The essence of the principle, especially regarding those levels of risk which justify action, was considered by the Court. The degree of uncertainty was indeed determinative: in particular, 'when the contested decision was adopted, there was great uncertainty as to the risks posed by live animals, bovine meat and derived products', and, given the uncertainty as to the existence or extent of risks to human health, 'the institutions may take protective measures without having to wait until the reality and seriousness of those risks become fully apparent'.[153] Invoking the soft law principles under the Treaty, the court ruled that its approach was borne out by Article 174.1 of the Treaty, according to which Community policy on the environment is to pursue the objective *inter alia* of protecting human health; and under Article 174.2, which 'provides that that policy is to aim at a high level of protection and is to be based in particular on the principles that preventive action should be taken and that environmental protection requirements must be integrated into the definition and implementation of other Community policies'.[154] Finally, 'in view of the seriousness of the risk and the urgency of the situation, the Commission did not react in a manifestly inappropriate manner by imposing, on a temporary basis and pending the production of more detailed scientific information, a general ban on exports of bovine animals, bovine meat and derived products', and in not pursuing alternative, lesser measures.[155]

---

148 Cases C-157/96; C-180/96, final judgment, at paras 96–111.
149 Case C-331/88, *Fedesa* [1990] ECR I-4023, para 13; Cases C-133/93, C-300/93, C-362/93, *Crispoltoni* [1994] ECR I-4863, para 41.
150 Cases C-157/96; C-180/96, interim judgment, at para 73.
151 *Ibid*, interim judgment, at para 74.
152 *Ibid*, final judgment, at para 63; and see Case 37/83, *Rewe-Zentrale v Landwirtschaftskammer Rheinland* [1984] ECR 1229, para 19.
153 *Ibid*, final judgment, at paras 98, 99.
154 *Ibid*, final judgment, at para 100.
155 *Ibid*, final judgment, at para 110.

4 SEEKING SOLUTIONS

This concluding section seeks a synthesis of the present discussion, suggesting approaches to consideration of risk and uncertainty on the part of policy makers and environmental and other regulators. There have been references throughout this book to the externalities which we impose upon one another. They can be complex and non-localised. Moreover, scientific progress and technological development, as discussed above, have brought about an increase in levels of risk and engendered doubts as to our institutional capacities to seek out optimal decisions. In particular, lessons are drawn from the administrative fiasco of the BSE tragedy. Conclusions reach beyond questions of public trust, to the importance of establishing a proper role for 'sound science' and clear expectations for the political process, emphasising transparency and accountability.

4.1   Politics and technocratic structures

The emergence of the risk society carries with it greater public scepticism of the acceptability of scientific solutions. Despite the need for science to be communicated widely within the community, scientists are increasingly mistrusted. This process is exacerbated where they rely (as most must) upon government or industry for funds.[156] Piller refers to 'powerful ... political and market influences over the course of research funding, and, consequently, the overall directions and priorities of science'.[157] This may contribute to the reluctance of scientists directly to speak out in public on policy issues.[158] Scientist can speak internally unto scientist, through written, published discourse (when scientists feel that they are ready to release their findings). The scientific community is left its internal world, according to Mukerji, 'just as 19th-century women were given the domestic sphere to run ... But structural dependence is a source of constraint. And in the relationship between science and the State ... the scientific establishment routinely gives away one of its greatest assets: its voice'.[159] Even where the community feels willing to rely upon objective science, whilst once scientists could be described as largely beyond critical public scrutiny, there is now a gulf in understanding.[160] Largely as a result of the reductive nature of scientific method (so crucial to the pace and sheer scale of progress) the process of separation affects scientists as well as citizens. Roszak has described two distinct consequences for society: first, where 'public appreciation of science grows ever more vicarious'; and, secondly, he asks 'where everything ... has been staked out as somebody else's specialized field of knowledge, what is the thinking of ordinary people worth? Precisely zero'.[161]

Yet uncertainty afflicts science also. The BSE crisis has proved emblematic of ways in which political processes should not respond when faced with a high degree of uncertainty as to the nature of risk (in this case to public health) and establishing

---

156 See Barlow, 1999.
157 Piller, 1991, p 200.
158 Mukerji, 1989, p 196.
159 Mukerji, 1989, p 203.
160 See Piller, 1991, p 31.
161 Roszak, 1972, pp 257–58.

appropriate responses. The Phillips Inquiry into BSE was set up by the incoming Labour government in 1997, and reported in October 2000. Important lessons were drawn by the report, especially as to the use made of technical advice, and the dangers of secrecy even in the face of technical uncertainty. Whilst the report avoided allocation of individual blame, and accepting that it was necessarily undertaken in hindsight, stark conclusions were reached, in light of the detailed review of the use of the key advisory committees, namely the original Southwood Working Party, the Tyrell Committee and the Spongiform Encephalopathy Advisory Committee.[162] The problems investigated are especially difficult in circumstances of uncertainty, as indeed during the long time which elapsed before a link between BSE and human health could be established. Lessons drawn in effect suggested that policy makers should approach the technical aspects of policies neither in the fashion of Pontius Pilate nor by way of convenient affirmation, however strained, of their preferred agendae. The report raised further issues such as the potential conflict of interest on the part of the responsible ministry, concerned at 'alarmist' consumer reactions causing harm to producers. This has apparently been borne out by a highly critical subsequent internal Whitehall report, leading Bevins to conclude that the Ministry of Agriculture, Fisheries and Food appeared preoccupied with farming and costs rather with people and welfare.[163]

On the question of demarcation between scientists and decision makers, what emerges from the report is a thorough critique of the use made by administrators of advisory committees.[164] This extended even to lack of clarity as to what is expected of expert advisers. Thus, for instance, lessons drawn as to the setting up of advisory committees included the following: areas of required advice should be identified as precisely as possible in advance; terms of reference should be specified with as much precision as possible; committees should include experts in required areas of advice and also lay membership; conflicts of interest should be declared and registered. As to role, emphasis was placed upon the subject matter on which advice was to be required, by reference to the role of the committee in setting out policy options; the circumstances where there would be little alternative but to follow advice; and clarity as to the committee's limits of expertise. Crucially, the report went on to conclude that questions need to be formulated with precision in order to be brought within the particular expertise of the committee; there should also be dialogue with administrators, so that implications of options or decisions, practical and otherwise, are made clear.

The other major criticism related to what was shown to be a severe lack of transparency as to the nature and context of the advice given to decision makers. Thus the administration issued statements that were at best highly ambiguous, and at worst misleading. For instance, in the chapter dealing with human health, the report refers to public statements, respectively in March 1993 and January 1994, when reports were circulating about illnesses and possible transmission of BSE in individual cases. In the first instance, the Chief Medical Officer (CMO) had issued a statement emphasising that 'there is *no* scientific evidence of a causal link between BSE in cattle and CJD in humans ... The advice (previously given) that beef can be eaten safely by everyone, both adults

---

162 Phillips Report, 2000, Vols 4 and 11.
163 Bevins, 1999, p 52.
164 Phillips Report, 2000, Vol 1, para 1290.

and children, including patients in hospital, remains valid'.[165] In the second, a statement was issued to the effect that upon 'the basis of the work done so far, there is no evidence whatever that BSE caused CJD and, similarly, not the slightest evidence that eating beef or hamburgers causes CJD'.[166] In respect to the former statement, the report concluded that the CMO's 'contemporary appreciation of the risk that BSE might be transmissible to humans was sound ... This, however, was never made clear to the public. The repetition of the same message – "it is safe to eat beef" – as a response to what were legitimate public concerns was misleading'.[167] It had been asserted in evidence that the statement had been premised upon an assumption of measures in place for removal of potentially infective meat ('Specified Bovine Offal') from the food chain, being effective. Here the Report states that this 'is no answer to our concern. He should have made it plain that it was on this basis that he was prepared to advise that it was safe to eat beef. We bear in mind the difficulties facing those called upon to make statements about BSE and the natural anxiety not to alarm the public. It was, however, important that a public statement by the CMO should deal with the risk posed by BSE clearly and accurately. Dr Calman erred in not painting the full picture and, in consequence, gave a picture that was misleading. In so doing, he fell short of the standard reasonably to be expected of the CMO'.[168] Yet the content of such statements readily testifies to the problems of communication for the scientist, or perhaps the scientist-administrator. The report concluded here that the statement 'was somewhat more emphatic than was desirable, but not to the extent that it would be right to criticise Dr Calman for his choice of language'.

The dominant justification of numerous actors in the process appeared to be a perceived need to reassure the public. In the political resolution of these questions, it seems that the precautionary principle received scant attention. Questioning the campaign of reassurance, the report castigates what seemed to be an obsession with avoiding public alarm. This had one especially undesirable consequence in that the precautionary measures in due course introduced (especially into meat processing) 'called for care and diligence in their implementation and enforcement' whereas in the event 'lack of diligence in implementing regulations and lack of urgency in other areas of response to BSE were attributable, in part, to the success of continuous efforts to make sure that news about BSE did not give rise to public concern'.[169] The emphasis upon lack of risk to health became a political canon. For instance, when higher levels of offal infectivity in calves had been established than was previously believed to be the case, Cabinet minutes for 30 June 1994 concluded that subsequent briefings 'should emphasise that eating beef presented no risk to human health' (although, creditably, the Secretary of State for Health, in subsequent announcements, did refer to the existence of risk, albeit one described as 'miniscule').[170] The problems therefore were not so much scientific or even legal, but were essentially political.[171] The domination by politicians and

---

165 Phillips Report, 2000, Vol 6, s 5.331.
166 Phillips Report, 2000, Vol 6, s 5.374.
167 Phillips Report, 2000, Vol 6, s 5.344.
168 Phillips Report, 2000, Vol 6, s 5.348–5.349.
169 Phillips Report, 2000, Vol 1, para 1186.
170 Phillips Report, 2000, Vol 6, s 5.385–5.387.
171 Elworthy and McCulloch, 1996, pp 742–43.

administrators operates not only within decision making, but also over public debate. It is the policy makers who control the processes whereby accumulating evidence enters the public domain. Scientific evidence, according to the plea of a *Financial Times* editorial, 'should be published, with all its uncertainties exposed. And scientists must never be encouraged to produce reassuring soundbites for ministers'.[172]

In all of the above, it is the crucial element of public awareness that was lacking. Ironically as Phillips points out, in the end the BSE story was one in which the government 'was driven not by its own, and its advisers', assessment of risk, but by the public's perception of risk ... The media played a valuable role in reflecting and stimulating public concerns which proved well founded and which had a beneficial influence on government policy'.[173] Yet, at most of the crucial times, the BSE crisis exemplified that it is politicians, rather than the scientists, who act as mediators with the public. There is a constant need for mediators linking the scientific community with the rest of society. Mukerji has referred to 'boundary objects', which are simpler images of the natural world, based on science but more accessible to outsiders, 'using specifically designed representations of scientific research that are cleaned of many of the technical issues that are central to the activities of researchers but not important to outsiders'.[174] The crisis facing scientists is that their detachment is perceived to be deneutralised, in the sense that it is available for use by the political mediators. Thus scientists become 'a central policy tool' offering 'politicians a powerful resource for legitimating their policies'.[175] The result is that government officials 'exhort the language of science and scientists' analytic skills to do their political jobs. Scientists are made mostly mute, except where politicians find their voices useful'.[176] In consequence there is a cost for both the scientific community and the public, in that 'scientists cultivate an expertise that empowers someone else'.[177] Mukerji contends therefore that scientific advice to government 'empowers the State' in that it tends to be oral, interactive, and located in 'a private sphere incorporated within the institutions of government', thereby vesting 'greater control' in government.[178]

If decisions are not for scientists alone, therefore, it is likewise important that politicians and administrators are constrained from blurring the science. Involvement of experts recommended by Phillips seems to have occurred, as in the case of seeking the advice of epidemiologists at an earlier stage of the Foot and Mouth crisis in 2001 than had been so in the case of BSE. On the other hand, there has been some public scepticism as to the lack of cattle inoculation, and as to whether (despite its own potential drawbacks) this policy was driven by the demands of securing future access to foreign markets. Yet, as stated above, science may be able to deliver neither the basic information nor the certainties which are the stock-in-trade of administrators. This leaves decision makers 'to

---

172 (2000) *Financial Times*, 27 October.
173 Phillips Report, 2000, Vol 1, para 1190.
174 Mukerji, 1989, p 193.
175 Mukerji, 1989, p 195.
176 Mukerji, 1989, p 198.
177 Mukerji, 1989, p 197.
178 Mukerji, 1989, p 201; see, further, Habermas, 1981.

make crucial decisions from fragmentary and disputable information'.[179] Indeed, Dales, arguing for charging systems for external damage caused by diffuse pollution, points out that politicians 'must decide what the public wants and stake their political lives on their decision; they are in a much better position to assess the benefit and cost of their action (or inaction) than any body of experts'.[180] The cost benefit process offers a framework for political decision making: 'an orderly way of thinking about pollution problems, and not trying to make it into an all-purpose decision making machine.'[181] It thus increases the sum of data available to the policy makers and to those responsible for the regulatory process. Johnson describes its value in that 'it injects rational calculation into a highly emotional subject ... It offers you a range of alternatives. Without stringent analysis, nobody knows whether costs imposed by the regulatory process are money well spent'.[182]

Crucial to this process is that institutional arrangements are able to offer optimum use of scientific advice. Whilst the process of formal assessment in principle offers clarity and consistency, it is therefore the responsibility of government 'to evaluate all the pros and cons of a particular approach'.[183] Yet assessment and management processes are inextricably linked, and in this respect, the former Chief Scientific Adviser's 2000 report on food safety reflected themes emphasised in the Phillips Report. The subsequent report concludes that 'some consideration of the ways in which a risk might be managed is necessarily part of assessment and communication. So while committees are not responsible for risk management as such, it may often be appropriate to ask them to consider and advise on options for managing the risk. It is also important that committees make clear to policy makers the assumptions and uncertainties underlying their advice. These principles are especially important for policy makers when evaluating options for risk management and the consequent implications of emerging evidence from monitoring activities'.[184]

4.2   Establishing a discourse as to risk

The essential risk problematic arises, as seen in this chapter and previously, from numerous factors. First, the processes of inexorable growth, and much of the attendant advances in technology, have led to high levels of fossil fuel use and its depletion. Incidents of these processes, including discharge of waste matter into the atmosphere and elsewhere, and development of artificial chemical compounds, often persistent as waste, has led to a continuing trend towards heightened risk to the ecosystems upon which our survival depends, as well as to novel forms of risk to health. Secondly, whilst these trends have been matched by staggering advances in science and technology, we are seeing a new era of scientific development, especially in the biological sciences and genetics. What might be regarded as 'traditional' fears, as to health consequences of, for instance,

---

179 Rosenbaum, 1991, p 145.
180 Dales, 1968, p 105.
181 Dales, 1968, p 38.
182 Johnson, 1980, p 17 (cited by Rosenbaum, 1991, p 130).
183 Office of Science and Technology, 2000, para 13.
184 Office of Science and Technology, 2000, para 14.

emissions and waste from nuclear power facilities, and even fluoridisation of water supplies, have now given way to a new generation of fears. Examples include fears concerning radio frequency radiation (as from mobile telephones), antibiotics in animals bred for meat, and the implications of GM foods. We are on the verge of major new fears and regulatory challenges, for instance as to GM animals and animal organ transplants into humans (xenotransplantation). It is quite possible that in the (near) future, we can expect tampering with the reproductive processes of humans, for instance through stem cell technology, cloning, and introducing genetic modifications into reproductive cells (germ-line engineering). The third factor arises for the most part in response to the above, and concerns the increasing scepticism, or at times outright hostility, towards much of the science which is making such changes possible. The current hostility within the UK to GM food cannot be divorced from experiences of BSE and other health scares such a E-coli outbreaks. Indeed, in the aftermath of the 2001 Foot and Mouth outbreak, there appeared to be a growing distrust of modern domestic farming practices.

Arrangements need to be established in which there is more informed translation of science into the public domain. Scientists are increasingly aware of the need to address the wider public, as can be seen in the work of the Committee on the Public Understanding of Science. Perceived problems as to independence can be further countered not only by peer review and the encouragement of earliest possible publication into the public domain, but also by open declarations of affiliations and sponsorships.[185] There are also supportive mechanisms, such as those introduced by the need for declarations as to approaches to public communication when making applications for research council grant funding. Wider calls for training towards achieving improved communication have been made. In the light of polling evidence from amongst scientists, Worcester has concluded that 'while many scientists feel that they should take part in the dialogue between Science and Society, few feel equipped to do so, especially in the moral and ethical issues surrounding their work, and fewer still have had the training to do so'.[186]

Yet it is important that economists and scientists should not alone define the problems and solutions, for as Barry points out, echoing Wynne, distinctions between the technical and the non-technical need to be determined not merely technically, but also politically.[187] Indeed, as 'the ecological crisis is not just a technical matter but requires both claims of knowledge and ethical judgment, it cannot be reduced to a question of instrumental or technical manipulation to be left to experts'.[188] The irony with regard to risk is that – whatever the claims of politicians – a lack of certainty must be accommodated not only in the social, but also the natural, sciences.[189] Scientists too, as seen above, have their individual values, often deeply held. The calculation of risks associated with the cultivation and ingestion of GM foods is for instance 'coloured by intuition, experience and opinion, in addition to what there is by way of hard, scientific fact. Scientists used to working in this particular area are likely to support the production

---

185 House of Lords, 2000, paras 4.19, 4.24.
186 Worcester, 2001, p 27; see MORI/Welcome Trust, March 2000:
www.wellcome.ac.uk, www.mori.com.
187 Barry, 1999, p 199.
188 Barry, 1999, p 200.
189 See Popper, 1962.

of GM crops. But their opinions are formed not from grubby self-interest ... but because they are excited about the science, because they believe in the science, and because, being accustomed to the science, they have acquired a different perspective on the potential risks from that held by a confused public'.[190] Therefore, once the inherent uncertainty of much analysis in the environmental arena is accepted, the process of establishing methods of prioritising is crucial in order to counteract imbalances in the market place. This can mean that scientific method should be 'constructed as no more legitimate an activity than many other social activities, each of which involves different forms of judgment'.[191]

Such an assertion does not necessarily require acceptance of post-modern approaches which promulgate acceptance of a plurality of equal knowledge claims.[192] As has been seen above, the idea of reflexivity has been interpreted as consisting 'of social practices being constantly examined and reformed in the light of incoming information received about those very practices thus constitutively altering their character'.[193] Wider notions of risk need to be accommodated and extended to include the broader implications affecting responses. A current illustration can be found in the concerns today at GM crops, where legitimate concerns such as to transparency (labelling to assist consumer choices) and more fundamental, ethical arguments need to be taken into account.[194] Policy makers seeking public support where science is in issue must ensure that 'the public's attitudes and values are recognised, respected and weighed in the balance along with the scientific and other factors'.[195]

Those reports which have recently considered the relationship between scientific advice and policy making, from such as the House of Lords Select Committee on Science and Technology, the Phillips Inquiry, and the former Chief Scientific Adviser, show general concurrence as to principles which should underlie the process. Fundamental to ensuring effective discourse as to risk, and thereby rational policy making, is the need for openness. Thus, with a view to producing the best possible technical advice, it is important to consult widely to involve relevant and best expertise and to seek to include experts from other fields and lay representation, so as to secure a broad questioning of conclusions. Furthermore, as to the communication of information, it is important to share data, to acknowledge uncertainty, and to operate advisory and decision making processes openly.

Much of the above argument suggests that it is necessary to so order technical and policy making processes that democratic values are applied to the assessment of risk. Events cited above, particularly the BSE story, are illustrative of just how fragile are opportunities for ensuring accountability within a democratic system such as that of the UK. The democratic process can be threatened by the impenetrability not only of the problems but likewise of the solutions proffered by risk assessment. Shere has categorised this as follows: 'the citizen's job is only to brace himself for the next announcement of

---

190 Barlow, 1999, p 40.
191 Macnaghten and Urry, 1998, p 26.
192 See, eg, Lyotard, 1975.
193 Giddens, 1990, p 38.
194 Global Environmental Change Programme, 1999.
195 House of Lords, 2000, para 2.66.

dangers uncovered by unverifiable expert analysis.'[196] Yet whilst regretting the loss of the capacity to reach social consensus on environmental policy, Ruckelshaus suggests that the creation of formal rules under the risk assessment process can take account of best scientific findings in guiding inferences and assumptions, and should reduce the possibility of administrative manipulation.[197] This should have an educational function for governors as well as for the governed. Ideally, community-based standards should operate across research priorities. Risk assessment would therefore require a new balance, whereby, for instance, products and technologies could be reviewed to assess their 'socially valuable goals'.[198] Markets are not always efficient, and it has for example been alleged that solar power has received little investment by comparison with nuclear power 'because solar's decentralized nature makes it less amenable to centralized control by corporate owners; control that is essential to a stable flow of profits'.[199]

Questioning the scientific assumptions of risk assessment, therefore, has led to calls for wider, participatory forms in devising solutions to the problem of weighing economic gains against environmental costs. Hence Beck's emphasis upon the imperative of democratic regulation of risk, through the self-reflexive society.[200] This requires an institutionalising of processes which openly demand objective and transparent deliberation, reflecting 'the need for constant self-interrogation'.[201] Such a review would necessitate structural change, and the creation of a procedural context in which information can be shared and policy made in the face of a risk environment, a prerequisite for which would be 'democratic, open-ended decision making procedures'.[202] This is not to say that science is anti-democratic. However, its neutrality must constantly be scrutinised. Giddens speaks of a 'constant revolutionising of technology' which 'gains some of its impetus from the imperatives of capitalist accumulation and from military considerations, but once under way has a dynamism of its own'.[203] This is a very difficult task, but he argues that 'the logic of unfettered scientific and technological development will have to be confronted if serious and irreversible harm is to be avoided. The humanising of technology is likely to involve the increasing introduction of moral issues into the now largely "instrumental" relation between human beings and the created environment'.[204]

Yet democracy does not necessarily guard us from misconceptions about risk. Indeed, levels of participation are problematic and varied. One of Ibsen's anti-heroes, Dr Tomas Stockmann, asked what 'sort of truths do the majority always rally round? Why, truths so stricken with age that they're practically decrepit! But when a truth's as old as that, gentlemen, it's well on the way to becoming a lie ... [and] although those elderly truths

---

196 Shere, 1995, p 491.
197 Ruckelshaus, 1997, pp 50–51.
198 Piller, 1991, p 199.
199 Piller, 1991.
200 Beck, 1992.
201 Saward, 1993, p 77.
202 Barry, 1999, p 203.
203 Giddens, 1990, p 169.
204 Giddens, 1990, p 170.

are always shockingly scrawny, it isn't till then that the majority takes them up and recommends them to society'.[205] For instance, where individual developments are projected, NIMBYism may even stymie the most carefully structured schemes for participation. Piller cites the untimely end of a North Carolina statewide board to decide on the location of hazardous waste dumps.[206] Breyer suggests that better risk communication may not create higher levels of consensus, but may continue to confirm protagonists' prior view, and as scientific recognition of risks grows then the greater the problem may be. Although pessimistic as to their likely success, he points to two available responses: 'to institute widespread public education in risk analysis or generate greater public trust in some particular group of experts or the institutions that employ them'.[207]

Institutional trends therefore, such as the creation of a Food Standards Agency in the UK, may be a rational response to the risk society. The Global Environmental Change Programme has proposed more effective ways of handling political decisions in the face of uncertainty. The central conclusion concerns the need for public involvement in issues that are inherently ethical in nature rather than purely scientific. Thus there are calls for 'a sharing of power over the process and possible outcomes, although this short term sharing of power should ultimately result in enhanced powers to act. The consequences of this logic have not been fully accepted in political and scientific advisory circles, with the result that entrenched but manifestly unsuccessful approaches prevail'.[208] These issues must be further considered in the context of the discussion of democracy and environmental change in Chapter 10.

205 Ibsen, 1882 (translation, 1964), p 186.
206 Piller, 1991, p 187.
207 Breyer, 1997, p 70.
208 Global Environmental Change Programme, 1999, p 4.

CHAPTER 9

HUMAN RIGHTS AND THE ENVIRONMENT

No man is an Iland, intire of itselfe; every man is a peece of the Continent, a part of the maine; ... any man's death diminishes me, because I am involved in Mankinde; And therefore never send to know for whom the bell tolls; it tolls for thee.[1]

Before tackling the multifaceted theme of political structures in the final chapter, attention is now given to the relationship between human rights notions and environmental protection. Following consideration of intragenerational equity in the context of the environmental justice movement, the argument proceeds to consider broad human rights structures and to analyse their relevance to environmental protection issues. Reference is made to notable instances to date of recourse to human rights mechanisms within the European regional framework, and consideration is accorded to their relevance and potential impact. This is more especially relevant in the light of the introduction of the European Convention on Human Rights into the UK domestic legal process. This will inevitably have an impact upon the scrutiny of regulatory systems. For instance, procedural grounds of challenge appear likely to be a fertile ground of third party challenge, given the blurred edges between administrative and adjudication functions within the land use planning regime, and especially within appellate and planning inquiry processes.

How far human rights perspectives offer a viable contribution to finding effective counters to environmental degradation is an aspect of the environmental debate that has proved highly contentious. Issues of individual and community justice remain generally within the parameters of national laws, which as we have seen may be augmented by reference to broader concepts, derived from both international law and otherwise.[2] The relatively unreliable and unstructured nature of this process has fuelled arguments for the integration of environmental protection principles within international human rights mechanisms. There is, however, serious contention as to whether the human rights dynamic is appropriate, especially in the terrain of international law. Aside from a residual argument, to the effect that any conceptual apparatus at all which tends to the improvement of opportunities for enforcement is to be welcomed, there is debate as to the viability of human rights routes in this context. Moreover, there is a distinct counterpoint with the kinds of civil and political or public law solutions explored throughout this book and synthesised in the next chapter. These, it is argued, flow more naturally from what has been said above than do solutions based upon ratcheting international mechanisms up a further, rights-based notch.

In the conclusion to the preceding chapter, reference was made to democratic limitations in processes of decision making. This is exemplified by questions of environmental justice, to which consideration now turns.

1　Donne, from *Devotions*, 1624, 1987 edn.
2　Eg, *Minors Oposa v Secretary of the Department of Environment and Natural Resources* (1994) 33 ILM 173.

1 THE ENVIRONMENTAL JUSTICE MOVEMENT

A powerful illustration of national responses can be seen in the environmental justice movement in the United States. The movement is rooted in the idea of inequitable treatment of vulnerable communities in the siting of polluting installations. It can be described as a political manifestation of the idea that interests should be infringed equally in conditions of scarcity.[3] The movement has been a major force in the United States, and has been incorporated into the processes of environmental and land use regulation, particularly through President Clinton's Executive Order of 1994, Outlining Policy on Environmental Justice.[4] The order requires the general recognition of the importance of environmental justice considerations in federal agency decision making.[5] Whilst Lyle offers an illustration of developers being pressured into changing siting plans and looking elsewhere, she adds that the Environmental Protection Agency is yet to overturn a state agency decision under federal licence on the basis of breach of the environmental justice criteria contained in its Interim Guidance.[6]

The movement was borne largely out of dissatisfaction with the alleged orientation of traditional (middle class) environmental organisations towards compromise by negotiated trade-offs, through lobbying and shaping of legislation, supported intermittently by taking out citizen suits. It is asserted that these result in severe distributional consequences for the poorest communities, which, 'located nearest to industrial facilities, hazardous waste sites, and other risk-producing land uses, paid the environmental price'.[7] Even what is termed in the States a civic republican approach, for all its improved participation, masks underlying private interests, failing to recognise that economic and other goods have consequences for environmental justice. The argument for direct participation by communities bearing the greatest environmental risk counters the ruling utilitarian approach, embodying the idea of aggregated self-interest, supported by cost benefit applications. Results are allegedly unfair, just as the scientific or technical approach is likewise not value-free. Proponents accordingly demand fair environmental protection, which Gauna categorises as follows: 'This injection of fairness into a discourse oriented toward the negotiated trade-off or technical requirements is profoundly disruptive, challenging the fundamental assumptions that support the current process.'[8]

In a system premised upon allowing acceptable pollution levels, Layard argues that the environmental justice movement's focus on distributional and spatial justice is not misplaced in its assertion that 'some communities are more polluted than others and that this is "unjust" (however this is defined). This is an issue not so far addressed by conventional interpretations of environmental rights'.[9] Thus, overall, environmental standards tend not to recognise sub-populations, who may suffer from the cumulative effects of pollution, the according of special conditions to existing polluting facilities, and

---

3   Layard, 1999, p 176.
4   US Executive Order, 1994.
5   Also, Environmental Protection Agency, 1998.
6   Lyle, 2000, p 706.
7   Gauna, 1998, pp 10–11.
8   Gauna, 1998, p 15.
9   Layard, 1999, p 175.

a lack of clout in the disposition of enforcement and other resources. Lazarus points to standard environmental law approaches 'not adequately accounting for distributional equity'.[10] Using the metaphor of water flow searching for its natural bed, he asserts that 'pollution in our regulatory environment finds the pathway of least resistance. It finds those places where the laws are least enforced and least understood'.[11]

There is a vital nexus between claims to environmental justice and land use. The idea of environmental justice seeks, for instance, changes of mindset within processes for the siting of toxic dumps. This may 'involve an analysis as to whether planning policies seek to redistribute the benefits of resource use and development and reduce the impact of adverse developments on poorer communities'.[12] Swanston argues that a need exists for environmental justice advocates to shift their focus away from pollution and towards land: 'environmental justice is, at its most basic level, about land. It is about public and private land ownership, land use, access to land, and land management and policy, including the substantive and enforcement decisions affecting land and environmental media.'[13] The argument underlying the movement is at root that benefits as well as burdens should be distributed fairly, and there is therefore a link to assertions of rights and interests related to private property, and in public response to land use planning regulation. Lazarus picks up the point by reference to brownfield initiatives (that is, funding support), which exemplify environmental justice and protection: appreciating that there are economic reasons for this, namely the combating of urban decline.[14]

As regards siting, however, the arguments of the environmental justice lobby are problematic. Been suggests that the seminal studies, for instance by Bullard,[15] ignore that areas were not minority areas at time of siting, but that demographic changes follow subsequently.[16] Lambert and Boerner agree, concluding that 'a static analysis of environmental equity concerns simply does not provide sufficient information to develop workable solutions and may often mistake disparities for discrimination'.[17] These authors refer to the co-existence of minority populations as the effect of the arrival of facilities, rather than being the cause, the poor being most exposed, with limited employment opportunities and reduced escape capability. In contrast, they instance 'white flight' (middle class outward migration) and reduced house prices (which in turn encourages inward industrial migration). On this basis, they argue that the problems are fundamentally economic in nature. Their own analysis (in St Louis) led to a conclusion that empirical support was provided 'for the theory that housing values are clearly related to existing environmental inequities, raising the possibility that siting decisions caused an influx of minority and poor residents'.[18] Following the logic of Lambert and

---

10 Lazarus, 1997, p 712.
11 Lazarus, 1997, p 714.
12 Macnaghten and Pinfield, 1999, p 22.
13 Swanston, 1999, p 546.
14 Lazarus, 1997, p 716.
15 Bullard, 1982; US General Accountancy Office, 1983.
16 Been, 1993.
17 Lambert and Boerner, 1997, pp 199–200.
18 Lambert and Boerner, 1997, pp 202, 204.

Boerner's argument, encouraging such development in wealthier areas can only be a short term fix.

Siting decisions can be brought more fully into accord with notions of fairness. In the United States for instance there are market mechanisms for *ex ante* compensation.[19] Sums can be paid to ensure professional advice and support say in the evaluation of cost benefits. They can take the form of direct payments to landowners, or specific hypothecated grants, or direct provision of amenities, or payment into community general revenue funds.[20] However, these are criticised, in the light of the negotiative weakness of poor communities, which may be more likely to accept compensation packages, through negotiation processes which reflect imbalances of power.[21] Moreover, there will be problems in assuring true freedom of action on the part of all members of a community, as well as obstacles posed by lack of understanding on the part of participants of the complex issues forming part of the process. The process of trade-off has been categorised as environmental blackmail, for instance by Bullard.[22] More trenchantly, such approaches have been described as a 'deliberate attempt by a bigoted and selfish white middle-class society to perpetuate its own values and protect its own lifestyle at the expense of the poor and underprivileged'.[23]

Whilst these issues have not surfaced in the United Kingdom in this context, the issues which environmental justice raises are part of the wider debate as to participation and inclusive structures. As Layard points out, there is no sure protection in expressing environmental justice in rights terms, such as that 'no segment of the population is to suffer disproportionately from adverse health effects of pollution, and all people should live in clean, healthy and sustainable communities'.[24] She concludes that some mechanism is necessary to decide not only which but also whose interests are to be infringed. Such disparities will inevitably impact upon opportunities for litigation – especially as to information provision and community responsiveness.[25] Thus even in the US, where there are added opportunities for constitutional arguments,[26] there is limited environmental justice case law. Austin and Schill refer to a 'certain scepticism about the efficacy of litigation in advancing the goals of minority grassroots environmentalism'.[27] Lyle points to a reason for this in that 'community members feel an alienation from and distrust of the judicial system',[28] quoting the conclusions of a practitioner experienced in such causes: 'litigation serves as one of the least useful strategies for grassroots organizations.'[29]

---

19 Layard, 1999, p 179.
20 Lambert and Boerner, 1997.
21 Schrader-Frechette, 1991, p 213; and see Layard, 1999, p 178.
22 Bullard, 1994, p 15.
23 Smith, 1974, pp 1–2.
24 Layard, 1999, p 174.
25 See Schiffer and Dowling, 1997.
26 See, eg, Title VI anti-discrimination provision, 42 USC para 2000d–d-7, 1944.
27 Austin and Schill, 1994, pp 63–64; for a UK perspective, see Shiner and Wallace, 1998.
28 Lyle, 2000, p 706.
29 Cole, 1994, p 524.

2 HUMAN RIGHTS UNDER INTERNATIONAL LAW

2.1 The separateness of human rights mechanisms from the environment

Despite the scepticism at the value of litigation referred to above, and before turning to a chapter which is devoted to the relationship of citizen participation and democratic processes to the objective of securing environmental improvements, the potential contribution of a litigated international human rights perspective is now considered. The issue of human rights in the context of the environment has not been a main theme of this book. Environmental rights have recently been considered most persuasively elsewhere, and for instance Miller accounts for an unrealised potential of a rights approach to environmental protection.[30] Indeed instances of applications of human rights doctrine in the environmental context have been limited. Whilst proposing an article devoted to a fundamental human right 'to an environment adequate for their health and well-being', the United Nations Experts' Group also recognised that little progress had been made towards the ideal.[31] No reference to human rights appeared in the eventual Rio Declaration. Yet although there is a distinct absence of (especially UN) treaty provisions explicitly containing a human right to an adequate environment, as referred to in Chapters 1 and 2 above, there are abundant examples of enactments in national legislation.[32] Moreover, the idea is alive at the UN, as illustrated by a 1994 report produced to the UN Sub-Commission on Prevention of Discrimination and Protection of Minorities, which contained a draft Declaration of principles on human rights and the environment.[33]

States espousing the western liberal tradition provided the original impetus behind the international development of human rights laws. There has been a traditional liberal emphasis upon the need for state neutrality on the question of 'the good life'.[34] Yet, liberal theory has generally been willing to accommodate certain basic rights, in accordance with the primacy of moral values.[35] According to Johnston, certain 'basic rights and rules of conduct, whether we call them commandments of God or human rights, must be above and outside the scope of the democratic decision making process. Some decisions must be "unlawful" no matter how big a majority votes for them'.[36] A main catalyst for the acceptance of human rights norms was the experience of catastrophic abuses in the Western world, particularly in the middle of the 20th century (sadly, by contrast, colonial abuses a century earlier, and modern abuses at the turn of the 21st century, have proved seemingly less affecting). There is therefore a temporal gap between human rights treaties, most of which date from the aftermath of the Second World War, and the relatively recent development of an environmental consciousness. There is also a particular dissonance between human rights laws and environmental protection.

---

30 Miller, 1998, Chapter 1.
31 Munro and Lammers, 1987, pp 38–42.
32 See Weiss, 1989; Popovic, 1996, pp 506–08.
33 Human Rights and the Environment Report of Special Rapporteur, UN DX E/CN 4/Sub 2/1994/9 (July 1994); see also, generally, Popovic, 1996.
34 Eg, Dworkin, 1978, p 127.
35 Eg, Rawls, 1993.
36 Johnston, 1994, p 192.

Acceptance and enforcement, in the international context of traditional human rights protections, is far advanced, both doctrinally and institutionally. This contrasts with the largely indistinct notions of international environmental law, previously discussed in Chapter 2. Such environmental commitments remain problematic in the face of those established in the human rights domain, where treaty provisions have variously been accorded with features of normative value systems.

In contrast, given the nature of international environmental law, and its main areas of growth, it is unsurprising that it has not explicitly recognised the area of human rights. A problem with human rights discourse is that protections have required approaches inimical to the main inter-state normative functions of international law.[37] Moreover, five illustrations of conceptual limitations can be offered. First, there is thus far extremely limited recognition of human rights in international environmental law. Secondly, human rights perspectives are of questionable value in the environmental context, given the technical complexity and macro-spatial implications of the political and economic issues at stake. Thirdly, as has been seen in earlier contexts, the justiciability of principles based upon environmental harm, with a view to enforcement, is inherently problematic. Fourthly, there is an uncomfortable fit of human rights with the communal, if not always ecological, perspectives at work within environmental law. As was seen in Chapter 2, the sustainable development debate is reflected in its growing recognition in treaties establishing a nexus between environmental protection and international law mechanisms. The focus is quite different as compared with those provisions whose direct concern is with human rights. Environmental concerns require a balancing of essentially polycentric interests and are not readily identifiable with the anthropocentric essence of human rights treaties, especially at an institutional level.[38] The competing environmental interests demand a more sophisticated focus upon the general, or collective, interest.[39] Thus Birnie and Boyle have pointed to 'the inappropriateness of human rights institutions, with their more limited perspective, for the task of supervision and balancing', and suggested a need for an 'alternative institutional machinery ... able to take a more holistic view, however difficult this may be to achieve in practice'.[40]

Finally, there are also more fundamental criticisms of 'rights talk', as in modern Kantian ontological perspectives, abjuring the need to accord rights in circumstances where man is subject to aspects of moral duty.[41] The expression of priorities in terms of rights is not necessarily conducive to environmental protection. Glendon accordingly criticises what she refers to as rights talk amongst three separate, powerful, groups. These include, first, those who rely upon science and economic growth both to cure environmental problems and to provide for posterity. Secondly, there are those who insist on a linkage through the market between the individual and the State, to the exclusion of other social networks. Thirdly, there are those who see adjudication as a replacement for a defective political and legislative process. She applies an ecological analogy when discussing the inadequacy of public discourse to focus upon solutions to social issues

---

37 See Handl, 1992.
38 Boyle, 1996, pp 51–53.
39 Eg, Woolf, 1992.
40 See Birnie and Boyle, 1992, p 194.
41 Eg, Lomasky, 1987, pp 224–25.

258

such as isolation and fragmentation: 'it borders on the bizarre to solemnly declare whether animals and trees have rights, at a time when all interdependent life on the planet is threatened by systematic degradation of the environment – a degradation that is often defended in the name of economic rights'.[42] Rights dialectic can be perceived as a distraction from a reformed, reflexive political arena where solutions are to be found: for 'simplistic rights talk regularly promotes the short run over the long term, sporadic crisis intervention over systematic preventive measures, and particular interests over the common good'.[43] Related questions have been discussed in the land use planning and wider regulatory contexts previously, and questions concerning the effective application of rights through the political process are considered further in Chapter 10.

2.2 Asserting a role for human rights doctrine in environmental protection

Space constrains the offering of more than an indication of the response of those who have challenged reservations such as those referred to above. Traditional international law approaches have however been criticised as operating largely through bilateral State relations and offering neither an effective legal and institutional framework for redressing environmental harm in an effective way.[44] In contrast, it has been propounded that human rights environmental perspectives can be found in established principles of customary international law, which are sufficiently defined to enable recognition of clear, enforceable standards for State obligations.[45] An alternative approach argues that an expansive right to environment is supported implicitly in human rights measures, that in any event existing enactments can be reinterpreted and expanded, and that environment is another of the solidarity rights (along with civil protection, social, economic and cultural rights) which are coming to be recognised as third generation rights.[46] There remains a need to keep such claims (in default of further treaty developments) within credible limits.[47] Lee has suggested that a degraded environment can be referable to either serious health consequences for a specific group of people or disruption of a people's way of life.[48]

The setting of human rights standards may likewise prove a valuable tool for domestic environmental protection, as in reporting requirements in treaties, the formal incorporation of input from non-governmental organisations, and individual complaints arrangements.[49] In regard to the latter, however, there has been limited experience of individual complaints under UN human rights mechanisms. Not only are decisions of treaty bodies non-binding, but given the requirement to establish that an applicant has been the victim of harm, standing has proved to be a particular difficulty. For instance, the UN Human Rights Committee dismissed a challenge to nuclear testing at Muroroa Atoll

---

42   Glendon, 1991, p 120.
43   Glendon, 1991, p 15.
44   Palmer, 1992.
45   See Lee, 2000b.
46   Rodriguez-Rivera, 2001, pp 18–23, 40–44.
47   Alston, 1984.
48   Lee, 2000b, p 285.
49   Dommen, 1998.

in the South Pacific, on grounds that the applicants could not be classified as victims.[50] There have been numerous cases under the UN International Covenant on Economic, Social and Cultural Rights,[51] but these have been concerned with economic rights, environmental in the sense only that arguments concern the question of availability of resources to indigenous peoples in traditional ways.[52] Most proponents presently need to fall back upon illustrations of human rights approaches in national court settings, in order to argue that such recognition is 'evidence of a general principle of law'.[53]

Nevertheless wider benefits can follow in the train of a rights-based approach. Thus, despite the problems of definition and implementation in respect of a healthy environment, Birnie and Boyle are unwilling to reject such formal statements, generally for the reason that 'the existence of individual procedural rights helps shape domestic environmental policy and facilitates the resolution of transboundary conflicts through equal access to the same private law procedures. It gives NGOs an opportunity to bring legal proceedings or to challenge proposed developments on a public interest basis. It would be entirely realistic for international law to encourage these trends'.[54] Shelton has argued that solutions found in those instruments providing such rights as to information and participation need to be coupled with substantive international recognition, through such means as the creation of human rights in this context.[55] Likewise Popovic has emphasised that the potential of a recognition of human rights principles through customary international law lies in the consequent impact also upon national laws, by advancing a standard-setting process, involving a wide range of international agencies and organisations and encouraging the mobilisation of public pressure.[56] Redgwell broadens the point, referring to what amounts to a fortuitous spill-over effect: she argues that precisely because of 'an increasing awareness of the interconnectedness of human beings and the environment and the intrinsic value of the latter, it is unlikely that the recognition of a human right to a clean, healthy, or decent environment will have as its necessary corollary the denial of non-human rights'.[57]

There are indeed analogies to be drawn as between human rights law and current environmental developments. Robinson has pointed to the widespread creation of human rights laws and enforcement mechanisms having followed on from processes originating under the Universal Declaration in 1948.[58] This has occurred despite the declaration having been 'a carefully negotiated statement of "soft law", a moral call which by itself did not legally oblige changes in how nations behaved'.[59] He has suggested that greater environmental protection could be generated in a similar fashion by human rights

---

50 *Bordes v France*, UN Human Rights Committee, Communication No 645/1995 (1997) 18 Human Rights LJ 36; but see Kamminga, 1996.
51 (1996) 6 ILM 360.
52 Dommen, 1998, pp 23–25.
53 Lee, 2000b, p 319.
54 Birnie and Boyle, 1992, p 196.
55 Shelton, 1991.
56 Popovic, 1996, p 603.
57 Redgwell, 1996, p 87.
58 UN, Universal Declaration of Human Rights, GA Res 217A (III0, UN GAOR, 3d Sess, UN Doc A/810) (1948).
59 Robinson, 1998, p 33.

approaches. Dias likewise calls for the further development of the idea of stewardship through human rights notions, calling for environmental rights mechanisms similar to those treaty-based mechanisms that have led to enhanced protection of human rights.[60] Each faces serious practical difficulties in terms of securing legal objectives. It has, for instance, been said that human rights provisions, whether in declarations, treaties or national constitutions, 'are conceptual ideals which typically structure behaviour at an abstract, political level. At the experiential level, prejudices, conflicting interests, greed, and simple brutality intercede between law and practice'.[61] Likewise, differential experiences of environmental degradation survive even in the context of law making to protect environmental quality, just as 'human rights are abused when cultural forces and economic greed co-opt and corrupt the implementation of legal structures'.[62]

3 THE EUROPEAN CONVENTION ON HUMAN RIGHTS

3.1   The European Convention and the United Kingdom

Contrasting with the lack of any substantial development in human rights approaches discussed above, the type of ready-made adjudicative and institutional processes afforded at a regional level by a treaty such as the European Convention is more likely to have been called upon to address environmental claims. The discussion now therefore focuses upon the European Convention on Human Rights, to which the UK was an original signatory.[63] The provisions of the Convention have accordingly had a binding effect upon the UK under international law. Until the coming into force, on 2 October 2000, of the Human Rights Act 1998, the Convention had not however been part of UK domestic law. The most that can be said is that judicial approaches to interpretation had gradually become more accommodating, where the construction of substantive domestic law could bear such interpretation.[64] Yet the obstacles to a litigant have been significant. Although an optional right of direct complaint was accorded by the government to UK citizens in 1966, a complainant taking a case to Strasbourg, following an exhaustion of domestic remedies, has faced considerable cost and delay. For the State, there have been disadvantages too: perhaps in particular in the pathological obsession with a 19th century constitutional framework,[65] with limited reform deliberations skewed reactively towards damage limitation where the Strasbourg process has found domestic laws to be wanting.[66]

Unsurprisingly, planning and environmental decisions have seldom been the subject of scrutiny under the terms of the Convention. This is, however, now set to change, in

---

60   Dias, 1998, p 47.
61   Johnston, 1994, p 10.
62   Johnston, 1994, p 12.
63   Rome, 4 November 1950, TS 71 (1953): Cmd 8969.
64   See, eg, *R v Secretary of State for the Home Department ex p Brind* [1991] 1 AC 696; *R v Ministry of Defence ex p Smith* [1996] 1 All ER 257; *R v Secretary of State for the Home Department ex p McQuillan* [1995] 4 All ER 400.
65   Hutton, 1996, Chapter 11.
66   See Hart, 2000, p 118.

both substantive and procedural contexts. The consequences are twofold. The first consequence concerns a greater judicialisation over outputs of the legal and political process, especially as to the acceptability of traditional forms of decision making and dispute resolution. In discussing human rights below, it is notable how the action of the UK Parliament in passing the Human Rights Act has promoted a more reflective balancing of interests than has previously been the case. This sweeps away the previous incremental, but fundamentally restrictive, judicial infusion of Convention principles referred to above. The process may encourage a more bottom-up approach to constitutional reform. It may be said that a reformist, even reflective, approach is long overdue. But the locus for the development, having been kick-started by a Parliament which is preternaturally averse to considering issues in (at any rate post-Diceyan) constitutional terms, will have unleashed a strange new power through a judiciary which in turn will need to reinvent itself.

Secondly, there may be important implications for the level and quality of the democratic and participative processes which it is argued in Chapter 10 are essential to the development of a sustainable agenda. We remain a long way from the kind of rights fatigue inherent in Glendon's critique of the articulation of concerns through rights systems. The values of expression in terms of rights have at least a rhetorical value, in default of an alternate vocabulary.[67] Such expression may lend further encouragement to powerful actors in the system, in particular those engaged in the judicial process, to seek more environmentally friendly solutions.[68] Moreover, the assertion of rights is an important adjunct to the realisation of access to justice in the context of environmental protection.[69]

3.2   'Environmental' human rights in Europe?

Yet any assertion of environmental rights generally operates in this context by a process of shoehorning into human rights provisions determined generically in different times, and with different priorities in view.[70] Thus the European Convention makes no reference to the environment at all. Therefore the Convention cannot be applied in support of domestic public law processes as part of an all-purpose public interest challenge to environmental threats generally.[71] Without wholesale reform at international and national levels, the human rights route remains unconvincing as compared with the more direct conceptual approaches argued for elsewhere in this book. Miller for instance has concluded that past experience of the assertion of environmental rights makes it 'unwise to place too much confidence' in recourse to human rights strategies.[72] Still, as will be seen below, there are under the European Convention certain substantive provisions that might be called upon, in particular, under Article 8, but also Articles 2 and 14, and Article

---

67   See Redgwell, 1996, p 81.
68   See Stone, 1972.
69   Schwartz, 1993.
70   See Anderson, 1996, pp 4–10.
71   See *X and Y v Germany* (1976) 5 D & R 161.
72   Miller, 1998, p 22.

1 of the First Protocol.[73] Indeed, reflecting the potential unlocking of Convention-based challenges in domestic courts, it has been asserted that it would be 'unreal to continue to develop the law on the protection of the environment, and the balancing of the competing interests involved, without reference to the general principles of human rights'.[74]

Moreover, the role of the European Convention as a vehicle for the idea of balancing of the respective interests has recently been asserted with some success, as discussed below. Save where absolute rights are accorded, such as the right to life,[75] most Convention rights are expressed in qualified form. Any enforcement of recognised rights must therefore be placed in the context of European Court of Human Rights (ECHR) jurisprudence, particularly in its approaches to securing a balancing of interests. Successful applications have made especial reference to Article 8 of the Convention, which provides as follows:

1   Everyone has the right to respect for his private and family life, his home and his correspondence.

2   There shall be no interference by a public authority with the exercise of this right, except such as is in accordance with the law and is necessary in a democratic society in the interests of national security, public safety or the economic well-being of the country, for the prevention of disorder or crime, for the protection of health or morals, or for the protection of the rights and freedoms of others.

The right to respect for private and family life has been held to extend both to qualitative threats (ordinarily expressed under nuisance principles) as well as to physical threats to well-being.[76] In the ground-breaking *Lopez Ostra* case,[77] the applicant was successful with a claim based upon Article 8. Here, the municipality had permitted (indeed subsidised) the construction of a waste treatment plant a few metres away from the applicant's home, which had caused severe pollution and threats to health. The ECHR found that 'severe environmental pollution may affect individuals' well-being and prevent them from enjoying their homes in such a way as to affect their private and family life adversely, without, however, seriously endangering their health ... [and] regard must be had to the fair balance that has to be struck between the competing interests of the individual and of the community as a whole'.[78] The basis of the breach in this case was the authorities' failure to strike such fair balance as between the applicant's rights under the Convention and the local economic interest. Subsequently, in *Guerra v Italy*, the court has ruled that Article 8 was breached by failure to provide essential information to enable the applicants 'to assess the risks they and their families might run if they continued to live [in] ... a town particularly exposed to danger in the event of an accident at the factory [a fertiliser plant]'.[79]

In *Guerra*, the applicants also sought to rely upon the terms of Article 2, concerning the right to life:

---

73   See Churchill, 1996.
74   Upton, 1998, p 320.
75   Under Article 2.
76   *Powell and Rayner v UK* (1990) 12 EHRR 355, para 41.
77   *Lopez Ostra v Spain* (1995) 20 EHRR 277.
78   *Ibid*, para 51.
79   Case 116/1996/735/932, *Guerra v Italy*, 4 BHRC 63, para 60.

1   Everyone's right to life shall be protected by law. No-one shall be deprived of his life intentionally save in the execution of a sentence of a court following his conviction of a crime for which this penalty is provided by law.

2   Deprivation of life shall not be regarded as inflicted in contravention of this Article when it results from the use of force which is no more than absolutely necessary:

   (a) in defence of any person from unlawful violence;

   (b) in order to effect a lawful arrest or to prevent the escape of a person lawfully detained;

   (c) in action lawfully taken for the purpose of quelling a riot or insurrection.

Having regard to its conclusion that there had been a violation of Article 8, the court found it unnecessary to consider the case under Article 2.[80] Whilst concurring, Judge Jambrek, referring to the release of harmful substances into the environment, considered the protection of health and physical integrity to be closely associated with both the right to life and respect for private and family life. Thus, where 'information is withheld by a government about circumstances which foreseeably, and on substantial grounds, present a real risk of danger to health and physical integrity, then such a situation may also be protected by Article 2 of the Convention'.[81]

Therefore, whether under Article 8 or Article 2, the principle appears to have been established that duties may arise whereby a responsible public authority must seek upon a proactive basis to provide information about environmental dangers and its regulatory responses taken. Thus, failure in this respect can amount to interference with private or family life: 'although the object of Article 8 is essentially that of protecting the individual against arbitrary interference by the public authorities, it does not merely compel the State to abstain from such interference: in addition to this primarily negative undertaking, there may be positive obligations inherent in effective respect for private or family life.'[82] The ECHR has similarly ruled that such obligations extend to the provision of information concerning hazardous activities (connected with exposure to radiation) which is available to the authorities.[83] These approaches impose a significant obligation upon authorities with regard to the provision of information, which is in accord with the requirements of the Aarhus Convention discussed in Chapter 10.[84] As a consequence, Hart suggests a potential for 'great pressure to produce continuing environmental data responsive to the concerns of objectors, over and above the environmental statement needed at the introduction of the new process'.[85]

The rulings in *Lopez Ostra* and *Guerra* might suggest considerable opportunity for reliance upon Convention principles. However, there is a lack of specificity as to the basis upon which a court with human rights jurisdiction might question the legality of private

---

80   Case 116/1996/735/932, *Guerra v Italy*, 4 BHRC 63, para 62.

81   See also concurring speech of Judge Walsh.

82   Case 116/1996/735/932, *Guerra v Italy*, 4 BHRC 63, para 58.

83   *LCB v UK* (1998) 4 BHRC 447; *McGinley and Egan v UK* (1998) 27 EHRR 1.

84   United Nations Economic Commission for Europe (UNECE), Convention on Access to Information, Public Participation in Decision-Making and Access to Justice on Environmental Matters 1998, especially Article 5(1).

85   Hart, 2000, p 123.

and public regulatory systems on grounds of overriding individual interests. The extent, indeed wisdom, therefore, of their application to environmental issues remains uncertain. Welcoming the *Lopez Ostra*, Sands has nevertheless cautioned that 'in most cases it will be difficult to predict whether the nature and extent of environmental harm upsets the balance which the court seeks to maintain between individual and community interests in Article 8'.[86] Miller has expressed the concern that a human rights court, as in *Lopez Ostra*, can in such circumstances replicate the role of a national civil court in determining what is a fair balance between conflicting uses. This becomes 'in effect, another court of appeal', and he suggests that such overturning of national decisions should not be reached lightly by an extra-jurisdictional court, save in cases which 'violate any notion of reasonableness'.[87] In any event, such an applicant would have the opportunity of a claim in nuisance, although this would be less likely to lie against the authority. On the other hand, the ECHR has been extremely cautions in other circumstances: as in its rejection of an argument that the restrictive common law approach to a cause of action in nuisance, also applied in the light of a special statutory planning regime, was a disproportionate response.[88] In a regulatory context, there may alternatively be State liability under EC law in the event of a breach by a public body, under *Francovich* principles.[89] This suggests an analogous approach to that of the ECHR in *Lopez Ostra*, although principles under the Convention as to compensatory awards are somewhat inchoate.[90] This suggests perhaps that the quality of regulatory action or indeed inaction are each vulnerable to challenge. Even so, this is problematic, given the potential availability of domestic remedies under administrative law, and the best conclusion may be that the situations litigated in the cases of *Lopez Ostra* and *Guerra* offer extreme examples of unacceptable breaches of Article 8 in the environmental context.

3.3   Securing a balance of interests

The question of securing a balancing of interests under the Convention in an environmental context has been considered mainly in connection with Articles 8 and 14, and Article 1 of the First Protocol. First, under Article 8, the ECHR ruled in *Lopez Ostra* that 'regard must be had to the fair balance that has to be struck between the competing interests of the individual and of the community as a whole, and in any case the State enjoys a certain margin of appreciation'.[91] Finding a fair balance generally requires an application of the jurisprudence of the court as to whether the public authorities' response (if any) was a proportionate one. Closely related, the idea behind the margin of appreciation (which may not transpose into a domestic court setting) is that the State is *prima facie* in a better position to adjudge the need for an interference with a right than is the court in Strasbourg.[92] For instance, it has been held that that whilst aircraft noise could constitute a violation of Article 8, the balancing process must take account of the

---

86   See Sands, 1996b, p 618.

87   Miller, 1998, pp 18–19.

88   *Khatun v UK* (1998) 26 EHRR CD 212; see *Hunter v Canary Wharf Ltd* [1997] AC 655.

89   Cases C-6 and 9/90, *Francovich v Italy* [1992] IRLR 84; see, eg, *Bowden v South West Water* [1998] Env LR 445; [1999] Env LR 438.

90   See eg Hart, 2000, p 125.

91   *Lopez Ostra v Spain* (1995) 20 EHRR 277, para 51.

92   *Handyside v UK* (1976) 1 EHRR 737.

economic contribution of an international airport such as Heathrow.[93] In contrast, finding that a breach of Article 8 had occurred in *Lopez Ostra*, the ECHR ruled that 'despite the margin of appreciation left to the respondent State, the court considers that the State did not succeed in striking a fair balance between the interest of the town's economic well-being – that of having a waste-treatment plant – and the applicant's effective enjoyment of her right to respect for her home and her private and family life'.[94] More generally still, the deleterious consequences of another's planning permission, in terms of amenity or even a devalued private property, may remain extremely difficult to challenge on substantive grounds, especially in the likely event of the public interest being part of the decision making process.[95]

Secondly, a similar reticence can be illustrated in connection with Article 14. This provides as follows:

> The enjoyment of the rights and freedoms set forth in this Convention shall be secured without discrimination on any grounds such as sex, race, colour, religion, political or other opinion, national or social origin, association with a national minority, property, birth or other status.

As well as Article 8, Article 14's specific concern with freedom from discrimination had been in issue in *Buckley*. The ECHR there stated that 'national courts are in principle better placed than an international court to evaluate local needs and conditions. In so far as the exercise of discretion involving a multitude of local factors is inherent in the choice and implementation of planning policies, the national authorities in principle enjoy a wide margin of appreciation'.[96] It is necessary for a *prima facie* breach of another Article to be established.[97] Here, the ECHR held that planning legislation, in prohibiting gypsies from following their traditional way of life by the siting of caravans on unoccupied land, was not discriminatory. Miller's conclusion is that this case offers 'a particularly cogent reminder that owners of land have no automatic right to use their land – even for the creation of a family home – as they might wish'.[98] He suggests that it is distinguishable from *Lopez Ostra*, in which case there were both health effects and a breach by the regulator of local regulations.

Thirdly, attached to the Convention is a controversial provision, concerned with the protection of property: the State is prohibited from depriving citizens of their property, save in accordance with law, and subject to such controls as are in accordance with the general interest.[99] The terms of Article 1 of the First Protocol are as follows:

> Every natural or legal person is entitled to the peaceful enjoyment of his possessions. No-one shall be deprived of his possessions except in the public interest and subject to conditions provided for by law and by the general principles of international law. The

---

93 *Powell and Rayner v UK* (1990) 12 EHRR 355; cf *Arrondelle v UK* (1980) 23 YB Eur Con HR 166 (App 7889/77).

94 *Lopez Ostra v Spain* (1995) 20 EHRR 277, para 58.

95 *S v France* (1990) 65 D & R 250 (App 13728/88).

96 *Buckley v UK* [1996] JPL 1018, 1039.

97 *Pine Valley Developments v Ireland* (1991) 14 EHRR 319.

98 Miller, 1998, p 51.

99 *James v UK* (1986) 8 EHRR 123.

preceding provisions shall not, however, in any way impair the right of a State to enforce such laws as it deems necessary to control the use of property in accordance with the general interest or to secure the payment of taxes or other contributions or penalties.

This element of the Convention is some way removed from substantive environmental protection, given that the protection of private property is in many contexts quite inimical to the imperative of sustainability, as has been considered in Chapter 3. This Article therefore suggests in vivid form the limitations inherent in human rights solutions.[100] It has even been argued that the First Protocol may eventually 'be the equivalent for free marketeers in the UK that the takings clause has been for their equivalents in the USA'.[101] However, the specific recognition of community interest in the balancing processes, and the greater acceptance of the conditionality of landholding in English (and indeed European) jurisprudence, suggests that the takings analogy is inappropriate.[102]

There is nevertheless potential for argument in the context of challenges to planning and environmental decisions, as in the case of prejudice caused by delays in planning process and compensation upon compulsory purchase.[103] As Grant has opined, 'there is a balance to be struck, and a test of proportionality to be applied when comparing the public objective and the private cost'.[104] Indeed, the application of the principle of proportionality, analogous to general principles of Community law developed by the European Court of Justice, as discussed in the previous chapter, suggests that the courts may become involved in the question as to whether less restrictive measures should have been applied.[105] The principle requires that measures adopted do not exceed the limits of what is appropriate and necessary in order to attain the objectives legitimately pursued by the legislation in question; when there is a choice between several appropriate measures recourse must be had to the least onerous; and the disadvantages caused must not be disproportionate to the aims pursued.[106] As a consequence, an interference with property rights may be unlawful and in principle compensable.[107] Overall, the wording of the provision expressly accepts the right of the State to control the use of property in accordance with the general interest. This suggests that interference would need to be so substantial as to amount to a deprivation. Thus, for instance, a revocation of a mineral extraction licence, on environmental grounds of nature conservation, has been held to be justified as being in the general interest.[108]

100 See, eg, Curtis, 1989.

101 McCrudden, 1999, p 290.

102 See Purdue, 1995.

103 *Lithgow v UK* (1986) 8 EHRR 329; *Sporrong and Lonroth v Sweden* (1982) 5 EHRR 356.

104 Grant, 2000a, para 1.2.2.4.

105 Eg, Case C-302/86, *Commission v Denmark* [1988] ECR 4607, paras 20–21.

106 See, eg, Case C-331/88, *Fedesa and Others* [1990] ECR I-4023, para 13; Cases C-133/93, C-300/93, C-362/93, *Crispoltoni* [1994] ECR I-4863, para 41.

107 *Booker Aquaculture v Secretary of State for Scotland* (1998) Times LR, 24 September.

108 *Fredin v Sweden* (1990) 13 EHRR 784.

3.4 'Procedural' requirements under the Convention

The most lasting impact may lie in the more indirect influences of due process, and procedural fairness, by reference to Article 6 of the Convention. By Article 6.1, it is provided that:

> In the determination of his civil rights and obligations or of any criminal charge against him, everyone is entitled to a fair and public hearing within a reasonable time by an independent and impartial tribunal established by law. Judgment shall be pronounced publicly but the press and public may be excluded from all or part of the trial in the interest of morals, public order or national security in a democratic society, where the interests of juveniles or the protection of the private life of the parties so require, or to the extent strictly necessary in the opinion of the court in special circumstances where publicity would prejudice the interests of justice.

Whilst in respect of the question of rights to silence on the part of those under investigation the Convention is itself silent, the ECHR has been willing to develop its jurisprudence under Article 6.[109] The Court's general position is that 'although not specific there can be no doubt that the right to remain silent under police questioning and the privilege against self-incrimination are generally recognised international standards which lie at the heart of the notion of a fair procedure under Article 6'.[110] The privilege against self-incrimination covers a range of cognate principles.[111] It may be the subject of a claim by a party subject to an environmental enforcement process, and it is therefore quite possible that the objectives of environmental regulation may be considered secondary to the assertion of a general procedural protection.[112] Indeed, the UK has been required to review the impact of its companies' legislation in the light of a finding by the ECHR.[113] Thus it was held that a need to combat fraud, albeit in the public interest, did not justify the use of answers compulsorily obtained in a non-judicial investigation to incriminate an individual at a later trial.[114] Yet it remains unclear how the expansive rights-based reach of the Court in the context of evidence gathering by regulators can be sensibly rationalised.

Inevitably such problems of balancing of private and wider public interests arise across a wide range of areas of commercial regulation. The House of Lords has been called upon to rule thus far just once in the environmental context.[115] In the case, following the discovery of unlawful depositing of waste, the applicants had refused to comply with requisitions for information mandated by statute, and relied unsuccessfully upon the privilege against self-incrimination.[116] This approach to gathering of information is essential to regulatory investigations, given the numerous, often complex objectives being pursued. It may, however, come into conflict with that of ECHR

---

109 See Munday, 1996, p 384.
110 *Murray v UK* (1996) 22 EHRR 29, para 45.
111 See the summary classification of Lord Mustill in *R v Serious Fraud Office ex p Smith* [1993] AC 1, 30–311.
112 Eg, *Zander v Sweden* (1993) 18 EHRR 175.
113 *Saunders v UK* (1996) 23 EHRR 313.
114 *Ibid*, para 74 *et seq*.
115 *R v Hertfordshire CC ex p Green Environmental Industries* [2000] 1 All ER 773.
116 See EPA 1990, ss 69, 71.

jurisprudence, given the latter's approach to enforcement of rights implicitly recognised under Article 6. It seems that a violation may follow, whatever the nature of the evidence disclosed in the investigative process, and that this might as a matter of logic extend to information arising indirectly from any such evidence.[117] Where important public interest issues are at stake, a conceptual framework must be found for resolving uncertainties as to the rights afforded under the Convention, especially in light of the degree of risk involved and the importance of the evidence to secure its control.[118] Regulation is moreover qualitatively different from other public enforcement processes. The relationship between regulator and regulated is generally of a negotiative nature, based upon compliance strategies, with a heavy reliance upon information availability.[119]

In the present context, therefore, the assertion of Article 6 might not necessarily be of environmental benefit, for even decisions of public bodies taken for environmental purposes are in principle subject to the assertion of rights under Article 6.[120] There are ECHR authorities which appear to establish a broad right of access to review procedures under Article 6. For instance, the court has recognised that rights of challenge under Article 6(1) can apply to a person who objects to the grant of planning permission to another in accordance with a Development Plan.[121] Likewise, neighbouring property owners have been able to assert a right to a judicial review of a decision to grant a waste licence.[122] Yet the rationale for the ECHR's interpretation of Article 6 has proved both complex and contentious, both in this field and elsewhere. Extreme conceptual difficulties have been encountered in deriving a principled basis for incursions into questions concerning the acceptability of domestic provisions which have the effect of excluding a litigant from the assertion of a civil entitlement at all.[123] This has resulted in quite opaque distinctions being drawn between substantive and procedural grounds of challenge.[124]

The ECHR has been called upon to rule on the planning system's intricate mix of participative rights and, ultimately, administrative decision making. In *Bryan*, the applicant's challenge to planning enforcement proceedings had been dismissed by a planning inspector upon appeal. Called upon to consider whether an inspector was an independent and impartial tribunal, under Article 6, the ECHR concluded that the remedies available to the applicant under UK planning law satisfied the requirements of the Convention.[125] In ruling upon such questions, established case law required that regard must be had to factors such as the manner of appointment of the tribunal, terms of office, the existence of guarantees against outside pressures, and whether the body presents an appearance of independence.[126] Here, although an inspector was under a duty to decide an enforcement appeal in a quasi-judicial manner by exercising

---

117 See Stallworthy, 2000.
118 See Dennis, 1995, p 375.
119 See eg Ogus, 1994, Chapter 5.
120 See *Fredin v Sweden* (1990) 13 EHRR 784; also *Bentham v Netherlands* (1985) 8 EHRR 1.
121 *Ortenberg v Austria* (1994) 19 EHRR 524.
122 *Zander v Sweden* (1993) 18 EHRR 175.
123 See *Osman v UK* (1998) 29 EHRR 245.
124 See Gearty, 2001.
125 *Bryan v United Kingdom* [1996] 1 PLR 47.
126 *Langborger v Sweden* (1990) 12 EHRR 416.

independent judgment free of any improper influence, the Secretary of State could at any time issue a direction revoking the inspector's powers to determine an appeal. The ECHR was accordingly satisfied that for the purposes of such planning appeals 'the very existence of this power available to the executive, whose own policies may be in issue, is enough to deprive the inspector of the requisite appearance of independence, notwithstanding the limited exercise of the power in practice and irrespective of whether its exercise was or could have been in issue in the present case'.[127] However, the Court ruled that such defects could be overcome where such tribunal is subject to supervision by a judicial body, with full jurisdiction, and which itself satisfies the requirements of the Convention.[128] Here, a right of appeal existed to the High Court against an enforcement appeal decision.[129] Although it was limited to points of law, and therefore would not embrace all the issues raised by an enforcement notice, domestic grounds of judicial review were held to be wide enough to provide the necessary safeguards.[130]

Indeed, as to the limitation of review to matters of law, the ECHR recognised that the substitution by courts of own findings of fact, over those derived through administrative systems, is typically denied in numerous judicial review jurisdictions. Thus 'the subject matter of the contested decision by the inspector was a typical example of the exercise of discretionary judgment in the regulation of citizens' conduct in the sphere of town and country planning'.[131] And yet it appears that, as seen above, this recognition may not prevent decision making, for this is a policy-laden area, coming under increasing challenge by reference to the principles implied under Article 6.

4 THE OPERATION OF THE CONVENTION WITHIN UK LAW

4.1 The Human Rights Act 1998

The coming into force of the Human Rights Act 1998 will have profound implications throughout private and public law processes within the UK, and may lead to a significant reappraisal in key areas of planning procedure.[132] The Act has secured the incorporation into domestic law of rights under the European Convention.[133] It is thus unlawful for a public authority to act in a way that is incompatible with a right under the Convention, and a victim may bring proceedings in reliance upon this.[134] 'Public authority' is defined generally by deference to bodies 'certain of whose functions are functions of a public nature'.[135] There remain outstanding queries as to the status of privatised bodies such as water companies, although the regulatory apparatus would generally ensure that a complaint might lie against a public body in terms of positive obligations to take

127 *Bryan v United Kingdom* [1996] 1 PLR 47, at p 58.
128 *Albert and Le Compte v Belgium* (1983) 5 EHRR 533.
129 Under TCPA 1990, s 174.
130 *Bryan v United Kingdom* [1996] 1 PLR 47, paras 44–46.
131 *Ibid*, para 47.
132 See, eg, Grant, 2000c.
133 Human Rights Act (HRA) 1998, s 1.
134 *Ibid*, s 6(1).
135 *Ibid*, s 6(3)(4).

appropriate measures to safeguard Convention rights against prejudice by others.[136] Where it is asserted that a public authority has acted or proposed to act unlawfully, a litigant may issue proceedings against the authority,[137] or rely upon the Convention in any proceedings.[138] Legislation must henceforth be interpreted in a manner compatible with rights under the Convention, and in accordance with ECHR jurisprudence.[139] It is expressly stated that courts and tribunals are public authorities and required to apply the Convention.[140]

The nature of an horizontal effect, as seen elsewhere in the context of environmental impact assessment in Chapter 5, is that private parties are affected, and it appears inevitable that the new legislation will impact upon the common law. It is unlikely that as a matter of interpretation any new cause of action against a private party may be founded, as for instance where a polluter has breached terms of regulatory consents and the regulatory action has not taken appropriate enforcement action.[141] However, Hart points to 'the intriguing possibility that, for example, the law of nuisance as between individuals may be further developed in order better to protect the rights of the claimant in respect of his home (and) ... it seems inevitable that, whether in leaps and bounds or imperceptibly the common law will be brought in conformity with Convention principles'.[142] This points to a further possibility of individual challenges to alleged nuisances caused by regulatory decisions on grounds of environmental justice, under Article 14 and by reference to Article 8. A public authority does not however act unlawfully if, as the result of primary legislation, it could not have acted differently, or where such provisions cannot be read or given effect in a compatible way, the authority acted to give them effect.[143] Thus, the legislation ensures that, in compliance with the abiding fundamental principle of Parliamentary sovereignty, there is no judicial power to rule primary domestic legislation invalid. Instead, in the event that such legislation is found to be incompatible with the Convention a 'declaration of incompatibility' may be issued.[144] Should the government respond by seeking to rectify the position, an expedited procedure is available for the introduction of legislation into Parliament.[145]

Transposition of the principles underlying the Convention into the laws of the UK will have significant impacts in the arena of planning and environmental controls. Grant anticipates that the legislation 'will bring new reinforcement to the process by introducing, in appropriate cases where human rights are at stake, a heightened degree of scrutiny not only of the processes through which official decisions are made, but also their substantive outcomes. Hence the balance of power is shifting, from the somewhat closed administrative process of 50 years ago, to a system in which in human rights cases the courts are now given, effectively, the final say, and not just a power to quash and

---

136 Eg *Lopez Ostra v Spain* (1995) 20 EHRR 277.
137 HRA 1998, s 7(1)(a).
138 *Ibid*, s 7(1)(b).
139 *Ibid*, ss 2, 3.
140 *Ibid*, s 6(3).
141 See *Blackburn v ARC Ltd* [1998] Env LR 469.
142 Hart, 2000, p 119.
143 HRA 1998, s 6(2).
144 *Ibid*, s 4.
145 *Ibid*, s 11.

remit'.[146] However, he also points out that the effect the legislation upon UK planning and environmental practice 'depends on how far our own judges are willing to go in the same direction, and to spell new rights out of the unpromising material the Convention hands them. And that in turn depends upon practitioners coming to grips with the requirements of the Act and the opportunities it offers for new approaches to the redress of grievances'.[147] Moreover, entitlement to bring proceedings against a public authority is only available, in accordance with the Convention, to 'a victim' of the act the subject of the challenge.[148] This appears narrower than recent interpretations of 'sufficient interest' for the purposes of standing under domestic law.[149] There may therefore be difficulties in the way of assertion of collective rights, such as a right to seek protection of the environment.[150] It appears necessary to establish that the applicant is actually and directly affected by the alleged breach.[151] In one application under Article 6, members of a community surrounding a nuclear power plant opposed an extension of an operating licence on grounds of alleged risks to the life and health of the local population. The application was dismissed by the ECHR on the grounds of a failure to 'establish a direct link between the operating conditions of the power station ... and their right to protection of their physical integrity ... [from a threat that] exposed them personally to a danger that was not only serious but also specific and, above all, imminent'.[152] The Court, significantly, was split, and the dissent emphasised that, in determining the available right and whether the executive apparatus constituted an independent and impartial administrative or judicial tribunal, reference to the precautionary principle was necessary.[153]

4.2   Policy making, decision making and review

Whilst domestic courts may nevertheless apply purposive approaches in the face of collective action, access to the Convention through the 1998 Act raises obvious questions concerning the operation of quasi-judicial and judicial processes under planning and environmental legislation. Here, the approach of the High Court, discussed below, in the first significant test, suggested a purposive approach in the context of individual assertions of rights.[154] The first question to arise in this context has been how far acceptance, in principle of the process allowing a right of appeal to the court against an inspector's appeal finding, pursuant to the ruling in *Bryan*, extends where direct ministerial powers, such as to recover jurisdiction, are exercised. Challenges to such call-in and related powers resulted in the High Court's first declaration of incompatibility with the Convention, in *ex p Alconbury Developments Ltd*, although the ruling was

---

146 Grant, 2000a, para 12.10.17.

147 Grant, 2000a, para 1.2.2.1.

148 See HRA 1998, s 7.

149 *R v Her Majesty's Inspectorate of Pollution ex p Greenpeace (No 2)* [1994] Env LR 76; *R v Somerset County Council ex p Dixon* [1997] JPL 1030.

150 *Greenpeace Schweiz v Switzerland* (1998) 23 EHRR CD 116.

151 *Tauiria v France* (1995) D & R 83-A 113 (1995/28204/95).

152 *Balmer-Schafroth v Switzerland*, 26 August 1997 (67/1996/686/876), para 40.

153 See Grant, 2000a, para 1.2.2.3.

154 And see, eg, *Britton v Secretary of State for the Environment* [1997] JPL 617.

subsequently reversed by the House of Lords.[155] The conjoined cases concerned various powers deriving from the Town and Country Planning Act 1990, to call in and determine applications for planning permission and to recover and determine appeals,[156] as well as to confirm compulsory purchase and related orders under the Highways Act 1980 and to make orders under the Transport and Works Act 1992. Central government is inevitably interested in such cases, given that the context is the implementation of planning and transport policies for developments with more than local implications, such as the green belt, and also respectively where the centre is itself promoting the necessary orders and where development land would produce financial reward for the State.[157]

The process aspect called into question in the litigation lies, therefore, at the foundation of regulatory policy, namely the formulation and promotion of policy and related powers of implementation. Thus the planning system, as Tuckey J in the High Court pointed out:

> ... provides strategic direction for the use of land and control over individual development with the aim of securing the most efficient and effective use of land in the public interest ... The policy is promoted by national guidance issued centrally and regional guidance ... Local planning authorities are required to work within this wider policy framework when formulating detailed development plans for their areas. Wide requirements of public participation and consultation are built into the system to ensure that the formulation of policy at every level is democratic. The position is similar for transport policy.[158]

The cases likewise go to the root of judicial restraint. In planning law, judicial discretion in determining what may be a material consideration does not in principle admit of policy review, this being 'only one aspect of a fundamental principle of British planning law, namely that the courts are concerned only with the legality of the decision making process and not with the merits of the decision. If there is one principle of planning law more firmly settled than any other, it is that matters of planning judgment are within the exclusive province of the local planning authority or the Secretary of State'.[159] It is accepted, therefore, that the scope of judicial review of a decision's legality does not extend so far as to allow a court 'to examine the evidence to form its own view about the substantial merits of the case. The merits of the case and questions of planning judgment are for the determining authority, not for the court'.[160]

Applying standard principles, the High Court acknowledged that the minister 'has a wide discretion whether or not to call in an application which he has to exercise on a case-by-case basis. We do not consider that it can be said that his decision to call in ... was arbitrary, nor can it be said to be perverse or irrational'.[161] Moreover, there was no statutory requirement for him to give reasons for a decision whether or not to call in. Guidance suggests that:

---

155 R (on the application of Alconbury Developments Ltd, Holding and Barnes plc, Premier Leisure UK Limited, Legal and General Assurance Society Limited) v Secretary of State for Environment Transport and the Regions [2001] 2 All ER 929.

156 TCPA 1990, s 77.

157 [2001] 2 All ER 929, 945 (para 55).

158 Ibid, 944–45 (para 54).

159 Tesco Stores Ltd v Secretary of State for the Environment [1995] 2 All ER 636, 657, per Lord Hoffmann.

160 [2001] 2 All ER 929, 958 (para 92).

161 Ibid, 962 (para 113).

why called in

The policy of the Secretary of State is to be very selective about calling in planning applications, and such action is generally taken only if planning issues of more than local importance are involved. Examples are applications which raise significant architectural and urban design issues, which could have wide effects beyond their immediate locality, which give rise to substantial national or regional controversy, which may conflict with national policy on important matters, or where the interests of foreign governments may be involved.[162]

The court noted that clear reasons had been given 'as to why he had decided to call in the application and there was no need for him to go any further than that', for in particular there was no 'duty to explain whether or not he considered the application to come within the generality of the policy in the sense of involving issues of more than local importance'.[163] Accordingly, but for the impact of Article 6, such call-in decisions could not be challenged on traditional grounds of judicial review.

The principal question requiring determination was whether the minister as decision maker was in such circumstances sufficiently independent and impartial, so as to comply with Article 6. The foundation for the High Court judgment was the determination of a distinction between the minister and the inspector, in which latter respect, following the ECHR ruling in *Bryan*, the safeguards of the inquiry process and role of the inspector were considered ultimately to ensure a fair and public hearing of issues of fact and law. Here the Court considered that the judicial power of review was too restricted, in circumstances of the minister's reaching his own decision after taking account of internal legal and policy elucidation and the recommendation of the decision officer, not seen by the parties.[164] This led the Court to conclude that 'the decision on the merits, which usually involves findings of fact and planning judgment, has not been determined by an independent and impartial tribunal or anyone approaching this, but by someone who is obviously not independent and impartial'.[165] The processes involved were thus not compatible with Article 6(1), given that such decision making powers operated where the minister's own policies were in issue. The minister was therefore not only not an independent and impartial tribunal but also a judge in his own cause as both policy maker and decision taker. The available process of judicial review was not sufficiently wide to afford a sufficient remedy for these defects.

constitutional

The House of Lords was, however, unanimous in rejecting this application of the Convention. A fundamental counter argument to the High Court's approach to interpretation concerns the implications of a widened nature and role for judicial review. This extension arguably suggests a subversion of the self-restraining constitutional role of the courts. This appeared to be the main rationale underlying the House of Lords' drawing back from a potential unravelling of the decision making structures that have arisen under planning legislation. The implications of this early test for our quasi-judicial administrative arrangements deserve space which is not presently available. However, the rest of this section offers an attempt to chart the more significant features, which are likely to require consideration in the future.

---

162 See DoE, PPG 1, 1997a, Annex D, para D7; also, DETR, Circular 07/99, Circular 5/2000: *Planning Appeals: Procedures.*
163 [2001] 2 All ER 929, 962 (para 112).
164 *Ibid*, 958 (para 94).
165 *Ibid*, 958–59 (para 95).

First and, as indicated above, crucially, following traditional understandings of constitutional relationships, the House of Lords was unwilling to accept the High Court's expansive view as to the implications of the introduction of the European Convention into domestic law. Moreover, references to democratic accountability pepper the speeches.[166] Secondly, as to the implications of 'full jurisdiction' for judicial review, their Lordships did not accept that ECHR jurisprudence required that this extend to review of decisions on their merits.[167] Lord Hoffmann pointed out the inherent limits of the notion, whereby it meant 'full jurisdiction to deal with the case as the nature of the decision requires'.[168] As to a third issue, on the narrower question of authority, whilst accepting the relevance of Article 6.1 and the lack of neutrality on the part of minister or inspector, it was held that the authority of *Bryan* should not be distinguished. Whether an inspector or minister decided the issue, the scope of judicial review was therefore sufficient for the purposes of the Convention.[169] In each case, whilst matters of fact and degree were reviewable, policy determinations were not.[170] In other words, policy issues are for the executive, as described in ECHR jurisprudence as matters of expediency.[171] The subject matter of the present appeals was one of policy, therefore, to which judicial restraint did not extend.[172] Disapproving the approach of the High Court, Lord Hoffmann stated that 'the question is not whether he (the minister) should be a judge in his own case. It is whether he should be a judge at all'.[173]

Two ancillary – indeed constitutional – questions arose in conjunction with the consideration by the High Court of the impact of the 1998 Act. First, the government submitted that a broader judicial approach to the review process, in conformity with the court's obligations as a public authority not to act in a way which is incompatible with the Convention, and to interpret the legislation accordingly, could cure any defects in process.[174] Such a view would inevitably mean a broader power of review over factual questions, whilst presumably in some way steering just clear enough of policy questions. The court rejected the argument, declining to accede to the suggestion that it remedy this itself by the stratagem of enlargement of its powers beyond the traditional understanding of judicial review. It was not possible 'to read and give effect to the legislation which quite plainly precludes full appeals or appeals against findings of fact to accommodate any enlarged power of review and it would not be right to do so by the back door of judicial review. Judicial review is a review and not a full appeal. The court's powers to review findings of fact are circumscribed by the nature of the process'.[175] Moreover, the court took the view that in the new circumstances available judicial remedies might not be

---

166 [2001] 2 All ER 929, 978 (para 60), *per* Lord Nolan; 982 (para 76), *per* Lord Hoffmann; 995 (para 129), *per* Lord Hutton.

167 [2001] 2 All ER 929, 976 (para 50), *per* Lord Slynn; see, eg, *Albert and Le Compte v Belgium* (1983) 5 EHRR 533, para 29; *Le Compte, van Leuven and de Meyere v Belgium* (1981) 4 EHRR 1; *Golder v UK* (1975) 1 EHRR 524; *Kaplan v UK* (1980) 4 EHRR 64.

168 [2001] 2 All ER 929, 985 (para 87); see *Zumtobel v Austria* (1993) 17 EHRR 116; *ISKCON v UK* (1994) 76A DR 90, E Com HR.

169 [2001] 2 All ER 929, 975 (para 49), *per* Lord Slynn.

170 *Ibid*, 991 (para 110), *per* Lord Hoffmann.

171 *Ibid*, 992 (para 117), *per* Lord Hoffmann.

172 See further *Chapman v UK* (2001) 10 BHRC 48.

173 [2001] 2 All ER 929, 994 (para 124).

174 HRA 1998, ss 6, 3(1).

175 [2001] 2 All ER 929, 960 (para 100), *per* Tuckey LJ.

effective. Because judicial powers, both under the legislation and on judicial review, are limited to quashing the decision in question, such cases could only go back for re-decision by the Secretary of State, once again in breach of Article 6. This indeed accords with previous ECHR authority, that Article 6 was breached where the High Court could only quash the decision in question, so that the matter would have to go back for decision by the same non-impartial authority.[176] The point would thus have been more comfortably resolved if the court were able to exercise jurisdiction by way of a declaration requiring for instance that the matter be remitted to the planning authority.[177]

Secondly, it was held that the novel order made – a declaration of incompatibility – did not affect the lawfulness of the incompatible provision, and there were therefore no grounds for an interim injunction.[178] In the government's reaction to the ruling, a Minister of State stated in a written Parliamentary answer that 'the existing primary legislation continues to apply and the Secretary of State has a duty to continue determining cases which have been called in and appeals that have been recovered, and to fulfil his statutory functions in relation to orders made, for example, under the Transport and Works and Highways Acts and under Compulsory Purchase legislation. He will continue to exercise his discretion – for example, as to whether to call in planning applications – as before. In all cases, he will proceed in accordance with his usual practice. Pending final decisions on the appeals, in deciding whether to call in or recover cases for his own decision, he will take account of the fact that call in and recovery, although lawful, have been declared incompatible with the Convention by the Divisional Court'.[179] Even though guidance emphasises criteria including that matters involved are of more than local importance or that a departure from development plan policy is proposed, it must be assumed that at the very least the Secretary of State would have been increasingly selective in such actions. In the event, the ruling of the House of Lords has for the present protected the executive from the consequences of such a declaration.

The *Alconbury* litigation is unlikely to be the last word. On the face of it, the jurisprudence of the ECHR cited in this chapter has set numerous rights-based hares running which need in individual cases to be pursued and subjected to stringent analysis. Article 6 should not, however, be accorded such a broad remit that it comes to dominate areas of executive policy making and its administration. Indeed, Lord Hoffmann must have had this in mind in *Alconbury*, when he questioned the premise on which policy decisions as to the public interest such as these should be regarded at all as the determination of a right.[180] Moreover, from the perspective of the relationship between public interests and the environment, as seen above, and indeed elsewhere in this book, rights-based approaches can be both inappropriate and unhelpful. However, it is the nature of regulation that the lines of demarcation as between administrative and adjudicative determinations may not be clearly defined. A significant benefit from the introduction of the Human Rights Act within UK domestic law, therefore, is that it may usher in the development of coherent legal principles with a view to ensuring that such

176 *Kingsley v UK* (2001) Times LR, 9 January.
177 Casely-Hayford and Leigh, 2001, p 10.
178 Section 4(6).
179 19 December 2000, quoted [2001] JPL 255, 256.
180 [2001] 2 All ER 929, 981–82 (para 74).

rulings by the executive can be justified. If they can, and the Lords are indeed right in incanting recourse to democratic accountability, then this itself must likewise be subject to appropriate scrutiny. As will be seen in the next chapter, legal processes should not be too readily excluded from that exercise.

5 ACCOMMODATING HUMAN RIGHTS PRINCIPLES INTO THE UK REGULATORY CONTEXT

The concluding section to this chapter considers the legal bases for challenge to unsatisfactory operation of regulatory controls, and for third party challenges to planning decisions. However inappropriate it can often be, the human rights context does offer a normative basis upon which such arguments can be raised. Ironically, human rights approaches may prove inimical to more sustainable solutions. They may however offer a useful contributory perspective as the development of policies becomes subject to more rigorous levels of transparency and participation, and rights of challenge become recognisably a part of that process.

5.1 Addressing unsatisfactory regulatory control

We are yet to see substantive challenges, for instance on the basis of unsatisfactory regulatory control and enforcement in the UK. Most jurisprudential debate in this area has concerned the availability of challenges to Member States for defective implementation or enforcement of EC environmental directives. The reason for this is that EC legislation has been responsible for the widespread imposition of required environmental quality standards. However, the opportunities for individual and group challenge have been limited. This is due not only to domestic standing restrictions, but also the nature of these directives. As we have seen, these tend to be of a framework nature, according considerable levels of discretion as to such matters as designation and other aspects of further implementation by the responsible authorities. This has further militated against recognition of direct effect, whereby individuals may rely upon a directive against a State where the State has failed to implement them correctly or at all.[181] For instance, standard criteria for direct effect require subject matter to be unconditional, that is, not subject, in its implementation or effects, to the taking of any measure either by the institutions of the Community or by the Member States,[182] as well as sufficiently precise, that is set out in unequivocal terms.[183] Thus far enforcement appears to be potentially available in only restricted circumstances, where the measure is designed to protect individuals, such as the protection of health and life, or otherwise under standard categories of more recognisably 'public' grounds of challenge, as for instance under the grant of procedural rights.[184]

---

181 Case 8/81, *Becker v Finanzamt Munster-Innenstadt* [1982] ECR 53; Case 103/88, *Fratelli Constanzo v Commune di Milano* [1989] ECR 1839; Case C-236/92, *Comitato di Coordinamento per la Difesa della Cava v Regione Lombardia* [1994] ECR I-483.

182 Case 28/67, *Molkerei-Zentrale Westfalen v Hauptzollamt Paderborn* [1968] ECR 143.

183 Case 152/84, *Marshall v Southampton and South-West Hampshire Health Authority (No 1)* [1986] QB 401.

184 Case C-72/95, *Aannemersbedrijf PK Kraaijevelt BV v Gedeputeerde Staten van Zuid-Holland* [1996] ECR I-5403.

Yet, restrictions upon individual challenge may be diminished where, pursuant to the positive obligations required by the ECHR in *Guerra*, a litigant could argue that regulatory implementation and enforcement is required in order to comply with Article 8 of the Convention. Despite the reference earlier in this chapter to the possibly arguably extreme nature of the circumstances in both *Lopez Ostra* and *Guerra*, and the tendency of balancing processes applied by the ECHR to accord respect for general public interests as pursued by the State, it has been said that the UK courts 'will not labour under the same concerns and may well prove more robust in their approach'.[185] In particular, Thornton and Tromans have argued that Article 2 might have the greatest impact on domestic environmental law. Thus it has the potential for being invoked 'by workers claiming exposure to the risk of industrial accidents as a result of poor management systems or the use of chemicals whose toxicity is unknown. Similar principles could apply to risks from chronic pollution, as for example asthma caused by traffic or even inhalation of cigarette smoke'.[186]

However, recourse to rights under the Convention cannot obviate general difficulties faced in the context of private environmental litigation. As has been seen previously, these difficulties extend to problems in establishing the nature of alleged harm for the purposes of reliance upon a recognised cause of action. In considering whether there is evidence of damage, it is necessary to establish a relationship to the relevant act or omission under recognised principles of causation.[187] A restrictive approach to the interpretation of available epidemiological studies can severely constrain opportunities for a successful action.[188] Particularly in the case of negligence, assuming that a breach can be identified, a potential multiplicity of pollution victims prompts limits upon judicial sympathy.[189] In cases of diffuse pollution, there may even be problems of finding an appropriate defendant. Novel approaches have been suggested, such as applying the precautionary principle in determining the availability of a remedy, and imposing reduced burdens of proof on plaintiffs.[190] Yet principles such as the precautionary principle have not been applied successfully in such settings.[191] Whilst it would be too much to expect the Convention based as it is on human rights to resolve these difficulties, it may be that the duty placed upon domestic courts to take the Convention into account will lead to broader approaches, as in the application of the precautionary principle,[192] or, say, where harm is suffered as a result of diffuse pollution.[193]

---

185 Thornton and Tromans, 1999, p 53.

186 Thornton and Tromans, 1999, p 54.

187 *Graham and Graham v Rechem* [1996] Env LR 158.

188 *Reay & Hope v BNFL* [1994] Env LR 320.

189 See Miller, 1995, p 386.

190 See Holder, 1994, p 305.

191 Case 379/92, *Peralta* [1994] ECR I-3453; *R v Secretary of State for Trade & Industry ex p Duddridge* [1995] Env LR 151.

192 See *Zander v Sweden* (1993) 18 EHRR 175.

193 See, eg, Case 361/88, *European Commission v Germany* [1991] ECR I-2567, concerning the Sulphur Dioxide Directive 80/779.

5.2 Applying human rights principles in the policy context

The *Alconbury* litigation is but one instance of a number of potential Convention-based challenges in domestic litigation. Even in the unlikely event of the number of call-ins per annum (at around 130) being regarded as *de minimis*, the current admixture of policy and decision making is unlikely long to withstand challenge and serious scrutiny. The situation is redolent of the quite inadequate political preparation, in a different context, given to the implications of the UK's accession to what was then the European Economic Community in 1973.[194] There, it was two decades later when the extent of the departure from the doctrine of Parliamentary sovereignty was finally pronounced by the House of Lords.[195] Notwithstanding the successful appeal in *Alconbury*, as Casely-Hayford and Leigh have stated, 'the government must thoroughly investigate the administrative procedure where it involves the minister, as part of the executive, making judgments in effect in his own cause ... A planning application which by definition should concern itself principally with land use matters may of course involve a balancing or judgment of political interests but at both local and central level requires the necessary guarantees that Article 6 of the Convention seeks as assurance that individual rights are not being subjugated to the attainment of unrestrained political objectives'.[196] A narrowly compliant response following the determination of the Lords in this case would be incremental and deeply unsatisfactory. By contrast, beneficial consequences of a requirement for fuller review may follow, for the situation may hasten the introduction of an Environmental Court jurisdiction. This is considered in further detail in the next chapter.

There are other current (or prospective) approaches that might be in breach of the Convention, and may therefore be subject to challenge under the 1998 Act.[197] The implications are extremely wide ranging. For instance, although there is authority that compliance can be achieved through a written hearing,[198] proposals to speed up the appeals process by instituting a ministerial power to determine when a right to be heard should be available might be challenged.[199] This issue should not however raise the same quandaries as are apparent with regard to ministerial call-ins, for the Convention 'is not prescriptive about the type of hearing, and there is no reason to doubt that an informal hearing is taken by any less independent or impartial a tribunal as a public local inquiry. The question of whether the proceedings are "fair" an aggrieved appellant has a right to test by appeal to the High Court'.[200] It may even prove that the current requirement to obtain leave from the High Court,[201] in order to further appeal an unsuccessful enforcement appeal, is open to challenge. Once again it has been pointed out that the need for leave 'is not an obstruction to meritorious cases proceeding, but a filter

---

194 See European Communities Act 1972, s 2.
195 *R v Secretary of State for Transport ex p Factortame (No 2)* [1991] 1 AC 603.
196 Casely-Hayford and Leigh, 2001, p 11.
197 See Grant, 2000a, para 1.2.2.2.
198 *Jan Ake Andersson v Sweden* (1991), cited by Corner, 1998, p 309.
199 Department of the Environment Consultation Paper, *Planning Appeals*, 1997.
200 Grant, 2000a, para 1.2.2.2; see *Dyason v Secretary of State for the Environment* [1998] 2 PLR 54.
201 TCPA 1990, s 289(6).

mechanism, intended to prevent appellants from buying further time for unlawful activity by keeping proceedings alive. It is unlikely to be seen as a dilution of the supervisory powers of the High Court'.[202] Then, current inquiry procedures may be impugned if an individual or group is able to assert that parts of the local plan come in due course to be inserted without due regard for Article 6.[203] Likewise, the Planning Inspectorate determines whether appeals are to go to inquiry or be determined by informal hearing, and with other parties in mind, there may be challenges where no public inquiry takes place.[204]

This touches upon a question of perhaps greater significance for the relationship between planning and environmental protection, and participative processes. In *Bryan*, it will be remembered that the applicant failed in essence because of the availability of both enforcement appeal to the inspector, and, importantly, a statutory right to a judicial review thereafter. Such opportunities are not available to a third party, who may only have judicial review available, on ordinary principles.[205] Domestic legislation includes no third-party rights of appeal. Against this the citizen has only the limited protection of information access rights,[206] and over a very short time scale, which contrasts markedly with the influence of regulators and regulated over the process. Whilst access to information can be seen as part of the political and legal structure for ensuring accountability, 'registers offer an easy option for seeming to meet the pressure for greater public access to environmental information without actually achieving very much. They amount to little more than a gesture to promoting public access'.[207] The Rio Declaration recognised explicitly the importance of access: 'Environmental issues are best handled with participation of all concerned citizens, at the relevant level. At national level, each individual shall have appropriate access to information concerning the environment that is held by the public authorities, including information on hazardous materials and activities in their communities, and the opportunity to participate in the decision making processes. States shall facilitate and encourage public awareness and participation by making information widely available.'[208] In this respect, rights will be rendered more substantial upon the transposition of the Aarhus Convention, discussed in Chapter 10. But if operated in conjunction with a third party right of appeal (and that Convention also requires increased access to justice provisions, although there are as yet no domestic implementation proposals) then readier access to information would become a much more potent right.

The picture is therefore extremely mixed when viewing the record of jurisprudence under the Human Rights Convention where environmental matters are at stake. Indeed, especially in the light of expansive interpretations of Article 6 by the ECHR, and despite the decision of the House in *ex p Green*, environmental defaulters may seek protection under the Convention when faced with regulatory investigation. In this respect, it is

---

202 Grant, 2000a, para 1.2.2.2.

203 See Kitson, 1998.

204 See DoE, 1996c, Circular 15/96, para 15.

205 Cf *R v Secretary of State for Wales ex p Emery* [1996] 4 All ER 1.

206 Environmental Information Regulations 1992 (SI 1992/3240).

207 Rowan-Robinson, Ross, Walton and Rothnie, 1996.

208 Principle 10.

ironic that 'the Convention will not necessarily benefit the environment or the public interest'.[209] Yet, as discussed above, this is perhaps an inevitable incident where recourse under human rights principles is made available. After all, interpretation of the Convention will tend to lean towards requiring a clearer recognition of individual interests within the balancing process. In contrast, it is unlikely that a successful challenge could be mounted on the basis of the policy foundations, and therefore essentially discretionary nature of planning decisions. Whilst there is thus far little evidence of this, and none in the domestic setting, it is arguable that substantive claims may burgeon. Hart has asserted for instance that especially in the context of health risk and rights to information, there is 'the prospect that the local authority or regulator might be held liable for the unwise grant of consent or the lax regulation thereafter'.[210]

Moreover the ruling approach in the UK, despite the eventual ruling in the *Alconbury* case, may require reconsideration. It may therefore be that the non-invasive rationale of the ECHR in *Bryan* is itself on shaky foundations, especially in the light of broader interpretations of Article 6(1) in other contexts. The public interest foundations of domestic planning and environmental law are quite far removed from priorities accorded by the Convention to personal circumstances.[211] A changed approach to planning control may be required, and perhaps even aspects of the development planning process itself. Indeed, it remains difficult to see how the heavy policy emphasis can be sustained without a different body to hear appeals or to make binding determinations following inquiries. A revamped Planning Inspectorate is one potential solution, although constitutionally, once again, 'a right of appeal on the merits to an independent tribunal, or even one with some, but not total, independence such as an inspector, would appear to be usurping the power of government to make and apply policy'.[212]

Finally, it is necessary to recall concerns expressed earlier in this chapter in respect of applying anthropogenic or right-based solutions to problems which demand separate paradigms. In particular, human rights litigation under the European Convention, as Desgagne has stated, 'presents limited opportunities to foster the protection of the environment in general. Environmental protection has an important public facet that cannot be translated into an individual perspective and involves social choices that cannot be dealt with piecemeal. A system of protection of human rights, given its individualist bias, is not the best forum to further objectives that go beyond individual interests'.[213] Yet in the context of wider concerns at achieving sustainable solutions through traditional legal processes, a parallel with the earlier development of human rights laws may still be useful. For instance, in 1974, in the context of land use planning, critical of the obsession of legal theory and practice with the protection of private property, McAuslan called for a realisation by lawyers 'that the law has long-standing connections with human rights and civil liberties, and that a system of planning founded

---

209 Thornton and Tromans, 1999, p 49.
210 Hart, 2000, p 133.
211 But see *Westminster City Council v Great Portland Estates plc* [1985] AC 661, 669–70 (*per* Lord Scarman); cf *Britton v Secretary of State for the Environment* [1997] JPL 617.
212 Corner, 1998, p 308.
213 Desgagne, 1995, p 294.

on those principles might make a better contribution to the solution of urban problems than are founded, as now, on property'.[214] The more effective components remain those founded upon the processes of informed public discourse and participation. These are considered as part of the discussion of environment and democracy in the following chapter.

214 McAuslan, 1974, p 152.

CHAPTER 10

SUSTAINABILITY, LAW AND DEMOCRATIC POLITICS

Economic efficiency is a necessary element in the life of any sane and vigorous society, and only the incorrigible sentimentalist will depreciate its significance. But to convert efficiency from an instrument into a primary object is to destroy efficiency itself. For the condition of effective action in a complex civilization is co-operation. And the condition of co-operation is agreement, both as to the ends to which effort should be applied, and the criteria by which its success is to be judged.[1]

Whatever the degree of movement towards subjective agreement or objective uncertainty as to risk, or towards more environmentally informed legal approaches, sustainability demands political solutions. Solutions, in order to be viable, require that limitations upon environmental perspectives, both institutional and within ourselves, be challenged and overcome. The argument now goes on to consider the contribution that might be made by reformed democratic approaches to these questions, by reference to participative arrangements and legal structures.

1 SUSTAINABILITY AND DEMOCRACY

1.1 Limitations upon sustainable decision making in the liberal State

As citizens we both compete and co-operate in civil society through processes overseen by the State. Sagoff offers a coherent description of liberalism by reference to the contention that 'political and social institutions should be structured to allow free and equal individuals the widest opportunities, consistent with the like opportunity of others, to plan their own lives, and to live the lives they plan'.[2] Whilst there is inevitably some confusion, given the use of the word liberal in rights-based discourse, the linkage between liberalism and the economic order are dominant features of our culture. The emergence of liberal democracy has rested upon not only the relationship of welfare and liberty, but also the commitment to economic growth, and as explored in Chapter 3 the idea of the minimal State. Dobelstein points out that the 'classical liberal view of individuality merged easily with economic rationality, and together these two ideologies spoke against any intervention by government except to ensure the fair and efficient functioning of markets'.[3] Democratic notions have been likewise conditioned. In consequence, they are in the main a 'social consequence of our corporate and consumerist culture,' in which a liberal individualism remains the dominant feature, with 'possessive and individualist assumptions appropriate to an age of rising market society'.[4]

---

1   Tawney, *Religion and the Rise of Capitalism*, 1926, 1984 edn, p 277.
2   Sagoff, 1988, p 151.
3   Dobelstein, 1980, p 109.
4   Westra, 1998, p 76.

In the environmental context there are three main critiques of this view of the liberal order. In the first place, the liberal State expresses values as personal wants, and in its most extreme form espouses the idea of there being no such thing as society. Sagoff describes this as the view that community values amount to an 'illegitimate meddling in other people's affairs'.[5] Public policy comes to be severely circumscribed by its being thus regarded as 'similar in kind to private or corporate policy, though different in degree', with society 'as the sum of its individual decision making parts'.[6] Secondly, the liberal State is dominated by the application of economic values. Sagoff contrasts the economics of preferences, consumerism, and a dogmatic pseudoscience with environmental claims rooted in ethics, citizenship and deliberation. At heart, he argues for a Kantian ethical imperative, which in a world of scarce resources cannot easily accommodate the insistence upon preference. Partridge has offered a further critique of such central tenets as value-free cost benefit analysis, in the substitution of measurable market costs for qualitative values, resulting in non-impartial methods of discounting future costs and benefits as discussed in Chapter 2.[7] Thus what emerges has been described as 'a weird sort of intangible that deserves a surrogate market price'.[8] A third critique suggests that liberal conceptions of democracy are misconceived. This reflects the irony that the liberal consensus conceives of democracy as 'demanding indefinite respect for the cultural plurality of needs ... and conceptions of the "good life"' whilst simultaneously encouraging consumption patterns which are destructive of cultural diversity'.[9] Thus it has been asserted that liberal notions are actually 'inimical to the further development of democracy. In some senses liberal democracy may be more "liberal" than "democratic"'.[10]

Steering the liberal State, the craft of politics lies in its role as mediating process, as discussed in connection with risk in Chapter 8. The expression of sustainability as a norm offers a way of applying a more democratic calculus and divesting technocratic views of their established primacy. Sustainability accordingly also depends upon the ability of policy makers to recognise such factors as 'the moral presuppositions and the motives that underlie and direct the selection and evaluation' of technical information.[11] In this way the process, whether through engagement or neglect, impacts upon social structures and behaviours, for good or ill in terms of sustainability. Political arrangements offer 'an arena to consider options, to transform perceptions of individual and collective interest, and to manage conflict, as well as a means to modify regulatory frameworks which circumscribe individual and collective action'.[12] Operational systems flow through institutions, and the nature of democratic arrangements is that these have limited powers. Within the UK, as a matter of constitutional law, the capability of notions of legal constraint to exert normative influences upon the process is traditionally limited. Advocates of law-based, normative controls charge those who emphasise the political nature of restraint as 'tending to weaken the fabric of democratic procedure at a very

---

5   Sagoff, 1988, p 147.
6   Partridge, 1981, p 15.
7   Partridge, 1981, p 14.
8   Sagoff, 1988, p 147.
9   Soper, 1997, p 47.
10 Barry, 1999, p 198.
11 Partridge, 1981, p 14.
12 Lafferty and Meadowcroft, 1996, p 3.

important point; and doing so in favour of what are likely to be, in effect, random ephemeral local interest'.[13] By this rationale, the UK's system fails Mayo's objective test of 'social performance' by reference to the existence of controls beyond current policy content or purposes of government.[14] Nevertheless, wherever the balance of restraint operating within a democracy lies, the political establishment, in the endeavour to gain or to retain political power, has generally been unable meaningfully to address the sustainability crisis. Lazarus has accordingly spoken of the executive being generally more concerned about the impact of environmental laws on national economic indicators.[15] This has been discussed previously, as in the context of cost benefit analysis, where an essential problem lay in the temporal gap between cost incurred and resulting environmental benefit.

A number of limitations confront the process, four broad themes of which are identified below. First, environmental factors appear insubstantial in political terms. Sagoff has referred to the 'category mistake' in classical economic analysis of according preference on the basis of willingness to pay, whereas it is necessary to separate subjective wants from objective beliefs, which respectively can and cannot be priced.[16] Yet both policy makers and citizens have tended to recoil from responsible environmental decisions in the face of such factors as altered habits and expectations demanded of producer practices and consumer lifestyles. The problem has been compounded by the complexity and uncertainty of key environmental questions, as well as the temporal gap referred to above. The question of the rights of future generations, and the difficulties in the way of setting up a regime which recognises intergenerational rights, was discussed in Chapter 2. The result of a widening of the debate to include future generations is that politicians are likely to offer their rhetorical support alone. As Lem has dramatically put it: 'democracy is a form of terror against the unborn ... The question is whether it is possible to get the democracies to accept self-imposed limitations which cannot be removed at the next election.'[17] The problem subsumes those of science and technology. Barry has argued that sustainability and sustainable development 'share a fundamental characteristic of having normative and scientific dimensions ... It embodies a particular moral attitude to the future, expressing, for example, how much the present generation care and are willing to make sacrifices for descendants and how, and to what degree, non-humans figure in this process'.[18] The political process is inevitably replete with Faustian bargains which divert attention from such imperatives.

Secondly, as discussed in Chapter 1, spatial limitations proliferate, especially given that much of the environmental debate concerns problems that extend beyond the jurisdictions of mere nation States. Moreover, policy makers, producers and consumers operate within the prevailing liberal system and the limitations of markets, which themselves have become increasingly globalised. Democratic institutions suffer severe handicaps in constraining the activities of multinational corporations.[19] Environmental

---

13 Murdoch, 1993, p 359.
14 Mayo, 1960, p 213.
15 Lazarus, 1991, pp 222–24.
16 Sagoff, 1981, pp 1411–12.
17 Lem, 1944, p 148 (translation quoted by Lafferty and Meadowcroft, 1996, p 14).
18 Barry, 1999, p 206.
19 See Donaldson and Werhane, 1993.

critics may argue that corporations are subject to 'an obligation to guarantee equal protection from risk across national boundaries',[20] but that is plainly not what political and legal structures generally require of them. Regulators accordingly struggle to impose standards effectively.[21] As for the regulated, markets offer surrogate regulation of a different kind: as various interests, such as the securities markets, finance houses, and even potential corporate predators, dictate obsessions with profitability (the bottom line) and a general predisposition to short-termism. This can be seen in the context of the pressures placed upon a 'primary' industry such as farming by the increasing globalisation of food supply, and market responses by consumers in the wake of recurrent food health scares. BSE, discussed in Chapter 8 in the context of risk, is an illustration, as also is the relationship between the market and the putatively 'Act of God' crisis of Foot and Mouth disease, which spread with extreme, arguably market-assisted, speed across much of the UK early in 2001.

Thirdly, accountability restraints have become increasingly tenuous under prevailing liberal approaches.[22] Westra goes so far as to conclude that 'it is precisely the unquestioned acceptance of the primacy of the democratic institutions that presents the major obstacle to the prevention of public harms, particularly environmentally induced risks to public health'.[23] In a State such as the UK, projects for devolution in Scotland, Wales and Northern Ireland, and in contrast slow progress towards regional assemblies in England (just as reforms to the Upper Chamber in the Westminster Parliament), have not as yet resulted in a reformed framework for accountability, especially of the retained government at the centre. Meanwhile the State performs ever-reducing roles in major development projects. Although it is argued that public-private partnerships offer a different way forward – and at root disputes as to great infrastructure projects such as the renewal of the London Underground system are fought over just such territory – it remains the case that publicly funded projects are on the wane.[24] In trivial (in terms of infrastructure) but momentous (in terms of what it tells us of our political leaders) contrast is the one-year Millennium Dome extravaganza at Greenwich in London. Referring to the (original) commitment of £550 million of lottery funds to the project, Young has asserted that the project 'was built with funny money, for which nobody is accountable. The Treasury would never have countenanced tax money being used. No business could have defended such folly to its shareholders. Lottery money, falling outside either discipline, was made available as a plaything for egotistical wasters who invented a national purpose that did not exist'.[25] Central government's apparent impotence in the face of the crisis which afflicted the national rail infrastructure from the autumn of 2000 (only partly potentially assuaged by a Strategic Rail Authority under the Transport Act 2000) is an illustration of reduced responsibility and diluted accountability. It is in such an era of political washing of hands that the ultimate questions posed by sustainability must be addressed.

---

20   Schrader-Frechette, 1991, p 148.
21   See Hawkins, 1984.
22   See Lafferty and Meadowcroft, 1996.
23   Westra, 1998, p 58.
24   Cf Hutton, 2000b.
25   Young, 2000.

Fourthly, politicians in liberal democracies are themselves geared to the short-termism imposed by the regular challenges of the ballot box. As Lindblom has pointed out, 'political will is often ... characterised by short term thinking, by domination of partial interests (especially interests with a powerful market position) and, in general, by "disjointed incrementalism"'.[26] A major problem confronting possibilities for achieving sustainability is that 'the current pattern of economic gain and political power is institutionally ensnared in non-sustainable development. Arguably, it is the non-sustainability that retains this institutional order, so one can hardly expect it to write its own epitaph in the interests of a contradictory and ambiguous goal'.[27] Fiscal controls, with few exceptions, have thus far played a minor role in pointing to environmental solutions. Indeed perhaps the opposite is the case, given the levels of resourcing required to achieve significant realignment in economic processes. Related measures, such as anticipated trading regimes for carbon emissions, both domestically and under the Kyoto Agreement, may be perceived as obviating or reducing the pressure on governments to deliver other key decisions. The UK's petrol prices conflict in the autumn of 2000, and so-called taxpayers' revolt, as well as the government's response, was a bleak indication of the peripheral nature of environmental arguments in such debates.[28]

1.2   Citizens, consumers and consensual risk takers

The nature of democratic consent is another prism through which to view the problematic relationship of risk and harm. The difficulties of risk assessment in the environmental context, seen in Chapter 8, were categorised by reference to the serious obstacles to perceptions of risk, including deficiencies in scientific predictive capacities, problems of cumulative effect, necessarily long time frames, and the underresearched introduction and use of substances and processes.[29] A lack of convergence with capacities for risk allocation at common law, especially where issues of liability depend upon the establishment of fault and levels of foreseeability,[30] has also been discussed. For their part, democratic processes may fail in ways that are both latent and apparent. For instance, the notion of individual consent is eroded where risk is undisclosed. Moreover, constraints upon the assertion of preferences may be less than open. For instance, it has been estimated that public relations press releases are responsible for around 40% of news content in the United States.[31] Likewise, Westra refers to preferences being 'manipulated by advertising campaigns, financed by public relations ... there seems to be little if anything left of our "preferences" or of "us" as individuals or even as community or national groups that is either distinctive or truly autonomous, while we change from multidimensional, rational individuals into mere "consumers"'.[32]

---

26 Lindblom, 1977.
27 O'Riordan, 2000, p 30.
28 See, eg (2001) *The Independent*, 22 February and 8 March.
29 See Westra, 1998, p 58; also, Colborn, Dumanoski and Myers, 1996.
30 *Cambridge Water Company v Eastern Counties Leather plc* [1994] 2 AC 264, *Wagon Mound (No 2), Overseas Tankship (UK) Ltd v Miller Steamship Co Pty Ltd* [1967] 1 AC 617.
31 Korten, 1995, p 146.
32 Westra, 1998, p 5.

Yet markets, so close to liberal conceptions of democracy, have delivered economic development and prosperity (for the north of the planet in any event). It is not only organised commercial pressures which threaten the environment. Albeit for different, though related, reasons, resistance to environmental protection measures can be detected within the population at large. This can be seen in middle-class values (witness the UK petrol price 'revolt' referred to above) but is inevitably marked in deprived urban areas. There, issues typically resolve themselves into economic imperatives, such as a paramount need for jobs. Even where concerned at pollution, deprived communities identify less with perceived white, middle class values such as 'preservation of wildlife and wilderness'.[33] The task of re-evaluating our political as opposed to our market selves is a major obstacle to the democratic generation of change. Thus it is argued that in judging democracy, the link to happiness is a further category mistake. Democracy, according to Barry, 'as a political decision making system, after all, is a procedure for making political decisions: that democratic decisions are to make people happy is not to judge the procedure but the product'.[34] It is a problem, however, that between the political deliberative processes and market achievement of aggregated preferences, a citizen-consumer distinction is maintained.[35] Achterberg concludes that our exposure to market society 'moulds our identity in a manner which cannot easily be neutralised merely by taking part in conventional representative democratic politics'.[36]

Self-regard appears therefore to be ingrained, with effects that are both intra- and intergenerational. This is institutionalised in the economic and social foundations, with concerns focused upon economic well-being.[37] One consequence is a discounting of future impacts through cost benefit criteria which are premised on 'the assumption that the value of future costs and benefits is directly proportional to their *proximity* in the future'.[38] This can be seen in the paucity of concern with respect to non-renewable resources.[39] It is hard to feel confident that arguments in favour of significant energy conservation will readily engender solid electoral support.[40] The difficulties in the face of the achievement of such changes are considerable. In order to counter such cultural resistance, it remains necessary to bring about a revolution in government processes, and in their acceptance, by producers and consumers alike. Invoking citizen commitment is crucial. Not only is there a distrust of the State's attitude towards sustainability, but there is a deeper problem of disengagement on the part of citizens. Macnaghten and Urry concluded from empirical studies investigating levels of trust and commitment that 'people's own sense of agency in relation to the problems was extremely weak. Most accepted some individual responsibility as morally responsible citizens, but felt that what they could do on a personal level was extremely limited. However, their lack of trust in government meant that "political" action would also be ineffective'.[41] It has accordingly

---

33 Lyle, 2000, p 703.
34 Barry, 1999, p 196.
35 Sagoff and Miller, 1992.
36 Achterberg, 1996, p 164.
37 Dunlap, 1989, p 130.
38 Partridge, 1981, p 15.
39 Wright, 1988, p 67.
40 Barry, 1977, p 270.
41 Macnaghten and Urry, 1998, p 231.

been argued that any State promotion of environmental initiatives 'will have to prove exemplary intent to a highly sceptical public ... [and] will have to recognise too that plans for a sustainable future cannot rely on existing methods of consultation or on existing reliance on expert knowledge'.[42]

Yet there is also the limitation inherent in the absence of incentive at the top, amongst the political elite. This appears to be NIMBYism writ large. Dobson has gone further, suggesting that a 'significant and influential proportion of society ... has a material interest in prolonging the environmental crisis because there is money to be made from managing it. It is Utopian to consider these people to be part of the engine for profound change'.[43] The problems of persuasion would perhaps deserve a lengthy discourse upon class theory, and Dobson points to critiques of the efficacy of broad appeals to society at large, as classically in Marx's insistence upon attracting a class with an interest in change.[44] The notion of identification with an appropriate class may appear ironic to ecologists, but seeking to avoid disproportionate burdens is a comparable process. Moreover, it has been argued that the middle classes might press for change, given 'the flexibility and security to act upon such (environmental) insights'.[45] Yet the same criticism of the movers and shakers referred to above would quite likely adversely dispose those benefiting from higher standards of living under the prevailing liberal consensus.

2 ENVIRONMENTAL CHALLENGES TO DEMOCRATIC LIMITATIONS

2.1   Reforming democratic structures

In this section, consideration is given to current conceptions of democracy and their determinist nexus with lifestyle. Following this, there will be discussion of the potential for institutional change towards 'green' democratic processes. There will be only limited mention of rights below, for the focus is upon structures, both political, and in the following section legal, which can inform the political process in a quest for greater sustainability. It may indeed be that human-rights-based perspectives can have more than a residual impact towards unlocking a more sustainable use of resources, although this point is returned to below. Despite the scale of the task, given current realities of the political State, it is to the policy arena that we must look for change. Solutions must be premised upon changes to political as well as legal structures. It is however necessary to pursue caution in pursuit of political solutions. To advocate democracy, as Goodin has it, 'is to advocate procedures, to advocate environmentalism is to advocate substantive outcomes: what guarantee can we have that the former procedures will yield the latter sort of outcomes?'.[46] Thus far the settled procedures of the democratic polity have not come under any serious challenge in the cause of sustainability. Yet without an attempt at

---

42   Macnaghten and Pinfield, 1999, pp 30–31.
43   Dobson, 2000, p 146.
44   See Lewis, 1957, Chapter 2.
45   See Porritt, 1984, p 116.
46   Goodin, 1992, p 168.

such restructuring, the assertion of the democratic 'will' appears likely to remain an obstacle to achievement of any meaningful realignment.

It is commonly argued that a sustainable society is also a democratic society.[47] The workings of democracy appear to favour conditions of prosperity. It has therefore been suggested that ecological values and democracy are incompatible.[48] Wilkinson points out that popular support 'for policies that are environmentally destructive but which provide tangible short term benefits is to be expected in a world of self-interested individuals'.[49] The task is to shift current liberal conceptions of democracy, and related electoral support, away from wealth perceptions as absolute values. The search to secure that the conditions to human survival are met requires changes to be made in our social recognition of need. Thus Soper has called for 'a rejection ... of consumerist perceptions of the good life in favour of modes of existence that place less stress on nature and are consistent with a more equitable distribution of resources'.[50] The introduction of ecological perspectives offers a radical challenge to current ways of thinking. It invokes 'a sort of communitarianism that is inconsistent with principles traditionally associated with a liberal State'.[51] Indeed it has been cogently argued that individualism, and current approaches to consumption and production, 'can sap the democratic vigour of a society even while maintaining democratic institutions'.[52]

Thus sustainability is predicated upon mandating lifestyle constraints with the objective of protecting those ecosystems upon which human kind depends, but which are often far removed from everyday perception and experience. The task entails a rejection of utilitarian approaches to resources, in which, for the majority, instrumental value outweighs intrinsic value.[53] This places great pressure on political structures, informed with liberal approaches, rooted in property, markets and choice. In light of the lack of progress to date, and problems such as State sovereignty, Westra concludes that the achievement of a re-evaluation of the majority preferences and choices inherent in nationalism and democracy demands international structures.[54] Indeed, even viewed from a national level, just as problems are global, patterns of living, as well as commerce, are non-local. Given the limitations operating upon the international arena, however, a starting point for analysis must be at the foundations of democracy (albeit uneven) which are rooted in most developed and other nation States.

A reworking of politics within a post-liberal democratic theory requires institutional change. Such change may encompass a questioning of democratic assumptions. This fact has led to the accusation that it signifies some form of ecological autocracy.[55] Ophuls, in emphasising a need for greater control over the distribution of scarce resources, rejects

---

47 Eg, Pearce, 1993, p 185.
48 See eg Saward, 1993.
49 Wilkinson, 1999, p 40.
50 Soper, 1997, p 46.
51 Sagoff, 1988, p 147.
52 Barry, 1999, p 212.
53 Hargrove, 1989, p 209.
54 Westra, 1993, p 125.
55 See Hardin, 1977; Heilbroner, 1980.

'the golden age of individualism, liberty and democracy ... In many important respects we shall be obliged to return to something resembling the pre-modern closed polity'.[56] A changed system which meets these demands would be 'much more oligarchic as well, with only those possessing the ecological and other competencies necessary to make prudent decisions allowed full participation in the political process'.[57] Whilst this view may be criticised as having an eco-authoritarian premise, as the welfare state consensus has shown, democratic values do not necessarily demand a rejection of all limits upon individual freedom to satisfy our wants. Nevertheless any process aimed at changing our perception of those wants looks potentially oppressive. As Huxley's Director for Hatcheries and Conditioning says: 'all conditioning aims at ... making people like their inescapable social destiny.'[58] Constraint is therefore where battle usually engages, especially as regards market ideologies, and, as discussed in Chapter 3, questions of autonomy of private property rights. Yet, even here, the idea of limits accords with Locke's notion of civil government, which allows for mutual constraint, whereby subject to the common good of 'the peace, safety and public good of the people' the individual is 'regulated by laws made by the society, so far forth as the preservation of himself and the rest of that society shall require'.[59] Thus given the gravity of the relatively newly identified threats to sustainability, the answer may be better found in seeking to justify further constraints.

There is a response which may produce a post-liberal (and green) democratic alternative, seeking a transformation in institutions and processes.[60] The achievement of sustainability, in both cultural consciousness and lifestyle, demands structural changes. Whilst institutional reforms may not be sufficient, they would be a necessary precondition to achieving deliverable change. In the wider cultural context, according to Barry, this offers 'a procedure within which cultural contradictions can be publicly raised, coped with and possibly resolved'.[61] Thus he asserts that 'macro- and micro-level reorganisation needs to be supplemented with changes in general values and practices. In short, institutional change must be complemented by wider cultural-level changes'.[62] The idea of associative democracy emphasises the plurality of involvement of forms of 'association' and looks to co-ordinating mechanisms, negotiation and decentralisation.[63] Achterberg points to the Dutch experience of central government entering into covenants with target groups, such as industry and public interest bodies.[64] He offers three transformations as structural responses to the liberal market economy, the first two of which suggest micro- and macro-economic approaches, and the third a more tentative recognition of issues of justice.

---

56 Ophuls, 1977, p 145.
57 Ophuls, 1977, p 163.
58 Huxley, 1932, p 24.
59 Locke, 1690, 1924 edn, Chapter ix, 'Of the ends of political society and government', paras 129, 131.
60 See Eckersley, 1992.
61 Barry, 1999, p 209.
62 Barry, 1999, p 228.
63 Eg, O'Neill, 1993; Hirst, 1994.
64 Achterberg, 1996, pp 168–71.

First, there would be a 'strategy of sustainability' with consequences for both technological and social adaptation.[65] Numerous strategies would be required, involving wide social groupings, including producers and consumers, employers and labour, industry and the environmental movement. These would aim co-operatively at an increased level of co-ordination of activities, enabling integral life-cycle management within management chains of production. Secondly, so as to counter the 'inherent tendency towards growth and expansion' and to effect further limits upon market activities, 'sustainability planning' would be introduced, by application of a sustainability criterion.[66] The objective would be that central government direction would 'determine an admissible level of environmental impact that will result from all economic activities taken together ... to prevent or manage environmental problems, conceived as negative side-effects generated by the economy. The instruments needed to give effect to sustainability planning would include physical regulation, financial incentives, public expenditure and persuasion based on appeals both to enlightened self-interest and to morality'.[67] Those excluded from the processes of production and consumption, such as the unemployed, remain likely (and justifiably so) to view material values as their dominant concerns. Therefore, in order to secure wide co-operation, the third measure suggested by Achterberg would be a more equal division of income.[68]

Such proposals face numerous obstacles. It is difficult to see how such changes would be sufficient to counteract the (global) market approaches which currently dominate, or avoid sectional interests in dictating progress. It is likewise difficult to formulate ways in which citizen-consumers can be successfully discouraged from market-based behaviour patterns. Indeed, notwithstanding partial successes such as Agenda 21 at a local level, the short-termism of politicians referred to above but mirrors that of citizens.[69] Macro-economic issues are still more problematic, although regulatory activity and alternative economic instruments are directed at producing environmental improvements. As to the achievement of greater equity, on the international stage the formal link between sustainability and development seeks to address this. However, if equity requires a reversal of growing disparities of wealth, subsequent events have not augured well. At national level, wealth redistribution is something which the majority of the electorate appears to view with unhealthy suspicion, so that any improvements tend to be both hidden and incremental. Moreover, it is at this point that the politics of the right (and increasingly the centre-left) appears to baulk. A resolution may lie not in the absolute level of wealth but rather in levels of its distribution. A reformed view of distribution is thus based on the notion that democracy is linked with 'economic security rather than affluence' and that the former compensates the latter by what Barry terms 'an increase in liberty and self-determination'.[70] The political order could therefore it is argued, withstand, even benefit from, reformed principles of redistribution, for 'social solidarity need not be threatened by this so long as the costs are shared equitably throughout the whole society'.[71]

---

65 Achterberg, 1996, p 161.
66 See Jacobs, 1991.
67 Achterberg, 1996, p 163.
68 Achterberg, 1996, p 165.
69 See Meadows, Meadows, Randers and Behrens, 1972, p 19.
70 Barry, 1999, pp 196–67.
71 Barry, 1999, pp 213–34.

2.2 Changes and the individual

Democratic systemic responses, with an emphasis upon participation, supported by public law process reforms, as outlined below, need to address cultural limitations. Any progress towards sustainable solutions requires broad social consensus and individual commitment. This is especially the case under democratic arrangements, where (on most issues) politicians are extremely sensitive to public demands. For all the 'greening' of debate, when exposed to costs, it seems that the public shows markedly reduced interest. Lazarus suggests that 'public aspirations for environmental protection, which have been uncompromising, have collided with the public's unwillingness to pay the costs associated with that change'.[72] As Naess put it, 'environmental measures which are popular are those which are not perceived as a threat to the consumption and behavioural patterns of each individual'.[73] Dobson points to the difficulty for the green movement in 'simultaneously calling into question a major aspiration of most people – maximising consumption of material objects – and making its position attractive'.[74] Without an alternative paradigm, it appears that pressure for change cannot be assumed, notwithstanding increased recognition of environmental threats. Communities accordingly 'deal with toxic exposure in ways that force them to continue participating in the system that caused the pollution', the process serving to 'institutionalize and legitimate as a problem what might otherwise be viewed as a fundamental crisis and, thus, a challenge to our modern, industrial way of life'.[75] More worryingly, as Edelstein has concluded, the adoption by the majority of a generalised concern for the environment 'reflects their attitudes and not their values. Their lives are so compartmentalised that they live a lifestyle that supports the pollution habit, without ever seeing the contradiction. Pollution is seen as an abstract "issue" – a problem to be solved – not as a personal problem to address'.[76]

The task is therefore to seek a realignment in perceptions of wants and needs, in order to encourage a change in (what are generally fixed) values. There are some indications that the UK Government is willing to open a debate on this question. In its recent white paper devoted to rural problems, it quoted earlier research evidence concerning public concern for the environment: 'few discriminate in their purchasing of food or travel in a way that would directly sustain the landscapes and bio-diversity they value ... [It appears that] high levels of public concern about the environment co-exist with a deep-seated reluctance to support measures to reduce the impact of their own lifestyles on environmental quality.'[77] The problem is that the ruling canons of efficiency and progress remain in place. In some areas, there are signs of greater maturity amongst the population, as for instance in the genetically modified food debate. This has been described as having thus far been 'so controversial not least because of the deep cultural significance of food and the changes that genetic engineering promises to bring culturally and socially. Our evidence shows that many people are increasingly unwilling simply to

---

72 Lazarus, 1994, p 876.

73 Naess, 1993, p 329.

74 Dobson, 2000, p 16.

75 Edelstein, 1988, p 194.

76 Edelstein, 1988, p 194.

77 DETR/MAFF, 2000, para 1.9; see generally, UK Government, 1998.

accept such revolutionary changes without a genuine debate about the options society faces'.[78] It may also be that the more direct the perceived threat to our own health (and comfort) then the more likely are we actively to respond.

Consideration of spiritual dimensions may also play a part in the process of change. Porritt suggests that 'without some huge groundswell of spiritual concern the transition to a more sustainable way of life remains utterly improbable'.[79] The nature of the crisis for humankind, given its link with our willingness to commodify and exhaust resources, can be said to be most manifest at an individual level. This need not be perceived as a spiritual matter, in the sense of ethereal or pseudo-religious. The idea underlying Gaia, of earth as a super organism, ultimately asserts the interactive nature of the ecosystems by which it exists, based upon objective, that is scientific, factors.[80] Porritt accordingly describes such a view of the planetary processes as 'a powerful secular alternative to the kind of dominant humanism that continues to put the human species at the very apex of life on earth, contrary to all scientific evidence about evolution'.[81] The crisis can be perceived as concerning the way we as humankind think, and see ourselves, and demands a reassessment of normative processes by which value judgments influence all human endeavour.[82] Central to Roszack's thesis is the notion of repairing our connectedness with our culture and our past, challenging the endless movement and rejection of fixed points implicit in modern science: the sense of who we are. Whilst perhaps it would be better to read his use of the word 'urban' as a metaphor for consumption patterns generally (especially given the need for urban solutions in the light of population levels), he speaks of 'an urban population no longer in vital touch with the true conditions of its survival'.[83] Finally, he prescribes fundamentally ecological solutions in 'scaling down, slowing down, democratization and decentralization'.[84]

The fundamental ecological contribution is therefore the emphasis upon our being a part of nature and that even commerce must depend 'on wise, respectful interaction with our biosphere'.[85] Appleyard suggests that reliance upon the transforming truths offered by science, in which liberal society's belief-free cultural relativity colludes, has resulted in a loss of awareness of ourselves and our cultures.[86] Likewise, Porritt argues that modern evolutionary theory has become unnecessarily enmeshed in a similar mechanistic, value-free vision, which leads to a 'desacralized' approach to ourselves.[87] Environmentalism (in a broad sense) may be accused of collusion, in similarly ignoring the question of reason and purpose, namely to go beyond an obligation to survive.[88] Yet it is with such ruling perceptions that liberal democracy currently identifies, and hence the scale of the task of realignment. Furthermore, science is ever-more straining upon the leash of institutional

---

78 Global Environmental Change Programme, 1999, p 20.
79 Porritt, 1984, p 210.
80 Lovelock, 1979 and 2000; also Margulis, 1998.
81 Porritt, 2000, p 125.
82 See Sherrard, 1992, pp 9–10.
83 Roszack, 1992, p 308.
84 Roszack, 1992, p 311.
85 Spretnak and Capra, 1985, p 28.
86 Appleyard, 1992, pp 231–37.
87 Porritt, 2000, pp 120–21.
88 Appleyard, 1992, pp 228–29.

control. Appleyard points to the shifting limits of ethical acceptability, with a tendency for boundaries 'to move further and further over to the scientific lobby'.[89] An ironic illustration is that for all the risks introduced under intensive agriculture, it is the very chemical companies that gave us chemical solutions which are now mutating into biotech companies.[90]

3 SUSTAINABILITY, DEMOCRACY AND PARTICIPATION

3.1 Participation within a reflexive society

Yet despite the apparent gap between lifestyle and progress towards sustainability, it is argued below that securing a meaningful transformation depends upon encouraging more genuine, informed, participatory mechanisms. This is encapsulated under Principle 10 of the Rio Declaration, providing as follows:

> Environmental issues are best handled with the participation of all concerned citizens, at the relevant level. At the national level, each individual shall have appropriate access to information concerning the environment that is held by public authorities, including information on hazardous materials and activities in their communities, and the opportunity to participate in decision making processes. States shall facilitate and encourage public awareness and participation by making information widely available. Effective access to judicial and administrative proceedings, including redress and remedy, shall be provided.

It has been claimed that, together with the right to live in an environment that does not damage one's health, the right to participate in decision making about the environment in which one lives is one of two fundamental environmental rights.[91] However, participation mechanisms can perhaps be contrasted with a somewhat narrower concentration upon rights, which in United States political discourse has been described as 'vacuous, hard-edged, and inflexible, just when it is called upon to encompass economic, social, and environmental problems of unparalleled difficulty and complexity'.[92] Asserting a need for explicit processes, Gedicks states that it is necessary to shift the 'focus of the debate ... from *how* this project will be developed, to who will be involved in the decision making process'.[93] Towards this end, participation offers valid forms of collective responsibility.

Much in the way that public health demands were a catalyst for the development of planning controls in the 19th century, commitments to sustainable development have the potential of bringing the idea of participatory purposes once more to the fore.[94] It will be recalled that McAuslan famously identified that the purposes of planning law could be

---

89 Appleyard, 1992, p 234.

90 McCarthy, 2001.

91 Freudenberg, 1984, p 261.

92 Glendon, 1991, p 172.

93 Gedicks, 1993, p 204.

94 See Simmie, 1994, p 3.

made to pursue one of three ideologies.[95] The first, an ideology of private property, accords priority to the protection of the private interest, so that property interests prevail over public control. Secondly, an ideology of public interest allows property rights to be overridden, on the basis of administrative decisions, reached in accordance with technical advice. A more radical third ideology is based upon the idea of participation, according the citizen opportunities to influence and to challenge official policy, thereby factoring in wider considerations which lie beyond those determined as a matter of administrative discretion. Likewise, political discourse in the United States has produced three broadly similar models of administrative discretion – an expertise model, a pluralist model and a civic republican model. Under the latter, similarly, the determination of the public interest is not confined within a technocratic magic circle. Instead, 'citizen inclusion is a regulatory ideal but is employed to achieve a form of deliberation focusing on true public good solutions rather than utility maximization'.[96]

Sustainable policy making requires that we accord primacy to participatory processes. On this basis, in light of the demands of sustainable development, Macnaghten and Pinfield argue for 'qualitative planning', evincing a greater understanding of people's needs, or their quality of life. This implies a more direct relationship with the public in policy making, which must operate on two levels: 'not simply adopting new processes of listening to what people want or need in their day-to-day lives, but also the formation of partnerships between planners and health professionals, community groups, community development professionals and social scientists.'[97] This form of associative democracy appears close also to what Rydin refers to as 'collaborative planning'. This operated through 'specific institutions to support communities and ... formal policy safeguards within the policy process on: access to information and decision making arenas; recognition of status within the policy process; and rights of redress, safeguards which allow action against professionals within the policy process'.[98]

Just as in the uncertain contexts of risk, the ultimate task is to achieve political 'closure' on policy decisions, and this demands citizen participation. It has been argued that such indeterminacy *a fortiori* 'calls for citizen deliberation, while its translation into policies and laws calls for their consent and, equally important, their participation in achieving it'.[99] A way forward is offered by modern commentators on risk construction. The necessary evolution towards fundamental transformation in social and political values requires institutional changes. This would be premised by Beck upon a new social relationship between the individual and society, including greater democracy and participation, through adherence to deliberative processes, and pursuing a precautionary approach, prioritising strategic and long term approaches. Such a view is useful for pointing to the need for the open acknowledgement of contingency, and longer term consequences of risk, within the political framework.[100] The principles offered in Beck's thesis of reflexivity may be applied across this wider democratic terrain. The report of the

---

95 McAuslan, 1980, pp 2–6.
96 Gauna, 1998, p 17.
97 Macnaghten and Pinfield, 1999, pp 21–22.
98 Rydin, 1998, 361.
99 Barry, 1999, p 206.
100 Eg, Beck, 1998.

Global Environmental Change Programme has argued for participatory methods on grounds of allowing a wider range of factors to be taken into account, with greater legitimacy for decisions than where based purely on 'sound science'. It concludes that 'participatory methods of public engagement are intrinsically open-ended. In the presence of profound uncertainties and "ignorance", they will also remain imperfect'.[101] Giddens develops the argument for a deliberative conception of democracy, which requires that decisions be made 'on the basis of a more or less continuous reflection on the conditions of one's action'.[102] The notion of reflexivity refers in this context 'to the use of information about the conditions of activity as a means of regularly re-ordering and redefining what that activity is'.[103] Myerson and Rydin eloquently suggest that 'the heroine of the story could be a new democracy, a democracy giving expression to plural enlightenment, a democracy whose principle is open-ended discussion, not single verdicts. It could be a story of enlightened uncertainty, the birth of democratic culture'.[104]

A final advantage of participation lies in the aspect of stakeholding. Whilst recognising the contested nature of sustainability issues, this for instance accords roles in the decision making process to those who are regulated, but also to those who claim to be adversely affected or otherwise in opposition. The environmental ethic underlying sustainable policy making demands an integration of environmental priorities into the political process. It has been said that the democratic liberal State can hold together multi-cultural societies only if it can deliver social and cultural rights, as well as liberal and political rights.[105]

Ideas based upon stakeholding need to address problems posed by obstructionism from powerful vested interests. Returning to the issue of risk, Edelstein expresses the distinction in terms of technocratic and democratic decision making paradigms. When the conflicts are exposed, the institutional influence of the engines of economic growth become apparent, with the desire to protect the business community from adverse impacts which is 'basic to the modern concept of regulation ... [and] creates regulations based on risk estimates that equate "caution" with steps that least threaten the private sector. The significance of claims by the victims of corporate pollution must be certified by experts to have legitimacy. For controlling risks, the marketplace is preferred to regulation'.[106] He further draws an interesting comparison, citing NIMSS (Not in My Smoke Stack) industry challenges to regulation: 'Through political action committees, industrial lobbying groups, the sense of shared self-interest among the elite, and, finally, the collusion of the consumer, the NIMSS movement is viewed as enlightened self-interest.'[107] The political forces in the UK which seek to undermine the climate levy (though its cautious introduction has been broadly accepted by industry) are a cynical illustration of this phenomenon.[108] Likewise, Rydin refers to a collective action problem, caused by the dominance of sectional interests involved in the process, so that other

---

101 Global Environmental Change Programme, 1999, p 20.
102 Giddens, 1994, p 113.
103 Giddens, 1994, p 86.
104 Myerson and Rydin, 1996, p 228.
105 See Weiss, 2000, p 370, citing Habermas, 1996, p 134.
106 Edelstein, 1988, p 129.
107 Edelstein, 1988, p 196.
108 Eg (2001) *The Guardian*, 25 April.

interests 'only achieve a place on the policy agenda if they do not challenge these interests fundamentally'.[109] For the policy maker, processes of participation can even be perceived as standing in the way of strategic progress. An even wider problem is that lay perceptions are reflexive in the sense that as seen for instance in Chapter 8, they are a response to levels of trust, or distrust, of policymakers and expert advisers.[110]

A further factor is the strain that can arise around community opposition to the siting of unpopular developments. NIMBYism connects with wider problems of environmental justice already discussed in the previous chapter. Social strains have become more complex in this context, especially in the United States, as between traditional environmental groups and *ad hoc* grassroots movements. The reasons are many, and include the contrasting social backgrounds. The *ad hoc* groupings may even be less risk averse, given economic pressures and possible employment dependence upon a development. Conversely, they are a coalition of people who feel powerless to prevent toxic operations in their neighbourhoods. In this sense, aside from questions concerning the nature of environmental threats, and whether concerns are being heard and addressed, a 'reverse commons effect' has been suggested, with certain citizens required to bear disproportionate burdens.[111] Moreover, such grassroots concerns can be at once threatening and collusive towards broader strategies, for they are 'not global but specific and immediate. They seek personal protection, compensation for loss, and the ability to return speedily to the normative consumptive American lifestyle. They assert the rights of individuals to avoid toxic exposure. And they join together out of necessity, not voluntarily because of shared ideals'.[112]

It becomes essential to develop inclusive approaches whereby many of those categorised as NIMBY activists can be brought within participative processes. This is not a question of meeting all expressions of local self-interest, but of bringing issues of sustainability into the process in an open and structured way.[113] Such regulatory approaches would establish the wider construct explored in Chapter 8, more willing to apply the precautionary principle as part of the assessment.[114] As well as pre-emptive regulatory approaches, solutions in North America have been expanded to take the form of market approaches such as siting agreements and compensatory awards. However, as with participation generally much appears to depend upon trust, for instance 'when individual communities no longer feel dumped upon for arbitrary reasons but instead are part of a larger, multifaceted approach to waste management that involves multiple communities and broad sharing of burdens'.[115] It is upon the generation of such levels of trust that the implementation of the UK's new waste disposal policies (with heavy reliance upon incineration) will heavily depend. Rabe suggests that where a waste treatment development is under discussion, important factors extend to wider issues, such as the extent of participation and openness; local powers of determination, to the extent of holding a plebiscite; formal assurances that the development will not make the

109 Rydin, 1998, p 356.
110 See discussion by Wynne, 1996; and Irwin, 1995.
111 Edelstein, 1988, p 185.
112 Edelstein, 1988, p 166.
113 See O'Hare, Bacon and Sanderson, 1983, p 149.
114 See further Dickson, 1981.
115 Rabe, 1994, p 57.

district a magnet for like sitings in the future; and continued participation once the scheme is operating.[116] This might involve ensuring that agreed criteria be reflected in planning conditions, with community involvement in monitoring and a threat of closure in the event of serious breaches. Most importantly, aside from technocratic bases for decisions, therefore, solutions are to be found 'in openness, communication and empowerment'.[117]

3.2   Sustainability and political responsibility

The emphasis upon participation in this section is aimed fundamentally at engaging the community in a shift towards sustainable solutions. Wider participation requires openness and maximising of opportunities for information and responses. Giddens comments on the trend towards democratic participation, and this condition endures because 'rulers of modern States discover that effective government demands the active acquiescence of subject populations in ways that were neither possible nor necessary in pre-modern States'.[118] He indicates trends towards a notion of polyarchy, defined as 'the continuing responsiveness of the government to the preferences of its citizens considered as political equals'.[119] Healey and Shaw place overriding emphasis upon land use planning judgments being a political question which cannot be left to administrative, technical, legal or economic parties. They conclude that the issue of democratic decision making frequently arises in connection with debates on environmental issues precisely because 'if there is to be any chance of "entrenching" environmental criteria in stable and legitimate spatial planning strategies which are sustained on implementation, the making of difficult, risky decisions needs to be widely shared among the diverse interests of a community'.[120] The breadth of the task is recognised by Korten, who argues beyond the creation of counter-cultures, to creation of what he terms a just, sustainable, and compassionate post-corporate world operating through a new core culture, a new political centre, and a new economic mainstream, with participation operating in densely interconnected communication networks.[121]

The question of 'carrying the people' remains the most intractable. It is nevertheless essential. The problem may perhaps be rooted in selfishness, but it is difficult to conceive of rational ways forward unless we are able to afford transparent opportunities for a reconsideration of our values and preferences. However convincingly the imperative values of the environment can be argued, it is necessary to address the implications caused by perceptions of threat. Solutions that can be offered focus upon so directing legal and political structures that they foster participation, and for this publicly accessible information and public education are essential. First, as we have seen, legal solutions are gradually emerging, under international processes, regionally and domestically. Given its declaratory value and capacity to project beyond cultural norms, it can encourage revised

---

116 Rabe, 1994, Chapter 3.
117 Edelstein, 1988, p 188.
118 Giddens, 1990, p 167.
119 Giddens, 1990, pp 167–68.
120 Healey and Shaw, 1994, p 436.
121 Korten, 1999, Chapter 14.

modes of conduct. Deeper engagement within legal mechanisms will assist this process by contributing to a normative re-evaluation.[122] Even without going so far, the varied terminology of the law, particularly in emphasising obligations to nature, may encourage transformation in personal values.[123] Further consideration of the prospects for such development in environmental law, in the realms of adjudication and contribution to policy making, appears below.

A second structural challenge lies in the question of public awareness. This is at heart a problem of good governance. Reference has been made to problems of accountability, and in this present context there is a need to address declining levels of trust. The point may be illustrated by reference to the BSE crisis. Hutton has pointed to the creation of:

> ... a trust gap between the public and their governors that will not be readily closed; the Phillips inquiry has revealed the degree of inbuilt official secrecy that lay behind a decade of bungled decision making which the public properly suspect. But paradoxically, the inquiry itself, failing cruelly to draw the tough conclusions from its own fastidious analysis, revealed another weakness of the British system – the quixotic, ad hoc nature of judge-led public inquiries whose results reflect the personal character of their chair and whose recommendations the government of the day, exercising its prerogative and secretive powers, may or may not accept ... Now we have an inquiry into BSE priding itself on its refusal to hold individuals to account for their actions. It is time to make the whole inquiry process systematic and independent.[124]

The above analysis suggests the need for an independent inquiry commission, just as, in a broader environmental context seen below, a standing specialist adjudicative body has been proposed. But the critique is also rooted in the general question of what amounts to public awareness, and therefore education.

In this third area, therefore, politicians are required to give a lead in terms of education of the population as to the risks of not acting sustainably, and how individual citizens can respond. It may be that only through increased participation can the necessary changes be brought about in ourselves as citizens.[125] There are limited signs that this is gradually happening, as under initiatives such as Local Agenda 21. Any progress needs however to be translated into wider political discourse. It is only in this way that the importance of sustainability can be clarified and concerns for perceived economic well-being and maximising personal disposable income addressed. In order to achieve the fundamental changes required in everyday life, higher levels of awareness as to external costs must be generated. Government must give the public more information about environmental costs of personal consumption, as for instance the true cost of motor cars. Even more difficult within current political structures, attention must be given to intragenerational equity, protecting those groups most vulnerable to change, with positive policy strategies to alleviate the consequences. Structural changes must likewise accommodate the interests of future generations, given the implications of non-justified discounting. If there are unpalatable messages which must be explained, then perhaps ironically reliance on 'sound science' will give the politicians the platforms that they

---

122 See Stone, 1988.
123 See Wilkinson, 1999, p 42.
124 Hutton, 2000a.
125 Hayward, 1995.

require. Likewise, wider recourse to risk assessment in the development and policy making process, reflecting the political dimensions of risk, can engage public involvement and also provide a learning curve for the wider community.

Solutions require open processes, not only in enabling wider access to justice, but in the arena of political debate. Secretive approaches have been gradually broken down, as for instance information has become more available, consequent upon the requirements of EC legislation.[126] A culture of selective disclosure has been replaced by the recognition of general rights to information, independent of any procedure, process or interest. Kimber has concluded that the nature, type and extent of information that can be requested or retrieved from public bodies is 'determined by the requester rather than the provider and is not dependent on having any interest, nor dependent on a link to any process or procedure'.[127] However, numerous studies point to an enduring lack of public exercise of rights, and problems in awareness and interpretation of accessed data.[128] It remains to be seen what effect the new Freedom of Information Act 2000 has. In the lead up to the introduction of the Bill, the Home Office, explaining the proposed replacement of previous information arrangements by a general right, gave an assurance that this would be modified where necessary in order to give effect to the provisions of both the Directive and the Aarhus Convention.[129] Under the Act, environmental information is to be treated as distinct from information generally.[130] There is specific power accorded for the Secretary of State to make provision relating to environmental information, by implementing the Convention (though only insofar as it relates to the access to environmental information).[131] It is suspected that at governmental, as opposed to regulatory, level, the eventual provisions will allow significant degrees of ministerial discretion as to matters of advice and factual information, including as to the availability or otherwise of executive reports.

4 THE IMPORTANCE OF ADJUDICATIVE STRUCTURES

4.1 Access to justice

Inclusive answers demand the assertion of participative processes, and these can be unlocked politically, as discussed above. But the legal process can be a catalyst for this change. As seen elsewhere in this book, policies of access to justice require greater attention in the context of environmental harm. To recognise the fact that environmental questions fit uneasily into private law processes is also to accept that the contribution of the citizen to environmental protection depends upon the scope and extent of the processes of public law. Likewise, accepting a continuing role for environmental

---

126 See Directive 90/313 on Public Access to Information on the Environment (OJ L158/56, 23 June 1990), transposed under the Environmental Information Regulations 1992 (SI 1992/3240).

127 Kimber, 1997.

128 See Rowan-Robinson, Ross, Walton and Rothnie, 1996.

129 Home Office, 1999, para 54; see United Nations Economic Commission for Europe (UNECE), Convention on Access to Information, Public Participation in Decision-Making and Access to Justice on Environmental Matters, 1998.

130 Freedom of Information Act 2000, s 39.

131 *Ibid*, s 74.

regulation (and a limit to the utility of economic and other alternatives) suggests that more root and branch reforms of adjudicative processes are called for. It is important to realise the wider impact of broader opportunities for citizens and groups in public law arenas. There have been signs that wider access is developing in the UK, especially for the purposes of challenge by way of judicial review. Domestic rules have become less restrictive and the notion of sufficient interest has moved away from inflexible proprietory interest requirements, opening up opportunities especially for established interest groups. In public law litigation, therefore, access opportunities have increased as obstacles as to standing have reduced. As discussed in Chapters 2 and 9, although not wholly resolved, it appears that there is now a judicial recognition that satisfying the test of sufficient interest includes such factors as vindication of the rule of law, importance of the issue raised, absence of any other responsible challenger, and nature of the breach of duty under challenge.[132] Whilst there are greater opportunities available in particular for actions by public interest groups, as seen in the brief discussion in Chapter 9, doubts persist as to the attractiveness of resort to challenge by way of judicial review in the face of more direct political and protest activities.[133]

Reflecting perhaps a supra-national administrative preference for seeing its legislation implemented and enforced by Member States, the European Commission has recognised the need for citizen participation in the adjudicative process, and further legislation is likely.[134] The Commission has now proposed that the Community accede to the Aarhus Convention, referred to in the previous section.[135] The whole thrust of the Convention is to enable greater access to justice and citizen participation: that environmental protection is not a matter for the sole jurisdiction of the State. The Convention's underlying objective is expressed as follows: 'In order to contribute to the protection of the right of every person of present and future generations to live in an environment adequate to his or her health and well-being, each Party shall guarantee the rights of access to information, public participation in decision making, and access to justice in environmental matters in accordance with the provisions of this Convention.'[136] There is an explicit requirement for 'adequate and effective remedies, including injunctive relief as appropriate, and ... fair, equitable, timely and not prohibitively expensive'.[137] To this end, it seeks to impose three duties. First, it requires rights of access to environmental information to be supported by access to a speedy and inexpensive legal review procedure, whether to require reconsideration by a public authority or by external review of the decision by an independent and impartial body.[138] Secondly, there is a requirement to ensure access to a review procedure to bring a challenge before a court or another independent and impartial body of the substantive and procedural legality of any decision, act or omission

---

132 *R v HM Inspectorate of Pollution ex p Greenpeace (No 2)* [1994] Env LR 76; *R v Secretary of State for Foreign and Commonwealth Affairs ex p World Development Movement* [1995] 1 WLR 386; *R v Somerset CC ex p Dixon* [1997] JPL 1030; see Hilson and Cram, 1996.

133 See, eg, Shiner and Wallace, 1998; Carney, 1997; also, Justice/Public Law Project, 1996; cf Harlow and Rawlings, 1992; Cane, 1995.

134 European Commission, 1996b, para 43.

135 Draft Directive Com(2000) 839; United Nations Economic Commission for Europe (UNECE) 1998.

136 *Ibid*, Art 1.

137 *Ibid*, Art 9.

138 *Ibid*, Art 4.

that is subject to environmental assessment, or other relevant provisions of the Convention.[139] Thirdly, it mandates access to a review procedure available to citizens and bodies, before a court of law and/or another independent and impartial body established by law. This is made subject to the meeting of national criteria such as establishing a sufficient interest or maintaining impairment of a right, although the interest of environmental NGOs is to be regarded as sufficient to satisfy the interest requirement.[140]

Ultimately, a system of judicial review depends upon the extent to which identifiable obligations are provided for, as in objectives or standards set or procedures to be applied. Carnwath has concluded as follows:

> For legislation to be worth the paper it is written on, it is not enough to state objectives and matters to be taken into account. It needs to define specific circumstances, in which specific remedies will be activated, in the form of obligations imposed upon defined enforcing authorities, or other specific remedies, by way of coercion or compensation, public or private. Without legislative underpinning of that kind, attempts through the courts to enforce the laudable aspirations which lie behind much environmental legislation, are doomed to failure.[141]

Increased access to justice was one of the themes which underlay Lord Woolf's review of the civil justice system, the final report for which was published in 1996.[142] He has elsewhere devoted specific attention to environmental questions, advocating acceptance of a general responsibility for overseeing and enforcing regulatory safeguards for the protection of the environment, and arguing that consideration be given to multifunctional, multidisciplinary and inquisitorial adjudicative panels.[143] Yet there remains a serious costs disincentive, especially given that costs tend to follow the event in English courts. To address this, a House of Lords Select Committee has recommended that courts should have power to award costs even to losing parties out of public funds, in cases considered to be in the public interest.[144] Likewise, Law Commission reform proposals have pressed for change, including a form of allocation of public funds to counter the risk of costs awards against applicants in approved circumstances.[145] Moreover, Grant has suggested that greater judicial activism, likely to be reinforced under the Human Rights Act 1998, will contribute to a shift in the system's balance of power, from one where the 'most distinctive characteristic lies in the lines of political accountability', to one which 'will bring new reinforcement to the process by introducing, in appropriate cases where human rights are at stake, a heightened degree of scrutiny not only of the processes through which official decisions are made, but also their substantive outcomes'. As has already been seen in Chapter 9, in cases calling for interpretation of the 1998 Act, the courts have potentially been given a wider role in determining issues of legality. This suggests an extension beyond standard remedial powers under judicial review such as to quash and remit decisions in relatively restricted circumstances.[146]

---

139 Draft Directive Com(2000) 839, Art 6.
140 *Ibid*, Art 9.
141 Carnwath, 1999, p 9.
142 Woolf, 1996.
143 Woolf, 1992.
144 See House of Lords Select Committee, 1997–98, para 103.
145 See Law Commission, 1994, paras 5.20–5.22; 103.
146 Grant, 2000a, para 12.10.17.

4.2 Changed adjudicative structures

The rest of this section is mainly devoted to the suggestion for an Environmental Court for England and Wales and to its potential impact on the issues under consideration. There is growing experience internationally, for instance in Australasian jurisdictions and in India, of the idea of specialist environmental tribunals. A radical report, published in 2000, and produced for the DETR, has proposed an Environmental Court.[147] English judicial approaches assert a traditionally rigorous maintaining of a formal distinction between policy and adjudication. Whilst this is a contentious area, the distinction means that in principle decisions by public bodies should not be reviewable on the policy merits.[148] In the context of planning law, for instance, Lord Hoffmann has stated that 'no English court would countenance having the merits of a planning decision judicially examined ... The result may be some lack of transparency, but that is a price which the English planning system, based upon central and local political responsibility, has been willing to pay for its relative freedom from judicial interference'.[149] More generally, the scope for administrative law challenge has been expressed in the following way:

> Judicial review involves a challenge to the legal validity of the decision. It does not allow the court of review to examine the evidence with a view to forming its own view about the substantial merits of the case. It may be that the tribunal whose decision is being challenged has done something which it had no lawful authority to do. It may have abused or misused the authority which it had. It may have departed from the procedures which either by statute or at common law as a matter of fairness it ought to have observed. As regards the decision itself it may be found to be perverse, or irrational, or grossly disproportionate to what was required. Or the decision may be found to be erroneous in respect of a legal deficiency, as, for example, through the absence of evidence, or of sufficient evidence to support it, or through account being taken of irrelevant matter, or through a failure for any reason to take account of a relevant matter, or through some misconstruction of the terms of the statutory provision which the decision maker is required to apply. But while the evidence may have to be explored in order to see if the decision is vitiated by such legal deficiencies, it is perfectly clear that in a case of review, as distinct from an ordinary appeal, the court may not set about forming its own preferred view of the evidence.[150]

Grant has expressed this approach in terms of 'the dominant role of central government, and the historical preference in Britain for systems of political accountability over law-based systems of public administration. The balance of power in administrative decision making lies with politicians and their officials, and not with courts ... the High Court is steadfast in its refusal to review the merits of the case. It is a trade-off, in which political accountability triumphs over legal transparency'.[151] The proposed reform would therefore require a fundamental review of this approach.

---

147 Grant, 2000a, para 13.14.10.

148 See *Malster v Ipswich BC and Ipswich Town FC* (2001) unreported, 17 August (Sullivan J), paras 59-63; cf Griffith, 1997.

149 *Tesco Stores Ltd v Secretary of State for the Environment* [1995] 2 All ER 636, 659.

150 *Reid v Secretary of State for Scotland* [1999] 2 AC 512, 541 (Lord Clyde).

151 Grant, 2000a, para 12.10.12.

The proposed Environmental Court would become a standing tribunal, hearing appeals on their merits in planning and environmental matters. Despite the heavy reliance of regulatory law in the UK upon criminal enforcement processes, the proposed court would have no criminal jurisdiction.[152] Likewise, it would not have a general civil jurisdiction in civil law matters, such as toxic tort actions. Such a cautious remit appears mainly due to the likely resource demands, although this would be subject exceptionally to a possibility of transfer of cases at the instance of the High Court. This would allow a referral in order to access the technical expertise available within the new court. The reasons for the civil bifurcation are described as both doctrinal and pragmatic: 'doctrinal, in the sense that there is not always any valid distinction between an environmental civil action and any other; and pragmatic, in the sense that one or two heavy civil actions could quickly consume such a high proportion of the resources available to the court as to disable it from undertaking its other responsibilities.'[153]

Central to the reform would be the extension of public access and a more comprehensive environmental jurisdiction. In 1992, Carnwath proposed a two-tier environmental court, especially with the administrative and public law jurisdiction of a division of the High Court (to include the Planning Inspectorate).[154] The proposed court would also be a two-tier body (partially analogous to specialist employment law jurisdiction), which, it is argued, would have greater status and capacity to develop a consistent body of environmental law, as well as affording extended public access.[155] Its overriding objective has been expressed as being 'to avoid technicality, by avoiding any prior definitions of respective jurisdiction; to promote public access rather than inhibit it; and to provide an inexpensive and quick remedy'.[156] Its standing jurisdiction would 'enable it to make the appropriate balance between justice and delay, and to apply a filter mechanism to weed out clearly unmeritorious cases, make directions for exchange of documents and expedited hearings, and generally apply a tight style of case management to prevent the long and costly delays that are widely feared would result from the introduction of third party appeal rights'.[157] As to costs, discussed above, the court would have jurisdiction to waive the normal rule on public interest grounds. No recommendation is made, however, as to whether there would be power to make awards of from public funds in public interest cases, on grounds that this question must be resolved as a general matter of public law jurisdiction.[158]

Grant concludes that the court could operate a reformed judicial review jurisdiction, described presently as 'a blunt instrument' which can result in lengthy delays, and whose effects are divorced from the merits. Whilst maintaining 'as strict an approach to case management in judicial review applications as it would in the rest of its work' it might 'see judicial review and third-party merits appeals being brought together, in a fast-track procedure, which would allow all the issues to be combined in a single hearing'.[159]

152 Grant, 2000a, para 13.14.6.
153 Grant, 2000a, para 13.14.8.
154 Carnwath, 1992, pp 807–08.
155 Grant, 2000a, para 13.15.
156 Grant, 2000a, para 13.14.1.
157 Grant, 2000a, para 13.14.
158 Grant, 2000a, para 13.14.2.
159 Grant, 2000a, para 13.14.7.

Crucially, the enhanced jurisdiction 'would provide a powerful antidote to the present regulatory monopoly over enforcement, and, properly designed and implemented, would meet the requirements of the Aarhus Convention, Article 9'.[160] It might therefore allow regulatory bodies to be more easily challenged on the merits. This does not amount to third party citizen suits seeking civil penalties.[161] Rather, any person or body would have the right to seek an order to enforce requirements of planning or environmental law.

The structure would enable the exercise of greater control over the current public inquiry process. Yet the report suggests that ultimate decision making responsibility would be unchanged. There is a conundrum here, for, as the report makes clear, there is a 'fictional character' to the legal relationship between the planning inspectors' functions and those of the Secretary of State:

> Formally securing an inspector's independence and impartiality from the Secretary of State could be achieved in the great bulk of cases by allocating all planning appeals wholly to inspectors (or, preferably, to the Planning Inspectorate). If necessary, those falling within certain pre-defined categories could be assigned instead to the Secretary of State (though the question still remains whether, even in high-policy cases, decisions can better be taken by inspectors who have seen the site and heard the parties, than by ministers and civil servants who have not).[162]

Moreover, as has been seen already in Chapter 9, human rights challenges are inevitable given the extent of reliance upon quasi-judicial procedures and the role of both the Secretary of State and planning inspectors in the process. Returning to the theme of the Human Rights Act, the report emphasises that positive rights are conferred, which should enable easier assertion of rights under the European Convention. It then goes on to point out that despite the binding nature of the new arrangements upon adjudicating bodies, such as planning inspectors and the courts, requiring that Convention rights be taken into account, 'the constitutional reality remains that it is an agency based within the government department which has administrative supervision of the planning and environmental protection systems for England, and is *de jure* subject to the direction of the Secretary of State'.[163] The position might change markedly, depending upon a new court's jurisdiction. As the report proposes, the role of the court, 'would be to undertake the most rigorous review of the arguments and the evidence behind them, and to come to conclusions about levels of advantage and risk upon which informed judgement could then be made, either by government or Parliament. It is in the evaluative process that it is important for the government to ensure impartiality, openness and fairness, and these are qualities which members of the Environmental Court should possess'.[164] Deeper issues are therefore at stake, for seemingly merits appeals might be available to the inspectorate tier, rather than the full court. This may further result in a movement of such forming of regulatory arrangements affecting land use towards more binding rules with which to inform the application of policy in specific circumstances. Yet, if the above concerns delivery, it is to the question of accountability of the policy making processes that the concluding arguments now turn.

---

160 Grant, 2000a, para 13.14.1.
161 See Miller, 2000; cf Healey, 1997.
162 Grant, 2000a, para 1.2.2.2.
163 Grant, 2000a, para 1.2.2.5.
164 Grant, 2000a, para 13.14.5.

5 CONCLUSION

5.1 Securing sustainability through the processes of politics and law

Owens has pointed out that 'the planning system constitutes the political process through which many land use decisions are made and therefore represents 'important institutional terrain for the contestation of the meaning and relations of the "natural environment"'.[165] Upon an institutional level, it has been argued that there is a 'control crisis', whereby large-scale systems remain locked into an obsession with economic growth.[166] Institutional transformation is required, given that 'the configuration of inherited institutions *shapes* any subsequent process of amendment by constraining the choices available, moulding the preferences of actors, and thereby lending policy a path-dependent character'.[167]

The tension between responsibilities at the various levels of political organisation has been a recurrent theme of this book. Thus national targets, say, for housing developments, waste disposal or air quality, may meet local resistance. The Royal Commission, reporting on responses to its consultation, pointed to 'the inherent tension between delivering national policy targets and ensuring adequate local accountability in the vicinity of the development'.[168] The most viable solution is to seek to improve levels of participation already prevalent in planning procedures. It is also necessary to investigate how a further opening of participative processes can be achieved in respect of wider environmental controls. McAuslan has pointed to environmental management in the UK taking 'the form of a predominantly secretive closed system of regulation in which great power is vested in officials to control emissions of pollutants and achieve higher environmental standards in industrial land uses'.[169]

Yet increased participation would not sufficiently address the tensions referred to above. Participation has traditionally been more achievable at local levels, and yet sustainability targets must ultimately be matters of national (or, as we have seen, international) determination. In so far as decisions must therefore be made at higher levels of government, solutions may lie in the emergence of a stronger regional planning base. Government guidance suggests a willingness to extend the participatory process in the context of development planning and in particular at the emerging regional level. For instance, by way of a start, the preparation of new Regional Planning Guidance was mandated to be a more inclusive process, 'involving key stakeholders ... with public examinations ... and independent panel reports'.[170] Moreover, housing guidance states that 'RPBs (Regional Planning Bodies) should be prepared to justify their views fully in public at the examination of the draft RPG'.[171] Thus, beyond Development Plans and RPG, the accountability of local (not national) government is emphasised, and engaging

---

165 Owens, 1994, p 440.
166 See Decleris, 2000.
167 O'Riordan and Jordan, 1999, p 83.
168 See RCEP, Environmental Planning Study, 2000 (at www.rcep.org.uk/epissues.html).
169 McAuslan, 1991, p 199.
170 DETR, 2000c, para 4.27.
171 DETR, PPG3, 2000a, para 5.

local communities through Community Planning innovations envisaged.[172] This is part of a proposed new legal framework that requires new duties of consultation to consult people locally, and to produce a Community Strategy, alongside new powers to promote economic, social and environmental well-being.[173]

Turning to the processes of participation, the Global Environmental Change Programme report itemises a series of priorities. These are greater public interaction concerning policy processes surrounding new technologies, through genuine participatory methods, requiring a sharing of power which should enhance political powers of action; greater transparency both in their decision making and in their provision of information; and acceptance by participants of responsibilities to reach agreement. The report concludes with the rhetorical question: 'So a crucial issue is whether the social insights to emerge from inclusive procedures, such as citizens' juries and consensus conferences, will be treated seriously by those in power. How will they be related to other arrangements for scientific debate such as advisory committees, specialist panels and technology assessments?'[174]

There is, alas, no space to devote to the detailed consideration of the delivery of participative approaches. Local referenda have been widely used in the United States.[175] As seen in Chapter 8, there is at last official recognition of the value of broader involvement of specialist expertise, as well as lay contributions to expert panels and committees. There is a wide range of machinery for public engagement now available. An excellent example is the local level consultation carried out by Hampshire County Council concerning waste disposal facilities.[176] Participative arrangements now being practised include: consultation at local and national levels; deliberative polling; standing consultative panels; focus groups; citizens' juries; consensus conferences; stakeholder dialogues; internet dialogue; and the government's Foresight programme. An excellent review of the variety of mechanisms to involve the wider public is provided in the House of Lords Select Committee Report.[177] Yet such mechanisms often serve to emphasise tensions between democratic credentials and the macro-spatial complexities of sustainability issues. Such tensions are likewise fundamental to issues of environmental justice discussed above. Calling in 1980 for new legislation, institutions and procedures towards new decision making processes, more open government and more searching debate, McAuslan recognised a need for 'decisions being about positive discrimination in the allocation of resources in favour of deprived persons and groups in the community, and an institutional framework which allows those groups power, subject to appropriate safteguards, to determine their own future'.[178]

Law can nevertheless contribute to the necessary realignment, through normative recognition of ecological priorities, and opportunities for enforcement. A major question concerns how far the adoption of broad sustainability commitments can be translated into

---

172 DETR, 2000c, eg, paras 1.12–1.14.
173 DETR, 2000c, paras 3.15–3.16, 3.20; and see Local Government Act 2000, s 4.
174 Global Environmental Change Programme, 1999, p 20.
175 Freilich and Guemmer, 1989.
176 House of Lords, 2000, paras 5.3–5.37.
177 See House of Lords, 2000, paras 5.8–5.11.
178 McAuslan, 1980, p 272.

discussion of private rights and the public interest. There are some cogent arguments suggesting the incorporation of a constitutional right.[179] However, especially within the UK context, it is difficult to see how environmental questions can justifiably be brought out of the mainstream of legal hierarchies. The great advantage of the Environment Court proposal, and indeed of expectations under the Human Rights Act, is that progress can be achieved through reformed, though ultimately established, conceptual foundations.

The changed balance brought about by the Human Rights Act is likely to influence judicial approaches in indirect ways, as more rigorous review principles are developed. In the *Alconbury* judgment, the High Court accepted the idea of the Convention being 'concerned to maintain and promote the ideas and values of a democratic society. Planning and transport policy and decisions were often sensitive political issues for which governments are held responsible in democratic societies. Because judges were not accountable in this way, it was desirable for such decisions to be made by government without interference from the courts, provided they were made lawfully'. However, the lower court was unwilling to conclude from this that a remedy should be withheld. The remarkable potential for a change in mindset can be seen in the following passage:

> It is not for us to decide how the system needs to be changed in the light of our decision, although it is obvious that government has been considering the options for some time. Our decision should not be interpreted as a bid for more judge power. This is a specialist field in which most judges would be unqualified to make value judgments of the kind which have to be made. ... [Government] already has at hand a cadre of sufficiently independent specialists well equipped to make such decisions. As with the decisions they now make, they would be required to have regard to government policy.[180]

The development of an Environmental Court would further consolidate the process of change. The introduction of third-party rights of challenge would enhance the objectives of greater participation within the process, also upon the political level, and encourage greater openness in the regulatory process. Extra-judicial techniques may also contribute, provided that they are conducive to these same objectives.[181]

5.2   Transforming the citizen

Institutional change is essential to the achievement of the process of transformation, through finding the means to 'unravel people's social commitments from their environmental effects, and yet gain assent for structural changes beneficial to the environment but also undermining of our lifestyles'.[182] Lifestyle expectations must inevitably change in accordance with the fundamental premise of sustainability; natural resources are not mere commodities. Wilkinson argues that 'the institution of democracy is only compatible with a body of ecological law if ecological values are protected from

---

179 Eg, Hayward, 2000; cf Decleris, 2000.

180 *R (on the application of Alconbury Developments Ltd, Holding and Barnes plc, Premier Leisure UK Limited, Legal and General Assurance Society Limited) v Secretary of State for Environment, Transport and the Regions* [2001] 2 All ER 929, paras 97–98.

181 See Reid, 2000, pp 192–94.

182 Redclift, 1997, p 261.

democratic subversion'.[183] Referring to participatory democracy, Macpherson argued that two prerequisites are a change in consciousness and a reduction in social and economic inequality. In particular, he called for 'a change in people's consciousness (or unconsciousness) from seeing themselves and acting as essentially consumers to seeing themselves and acting as exerters and enjoyers of the exertion and development of their capacities. This is requisite not only to the emergence but also to the operation of a participatory democracy. For the latter self-image brings with it a sense of community which the former does not'.[184] Paehlke has described the contribution to the democratic process of the availability of information, together with opportunities for participation and conflict, as offering the best means of mobilising educated and prosperous populations to face environmental challenges.[185]

It is imperative that the above processes engage the citizen upon wider levels than the merely local. Glendon, in expressing her concerns at rights-based solutions, said of group assertion of rights upon a local basis:

> Like individuals and State, they too are subject to pathologies. Excessive pre-occupations with one's immediate community can foster intolerance or indifference to the general welfare, as witness the proliferation of NIMBY ... movements when new locations for prisons, group homes for the mentally retarded, and other public works are proposed ... What we need therefore is not a new portfolio of 'group rights', but a fuller concept of human personhood and a more ecological way of thinking about social policy.[186]

Yet it is necessary to engage with the public. The House of Lords Select Committee has concluded that the central challenge is this question of identification. Their report speaks of the need for 'genuine changes in the cultures and constitutions of key decision making institutions, where the need is to render these more accountable and open. Instead, they may well have a use as catalysts, to bring such changes about'.[187] Existing associative processes necessitate that groups, such as direct action movements, be brought further within the process. This challenges the dangers inherent in markets being the main mediating mechanism between individual and State: 'A nation can be maintained only if, between the State and the individual, there is intercalated a whole series of secondary groups near enough to the individuals to attract them strongly in their sphere of action and drag them, in this way, into the general torrent of social life.'[188] Returning to themes discussed earlier, such inclusive, collective responsibility must therefore extend to stakeholders on all levels:

> ... ordinary landowners and other citizens must be drawn into the processes by which land use decisions are made. Broad-based participation can diminish fears of exclusion. At the same time, such participation can help landowners become more knowledgeable about environmental problems. And the more knowledgeable people are, the more likely they are to see land use restrictions as legitimate responses to real problems, rather than as the corruption or dismantling of private rights.[189]

---

183 Wilkinson, 1999, p 17.
184 Macpherson, 1977, cited by McAuslan, 1980, p 273.
185 Paehlke, 1988, pp 294–45.
186 Glendon, 1991, p 137.
187 House of Lords, 2000, para 5.50.
188 Durkheim, 1964, p 28.
189 Freyfogle, 1998, p 307.

Such processes will further discourage the exercise of disproportionate influence by special interest groups over administrators and regulators.[190] Grove-White has pointed out that it is important to seek to harmonise the various coalitions if sustainability is to resonate sufficiently with the wider public.[191] Achieving greater participation can induce greater awareness of the requirements of sustainability, just as it has been argued that risk has political dimensions which demand greater openness and discussion.

The citizen 'must be treated as a resource for solving complex problems, rather than shunned as an obstacle to expedient solutions. The public must be valued as a key actor in a social process'.[192] Solutions must lie in what Glendon refers to as ' the effective conditions for deliberation'. She suggests that the 'greatest obstacle to political renewal under present circumstances may not be an "inert people" so much as the failure of persons in positions of leadership to provide models by personal example and to work actively to create opportunities for discussion'.[193] The solution lies somewhere in 'flexible, discriminating, and reasonably efficient public involvement in decision making regarding science and technology'.[194] The Select Committee has called for the UK to alter 'existing institutional terms of reference and procedures to open them up to more substantial influence and effective inputs from diverse groups'.[195]

Recalling the earlier discussion of the relationship between science, policy makers and the public, it is necessary to impose a sustainability, or public interest, rationale into the conflictual processes of environmental protection and land use control. A lesson of our evolutionary history is that humankind responds to the immediate, and May has pointed out that just as the Third World is an abstraction to most British consumers then distance into the future leads to public perceptions of problems (such as climate change) as abstractions also. For such a changed rationale to be brought about, therefore, it is essential that the electorate be informed, educated and led by policy makers who aspire to the long term. This can be achieved only through reformed political and legal processes. The achievement of sustainability is more than a matter of 'greener' science: it requires that we create and maintain greener institutional arrangements within which all levels of government and the citizen can engage.

---

190 Frazier, 1998, p 74.
191 Grove-White, 1996, pp 278–80.
192 Piller, 1991, p 205.
193 Glendon, 1991, p 179.
194 Piller, 1991, p 195.
195 House of Lords, 2000, para 5.46.

CHAPTER 11

AFTERWORD

THE POLITICAL CHALLENGES OF SUSTAINABILITY

The common resistance of environmental precepts to workable definition is true *a fortiori* of the notion of sustainability. As has been seen, this is especially the case when expressed in the more pragmatic, limited form of sustainable development. Such ideas are essentially value-laden, while they also are the stuff of long time frames and sit often at the very boundaries of human knowledge. Moreover, environmental threats span a wide continuum: from gradual, barely traceable forms of degradation of natural systems to extremely visible, high-impact, low incidence events which threaten our survival.

The search for solutions to present threats to sustainability must be found both through political processes and within ourselves. If the latter has a moralistic feel, then this at least can be seen as a counterweight to the stuff of politics, which is shot through with perceived limits upon what is achievable.

Problem solving on the scale required must be viewed against the broadest canvas of international relations, and a radical degree of co-operation between States. There remains an abiding need for international solutions to problems that transcend frontiers. Yet at the time of writing, upon the international stage the United States remains opposed even to the limited level of consensus so far achieved following the Kyoto Protocol.[1] Nevertheless, the process to secure international emissions controls has moved a stage further without the US, with the initial brokering of rules for implementation at Bonn in July 2001.[2]

Another challenge which currently stands even further from convincing international resolution is the use of economic instruments to secure environmental change. Modern preferences for economic instruments, ancillary to and in partial replacement for traditional regulatory approaches, demand reciprocity between States.[3] Yet thus far there has been an inability to develop coherent multilateral approaches to energy or pollution taxes (not even as part of the developing climate convention framework). For sure, the ability to raise taxes is traditionally among the most important powers of autonomous, sovereign States, and there is a reluctance to delegate to international bodies. And yet by contrast other processes, such as the opening of markets through the removal of tariffs, achieve much the same effect.[4]

International structures are insufficiently equipped for the task of creating enforceable environmental arrangements, with those in place being manifestly less robust than those which operate in relation to trade agreements. For instance, it appears that the implementation of Kyoto following the Bonn agreement will not have a binding compliance mechanism, but instead a compromise procedural package, with what

---

1   Browne, 2001.
2   ENDS Report 318, July 2001, 49; for an overview of the wider Kyoto process, see Grimeaud, 2001.
3   See O'Brien and Vourc'h, 2001.
4   Moomaw, 1997, p 14.

amounts to the potential for increased State targets post-2010 in the event of a State's non-compliance. Furthermore, the climate change debate inevitably cannot be seen in isolation. As pressures for industrialisation (including the intensification of agriculture) mount across the world, the global economy remains in the hands of the World Trade Organisation and other Bretton Woods institutions of global economic governance.[5] There are therefore major institutional challenges in the international environmental context, in order to confront the ruling ethos based upon growth and resource depletion.

This book has not been concerned with how the international community might fund the necessary changes. Yet a large body of opinion now asserts that meeting costs is an achievable objective. For instance O'Riordan, whilst expressing caution pending analysis of scientific implications and proper implementation of national strategies, has estimated a cost transition to sustainability at around $300 billion per annum. This figure he contrasts with worldwide figures, for military and narcotics spending respectively, of $780 and $400 billion.[6] It is notable that a commitment to support funding for incremental costs for developing countries is part of the Bonn agreement, set at $530 million per annum, one half of which must come from the European Union.[7]

Yet the logic of the notion of sustainable development cannot be corralled within the comparative political safety of international deliberating chambers. It has been seen that the genesis of a wider awareness, first developed at an international level, has since been progressed prominently at regional levels such as the European Union. Effective solutions however demand political commitment at the level of the nation State. Here, as has been seen, it is necessary for political and law making priorities to build upon what appears to be a heightened, if thus far fragile, degree of environmental consciousness within populations at large.[8] It remains problematic as to how to deliver the necessary changes in domestic politics. An optimistic view is that such changes can be brought about by the development of institutional and normative legal structures which expressly set sustainability objectives.

On the smaller political stage, the UK's 2001 general election was disappointingly fought with scant regard for environmental perspectives. The best that can be said is that the political party which was the main loser, the Conservative Party, contributed negligibly to what environmental debate there was. Yet the presiding New Labour Government appeared to sideline the environment as an election issue. This may be part of the oft-derided 'dumbing down' of politics in the UK. But the problem lies deeper, in that for all its rhetoric, national government is indeed ambivalent upon environmental issues. This is partly because growth remains its prime concern (and for the present government the main vehicle it seems for moving towards a promised increase in social justice). Of greater long term concern, however, is that the political roots for this ambivalent posture lie in the identification of political discomfort with environmental consciousness. Indeed there is a sad irony in comparing the sustainability debate with the attraction of the UK government to geopolitical affairs, and a proclaimed imperative for armed conflict in response to the savagery of global terrorism. It is not necessary to cede

---

5   See Gray, 2000 and 2001.
6   O'Riordan, 2000, pp 48–50 (based upon figures provided by the 1998 UN Development Programme).
7   See generally, as to incremental costs, Werksman 1993.
8   See, eg, ICM poll, 'The Great British 2001 Environmental Survey' (2001) 31 Ecologist, 33–39.

to anyone in expression of disgust and simple human shame at the atrocities that took place in New York, Washington and Pennsylvania on 11 September 2001 in order to point to the importance of continued commitments to values such as those of human rights. Likewise, environmental objectives must remain in place, for threats to sustainability demand forthright political commitment and action in no less degree than do more immediate, however fearsome, physical threats.

Returning to the question of growth, engagement with issues such as global warming has been extremely limited, and much of the UK's improvements to date can largely be ascribed to a large scale switching from coal to gas fired generation of energy. Indeed, on the supply side, there appears to be slow progress towards the current target of 10% of energy from renewable sources by 2010. To date there is little informed public discussion or political lead regarding either non-renewable resource questions or the true costs of fossil fuel energy.[9] Unsustainable transport patterns persist.[10] Yet the UK government's response to the so-called 'people's tax revolt' in the autumn of 2000 (for the most part led by sections from the freight industry supported by disparate disaffected agricultural interests) was an exercise in political finesse. This culminated in reductions in fuel duty (cynically linked to 'low sulphur' fuels already in course of being introduced), as well as large cuts in freight road fund licence taxation. The response in short appeared to be based upon avoidance of perceived political risks inherent in more open discussion of energy availability and environmental considerations within the wider policy context. This response has likewise put further at risk key climate change strategies.[11]

There is another point of comparison with increasing technical and political uncertainties, and fears for individual and community safety. As the reach of extreme forces of terrorism appears to have broken new ground, the result especially in the west is a greatly increased perception of vulnerability in the minds of rulers and ruled alike. It will be recalled that uncertainty likewise lies at the root of much of the sustainability debate, in which Jasanoff has defined risk as the organising concept underlying modern society.[12] Indeed it has been seen how environmental threats pose complex problems for legal responses. Levels of certainty expected by the law, both as to substance and process, are often illusory in this context. The nature of environmental harm can be deeply deceptive. Accommodating responses to apparently remote external hazards calls standard approaches into question. Moreover, questions of asset valuation and the need to accord special recognition or protections to natural capital are deeply problematic. Yet it is necessary to find rational ways of responding to the dilemmas encountered within the sustainability debate.

Questioning and uncertainty remain the stuff of science. Disputes persist in cognate fields, such as to the nature and range of threats to human health posed by artificial chemicals and changed methods for instance of food production.[13] Indeed, for all that there is a developing consensus in the area of global warming, scientific arguments

---

9   Brown, 2001.
10 Wallach and Sforza, 1999.
11 ENDS Report 308, September 2000, 19–21, *Climate Change and Transport Strategies at Risk in Fall-out From Fuel Crisis.*
12 Jasanoff, 1997, p 1.
13 Concerning food safety, see eg Bove and Dufour, 2001; Humphrys, 2001.

persist even here, and some scientists dispute accepted technical findings on the issue of climate change.[14] Inevitably others counter such sceptics, on the basis for instance that they accord insufficient allowance to threats to the recovery capacities of natural systems, and as being unrealistic in their future discounting assumptions.[15] Nevertheless, as to global warming, a considerable scientific consensus has emerged, and this needs to be met by international efforts to formulate appropriate political and legal responses, backed by increased transparency and efforts at securing enforcement.

This book has been largely concerned with the development especially within the UK of national structures and processes, and their potential for reform towards a more consistently sustainable agenda. At the political level, a dismantling of traditional conflictual perceptions is perhaps ultimately required. It is no longer a question of left and right, but rather a question of establishment priorities. This demands radical action amongst a ruling elite at once more comfortable in manipulating the levers of patronage and power, and looking to keep the majority reasonably happy for most of the time, especially in the economic arena. Yet a reformist sustainability agenda demands that radical political adjustments be made.

Thus, on the international plain, heightened wealth inequalities prejudice multilateral approaches to achieving necessary changes.[16] The environment is threatened by increased devastation unless we can adjust to the vast inequalities in wealth by finding different solutions beyond those offered by globalism: especially, in increased market access (if not opportunities) for all. Similar issues arise at the domestic level. The UK's recent urban and rural white papers evidence serious economic and cultural dislocation within a large proportion of the population. Yet poverty is traditionally seen as a justification of more of the same, growth-based economic strategies.[17] It may be that the poor may always be with us, but this does not absolve the majority (in the richer nation States) from an acceptance of the need for a readjustment on the part of those who have taken, and continue to consume, the most. Whatever the ethical arguments, there are now no valid reasons for a continued edging of environmental arguments to the outer margins of debate.

The unavoidable reality is that those citizens who are the main repositories of economic wealth – and in a State such as the UK there are many of us – must accept the responsibility to bring about and indeed 'subsidise' (if indeed it is within our gift) necessary lifestyle changes. If this leads to accusations of environmental autocracy referred to earlier in the book, then so be it. Moreover, pursuing the essential strands of Lockean analysis, the individualistic temptation to avoid these responsibilities, as by use of easy capital flight, should be prohibited. Where after all are those so inclined to take themselves and their capital? Assuming that there will be no 'sustainability havens', then to another planet?

---

14 Lomborg, 2001.
15 Eg McMichael, 2001.
16 Weiss, 2000, pp 370–71.
17 Perkins, 2001.

SEEKING OPENNESS, PARTICIPATION
AND INSTITUTIONAL CHANGE

It is necessary that debates concerning sustainability, upon production and consumption, upon markets, and upon related issues such as food safety, take place with the maximum degree of transparency and opportunities for genuine participation. Participation is expressed in numerous ways, including the according of wider opportunities for access to justice, and more proactively still in the context of policy-making.

As to access to justice, whilst such questions have been discussed, it must be allowed that, for all the caution previously advised, the accommodation of human rights approaches within environmental law is likely to become an influential factor in judicialised processes within the UK. The *Alconbury* litigation may result in pragmatic constraints upon the recognition of procedural rights to a hearing where essentially political and administrative decisions are being made. However, human rights principles can correlate closely with demands for environmental protection. Thus, for instance, an action has now been brought in the UK courts in the context of the right to respect for home and family life. Applying the ECHR authority of *Guerra*,[18] the High Court has found a breach of Article 8 of the European Convention, in circumstances of public agency inaction to improve water and sewerage infrastructure against increased natural flood risks to neighbouring land. Thus, despite the lack of any actionable right under common law or statute, the defendant water company was held to be in breach of its duty to comply with the Convention arising under the 1998 Human Rights Act.[19] It has moreover been further held that damages could lie.[20]

In any event, the impact of the Human Rights Act upon issues of procedure will inevitably be further tested in the future. For instance, there remains a significant disparity of rights of challenge as between the appeal rights available to developers and the limited opportunities for judicial review available to others. The distinction reflects a still prevailing ethos of private property, with the public interest reserved to public agencies. A right of third party appeal in planning matters would be a step towards a wider recognition of the precautionary principle and sustainable development objectives within the structures of development planning.

Going beyond the inevitable limitations of access to justice, into general areas of decision making, a transition to sustainability demands significant changes within ourselves as citizens, in our lifestyles, expectations and world views. There is a need for individual engagement with environmental problems. In particular, the Royal Commission has emphasised 'a change in public attitudes with people linking their own day to day use of energy with fossil fuel consumption and the threat of climate change, and a new cultural and institutional framework within which individuals will feel that they can make a difference'.[21] Moreover, as seen above, citizens of developed States must shoulder the main burdens, just as intra-State those best able to bear such responsibilities must contribute the most to the necessary adjustments.

---

18 *Guerra v Italy* 4 BHRC 63.
19 *Marcic v Thames Water Utilities Ltd* [2001] 3 All ER 698.
20 *Marcic v Thames Water Utilities Ltd (No 2)* [2001] 4 All ER 326.
21 RCEP, 2000, p 4, para 22.

It is important to recognise that co-operative conflict management processes demand active engagement with the public, across the range of levels of administration, and should include central government. Participative solutions will not necessarily resolve conflict, but they will tend to encourage decision making arrangements which maximise transparency. As discussed previously, NIMBYism (or 'why me?') is an inevitable incident of siting arguments, and there are for instance signs of local resistance to the siting of renewable energy sites such as wind farms. The most appropriate response must surely be to clarify the need for renewable energy supply in the minds of the public and then to proceed to match appropriate installation sites in a manner which pays regard to both reliable technical data and equitable treatment of communities. Moreover, the transparency inherent in genuine participation methods enables the educative process of encouraging the development of environmental awareness as indeed also the recognition of ambivalent views within the community. As has been said previously, local communities are subject to varying pressures, and local people may be suspicious of environmental group agendas.[22] The planning system can deliver, perhaps especially on a regional basis, although such problems serve to emphasise the importance of the development of a political and legal commitment to the ideas underlying strategic environmental assessment. Such structures should likewise encourage political decision making which looks beyond fear of the next election (or indeed the next opinion poll).

Yet participation is itself a contested area. Government has for instance proposed to confine participation levels through the planning inquiry process.[23] Whilst legislation is awaited, it appears that decisions in principle as to major projects are to be matters for Parliament, and local inquires are to be required to focus upon specific matters of detail. Whilst it has been argued above that there is a need for coherent spatial strategies, it is not self-evident that Parliament is the appropriate place where such decisions should be made. Yet this is not the only area where participation even as currently understood might be limited. Small, incremental shifts occur, as for instance in applications for authorisations under the new integrated pollution prevention and control processes, to be progressed first through the Environment Agency as pollution regulator, whereas waste regulation continues to require prior public consideration of applications for planning permission.

In order to be effective, participation demands coherent strategies: as in the development of priorities which recognise environmental capacities and the nature of natural capital, together with clarity as to the form and remit of public involvement, and responsive public authority management systems which ensure appropriate delivery.[24] As seen previously, there has been some discussion of participative opportunities in the context of the relationship between scientist and public, especially in the context of the Report of the House of Lords Select Committee.[25] These issues likewise increasingly inform discussions elsewhere, and a cross-jurisdictional project, responding to Beck's expression of the need for reflexive modernisation, and calling for increased participatory

22 See, eg, Burningham and Thrush, 2001.
23 ENDS Report 318, July 2001, 32, *Polarised Reactions to New Processes for Major Projects*; and see possible Commission proceedings, (2001) *Independent on Sunday*, 26 August.
24 See, eg, Spyke, 1999.
25 House of Lords, 2000.

techniques for the involvement of a range of (business and citizen) stakeholders, has concluded as follows:

> Assessments of global environmental problems have started with results from the natural sciences. Yet the complexity, uncertainty, and multiplicity of values that characterize this debate have led to an increasing awareness of the need to integrate expert assessments with problem framings of the lay public. Actions directed to mitigate global change will eventually impinge on stakeholder interests, personal lifestyles and public institutions ... In democratic contexts, new and imaginative channels for preventing the exclusion of lay public views in global change science and politics will have to be devised.[26]

There are indeed signs that the UK government wishes to progress in this direction in one crucial area. Its revised climate change programme contains a commitment to broadening processes of stakeholder participation in order for instance to seek to shift patterns of demand and consumption.[27]

It is perhaps at the institutional level that progress appears to be more limited. It seems for instance that for now the proposal for an Environmental Court, discussed above, has been rejected by government.[28] Yet this proposal offered the opportunity of a specialist, technically adept judicial process in matters affecting public law and the environment. This might have had a significant impact upon the quality of regulation and decision making. Indeed despite the *Alconbury* litigation referred to above it is likely that the quasi-judicial roles of Secretary of State and indeed the Planning Inspectorate will come under renewed scrutiny. Albeit coloured by an awareness of the nature of these roles, answers to key questions as to the validity of challenge will depend upon a range of circumstances, including the nature of any interest of decision-makers in development decisions, as well as the circumstances of any departures from the development planning process. Meanwhile, it is to be hoped that pressures on resources, including as to water and energy supply, and questions of true environmental costs of our production and consumption led society, including as to degradation caused by waste as well as emissions, will come under renewed public scrutiny through the new Commission on Sustainable Development.

The extent of the task faced in reducing energy demand and seeking substantially to increase use of renewable energy sources (without renewed recourse to nuclear power) has been emphasised by the Royal Commission. This question is emblematic of much of today's environmental quandaries. Thus, referring to a need to cut national emissions by as much as 60% by the middle of this new century, the Commission points out that politicians 'are seldom asked to look so far into the future; the quickening pace of change and the shrinking power of the nation State may make it increasingly difficult to do so'.[29] This powerlessness is indeed exacerbated by global processes beyond State control. Moreover, sustainable energy policy must meet numerous broader objectives, such as to 'protect the interests of generations to come, but it must also seek to achieve social justice, a higher quality of life and individual competitiveness today. Achieving the right balance is formidably difficult; current policies do not strike it'.[30]

---

26   See Kasemir, Dahinden, Swartling, Schule, Tabara and Jaeger, 2000.

27   DETR, 2000e.

28   DETR, Government's Response to the Environment Transport and Regional Affairs Committee Report, October 2000.

29   RCEP, 2000, p 9, para 51.

30   RCEP, 2000, p 1, para 1.

FINALLY

It is necessary to confront problems upon two key fronts: first, the ability of nation States to respond in sustainable ways in the face of global threats to sustainability; secondly, the willingness of those States to make radical political decisions with a view to a re-ordering of priorities. In terms of policy, it is essential that there be a reassessment of responsibilities for strategic decision making, and in specific circumstances attention must be given to the recognition of environmental priorities within institutional arrangements. Necessary shifts require increased involvement of the public and transparent, articulate mediation of scientific advice into the public domain. Participative, transparent solutions would be beneficial in addressing problems of accountability in this context. Yet threats to sustainability, such as from global warming, are closely tied to cultural lifestyles and aspirations. Individual attitudes are therefore central to all such projects. It is an essential task to counter widespread perceptions that environmental threats are removed from everyday experience.

Those concerned in these matters, across the disciplinary spectrum, can engage best by seeking to offer principled approaches which might be conducive towards the changed paradigms explored throughout this book. As for the environmental lawyer, there are inevitable concerns with the rights of individuals, due enforcement of standards, and the quality of inputs into decision making processes. Lord Woolf has reasoned that these concerns import a commitment 'to guarantee a greater openness and participation in environmental decision making'.[31]

And yet there are more fundamental processes still. The reorderings prompted by the sustainability debate must enjoin lawyers into more reflexive consideration of the normative underpinnings of legal content and process. In particular, it is necessary to review the nature of those rights which we seek to protect, as well as the quality of outcome of those decision making processes. In support of these objectives, it is moreover essential to encourage the creation of structures which maximise the likelihood that coherent, consistent attention can be devoted to the quality of environmental decision making in all its forms.

A learned discussion of democracy has it that it is necessary 'to explain how relevant information must be distributed in a political community if makers of law and policy are to be responsible to their subjects ... [including] what kinds of information are suited to different kinds of political decisions'.[32] In terms of environmental law and policy, the quality of informed debate and criticism that result from this process is essential. It is inescapable that wider issues explored in the context of environmental justice must be increasingly brought into this debate. Environmental solutions must address not only lack of voice but also lack of choice.

---

31   Woolf, 2001, p 9.
32   Plamenatz, 1973, p 177.

BIBLIOGRAPHY

Achterberg, W, 'Sustainability and associative democracy', in Lafferty and Meadowcroft, *Democracy and the Environment: Problems and Prospects*, 1996, Cheltenham: Edward Elgar

Ackerman, BA, *Social Justice in the Liberal State*, 1980, New Haven: Yale UP

Adams, J, 'What do mad cows, Brent Spar, the NHS and contaminated land have in common?', 1996 paper, Cambridge University

Adams, J, *Risk*, 1995, London: UCL

Adams, J, *The Social Implications of Hypermobility*, 1999, OECD Report (available at www.oecd.org/env/online-trans.htm)

Advisory Committee on Releases into the Environment, *Proposed Guidance on the Assessment of Risk to Wider Biodiversity from Proposed Cultivation of GM Crops*, 2000

Alder, J and Wilkinson, D, *Environmental Law and Ethics*, 1999, Basingstoke: Macmillan

Alder, J, 'Access to the courts: a conflict of ideologies' (1998) 10 JEL 161

Alder, J, 'Environmental impact assessment – the inadequacies of English law' (1993) 5 JEL 203

Allen, T, 'The Philippine children's case: recognising legal standing for future generations' (1994) 6 Georgetown Int Env LR 713

Allmendinger, P and Chapman, M, 'Planning in the millennium', in Allmendinger and Chapman, *Planning Beyond 2000*, 1999, Chichester: Wiley

Allmendinger, P and Chapman, M, *Planning Beyond 2000*, 1999, Chichester: Wiley

Alston, P, 'Conjuring up new human rights: a proposal for quality control' (1984) 78 AJIL 607

Anderson, MR, 'Human rights approaches to environmental protection: an overview', in Boyle and Anderson, *Human Rights Approaches to Environmental Protection*, 1996, Oxford: Clarendon

Applegate, JS, 'A beginning and not a end in itself: the role of risk assessment in environmental decision-making' (1995) 63 University of Cincinnati L Rev 1643

Appleyard, B, *Understanding the Present: Science and the Soul of Modern Man*, 1992, London: Picador

Ashworth, W, *The Genesis of Modern British Town Planning*, 1954, London: Routledge and Kegan Paul

Attfield, R, *The Ethics of Environmental Concern*, 1983, Oxford: Blackwell

Austin, R and Schill, M, 'Black, brown, red and poisoned', in Bullard, *Unequal Protection: Environmental Justice and Communities of Color*, 1994, San Francisco: Sierra Club

Ayres, I and Braithwaite, J, *Responsive Regulation*, 1993, Oxford: OUP

Babcock, RF and Feurer, DA, 'Land as a commodity "affected with a public interest"' (1977) 52 Washington L Rev 289

Bachtler, JF and Twok, I, *Coherence of EU Regional Policy: Contrasting Perspectives on the Structural Funds*, 1997, London: Jessica Kingsley

Baden, JA and Noonan, DS, *Managing the Commons*, 2nd edn, 1998, Bloomington, Indiana: Indiana UP

Baird Callicott, J, 'Animal liberation: a triangular affair', in Sober, *Environmental Ethics*, 1995, Oxford: OUP

Baker, S, Kousis, M, Richardson, D and Young, S, *The Politics of Sustainable Development: Theory, Policy and Practice Within the European Union*, 1997, London: Routledge

Barlow, J, Cocks, R and Parker, M, *Planning for Affordable Housing*, Department of the Environment, 1994, London: HMSO

Barlow, T, 'Science plc' [1999] Prospect 36 (August/September)

Barnes, J, 'The survivor', in *The History of the World in 10 and a half Chapters*, 1989, London: Picador

Barresi, PA, 'Beyond fairness to future generations: an intragenerational alternative to intergenerational equity in the environmental arena' (1997) 11 Tulane Env LJ 59

Barry, BM, 'Justice between generations', in Hacker and Raz, *Law, Morality and Society: Essays in Honour of HLA Hart*, 1977, Oxford: Clarendon

Barry, J, *Rethinking Green Politics*, 1999, London: Sage

Beck, 'Risk society and the provident state', in Lash, Szerszynski and Wynne, *Risk, Environment and Modernity*, 1996, London: Sage

Beck, U, *Democracy Without Enemies*, 1998, Cambridge: Polity

Beck, U, *Risk Society: Towards a New Modernity*, 1992, London: Sage

Beckerman, W, *Small is Stupid: Blowing the Whistle on the Greens*, 1995, London: Duckworth

Been, V, 'What's fairness got to do with it? Environmental justice and the siting of locally undesirable land uses' (1993) 78 Cornell L Rev 1001

Bell, S and McGillivray, D, *Ball and Bell on Environmental Law*, 5th edn, 2000, London: Blackstone

Benton, T, 'Ecology, community and justice', in Hayward and O'Neill, *Justice, Property and the Environment*, 1997, Aldershot: Ashgate

Betjeman, J, *Collected Poems*, 1970, London: John Murray

Betlem, G, 'Standing for ecosystems – going Dutch' [1995] CLJ 153

Bevins, A, 'Special report: science and government' [1999] Prospect 52 (April)

Biermann, F, 'The rising tide of green unilateralism in world trade law' (2001) 35 J World Trade 421

Birnie, PW and Boyle, AE, *International Law and the Environment*, 1992, Oxford: OUP

Blowers, A and Evans, B, *Town Planning into the 21st Century*, 1997, London: Routledge

Blowers, A, 'Society and sustainability, the context of change for planning', in Blowers, A and Evans, B, *Town Planning into the 21st Century*, 1997, London: Routledge

Blowers, A, *Planning for a Sustainable Environment*, 1993, London: Earthscan

Bove, J and Dufour, F, *The World is Not for Sale: Farmers Against Junkfood*, 2001, London: Verso

Bright, S and Dewar, J, *Land Law: Themes and Perspectives*, 1998, Oxford: OUP

Boyle, AE and Anderson, MR, *Human Rights Approaches to Environmental Protection*, 1996, Oxford: Clarendon

Boyle, AE and Freestone, D, *International Law and Sustainable Development: Past Achievements and Future Challenges*, 1999, Oxford: OUP

Boyle, AE, 'Creation of international environmental law and the International Law Commission: injurious consequences revisited', in Boyle and Freestone, *International Law and Sustainable Development: Past Achievements and Future Challenges*, 1999, Oxford: OUP

Boyle, AE, 'Saving the world? Implementation and enforcement of international environmental law through international institutions' (1991) 3 JEL 229

Boyle, AE, 'The role of international human rights law in the protection of the environment', in Boyle and Anderson, *Human Rights Approaches to Environmental Protection*, 1996, Oxford: Clarendon

Braithwaite, J and Pettit, P, *Not Just Deserts: A Republican Theory of Criminal Justice*, 1992, Oxford: Clarendon

Bramley, G and Watkins, C, *Steering the Market: New Housebuilding and the Changing Planning System*, 1996, Bristol: Policy

Brearley, C, 'Integrated transport policy: the implications for planning' [1999] JPL 408

Breheny, M and Hall, P, 'National questions, regional answers', in Breheny and Hall, *The People – Where Will They Go?*, 1996, London: Town and Country Planning Association

Breyer, S and Heyvaert, V, 'Institutions for regulating risk', in Revesz, Sands and Stewart, *Environmental Law, the Economy, and Sustainable Development*, 2000, Cambridge: CUP

Breyer, S, 'Breaking the vicious circle: toward effective risk regulation', in Revesz, *Foundations of Environmental Law and Policy*, 1997, New York: OUP

Brown, DA, 'Superfund cleanups, ethics and environmental risk assessment' (1988) 16 BC Env Aff L Rev 181

Brown, LR, *Building a Sustainable Society*, 1981, New York: Norton

Brown, MD, 'Time to look again at judicial review and planning decisions and to allow third party rights of appeal' [2001] JPL 1043

Brown, P, 'Waste of energy' (2001) *The Guardian*, 7 February

Browne, A, 'Greenhouse gas emissions soar in defiant US' (2001) *The Guardian*, 1 July

Brownlie, I, *Principles of Public International Law*, 4th edn, 1990, Oxford: Clarendon

Brubaker, E, 'The common law and the environment: the Canadian experience', in Hill and Meiners, *Who Owns the Environment?*, 1999, Lanham MD: Rowman and Littlefield

Bruggemeier, G, 'Enterprise liability for environmental damage: German and European law', in Teubner, *Environmental Law and Ecological Responsibility*, 1994, Chichester: Wiley

Brundtland, GH, 'Economia ecologica' (1999) *El Pais* 4, 30 March

Bryant, B, *Twyford Down – Roads, Campaigning and Environmental Law*, 1996, London: E & FN Spon

Buckingham-Hatfield, S and Evans, B, 'Achieving sustainability through environmental planning', in Buckingham-Hatfield and Evans, *Environmental Planning and Sustainability*, 1996, Chichester: Wiley

Bullard, RD, 'Solid waste sites and the black Houston community' (1982) 53 Soc Inquiry 273

Bullard, RD, *Unequal Protection: Environmental Justice and Communities of Color*, 1994, San Francisco: Sierra Club

Bunyard, P and Morgan-Grenville, F, *The Green Alternative: Guide to Good Living*, 1987, London: Mandarin

Burnett, *A Social History of Housing 1815–1970*, 1978, Newton Abbot: David and Charles

Burningham, K and Thrush, D, *'Rainforests are a long way from here': The environmental concerns of disadvantaged groups*, Report for Joseph Rowntree Foundation, 2001, York: York Publishing Service

Butler, S, *Erewhon*, 1872, Mudford (ed), 1985 edn, Harmondsworth: Penguin

Byrne, JP, 'Green property' (1990) 7 Constitutional Commentary 239

CAG Consultants, *Environmental Planning, People's Values and Sustainable Development*, Report prepared for the Royal Commission on Environmental Pollution, 1999

Caldwell, LK, 'Rights of ownership or rights of use? The need for a new conceptual basis for land use theory' (1974) 15 William and Mary L Rev 759

Cameron, J and Abouchar, J, 'The status of the precautionary principle in international law', in Freestone and Hey, *The Precautionary Principle and International Law: The Challenge of Implementation*, 1996, The Hague: Kluwer

Cameron, J and Campbell, K, 'Challenging the boundaries of the DSU through trade and environmental disputes', in Cameron and Campbell, *Dispute Resolution in the World Trade Organisation*, 1998, London: Cameron May

Cameron, J and Makuch, Z, 'The UN Framework Convention on Climate Change: the European carbon/energy tax and its international trade law implications', in Cameron, Werksman, and Roderick, *Improving Compliance with International Environmental Law*, 1996, London: Earthscan

Cameron, J, Werksman, J and Roderick, P, *Improving Compliance with International Environmental Law*, 1996, London: Earthscan

Cancado Trindade, AA, *Human Rights, Sustainable Development and the Environment*, 1992, San Jose: Inst Interamericano de Derechos Humanos

Cane, P, 'Standing up for the public' [1995] PL 276

Carney, DP, 'Environmental interest groups and the litigation process: an overview of the experience in England and Wales', paper delivered at WG Hart Workshop, IALS, London, 1997

Carnwath, R, 'Environmental enforcement: the need for a specialist court' (1992) 4 JPEL 799

Carnwath, R, 'Environmental litigation – a way through the maze?' (1999) 11 JEL 3

Carnwath, R, 'The planning lawyer and the environment' (1991) 3 JEL 57

Carson, R, *Silent Spring*, 1965, Harmondsworth: Penguin

Cartledge, B, *Energy and the Environment*, 1993, Oxford: OUP

Casely-Hayford, M and Leigh, K, 'The birth of the Human Rights Act: the death of the planning call-in procedure?' [2001] JPL 7

Casey, HM and Morgante, A, *Human Rights, Environmental Law and the Earth Charter*, 1998, Cambridge, Mass: Boston Research Center for the 21st Century

Churchill, R, 'Environmental rights in existing human rights treaties', in Boyle and Anderson, *Human Rights Approaches to Environmental Protection*, 1996, Oxford: Clarendon

Coase, RH, 'The problem of social cost' (1960) 3 J Law and Economics 1

Cohen, LJ, *The Probable and Provable*, 1997, Oxford: Clarendon

Colborn, T, Dumanoski, D and Myers, JP, *Our Stolen Future*, 1996, New York: Dutton

Cole, LW, 'Environmental justice litigation: another stone in David's sling' (1994) 21 Fordham Urban LJ 523

Collison, DJ, 'The impact of the environmental agenda for business: an accounting perspective' (1998) 5 Env Liability 150

Commoner, B, *The Closing Circle: Nature, Man and Technology*, 1971, New York: Alfred A Knopf

Corner, T, 'Planning, environment and the European Convention on Human Rights' [1998] JPL 301

Council of Europe, Lugano Convention on Civil Liability for Damage Resulting from Activities Dangerous to the Environment, ETS No 150 (21 June 1993)

Coward, R, 'Time to back-track' (2000) *The Guardian,* 19 December

Cowell, R and Owens, S, 'Suitable locations: equity and sustainability in the minerals planning process' (1998) 32 Regional Studies 797

Craig, P and de Búrca, G, *EU Law: Text and Materials,* 2nd edn, 1998, Oxford: OUP

Craig, P and de Búrca, G, *The Evolution of EC Law,* 1999, Oxford: OUP

Crawford, C, 'Public law rules over private law as a standard for nuisance: OK?' (1992) 4 JEL 251

Cromer, J, 'Sanitary and phytosanitary measures: what they could mean for health and safety regulations under GATT' (1995) 36 Harvard J Int Law 560

Cullingworth, B, *British Planning: Fifty Years of Urban and Regional Policy,* 1999, London: Athlone

Cullingworth, JB and Nadin, V, *Town and Country Planning in the UK,* 12th edn, 1997, London: Routledge

Curry, N and Owens, S, *Changing Rural Policy in Britain: Planning Administration, Agriculture and the Environment,* 1996, Cheltenham: Countryside and Community

Curtis, J, 'Comparison of regulatory takings under the United States constitution and the European Convention on Human Rights' (1989) 14 European L Rev 67

D'Amato, A, 'Do we owe a duty to future generations to preserve the global environment?' (1990) 84 AJIL 190

Dales, JH, *Pollution, Property and Prices,* 1968, Toronto: Toronto UP

Daly, HE and Cobb, JB, *For the Common Good: Redirecting the Economy Toward Community, the Environment and a Sustainable Future,* 1989, Boston, Mass: Beacon

Daly, HE, 'Toward a stationary-state economy', in Harte and Socolow, *The Patient Earth,* 1971, New York: Rinehart & Winston

Davoudi, S, 'Sustainability: a new vision for the British planning system' (2000) 15 Planning Perspectives 123

Dawkins, R, *The Selfish Gene,* 1989, Oxford: OUP (originally published 1976)

De Alessi, 'Private property rights as the basis for free marker environmentalism', in Hill and Meiners, *Who Owns the Environment?,* 1999, Lanham MD: Rowman and Littlefield

De Souza, J and Snape, J, 'Environmental tax proposals: analysis and evaluation' (2000) 2 Env L Rev 74

de Witte, B, 'Direct effect, supremacy, and the nature of legal order', in Craig and de Búrca, *The Evolution of EC Law,* 1999, Oxford: OUP

Decleris, M, *The Law of Sustainable Development: General Principles,* Report produced for the European Commission, 2000

Dejevsky, M, Connor, S and McCarthy, M, 'Bush drops pledge on carbon dioxide emissions' (2001) *The Independent*, 15 March

Demetz, H, 'Towards a theory of property rights' (1967) 57 Am Ec Rev: Proceedings and Papers 347

Dennis, I, 'Instrumental protection, human right or functional necessity? Reassessing the privilege against self-incrimination' [1995] CLJ 342

Department of Health, Bulletin 2001/0068, 5 February 2001

Department of Health, Bulletin 98/005, 5 January 1998

Desgagne, R, 'Integrating environmental values into the European Convention on Human Rights' (1995) 89 AJIL 263

DETR, PPG13, *Planning Policy Guidance: Transport*, 2001a

DETR, *Guidance on Municipal Waste Management Strategies*, 2001b

DETR, PPG3, *Planning Policy Guidance: Housing*, 2000a

DETR, PPG11, *Planning Policy Guidance: Regional Planning*, 2000b

DETR, *Our Towns and Cities: The Future – Delivering and Urban Renaissance*, White Paper, 2000c

DETR, *Greenfield Housing Direction*, 2000d

DETR, *Climate Change: The UK Programme*, Cm 4913, London: HMSO, 2000e

DETR, *Good Practice Guide to Sustainability Appraisal of Regional Planning Guidance*, 2000f

DETR, *National Air Quality Strategy for England, Scotland, Wales and Northern Ireland*, Cm 4548, 2000g

DETR, *Transport 2010: The Ten-Year Plan*, 2000h

DETR, *Waste Strategy*, Cm 4693-I and II, 2000i

DETR, *Implementation of Directive 1999/31*, Consultation Paper, 2000j

DETR, *Contaminated Land*, Circular 02/2000, 2000k

DETR, *Environmental Impact Assessment*, Circular 02/1999, 1999a

DETR, PPG10, *Planning Policy Guidance: Planning and Waste Management*, 1999b

DETR, PPG12, *Planning Policy Guidance: Development Plans*, 1999c

DETR, *Limiting Landfill*, 1999d

DETR, *Modernising Planning*, 1998a, London: HMSO

DETR, *A New Deal for Transport: Better for Everyone*, Cm 3950, 1998b

DETR, *Planning for Sustainable Development: Towards Better Practice*, 1998c

DETR, *Planning and Affordable Housing*, Circular 06/98, 1998d

DETR, *Regional Development Agencies: Issues for Discussion*, 1997a, London: HMSO

DETR, *Air Quality and Traffic Management*, 1997b

DETR, *The UK National Air Quality Standards: Guidance for Local Authorities*, Circular 15/97, 1997c

DETR/Environment Agency/Institute for Environment and Health, *Guidelines for Environmental Risk Assessment and Management: Revised Departmental Guidance*, 2000

DETR/MAFF, *Our Countryside: The Future – A Fair Deal for Rural England*, Cm 4909, 2000, London: HMSO

Dias, CJ, 'Misconceptions and misunderstandings', in Casey and Morgante, *Human Rights, Environmental Law and the Earth Charter*, 1998, Cambridge, Mass: Boston Research Center for the 21st Century

Dickens, C, *Hard Times*, 1854 (ed Schlicke 1989), Oxford: OUP

Dickson, D, 'Limiting democracy: technocrats and the liberal state' (1981) 1 Democracy 61

Dobelstein, A, *Politics, Economics and Public Welfare*, 1980, Englewood Cliffs, NJ: Prentice Hall

Dobson, A and Lucardie, P, *The Politics of Nature: Explorations in Green Political Theory*, 1993, London: Routledge

Dobson, A, *Fairness and Futurity: Essays on Environmental Sustainability and Social Justice*, 1999, Oxford: OUP

Dobson, A, *Green Political Thought*, 3rd edn, 2000, London: Routledge

DoE, PPG1, *Planning Policy Guidance: General Policy and Principles*, 1997a

DoE, *Planning Obligations*, Circular 01/97, 1997b

DoE, PPG7, *Planning Policy Guidance: Countryside: Environmental Quality and Economic and Social Development*, 1997c, London: HMSO

DoE, *Air Quality and Land Use Planning Guidance*, Circular 15/97, 1997d

DoE, *Household Growth: Where Shall We Live?*, 1996a, London: HMSO

DoE, PPG6, *Planning Policy Guidance: Town Centres and Retail Developments*, 1996b

DoE, *Planning Appeals*, Circular 15/96, 1996c

DoE, *The Use of Conditions in Planning Permissions*, Circular 11/95, 1995a

DoE, PPG2, *Planning Policy Guidance: Green Belts*, 1995b

DoE, *Guide to Risk Assessment and Risk Management for Environmental Protection*, 1995c, London: HMSO

DoE, PPG23, *Planning Policy Guidance: Planning and Pollution Control*, 1994a

DoE, PPG15, *Planning Policy Guidance: Planning and the Historic Environment*, 1994b

DoE, PPG9, *Planning Policy Guidance: Nature Conservation*, 1994c

DoE, *Environmental Appraisal of Development Plans: Good Practice Guide*, 1993a

DoE, PPG22, *Planning Policy Guidance: Renewable Energy*, 1993b

DoE, PPG20, *Planning Policy Guidance, Coastal Planning*, 1992

DoE, *Planning and Affordable Housing*, Circular 7/91, 1991

DoE, PPG16, *Planning Policy Guidance: Archaeology and Planning*, 1990a

DoE, PPG14, *Planning Policy Guidance: Development on Unstable Land*, 1990b

DoE, *Environmental Assessment*, Circular 15/88, 1988

DoE/MAFF, *Rural England: a Nation Committed to a Living Countryside*, 1995, London: HMSO

Dommen, C, 'Claiming environmental rights: some possibilities offered by the United Nations human rights mechanisms' (1998) 11 Georgetown Int Env L Rev 1

Donaldson, T and Werhane, P, 'Moral dilemmas for multinationals', in Donaldson and Werhane, *Ethical Issues in Business*, 1993, Englewood Cliffs, NJ: Prentice Hall

Donne, J, *Devotions upon Emergent Occasions* (1624), Raspa, A, 1987 edn, Oxford: OUP

Donson, F, 'Planning in a sensitive environment – lessons from Twyford Down', paper given at the WG Hart Workshop, IALS, London, 1997

Douglas, M, *Risk and Blame: Essays in Cultural Theory*, 1994, London: Routledge

Driscoll, J, *What is the Future for Social Housing? Reflections on the Public Sector Provisions of the Housing Act 1996* (1997) 60 MLR 823

DTI, *Our Competitive Future: Building the Knowledge Driven Economy*, White Paper, 1998

DTLGR, PPG25, *Flood Risk and Development*, 2000

Dunlap, RE, 'Public opinion and environmental policy', in Lester, *Environmental Politics and Policy: Theories and Evidence*, 1989, Durham, NC: Duke UP

Durkheim, E, *On Morality and Society*, 1973 edn, Chicago: Chicago UP

Durkheim, E, *The Division of Labour in Society*, Simpson, G (trans), 1964, New York: Free

Duxbury, R, *Planning Law and Procedure*, 11th edn, 1999, London: Butterworths

Dworkin, R, 'Hard cases' (1975) 85 Harvard L Rev 1057

Dworkin, R, 'Liberalism', in Hampshire, *Public and Private Morality*, 1978, Cambridge: CUP

Dworkin, R, *Taking Rights Seriously*, 1977, London: Duckworth

Eckersley, R, *Environmentalism and Political Theory: Toward an Ecocentric Approach*, 1992, London: University of London

Edelstein, MR, *Contaminated Communities: the Social and Psychological Impacts of Residential Toxic Exposure*, 1988, Boulder: Westview

Elliott, R, *Environmental Ethics*, 1995, Oxford: OUP

Elson, M, Steenberg, C and Mendham, N, *Green Belts and Affordable Housing: Can We Have Both?*, 1996, Bristol: Policy

Elson, MJ and Ford, A, 'Green belts and very special circumstances' [1994] JPL 594

Elson, MJ, Macdonald, R and Steenberg, C, *Planning for Rural Diversification*, 1995, London: HMSO

Elson, MJ, Walker, S and Macdonald, R, *The Effectiveness of Green Belts*, 1993, London: HMSO

Elvin, D and Robinson, J, 'Environmental impact assessment' [2000] JPL 876

Elworthy, S and Holder, J, *Environmental Protection: Text and Materials*, 1997, London: Butterworths

Elworthy, S and McCulloch, A, 'BSE in Britain: science, socio-economics and European law' (1996) 5 Env Politics 736

Environment Agency, *Risk from BSE via Environmental Pathways*, 1997

Environmental Protection Agency, *Interim Guidance*, 1998

Epstein, RA, *Takings: Private Property and the Power of the Eminent Domain*, 1985, Cambridge, Mass: Harvard UP

European Commission, Communication on *The Sixth Environment Action Programme of the European Community 'Environment 2010: Our Future, Our Choice*, COM(2001) 31 final, 2001a

European Commission, Consultation Paper, *The Preparation of a European Union Strategy for Sustainable Development*, SEC (2001) 517, 2001b

European Commission, Communication on *Bringing our Needs and Responsibilities Together – Integrating Environmental Issues with Economic Policy*, COM(2000) 576, 2000a

European Commission, White Paper, *Environmental Liability*, COM(2000) 66, 2000b

European Commission, Communication on *the Precautionary Principle*, COM(2000) 1, 2000c

European Commission, Communication on *Community Policies in Support of Employment*, COM(99) 167, 1999

European Commission, Communication on *Environment and Employment (Building a Sustainable Europe)*, COM(97) 592, 1997a

European Commisssion, Communication on *Environmental Taxes and Charges in the Single Market*, COM(97) 9, 1997b

European Commission, *Communication on Environmental Agreements* COM(96) 561 final, 1996a

European Commission, Communication on *Implementing Community Environmental Law*, COM(96) 500 final, 1996b

European Commission, Programme of Policy and Action in Relation to the Environment and Sustainable Development, *Towards Sustainability*, OJ C138, 1993a

European Commission, Green Paper, *Remedying Environmental Damage*, 1993b

European Economic and Social Committee, *Opinion on Commission Communication, Europe's Environment: What Directions for the Future? The Global Assessment of the European Community Programme of Policy and Action in relation to the Environment and Sustainable Development*, 'Towards Sustainability', 2000, CES 593/2000 E/O

Farber, DA and Frickey, PP, 'In the shadow of the legislature: the common law in the age of the new public law' (1991) 89 Michigan L Rev 875

Farber, DA, *Eco-pragmatism: Making Sensible Environmental Decisions an Uncertain World*, 1999, Chicago: Chicago UP

Farmer, A, Skinner, I, Wilkinson, D and Bishop, K, *Environmental Planning in the United Kingdom, Background Paper for the Royal Commission on Environmental Pollution*, 1999

Faure, MG and Grimeaud, D, *Financial Assurance Issues of Environmental Liability*, 2000, Maastricht: European Centre for Tort and Insurance Law

Feinberg, J, *Rights, Justice and the Bounds of Liberty*, 1980, Princeton: Princeton UP

Finger, M, 'Politics of the UNCED process', in Sachs, *Global Ecology: A New Arena of Political Conflict*, 1993, London: Zed

Fisher, R, *Improving Compliance with International Law*, 1981, Charlottesville, Va: Virginia UP

Fitzpatrick, B, 'Redressing the late implementation of the environmental impact assessment directive' (1994) 6 JEL 351

Frazier, TW, 'Protecting ecological integrity within the balancing function of property law' [1998] Env Law 53

Frazier, TW, 'The green alternative to classical liberal property theory' (1995) 20 Vermont L Rev 299

Freestone, D and Hey, E, 'Origins and development of the precautionary principle', in Freestone and Hey, *The Precautionary Principle and International Law: The Challenge of Implementation*, 1996, The Hague: Kluwer

Freestone, D and Hey, E, *The Precautionary Principle and International Law: The Challenge of Implementation*, 1996, The Hague: Kluwer

Freestone, D, 'The challenge of implementation', in Boyle and Freestone, *International Law and Sustainable Development: Past Achievements and Future Challenges*, 1999, Oxford: OUP

Freilich, RH and Guemmer, DK, 'Removing artificial barriers to public participation in land-use policy: effective zoning and planning by initiative and referenda' (1989) 21 Urban Lawyer 511

French, D, '1997 Kyoto Protocol to the 1992 UN Framework Convention on Climate Change' (1998) 10 JEL 27

Freudenberg, N, *Not in Our Backyards*, 1984, New York: Monthly Review

Freyfogle ET, 'Owning the land: four contemporary narratives' (1998) 13 J Land Use and Env Law 279

Freyfogle, ET, 'Ethics, community, and private land' (1996b) 23 Ecology LQ 631

Freyfogle, ET, 'Land use and the study of early American history' (1985) 94 Yale LJ 717

Freyfogle, ET, 'The construction of ownership' (1996a) 6 University of Illinois L Rev 173

Freyfogle, ET, 'The ethical strands of environmental law' (1994) 4 University of Illinois L Rev 819

Friedman, M, *Capitalism and Freedom*, 1962, Chicago: Chicago UP

Gaba, JM, 'Environmental ethics and our moral relationship to future generations: future rights and present virtue' (1999) 24 Columbia JEL 249

Gaines, SE, 'Rethinking environmental protection, competitiveness and international trade' [1997] University of Chicago Legal Forum 231

Galizzi, P, 'Globalisation, trade and the environment: broadening the agenda after Seattle?' (2000) 4 Env Liability 106

Gauna, E, 'The environmental justice misfit: public participation and the paradigm paradox' (1998) 17 Stanford Env LJ 3

Gauthier, DP, *Morals by Agreement*, 1986, Oxford: Clarendon

Gearty, C, 'Unravelling *Osman*' (2001) 64 MLR 159

Geddes, P, *Cities in Evolution*, 1915, London: Williams and Norgate

Gedicks, A, *The New Resource Wars*, 1993, Boston, Mass: South End

George, H, *Progress and Poverty: An Inquiry into the Cause of Industrial Depressions and of Increase of Want with Increase of Wealth*, 1884, London: William Reeves

Giddens, A, *Beyond Left and Right: The Future of Radical Politics*, 1994, Cambridge: Polity

Giddens, A, *The Consequences of Modernity*, 1990, Cambridge: Polity

Giddens, A, *The Renewal of Social Democracy*, 1998, Cambridge: Polity

Gilpin, A, *Environmental Impact Assessment (EIA): Cutting Edge for the Twenty-first Century*, 1995, Cambridge: CUP

Glendon, MA, *Rights Talk: The Impoverishment of Political Discourse*, 1991, New York: Free

Global Environmental Change Programme, ESRC Report, *The Politics of GM Food: Risk, Science and Public Trust*, 1999, Sussex: ESRC

Goodin, R, *Green Political Theory*, 1992, Cambridge: Polity

Gorz, A, *Critique of Economic Reason*, 1989, London: Verso

Grant, M, 'Compensation and betterment', in Cullingworth, *British Planning: Fifty Years of Urban and Regional Policy*, 1999, London: Athlone

Grant, M, 'Development and the protection of birds: the Swale decision' (1991) 3 JEL 135

Grant, M, 'Financial contributions: a global perspective' (2000b) 6 Env Liability 169

Grant, M, 'Human rights and due process in planning' [2000c] JPL 1215

Grant, M, *Environmental Court Project: Final Report*, London: DETR, 2000a

Grant, M, *Urban Planning Law*, 1982, London: Sweet & Maxwell

Gray, J, 'Wars of want' (2001) *The Guardian*, 21 August

Gray, J, 'Wild globalisation' (2000) *The Guardian*, 5 December

Gray, JS, 'Integrating precautionary scientific methods into decision-making', in Freestone and Hey, *The Precautionary Principle and International Law: The Challenge of Implementation*, 1996b, The Hague: Kluwer

Gray, KF and Gray, SF, *Elements of Land Law*, 3rd edn, 2001, London: Butterworths

Gray, MA, 'The international crime of ecocide' (1996a) 26 California Western Int LJ 215

Gray, R, *Accounting for the Environment*, 1993, London: Paul Chapman

Grayling, T, 'Drive on' (2001) *The Guardian*, 13 March

Grayling, T, Institute for Public Policy Research, 'Turbulence ahead', 2000, *The Guardian*, 13 December

Green, H Marlow, 'Common law, property rights and the environment: a comparative analysis of historical developments in the US and England and a model for the future' (1997) 30 Cornell Int LJ 541

Greenwood, B, *Butterworths Planning Law Guidance*, 2nd edn, 1999, London: Butterworths

Greve, MS, 'The private enforcement of environmental law' (199) 65 Tulane L Rev 339

Griffith, JAG, *The Politics of the Judiciary*, 5th edn, 1997, London: Fontana

Grimeaud, D J-E, 'An overview of the policy and legal aspects of the international climate change regime' [2001] 9 Env Liability 39

Grove-White, R, 'Environmental knowledge and public policy needs: on humanising the research agenda', in Lash, Szerszynski and Wynne, *Risk, Environment and Modernity*, 1996, London: Sage

Guest, A, *Oxford Essays in Jurisprudence*, 1961, Oxford: OUP

Gunningham, N, *Pollution, Social Interest and the Law*, 1974, London: Robertson

Habermas, J, 'The European Nation State: its achievements and its limitations on the past and future of sovereignty and citizenship' (1996) 9 Ratio Juris 125

Habermas, J, *The Theory of Communicative Action, Vol 1: Reason and Rationalization of Society*, 1981, Boston: Beacon

Hacker, PMS and Raz, J, *Law, Morality and Society: Essays in Honour of HLA Hart*, 1977, Oxford: Clarendon

Hajer, M, *The Politics of Environmental Discourse*, 1997, Oxford: OUP

Hall, D, Hebbert, M and Lusser, H, 'The planning background', in Blowers, *Planning for a Sustainable Environment*, 1993, London: Earthscan

Hall, P, *Cities of Tomorrow*, 1994, Oxford: Blackwell

Hall, P, Gracey, H, Drewett, R and Thomas, R, *The Containment of Urban England, Vols I and II*, 1973, London: George Allen and Unwin

Hampshire, S, *Public and Private Morality*, 1978, Cambridge: CUP

Handl, G, 'Human rights and protection of the environment: a mildly "revisionist" view', in Cancado Trindade, *Human Rights, Sustainable Development and the Environment*, 1992, San Jose: Inst Interamericano de Derechos Humanos

Hanley, N and Milne, J, 'Ethical beliefs and behaviour in contingent valuation surveys' (1996) 39 J Env Planning and Management 255

Hardin, G, 'The tragedy of the commons', in Baden and Noonan, *Managing the Commons*, 2nd edn, 1998, Bloomington, Ind: Indiana UP

Hardin, G, *The Limits of Altruism*, 1977, Indianapolis: Indiana UP

Hargrove, EC, *The Foundations of Environmental Ethics*, 1989, Englewood Cliffs, NJ: Prentice Hall

Harlow, C and Rawlings, R, *Pressure Through Law*, 1992, London: Routledge

Harrison, M, 'A presumption in favour of planning permission' [1992] JPL 121

Hart, D, 'The impact of the European Convention on Human Rights on planning and environmental law' [2001] JPL 117

Hart, HLA and Honore, T, *Causation in the Law*, 2nd edn, 1985, Oxford: Clarendon

Hart, HLA, 'Are there natural rights?', in Waldron, *Theories of Rights*, 1984, Oxford: OUP

Harte, J and Socolow, R, *The Patient Earth*, 1971, New York: Rinehart & Winston

Harte, J, 'The extent of the legal protection enjoyed by sites of special scientific interest in England and Wales' (1991) 3 JEL 293

Harvey, G, 'The blight on our landscape' (2001) *The Times*, 12 April

Haskins, C, 'The danger of being too careful' (2000) *Financial Times*, 27 October

Hawkins, K, *Environment and Enforcement*, 1984, Oxford: OUP

Hayek, FA, *Individualism and Economic Order*, 1949, London: Routledge and Kegan Paul

Hayward, BM, 'The greening of participatory democracy: a reconsideration of theory' (1995) 4 Env Politics 215

Hayward, T, 'Constitutional environmental rights: a case for political analysis' (2000) 48 Political Studies 358

Hayward, T, and O'Neill, J, *Justice, Property and the Environment*, 1997, Aldershot: Ashgate

Heal, G, 'Markets and sustainability', in Revesz, Sands and Stewart, *Environmental Law, the Economy, and Sustainable Development*, 2000, Cambridge: CUP

Healey, MP, 'Still dirty after twenty-five years: water quality standard enforcement and the availability of citizen suits'(1997) 24 Ecology LQ 393

Healey, P and Shaw, T, 'Changing meanings of "environment" in the British planning system' (1994) 19 Transactions of the Institute of British Geographers 425

Healey, P, Purdue, M and Ennis, F, *Negotiating Development: Rationales and Practice for Development Obligations and Planning Gain*, 1995, London: E & FN Spon

Health and Safety Executive, *Risk Criteria for Land Use Planning in the Vicinity of Major Industrial Hazards*, 1989

Heap, D, *An Outline of Planning Law*, 11th edn, 1996, London: Sweet & Maxwell

Hedemann-Robinson, M and Wilde, M, 'Towards a European tort law on the environment? European Union initiatives and developments on civil liability in respect of environmental harm', in Lowry and Edmunds, *Environmental Protection and the Common Law*, 2000, Oxford: Hart

Heilbroner, R, *An Inquiry into the Human Prospect*, 2nd edn, 1980, New York: Norton

Hencke, D, 'Watchdog admits ignorance of incinerator health risks' (2000) *The Guardian*, 29 November

Hession, M and Macrory, R, 'Maastricht and the environmental policy of the community: legal issues of a new environment policy', in O'Keeffe and Twomey, *Legal Issues of the Maastricht Treaty*, 1994, London: Chancery

Hetherington, P, 'Cold comfort for village as housing market woos outsiders' (2000a) *The Guardian*, 29 November

Hetherington, P, 'Councils can tax second homes at full rate' (2000b) *The Guardian*, 29 November

Hetherington, P, 'Divide and rule' (2001) *The Guardian*, 31 January

Higgins, R, 'Natural resources in the case law of the international court', in Boyle and Freestone, *International Law and Sustainable Development: Past Achievements and Future Challenges*, 1999, Oxford: OUP

Hill, PJ and Meiners, RE, *Who Owns the Environment?*, 1999, Lanham MD: Rowman and Littlefield

Hilson, C and Downes, T, 'Making sense of rights: Community rights in EC law' (1999) 24 Euro L Rev 121

Hilson, I and Cram, I, 'Judicial review and environmental law – is there a coherent view of standing?' (1996) 16 LS 1

Himsworth, C, 'Unsustainable developments in law-making for environmental liability?', in Hayward and O'Neill, *Property and the Environment*, 1997, Aldershot: Ashgate

Hine, J, 'Transport policy', in Allmendinger and Chapman, *Planning Beyond 2000*, 1999, Chichester: Wiley

Hirschliefer, J, 'Economics from a biological viewpoint' (1977) 20 J Law & Economics 1

Hirst, P, *Associative Democracy*, 1994, Cambridge: Polity

HM Customs and Excise, *Review of Landfill Tax*, 1998

Hobbes, T, *Leviathan*, 1651, Tuck, R (ed), 1996, Cambridge: CUP

Hockman, S, Trimbos, J *et al*, *Blackstone Planning Law and Practice*, 1999, London: Blackstone

Hodas, DR, 'The role of law in defining sustainable development: NEPA reconsidered' [1998] Widener Law Symposium J 1

Hohfeld, WN, *Fundamental Legal Conceptions*, 1919, New Haven CT: Yale UP

Holder, J and McGillivray, D, *Locality and Identity: Environmental Issues in Law and Society*, 1999, Aldershot: Dartmouth

Holder, J, 'The precautionary principle under UK environmental law', in Holder, *Impact of EC Environmental Law in the UK*, 1997, Chichester: Wiley

Holder, J, 'The Sellafield litigation and questions of causation in environmental law' [1994] CLP 287

Holland, A, 'Foreword', in Westra, *Living in Integrity: A Global Ethic to Restore a Fragmented Earth*, 1998, Lanham, Maryland: Rowman & Littlefield

Holland, MC, 'Judicial review of compliance with the national environmental protection act: an opportunity for the rule of reason' (1985) 12 Boston Col Env LR 743

Holmans, A, 'Housing demand and need in England to 2011: the national picture', in Breheny and Hall, *The People – Where Will They Go?* 1996, London: Town and Country Planning Association

Home Office, *Freedom of Information: Consultation on Draft Legislation*, Cm 4355, 1999

Honore, T, 'Ownership', in Guest, *Oxford Essays in Jurisprudence*, 1961, Oxford: OUP

Hornstein, DT, 'Reclaiming environmental law: a normative critique of comparative risk analysis' (1992) 92 Columbia L Rev 562

House of Commons Environment, Transport and Regional Affairs Committee, *Delivering Sustainable Waste Management*, HC 903-II, 2000a

House of Commons, Environment, Transport and Regional Affairs Select Committee, *Development on, or Affecting, the Flood Plain*, Session 2000–2001, HC 64, 20 December 2000

House of Lords Select Committee on the European Communities, *Community Environmental Law: Making it Work*, 2nd Report, Session 1997–98 (HL Paper 12)

House of Lords Select Committee on Science and Technology, *Science and Society*, 1999–2000, 3rd Report, 2000

Howard, E, *Garden Cities of Tomorrow* (originally *A Peaceful Path to Reform*, 1898), 1902, London: S Sonnenschein

Hughes, T, *Tales from Ovid: Twenty-four Passages from the Metamorphoses*, 1997, London: Faber and Faber

Humphrys, J, *The Great Food Gamble*, 2001, London: Hodder & Stoughton

Hutton, W, 'The state we can't escape' (2000a) *The Observer*, 29 October

Hutton, W, 'Why the tube is an issue for us all' (2000b) *The Observer*, 17 December

Hutton, W, *The State We're In*, 1996, London: Vintage

Huxley, A, *Brave New World*, 1932 (1955 edn), Harmondsworth: Penguin

Ibsen, H, 'A public enemy', 1882, in *Ghosts and Other Plays*, Watts, P (trans), 1964, Harmondsworth: Penguin

International Union for Conservation of Nature and Natural Resources (IUCN), *World Conservation Strategy: Living Resource Conservation for Sustainable Development*, 1980, Gland, Switzerland: IUCN

International Union for Conservation of Nature and Natural Resources (IUCN), *Caring for the Earth: A Strategy for Sustainable Living*, 1991, Gland, Switzerland: IUCN

Irvine, S and Ponton, A, *A Green Manifesto: Policies for a Green Future*, 1988, London: Macdonald Optima

Irwin, A and Wynne, B, *Misunderstanding Science? The Public Reconstruction of Science and Technology*, 1996, Cambridge: CUP

Irwin, A, *Citizen Science: A Study of People, Expertise and Sustainable Development*, 1995, London: Routledge

Jacobs, M, 'Sustainable development as a contested concept', in Dobson, *Fairness and Futurity: Essays on Environmental Sustainability and Social Justice*, 1999, Oxford: OUP

Jacobs, M, *The Green Economy*, 1991, London: Pluto

Jacobs, M, *The Politics of the Real World: Meeting the New Century*, 1996, London: Earthscan

Jans, J, *European Environmental Law*, 2nd edn, 2000, Amsterdam: Europa Institute

Jasanoff, S, 'Social learning in the risk society', 1997 paper, Cambridge University

Jasanoff, S, 'The songlines of risk' (1999) 8 Env Values 135

Jenkins, S, *Accountable to None: the Tory Nationalization of Britain*, 1995, Harmondsworth: Penguin

Jewell, T and Steele, J, 'Planning law and the environment: prospects for decision making', in *Law and Environmental Decision Making: National European and International Perspectives*, 1998, Oxford: Clarendon

Johnson, P, 'The perils of risk avoidance', Regulation, May/June 1980

Johnston, BR, *Who Pays the Price? The Sociocultural Context of Environmental Crisis*, 1994, Washington DC: Island

Jones, C and Watkins, C, 'Planning and the housing system', in Allmendinger and Chapman, *Planning Beyond 2000*, 1999, Chichester: Wiley

Jones, CE and Bull, TRT, 'Analysis of changing trends in United Kingdom environmental statements 1988–94' [1997] JPL 1091

Jordan, A and Voisey, H, 'The Rio process: the politics and substantive outcomes of Earth Summit II' (1998) 8 Global Env Change 93

Jordan, A and Werksman, J, 'Financing global environmental protection', in Cameron, Werksman and Roderick, *Improving Compliance with International Environmental Law*, 1996, London: Earthscan

Jouhar, AJ, *Risk in Society*, 1984, London: John Libbey

Juniper, T and Denny, C, 'Planet profit' (2000) *The Guardian*, 17 November

Justice/Public Law Project, *A Matter of Public Interest: Reforming the Law on Interventions in Public Interest Cases*, 1996, London: Justice, Public Law Project

Kamminga, MT, 'The precautionary principle in international human rights law: how it can benefit the environment', in Freestone and Hey, *The Precautionary Principle and International Law: The Challenge of Implementation*, 1996, The Hague: Kluwer

Kasemir, B, Dahinden, U, Swartling, AG, Schule, R, Tabara, D and Jaeger, CC, 'Citizens' perspectives on climate change and energy use' (2000) 10 Global Env Change 169

Kavka, G, 'The futurity problem', in Sikora and Barry, *Obligations to Future Generations*, 1978, Philadelphia: Temple UP

Kelman, S, 'Cost-benefit analysis: an ethical critique', in Revesz, *Foundations of Environmental Law and Policy*, 1997, New York: OUP

Kelsen, H, *Pure Theory of Law*, 1970, Berkeley: University of California

Kettle, J and Moran, C, 'Social housing and exclusion', in Allmendinger and Chapman, *Planning Beyond 2000*, 1999, Chichester: Wiley

Kimber, C, 'Access to justice and freedom of information', paper, IALS, London, 1997

Kimblin, 'Risk, jurisprudence and the environment' [2000] JPL 359

Kirkwood, G and Edwards, M, 'Affordable housing policy: desirable but unlawful?' [1993] JPL 317

Kitson, A, 'The European Convention on Human Rights and local plans' [1998] JPL 321

Klemma, HC, 'The enterprise liability theory of torts' (1976) 47 Colorado UL Rev 153

Kohler, P, 'Common property and private trusts', in Holder and McGillivray, *Locality and Identity: Environmental Issues in Law and Society*, 1999, Aldershot: Dartmouth

Korten, AD, *The Post-Corporate World: Life After Capitalism*, 1999, West Hartford, Ct: Kumarian

Korten, DC, *When Corporations Rule the World*, 1995, West Hartford, Ct: Kumarian

Lafferty, WM and Meadowcroft, J, 'Democracy and the environment: congruence and conflict – preliminary reflections', in Lafferty and Meadowcroft, *Democracy and the Environment: Problems and Prospects*, 1996, Cheltenham: Edward Elgar

Lafferty, WM, and Meadowcroft, J, *Democracy and the Environment: Problems and Prospects*, 1996, Cheltenham: Edward Elgar

Lambert, T and Boerner, C, 'Environmental inequity: economic causes, economic solutions' (1997) 14 Yale J on Regulation 195

Land Use Consultants, *The Use of the Land Use Planning System to Achieve Non-Land Use Planning Objectives, Background Paper for the Royal Commission on Environmental Pollution*, December 1999

Langhelle, O, 'Sustainable development and global justice: expanding the Rawlsian framework of global justice' (2000) 9 Env Values 295

Larkin, *Collected Poems*, Thwaite, A (ed), 1990, London: Faber and Faber

Lash, S and Urry, J, *The End of Organised Capitalism*, 1987, Cambridge: Polity

Lash, S, Wynne, B and Szerszynski, B, *Risk, Environment and Modernity*, 1996, London: Sage

Latin, HA, 'Environmental deregulation and consumer decisionmaking under uncertainty' (1982) 6 Harvard Env L Rev 187

Laurance, J, 'Traffic fumes linked to 6% of deaths in Europe' (2000) *The Guardian*, 1 September

Law Commission, Report No 226, *Administrative Law: Judicial Review and Statutory Appeals*, 1994

Layard, A, 'Environmental justice: the American experience and its possible application to the United Kingdom', in Holder and McGillivray, *Locality and Identity: Environmental Issues in Law and Society* 1999, Aldershot: Dartmouth

Lazarus, RJ, 'Assimilating environmental protection into legal rules and the problem with environmental crime' (1994) 27 Loyola of Los Angeles L Rev 867

Lazarus, RJ, 'Changing conceptions of property and sovereignty in natural resources: questioning the public trust doctrine' (1986) 71 Iowa L Rev 631

Lazarus, RJ, 'Fairness in environmental law' (1997) 27 Env Law 705

Lazarus, RJ, 'The neglected question of congressional oversight of EPA: *quis custodiet ipso custodes* (who shall watch over the watchers themselves)?' (1991) 54 Law & Contemporary Problems 205

Lea, A, 'Environmental impact assessment – should the regulations apply to reserved matters applications?' (2000) 2 Env L Rev 131

Lee, J, 'The underlying legal theory to support a well-defined human right to a healthy environment as a principle of customary international law' (2000b) 25 Columbia JEL 283

Lee, P and Murie, A, *Poverty, Housing Tenure and Social Exclusion*, 1997, Bristol: Policy

Lee, P, Murie, A and Marsh, A, *The Price of Social Exclusion*, 1995, London: National Federation of Housing Associations

Lee, RG, 'From the individual to the environmental: tort law in turbulence', in Lowry and Edmunds, *Environmental Protection and the Common Law*, 2000a, Oxford: Hart

Legrain, P, 'Against globaphobia', Prospect, May 2000, 30

Lele, S, 'Sustainable development: a critical review' (1991) 19 World Development 607

Lem, S, *Den Tause Krigen (The Silent War)*, 1944

Leopold, A, *A Sand County Almanac*, 1949, 1966 edn, New York: OUP

Lester, JP, *Environmental Politics and Policy: Theories and Evidence*, 1989, Durham, NC: Duke UP

Lewis, J, *Marxism and the Open Mind*, 1957, London: Routledge and Kegan Paul

Lindblom, CE, *Politics and Markets*, 1977, New York: Basic

Local Government Management Board, *Sustainable Local Communities: Some Model Approaches to Strategy Development – A Guide to Preparing Local Agenda 21 Strategies by the Year 2000*, 1998

Locke, J, *Second Treatise of Government, Book II: The True Original Extent and End of Civil Government* (1690), Carpenter, WS (ed), 1924, London: PMDent

Logan, JR and Molotch, HL, *Urban Fortunes: The Political Economy of Place*, 1987, Berkeley: University of California

Lomasky, LE, *Persons, Rights and the Moral Community*, 1987, Oxford: OUP

Lomborg, B, *The Skeptical Environmentalist: Measuring the State of the World*, 2001, Cambridge: CUP

Lovelock, J, *Gaia: A New Look at Life on Earth*, 1979, Oxford: OUP

Lovelock, J, *Homage to Gaia: The Life of an Independent Scientist*, 2000, Oxford: OUP

Lowe, 'Sustainable development and unsustainable arguments', in Boyle and Freestone, *International Law and Sustainable Development: Past Achievements and Future Challenges*, 1999, Oxford: OUP

Lowry, J and Edmunds, R, *Environmental Protection and the Common Law*, 2000, Oxford: Hart

Lyle, JM, 'Reactions to EPA's interim guidance: the growing battle for control over environmental justice decision-making' (2000) 75 Indiana LJ 687

Lyotard, J-F, *The Post-Modern Condition: A Report on Knowledge* (1975), Bennington, G and Massumi, B, 1984, Manchester: Manchester UP

Macdonald, R and Heaney, D, 'Environmental policy in the new millennium – does planning have a role in achieving sustainable development?', in Allmendinger and Chapman, *Planning Beyond 2000*, 1999, Chichester: Wiley

MacGillivray A and Zadek, S, *Accounting for Change: Indicators for Sustainable Development*, 1995, London: New Economics Foundation

MacLean, D and Brown, P, *Energy and the Future*, 1983, Totowa, NJ: Rowman & Littlefield

Macloughlin, JB, *Urban and Rural Planning: A Systems Approach*, 1969, London: Faber

Macnaghten, P and Pinfield, G, 'Planning for sustainable development: prospects for social change', in Allmendinger and Chapman, *Planning Beyond 2000*, 1999, Chichester: Wiley

Macnaghten, P and Urry, J, *Contested Natures*, 1998, London: Sage

Macpherson, CB, *The Life and Times of Liberal Democracy*, 1977, Oxford: OUP

Macrory, R, 'Environmental assessment and community law' (1992) 4 JEL 289

Macrory, R, 'Environmental citizenship and the law: repairing the European road' (1996) 8 JEL 219

Margulis, L, *The Symbiotic Planet: A New Look at Evolution*, 1999, London: Phoenix

Marr, A, *Ruling Britannia: The Failure and Future of British Democracy*, 1996, Harmondsworth: Penguin

Matthews, P, 'The new trusts: obligations without rights?', in Oakley, *Trends in Contemporary Trust Law*, 1996, Oxford: Clarendon

Mayo, HB, *An Introduction to Democratic Theory*, 1960, New York: OUP

Mazur, A, *The Dynamics of Technical Controversy*, 1981, Washington DC: Communications

McAuslan, P, 'Planning law's contribution to the problems of urban society' (1974) 37 MLR 134

McAuslan, P, 'The role of courts and other judicial type bodies in environmental management' (1991) 3 JEL 195

McAuslan, P, *The Ideologies of Planning Law*, 1980, Oxford: Pergamon

McCarthy, M, 'Government advisers split over GM trials' (2001) *The Independent*, 12 May

McCarthy, M, 'Hidden cost of the freight trade: pollution in the air, congestion in the cities and danger on the roads' (2000b) *The Independent*, 11 November

McCarthy, M, 'Network of massive waste incinerators planned' (2000a) *The Independent*, 24 January

McCrudden, C, 'Social policy and economic regulators: some issues from the reform of utility regulation', in McCrudden, *Regulation and Deregulation: Policy and Practice in the Utilities and Financial Services Industries*, 1999, Oxford: Clarendon

McCrudden, C, *Regulation and Deregulation: Policy and Practice in the Utilities and Financial Services Industries*, 1999, Oxford: Clarendon

McGillivray, D and Wightman, J, 'Private rights, public interests and the environment', in Hayward and O'Neill, *Justice, Property and the Environment*, 1997, Aldershot: Avebury

McGregor, JL, 'Property rights and environmental protection: is this land made for you and me?' (1999) 31 Arizona State LJ 391

McLaren, JPS, 'Nuisance law and the industrial revolution' [1983] OJLS 155

McMichael, AJ, *Human Frontiers, Environments and Disease: Past Patterns, Uncertain Futures*, 2001, Cambridge: CUP

Meadows, DH, Meadows, DL and Randers, J, *Beyond the Limits: Global Collapse or a Sustainable Future*, 1992, London: Earthscan

Meadows, DH, Meadows, DL, Randers, J and Behrens, WW, *The Limits to Growth*, 1972, London: Earth Island

Mee, LD, 'Scientific methods and the precautionary principle', in Freestone and Hey, *The Precautionary Principle and International Law*, 1996, The Hague: Kluwer

Merrett, S, *State Housing in Britain*, 1979, London: Routledge and Kegan Paul

Merrills, JG, 'Environmental protection and human rights: conceptual aspects', in Boyle and Anderson, *Human Rights Approaches to Environmental Protection*, 1996, Oxford: Clarendon

Mertz, SW, 'The European Economic Community Directive on Environmental Assessments: how will it affect United Kingdom developers?' [1989] JPL 483

Miles, I and Irvine, J, *The Poverty of Progress: Changing Ways of Life in Industrial Societies*, 1982, Oxford: Pergamon

Miller, C, 'Environmental rights: European fact or English fiction?' (1995) 22 J Law & Soc 374

Miller, C, *Environmental Rights: Critical Perspectives*, 1998, London: Routledge

Miller, C, *Planning and Pollution Revisited, a Background Paper for the Royal Commission on Environmental Pollution*, 1999

Miller, JG, 'The standing of citizens to enforce against violations of environmental statutes in the United States' (2000) 12 JEL 370

Millichap, D, 'Sustainability: a long-established concern of planning' [1993] JPL 1111

Millichap, M, 'Real property and its regulation; the community rights rationale for town planning', in Bright and Dewar, *Land Law: Themes and Perspectives*, 1998, Oxford: OUP

Mitchell, RB, 'Compliance theory: an overview', in Cameron, Werksman and Roderick, *Improving Compliance with International Environmental Law*, 1996, London: Earthscan

Moffatt, I, *Sustainable Development: Principles, Analysis and Policies*, 1996, London: Parthenon

Monk, S, Whitehead, C, Jarvis, H and Russell, W, 'The use of residential land and house prices as a planning tool', RICS conference, *The Cutting Edge*, Cambridge, 1999

Moomaw, WR, 'International environmental policy and the softening of sovereignty' (1997) 21 Fletcher Forum of World Affairs 7

Moore, G, *Principia Ethica*, 1959, Cambridge: CUP

Moore, V, *A Practical Approach to Planning Law*, 7th edn, 2000, London: Blackstone

Morelli, L, 'Citizen suit enforcement of environmental laws in the United States: an overview' (1997) 5 Env Liability 19

Morris, J, *Climate Change: Challenging the Conventional Wisdom*, 1997, London: Institute of Economic Affairs

Mugwanya, GW, 'Global free trade vis-à-vis environmental regulation and sustainable development: reinvigorating efforts towards a more integrated approach' (1999) 14 JEL and Litigation 401

Mukerji, C, *A Fragile Power: Scientists and the State*, 1989, Princeton, NJ: Princeton UP

Munday, R, 'Inferences from silence and human rights law' [1996] Crim LR 370

Munro, RD and Lammers, JG, *Environmental Protection and Sustainable Development: Legal Principles and Recommendations Adopted by the Experts' Group on Environmental Law of the World Commission on Environment and Development*, 1987, London: Graham & Trotman

Murdoch, I, *Metaphysics as a Guide to Morals*, 1993, Harmondsworth: Penguin

Murdoch, J and Marsden, T, *Reconstructing Rurality: Class Community and Power in the Development Process*, 1994, London: UCL

MVA Consultancy, *The London Congestion Charging Research Programme: Report*, 1996, London: HMSO

Myerson, G and Rydin, Y, *The Language of Environment: A New Rhetoric*, 1996, London: UCL

Naess, A, 'Can urban development be made environmentally sound?' (1993) 36 J Env Planning and Management 301

Naess, A, 'The shallow and the deep, long-range ecology movement: a summary' (1973) 16 Inquiry 95

Newby, H, *Green and Pleasant Land? Social Change in Rural England*, 1979, London: Hutchinson

Nollkaemper, A, '"What you risk reveals what you value", and other dilemmas encountered in the legal assaults on risks', in Freestone and Hey, *The Precautionary Principle and International Law: the Challenge of Implementation*, 1996, The Hague: Kluwer

Norton, BG, 'Environmental ethics and the rights of future generations' (1982) 4 Env Ethics 319

Norton, BG, *Towards Unity Among Environmentalists*, 1991, Oxford: OUP

Nozick, R, *Anarchy, State and Utopia*, 1974, New York: Basic

O'Hagan, A, *Our Fathers*, 1999, London: Faber and Faber

O'Hare, M, Bacon, L and Sanderson, D, *Facility Siting and Public Opposition*, 1983, New York: van Nostrand Reinhold

O'Keeffe, D and Twomey, P, *Legal Issues of the Maastricht Treaty*, 1994, London: Chancery

O'Neill, JO, *Ecology, Policy and Politics: Human Well-Being and the Natural World*, 1993, London: Routledge

O'Riordan, T and Cameron, J, *Interpreting the Precautionary Principle*, 1994, London: Earthscan

O'Riordan, T and Jordan, A, 'Institutions, climate change and cultural theory: towards a common analytical framework' (1999) 9 Global Env Change 81

O'Riordan, T and Voisey, H, *The Transition to Sustainability: The Politics of Agenda 21 in Europe*, 1998, London: Earthscan

O'Riordan, T, 'The politics of sustainability', in Turner, *Sustainable Environmental Economics and Management: Principles and Practice*, 1993, London: Belhaven

O'Riordan, T, *Environmental Science for Environmental Management*, 2nd edn, 2000, Harlow: Prentice Hall

O'Riordan, T, *Globalism, Localism and Identity: Fresh Perspectives on the Transition to Sustainability*, 2001, London: Earthscan

Oakley, AJ, *Trends in Contemporary Trust Law*, 1996, Oxford: Clarendon

O'Brien, PS and Vourc'h, A, 'Encouraging environmentally sustainable growth: experience in OECD countries', OECD Economics Department Working Paper No 293, 2001, Paris: OECD

OECD/European Conference of Ministers of Transport, *Urban Travel and Sustainable Development*, 1995, Paris: OECD/ECMT

Oesterle, DA, 'Just say "I don't know": a recommendation for WTO panels dealing with environmental regulations' (2001) 3 Env L Rev 113

Office of Science and Technology, *Guidelines on the Use of Scientific Advice in Policy Making*, 1997

Office of Science and Technology, *Implementation of the Guidelines on the Use of Scientific Advice in Policy Making: First Annual Report*, 1998

Office of Science and Technology, *Review of Risk Procedures Used by the Government's Advisory Committees Dealing With Food Safety*, 2000

Office of Science and Technology, *The Use of Scientific Advice in Policy Making: Implementation of the Guidelines*, 1999

Ogus, AI and Richardson, GM, 'Economics and the environment: a study of private nuisance' (1977) 36 CLJ 284

Ogus, AI, *Regulation: Legal Form and Economic Theory*, 1994, Oxford: Clarendon

Ophuls, W and Boyan, AS, *Ecology and the Politics of Scarcity Revisited: The Unravelling of the American Dream*, 1992, New York: WH Freeman

Ophuls, W, *Ecology and the Politics of Scarcity*, 1977, San Francisco: Freeman

Ost, F, 'A game without rules? The ecological self-organization of firms', Fraser, I (trans), in Teubner, Farmer and Murphy, *Environmental Law and Ecological Responsibility: The Concept and Practice of Ecological Self-Organization*, 1994, Chichester: Wiley

Owens, S, 'Land, limits and sustainability: a conceptual framework and some dilemmas for the planning system' (1994) 19 Transactions of the Institute of British Geographers 439

Paehlke, RC, 'Democracy, bureaucracy, environmentalism' (1988) 10 Env Ethics 294

Paehlke, RC, *Environmentalism and the Future of Progressive Politics*, 1989, New Haven CT: Yale UP

Pallemaerts, M, 'International environmental law from Stockholm to Rio: back to the future?', in Sands, *Greening International Law*, 1994, New York: New

Palmer, G, 'New ways to make international environmental law' (1992) 86 AJIL 259

Parfit, D, 'Energy policy and the further future: the identity problem', in MacLean and Brown, *Energy and the Future*, 1983, Totowa, NJ: Rowman & Littlefield

Parkin, J, *Judging Plans and Projects: Analysis and Public Participation in the Evaluation Process*, 1993, Aldershot: Avebury

Partridge, E, *Responsibilities to Future Generations: Environmental Ethics*, 1981, New York: Prometheus

Passmore, J, *Man's Responsibility to Nature: Ecological Problems and Western Traditions*, 1974, London: Duckworth

Pearce, D and Barbier, EB, *Blueprint for a Sustainable Economy*, 2000, London: Earthscan

Pearce, D, *Blueprint 3: Measuring Sustainable Development*, 1993, London: Earthscan

Penner, JE, 'Nuisance and the character of the neighbourhood' (1993) 5 JEL 1

Pepper, D, *The Roots of Modern Environmentalism*, 1984, London: Croom Helm

Perkins, A, 'Poor need cheap food, says Blair's rural aide' (2001) *The Guardian*, 13 August

Petts, J, Cairney, T and Smith, M, *Risk Based Contaminated Land Investigation and Assessment*, 1997, Chichester: Wiley

Philbrick, F, 'Changing conceptions of property in law' (1938) 86 U Pa Law Rev 698

Phillips Report, *Report of the Inquiry into BSE and Variant CJD in the UK*, 2000, London: HMSO

Piatt, A, 'Public concern a material consideration?' [1997] JPL 397

Piller, C, *The Fail-Safe Society*, 1991, New York: Basic

Pipes, R, *Property and Freedom*, 1999, London: Harvill

Plamenatz, J, *Democracy and Illusion*, 1973, London: Longman

Popovic, NAF, 'In pursuit of environmental human rights: commentary on the Draft Declaration of Principles on Human Rights and the Environment' (1996) 27 Columbia Human Rights L Rev 487

Popper, K, *Conjectures and Refutations*, 1962, London: Routledge

Porritt, J, 'Sustainable development: panacea, platitude or downright deception', in Cartledge, *Energy and the Environment*, 1993, Oxford: OUP

Porritt, J, *Playing Safe: Science and the Environment*, 2000, London: Thames & Hudson

Porritt, J, *Seeing Green: The Politics of Ecology Explained*, 1984, Oxford: Blackwell

Posner, R, *Economic Analysis of Law*, 4th edn, 1992, Boston: Little Brown

Purdue, M, 'Integrated pollution control in the Environmental Protection Act 1990: a coming of age for environmental law?' (1991) 56 MLR 534

Purdue, M, 'The case for third party planning appeals' (2001) 3 Env L Rev 83

Purdue, M, 'The impact of EC environmental law on planning law in the UK', in Holder, *The Impact of EC Environmental Law in the UK*, 1997, London: Wiley

Purdue, M, 'The relationship between development control and specialist pollution controls: which is the tail and which is the dog?' [1999] JPL 585

Purdue, M, 'When a regulation of land becomes a taking of land' [1995] JPL 279

Rabe, BG, *Beyond Nimby: Hazardous Waste Siting in Canada and the United States*, 1994, Washington DC: Brookings Institution

Rabin, RL, 'Environmental liability and the tort system' (1987) 24 Houston L Rev 27

Radford, T, 'Juggling life's comical odds' (1997) *The Guardian*, 5 December

Radford, T, 'They don't know, you know' (1999) *The Guardian*, 23 February

Raff, M, 'Environmental obligations and the western liberal property concept' (1998) 22 Melbourne UL Rev 657

Rawls, J, *A Theory of Justice*, 1973, Oxford: OUP

Rawls, J, *Political Liberalism*, 1993, New York: Columbia UP

Reagan, R, *Speaking My Mind*, 1990, London: Hutchinson

Redclift, M, 'Sustainable development in the twenty-first century: the beginning of history?', in Baker, Kousis, Richardson and Young, *The Politics of Sustainable Development: Theory, Policy and Practice within the European Union*, 1997, London: Routledge

Redgwell, C, 'Life, the universe and everything: a critique of anthropocentric rights', in Boyle and Anderson, *Human Rights Approaches to Environmental Protection*, 1996, Oxford: Clarendon

Redgwell, C, *Intergenerational Trusts and Environmental Protection*, 1999, Manchester: Manchester UP

Reich, CA, 'The new property' (1964) 73 Yale LJ 733

Reid, C, 'Environmental citizenship and the courts' (2000) 2 Env L Rev 177

Revesz, RL, *Foundations of Environmental Law and Policy*, 1997, New York: OUP

Revesz, RL, Sands, P and Stewart, RB, *Environmental Law, the Economy, and Sustainable Development*, 2000, Cambridge: CUP

Rifkin, J, *The Biotech Century: How Genetic Commerce Will Change the World*, 1999, London: Phoenix

Roberts, J, Cleary, J, Hamilton, K and Hanna, J, *Travel Sickness – The Need for Sustainable Transport Policy for Britain*, 1992, London: Lawrence and Wishart

Robinson, NA, 'The Draft Convention on Environment and Development: a sustainable model for international lawmaking', in Casey and Morgante, *Human Rights, Environmental Law and the Earth Charter*, 1998, Cambridge, Mass: Boston Research Center for the 21st Century

Rodriguez-Rivera, LE, 'Is the human right to environment recognised under international law? It depends on the source' (2001) 12 Colorado J Int Env Law & Policy 1

Rogers, R, Urban Task Force Report, *Towards an Urban Renaissance*, 1999

Rose, C, 'The comedy of the commons: custom, commerce, and inherently public property' (1986) 53 University of Chicago L Rev 711 (1986)

Rose, C, *Property and Persuasion: Essays on the History, Theory, and Rhetoric of Ownership*, 1994, Oxford: Westview

Rose, CM, 'Environmental Faust succumbs to temptations of economic Mephistopheles, or, value by any other name is preference' (1989) 87 Michigan L Rev 1631

Rosenbaum, W, *Environmental Politics and Policy*, 2nd edn, 1991, Washington DC: CQ

Roszack, T, *The Voice of the Earth*, 1992, New York: Simon & Schuster

Roszak, T, *Where the Wasteland Ends*, 1972, New York: Doubleday

Rousseau, J-J, *Discourse on Inequality*, Part 2 (1755), Vaughan, CE (ed), *The Political Writings of Jean Jacques Rousseau*, Vol 1, 1962, Oxford: Blackwell

Rousseau, J-J, *The Social Contract* (1743), Cranston, M (trans), 1968, Harmondsworth: Penguin

Rowan-Robinson, J, Ross, A, Walton, W and Rothnie, J, 'Public access to environmental information: a means to what end?' (1996) 8 JEL 19

Rowan-Robinson, J, 'Sustainable development and the development control process' (1995) 66 Town Planning Rev 269

Rowan-Robinson, R and Durman, RF, 'Conditions or agreements' [1992] JPL 1003

Rowley, CK, *Property Rights and the Limits of Democracy*, 1993, Aldershot: Edward Elgar

Royal Commission on Environmental Pollution (RCEP), 'Setting out objectives', seminar, February 2000

Royal Commission on Environmental Pollution, 1st Report, Cmnd 4585, 1971

Royal Commission on Environmental Pollution, 5th Report, *Air Pollution: An Integrated Approach*, Cmnd 6371, 1976

Royal Commission on Environmental Pollution, 12th Report, *Best Practicable Environmental Option*, Cmd 310, 1988, London: HMSO

Royal Commission on Environmental Pollution, 22nd Report, *Energy: The Changing Climate*, 2000

Royal Commission on Environmental Pollution, 21st Report, *Setting Environmental Standards*, Cm 4053, 1998

Royal Commission on Environmental Pollution, 18th Report, *Transport and the Environment*, 1994, Cm 2674

Ruckelshaus, WD, 'Risk, science, and democracy', in Revesz, *Foundations of Environmental Law and Policy*, 1997, New York: OUP

Rydin, Y, *Urban and Environmental Planning in the UK*, 1998, Basingstoke: Macmillan

Sachs, W, *Global Ecology: A New Arena of Political Conflict*, 1993, London: Zed

Sager, T, *Communicative Planning Theory*, 1994, Aldershot: Avebury

Sagoff, M and Miller, D, *Market, State and Community*, 1992, Oxford: Clarendon

Sagoff, M, 'Economic theory and environmental law' (1981) 79 Michigan L Rev 1393

Sagoff, M, 'The economy of the earth: philosophy, law, and the environment', in Revesz, *Foundations of Environmental Law and Policy*, 1997, New York: OUP

Sagoff, M, *The Economy of the Earth: Philosophy, Law and Economics*, 1988, Cambridge: CUP

Salzman, J, 'Valuing ecosystem services' (1997) 24 Ecology LQ 887

Sanders, JT, 'Justice and the initial acquisition of property' (1987) 10 Harvard J Law & Public Policy 367

Sandman, PM, *Responding to Community Outrage: Strategies for Effective Risk Communication*, 1993, Fairfax, Va: American Industrial Hygiene Association

Sands, *Greening International Law*, 1994, New York: New

Sands, P, 'Compliance with international environmental obligations: existing international legal arrangements', in Cameron, Werksman and Roderick, *Improving Compliance With International Environmental Law*, 1996c, London: Earthscan

Sands, P, 'Environmental protection in the twenty-first century: sustainable development and international law', in Revesz, Sands and Stewart, *Environmental Law, the Economy, and Sustainable Development*, 2000, Cambridge: CUP

Sands, P, 'Human rights, environment and the *Lopez Ostra* case: context and consequences' (1996b) 6 EHRLR 597

Sands, P, 'International environmental litigation: what future?' (1998) 7 Review of European Community and Int Env Law 1

Sands, P, 'The environment, community and international law' (1989) 30 Harvard Int LJ 392

Sands, P, 'The International Court of Justice and the European Court of Justice', in Werksman, *Greening International Institutions*, 1996a, London: Earthscan

Sands, P, *Principles of International Environmental Law, Part I: Frameworks, Standards and Implementation*, 1995, Manchester: Manchester UP

Saward, M, 'Green democracy?', in Dobson and Lucardie, *The Politics of Nature: Explorations in Green Political Theory*, 1993, London: Routledge

Sax, JL, 'The public trust doctrine in natural resource law: effective judicial intervention' (1970) 68 Michigan L Rev 471

Sax, JL, 'Using property rights to attack environmental protection' (1996) 14 Pace Env L Rev 1

Schaffer, F, *The New Town Story*, 1970, London: MacGibbon and Kee

Schiffer, LJ and Dowling, TJ, 'Reflections on the role of the courts in environmental law' (1997) 27 Env Law 327

Schrader-Frechette, K, *Risk and Rationality: Philosophical Foundations for Populist Reforms* 1991, Berkeley: University of California

Schwartz, M Leighton, 'International legal protection for victims of environmental abuse' (1993) 18 Yale J Int Law 355

Scott, J, *EC Environmental Law*, 1998, London: Longman

Shaw, D, 'Whither rural planning?', in Allmendinger and Chapman, *Planning Beyond 2000*, 1999, Chichester: Wiley

Sheate, W, *Making an Impact – A Guide to EIA Law and Policy*, 1994, London: Cameron May

Shelton, D, 'Human rights, environmental rights, and the right to environment' (1991) 28 Stanford J Int Law 103

Shere, ME, 'The myth of meaningful risk assessment' (1995) 19 Harvard Env L Rev 409

Sherrard, P, *Human Image: World Image: The Death and Resurrection of Sacred Cosmology*, 1992, Ipswich: Golgonooza

Shiner, P and Wallace, A, 'Environmental protection judicial review and the community' [1998] Legal Action 23

Shucksmith, M, *Housebuilding in Britain's Countryside*, 1990, London: Routledge

Sikora, RI and Barry, B, *Obligations to Future Generations*, 1978, Philadelphia: Temple UP

Simmie, J, *Planning London*, 1994, London: UCL

Sjoberg, H, 'The global environment facility', in Werksman, *Greening International Institutions*, 1996, London: Earthscan

Skeffington, AM, *People and Planning: Report of the Committee on Public Participation in Planning*, 1969, London: Ministry of Housing and Local Government

Smith, A, *Wealth of Nations* (1776), Cannan, E (ed), 1976, Chicago: University of Chicago

Smith, JN, 'The coming of age of environmentalism in American society', in Smith, *Environmental Quality and Social Justice in Urban America*, 1974, Washington DC: Conservation Foundation

Smith, SL, 'Ecologically sustainable development: integrating economics, ecology and law' (1995) 31 Williamette L Rev 261

Smith, Turner T, 'Regulatory reform in the USA and Europe' (1996) 8 JEL 257

Sober, E, *Environmental Ethics*, 1995, Oxford: OUP

Soper, K, 'Human needs and natural relations: the dilemmas of ecology', in Hayward and O'Neill, *Justice, Property and the Environment*, 1997, Aldershot: Ashgate

Spretnak, C and Capra, F, *Green Politics*, 1985, London: Paladin

Spyke, NP, 'Public participation in environmental decision making at the new millennium: structuring new spheres of public influence' (1999) 26 BC Env Aff L Rev 263

Stallworthy, M, 'The regulation and investigation of commercial activities in the UK and the privilege against self-incrimination' [2000] Int Company & Commercial L Rev 167

Stanley, N, 'Contentious planning disputes: an insoluble problem' [2000] JPL 1226

Stanley, N, 'Is the town and country planning system an ineffective method of controlling hazardous development', WG Hart Legal Workshop, IALS, London, 1997

Stanley, N, 'Public concern: the decision-makers' dilemma' [1998] JPL 919

Steele J, 'Private law and the environment: nuisance in context' (1995) 15 LS 236

Steele, J and Jewell, T, 'Nuisance and planning' (1993) 56 MLR 568

Steele, J and Wikeley, N, 'Dust on the streets and liability for environmental cancers' (1997) 60 MLR 265

Steingraber, S, *Living Downstream: An Ecologist Looks at Cancer and the Environment*, 1999, London: Virago

Stone, C, 'Should trees have standing? Towards legal rights for natural objects' (1972) 45 So Cal L Rev 450

Stone, C, 'The law as a force in shaping cultural norms relating to war and the environment', in Westing, *Cultural Norms, War and the Environment*, 1988, Oxford: OUP

Sunstein, CR, *Free Markets and Social Justice*, 1997, New York: OUP

Suzuki, D, *The Sacred Balance: Rediscovering Our Place in Nature*, 1997, Vancouver: Greystone

Svedin, U, O'Riordan, T and Jordan, A, 'Multilevel governance for the sustainability transition', in O'Riordan, *Globalism, Locality and Identity*, 2001, London: Earthscan

Swanston, SF, 'Environmental justice and environmental quality benefits: the oldest, most pernicious struggle and hope for burdened communities' (1999) 23 Vermont L Rev 545

Symes, D, 'The rural community in lowland Britain: counting the garden gnomes', in Bowers, *Agriculture and Rural Land Use: Into the 1990s*, 1990, Swindon: ESRC

Tabb, WM, 'Environmental impact assessment in the European community: shaping international norms' (1999) 73 Tulane L Rev 923

Tawney, RH, *Religion and the Rise of Capitalism* (1926), Gore, C (ed), 1984, Harmondsworth: Penguin

Teubner, G, 'Environmental law and ecological responsibility', in Teubner, Farmer and Murphy, *Environmental Law and Ecological Responsibility: The Concept and Practice of Ecological Self-Organization*, 1994, Chichester: Wiley

Teubner, G, Farmer, L and Murphy, D, *Environmental Law and Ecological Responsibility: The Concept and Practice of Ecological Self-Organization*, 1994, Chichester: Wiley

Therivel, R, Wilson, E, Thompson, S, Heaney, D and Protchard, D, *Strategic Environmental Assessment*, 1992, London: Earthscan

Thornley, A, *Urban Planning Under Thatcherism: The Challenge of the Market*, 1991, London: Routledge

Thornton, J and Tromans, S, 'Human rights and environmental wrongs' (1999) 11 JEL 35

Tietenberg, T, *Environmental and Natural Resource Economics*, 5th edn, 2000, Harlow: Addison-Wesley Longman

Tilleman, WA, 'Public participation in the environmental impact assessment process: a comparative study of impact assessment in Canada, the United States and the European community' (1995) Columbia J Transnational Law 337

Tromans, S and Guruswamy, LD, 'Towards an integrated approach to pollution control: the best practicable environmental option and its antecedents' [1986] JPL 643

Tromans, S and Turrall-Clarke, *Contaminated Land: The New Regime*, 2000, London: Sweet & Maxwell

Tromans, S, 'Alternatives to landfill – can the planning system deliver?' [2001] JPL 257

Tromans, S, 'High talk and low cunning: putting environmental principles into legal practice' [1995] JPL 779

Tromans, S, 'Nuisance – prevention or payment?' [1982] CLJ 87

Tromans, S, 'The Environmental Protection Act 1990: its relevance to planning controls' [1991b] JPL 507

Tromans, S, 'Town and country planning and environmnental protection', 1991a, Oxford: JPL Occasional Papers No 18

Tromans, S, *Best Practicable Environmental Option – A New Jerusalem?*, 1987, London: UKELA

Turner, RK, *Sustainable Environmental Economics and Management: Principles and Practice*, 1993, London: Belhaven

UK Government, *A Better Quality of Life: A Strategy for Sustainable Development for the United Kingdom*, Cm 4345, 1999

UK Government, Barlow Committee Report, *The Geographical Distribution of the Industrial Population*, Cmd 6153, 1940

UK Government, *Rural Spaces and Urban Jams, Social Attitudes Survey*, 1998

UK Government, Scott Committee Report, *Land Utilization in Rural Areas*, Cmd 6378, 1942b

UK Government, *Sustainable Development: The UK Strategy*, Cm 2426, 1994

UK Government, *This Common Inheritance: Britain's Environmental Strategy*, Cm 1200, 1990

UK Government, Uthwatt Committee Report, *Compensation and Betterment*, Cmnd 6386, 1942a

UK Round Table on Sustainable Development, *Indicators of Sustainable Development*, 2000b

UK Round Table on Sustainable Development, *Not Too Difficult! Economic Instruments to Promote Sustainable Development within a Modernised Economy*, 2000a

UK Round Table on Sustainable Development, *Planning for Sustainable Development in the 21st Century*, 2000c

United Nations Economic Commission for Europe (UNECE), *Convention on Access to Information, Public Participation in Decision-Making and Access to Justice on Environmental Matters*, 1998 (DOC ECE-CEP-43)

United Nations, *Climate Change 2001: Impacts, Adaptation, and Vulnerability, Contribution of Working Group II to the Third Assessment Report of the Intergovernmental Panel on Climate Change (IPCC)*, McCarthy, JJ, Canziani, OF, Leary, NA, Dokken, DJ and White, KS (eds), 2001b, Cambridge: CUP

United Nations, *Climate Change 2001: Mitigation, Contribution of Working Group III to the Third Assessment Report of the Intergovernmental Panel on Climate Change (IPCC)*, Metz, B, Davidson, O, Swart, R and Jiahua Pan (eds), 2001c, Cambridge: CUP

United Nations, *Climate Change 2001: The Scientific Basis, Contribution of Working Group I to the Third Assessment Report of the Intergovernmental Panel on Climate Change (IPCC)*, Houghton, JT, Ding, Y, Griggs, DJ, Noguer, M, van der Linden, PJ, Xiaosu, D, Maskell, K and Johnson, CA (eds), 2001a, Cambridge: CUP

United Nations, World Commission on Environment and Development, Brundtland Report, *Our Common Future*, 1987, Oxford: OUP

Upton, W, 'The European Convention on Human Rights and environmental law' [1998] JPL 315

US Executive Order, *Outlining Policy on Environmental Justice*, 12,898 – 3 CFR 859 or 59 Fed Reg 7629 (1994)

US General Accountancy Office, *Siting of Hazardous Waste Landfills and their Correlation with Racial and Economic Status of Surrounding Communities*, 1983

van Calster, G and Deketelaere, K, 'Amsterdam, the intergovernmental conference and greening the EU Treaty' (1998) 7 European Env L Rev 12

Vidal, J, 'Scientists question safety of GM maize' (2000) *The Guardian*, 4 November

Vogel, D, *National Styles of Regulation: Environmental Protection in Great Britain and the United States*, 1986, Ithaca: Cornell UP

Voisey, H and O'Riordan, T, 'Globalization and localization', in O'Riordan, *Globalism, Localism and Identity: Fresh Perspectives on the Transition to Sustainability*, 2001, London: Earthscan

von Moltke, K, 'The relationship between policy, science, technology, economics and law in the implementation of the precautionary principle', in Freestone and Hey, *The Precautionary Principle and International Law: The Challenge of Implementation*, 1996, The Hague: Kluwer

von Moltke, K, 'The Vorsorgeprinzip in West German environmental policy', in Royal Commission on Environmental Pollution, 12th Report, *Best Practicable Environmental Option*, 1988, London: HMSO

von Weizsacker, E, Lovins, AB and Lovins, LH, *Factor Four: Doubling Wealth, Halving Resource Use*, 1997, London: Earthscan

Wade, HWR and Forsyth, CF, *Administrative Law*, 8th edn, 2000, Oxford: OUP

Waldron, J, *The Right to Private Property*, 1988, Oxford: Clarendon

Waldron, J, *Theories of Rights*, 1984, Oxford: OUP

Walker, D, 'Urban plight' (2000) *The Guardian*, 29 November

Wall, D, *Green History: A Reader in Environmental Literature, Philosophy and Politics*, 1994, London: Routledge

Wallach, L and Sforza, M, *Whose Trade Organization? Corporate Globalization and the Erosion of Democracy: An Assessment of the World Trade Organization*, 1999, Washington DC: Public

Waltz, KN, *Theory of International Politics*, 1979, New York: Random House

Ward, A, 'The right to an effective remedy in European Community law and environmental protection: a case study of United Kingdom judicial decisions concerning the environmental assessment directive' (1993) 5 JEL 221

Ward, C, 'High density life' [2000] Prospect 38 (July)

Ward, D and Tindale, S, 'Can the left learn to love the car?' [2000] Prospect (November)

Ward, SV, *Planning and Urban Change*, 1994, London: Paul Chapman

Wathern, P, *Environmental Impact Assessment: Theory and Practice*, 1988, London: Unwin Hyman

Weale, A, *The New Politics of Pollution*, 1992, Manchester: Manchester UP

Weiss, E Brown, 'The rise or the fall of international law?' (2000) 69 Fordham L Rev 345

Weiss, E Brown, *In Fairness to Future Generations: International Law, Common Patrimony, and Intergenerational Equity*, 1989, Tokyo: United Nations University

Welford, R and Gouldson, A, *Environmental Management and Business Strategy*, 1993, London: Pitman

Wells, C, '"I blame the parents": fitting new genes in old criminal law' (1998) 61 MLR 724

Werksman, J, *Incremental Costs under the Climate Change Convention: The International Legal Context*, 1993, London: Foundation of Int Env Law and Development

Werksman, J, *Greening International Institutions*, 1996, London: Earthscan

Westing, A, 1988, *Cultural Norms, War and the Environment*, Oxford: OUP

Westra, L, 'The disvalue of "contingent valuation" and the problem of the "expectation gap"' (2000) 9 Env Values 153

Westra, L, 'The ethics of environmental holism and the democratic state: are they in conflict?' (1993) 2 Env Values 123

Westra, L, *An Environmental Proposal for Ethics: The Principle of Integrity*, 1994, Lanham, Maryland: Rowman & Littlefield

Westra, L, *Living in Integrity: A Global Ethic to Restore a Fragmented Earth*, 1998, Lanham, Maryland: Rowman & Littlefield

Wilkinson, D, 'Using environmental ethics to create ecological law', in Holder and McGillivray, *Locality and Identity: Environmental Issues in Law and Society*, 1999, Aldershot: Dartmouth

Williams, G, Bell, P and Russell, L, *Evaluating the Low Cost Housing Initiative*, 1991, London: HMSO (DoE)

Williams, MB, 'Discounting versus maximum sustainable yield', in Elliott, *Environmental Ethics*, 1995, Oxford: OUP

Winter, G, 'Perspectives for environmental law – entering the fourth phase' (1989) 1 JEL 38

Wintour, 'South MPs warn of "prosperity crisis" as more jobs force up house prices' (2000) *The Guardian*, 27 December

Wolf, H, *Environmental Risk: The Responsibilities of Law and Science*, July 2001, London: Environmental Law Foundation

Wolf, MA, 'Fruits of the "impenetrable jungle": navigating the boundary between land-use planning and environmental law' (1996) 50 J Urban and Contemporary Law 5

Wolmar, C, '£3 billion on road safety would save more lives' (2001) *The Independent*, 1 April

Wood, D, 'Challenging the ethos of the European Union: a green perspective on European Union policies and programmes for rural development and the environment', in Holder and McGillivray, *Locality and Identity: Environmental Issues in Law and Society*, 1999, Aldershot: Dartmouth

Wood, D, 'Looking to the future: politics and planning', 1995, Oxford: Papers from JPL Conference, 68

Woolf, H, 'Are the judiciary environmentally myopic?' (1992) 4 JEL 1

Woolf, H, *Access to Justice: Final Report to the Lord Chancellor on the Civil Justice System in England and Wales*, 1996, London: HMSO

Worcester, R, 'Science and society: what scientists and the public can learn from each other', paper delivered at *Projecting Science into Society*, Cambridge, March 2001

Wright, JC, *Future Generations and the Environment*, 1988, Canterbury, NZ: Centre for Resource Management

Wynne, B and Mayer, S, 'How science fails the environment: if politicians don't like uncertainties and scientists often conceal them, how can we make policies that deal with the vagaries of the world around us?' (1993) 138 New Scientist, No 1876, p 33

Wynne, B, 'May the sheep safely graze? A reflexive view of the expert-lay knowledge divide', in Lash, Szerszynski and Wynne, *Risk, Environment and Modernity*, 1996, London: Sage

Young, H, 'The folly built by our leaders that makes fools of us all' (2000) *The Guardian*, 23 May